**N O V E L L ' S**

Guide to

LAN/WAN Analysis:

IPX/SPX™

NOVELL'S

# Guide to LAN/WAN Analysis: IPX/SPX™

LAURA A. CHAPPELL

Novell Press, San Jose

Novell's Guide to LAN/WAN Analysis: IPX/SPX™

Published by
**Novell Press**
**2180 Fortune Drive**
**San Jose, CA 95131**

Library of Congress Catalog Card No.: 97-77228

ISBN: 0-7645-4508-6

Printed in the United States of America

10 9 8 7 6 5 4 3 2 1

1B/RX/QT/ZY/FC

Distributed in the United States by IDG Books Worldwide, Inc.

Distributed by Macmillan Canada for Canada; by Transworld Publishers Limited in the United Kingdom; by IDG Norge Books for Norway; by IDG Sweden Books for Sweden; by Woodslane Pty. Ltd. for Australia; by Woodslane New Zealand Ltd. for New Zealand; by Addison Wesley Longman Singapore Pte Ltd. for Singapore, Malaysia, Thailand, and Indonesia; by Distribuidora Norma S.A.-Columbia for Columbia; by Intersoft for South Africa; by International Thomson Publishing for Germany, Austria, and Switzerland; by Toppan Company Ltd. for Japan; by Distribuidora Cuspide for Argentina; by Livraria Cultura for Brazil; by Ediciencia S.A. for Ecuador; by Addison-Wesley Publishing Company for Korea; by Ediciones ZETA S.C.R. Ltda. for Peru; by WS Computer Publishing Corporation, Inc., for the Philippines; by Unalis Corporation for Taiwan; by Contemporanea de Ediciones for Venezuela; by Computer Book & Magazine Store for Puerto Rico; by Express Computer Distributors for the Caribbean and West Indies. Authorized Sales Agent: Anthony Rudkin Associates for the Middle East and North Africa.

For general information on IDG Books Worldwide's books in the U.S., please call our Consumer Customer Service department at 800-762-2974. For reseller information, including discounts and premium sales, please call our Reseller Customer Service department at 800-434-3422.

For information on where to purchase IDG Books Worldwide's books outside the U.S., please contact our International Sales department at 650-655-3200 or fax 650-655-3297.

For information on foreign language translations, please contact our Foreign & Subsidiary Rights department at 650-655-3021 or fax 650-655-3281.

For sales inquiries and special prices for bulk quantities, please contact our Sales department at 650-655-3200 or write to the address above.

For information on using IDG Books Worldwide's books in the classroom or for ordering examination copies, please contact our Educational Sales department at 800-434-2086 or fax 817-421-5012.

For press review copies, author interviews, or other publicity information, please contact our Public Relations department at 650-655-3000 or fax 650-655-3299.

For authorization to photocopy items for corporate, personal, or educational use, please contact Copyright Clearance Center, 222 Rosewood Drive, Danvers, MA 01923, or fax 978-750-4470.

For general information on Novell Press books in the U.S., including information on discounts and premiums, contact IDG Books at 800-434-3422 or 650-655-3200. For information on where to purchase Novell Press books outside the U.S., contact IDG Books International at 650-655-3021 or fax 650-655-3295.

John Kilcullen, *CEO, IDG Books Worldwide, Inc.*
Steven Berkowitz, *President, IDG Books Worldwide, Inc.*
Brenda McLaughlin, *Senior Vice President and Group Publisher, IDG Books Worldwide, Inc.*

The IDG Books Worldwide logo is a trademark under exclusive license to IDG Books Worldwide, Inc., from International Data Group, Inc.

KC Sue, Publisher, Novell Press, Inc.

Novell Press and the Novell Press logo are trademarks of Novell, Inc.

## Welcome to Novell Press

**N**ovell Press, the world's leading provider of networking books, is the premier source for the most timely and useful information in the networking industry. Novell Press books cover fundamental networking issues as they emerge—from today's Novell and third-party products to the concepts and strategies that will guide the industry's future. The result is a broad spectrum of titles for the benefit of those involved in networking at any level: end user, department administrator, developer, systems manager, or network architect.

Novell Press books are written by experts with the full participation of Novell's technical, managerial, and marketing staff. The books are exhaustively reviewed by Novell's own technicians and are published only on the basis of final released software, never on prereleased versions.

Novell Press at IDG Books Worldwide is an exciting partnership between two companies at the forefront of the knowledge and communications revolution. The Press is implementing an ambitious publishing program to develop new networking titles centered on the current version of IntranetWare, GroupWise, BorderManager, ManageWise, and networking integration products.

Novell Press books are translated into 14 languages and are available at bookstores around the world.

KC Sue, Publisher, Novell Press, Novell, Inc.

## Novell

**Publisher**
*KC Sue*

**Marketing Manager**
*Marcy Shanti*

**Web Specialist/Publisher Support Liaison**
*Robin Wheatley*

## IDG BOOKS WORLDWIDE

**Acquisitions Editor**
*Jim Sumser*

**Development Editors**
*Jennifer Rowe*
*Claire Keaveney*

**Copy Editors**
*Robert Campbell*
*Nicole Fountain*
*Larisa North*
*Ami Knox*
*Carolyn Welch*

**Technical Editors**
*Alampoondi Natarajan*
*Roger Spicer*

**Production Coordinator**
*Susan Parini*

**Graphics and Production Specialists**
*Linda Marousek*
*Hector Mendoza*
*Maureen Moore*
*Dina F Quan*

**Quality Control Specialists**
*Mick Arellano*
*Mark Schumann*

**Illustrator**
*David Puckett*

**Proofreader**
*Christine Sabooni*

**Indexer**
*Donald Glassman*

## About the Author

Laura Chappell is a Protocol/Network Analyst for ImagiTech, Inc., based in Milpitas, California. She is a member of the IEEE (Institute for Electrical and Electronics Engineers) and is also a Certified Novell Instructor (CNI) and a Certified NetWare Engineer (CNE). Laura travels worldwide providing on-site communications analysis sessions and protocol analysis training seminars as a member of the NetWare Users Association and Network Professional Association. She is a regular speaker at the NUI conferences and BrainShare. Laura also writes about network communications, protocols, analysis, troubleshooting, testing, and optimization for *NetWare Connections* magazine.

Other titles by Laura Chappell include: *Novell's Guide to NetWare LAN Analysis, Novell's Guide to Multiprotocol Internetworking, Novell's Guide to Internet Access,* and *The Complete Guide to NetWare Communications.*

For more information, refer to www.imagitech.com or send an e-mail to info@imagitech.com.

*This book is dedicated to my daughter, Ginny, and her namesake, my Mom.*
*Someday, we'll play a mean three-way Rummicubes game!*

# Preface

**Y**ou cannot truly understand how your network is working unless you look under the hood at the communications that cross the cabling system. These packet-level communications are the lifeblood of the network. Even a quick perusal of the packet flow can indicate whether preventive or troubleshooting steps should be taken.

People are usually amazed at the type of information they can gather on their network through a simple afternoon of analysis (sure, call me a nerd . . .).

- ▶ Do you have any network errors?

- ▶ Are there too many broadcasts on your network?

- ▶ Are your applications configured properly?

- ▶ Is your cabling system healthy?

- ▶ Any problems with parallel routes/routing loops?

- ▶ Are your users connecting correctly?

- ▶ Is your file transfer process as fast as it can be?

- ▶ What causes that "cursor hang" suddenly?

- ▶ Why does printing take so long?

- ▶ What happens when the users lose connectivity to the server?

- ▶ How much overhead is caused by running Windows off a server (ouch)?

- ▶ What's the utilization percentage caused by NDS updates?

- ▶ Are you using efficient packet sizes?

- ▶ Do your users experience any hidden failures when they ask for network resources?

> ► Which users are taking up the most bandwidth?

> ► Would installing a switch help your network bandwidth problems?

> ► Is your idle backup link really idle?

> ► Would installing a secondary redundant router really help performance?

> ► What will happen if you add five more users to this segment?

In fact, you can use an analyzer to get the final answers on questions such as, "Which client is better—the Microsoft Client for NetWare Networks or Novell's Client 32?" When NetWare 5 with Native IP services is released, we'll be using analyzers to answer the question "What's the difference in performance between IPX/SPX and TCP/IP as a NetWare transport?"

## It's Not Rocket Science—Really!

Although you may shy away from protocol/network analyzers, you'd be surprised how easily you can pick up and use the most basic analyzers to spot network problems. Be certain you get an analyzer that has a nice, easy interface and decent documentation of any alarms. Chapter 4 includes information about analysis offerings and tips on selecting an analyzer that suits your needs.

## Who Should Read This Book

*If you have never looked at an analyzer, this book is for you.* We've provided a very graphical reference to how NetWare communicates and what you should (and shouldn't) be seeing on the cabling system. You might want to start with the media access layer analysis and troubleshooting information contained in Chapters 2 and 3. Probably the best way to delve into this stuff is just to plug in an analyzer and watch what happens when you execute various commands on your NetWare client.

*If you're relatively new to network analysis, this book is for you.* I've provided step-by-step gradual introductions and transitions from the basic protocol analysis techniques to the more advanced techniques. Take a look at the step-by-step decoded login process shown in Chapter 13.

*If you're an experienced network analyst, this book is for you.* I've included the latest and greatest packet structures, field values, and troubleshooting tips to help you identify network problems and unusual sequences. Of special note is the NCP description list in Appendix G. You might also want to take a look at the trace files included on the CD-ROM and listed in Appendix H.

Novice through geek, you'll find many interesting facts about NetWare IPX/SPX communications in these pages.

## How This Book Is Organized

This book is separated into three distinct parts: analysis and lower-layer information (Chapters 1–5), NetWare protocol information (Chapters 6–14), and supplemental information (appendixes). Here's a quick description of each chapter contained herein.

**CHAPTER 1: Fundamentals of Analysis**     This chapter defines the purpose of analysis and provides you with a starting point if you are going to begin analyzing your network. Follow the list of trends to track and test your application overhead as defined in this chapter.

**CHAPTER 2: Analysis 101 for Ethernet Networks**     This chapter lists the basic Ethernet network errors to watch out for and identifies their causes and how to track down the source of errors. Also illustrated are the various points to "tap in" to an Ethernet network with an analyzer.

**CHAPTER 3: Analysis 101 for Token Ring Networks**     This chapter defines basic Token Ring functionality, examines the fault isolation process, and also illustrates where you can tap into a Token Ring network for best traffic viewing.

**CHAPTER 4: Selecting an Analysis Solution**     Here, I list many of the features available from various protocol analyzers. I also provide examples of how the features can be used and which vendors provide various functions. This is a good place to look if you're thinking about buying an analyzer.

**CHAPTER 5: Analyzer Product Listing**   In this chapter, I've listed some of the analyzers that were used to research and develop this book, or analyzers that have interesting characteristics or features. I include contact information and basic feature sets and product descriptions.

**CHAPTER 6: Overview of NetWare Protocols**   Here, I give a brief overview of the entire NetWare protocol stack including IPX, SPX, SAP, RIP, NCP, and NLSP. For first-time analysts who are ready to dig into the technical materials, this is the place to look.

**CHAPTER 7: NetWare IPX**   This chapter provides complete details on Novell's Internetwork Packet Exchange protocol (IPX), along with sample communications showing the values of each IPX header field. It also illustrates how routers use IPX information to make their forwarding decisions.

**CHAPTER 8: NetWare SPX and SPX II**   This chapter provides complete coverage of the Sequenced Packet Exchange (SPX) connection-oriented protocol. It also details the types of programs that use SPX, discusses how to avoid SPX timeouts or WAN link problems caused by SPX watchdog, and explains the SPX II protocol that enables multiple outstanding packets in a single transaction.

**CHAPTER 9: NetWare SAP**   Here, I elaborate on Novell's Service Advertising Protocol (SAP) functionality and packet structures. Starting with an overview of SAP's use in getting a connection (get nearest server requests) and moving on to the maintenance of the server information table (SIT), I provide complete details on service discovery and registration. (Refer to Appendix E for the SAP number list.)

**CHAPTER 10: NetWare RIP**   This chapter details Novell's Routing Information Protocol (RIP) functionality and packet structures. It covers various routing situations, including parallel networks and parallel routers, to identify how RIP routers determine the best path to use. Special notes about third-party integration are also included in this chapter.

**CHAPTER 11: NetWare NLSP**   You can find in-depth coverage of Novell's NetWare Link Services Protocol (NLSP) functionality and packet structures in this chapter. This section illustrates the initial startup sequence of a link state network and includes information on the maintenance of the Link State database. This chapter also includes information on RIP/NLSP coexistence and migration.

**CHAPTER 12: NetWare IPXWAN2**   Here, I cover IPXWAN2, Novell's WAN timing and information exchange protocol for remote routers, as well as IPXWAN functionality and packet structures.

**CHAPTER 13: NetWare NCP (including NDS)**   This comprehensive chapter covers Novell's NetWare Core Protocol (NCP) and NetWare Directory Services (NDS) packet formats and functions. The text provides details on the process of connecting to a server, logging in, copying a file, reading/writing burst mode transactions, and disconnecting from a server. Also included is a quick reference list of NCP function, subfunction, and verb numbers. (Appendix G includes a description of each NCP function.)

**CHAPTER 14: NetWare Diagnostic Responder and IPX Ping**   The last chapter covers Novell's Diagnostic Responder and IPX Ping protocols, and defines how they can be used to time WAN data paths and test local machines and networks. Here, I include a matrix of devices that will and will not respond to these packets.

**APPENDIXES**   The appendixes in this book contain reference materials that are required for network analysis. These appendixes include:

Hex-Decimal-Binary Conversion Chart (Appendix A)
IPX MIB (Appendix B)
RIP/SAP MIB (Appendix C)
NLSP MIB (Appendix D)
SAP Number List (Appendix E)
Socket Number List (Appendix F)
NCP Descriptions (Appendix G)
About the CD-ROM (Appendix H)

## CONTACTING THE AUTHOR

My primary job these days is to study, document, and present details about network protocol performance, troubleshooting, and optimization. It's something I really love to do (you may have picked that up at one of the BrainShare presentations or perhaps an NUI conference). As a network analyst I often get to see the underpinnings of the network and look for analyzing projects to do for fun. If there's a process you'd like to understand more completely, please feel free to drop me an e-mail message at chappell@imagitech.com. You can also go out on our Web site, www.imagitech.com, for more details on analysis project results, analysis services, and presentation services. I look forward to hearing from you.

# Acknowledgments

This book was a collaborative effort by many people who helped organize content, gather information, research findings, input pages, format text and graphics, keep the fridge stocked with beer (grin), and provide myriad other support processes.

First and foremost, I'd like to thank Jill Poulsen, who arranged, unarranged, and rearranged my book materials and kept track of my chapters (and sometimes my brain) when I couldn't find either. Your help on this book (and all my projects) is invaluable. Next time, we'll work on a book when we're *not* pregnant, okay? (puff, puff) Thanks also to Roger Spicer for putting up with my obsession on this book by reviewing my numerous reworkings of the book outline. Roger, your advice and technical eye are appreciated! Special thanks also to Jessica Pleasant who has kept the kids smiling for the last several years! You're one of the family, you poor girl! (grin) Special thanks to my dad for all his support and enthusiasm over the years.

Very special thanks to Jim Sumser of IDG Books Worldwide, who allowed this book to "bake" for the required time and always sent humorous e-mails regardless of the deadline pressures. Thanks for putting up with my conflicting passion for documenting this stuff and staying on top of a hectic schedule. I sincerely hope this project is the first in a long line of collaborative book efforts — what's next?

Special thanks to Novell Press and the IDG Books team for really putting this book together and believing that I'd finish it before the millennium. Thanks to Lois Dudley (Novell) for your persistence when doors were closed, Robin Wheatley (Novell) for providing the products I requested in such a timely fashion, Ron Hull (IDG Books) for hanging in there while the book changed shape and form so often, and Jennifer Rowe (IDG Books) for your superb editing eye and organization. Special thanks to the editorial team that went beyond the call of duty to get this book to press: Claire Keaveney, Robert Campbell, Nicole Fountain, Larisa North, and Ami Knox. I appreciate all the extra effort to pull this book out of the fire.

My sincere gratitude goes to the many technical editors, advisors, and consultants who continually answered my (often hounding) questions on my analysis findings. Thanks to Kevin Baker, Norman Chin, Tim Delaney, Colin Dixon, Kyle Flindt, Ben Hendrick, Pat Holman, Jeff Hughes, Greg Hundley, Kathy Jensen, To-Choi Lau, LaMont Leavitt, Mason Lee, Juan Luciani, Alan Mark, Ginger

Munk, A. E. Natarajian, Jim Norman, Radia Perlman, Jon Rosdahl, Todd Ruppert, Jay Sevison, Kurt Voutaz, and John Wright. Ready for the next project? Special thanks to Adam Jerome for helping grease the wheels at Novell when I thought they'd rusted completely. (groan)

I would also like to acknowledge the many instructors, students, and technicians/engineers who helped steer the content of this book. Thanks to Silvia Hagen, Art and Barbara Lamb, Mason Lee, and Gary Porter for reviewing the early outlines and providing honest feedback. I'll get the next book outlines to you a.s.a.p. Thanks also to the many conference attendees who have shared their insights and experiences with me over the years.

To the many vendors who supported this effort and supplied their products, I thank you. I look forward to working with you all again on another project. Thanks to Nicole Martin (AG Group, Inc.), Caroline Pasquesi and Lisa Hamilton (Cinco Networks, Inc./Network General/Network Associates), Sujit Purkayasta (Digital Technology), Adele Annesi, Dave Ushler (DigiTech Industries), Paul Stone (Fluke Corporation), Tom Woolf (Ganymede Software), Rick McKenna, David Lavenda (Imagenet, Inc.), Jeff Erwin, Jennifer Guimond (Kaspia Systems, Inc.), Paul Czarnick (LANQuest), Roger Wood (NETSYS Technologies, Inc.), Margo Lindenmayer, Cheryl Haines (Network General/Network Associates), Nicolet Gibson (Optimal Internet Monitors), and Jim McDonald (Tinwald Networking Technologies).

# Contents at a Glance

# Part III    Appendixes

# Contents

# Basics of Analysis

**P**rotocol *analysis* may sound intimidating to many people—but don't let it detract you from jumping into network communications analysis. Believe me, many people have gone through my training sessions to find that they can and do understand how to catch network communication errors without obtaining a Ph.D. in electrical engineering. In fact, dare I say, it can even be fun! (OK, that's pushing it a bit for most folks.)

The "stickiest" areas of analysis are often the product evaluation process, system integration, and placement of the analyzer to ensure you are getting a "complete" picture of your network traffic. Part I of this book focuses on those areas as well as the basic analysis techniques used to identify and resolve Ethernet and Token Ring errors, test applications, troubleshoot network communications, and plan for growth.

Although you may want to delve directly into the heart of the NetWare communications system, I recommend that you peruse this part of the book for some analysis options and techniques.

# CHAPTER 1

# Fundamentals of Analysis

**T**his chapter defines the fundamentals of network analysis for all versions of NetWare (2.*x*, 3.*x*, and 4.*x*) and provides step-by-step details of NetWare performance baselining techniques. By providing real-world examples of how analyzers can be used, we'll examine how to test an application, stress-test devices and the network itself, and check router/server capabilities. In this chapter, you'll also learn how to use an analyzer to plan for network growth.

A *network analyzer*, often called a *protocol analyzer*, is a device that listens in to the network traffic to determine if there are errors in the communications process and to determine the health of the network communications channel. Using a network analyzer is similar to eavesdropping on a conversation to observe the communications process and determine if the two parties conversing are able to hear each other and respond correctly using the appropriate language and proper etiquette.

An analyzer can be used to:

- ▸ Troubleshoot media access control (such as Ethernet and Token Ring) errors

- ▸ Troubleshoot network protocol errors

- ▸ Baseline network and device performance

- ▸ Test new applications

- ▸ Stress test the network and network devices

- ▸ Check router and server abilities

- ▸ Learn how protocols interoperate

## Using an Analyzer to Troubleshoot Media Access Control Errors

Ethernet's CSMA/CD (Carrier Sense Multiple Access/Collision Detection) and Token Ring's token passing system are *media access control* (MAC) methods. They define how the connected devices control access to the media (cabling system).

Using an analyzer, we can detect the MAC-layer errors that occur on these networks. For example, when an Ethernet station has a faulty NIC, it can transmit invalid frames. With an analyzer, we can view these invalid frames to locate the faulty NIC. In the case of Token Ring networks, we can listen in on stations reporting errors in order to identify the problems on the network. (In Token Ring, every station "rats" on its neighbor.)

What types of errors should you be concerned about and track on your network? The following list serves as a checklist of Ethernet MAC errors to watch for:

▶ CRC/alignment errors

▶ Collisions (local/remote/late)

▶ Jabber

▶ Long/short packets

**NOTE** **Each of the preceding errors indicates a possible problem with a network interface card, the cabling system, or the LAN driver. Some errors can be caused by overloading the network, as well.**

The following list constitutes a checklist of Token Ring errors to watch for:

▶ Line errors

▶ Beaconing

▶ Token errors

▶ Frequency errors

- ▸ Frame copied errors

- ▸ Internal errors

- ▸ Lost frames

**NOTE**

**Due to each Token Ring card's natural behavior of blaming its upstream neighbor for problems seen on the ring, an analyzer can plug in to the ring and see who's complaining to determine the status of the ring. The analyzer doesn't need to actually witness the errors to know they've occurred.**

**X-REF**

**For more information on Ethernet and Token Ring MAC-layer troubleshooting techniques, refer to Chapter 2 and Chapter 3.**

## Using an Analyzer to Troubleshoot Protocol Errors

There are times in networking when you just plain have to use an analyzer to look at the cabling system to see what's going on. What is the client "saying" to the server? What is the server answering — if it is answering at all?

I have seen countless situations where a problem has gone unresolved for days, weeks, even months, because no error message or alert defined the problem from the client side, the server side, or intermediary device (such as a router). That's why an analyzer can be a handy tool.

Using an analyzer is similar to having a stethoscope to take vital signs of a patient. By listening in on the various conversations, you can isolate and identify a tremendous number of errors and problems, including those dealing with:

- ▸ Routing

- ▸ Service advertising

- ▸ Connection setup

- ▸ Logging in

► NDS replication

► Printing

► Data transfer

► Wide-area network (WAN) communications

► Server response

The following are representative signs and symptoms of common problems in those areas:

► *Routing.* A network that grew in a mesh design seemed to be unusually sluggish after a redundant link was installed between the two main network backbones. The clients immediately noticed a degradation in performance of about 40 percent.

► *Service advertising.* A client boots up and automatically attaches to a server that is on the other side of a WAN link, not the local server on his local network.

► *Connection setup.* Two identically configured stations have dramatically different performance rates even though they are accessing the same server and are using the same applications.

   A client receives an "unknown preferred server" error message today when booting up — yesterday the network was fine.

   You update an old NetWare client from NETX to the VLMs and find that the connection sequence is noticeably slower. What happened?

► *Logging in.* You've just configured a new container login script, but users complain that their startup time is now too slow.

   Your servers are unable to successfully complete the NDS synchronization process.

▸ *Printing.* Your printing solution across the WAN link is too slow, and you're losing connections between your remote printers and the print servers.

▸ *Data transfer.* A customer database application seemed to corrupt data that it wrote to one NetWare 4.11 server, but not another.

A backup solution performs about 400 percent faster when it accesses a NetWare 4.11 server than when it accesses a NetWare 3.11 server.

▸ *WAN communications.* A dial-on-demand ISDN link stays up 24 hours a day, 365 days a year, even though no one is logging in and using services across the WAN link.

▸ *Server response.* Your client stations seem to "hang" momentarily at random times during the day. Clients believe the server is slowing down.

## Using an Analyzer to Baseline Network and Device Performance

A *baseline* is a snapshot that depicts how a network or device typically performs. The baseline is developed in the form of a report that may or may not include network trend graphs and may even have disks attached that contain sample communication sessions. A good baseline report consists of data collected over at least a two-week period. A better baseline would define performance over an entire month (as many networks experience peaks during the "end-of-month report" time).

To run a baseline, place an analyzer or analyzer agent that collects trend data (detailed in the next section) on each network segment that you want to monitor. Check the analyzer frequently to ensure it is still powered on and capturing trend information.

At the end of the baseline time, print trend graphs, reports, and so on, to create your baseline report.

## LONG-TERM TRENDS YOU SHOULD TRACK

There are a number of network characteristics that you should document in a baseline report. They include:

- ▶ Utilization percentage

- ▶ Packets per second

- ▶ Errors per second

- ▶ Protocols in use

- ▶ Most active devices

- ▶ Broadcasts per second

- ▶ Multicasts per second

- ▶ Average packet size

### Utilization Percentage

*Utilization percentage* represents the average utilization of the cabling system. Analyzers derive this number by counting the number of bits per second transmitted on the network and defining that number as a percentage of the total possible bits per second that the media access control method (such as 10 Mbps Ethernet and 4 Mbps Token Ring) will support.

### Packets per Second

*Packets per second* is the average number of packets (regardless of protocol or destination) that occur on the network cable every second. Check your analyzer to determine if this number includes error packets or only good packets. Ideally, you want to know both error packet averages and good packet averages for your baseline.

### Errors per Second

*Errors per second* is the average number of errors per second that the analyzer has noticed. Check your analyzer documentation to determine which errors are tracked and included in the errors per second packet counter.

**TIP**

**If the average error per second value is one error per second or greater on a long-term trend graph, you should examine the cause of errors on your network before you complete your baseline. One error per second (average) is very high for long-term trending and indicates a possible communications problem.**

### Protocols in Use

*Protocols in use* is the distribution of protocols on the network, that is, how much of the network traffic is in use by NetWare's IPX/SPX, TCP/IP, AppleTalk, SNA, or other protocols.

### Most Active Devices

The *most active devices* are the devices that transmit the most packets per second and use the highest average bandwidth on the network. If possible, it is always a good idea to print out a master list of all devices communicating on the network, their node addresses, and protocols spoken, as shown in Figure 1.1.

### FIGURE I.I

*The most active devices list should also list the station's node address and protocols spoken, if the analyzer supports this function.*

**Station Monitor - 9 Stations**

| Station | Pkts/s In | Pkts/s Out | Pkts Out | Pkts In | Errors | Kbytes Out | Kbytes In | Bytes/s Out | Bytes/s In | Protocols | Address |
|---------|-----------|------------|----------|---------|--------|------------|-----------|-------------|------------|-----------|---------|
| SERV1 | 1 | 2 | 52,133 | 53,064 | 0 | 4,889 | 6,823 | 123 | 145 | NetWare | 00-00-1B-32-0A-B5 |
| ADMIN | 0 | 0 | 48,801 | 48,930 | 0 | 3,733 | 4,253 | 0 | 0 | NetWare | 00-20-C5-00-E4-21 |
| This_Workstation | 0 | 0 | 3,749 | 2,226 | 0 | 3,023 | 540 | 0 | 0 | NetWare,AppleTal | 00-80-C7-67-A0-93 |
| SERV2 | 1 | 1 | 2,240 | 2,111 | 0 | 212 | 194 | 145 | 62 | NetWare | 00-80-5F-14-04-51 |
| CORP-FS1 | 0 | 0 | 1,472 | 1,308 | 0 | 140 | 104 | 0 | 0 | NetWare,AppleTal | 00-20-AF-63-EB-2B |
| 00-20-78-10-42-B4 | 0 | 0 | 69 | 69 | 0 | 4 | 4 | 0 | 0 | NetWare | 00-20-78-10-42-B4 |
| ATalk_Bcast | 0 | 0 | 0 | 169 | 0 | 0 | 10 | 0 | 0 | None Spoken | 09-00-07-FF-FF-FF |
| 09-00-07-00-00-14 | 0 | 0 | 0 | 2 | 0 | 0 | 0 | 0 | 0 | None Spoken | 09-00-07-00-00-14 |
| Broadcast | 1 | 0 | 0 | 585 | 0 | 0 | 71 | 0 | 62 | None Spoken | FF-FF-FF-FF-FF-FF |

### Broadcasts per Second

*Broadcasts per second* is the average number of packets per second that are transmitted to the generic broadcast address (0xFF-FF-FF-FF-FF-FF). If you are using Token Ring networks, you may also want to track the number of packets sent to the Token Ring broadcast address (0xC0-00-FF-FF-FF-FF). AppleTalk also supports a special broadcast address, 0x09-00-07-FF-FF-FF.

### Multicasts per Second

*Multicasts per second* is the average number of packets per second that are transmitted to a group of devices by using multicast addressing. The following is an example of some multicast addresses you might see on your network:

0x09-00-1B-FF-FF-FF: NLSP routers (IEEE 802.3 and FDDI networks)
0xC0-00-10-00-00-00: NLSP routers (IEEE 802.5 networks)

0xC0-00-00-00-00-01: Active Monitor (Token Ring)
0xC0-00-00-00-00-02: Ring Parameter Server (Token Ring)
0xC0-00-00-00-00-08: Ring Error Monitor (Token Ring)
0xC0-00-00-00-00-10: Configuration Report Server (Token Ring)
0xC0-00-00-00-01-00: Source Routing Bridge (Token Ring)

### Average Packet Size

*Average packet size* is the average size in bytes of all packets that cross the network. You may also want to track the average packet size for each network protocol in use.

## USING YOUR BASELINE REPORT

Keep your baseline report handy — you'll use it to check current network performance and prepare your network for growth. You can use your baseline report for the following purposes:

> ▸ *Maintaining a troubleshooting reference.* If you spot a problem in network communications, you can refer to your original communications patterns to determine what has changed. For instance, if you notice that the network clients are regularly loosing network connections, check the current network error level against your baseline. If the error level has increased dramatically, that could be the cause of the client connectivity problems.

> ▸ *Planning for growth.* Your baseline report shows how much network bandwidth is currently in use and which devices are the most active. If you plan to add a few new clients, you can use your baseline report to determine how to split your network devices across a router or switch to enhance performance.

> ▸ *Spotting new/unusual traffic patterns.* If you suddenly spot a high number of small packets on the network, you can check this traffic pattern against your baseline report to see if this is typical of your network's performance. If not, you might want to know why your network performance has changed.

▶ *Optimizing network performance.* If your baseline reveals that your network typically supports small packet sizes, an excessive number of broadcast packets, and problems with SPX-based communications, you might consider upgrading the client software you are using to enhance performance.

▶ *Scheduling network maintenance tasks.* If the baseline report shows high network utilization between 4:30 P.M. and 7:00 P.M., you can use this information to schedule routine backup tasks and heavy printing loads for a later time.

## PLANNING FOR GROWTH/BUILDING A SUCCESSFUL LAN AND WAN

In order to grow a network that supports added segments, devices, programs, and links, you must understand how your current communications system works. Once you understand your current communications pattern, the communications parameters available for NetWare, and network traffic patterns defined by internetworking devices (such as hubs, bridges, switches, and routers), you can plan for the successful growth of your network. You can use the information gathered during the baseline process to determine which of the following actions may be needed on your growing network:

▶ *Splitting overloaded segments.* If your baseline report indicates that the current network is experiencing relatively high utilization, you can use the most active stations information to determine how you should rearrange network devices to load-balance communications. For example, you could determine the top 20 network clients and run 10 of them off one network interface card in the server and the other 10 off the other card.

▶ *Changing default packet sizes.* If your baseline indicates that your typical packet size is 576 bytes even though your network supports 1,518-byte packets, you may want to investigate why your network supports smaller packet sizes. A protocol called LIP (Large Internet Packet) includes functionality that ensures clients don't default to minimum packet sizes unnecessarily.

**X-REF**

**Refer to Chapter 13 for more information.**

▶ *Placing servers close to their respective clients.* If your baseline indicates that most communications are coming from remote segments perhaps you should consider moving your NetWare server closer to the clients that use it most. You must reference the IPX header Hop Count field to determine how far the packet has traveled.

**X-REF**

**For more information on the IPX header Hop Count, refer to Chapter 7.**

▶ *Controlling traffic patterns.* If you need to grow your network to support more traffic, refer to your baseline report to determine which devices should be placed off a network switch, bridge, or router.

## Using an Analyzer to Test New Applications

Your analyzer can be used to determine how new applications will affect network performance. For example, if you are considering loading Windows off the file server, you can analyze a single user loading Windows off the server first. Look at the utilization and packet per second rate that the load sequence places on the network. Multiply the results by the number of stations that will be loading Windows off the server to determine if the network can support the additional traffic.

Use the following five-step process to analyze the effect of network applications before full deployment:

1 • Set up a capture filter on the analyzer. Look for all traffic to and from the test station.

2 • Start capturing packets.

**3** · Launch the application on the test station. Run through the basic set of operations for at least 15 minutes.

**4** · Stop the analyzer and examine the trend detail information for utilization and packets per second. Many analyzers, such as LANalyzer for Windows and the ManageWise LANalyzer Agent, can graph the usage statistics for the filtered station's traffic.

**5** · Multiply the single test station's traffic by the number of stations that will be using the application on the network. Can your network communications system support the additional load? Do you need to segment the LAN to allow for the additional traffic? Will your WAN support the additional load if the applications are run from remote stations?

## Using an Analyzer to Stress-Test the Network and Network Devices

Some analyzers and analyzer add-ons enable you to transmit packets onto the network for testing purposes. This capability is used to test the network devices and the network itself. There are two types of packets that you can transmit to test the network and devices — a *dumb load* and an *intelligent load*.

A dumb load is addressed to a fictitious address and won't be actually answered by any device. This way we can send the traffic out onto the cabling system and be certain that no devices are being stress-tested by processing those packets.

An intelligent load is addressed to a specific device (or devices using multicast addresses). Intelligent loads require more work to transmit because you have to know the internetwork address of the destination device.

LANQuest's LANload for LANalyzer enables you to build an intelligent load by addressing packets to a specific device on the network, as shown in Figure 1.2. LANLoad for LANalyzer is used only to transmit packets, not to receive packets. You must use another analyzer, such as LANalyzer for Windows, to receive packets. LANQuest also has a product called Net/WRx that transmits and receives network packets.

**TIP**

**For more information on LANQuest's products, visit**
`www.lanquest.com.`

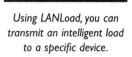

F I G U R E   1.2

*Using LANLoad, you can transmit an intelligent load to a specific device.*

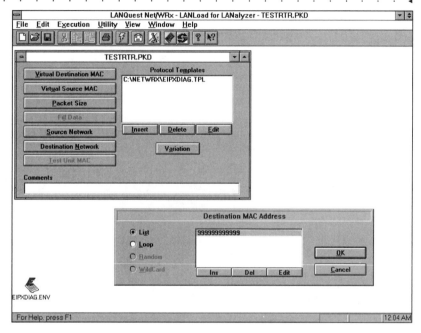

**X-REF**

**For more information on LANQuest LANLoad, refer to Chapter 5.**

## Using an Analyzer to Test the Network

You can use some analyzers to transmit a set of nondescript packets onto the network cabling system. This enables you to see how much extra traffic your network can support before clients begin to timeout and users complain of poor performance. In order to perform this type of testing, you must configure your analyzer to transmit packets addressed to a nonbroadcast, unused node address (this ensures that you are not stressing a specific network device so that it cannot communicate in a typical manner). For example, you might send packets to node address 0x99-99-99-99-99-99 and then view the trend information for utilization percentage and error information.

For example, suppose you are adding twenty new stations to your network and you want them to load Windows 95 off a NetWare server. In order to see how the network reacts to the additional traffic, you can transmit a dumb load that matches the average utilization percentage placed on the network by the twenty new stations:

**1** • Load a single Windows 95 station from a NetWare server and prefilter its packets.

**2** • Determine the average utilization percentage placed on the network from that load sequence ($z$%).

**3** • Transmit a dumb load equal to 20 times $z$% and look for an increase in any MAC or protocol-layer errors.

## Using an Analyzer to Test Network Devices

By transmitting packets to a specific device, you can determine if the device can handle additional loads as the network continues to grow. Many analyzers and some analyzer add-on products, such as LANLoad by LANQuest, can be used to test a NetWare server by transmitting a burst of NetWare Diagnostic Responder packets to the server. All versions of the NetWare OS must respond to these types of packets. If a server cannot respond properly because it is overloaded, perhaps you should avoid placing additional NLMs and functions on that server.

**X-REF**

**For more information on the NetWare Diagnostic Responder, refer to Chapter 14. For more information on LANLoad by LANQuest, refer to Chapter 5.**

## Using an Analyzer to Check Router and Server Capabilities

You can use your analyzer to check server and router abilities by manually transmitting function request packets to the device and watching the device reactions. For example, if you are unsure how a NetWare server will react to a Packet Burst connection request, you can transmit a test packet to the server. The server's response indicates whether or not the server can provide Burst Mode connectivity. In Figure 1.3, a server indicates that it does not support Burst Mode connectivity in Packet 26. This is a NetWare 3.11 server that does not have the add-on NLM loaded to support burst mode.

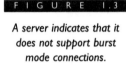

F I G U R E    1.3

*A server indicates that it does not support burst mode connections.*

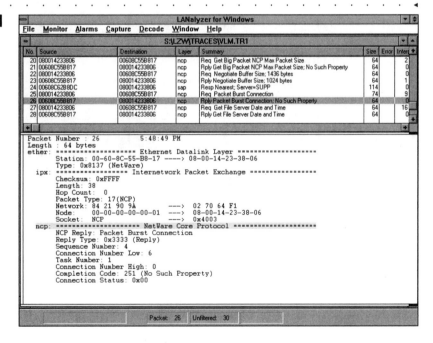

## Using an Analyzer to Learn How Protocols Interoperate

Finally, you can use a network analyzer to find out how network protocols actually operate. It is not unusual to find that network documentation is sketchy, incorrect, or too difficult to follow. With an analyzer, you can see the protocols operate and get a much better handle on how clients connect to servers and access file and print services.

## Summary

In this chapter, we've examined the need for a thorough baseline to define current network health, as well as the necessary steps for growth planning. We've seen how an analyzer can isolate network problems associated with the media access control, network hardware, and network software. In the next chapter, we'll take a look at how you can use an analyzer to identify errors that occur on a typical Ethernet network as well as where to place an analyzer on an Ethernet network.

# CHAPTER 2

# Analysis 101 for Ethernet Networks

**A** number of events can occur on an Ethernet network that signal trouble. Using an analyzer, we can "listen in" on the communications and spot problems such as faulty drivers and network interface cards or an overloaded cabling system. This chapter focuses on:

▸   How Ethernet communications work, including the Ethernet Carrier Sense Multiple Access/Collision Detection (CSMA/CD) method and Ethernet frame types

▸   The types of errors that occur on an Ethernet network

▸   Where to place an analyzer to get a complete picture of your Ethernet network communications

## How Ethernet Communications Work

Before we can define what the problems are, let's take a brief look at how communications should look on a healthy Ethernet network. Just as Token Ring networks rely on a token-passing scheme for information flow, Ethernet communications are based on Carrier Sense Multiple Access/Collision Detection (CSMA/CD) and Ethernet frames structures.

### CARRIER SENSE MULTIPLE ACCESS/COLLISION DETECTION

The access method used by Ethernet networks is Carrier Sense Multiple Access/Collision Detection. This simply means that stations must listen before they transmit — if the cable is busy, they must defer (wait) and try retransmission later, when the cable is free.

On an ideal Ethernet network, each station waits when the medium is busy but still gets to transmit often enough that the upper-layer applications (such as the NetWare shell or requester) can communicate without timing out. On this same ideal network, the transmitting station knows that when it transmits a packet, it has total control of the cabling system and no other station would dare to transmit at the same time — thereby causing packets to collide on the cabling system.

Unfortunately, it is not an ideal world, and as networks grow in size and applications increase their need for bandwidth, the CSMA/CD model begins to moan and groan and creak at the seams.

Before we look at the various problems that can occur on an Ethernet network, let's look at the frame structures supported by NetWare.

## ETHERNET FRAME STRUCTURES

On NetWare LANs you can find up to four Ethernet frame structures:

▸ Ethernet_802.3 (often referred to as the "raw" frame format)

▸ Ethernet_802.2

▸ Ethernet_SNAP

▸ Ethernet_II

The type of frame you use is based on the protocols you are running and the frame type(s) they support.

**NOTE**

**Be aware that enabling your server to use more frame types than are absolutely necessary for NetWare communications can be detrimental to network performance. Certain protocols, such as Service Advertising Protocol (SAP) and Router Information Protocol (RIP), send broadcast packets out using each frame type that has been enabled for IPX. If you use all four Ethernet frame types on one network interface card, you have quadrupled your SAP and RIP broadcast traffic.**

**X-REF**

**For more information on SAP and RIP broadcasts, refer to Chapter 9.**

Let's examine each of these frame types and see how they are displayed on an analyzer screen.

### Ethernet_802.3

This frame structure was the default Ethernet frame used with NetWare 2.*x* and 3.11 and the NETX client software. The frame has one fatal flaw — it does not have the Logical Link Control (LLC) portion that the Institute of Electrical and Electronic Engineers (IEEE) 802.3 specification requires. As you can see in Figure 2.1, there is no "protocol ID" or "protocol type" field to identify the upper-layer protocol that this packet should be handled by.

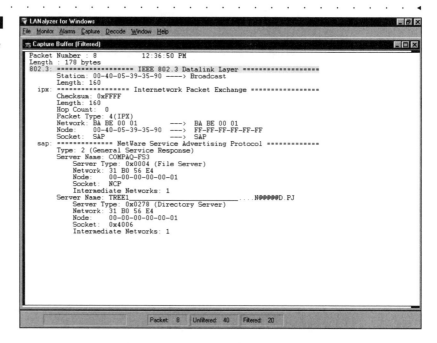

FIGURE    2.1

*The Ethernet_802.3 frame structure is missing a protocol type field.*

This frame type was selected for use by Novell at a time when multiprotocol LANs were unheard of. Therefore, a protocol type field was considered quite unnecessary overhead. Of course, as the networking industry matured, this frame type did not work on multiprotocol networks that expected the type field to follow the length field.

This frame type can be bound only to the Internetwork Packet Exchange (IPX) protocol stack.

**Ethernet frames start with an eight-byte preamble field that indicates where the frame starts and establishes the timing. The frames also contain a four-byte Frame Check Sequence field at the end that is used for error checking. Analyzers do not show you these fields because they are stripped off by the Ethernet card.**

### Ethernet_802.2

This frame structure is the default Ethernet frame used with NetWare 3.12 and 4.x and the VLM clients. It does contain the LLC portion that the IEEE 802.3 specification requires. The protocol in use is specified in the "protocol type" field in the LLC portion of the frame structure, as shown in Figure 2.2.

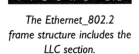

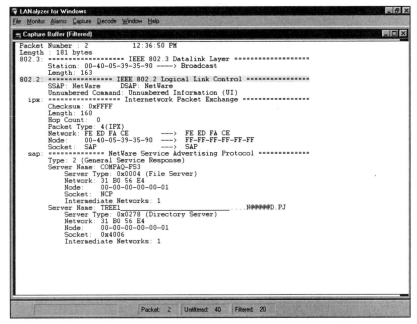

The Ethernet_802.2 frame structure includes the LLC section.

This frame type is more appropriate as a default frame type, since it is IEEE 802.3–compliant and not considered proprietary to the NetWare protocol.

This frame type can be bound to Novell's IPX/SPX protocol stack or the FTAM (File Transfer Access Management) protocol stack.

### Ethernet_SNAP

This frame type has the largest header structure of the four Ethernet frame types and is based on the Ethernet_802.2 frame structure. As shown in Figure 2.3, there is an Ethernet type field embedded in the LLC layer. This Ethernet type field indicates the upper-layer protocol in use.

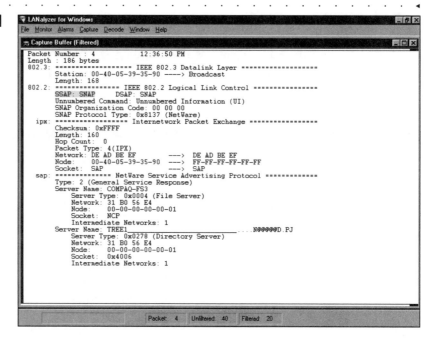

This frame type can be bound to Novell's IPX/SPX protocol stack, AppleTalk Phase II, or TCP/IP.

### Ethernet_II

This frame type is typically seen on TCP/IP networks and is shown in Figure 2.4. The type field follows the destination and source address fields and indicates the upper-layer protocol in use.

FIGURE 2.4

*The Ethernet_II frame structure has a type field directly after the source address field.*

```
LANalyzer for Windows                                          _ 8 X
File  Monitor  Alarms  Capture  Decode  Window  Help
Capture Buffer (Filtered)                                     _ □ X
Packet Number : 6              12:36:50 PM
Length : 178 bytes
ether: ==================== Ethernet Datalink Layer ====================
        Station: 00-40-05-39-35-90 ----> Broadcast
        Type: 0x8137 (NetWare)
ipx:   ================= Internetwork Packet Exchange =================
        Checksum: 0xFFFF
        Length: 160
        Hop Count:  0
        Packet Type: 4(IPX)
        Network: BA BE BA BE          ---> BA BE BA BE
        Node:    00-40-05-39-35-90   ---> FF-FF-FF-FF-FF-FF
        Socket:  SAP                 ---> SAP
sap:   ============= NetWare Service Advertising Protocol =============
        Type: 2 (General Service Response)
        Server Name: COMPAQ-FS3
            Server Type: 0x0004 (File Server)
            Network: 31 B0 56 E4
            Node:    00-00-00-00-00-01
            Socket:  NCP
            Intermediate Networks: 1
        Server Name: TREE1_____....N@@@@@D.PJ
            Server Type: 0x0278 (Directory Server)
            Network: 31 B0 56 E4
            Node:    00-00-00-00-00-01
            Socket:  0x4006
            Intermediate Networks: 1



                    Packet:  6    Unfiltered:  40    Filtered:  20
```

This frame type can be bound to Novell's IPX/SPX protocol stack, TCP/IP, or AppleTalk Phase I.

**NOTE**

**Most analyzers reverse the destination and source fields in their packet displays to make the display more esthetically pleasing: People want to see source information on the left side of the screen and destination information on the right side of the screen, as shown in Figures 2.1–2.4. This is a cosmetic display of the packet contents only and does not change the meaning of the fields.**

# Ethernet Network Problems

Problems that occur on Ethernet networks have three primary causes:

▸ Overloaded networks

> ▸ Faulty networks

> ▸ Frame problems

## THE OVERLOADED ETHERNET NETWORK

On a very busy network, it is common to see multiple stations involved in a *collision* on the wire. Stations listen to the cable at the same time, build a packet, and then transmit. When they were listening, the cable was free, right?

 **Don't confuse network utilization (how busy the medium is) with server utilization (how busy the processor is). In this section, we are talking about the level of activity on the network media.**

NOTE

After being involved in a collision, the stations must perform a function, called the *backoff algorithm,* to determine possible retransmission times. It is possible that when they retransmit they could retransmit at the same time as other stations, thereby causing another collision.

To ensure that stations do not get into an endless loop of colliding, the backoff algorithm enables stations to get a much larger choice of retransmission times: It would be very unusual if three stations selected the same retransmission time when they have performed the backoff algorithm three times already.

Besides a higher number of collisions, the busy Ethernet network will also have an increase in utilization percentage. The utilization percentage indicates the amount of total bandwidth in use. On a 10BaseT or 10Base2 network, 10 Mbps is the available bandwidth. If your Ethernet segment is currently registering 20 percent utilization, this means that 2 Mbps is in use and 8 Mbps is still available.

### The Collision Domain

The *collision domain* is the entire cabling and device area where collisions can occur. For example, on a 10Base2 network (thin coaxial Ethernet network in a linear bus configuration), as shown in Figure 2.5, the collision domains include all the cabling on each side of the bridge. Any packet transmitted into a collision domain has a chance of colliding with a packet transmitted from the other devices in the domain. A larger collision domain means a greater chance of collisions; a smaller collision domain means a lower chance of collisions.

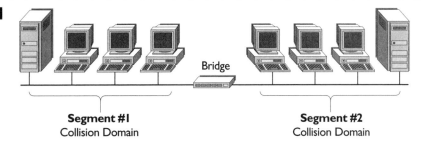

FIGURE 2.5

There are two separate
collision domains on this
10Base2 network.

**Segment #1**
Collision Domain

**Segment #2**
Collision Domain

On a 10Base2 network, all devices attached to the common coaxial cable are in the same collision domain. On a 10BaseT network, the collision domain includes all devices that transmit through a hub or set of hubs with no other intermediary device (such as a bridge or router). Figure 2.6 depicts a 10BaseT network that supports two separate collision domains.

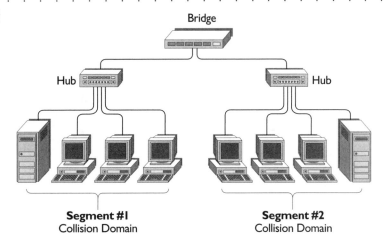

FIGURE 2.6

A 10BaseT network
with two separate
collision domains

Bridge

Hub

Hub

**Segment #1**
Collision Domain

**Segment #2**
Collision Domain

### How High Is Too High for Utilization?

This question comes up all the time in discussions about utilization statistics. The answer varies from network to network. How much activity can your network handle before people start to complain about the performance or applications begin to time out and attempt retries? A good ballpark number to use as a utilization alarm threshold is 35 percent. If your network consistently maintains 35 percent usage, you may consider splitting the network.

### Segmenting Ethernet Traffic

One way to reduce the amount of utilization on an Ethernet network is to segment traffic using a bridge, router, or switch.

**Bridges**   A *bridge* isolates traffic between stations based on their MAC (Media Access Control) address. Bridges connect multiple network segments and are the predecessors of today's switches, which also make forwarding decisions based on MAC addresses. Bridges learn the MAC address of stations on each side and forward packets addressed to stations on the other segment only when necessary. In Figure 2.7, for example, if Station A (MAC address 0x00-00-1B-23-23-12) sent a packet to Station B (MAC address 0x00-00-1B-67-4A-22), the bridge would not forward the packet to Segment 1.

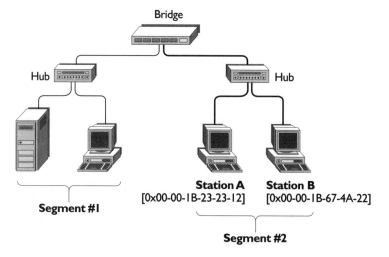

**FIGURE 2.7**

*Bridges will forward only traffic addressed to other network segments.*

Unfortunately, if a bridge does not know the location of the device defined in the destination address field of a packet, it must forward the packet out all connected ports. The same is true of broadcast packets. Bridges cannot control broadcast traffic, connect different networks, or make routing decisions. Routers provide that level of functionality.

**Routers**   *Routers* can be used to connect two or more separate networks and make forwarding decisions based on a network address. Routers are able to isolate broadcast traffic that is destined to all nodes on one network, make intelligent routing decisions, and depending on the routing protocol used, perform some level of load balancing.

Figure 2.8 shows a router that connects two LANs and one WAN. Traffic between Stations A and B remains on Network 2. Station A can transmit broadcasts to all devices on Network 2; those broadcasts are not forwarded to Network 1 or across the WAN link because the destination network address is all nodes on Network 2.

FIGURE 2.8

*Routers can make intelligent forwarding decisions and permit local broadcasting.*

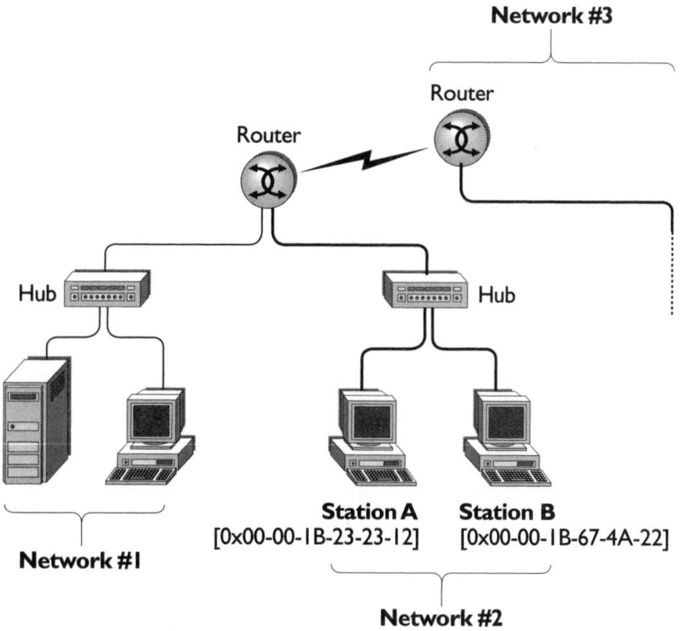

**Switches** *Switches* are similar to bridges, except they have the capability to connect to various devices or network segments, as shown in Figure 2.9. (Bridges connect to segments only.)

Switches create a virtual circuit between the sending and receiving devices connected. This enables a client to have full use of the bandwidth — they do not have to share the collision domain or available bandwidth with other users.

Ethernet switches can begin forwarding packets at wire speed (10 Mbps) after the destination address has been received. The packet is still being received on one port while the packet is being transmitted out another port at the same time. This is called *cut-through switching.*

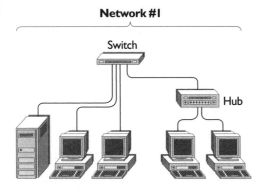

*Switches can connect to devices or network segments and can forward packets as they are being received.*

This ability to forward packets as they are still arriving has a drawback, however. What if the packet has an error (as defined by an algorithm performed on the Frame Check Sequence field at the end of the packet)? The error packet would be forwarded on to the other port. Because of this potential problem, switch manufacturers often provide *store-and-forward capability*, which enables the switch to hold the entire packet and check its integrity before forwarding it. Some manufacturers also provide *adaptive switches*; such a switch starts as a cut-through switch and, if a certain number of error packets have been forwarded through the port, changes over to store-and-forward mode until the problem is resolved.

Utilization is a network statistic that should be tracked regularly. Keep in mind that new users and new applications can affect network utilization. New devices (such as a print-serving device) can also affect network utilization.

## THE FAULTY ETHERNET NETWORK

Corrupted packets are a sign of a faulty Ethernet network — one that is experiencing cable, card, or driver problems. A good indication of a faulty Ethernet network is when the number of errors increases dramatically but the average utilization percentage remains low (as shown in Figure 2.10).

As you can see in the figure, the overloaded Ethernet network has a high utilization percentage, along with a high error rate — most of these errors are fragments caused by collisions on the busy cable segment. The faulty network, however, has a lower utilization percentage with the same high error rate — most of these errors are CRC errors and indicate a faulty network interface card.

FIGURE 2.10

*Differentiating between a faulty Ethernet network and an overloaded Ethernet network*

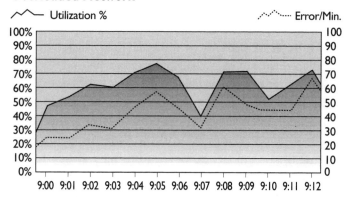

**Overloaded Network**

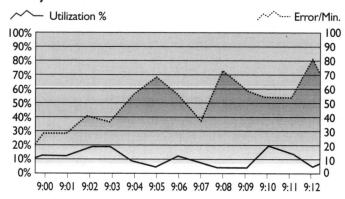

**Faulty Network**

### Ethernet Errors to Track

A variety of errors and faults can occur on an Ethernet network. Some of the most common Ethernet errors that can be located with most network analyzers are:

▸ Fragments

▸ CRC errors

▸ Jabber

> ▸ Oversized/long packets

> ▸ Undersized/short packets

**Fragments** *Fragments* are the result of a collision on the network. As mentioned earlier in this chapter, a collision occurs when more than one station transmits at the same time (or approximately the same time) onto the cabling system.

If fragments occur at the same time that utilization peaks, the network segment is becoming overloaded. The cabling system is the bottleneck. If this condition becomes typical of your network, consider using a router to split network traffic into multiple segments or look into using a switch to provide devices with a 10 Mbps throughput individually.

If utilization is low but the fragment errors are high and do not peak in relation to any utilization spikes, look for a problem component. For example, you might see this error if a station acts like a "deaf node" and does not follow the rules of "carrier sense" before transmission. A deaf node may transmit bits on the wire when the medium is busy. To isolate a deaf node, capture and display packets. Analyze the contents of the packet capture buffer to determine the station that most often retransmits on the network immediately after these fragments are observed. Replace that station's network board.

Some problems have also occurred over the years with some Ethernet chipsets that "dribbled" bits onto the wire. These cards cause random collisions on the network and must also be replaced. Unfortunately, these cards are not as easy to spot, since they really don't have anything queued up waiting to transmit. You might actually catch one of these stations by observing the time of day that collisions begin to occur and checking the login time of the stations. Check with your hardware manufacturer to see if they are aware of and have experienced this problem with any of their chipset revisions.

**CRC Errors** A CRC (cyclical redundancy check) operation is the error-checking operation Ethernet network interface cards perform before transmitting packets onto the wire. Upon completion of this CRC check, a network interface card places the CRC value into the last field of the Ethernet frame, the Frame Check Sequence (FCS) field.

Upon receipt of a packet, the destination station's network interface card performs the same CRC equation and checks the FCS field value of the packet to see if it comes up with the same result. Identical results indicate the packet is valid; differing results indicate the packet is corrupt.

If CRC errors are attributed to a single station, the station's network board or transceiver is faulty. Replace the faulty component. If the CRC errors are attributed to numerous stations or no specific stations, there may be a cabling problem, electromagnetic interference (EMI), or improper grounding. Check your cabling system to ensure that it is within specification limitations and that it does not contain shorts or other faults.

**Jabber Errors**   A *jabber* is a packet that is greater than 1,518 bytes (the maximum legal packet length in Ethernet) and contains a CRC error.

A jabber error can be caused by faulty hardware, for example, a faulty transceiver (on-board or external). Use an analyzer that can detect jabber errors and associate a source station with the error (if possible). Replace the network board or transceiver of the station transmitting the jabber error.

**Oversized Packets/Long Packets**   An *oversized* packet contains more than 1,518 bytes but is otherwise well-formed with a valid CRC value. This error is typically caused by a driver bug; replace the LAN driver of the transmitting device.

**Communications may work fine with oversized packets, but you should consider updating the driver when you get a chance. It is never a good idea to use a product that communicates "out of spec." Not all Ethernet products are tolerant of these types of communications. Therefore, when you mix these products with other vendors' products, unpredictable results may occur.**

TIP

**Undersized Packets/Short Packets**   An *undersized* packet contains less than 64 bytes but is otherwise well-formed with a valid CRC value.

This error is typically caused by a driver problem and can be resolved by replacing the LAN driver of the transmitting device.

**As with oversized packets, your communications may work fine with undersized packets, but you should consider updating the driver when you get a chance. It is never a good idea to use a product that communicates "out of spec."**

TIP

### Frame Problems

We've already seen a number of Ethernet network problems that cause corrupt frames or frames of illegal length. Frame problems, however, can also be caused by frame mismatches on the cabling system. Unfortunately, this is all too often seen on NetWare LANs.

Consider a protocol that is bound to a frame type as a single logical network. If you bind the protocol to another frame type, it is another logical network. Bind it a third and fourth time, and you have four logical networks, as shown in Table 2.1

| TABLE 2.1 | LOGICAL NETWORK | PROTOCOL | FRAME NETWORK ADDRESS |
| --- | --- | --- | --- |
| Binding a protocol to a frame type creates a logical network | A | IPX/SPX | Ethernet_802.3 | AA-AA-AA-AA |
| | B | IPX/SPX | Ethernet_802.2 | BB-BB-BB-BB |
| | C | IPX/SPX | Ethernet_II | CC-CC-CC-CC |
| | D | IPX/SPX | Ethernet_SNAP | DD-DD-DD-DD |

Type **CONFIG** at the NetWare console to see if you have multiple frame types bound, as shown in Figure 2.11. We can see by the network card settings that we are looking at only a single card that is bound twice, once to the Ethernet_802.2 frame type and again to the Ethernet_802.3 frame type.

FIGURE 2.11

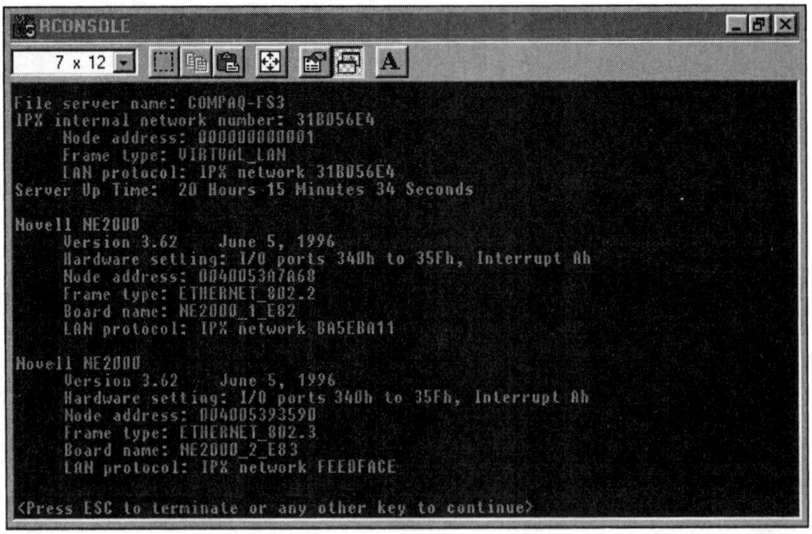

Type **CONFIG** to determine if you have multiple logical networks.

Frame mismatches generally cause more traffic on the wire and may use precious routing resources of a device on the network. The following are examples of frame mismatches:

**No Server Found** A frame mismatch can occur when a client communicates using one frame type (Ethernet_802.3, for example) and the server uses another frame type (Ethernet_802.2, for example), as shown in Figure 2.12.

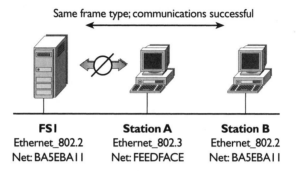

Same frame type; communications successful

**F I G U R E   2.12**

*A NetWare client using the Ethernet_802.3 frame cannot communicate with a server that supports only the Ethernet_802.2 frame type.*

| **FS1** | **Station A** | **Station B** |
|---------|---------------|---------------|
| Ethernet_802.2 | Ethernet_802.3 | Ethernet_802.2 |
| Net: BA5EBA11 | Net: FEEDFACE | Net: BA5EBA11 |

**Server Performs Frame Translation Routing** If a client is on a network that has a server with the same frame type and the desired frame type, that server can actually become a router to the intended server, as shown in Figure 2.13. In Figure 2.13, the client sends 802.3 frames to FS2. FS2 sees that the packet is addressed to the other logical network (the one that supports Ethernet_802.2), and it routes it back onto the same cabling system with the new frame. The server FS1 transmits its reply to FS2 using the Ethernet_802.2 frame type. FS2, in turn, routes the packet onto the Ethernet_802.3 network to the requesting client station.

Frame translation problems are generally easy to catch. On the network, you will see two requests followed by two replies. If you look inside the packets at the IPX layer, you can see the only differences between the requests are that the frame types and the hop count will be one higher on the second request packet (because the packet has been routed from one logical network to another). Of course, the MAC addresses are different, as well.

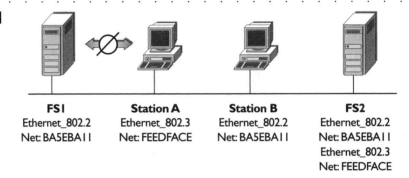

**FS1**
Ethernet_802.2
Net: BA5EBA11

**Station A**
Ethernet_802.3
Net: FEEDFACE

**Station B**
Ethernet_802.2
Net: BA5EBA11

**FS2**
Ethernet_802.2
Net: BA5EBA11
Ethernet_802.3
Net: FEEDFACE

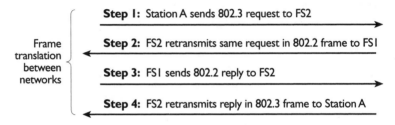

Frame
translation
between
networks

**Step 1:** Station A sends 802.3 request to FS2

**Step 2:** FS2 retransmits same request in 802.2 frame to FS1

**Step 3:** FS1 sends 802.2 reply to FS2

**Step 4:** FS2 retransmits reply in 802.3 frame to Station A

Overloaded networks, faulty networks, and frame errors are the three types of errors that you should look for when you check out the health of your network. Next, let's look at where to place your analyzer to ensure that you are seeing all the network communications and forming an accurate opinion as to the LAN/WAN state.

## Where to Place Your Analyzer on an Ethernet Network

The ideal location for your analyzer varies depending upon the layout of your network cabling system and interconnecting devices. By knowing which devices "localize" traffic, you can determine where analyzers or analyzer agents should be placed.

## DEVICES AFFECTING PLACEMENT

The following interconnecting devices affect the placement of your analyzer:

- ▸ hubs/repeaters

- ▸ bridges

- ▸ routers

- ▸ switches

### Hubs/Repeaters

As shown in Figure 2.14, typical hubs and repeaters forward all bits from one port to the other ports. This enables you to place a single analyzer or analyzer agent on one port and see all communications that travel on any attached segment.

**NOTE**

**Some intelligent hubs can "partition off" ports that are injecting errors onto the network. When a port is partitioned, it is logically separated or removed from the network, so you can no longer see their communications with an analyzer. Generally, these hubs include some management software or error light system to alert you to partitioned ports.**

**F I G U R E   2.14**

*Hubs forward all packets to all connected devices.*

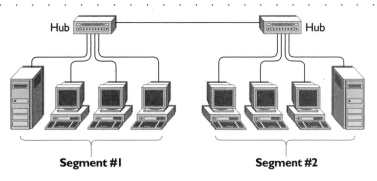

Segment #1    Segment #2

Segment #1 traffic = Segment #2 traffic

### Bridges

Bridges do not forward all traffic onto all attached segments, as shown in Figure 2.15. Unlike with a completely hub-based solution, traffic between the clients and server on Segment 1 is not forwarded through the bridge to the devices on Segment 2. Bridges do forward broadcasts, packets transmitted to an unknown hardware address, and packets destined to devices on the other side of the bridge, based on the station's MAC address.

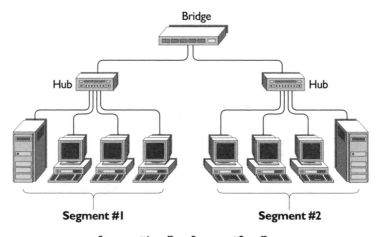

Segment #1 traffic ≠ Segment #2 traffic

### Routers

As shown in Figure 2.16, routers forward only packets addressed to another network. For example, when a client sends packets from Network 1 to a server on Network 3, the router examines the routing information contained in the packet to make forwarding decisions. The router does not contain a list of MAC addresses — it contains a list of network addresses. This type of forwarding is much more efficient on larger networks.

Another great benefit of a routed environment is that the routers can control broadcasts. Routers do not typically forward broadcast packets; they have the ability to answer a broadcast request directly.

*Routers forward only packets destined for another network.*

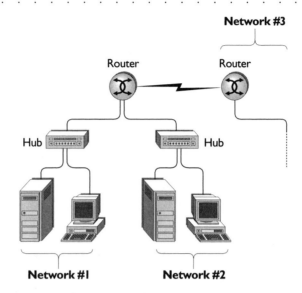

Network #1 traffic ≠ Network #2 traffic ≠ Network #3 traffic

### Switches

Like bridges and routers, switches do not forward all traffic onto all attached segments. For example, as shown in Figure 2.17, when a client on Port 3 communicates with the server on Port 1, a switch creates a virtual circuit between the two ports. The client's packets are sent only to the server, not to any other device on the switch. Switches are very similar to bridges in the forwarding decisions they make. Some switches, however, can begin forwarding packets upon receipt of the first 14 bytes (the 8-byte preamble and the 6-byte destination address field) and may forward fragments onto all attached ports. Store-and-forward switches, however, buffer packets to ensure fragments and error packets are not forwarded.

Unfortunately, some aspects of switching can cause problems. Switches forward broadcasts, multicasts, and packets to unknown addresses. They may also forward fragments onto all attached ports. Several switch vendors provide broadcast control and fragment control switches that help control this type of traffic.

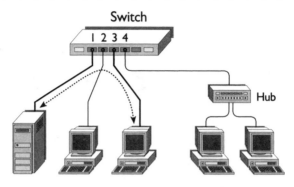

*Switches are similar to
bridges; they forward based
on the destination
MAC address.*

Port 1 to Port 3 traffic is local only

## ANALYSIS SETUPS: 10BASET NETWORKS

10BaseT networks use a twisted-pair cabling system in a star-layout design. When a NetWare client connected to the hub transmits a packet to a server, the hub acts as a multiport repeater, repeating the packet down each active port.

Figure 2.18 depicts a simple 10BaseT network segment with a stand-alone analyzer connected to one of the hub ports.

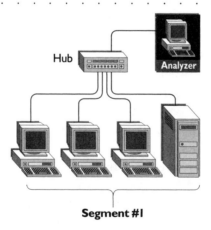

*A simple 10BaseT network
segment with a
standalone analyzer*

**Segment #1**

This network is easy to analyze because the hub repeats all packets down all connected ports. Hooking an analyzer to any port enables you to monitor all communications.

### Repeated 10BaseT Networks

As a 10BaseT network grows, one option for expansion is to daisy-chain the 10BaseT hubs together, as shown in Figure 2.19.

**NOTE** **Remember, hubs do not make any forwarding decisions; they simply repeat all signals received from one direction on to the other directions.**

As shown in Figure 2.19, you can leave the analyzer plugged into either hub and still monitor all network conversations, since the hubs just repeat all packets down all attached ports.

FIGURE 2.19

*A repeated 10BaseT network with a standalone analyzer*

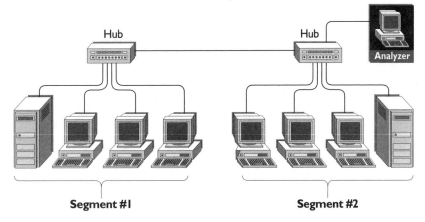

Segment #1 traffic = Segment #2 traffic

### Bridged 10BaseT Networks

Because bridges do not forward all packets as hubs and repeaters do, you must look at the communications on each side of the bridge to get a complete picture of the communications.

As shown in Figure 2.20, you can hook up multiple stand-alone analyzers to see communications on both sides of the bridge. If your network is large, however, this is not a cost-effective or time-efficient design. You might be better off using a distributed analysis solution.

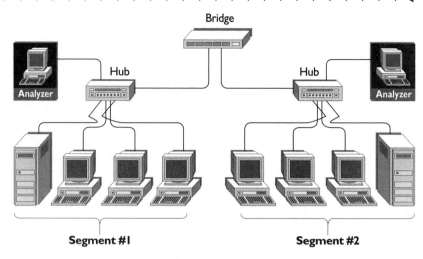

*A bridged 10BaseT network with a standalone analyzer solution*

Segment #1 traffic = Segment #2 traffic

In Figure 2.21, an analysis console is located on one side of the bridge, and analysis agents are located on both sides. The agents monitor and capture packets as defined by the console. From the console, you can see all network traffic. This is the great advantage of a distributed analysis solution.

### Routed 10BaseT Networks

Because routers also keep some traffic on the local network, an analyzer must be placed on each side of the routing device to ensure you are getting a complete picture of network communications.

As shown in Figure 2.22, several standalone analyzers — one for each network on the entire internetwork — must be placed on the routed network to ensure you can see all traffic. On a large network, this can become very costly. And moving about from one analyzer to the next is a big waste of time!

FIGURE 2.21

*A bridged 10Base2 network with a distributed analyzer solution*

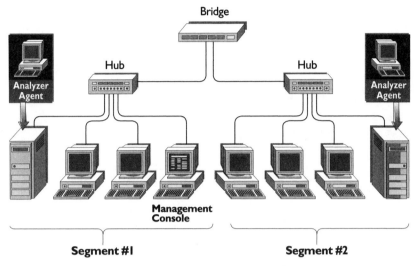

Segment #1 traffic ≠ Segment #2 traffic

FIGURE 2.22

*A routed 10BaseT network with a standalone analyzer*

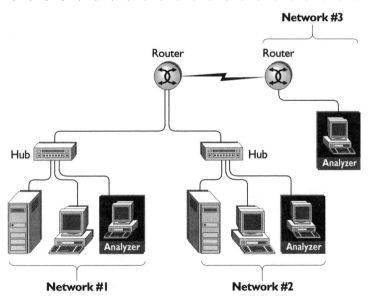

Network #1 traffic ≠ Network #2 traffic ≠ Network #3 traffic

A distributed analyzer solution, as shown in Figure 2.23, is a more cost-effective and time-efficient way of managing a large routed network. The analysis agents track communications on the local network and send the information to the management console.

FIGURE 2.23

*A routed 10BaseT network with a distributed analyzer solution*

Network #1 traffic ≠ Network #2 traffic ≠ Network #3 traffic

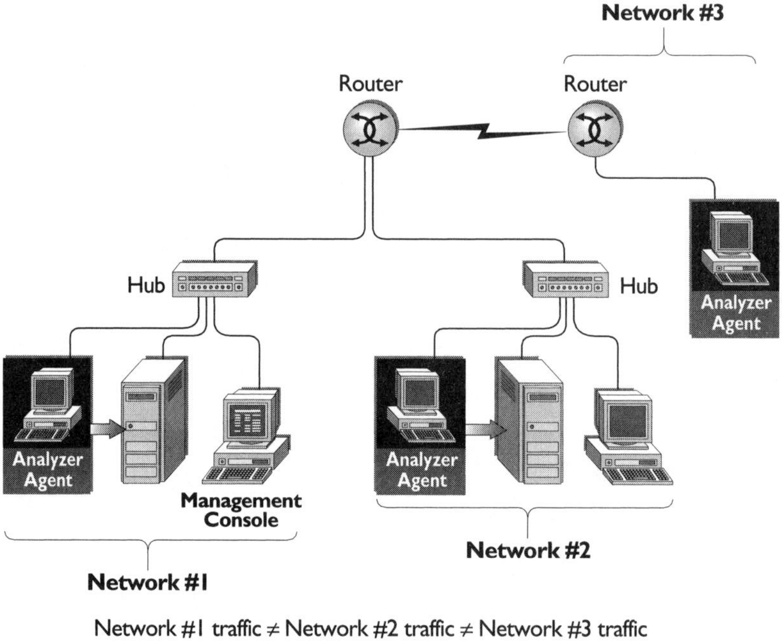

In the case of a very large network, you may find that you need multiple management consoles. This allows simultaneous monitoring of the network by two or more network technicians.

### Switched 10BaseT Networks

Switched technology enables you to reduce overall network load by connecting clients to a virtual network segment. When a client sends a request to a server, the switch does not repeat the packet on all active ports as a hub does. The switch only forwards the packet to the destination port. If the packet is destined to the broadcast address or an unknown destination address, however, it is forwarded to all attached ports.

Switched networks present a problem to the typical analyzer. If you connect a typical analyzer into one of the switch ports, you cannot "eavesdrop" on conversations. You have three primary ways of monitoring switched traffic.

A distributed analyzer solution that places an agent on the NetWare server, such as ManageWise, enables you to listen to all communications to and from that server, as shown in Figure 2.24. On a switched network, this is the best way to monitor all NetWare traffic, but it does not enable you to see all peer-to-peer traffic between clients.

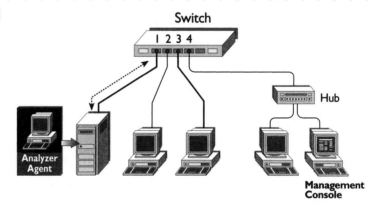

FIGURE 2.24

*A switched 10BaseT network segment with a distributed analyzer*

Standard NetWare file reads and writes use a client-server type of communication architecture in which NetWare clients send requests to the NetWare servers and the servers send reply packets back. By tracking all traffic to and from the server, you can see most NetWare communications. Not all applications and protocols are designed that way, though.

Some applications, such as FTP (File Transfer Protocol), allow the serving software (daemon) to sit on a client station. When another client wants to transfer a file using FTP, the communications flow directly from station to station, bypassing the NetWare server. You cannot track this type of communication by using an analysis agent on the NetWare server — the server cannot see the communication through the switch.

### Switch Monitoring

Many switches include the ability to configure a monitor port, allowing you to plug an analyzer directly into that switch port to see traffic that it is handling.

Three levels of switch monitoring are possible: port monitoring, circuit monitoring, and switch monitoring.

> ▸ *Port monitoring.* Port monitoring enables you to focus on all packets to and from a specific port. For example, if you wanted to track all communications to and from SERV1, you could choose to monitor that specific port only.

> ▸ *Circuit monitoring.* Circuit monitoring is used to track a specific conversation between devices connected to a switch. For example, if you wanted to track all communications between SERV1 and Fred, you could monitor a circuit that included ports 1 and 3 on the switch.

> ▸ *Switch monitoring.* Switch monitoring enables you to watch all communications flowing through a switch regardless of source or destination port.

In order to monitor a switched environment, you could connect an analyzer, such as Network General's Sniffer, directly into a switch's monitor port as shown in Figure 2.25.

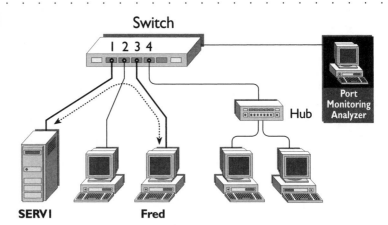

Switch

1 2 3 4

Hub

Port Monitoring Analyzer

**SERV1**    **Fred**

**TIP**

**If you typically use more than one analyzer simultaneously, you can connect a four-port hub to the monitor port through a crossover cable (or use a hub with a single crossover port and connect that port directly to the monitor port) and then plug your analyzers into the hub to capture all traffic simultaneously.**

**X-REF**

**For more information on Network General products, refer to Chapter 5.**

As shown in Figure 2.26, you can work around the switched network problem by extending your NetWare servers and a standalone analyzer off a 10BaseT hub. This is not the cleanest approach, but you will be able to see all traffic to and from the server simply by using a standalone analyzer.

*A switched 10BaseT network segment with a standalone analyzer*

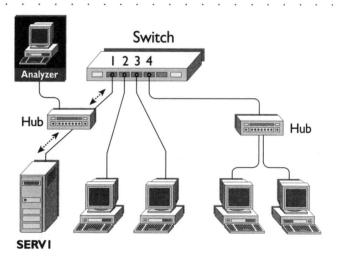

## ANALYSIS SETUPS: 10BASE2 NETWORKS

While 10BaseT is designed as a distributed star, 10Base2 networks are designed in a linear bus. When you connect an analyzer into a 10Base2 network, you can see all communications exchanged between devices on the local side of bridges, routers, and switches, just as with 10BaseT.

Figure 2.27 shows a stand-alone analyzer connected to a single-segment 10Base2 network. Since there are no bridges, routers, or switches on this network, we can see all communications from this one standalone analyzer.

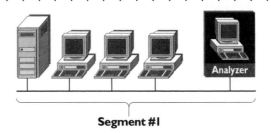

**FIGURE 2.27**

*A simple 10Base2 network segment with a standalone analyzer*

Segment #1

### Repeated 10Base2 Networks

10Base2 repeaters simply do what their name implies: they repeat. They repeat bits from one segment of the network to the other segment of the network. As shown in Figure 2.28, we can connect the analyzer to either segment to track communications.

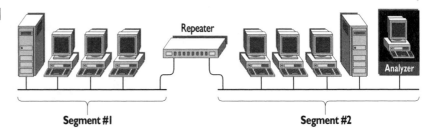

**FIGURE 2.28**

*A repeated 10Base2 network with a standalone analyzer*

Segment #1          Segment #2

### Bridged 10Base2 Networks

Because bridges do not forward all packets onto attached networks, we must place a standalone analyzer (as shown in Figure 2.29) or an analyzer agent (as shown in Figure 2.30) on each side of the bridge.

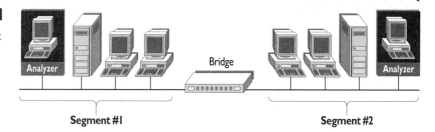

**FIGURE 2.29**

*A bridged 10Base2 network with a standalone analyzer solution*

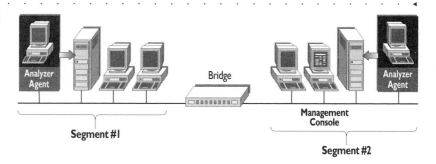

**FIGURE 2.30**

*A bridged 10Base2 network with a distributed analyzer solution*

### Routed 10Base2 Networks

Routers forward only packets that are destined to another network; therefore, we must place an analyzer on each side of a routing device, as shown in Figure 2.31.

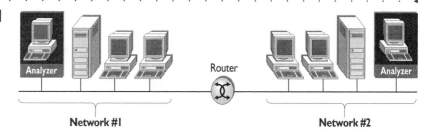

**FIGURE 2.31**

*A routed 10Base2 network with a standalone analyzer*

Using a distributed solution, you can place a management console anywhere on the network as long as an analysis agent is located somewhere on each network, as shown in Figure 2.32. The analysis agents track traffic and report communication information to the management console regardless of its location.

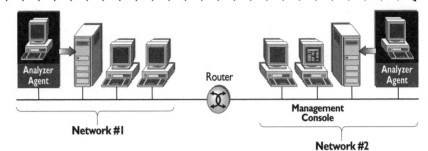

F I G U R E    2.32

*A routed 10Base2 network with a distributed analyzer solution*

## Summary

As we've discussed in this chapter, there are a number of reasons to place an analyzer on an Ethernet network — and several ways to design your analysis solution.

**For more information on the different types of analyzers (standalone, distributed, and port-attached), refer to Chapter 4.**

X-REF

In the next chapter, we'll focus on Token Ring networks and how to design an appropriate analysis solution for a token-passing ring system.

# CHAPTER 3

# Analysis 101 for
# Token Ring Networks

**A**aaaah, good old Token Ring. There are two distinct camps on the Token Ring issue: those who hate Token Ring with a passion and think it should be banned from all networks in existence, and those who have a healthy respect for its robust self-managing (and sometimes suicidal) nature. I definitely fit in the latter category. I have long maintained that if you can successfully troubleshoot a Token Ring network, you'll never be unemployed.

In this chapter, we'll examine the Token Ring events that can occur that might signal trouble. Interestingly, Token Ring networks have the inherent ability to spot a number of problems and resolve them through the Token Ring protocol. For example, if a Token Ring device is transmitting bad frames, it will remove itself from the ring to perform a self-test. If the device fails the self-test, it remains off the ring. If the device can reset itself and fix its problem, it may return to the ring. As a protocol analyst, you can see this process occurring, but you don't have to take any action.

## How Token Ring Communications Work

Let's take a brief look at how the communications should look on a healthy Token Ring network. First, we'll examine how the token-passing system works and examine the types of Token Ring networks available today. Then we'll look at the two Token Ring frame types and the types of management processes that occur on a typical ring. Finally, we'll examine the errors that you should look for on your Token Ring network and the various methods for problem resolution.

### TOKEN-PASSING RING TECHNOLOGY

On a Token Ring network, a station or device must receive a token before it can transmit onto the cable. A properly performing ring only has a single token on it at any time. The token travels in a counterclockwise direction around the ring, as do all other Token Ring communications.

When a station has something to transmit (data or a management frame), it waits for a token. Upon receipt of a token on the cable, the station is allowed to transmit a single frame.

Each active Token Ring station acts as a repeater. When a data frame is transmitted by a station, as shown in Figure 3.1, it travels counterclockwise around the ring and is repeated by Stations B, C, and D. As the frame is repeated, the stations view the frame's contents to see if it is addressed to them. If the frame is addressed to Station C, for example, Station C buffers a copy of the frame and toggles a set of four bits of the original frame before repeating it back out on the wire. The bits that Station C toggles indicate that Station C recognized its address and copied the frame; these are called the address recognized indicator (ARI) and frame copied indicator (FCI) bits.

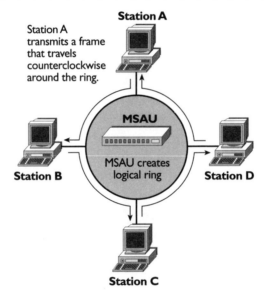

**FIGURE 3.1**

*Frames and tokens always travel counterclockwise around the ring.*

Station A transmits a frame that travels counterclockwise around the ring.

**Station A**

**MSAU**

MSAU creates logical ring

**Station B**

**Station D**

**Station C**

When the original sender, Station A, receives the frame back, it strips the frame from the ring and releases a token. As you will learn later in this chapter, a technology called Early Token Release (ETR) enables a station to transmit a token onto the ring immediately following transmission of the frame, without waiting for the frame to return.

Unlike Ethernet networks, Token Ring networks support a variety of management communications that use special Media Access Control (MAC) frames. These communications can enable a faulty ring to restart itself, pull off a bad network interface card, and even point directly to the location of a network problem (the fault domain). We'll take a look at these management processes and frame structures later in this chapter.

## TYPES OF TOKEN RING NETWORKS

Three basic types of Token Ring networks are commonly seen in our industry. The type of ring you are running is determined by the network cards you use, the LAN drivers you load, and the interconnecting devices installed.

**WARNING**

**Don't mix and match the three types of Token Ring cards on a single ring! They are different beasts and do not get along well with each other.**

▶ *4 Mbps Token Ring.* Still seen in a number of companies, this is the old workhorse Token Ring network. All data and tokens travel at a rate of 4 Mbps around the ring.

▶ *16 Mbps Token Ring.* The basic functionality is the same as 4 Mbps Token Ring, but the data rate is now 16 Mbps.

▶ *16 Mbps Token Ring with Early Token Release (ETR).* Early Token Release technology enables a ring station to transmit a free token immediately after a frame. The next station in the ring repeats the frame, as usual, and can then use the token following it to pop another frame onto the network. The second station places a token on the ring immediately following the new frame. ETR enables a large ring to have multiple data frames on the ring simultaneously.

## TOKEN RING FRAME, TOKEN, AND ABORT DELIMITER STRUCTURES

Unlike Ethernet, which has only four different frames that travel on a NetWare network, Token Ring has a mixture of communications that occur. These include Token Ring data frames (with or without source routing fields), Token Ring_SNAP data frames (with or without source routing fields), MAC (Media Access Control) or management frames, Tokens, and Abort Delimiters. Let's examine each of these Token Ring communications to see how they are displayed on an analyzer screen.

**NOTE**

**Typical analyzers don't capture or display tokens or abort delimiters.**

### Token Ring Frame Structure

The basic NetWare Token Ring frame format includes all the required 802.5 fields as well as the 802.2 Logical Link Control (LLC) fields. If this frame is used to transport NetWare data over IPX, the IPX header begins after the 802.2 fields, as shown in Figure 3.2.

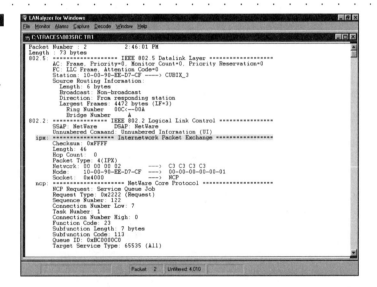

**FIGURE 3.2**

*If the Token Ring frame structure is used for NetWare data, the IPX header begins immediately following the 802.2 fields.*

If the frame is a MAC frame, the MAC information begins immediately following the 802.2 fields, as shown in Figure 3.3. No routing header is required for MAC frames because they are localized to the attached ring and cannot be forwarded or routed through the network by a bridge or router.

**NOTE**

**The standard Token Ring frame structure actually begins with a one-byte field called the Start Delimiter—this is similar to the Ethernet preamble in that it signals the beginning of the frame. Analyzers don't show you the contents of this field, but you can assume that it is there.**

FIGURE 3.3

*If the Token Ring frame structure is used for management information, the MAC information begins immediately following the 802.2 fields.*

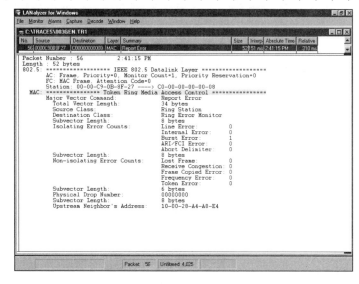

This frame type can be bound to Novell's IPX/SPX protocol stack or TCP/IP.

### Token Ring_SNAP Frame Structure

The SNAP frame structure also supports AppleTalk communications and includes the SNAP fields in the 802.2 portion of the header, as shown in Figure 3.4.

FIGURE 3.4

*If the Token Ring_SNAP frame structure is used for NetWare data, the IPX header begins immediately following the 802.2 SNAP fields.*

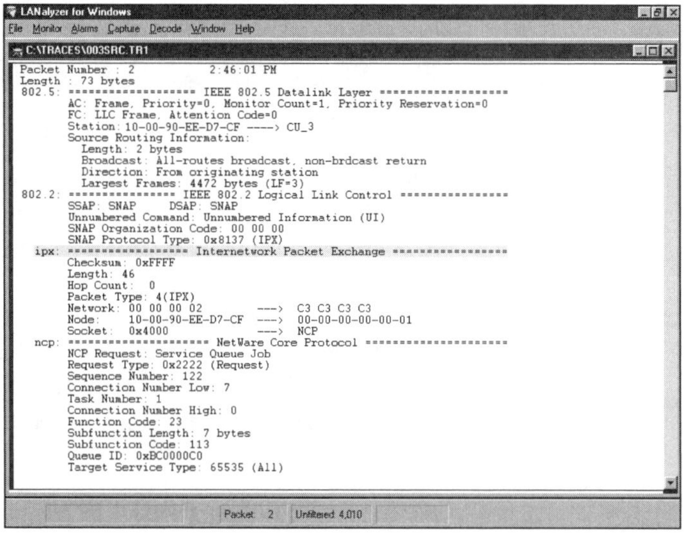

This frame type can be bound to Novell's IPX/SPX protocol stack, AppleTalk, or TCP/IP.

### Source Routing Frame Structure

Source route bridging, developed by IBM, requires that each device on a ring maintain a source route table and define the data path inside each frame it transmits. This does require additional software at each end of the communications (ROUTE.COM for 16-bit NetWare clients, SROUTE.NLM for 32-bit NetWare clients, and ROUTE.NLM on NetWare servers), as shown in Figure 3.5.

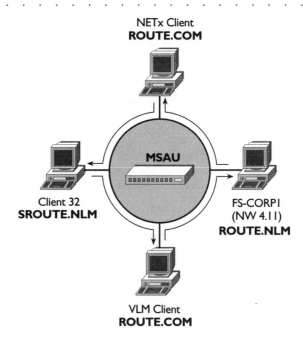

**F I G U R E   3.5**

*Each end of source-routed communications must load additional software to support source routing.*

NETx Client
**ROUTE.COM**

**MSAU**

Client 32
**SROUTE.NLM**

FS-CORP1
(NW 4.11)
**ROUTE.NLM**

VLM Client
**ROUTE.COM**

When source routing is used, the frame contains route information, as shown in Figure 3.6. The direction field (contained in the 802.5 portion of the header) indicates that this is coming from the originating station.

FIGURE 3.6

*The direction field indicates that this source-routed frame is coming from the originating station.*

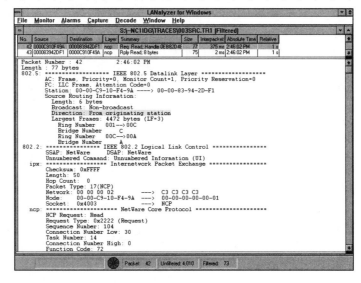

FIGURE 3.6

*The direction field indicates that this source-routed frame is coming from the originating station.*

When the receiver replies, it can simply change the direction field value to indicate that the frame is going the opposite direction along the same path from the responding station. Source route bridges will read the path information in reverse order, as shown in Figure 3.7.

FIGURE 3.7

*When the direction field indicates that the frame is from the responding station, source route bridges read the routing information in reverse order.*

Source routing information can be a tremendous help when you're analyzing Token Ring communications. Each frame contains the exact path that the frame took. For example, in Figure 3.8, we can draw a conceptual diagram of the frame's path, thereby giving us a good start on diagramming the network layout.

▶ . . . . . . . . . . . . . . . . . . . . . . . . . . . . . ◀

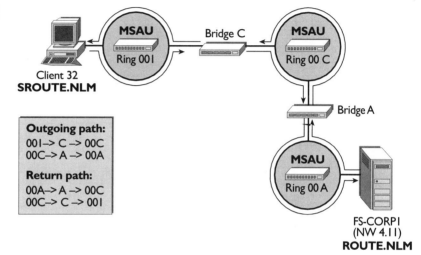

F I G U R E   3 . 8

*Based on the source routing information contained in a packet, we can create an initial drawing of the Token Ring network layout.*

## Token Ring Management Frames

Management frames, called MAC (Media Access Control) frames, enable Token Ring clients to report errors they have seen on the network, initialize their adapter parameters for the ring, and even test the integrity of the ring. You can see a total of 25 different MAC frames on your Token Ring network.

MAC frames contain management information immediately following the Token Ring header, as shown in Figure 3.9. The Major Vector Command field indicates the type of MAC frame being transmitted.

▶ • • • • • • • • • • • • • • • • • • • • • • • • • • • • • • • • • • • • ◀

**FIGURE 3.9**

*A Report Error MAC frame is sent from a ring station to the Ring Error Monitor; it indicates a Lost Frame count of 1.*

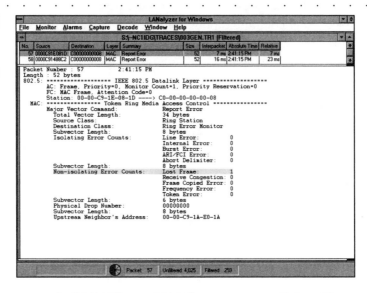

You can see a total of 25 different MAC frames on your Token Ring network. They are separated into four distinct categories, as shown here:

**Station Initialization**

> Lobe Media Test
>
> Duplicate Address Test
>
> Request Initialization
>
> Initialize Ring Station
>
> Change Parameters

**Media Control**

> Beacon
>
> Claim Token
>
> Ring Purge
>
> Active Monitor Present
>
> Standby Monitor Present

**Error Reporting**

> Report Error
>
> Report Monitor Errors
>
> Report Ring Poll Failure

### Station Management

>> Report New Monitor
>> Report SUA Change
>> Remove Ring Station
>> Transmit Forward
>> Report Transmit Forward
>> Response
>> Request Station State
>> Request Station Attachment
>> Request Station Address
>> Report Station State
>> Report Station Attachment
>> Report Station Address

You can always tell the type of frame by the Major Vector Command field in the MAC portion of the packet.

### Token Ring Functional Addresses and Broadcast Addresses

In Token Ring technology, a number of assigned addresses are used to address various functional Token Ring processes. These are referred to as *functional addresses*. These functional addresses include:

| | |
|---|---|
| C0-00-00-00-00-01 | Active Monitor |
| C0-00-00-00-00-02 | Ring Parameter Server |
| C0-00-00-00-00-08 | Ring Error Monitor |
| C0-00-00-00-00-10 | Configuration Report Server |

**NOTE**

**Only the Active Monitor process *must* be running on a ring. All other processes listed are optional and typically require you to purchase additional software to enable them.**

**Active Monitor.**   The Active Monitor process is required on each ring. This is a transparent function that is assumed by one ring station or device (usually the station or device that has been running the longest on the ring). The device that is acting as Active Monitor starts the Ring Poll process and constantly checks the integrity of the ring to ensure that a good token is released by stations on a regular basis.

**The Ring Poll process is covered later in this chapter.**

X-REF

The Active Monitor is selected through the Monitor Contention process (covered later in this chapter). There is always one Active Monitor for each ring of a Token Ring network.

**Ring Parameter Server.**   The Ring Parameter Server can provide startup configuration information to a ring station while the station is initializing onto the ring. For example, if you chose, you could have the Ring Parameter Server set the ring device's error reporting timer to every one minute (instead of the default two seconds).

The Ring Parameter Server is an optional function. Some ring management software and devices (such as a bridges) provide Ring Parameter Server functionality. Typically, however, it is unnecessary.

**Ring Error Monitor.**   The Ring Error Monitor acts as a Token Ring management data collector. By default, ring stations report any known errors they have seen in each two-second interval to the Ring Error Monitor. If the station has not seen an error within the two-second interval, it will not send a frame to the Ring Error Monitor.

The Ring Error Monitor is an optional function and typically exists on a ring only if you have purchased some ring management software or some device (such as a bridge) that might provide this functionality automatically.

**Configuration Report Server.**   Configuration Report Servers can be used to tweak the network's performance after stations have already initialized to the ring. Besides being able to set all the parameters that the Ring Parameter Server can, the Configuration Report Server can also remove stations from the ring and request information from stations (such as the station's state, address, and attachment information).

**Whereas IBM and IEEE refer to this function as the Configuration Report Server, Texas Instruments refers to this function as the Network Manager.**

NOTE

The Configuration Report Server is an optional function. If you've purchased ring management software or some device (such as a bridge) that provides this functionality, you may see more Configuration Report Server traffic.

**NOTE**

**One of my clients discovered that all their bridges were "chatting" on the wire consistently. We determined (using an analyzer) that the bridges shipped with the Configuration Report Server functionality enabled. The bridges were polling ring stations for attachment and address information every two seconds. This "feature" was not documented in any of the vendor literature and served no purpose on the network. The client upgraded the bridges to models that did not enable any functional communications by default.**

### Management Processes of the Ring

Token Ring networks also support a variety of error checking and management processes that help ensure the integrity of the ring. These processes include the Ring Station Initialization process, the Ring Poll process, the Monitor Contention process, the Ring Purge process, and the Beacon process.

Let's take a quick look at each of these processes and the resulting traffic on the ring.

**The Ring Station Initialization Process**   Token Ring adapters must perform an initialization process to ensure they are functioning properly and may be permitted onto the ring.

Before the adapter can even transmit onto the ring, it must perform a lobe media test by sending 2,047 Lobe Media management frames up the cable and one Duplicate Address management frame on the lobe loopback path. These frames simply travel up the cable to the Multistation Access Unit (MSAU) on the transmit cable pair and directly back to the adapter on the receive cable pair.

The purpose of this test is to ensure that the Token Ring adapter can transmit, receive, and recognize its own address.

Upon successful completion of this process, the adapter can then begin to enter the ring. In order to enter the ring, the adapter must activate the relays in the MSAU by sending an electrical current (the *phantom current*) to the MSAU. This opens the relays on that port.

The adapter waits for up to 18 seconds for either an Active Monitor Present frame, a Standby Monitor Present frame, or a Ring Purge frame to circle the ring. If the station does not see any of these frames, the station enters the Monitor Contention process to become the Active Monitor. The Monitor Contention process is covered later in this section.

If the adapter does see one of the required frames, it begins entering the ring by sending two Duplicate Address frames out onto the cabling system. A Duplicate Address frame is a management frame that is addressed back to the originating station's address, as shown in Figure 3.10. If another station buffers and copies this frame as if it were addressed to that station by setting the ARI/FCI bits to 1, there must be two Token Ring cards with the same address on a single ring. The entering station will not complete the Station Initialization process if this happens.

**FIGURE 3.10**

*The Duplicate Address management frame*

If the Duplicate Address management frames are received with the ARI/FCI bits set to 0, the station next transmits a Report SUA Change frame to the Configuration Report Server. This SUA (Stored Upstream Address) indicates that a new station has entered the ring and the station is reporting its new upstream neighbor's address. The station must participate in the Ring Poll process if it is in progress, and finally the station must transmit a Request Initialization frame to the Ring Parameter Server's functional address. If a Ring Parameter Server exists, it can set the adapter parameters at this time. Adapter parameters include:

▸ Physical Drop Number (default = 0)

▸ Local Ring Number (default = 0)

▸ Soft Error Report Timer (default = 2 seconds)

▸ Enable Function Class Mask (default = on)

▸ Allowed Access Priority (default = 3)

▸ All Error Counters (default = 0)

Figure 3.11 shows the entire process as it appears on an analyzer trace screen.

**FIGURE 3.11**

*The Station Initialization process as seen on an analyzer*

**The Ring Poll Process**    The Ring Poll process occurs every seven seconds and is used to ensure that every station in the ring knows the address of its *nearest active upstream neighbor* (NAUN), as shown in Figure 3.12. Why should every Token Ring station know its NAUN's address? Each station needs someone to blame if it spots a problem. Think of each ring station as a two-year-old child. If there's a problem, the ring station points to its NAUN and begins to wail that the NAUN caused the problem. Whether this is true or not, it is the nature of Token Ring (and two-year-olds).

*The Ring Poll process enables all stations on a ring to know their nearest active upstream neighbor.*

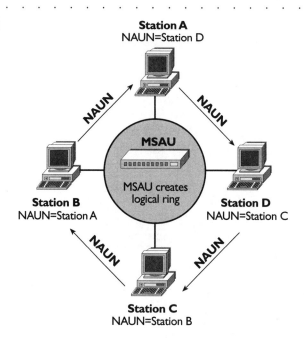

The Ring Poll process is started by the Active Monitor every seven seconds when the Active Monitor broadcasts an Active Monitor Present (AMP) frame onto the network, as shown in Figure 3.13. The next active station on the network, Station B, buffers the frame and changes the ARI/FCI bits to indicate that the frame has been received by the intended recipient. All other stations simply repeat the frame around the ring. Upon receipt of the AMP frame, the Active Monitor strips it off the ring and releases a token.

The station that buffered the AMP frame now knows that the AMP is its upstream neighbor (the ARI/FCI bits were set to 0 in the AMP, indicating that no other stations saw the frame before Station B). Station B now sends a Standby Monitor Present frame, as shown in Figure 3.14. The next station, Station C, buffers the frame, sets the ARI/FCI bits to 1, and repeats the frame back onto the ring.

FIGURE 3.13

The Active Monitor
Present frame

FIGURE 3.14

The Standby Monitor
Present frame

Upon receipt of its Standby Monitor Present frame, Station B strips the frame off the ring and issues a token. The next station, Station C, now transmits its own Standby Monitor Present frame.

This process continues until the Active Monitor sees a Standby Monitor Present frame with the ARI/FCI bits set to 0. The Active Monitor then assumes that the Ring Poll process is finished and all active Standby Monitor stations have participated.

Figure 3.15 shows what the Ring Poll process looks like on an analyzer. Notice that the process begins with an Active Monitor Present frame. This is followed by a Standby Monitor Present frame from each active station in the order their logical order on the ring. Another Active Monitor Present frame is sent exactly seven seconds after the first Active Monitor Present frame. The entire Ring Poll process must be able to be completed within a seven-second time frame for the ring to function properly.

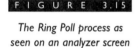

**F I G U R E  3.15**

*The Ring Poll process as seen on an analyzer screen*

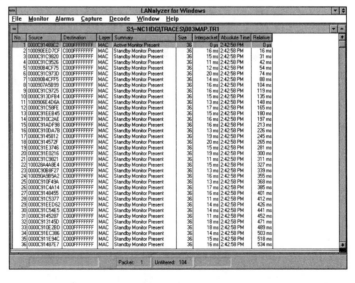

**The Monitor Contention Process**  The Monitor Contention process occurs when it appears that there is no Active Monitor on the ring or the Active Monitor appears to be failing. The first station that notices the Active Monitor's absence or faulty performance transmits a Claim Token frame.

NOTE
**The Claim Token is actually a management frame, as shown in Figure 3.16, not just a token. The term *token* denotes, however, that the frame can be transmitted without receiving a token first. Although all other communications require a token for "permission to transmit," the Monitor Contention process assumes there is no token available at the time the problem must be resolved.**

FIGURE 3.16

*The Claim Token frame*

In Figure 3.17, Station A has failed as the Active Monitor and Station B is transmitting a Claim Token. The Claim Token contains the address of the transmitting station. This address is used to determine which station should be the Active Monitor in the case of two or more aggressive stations that are configured to participate in the claiming process.

NOTE
**Most network interface cards are configured to be passive by default.**

The station will transmit at least three Claim Tokens onto the ring. All ring stations will repeat the Claim Token back onto the ring. When the originating station receives three of its own Claim Tokens back, it becomes the Active Monitor.

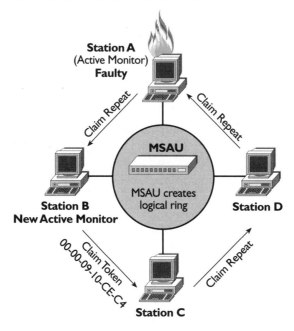

*The Monitor Contention process is started by the first station to notice that the Active Monitor is absent or not functioning properly.*

Figure 3.18 shows a sample Monitor Contention trace. The processes occurring after the three Claim Tokens indicate that a new Active Monitor has been selected. A new Active Monitor must clean up the ring (using the Ring Purge process) and report to the Configuration Report Server that it is the new Active Monitor.

*The Monitor Contention process as seen on an analyzer screen*

| No. | Source | Destination | Layer | Summary | Size | Interpacket | Absolute Time | Relative |
|-----|--------|-------------|-------|---------|------|-------------|---------------|----------|
| 22 | 0000C910CEC4 | C000FFFFFFFF | MAC | Claim Token | 36 | 0 µs | 3:19:32 PM | 34 s |
| 23 | 0000C910CEC4 | C000FFFFFFFF | MAC | Claim Token | 36 | 0 µs | 3:19:32 PM | 34 s |
| 24 | 0000C910CEC4 | C000FFFFFFFF | MAC | Claim Token | 36 | 0 µs | 3:19:32 PM | 34 s |
| 25 | 0000C910CEC4 | C000FFFFFFFF | MAC | Ring Purge | 36 | 0 µs | 3:19:32 PM | 34 s |
| 26 | 0000C910CEC4 | C00000000008 | MAC | Report Error | 52 | 0 µs | 3:19:32 PM | 34 s |
| 27 | 0000C910CEC4 | C00000000010 | MAC | Report New Monitor | 56 | 0 µs | 3:19:32 PM | 34 s |
| 28 | 0000C910CEC4 | C000FFFFFFFF | MAC | Active Monitor Present | 36 | 0 µs | 3:19:32 PM | 34 s |
| 29 | 0000C90869C1 | 0000C910CEC4 | MAC | Request Station Address | 26 | 6 s | 3:19:38 PM | 40 s |
| 30 | 0000C910CEC4 | 0000C90869C1 | MAC | Report Station Address | 56 | 0 µs | 3:19:38 PM | 40 s |

**M:\TRACES\CDBEACON.TR1**

**The Ring Purge Process**     The Ring Purge process is started by the Active Monitor when it notices a fatal flaw in the ring operation, such as the absence of a token or frame for a specified length of time—the *T(good_token) timer*. The

Active Monitor does not have to wait for a token to start this process—after all, we're assuming there may not even be a token on the ring.

**The T(good_token) timer value is 2.6 seconds.**

NOTE

The Ring Purge frame can be generated only by the Active Monitor. If a momentary break in the ring caused the problem, all stations repeat the Ring Purge frame, as shown in Figure 3.19. When the Active Monitor receives a Ring Purge frame that has circled the entire ring, it assumes the ring is now functional and releases a new token.

FIGURE  3.19

*Once a Ring Purge frame is received back by the Active Monitor, the Ring Purge process is completed.*

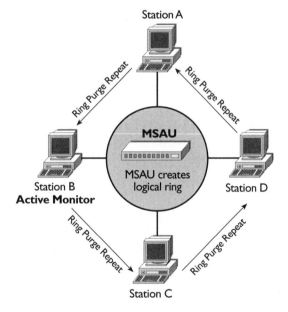

Station A

Ring Purge Repeat

Ring Purge Repeat

**MSAU**

MSAU creates logical ring

Station B
**Active Monitor**

Station D

Ring Purge Repeat

Ring Purge Repeat

Station C

**If your analyzer does not see any Ring Purge frames but you are certain that the Ring Purge process is under way, it is likely that your analyzer is downstream from the break in the ring.**

TIP

Seeing a small number of Ring Purge frames is normal—the ring is naturally broken when stations enter or leave the ring, as shown in Figure 3.20.

*The Ring Purge process as seen on an analyzer*

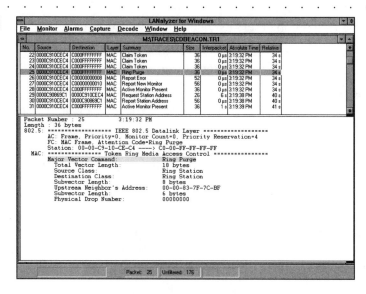

If the ring cannot recover from the Ring Purge process, the next step in recovery is the dreaded Beacon process.

**The Beacon Process**   If you've ever worked on a Token Ring network, you are probably familiar with the dreaded Beacon process. In fact, however, the Beacon process is one of the most powerful processes for getting a nonfunctioning ring back online.

Typically, the device that is directly downstream from a break in the ring notices that no data or management frames are traveling around the ring, and the device begins to *beacon*. Beaconing is simply the process of blaming your upstream neighbor for the problem. Every Token Ring station assumes that its upstream neighbor is at fault if an error occurs, as shown in Figure 3.21.

**Station Initialization processes cannot succeed once the beacon process has begun. That simply means that no new stations can enter a beaconing ring.**

NOTE

The Beacon frame contains the upstream neighbor's address, as shown in Figure 3.22, and is transmitted every 20 milliseconds without waiting for a token. All stations go into *Beacon Repeat* mode and repeat the Beacon frame back onto the ring. Once the upstream neighbor, such as Station A in Figure 3.22, receives eight Beacon frames, it must remove itself from the ring and perform a self-test.

F I G U R E   3.21

During the beaconing process, the station that detects the fault blames its upstream neighbor.

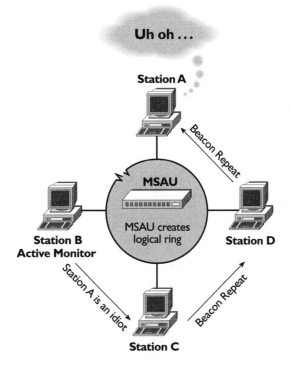

F I G U R E   3.22

A Beacon frame indicates the station that is being blamed for the problems.

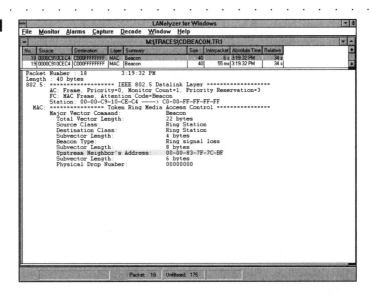

The self-test is simply the lobe media check described earlier in the "Station Initialization Process" section. There are three possible endings to the Beacon process:

1 • Station B fails its lobe media check and removes itself from the ring, thereby fixing the open ring. The beaconing station begins to receive its beacons back, stops beaconing, and enters Monitor Contention.

2 • Station B passes its lobe media check and reenters the ring in Beacon Repeat mode. Since there is still a break in the ring, however, the beacons are not received back by the beaconing station. After 16 seconds of beaconing, the beaconing station, Station C, removes itself from the ring and performs a lobe media check. If it fails, it remains off the ring. Station C's downstream neighbor, Station D, starts up the beaconing process after Station C removes itself from the ring. If Station C was the problem, Station D receives its own beacons, stops beaconing, and enters Monitor Contention.

3 • Station B and Station C pass their lobe media checks. When Station C reenters the ring, it continues to beacon until someone manually intervenes and fixes the break in the ring.

Stations and devices cannot enter a beaconing ring, so your analyzer must be on the ring and active in order to capture beacon packets.

The Beacon process can be seen on an analyzer, as shown in Figure 3.23. These processes are vital to maintaining the health of the ring. Using an analyzer, you can spot and document the recovery process your ring stations typically perform.

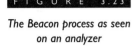

*The Beacon process as seen on an analyzer*

Now let's examine the process of reporting errors on the ring and isolating a fault domain.

# Identifying and Isolating Token Ring Errors

If you can view the communications on any Token Ring network and interpret the errors that are being reported by ring stations, you can define the health of the ring. First, however, you must understand the types of problems that typically occur on a Token Ring network and their tell-tale sign—the errors they cause. Finally, you must use the information provided by your analyzer to isolate the source of the error and pinpoint the device or process at fault.

## TOKEN RING NETWORK PROBLEMS

The most common Token Ring problems we deal with include the following: cabling issues that cause intermittent breaks in the ring, receiver congestion, misconfigured source routing, blatantly open rings, and faulty rings/excessive errors.

### Cabling Issues That Cause Intermittent Breaks in the Ring

If a Token Ring network has a faulty cabling system that causes intermittent breaks in the Token Ring protocol, ring stations will track the resulting errors as *line errors*. An excessive number of line errors reported by numerous stations on the ring indicates problems in the cabling system.

**TIP**

**You may want to invest in a cable tester if your network problems center around the cabling system. Although many analyzer manufacturers claim their products have excellent cable testing features, few of them actually work well.**

### Receiver Congestion

Receiver congestion indicates that a station recognized that a frame was addressed to it by setting the ARI bits to 1, but it could not copy the frame (and therefore it left the FCI bits still set to 0). Typically, this indicates that the destination adapter did not have enough buffer space to allocate for the incoming frame. There could be several reasons for this:

▸ The adapter is older and does not have enough on-board buffer space available.

▸ The adapter has been misconfigured to segment on-board buffers into maximum sizes, thereby limiting the number of buffers available for the typically smaller incoming frames.

▸ The application that is running on the workstation is not pulling data from the buffer fast enough to free up buffers in time for the next incoming frame.

▸ A station is *flaming*, or bombarding another station with frames.

### Misconfigured Source Routing

Consider source routing frames as their own frame type. If you have a NetWare server and client that should communicate on the same ring, either load source routing for both or do not load source routing for either.

### Blatantly Open Rings

An open ring is a dead ring. An open ring causes beaconing and can be very difficult to troubleshoot. Where does the break exist? If you do not have an analyzer on the network already, you may not be able to look into the Beacon frames to define the fault domain. This is one of the big reasons to have an analyzer on each ring at all times—just let it continue to run so that when you need to capture Beacon frames, the analyzer's adapter is already in the ring and can show you who's being blamed for all the problems.

### Faulty Rings/Excessive Errors

Every two seconds (by default), Token Ring stations must report any errors they have seen on the network. They report these errors to a multicast address for the Ring Error Monitor (whether or not one exists). With an analyzer, you can listen in on the types of errors being reported on the ring. This is an essential step in locating the fault domain on the ring, as mentioned later in this chapter.

Figure 3.24 shows a Report Error frame addressed to the Ring Error Monitor's MAC address.

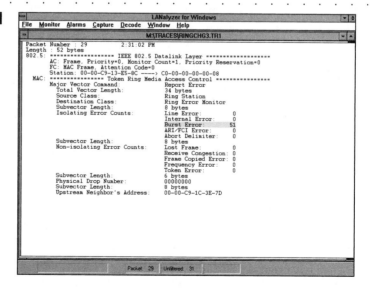

## COMMON TOKEN RING ERRORS

The following section provides a brief look at some of the most common Token Ring errors that are reported by ring stations or seen by most network analyzers. They are Abort Delimiter, A/C errors, Beaconing, Burst errors, Frame Copied errors, Frequency errors, Internal errors, Line errors, Lost Frames, Receiver Congestion, and Token errors. This section also provides basic troubleshooting tasks that should be undertaken when you identify one of these errors.

### Abort Delimiter

This error is transmitted by a station that is aborting a frame transmission because of a faulty transmission attempt (similar to a slight transmission "hiccup"). Token Ring stations can recover from this type of error without removing themselves from the Token Ring. If for some reason a station cannot recover automatically, it removes itself from the ring permanently. Replace the adapter of the station that is transmitting the abort delimiter.

### A/C Errors

A/C errors indicate that a station cannot set the Address Recognized Indicator (ARI) or Frame Copied Indicator (FCI) bits in a frame that it has recognized and copied. The error indicates a faulty adapter. Replace the adapter.

### Beaconing

Beacon frames typically indicate a serious problem on the network, such as a broken cable, port, or adapter of a station in the fault domain. Locate the station transmitting the beacons. The fault domain is between the beaconing station and that station's upstream neighbor. If beaconing is not automatically resolved, systematically check and (if required) replace the faulty component or cable in the fault domain.

### Burst Errors

Burst errors indicate that the cable "flatlined" or had no signal changes for five half-bit times (hence this error is also referred to as a Burst 5 error). This could be due to a brief disconnection in the cable, a surge of electronic noise, or a station entering or exiting the ring as its lobe attaches or removes itself from the ring.

Burst errors are considered normal on a Token Ring network because they occur when stations enter and exit the ring. If your Burst error counter is extremely high in one particular place and you are certain the upstream neighbor is not entering and exiting the ring frequently, you may want to check the integrity of the cable connected to the reporting station and its upstream neighbor.

### Frame Copied Errors

Frame Copied errors indicate the number of times a station detected a frame addressed to its specific address with either the Address Recognized Indicator (ARI) bit or the Frame Copied Indicator (FCI) bit, or both, set to 1. This condition indicates that two devices share the same address, and because of the Station Initialization process Duplicate Address Test, it should obviously never happen. If it does, replace the adapter in the station reporting the error.

### Frequency Error

This error indicates that the ring clock and the adapter clock differ by an excessive amount and the ring station must enter Monitor Contention to reestablish the integrity of the ring. This error indicates that the cabling system may be out of specification or exposed to electromagnetic interference (EMI). Check the cabling system to verify integrity and proper configuration.

### Internal Error

Internal errors are detected by a station's hardware or firmware. Stations detecting an Internal error remove themselves from the Token Ring. This message indicates that a ring station is in marginal operating condition. On an analyzer, you'll see the ring station inserting itself, removing itself and reinserting itself continuously into the ring. Replace the adapter.

### Line Errors

Line errors indicate that a station has seen a corrupt frame on the cable as the frame is copied or repeated. A high number of Line errors reported from a single station indicates a fault with the upstream neighbor's adapter—replace the adapter. A high number of line errors reported from a variety of stations indicates cabling faults—check the cable integrity.

### Lost Frames

Lost Frames indicates the number of times a station has transmitted a frame but failed to receive it back in its entirety. This could be seen in conjunction with intermittent opens (Burst 5 errors) or beacons. This is not an "isolating" error that indicates where to look for the problem, so look for other errors that occur in close time proximity with these lost frames.

### Receiver Congestion

Receiver Congestion results from a station recognizing its address in the destination field of a frame but being unable to copy the frame due to lack of buffer space. This might also signal that the destination system is hung. The system's adapter is still in the ring, but the PC is hung and does not service the network board.

Receiver Congestion might also signal a poorly configured on-board buffer or an older NIC. In this case, you could upgrade the card or reconfigure the on-board buffer space.

Be aware that some applications may also be causing this problem by not taking the data from the buffer area quickly enough. Watch the applications that are running when the Receiver Congestion errors are reported and look for a pattern.

### Token Errors

Token errors are reported only by the Active Monitor and can indicate that the Active Monitor has had to purge the ring because of one of three possible situations:

1 • The Active Monitor saw a frame or token with the Monitor bit set to binary 1, indicating it had already been repeated by the Active Monitor. This means that a token or frame has circulated the ring more than once. The Active Monitor will purge the ring and release a new token onto the ring.

2 • The Active Monitor saw a station transmit abort sequences because it detected a corrupt token or frame.

3 • The Active Monitor did not see a good token or frame within its good token timer value (typically 2.6 seconds).

## ISOLATING THE FAULT DOMAIN

By examining the errors reported on the ring, you can determine where the problems are on the ring. Typically, stations report errors that occur immediately upstream from them. For example, in Figure 3.25, if Station B continuously transmits Beacon frames onto the network, the fault domain lies between Station A's adapter and Station B's adapter.

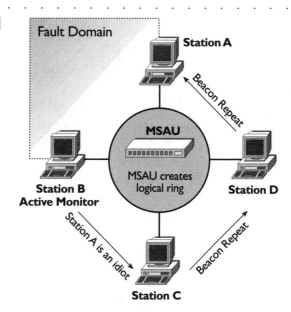

Use this simple technique when tracking the Token Ring error listed in the previous section.

# Where to Place Your Analyzer on a Token Ring Network

The ideal location for your analyzer depends on the layout of your Token Ring network. You must know which devices "localize" the traffic to determine where your analyzer or analyzer agents should be placed. The following interconnecting devices affect your analyzer placement: multistation access units/controlled access units, bridges, and routers.

Multistation access units (MSAUs) and controlled access units (CAUs) are very similar to Ethernet hubs in that they do not filter out any traffic. CAUs offer added intelligence and management capabilities beyond MSAU functions. In Token Ring, the signal from the devices, however, is not forwarded to all attached ports upon receipt, as it is in Ethernet. In Token Ring, the signal travels counterclockwise from active port to active port, as shown in Figure 3.26.

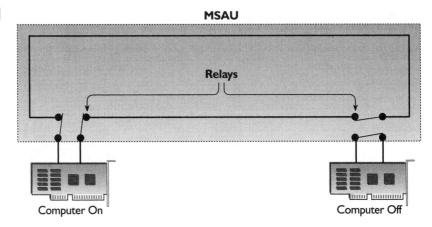

FIGURE 3.26

Frames and tokens travel counterclockwise from active port to active port.

**X-REF**

**In this chapter, we'll focus on how to set up an analysis solution for bridged and routed networks, but we do not delve into the functionality of bridges and routers. For more information on bridge and router functionality, refer to Chapter 2.**

## ANALYSIS SETUP: SINGLE RING

A single ring that uses one or more MSAUs and CAUs only requires a stand-alone analyzer. Because MSAUs and CSAUs do not filter any information from attached devices, you can place your analyzer anywhere on a MSAU and "listen in" on the frames as they circle the ring, as shown in Figure 3.27. You can use a single analyzer to monitor communications even if multiple MSAUs/CAUs are daisy-chained together using the Ring In/Ring Out ports.

FIGURE 3.27

*A single standalone analyzer can listen to all devices connected to MSAUs.*

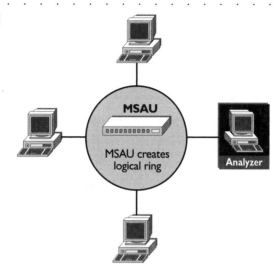

## ANALYSIS SETUP: BRIDGED RINGS

Bridges do not forward all traffic onto all attached rings. They do forward broadcasts, packets transmitted to an unknown hardware address, and packets destined for devices on the other side of the bridge, based on the station's MAC address.

Because the traffic is not the same on each attached ring, you must place an analyzer or analyzer agent on each side of the bridge, as shown in Figure 3.28.

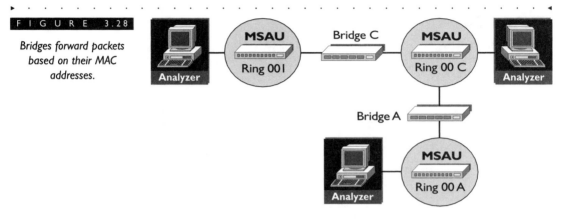

FIGURE 3.28

*Bridges forward packets based on their MAC addresses.*

Ring 001 traffic ≠ Ring 00C traffic ≠ Ring 00A traffic

## ROUTERS

Routers do not forward all traffic onto all attached rings, as shown in Figure 3.29. They only forward packets destined to other networks.

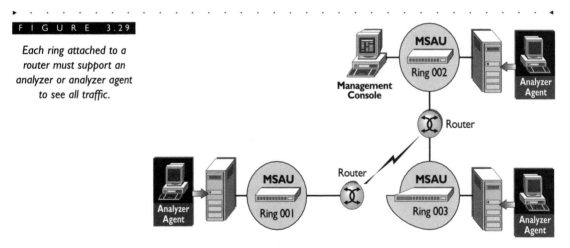

FIGURE 3.29

*Each ring attached to a router must support an analyzer or analyzer agent to see all traffic.*

Ring 001 traffic ≠ Ring 002 traffic ≠ Ring 003 traffic

## Summary

In this chapter I covered the basic analysis techniques and focus for Token Ring networks. In the next chapter, I'll examine analyzer qualities and solutions.

# CHAPTER 4

# Selecting an Analysis Solution

In this chapter, we examine the different qualities that distinguish various analyzers on the market, and we provide some details on the different types of analyzers—standalone, distributed, and port-attached. This chapter also addresses the issue of where to place your analyzer or management system for best results.

## Types of Analyzers

There are three general types of analyzers:

▸  Standalone analyzers

▸  Distributed analyzers

▸  Monitor-port analyzers

### STAND-ALONE ANALYZERS

Stand-alone analyzers capture information on the network segment they are located on, as shown in Figure 4.1. They cannot "see" across any type of device that is capable of filtering out traffic, such as a switch, a bridge, or a router. This type of analyzer is best for small to medium-sized networks without a lot of network segments. As your network begins to grow to include bridges, routers, and switches, however, you must keep in mind that a distributed analyzer or monitor port analyzer may be the best solution for your configuration.

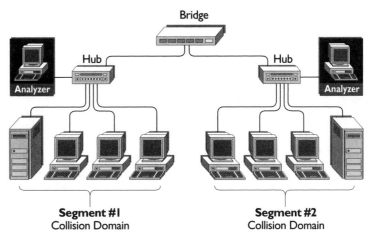

## DISTRIBUTED ANALYZERS

Distributed analyzers have a unique architecture that allows you to monitor a multisegment network from a single location— the *management console*, as shown in Figure 4.2. Distributed analyzer architecture includes both a management console and *analyzer agents*, which are deployed throughout the network on various segments. Although there are several variations on the theme of distributed analyzers, they all typically function by the same set of rules:

1 • Remote agents gather information and report traffic summary information to the console on a regular basis.

2 • If requested to by the management console, a remote analyzer agent will begin capturing network traffic.

3 • When the management console requests traffic information from the analysis agent, the agent sends the traffic summary to the console. When the management console requests a complete packet decode, the remote agent sends the entire packet selected.

Novell's ManageWise product and Network General's Distributed Sniffer provide distributed analysis solutions. Novell's ManageWise product, however, also maps the entire internetwork and provides server management agents that report statistics on server settings and performance.

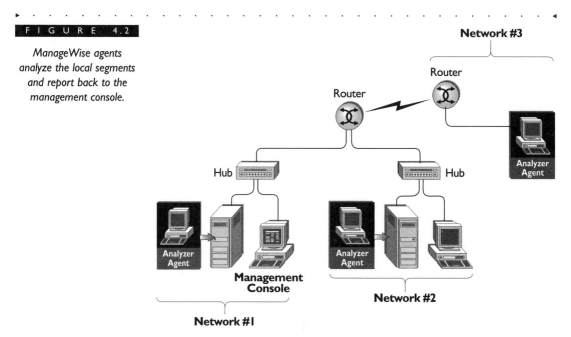

FIGURE   4.2

*ManageWise agents analyze the local segments and report back to the management console.*

Network #1 Traffic ≠ Network #2 Traffic ≠ Network #3 Traffic

**For more information on ManageWise or Distributed Sniffer, refer to Chapter 5.**

X-REF

## MONITOR-PORT ANALYZERS

Monitor-port analyzers have become a necessity for capturing and analyzing data flowing through a switch. Whereas all ports on a hub or repeater share a common backplane and any analyzer device plugged into the hub can "hear" all communications flowing between all the ports, a switch sets up a temporary circuit between the source port and destination port. Switches do not have a common backplane, and therefore they allow traffic to be isolated and thus to be hindered less by heavier traffic loads.

As shown in Figure 4.3, three types of analysis functions can be performed by monitor-port analyzers:

▸ *Port analysis.* Analysis of all traffic to and from a single switch port—a server's port, for example.

▸ *Circuit analysis.* Analysis of all communications between two specific ports—the server and Fred's workstation, for example.

▸ *Switch analysis.* Analysis of all traffic between all switch ports.

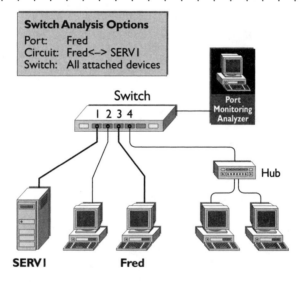

Keep in mind that there are some workarounds to placing a monitor-port solution on each switch in your internetwork. You could place analyzer agents on all NetWare servers—in the NetWare environment, just about all communications occur between clients and servers. If you analyze all traffic to your servers by placing agents on them, you are in effect seeing all NetWare traffic. You could also connect your servers, a stand-alone analyzer, and the switch into a three-port hub, as shown in Figure 4.4. This enables your LANalyzer for Windows device to monitor all traffic to and from the server without your having to install an agent on the server.

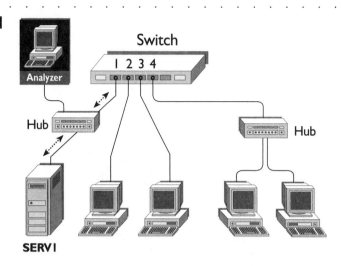

FIGURE 4.4

*You can hook up your server and a standalone analyzer to a three-port hub.*

## Choosing an Analyzer

Over the past two years, we've seen a tremendous number of network management and analyzer solutions surface in the industry. Some solutions are good; many are not so good. When you select an analyzer, keep in mind what you want to use the analyzer for and who will be using it.

**TIP**

**Make certain you get sufficient training on the analyzer operations to ensure that the analyzer is used frequently and properly. Too many analyzers sit idle in a wiring closet because no one understands how to define filters, capture packets, and print reports.**

When choosing your analyzer solution, you should consider the size of your network and the following product features:

▸ Promiscuous mode capability

▸ Media Access Control options

▸ Network size

▶ Packet monitoring

▶ Station monitoring

▶ Trending

▶ Alarm settings

▶ Packet transmit capability

▶ Filtering (pre- and post-)

▶ Portability

▶ Available decodes

▶ Expert system/interpretations

▶ Commodity-based components

▶ Interface/ease-of-use

▶ Report generation

▶ Cost

▶ Combined functionality

Let's examine each of these characteristics so that you can make an informed decision on your analyzer purchase.

## PROMISCUOUS MODE CAPABILITIES

Your analyzer station must be able to view and buffer all network communications—not just the communications addressed to the analyzer station or the broadcast address. Therefore, you want to use a promiscuous mode card and driver in that analyzer station. The term *promiscuous mode* is used to describe a network interface card and card driver characteristic that enables a device to view all traffic, including traffic destined to other devices on the network. Promiscuous mode cards/drivers should be able to buffer all network communications, including unicasts (from one single device to another single device), multicasts (from one device to a group of devices), and broadcasts (from one device to all devices).

Truly promiscuous cards/drivers should be able to monitor the following types of communications:

▶ Broadcast packets (packets addressed to all stations)

▶ Unicast packets (packets addressed to a single station)

▶ Multicast packets (packets addressed to a group of stations)

▶ Error packets (not required for Token Ring networks)

**WARNING**

**The NetWare 4.1x driver certification program required cards/drivers to buffer packets addressed to all stations, but it did not require that the card/driver pass error information to a higher layer. Although listed as "promiscuous mode" products, these cards/drivers may not work as analyzer solutions.**

The following drivers, which were shipped with LANalyzer for Windows, work with LANalyzer for Windows (versions 2.0, 2.1, and 2.2):

| VENDOR | PRODUCT |
| --- | --- |
| 3Com | 3C503 Etherlink II |
| | 3C505 Etherlink + Ethernet |
| | 3C523 Etherlink/MC |
| Cabletron | E20 |
| | E21 |
| | E2HUB |
| | EXOS |
| HP | HP MC Adapter/16 Ethernet |
| | HP PC Adapter/8, 16, 16+ Ethernet |
| IBM | PS/2 Ethernet |

| VENDOR | PRODUCT |
| --- | --- |
| Network Communications Corporation | LAN Network Probe LANalyzer Ethernet Board (LANZENET) |
| Madge | Smart 16/4 (Token Ring) |
| Anthem/Eagle/Novell | NE1000 |
|  | NE1500T |
|  | NE2_32 |
|  | NE2000 |
|  | NE2100 |
|  | NE3200 |
| SMC | Ethercard Plus |

**Contact your NIC vendor to determine if its card/drivers have the ability to work in promiscuous mode. If you are analyzing an Ethernet network, be certain to mention that you want to see errors.**

**TIP**

Remember that only your analysis-gathering system (stand-alone analyzer or analyzer agent system) needs to have a promiscuous mode card and driver. All other systems on your network can have non–promiscuous mode cards/drivers.

The ability to see errors is not required on Token Ring networks because of the natural tattle-tale behavior of Token Ring cards. By default, Token Ring cards consistently watch the network for any signs of trouble and report what they see to a Ring Error Monitor, whether or not it exists. If a card detects a potentially fatal error on the network, it begins to beacon, blaming the upstream neighbor it believes is at fault. This beaconing process helps you isolate the fault area (also referred to as the *fault domain*) on the ring.

**For more information on Token Ring, refer to Chapter 3.**

**X-REF**

## MEDIA ACCESS CONTROL OPTIONS

A variety of analyzers can be connected to Ethernet, Token Ring, FDDI, or other network types. Make sure you buy an analyzer that fits your network media access control method. Many analyzers can hook to more than one type of one network type. For example, one of our analyzers, a Network General Sniffer, supports Ethernet and Token Ring analysis. This portable analyzer has a Token Ring PCMCIA card and an Ethernet PCMCIA card installed.

By placing both cards in your analyzer system, you can connect to one network type to analyze it and then disconnect and reconnect via another a LAN driver and card to another network type, as shown in Figure 4.5.

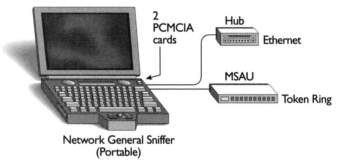

**FIGURE 4.5**

*Many analyzers, such as the Sniffer, support multiple access types.*

If you want to analyze WAN communications, look for an analyzer that can tap into your WAN link type, such as an ATM analyzer or a Frame Relay analyzer.

**Refer to Chapter 5, for more information on WAN analyzers.**

X-REF

## NETWORK SIZE

Your network size should affect your analysis device decision. Some analyzers are great for small to medium-sized networks. They can be moved from network segment to network segment to analyze the LAN. If you have a large network that makes moving from segment to segment impossible in a 24-hour workday (just kidding), you may want to consider a more robust distributed analyzer solution. Distributed analyzers are covered in more detail later in this chapter.

## PACKET MONITORING

Some analysis systems provide an overview of the communications on the network but do not actually capture and decode network packets for you. These products are typically cable testers that now support an LED display panel.

Although they can give you the current packet per second and utilization rates, they do not have the capability to provide you with a packet-by-packet breakdown of your network communications. (And who would want one on that tiny little screen, anyway, eh?)

Thorough network analysis requires you to be able to view packet sequences and structures.

## STATION MONITORING

It's great to have a solution that lists all stations talking on the network, as shown in Figure 4.6. Be certain that your analyzer can hold enough station information to list all devices that are communicating. For example, if the analyzer can list only the top 10 stations on a network segment that supports 89 communicating devices, you are not seeing most of the stations on the wire.

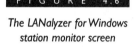

FIGURE 4.6

*The LANalyzer for Windows station monitor screen*

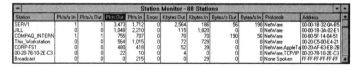

**TIP**

**It is also a good idea to get an analyzer that performs name gathering so that you can see login names rather than node addresses.**

## TRENDING

If you plan on using your analyzer to create baseline reports, make sure you find an analysis solution that provides adequate trending of network performance. An analyzer that provides only a 24-hour trend screen is not sufficient. Look for an analyzer that provides trend information for at least a one-month time period. Why do you need an analyzer that provides long-term trending? Every network experiences regular peaks in network activity. These peaks may occur on a nightly, weekly, or monthly basis. Long-term trending provides you with information for planning larger network tasks, such as full backup, updates and upgrades, and new application loading. Look for the low utilization times to add network load from these tasks.

Figures 4.7 and 4.8 depict trend screens from LANalyzer for Windows.

Figure 4.7 depicts a short-term trend screen from LANalyzer for Windows. Note that this screen details only 15 minutes of activity. Figure 4.8, on the other hand, is a long-term trend screen. By scrolling back and forth along this trend time line, we can determine the network load over a longer period of time and identify peak load times.

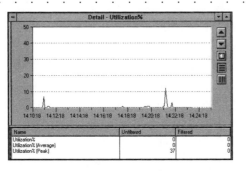

**FIGURE 4.7**

*Short-term trend screens indicate recent network activity levels.*

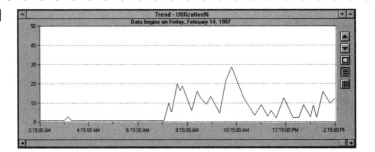

**FIGURE 4.8**

*Long-term trend screens should detail at least one month of activity.*

## ALARM SETTINGS

Make sure the analyzer you select provides alarms for both the most common and the most devastating types of network events. For example, a good analyzer should provide Ethernet alarm settings for CRC errors, utilization, and short/long packets, as well as server down/router down alarms. On Token Ring networks, a good analyzer would notify you immediately if the ring experiences burst errors (commonly seen when stations first enter the ring) or begins to beacon (a devastating event).

Figures 4.9 through 4.11 show various alarm definition screens. Figures 4.9 and 4.10 show the simpler point-and-click alarm setting system on LANalyzer for Windows. Figure 4.11 shows the more detailed alarm setting screen of Network General's Sniffer.

**FIGURE  4.9**

*The basic Ethernet alarm setting screen denotes errors that should be tracked and may indicate a problem.*

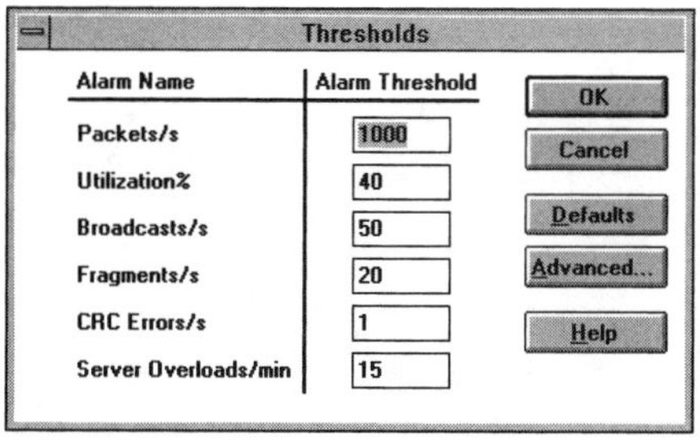

**FIGURE  4.10**

*The advanced alarm setting screen depicts errors that should never occur and may indicate more serious problems on the network.*

**FIGURE  4.11**

*More advanced analyzers, such as Network General's Sniffer, enable you to set alarm thresholds on application performance.*

## PACKET TRANSMIT

Some higher-end analyzers and analyzer add-ons can transmit packets onto the wire to test network cabling systems and devices. In order to really take advantage of this type of analysis product, you must have a thorough knowledge of networking protocols, packet structures, and addressing systems.

Figure 4.12 shows the Sniffer interface for building a packet. Figure 4.13 depicts the process of building a packet with LANQuest Net/WRx-LANLoad.

**For more information on NCC LAN Network Probe and Net/WRx, refer to Chapter 5.**

**X-REF**

▶ · · · · · · · · · · · · · · · · · · · · · ◀

F I G U R E   4.12

*Use the Sniffer's Traffic Generator to build a packet.*

▶ · · · · · · · · · · · · · · · · · · · · · ◀

F I G U R E   4.13

*LANQuest's Net/WRx was designed specifically for building and transmitting packets.*

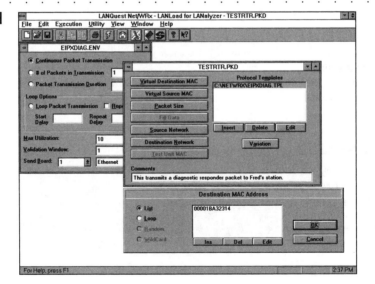

## FILTERING (PRE- AND POST-)

*Prefiltering* and *postfiltering* are used to narrow the number of packets kept in your buffer. You certainly don't want to sort through thousands of miscellaneous packets in order to determine the cause of a station disconnect.

Prefiltering enables you to decide what packets are captured and moved into a trace buffer. For example, perhaps you only want to capture packets between FRED and COMPAQ-FS1. With many analyzers, you can set up a prefilter, as shown in Figure 4.14.

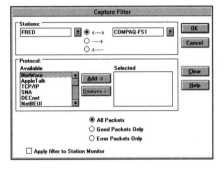

F I G U R E   4.14

Setting up a prefilter can be a simple way to streamline the analysis process.

Prefiltering (also referred to as *capture filtering*) can reduce the number of packets that you have to wade through when analyzing a communications session.

*Postfiltering* enables you to further define the packets that are viewed: Your postfiltered buffer is a subset of your prefiltered buffer, as shown in Figure 4.15.

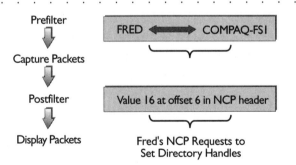

F I G U R E   4.15

The postfilter is a subset of your prefiltered buffer.

Some analyzers provide a very detailed level of postfiltering (to the binary level), whereas others provide a simple, predefined set of filters. LANalyzer for Windows, for example, has a predefined set of postfilters, which includes AppleTalk, NetWare, TCP/IP, Data Link, NFS (Network File System), NWIP (NetWare IP), SNA, and error packets. Filters can also be set for specific source and destination addresses, as well as specific values at defined locations within the packets.

In Figure 4.16, we have defined a postfilter (called a Display Filter in LANalyzer for Windows) that displays packets that meet the following criteria:

**Source and destination addresses:** To/From FRED and COMPAQ-FS1

**Protocol:** NetWare NCP

**Field Value:** 16 (hexadecimal) at an offset of six bytes from the protocol layer (NCP header start).

This postfilter will display all NCP requests from FRED to set a directory handle.

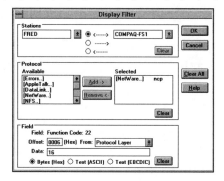

FIGURE 4.16

*Prefiltering and postfiltering help you isolate specific communications on the network.*

**X-REF**

**For more information on NCP, refer to Chapter 13.**

Don't be fooled by the simplistic titles of the filters—NetWare, TCP/IP, and so on. Each filter listed offers various options that enhance your filtering capability. For example, under the NetWare filter you can select:

- Broadcast

- Diagnostic responder

- IPX (Internetwork Packet Exchange)

- Lite Sideband Protocol (NetWare Lite)

- NetBIOS

- NCP (NetWare Core Protocol)

▸ NDS (NetWare Directory Services)

▸ NetWare Lite Protocol

▸ NLSP (NetWare Link Services Protocol)

▸ RIP (Routing Information Protocol)

▸ SAP (Service Advertising Protocol)

▸ SER (Serialization)

▸ Watchdog

More advanced analyzers, such as Network General Sniffer and NCC LAN Network Probe, enable you to set more advanced filters. For example, on the Sniffer you can set a binary filter indicating that you are looking for the bit pattern "1001" at a specific location within a packet, as shown in Figure 4.17. In the right-hand column, we have defined a pattern of 1001 at offset 0000 (the start of the packet), indicating that we are looking for a specific destination address bit sequence. Sniffer's powerful Boolean operands (AND/OR) enable us to really zoom in on our desired traffic type.

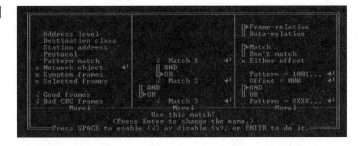

**F I G U R E    4.17**

*A binary filter indicates that we are looking for packets with the value 1,001 at the beginning of the frame in the destination address field.*

**X-REF**

**Binary filtering requires a thorough knowledge of the protocols and field values. Appendix A provides a hex-decimal-binary conversion chart that should help in setting up binary filters.**

## PORTABILITY

If you're planning on taking your analyzer to various sites that are not connected via WAN links or other media, portability is an important feature. For example, I go to a number of companies throughout the world and need a portable analyzer to take with me. Currently, I have three portable analyzers that I use most of the time. Following are the specs on each system.

**Portable No. 1**
**System:** Sharp 9030, Pentium 90MHz
**RAM:** 40MB
**Drive:** 1GB
**NIC:** Xircom Ethernet + 28.8 Modem
**Analyzer:** LANalyzer for Windows

**Portable No. 2**
**System:** Compaq 486, 33MHz Lunchbox
**RAM:** 32MB
**Drive:** 500MB
**NIC:** Analyzer (NCC LAN Network Probe) Ethernet and LANalyzer (NCC LAN Network Probe) 4/16 Token Ring cards
**Analyzer:** LANalyzer (NCC LAN Network Probe) and LANalyzer for Windows

**NOTE**

**NCC LAN Network Probe (formerly known as LANalyzer when it was owned by Novell) does not use PCMCIA cards, hence the need for the "luggable" Compaq system.**

**Portable No. 3**

 ▸ **System:** Toshiba T4700CS, 486 DX2 50MHz

 ▸ **RAM:** 24MB

 ▸ **Drive:** 250MB

 ▸ **NIC:** Sniffer (IBM) Ethernet Adapter and Sniffer (Madge) Token Ring adapter

 ▸ **Analyzer:** Sniffer Network Analyzer

Many analyzers use color-coded displays. If you are going to purchase your analysis software and a portable separately, check the system requirements for color needs.


## AVAILABLE DECODES

A *decode* is the text interpretation of the fields of a packet. If an analyzer has a decode for NetWare communications, each field should be defined and the contents interpreted whenever possible. For example, when the analyzer sees a destination socket number of 0x451 (hexadecimal), the analyzer should display the term "NCP" and break the packet down as an NCP packet, as shown in Figure 4.18.

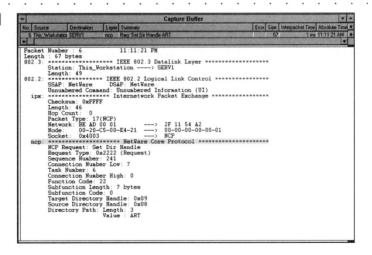

FIGURE 4.18

*A decoded NCP packet*

If an analyzer does provide a decode for a protocol, you do not get a nice clean breakdown of all the packet fields. Figure 4.19 shows a packet that is only partially decoded—LANalyzer for Windows does not know how to interpret the application layer communications.

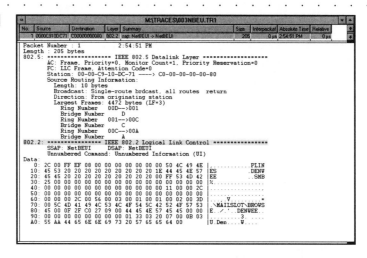

*A partially undecoded packet*

Some analyzers come bundled with all the decodes you could want; others sell a basic package and let you add on decodes as they are needed. For typical NetWare LANs, you probably want the NetWare decodes that include the more recent additions to the NetWare protocol stack, such as NetWare/IP, NLSP, and NDS communications. Check to make sure the analyzer provides decodes for packet burst technology, as well.

## EXPERT SYSTEM/INTERPRETATIONS

Now that the analyzer has presented you with all this information, how do you interpret it? That is the quandary in analysis. Some analyzers come with an "expert system" that makes judgments based on the traffic seen. This can be very helpful if their assumptions are correct and you can research the problems further to back up the assumptions.

One example is the NetWare Expert in LANalyzer for Windows, as shown in Figure 4.20. Upon selecting an error that has been defined in the error log, you can click the NetWare Expert icon to get the recommended steps for solving the problem.

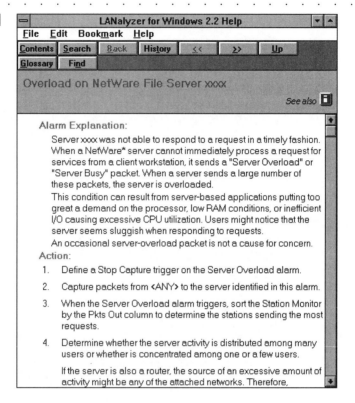

FIGURE 4.20

*LANalyzer for Windows NetWare Expert provides assistance with errors.*

Network General Sniffer also has an expert system that makes analysis judgments based on the sequence of events and of packets captured. Figures 4.21 and 4.22 show two screens of the Sniffer Expert system. Figure 4.21, the Expert Overview, indicates that there is one diagnosis of a problem (55 indications/symptoms have occurred). Figure 4.22 shows the Sniffer's diagnosis of excessive retransmissions. If we were to examine the packets in the buffer, we would find the server sending "server busy" packets to the client and the client retransmitting requests.

FIGURE 4.21

Sniffer's Expert Overview
System indicates one
problem has been
diagnosed—a
retransmission problem.

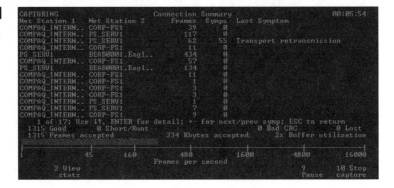

FIGURE 4.22

Sniffer's diagnosis: excessive
retransmissions

For more information on NetWare "server busy" packets, refer to
Chapter 13.

**X-REF**

## COMMODITY-BASED COMPONENTS

Consider whether you want an analyzer that is based on available commodities (that is, generally available network interface cards and the PC platform) or whether you can work with one of the dedicated, specialized network analysis systems. Commodity-based analyzers are often most convenient in case a component of the analyzer (such as a network interface card) fails. You can typically find a replacement within your own company or at a local network product dealer. The specialized systems are generally more expensive but can provide additional functionality (such as cable testing) through their proprietary hardware.

## INTERFACE/EASE OF USE

If the analyzer's interface doesn't feel intuitive and logical, don't buy it. Too often I hear people saying that they have an analyzer but they've never had the time to learn how to operate it. Your analyzer is no good sitting on a shelf. Fortunately, within the last few years, analyzer manufacturers have realized that a cryptic interface can deter a potential customer. A number of them have given their products point-and-click functions and have tried to appeal to you by modeling their interfaces after the control panel of a car—a very comfortable, nonthreatening interface for most people. LANalyzer for Windows is an example of a product that provides gauges and alarm lights similar to those found on your car dashboard, as shown in Figure 4.23. The Sniffer, on the other hand, has a text-based interface (as shown in Figure 4.24), but its Network Monitor application can be configured to display graphical interpretations of network traffic (as shown in Figure 4.25).

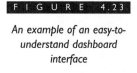

F I G U R E   4.23

*An example of an easy-to-understand dashboard interface*

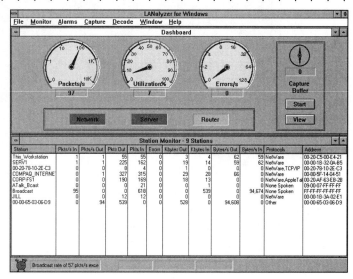

F I G U R E   4.24

*The Sniffer has a text-based interface.*

F I G U R E   4.25

*Sniffer's Network Monitor application can be configured to display graphical interpretations of network traffic.*

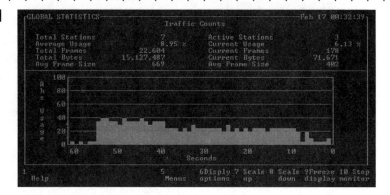

## REPORT GENERATION

Can your analyzer export information for report generation? This has typically been a weak spot for analyzers, although the ability to print reports and export data makes the task of cost-justifying the analysis product purchase much easier.

Figure 4.26 shows a product, Analyzer Companion, that creates reports based on the content of trace files. Analyzer Companion works with a variety of industry analyzers, including LANalyzer for Windows, Sniffer, and NCC LAN Network Probe.

FIGURE 4.26

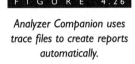

*Analyzer Companion uses trace files to create reports automatically.*

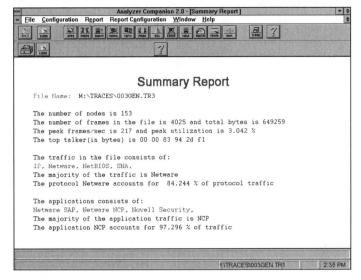

## COST

Of course, cost is an important consideration when you are selecting an analyzer. Analyzers can range in cost from $1,500 to $50,000. Some analyzers provide a "base cost" and charge you for each add-on protocol that you want to analyze.

Keep in mind that if you don't feel comfortable with the analyzer and use it, it won't be worth much. You should always consider the cost of training, which should ensure that you understand what the analyzer can do for you and should provide you with some hands-on experience in filtering, capturing packets, and configuring your alarm thresholds.

## COMBINED FUNCTIONALITY

Recently, a number of products have been released that are claimed to provide network analysis functions as well as another function, such as cable testing or RMON MIB querying and Internet map building. Provided the analysis function is robust enough to give you packet traces, you may be interested in exploring these tools further.

Novell's ManageWise is an example of a product that provides combined functionality. For more information on ManageWise, refer to Chapter 5.

**X-REF**

## Placing an Analyzer

When you are considering placement of the analyzer or analyzer agent, you must understand the nature of internetworking devices. Which ones filter out traffic? You must have an analysis process running on each network that is separated by a filtering device.

The typical devices found on networks include:

- Repeaters

- Hubs

- Multistation access units

- Switches

- Bridges

- Routers

- The management console

### REPEATERS

Repeaters do not filter out any network traffic; they simply repeat bits received from one port out the other ports, as shown in Figure 4.27. All communications occurring on Segment 1 are propagated onto Segment 2. Even Ethernet fragments (the result of a collision) are repeated onto Segment 2. You need only one analyzer to handle traffic on each side of a repeater.

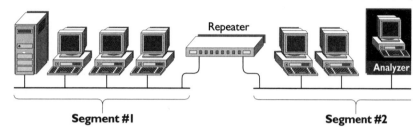

F I G U R E   4.27

*A repeated network requires only a single analyzer.*

Segment #1 Traffic = Segment #2 Traffic

## HUBS

Hubs do not filter out any network traffic either. In that sense, they are just like repeaters, but they do often have some intelligence and may partition off devices that are injecting errors (such as CRC errors) into the network, as shown in Figure 4.28. You need only one analyzer to handle traffic on both sides of a hub.

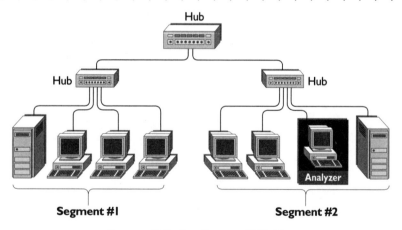

F I G U R E   4.28

*A 10BaseT hub repeated network requires only one analyzer to "see" all traffic.*

Segment #1 Traffic = Segment #2 Traffic

## MULTISTATION ACCESS UNITS

MSAUs, used in Token Ring networks, act like hubs. The nature of Token Ring communications, however, causes all communications to travel in a counterclockwise direction from station to station. By placing an analyzer in any port of a MSAU, you can see all traffic on the ring, as shown in Figure 4.29. You need only one analyzer to handle traffic throughout the MSAU and on any attached MSAUs (provided the MSAUs are not connected via switches, bridges, or routers). Keep in mind, however, that if your analysis station is directly downstream from a break in the ring, you may not see any traffic at all. Also remember that most analyzers cannot enter a beaconing ring: It is a good idea to keep an active analyzer or analyzer agent on your critical rings.

**X-REF**

**For more information on beaconing, refer to Chapter 3.**

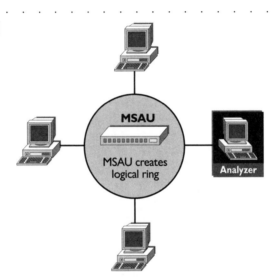

F I G U R E   4.29

*Token Rings connected through MSAUs need only one analyzer to "see" all traffic.*

## SWITCHES

Switches act as relaying devices, making temporary circuits between two communicating device ports. Although switches enhance communications throughput by directing most communications between devices connected, they can be very difficult for network analyzers. You must use either an analysis agent, an extended hub solution, or a monitor-port analysis solution (as mentioned earlier in this chapter) to see all communications traveling through to and from a NetWare server. Figure 4.30 shows a distributed analysis solution using a management console and an analyzer agent on the server. All traffic to and from the server can be viewed (typically sufficient for NetWare's client/server communications), but traffic between stations (peer-to-peer traffic) cannot be seen.

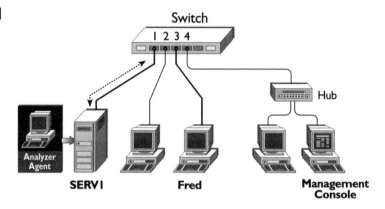

FIGURE 4.30

*A distributed analyzer solution can work for a switched NetWare network.*

**For more switched analysis solutions, refer to Chapter 2**

X-REF

## BRIDGES

Bridges build a forwarding table based on device node addresses (also referred to as *hardware addresses* or *network interface card addresses*), as shown in Figure 4.31. They forward all broadcast traffic but filter out traffic not destined to the attached network. In order to see all communications on each side of a bridge, you must place an analyzer or analyzer agent on each side of that bridge.

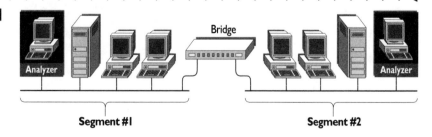

FIGURE 4.31

*A bridged network requires an analyzer or analyzer agent on each attached segment.*

## ROUTERS

Routers build forwarding tables based on network addresses. As packets arrive at the router, the router uses a routing information table to determine how to handle the packet. Packets that are not destined for another network are not forwarded. In order to see all communications on each side of a router, you must place an analyzer or analyzer agent on each side of the router, as shown in Figure 4.32.

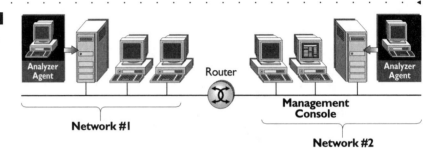

F I G U R E   4.32

*A routed network requires an analyzer or analyzer agent on each attached network.*

Analyzer Agent

Router

Analyzer Agent

Management Console

Network #1

Network #2

# Placing the Management Console

Because the analyzer agents must communicate with the management console to provide communications trend information, summary screens, and if required, packet traces, you should try to keep the path between the management console and analyzer optimal by centrally locating the management console, as shown in Figure 4.33.

If you are managing a very large network that is connected via WAN link, you may consider having two management consoles, one at each end of the WAN link. This helps cut down on the traffic introduced on the WAN by requiring local agents to communicate with local management consoles, as shown in Figure 4.34.

FIGURE 4.33

*Find a central location for your management console.*

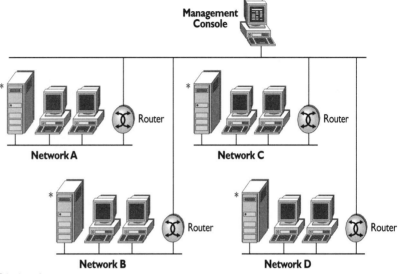

FIGURE 4.34

*Multiple consoles are used to manage a larger network.*

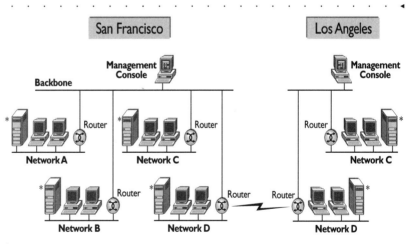

## Summary

In this chapter, we have examined the analyzer qualities that you should look for and several options for placing your analyzer/analyzer agents.

In the next chapter, we'll examine some analysis products that can be used to track and monitor NetWare LAN and WAN traffic.

# CHAPTER 5

# Analyzer Product Listing

If you don't have an analyzer—get one! You'll be amazed at all the information you can gather on your network's performance (good and bad). Placing a network analyzer on your cabling system is *the* quickest method for detecting network errors and classifying network performance. When you look into analyzers, keep in mind that they vary greatly in their abilities and their ease of use.

**NOTE**

**In this chapter, we'll examine some of the analyzer products that we use in our lab today. If you have an analyzer that you'd like reviewed for future revisions of this book, please send me information (chappell@imagitech.com).**

## The Best of All Worlds

In an ideal world, you should have both high-end and low-end analyzer solutions available to you. The high-end analyzers have more sophisticated alarm systems and can help you catch many upper-layer problems. Low-end analyzers are more affordable, typically easier to use, and easier to navigate quickly.

When I do an on-site visit, I take one high-end analyzer and one low-end analyzer. I plug in and just "feel" the network, capturing a general trace of all traffic. If there's a problem, one of the two analyzers is going to alert me. If I don't get an alarm message, then I begin to wade through packets to see what type of communications occur on the wire.

**TIP**

**For more information on how to perform an onsite analysis, browse our Web site at www.imagitech.com.**

## Author's Choice Product Review

Over the years, I've had the chance to work with various analyzers. Some have been good; many have been lousy. These are my favorites that I use in the lab. The best solution is to have one low-end analyzer with a very intuitive interface and one high-end analyzer to provide more detailed decodes and an expert system:

Here are my picks for analyzer products to look at:

- ▶ EtherPeek (AG Group)

- ▶ LAN Load (LANQuest Corporation)

- ▶ LAN Probe (Network Communications Corporation)

- ▶ LANalyzer for Windows (Novell, Inc.)

- ▶ ManageWise: LANalyzer Agents (Novell, Inc.)

- ▶ Sniffer Network Analyzer (Network General Corporation)

In this next section, we'll describe the analyzers listed and show screen shots so that you can take a look at the interface you'll be working with if you use any of these products. Contact information and approximate price categories (low through high) are also provided for your reference.

## ETHERPEEK (AG GROUP)

If you've been around analyzers a while, you may remember EtherPeek—it is a nice Macintosh-based analyzer. The AG Group that created EtherPeek for Macintosh has now released EtherPeek for Windows (95 and NT only). The product has a nice, easy interface, as shown in Figure 5.1, and installation is a snap.

If you want a product that's up and running this minute, EtherPeek is your best bet. Although I do miss the "dashboard" screen offered in LANalyzer for Windows, EtherPeek allows me to view packets while the capture process is still running in the background (one of my favorite features of this product).

During the writing of this book, EtherPeek for Windows underwent extensive upgrades quarterly (an aggressive development team is welcome). Besides the basic features added, focus was on stronger IP support to provide duplicate IP address detection, transaction-level details, Telnet text, TCP/SYN attack logging, ICMP logging, FTP download log, and newsgroup access logging.

▶ · · · · · · · · · · · · · · · · · · · · · · · · · · · · ◀

F I G U R E   5.1

*Etherpeek's summary screen and packet decode are well-designed.*

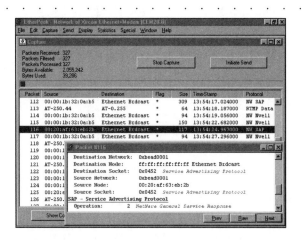

If the AG Group continues to develop their product at this rate, they may set the standard for all-in-one low-end analyzers. Keep your eye on their products, even if you don't buy one now.

> **The AG Group has released a *free* IP utility toolkit on its Website (www.aggroup.com).**
>
> **NOTE**

Decodes include: 802.1 Spanning Tree, AppleTalk (NBP, PAP, AFP), AARP, IP (TCP, UDP, IPv6), ARP, RARP, IPX, IPX-LSAP, IPX-SNAP, DECnet (Phase IV, LAT, MOP), NetBEUI/NetBIOS, OSI (LLC, ES-IS, IS-IS, TP), XNS, VINES-IP-LSAP, VINES-IP-SNAP, VINES-Echo, and Cisco Discovery.

> **For more information on EtherPeek, contact the AG Group at 800-466-2447 or 510-937-7900, or else browse their Web site at www.aggroup.com.**
>
> **TIP**

## NET/WRX 4.0—LANLOAD (LANQUEST CORPORATION)

Net/WRx is a nice utility to have in your toolkit if you need to work on Fast Ethernet, Gigabit Ethernet, Token Ring, ATM, and FDDI networks. You can use Net/WRx to test network products in various network scenarios to see how they'll perform. I use Net/WRx LANLoad to generate diagnostic responder packets (see Chapter 14) to test connectivity and round-trip times.

This product requires some knowledge of packet structures, as shown in Figure 5.2.

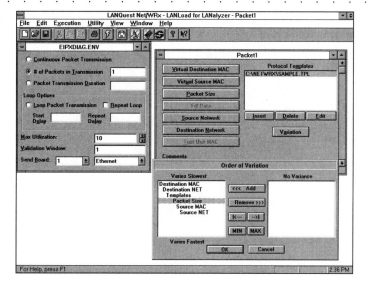

The Net/WRx features list includes:

▸ Automatic packet suite generation for IP and add-in protocols

▸ Multiple packet size generation options — fixed, random, stepped, and designated sizes

▸ Traffic generation on Ethernet, Fast Ethernet, Gigabit Ethernet, ATM, or Token Ring.

▸ Independent variation of source MAC, destination MAC, source network, and destination network addresses in packet descriptions

▸ Capability to vary protocols, packet sizes, and all addresses; and to fill data within packets during a single test

▸ IP, ICMP, TCP, and UDP checksum calculations

▸ Source route bridge testing

▸ A quick run option for fast, simple testing scenarios

▸ A send/receive/compare run-time option for comprehensive traffic testing

▸ Generation of comprehensive reports including packets sent, packets received, latency, miscompares, missing packets, and more

▸ Network monitoring

▸ Network learning

▸ Packet capture and high-level decodes

▸ A host table

▸ Specification of manufacturers' prefixes for MAC addresses

▸ A Windows GUI for traffic definition

▸ Custom traffic scripting for test scenarios

▸ Predefined sample transmit scripts

IP is included with the base product. IP suite includes HTTP, SMTP, NNTP, FTP, Finger, Telnet, and many other Internet-based templates. IPX, AppleTalk, DECnet, Vines, OSI, and XNS are available as add-ins.

**TIP**

**For more information on Net/WRx, call 800-487-7779 or 510-354-0940, or else browse LANQuest's Web site at** www.lanquest.com.

## LAN NETWORK PROBE (NETWORK COMMUNICATIONS CORPORATION)

Ahh, good ol' LAN Network Probe by NCC. This used to be the hardware/software "LANalyzer" product from Novell. This product is not cheap, folks—it's up there in the high-end analyzer range. It's worth every penny! The LAN Network Probe (we call it the LAN Probe) offers a DOS-based (that's right, it don't need no stinkin' Windows) analyzer with a huge range of decodes built in (Appletalk, Banyan, DEC Net, Microsoft, IBM, NFS, Novell, SMB, Sun NFS, TCP/IP, Token Ring/LLC, X-WINDOWS, and XNS). Figure 5.3 shows a sample screen with the NetWare "1st-Step" application running.

**F I G U R E   5.3**

*The LAN Network Probe contains many "canned" applications, such as "1st-Step."*

```
+-----------------------------------------------------------------------+
:01/02/98 15:32:49 Delays packet rate of 1 pkts/s exceeded threshold of 0 :
+-----------------------------------------------------------------------+
: Channel      Packets    Rate +------------------------------------------+ :
: Global        4448  100%     0 :_____       :
: Requests       865   19%     0 :_____                                    :
: Success        848   19%     0 :_____                                    :
: Failures        34    1%     0 :____                                       :
: Delays           3    0%     0 :                                           :
: RIP             40    1%     0 :__                                         :
: SAP             55    1%     0 :__                                         :
: Broadcst       162    4%     0 :___                                        :
: Other         2338   53%     0 :___                                        :
:                              +------+--------+--------+--------+-------++   :
:                              0      10       100      1000      10000:      :
:           0 Local Collisions/SQEs         Packets/Sec                      :
:           0 Remote Collisions                                              :
:           0 CRC/Alignment Errors        0 Packets Transmitted              :
:           0 Illegal Length Packets      0 Transmissions Deferred           :
:        4448 Good Packets                0 Transmitted with Collisions      :
:        -----                                                               :
:        4448 Total Packets Processed   1864 Packets Saved In Buffer         :
+----------------------------- Screen Function Keys ----------------------+
:F1   :F2    :F3     :F4    :F5    :F6     :F7     :F8    :F9    :F10       :
:Help :      :Global :Rate  :Util  :Station:TxStats:      :More  :Stop      :
```

**NOTE**

**It's true, I'm rather partial to this product since I "grew up" in the LANalyzer days. I'm accustomed to the interface and can work the product with my hands tied behind my back (kinda strange to type with your feet).**

You can easily cut and paste packets from a receive channel to a transmit channel and do simultaneous transmit and receive (unique to LAN Probe), and you can export LAN Probe data and run the included Excel macros to make some excellent charts/graphs depicting your findings, as shown in Figure 5.4.

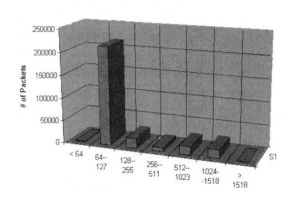

**F I G U R E   5.4**

Packet Size Distribution (szdist.xlc)

*An elegant packet distribution chart can be created with the Excel macros that ship with LAN Network Probe.*

Unfortunately, there aren't as many people skilled in the LAN Probe as there are in the Sniffer. Sniffer *owns* the high-end market. If you learn how to use the LAN Probe, however, you can really dig deep into the network workings and perform advanced features. For example, I recently received an e-mail message stating that NetWare 4.11 was vulnerable to a TCP/SYN Denial of Service (DOS) attack. I used LAN Probe to recreate the attack packet and pummel the server with SYN packets to see how the OS reacted. FYI, the server did just fine — no abend, no slow down, no utilization jump.

**If you're new to high-end analyzers, it's a good idea to spend some money on training. Typically, the more detailed the product, the less likely someone will know how to use it when you need it.**

TIP

**For more information on the LAN Probe, call 800-228-9202 or 612-844-0584, or else visit NCC's Web site at** `www.netcommcorp.com`.

TIP

## LANALYZER FOR WINDOWS (NOVELL, INC.)

I do love LANalyzer for Windows! The interface is easy to understand and intuitive. The navigation and alarms are a breeze. As a software-only analyzer, LANalyzer for Windows requires Novell's Client 32 and ODI (Open Datalink Interface) drivers to work.

The main window provides a dashboard for a quick look at overall network communications health, as shown in Figure 5.5.

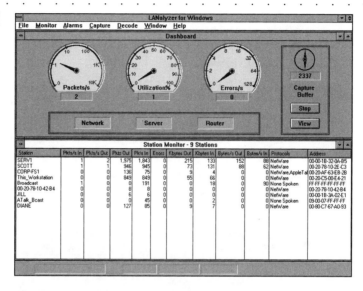

**F I G U R E   5 . 5**

*LANalyzer for Windows'
dashboard provides a quick
look at network
communications health.*

Decodes include IPX, TCP/IP, AppleTalk, and SNA.

**You can get the Native IP (NCP over IP) decode update from our Web site at** www.imagitech.com.

**TIP**

Because this book is full of LANalyzer for Windows screens, it seems redundant to place any more information here. If you want more information on LANalyzer for Windows, call your Novell reseller or check out Novell's Web site at www.novell.com.

## MANAGEWISE: LANALYZER AGENTS (NOVELL, INC.)

ManageWise offers distributed analysis using LANalyzer agents that reside on NetWare servers. The ManageWise console provides an interface similar to the LANalyzer for Windows dashboard.

The big strength of ManageWise, however, is not its distributed analysis solution as much as its NetWare server management offering. Take a look at ManageWise—it's grown up nicely.

**For more information on ManageWise, call your Novell reseller or check out Novell's Web site at** `www.novell.com`.

TIP

## SNIFFER NETWORK ANALYZER (NETWORK GENERAL CORPORATION)

Network General (purchased by McAfee and renamed to Network Associates in 1997) is definitely the leader in network analysis solutions with their Sniffer and Distributed Sniffer products. They currently offer stand-alone and distributed analysis solutions. I recommend that you take some courses to learn all the functions possible with the Sniffer—the interface takes some getting used to.

Sniffer's decodes are nicely done and resemble those of LANalyzer for Windows in their three-window display abilities, as shown in Figure 5.6.

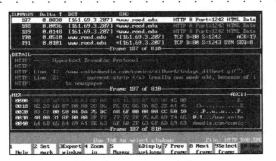

F I G U R E   5.6

*Sniffer can be configured to provide summary information, detail information, and hexadecimal decodes, if desired.*

One of the Sniffer's key selling points, however, is its expert system, which alerts you to problems on the network and provides a preliminary diagnosis of the problem, as shown in Figure 5.7.

Network General has Sniffer analyzers to support ATM, FDDI, Fast Ethernet, HSSI, and ISDN. They also have Oracle, Sybase, and Microsoft SQL database modules to enhance your Sniffer for troubleshooting these environments.

I should also mention that during the writing of this book, Network General began distributing NetXRay, a low-end Windows-based analyzer solution. NetXRay supports all major LAN topologies (Ethernet, Fast Ethernet, Token Ring, 100-VG/Any LAN) and can decode over 110 protocols including IPX/SPX, IP, AppleTalk, IBM/Microsoft, SNA, Banyan VINES, XNS, and DECnet.

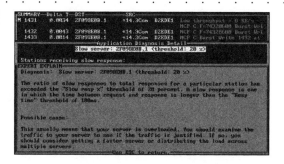

F I G U R E   5.7

*Sniffer's expert system is its key advantage over other analyzers.*

**TIP**

**For more information on the Sniffer or NetXRay, call 800-SNIFFER (800-764-3337) or 415-473-2000, or visit Network General/Network Associates' home page at www.ngc.com.**

## Summary

Purchasing an analyzer may seem like a daunting task—there are so many choices on the market these days. Try to create a list of the various functions you'd like to be able to perform on your network. Use Chapter 4 as a reference for the types of functions that you can perform with an analyzer. Ask other analyzer users and consider the experience and history of the vendors—many vendors have not kept up with the latest and greatest decodes (such as NDS). Finally, consider the "recommended training time" as an indication of the difficulty level of the product. You should spend the time (and probably money) to learn how to use your analyzer in order to get your money's worth.

Now that we've looked at the fundamentals of analysis, in Chapter 6 we'll take a look at how NetWare's IPX/SPX communications system works.

# PART II

# How NetWare Communicates

This part of the book is the real techno-meat for those of you who want to understand the NetWare protocol stack. Keep in mind that if you learn the basic functionality of one protocol stack in the industry, you have a good head start toward understanding other protocol stacks. There are some definite similarities among all the protocols, including TCP/IP, AppleTalk, and SNA.

This part begins with Chapter 6, which provides an overview of the entire NetWare protocol suite. This puts the NetWare communications system in perspective, and helps you understand the relationship between each NetWare function.

After the overview portion, we dive right into the protocols, starting with the network layer protocol, Internetwork Packet Exchange (IPX) in Chapter 7, and the transport layer protocols, Sequenced Packet Exchange (SPX) versions 1 and 2 in Chapter 8.

The next chapters deal with Novell's older protocols that provide service information and routing information on the network: Service Advertising Protocol (SAP) in Chapter 9 and Routing Information Protocol (RIP) in Chapter 10, respectively. These chapters provide troubleshooting tips and configuration options for enhancing RIP/SAP performance.

In Chapter 11, we focus on Novell's link state routing protocol, NetWare Link Services Protocol (NLSP). If you haven't yet taken a look at NLSP technology and become familiar with the pros and cons of it, this chapter is a must! By examining a sample NLSP network, you'll see the process that NLSP routers undergo to initialize the link state database and make forwarding decisions. You'll also learn how NLSP routers can coexist with RIP/SAP routing devices.

Chapter 12 focuses on IPXWAN2, Novell's protocol for supporting IPX across WAN routers. If you plan on having a WAN that communicates using IPX between locations, be sure to read this chapter thoroughly.

Chapters 13 focuses on the Novell "family jewels": NetWare Core Protocol (NCP) and NetWare Directory Services (NDS). In these chapters, we look at how NetWare clients request services, and how NetWare servers handle client NCP requests. We also look at a variety of processes including the login, file copy, application execution, and file read and write processes. This chapter includes a master list of NetWare NCP function, subfunction, and verbs, as well.

Chapter 14 focuses primarily on the Diagnostic Responder and IPX Ping programs.

# CHAPTER 6

# Overview of NetWare IPX/SPX Protocols

In this chapter, we focus on the basic NetWare protocols and their performance (including IPX, SPX, SAP, RIP, NCP, NDS, IPXWAN2, NLSP, NetWare/IP, Mobile IPX, Diagnostic Responder, Watchdog, and Serialization processes). This chapter provides a glimpse of the NetWare connection process to see the various protocols in use by default (IPX, SAP, RIP, NCP, and NDS) but defers to the chapters following it for detailed information on packet structures and performance.

## The NetWare IPX/SPX Protocol Stack

OK, OK, you've probably heard it before—Novell defined the IPX/SPX protocols after Xerox's XNS (Xerox Network System) protocol set had appeared. It's true! Why reinvent a completely new protocol when there seemed to be one that had a great start?

**NOTE**

**It's a major pain when analysis vendors use the Xerox protocol stack nomenclature (calling SPX "SPP," and so on) because you'll never be able to look up SPP setable parameters in the NetWare manuals. I strongly recommend that you seek out an analyzer that uses the correct Novell terminology.**

The NetWare protocol stack provides all the services required to access servers, files, print, route, synchronize NDS databases, and so on. As you can see from Figure 6.1, Novell's entire protocol suite consists of many individual protocols and functions.

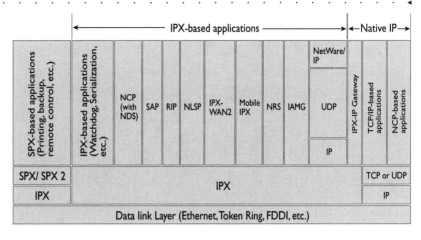

F I G U R E   6.1

*The Netware protocol stack consists of many individual protocols.*

Let's take a quick look at the services offered by each of the protocols. Remember, the protocols are covered in detail in the following chapters:

- ▸ Chapter 7: NetWare IPX

- ▸ Chapter 8: NetWare SPX/SPX 2

- ▸ Chapter 9: NetWare SAP

- ▸ Chapter 10: NetWare RIP

- ▸ Chapter 11: NetWare NLSP

- ▸ Chapter 12: IPXWAN2

- ▸ Chapter 13: NetWare NCP

- ▸ Chapter 14: NetWare Diagnostic Responder and IPX Ping

## Overview of Communication Protocols and Their Purposes

Each piece of the NetWare protocol stack provides a different service either between clients and servers or directly between servers. For example, when a Virtual Loadable Module (VLM) client requests a connection to a NetWare Directory Services (NDS) tree, it first uses the Service Advertising Protocol (SAP) to locate an NDS server. The client also uses the Routing Information Protocol (RIP), the NetWare Core Protocol (NCP), and NDS to locate routes, obtain the connection, and authenticate itself.

Let's examine the purpose of each of the protocols individually. This discussion should provide a solid understanding of the role each protocol plays in providing services on the network.

### INTERNETWORK PACKET EXCHANGE (IPX)

IPX was modeled after the Xerox Internetwork Datagram Packet (IDP) protocol and provides connectionless datagram services. The term *datagram* indicates that each packet is considered a separate entity, not referenced or related in any way to any other IPX packet. There is no sequencing of IPX packets either. If sequencing is required, another protocol (such as NCP) must provide it.

A connectionless service does not require the two sides of the communication to *handshake* or establish a logical connection ("I'm here, are you?") before transmitting data. IPX source and destination internetwork addresses contained in a packet (as an IPX header) are used by routing devices to forward packets to the appropriate network.

IPX does not offer any guarantee or verification of delivery. It must rely on other protocols above IPX (such as SPX) for guaranteed delivery. For an analogy, the U.S. Mail system uses an unguaranteed delivery system, by default. In the U.S., when you address a letter and place it in your mailbox, there is no guarantee or verification of delivery. If you must receive an acknowledgment for your letter, you should use Return Receipt Requested forms so that you know that your letter arrived. These forms require recipients to sign and return a form indicating they have received the letter.

Upper-layer applications (applications that reside above IPX, such as NCP) can provide a level of guarantee that is implied. For example, if I send an NCP request to open a file using IPX as the network layer protocol, and if I do not receive an NCP reply, I can assume that my request did not get there and retransmit the request. The upper-layer protocol, NCP, however, is waiting for a response and will take some action if no reply is forthcoming within its timeout parameters.

### What Applications Use IPX?

Over 90 percent of the applications written for NetWare's IPX/SPX stack are written to use connectionless IPX services. This is because of the low overhead of IPX — requiring no connection establishment (the handshake), no acknowledgment on a per-packet basis (let the upper-layer protocol reissue a request only when necessary), and a very small header structure in the packets (30 bytes overhead).

### A Glimpse at an IPX Header

An IPX header defines the packet source internetwork address and destination internetwork address as well as an indication of how far the packet has traveled based on the number of routers the packet has crossed. Communications that use IPX have an IPX header immediately following the header of the datalink layer (such as Ethernet or Token Ring). For example, Figure 6.2 shows a sample packet that contains an IPX header. This packet is an NCP packet used to "ping" for NDS services. As you can see, the IPX header is not very large — only 30 bytes total, in fact.

▶ · · · · · · · · · · · · · · · · · · · · · · · · · · · · · · · ◀

FIGURE  6.2

The IPX header follows
the datalink header.

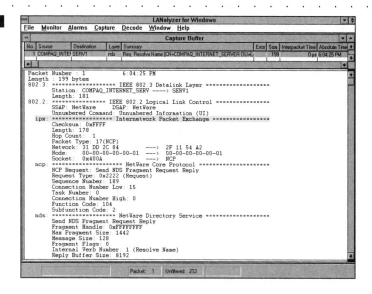

```
                                    LANalyzer for Windows
File   Monitor   Alarms   Capture   Decode   Window   Help
                                    Capture Buffer
No. Source        Destination    Layer Summary                                        Error Size Interpacket Time Absolute Time
   1 COMPAQ_INTEF SERV1          nds   Req Resolve Name [CN=COMPAQ_INTERNET_SERVER OU=L  199        0 µs 6:04:25 PM

Packet Number : 1              6:04:25 PM
Length : 199 bytes
802.3: ================= IEEE 802.3 Datalink Layer =================
       Station: COMPAQ_INTERNET_SERV ----> SERV1
       Length: 181
802.2: ================= IEEE 802.2 Logical Link Control ================
       SSAP: NetWare      DSAP: NetWare
       Unnumbered Command: Unnumbered Information (UI)
  ipx: ================= Internetwork Packet Exchange ================
       Checksum: 0xFFFF
       Length: 178
       Hop Count: 1
       Packet Type: 17(NCP)
       Network: 31 DD 2C 84      --->  2F 11 54 A2
       Node:    00-00-00-00-00-01 --->  00-00-00-00-00-01
       Socket:  0x400A           --->  NCP
  ncp: ================= NetWare Core Protocol ================
       NCP Request: Send NDS Fragment Request Reply
       Request Type: 0x2222 (Request)
       Sequence Number: 189
       Connection Number Low: 15
       Task Number: 0
       Connection Number High: 0
       Function Code: 104
       Subfunction Code: 2
  nds: ================= NetWare Directory Service ================
       Send NDS Fragment Request Reply
       Fragment Handle: 0xFFFFFFFF
       Max Fragment Size: 1442
       Message Size: 128
       Fragment Flags: 0
       Internal Verb Number: 1 (Resolve Name)
       Reply Buffer Size: 8192

                      Packet  1   Unfiltered  233
```

**X-REF**

**For detailed information on the functionality of IPX and the fields contained in the IPX header, refer to Chapter 7.**

## SEQUENCED PACKET EXCHANGE (SPX AND SPX II)

SPX was modeled after the Xerox Sequenced Packet Protocol (SPP) and is a connection-oriented transport protocol.

A *connection-oriented* protocol requires the two sides of the communication to set up a connection before they exchange any data. This process is often called the *handshake* process. The handshake is started by one side of a communication, which requests an SPX connection from the other side. If the other side has SPX connection slots available, it will respond. Now the first side can send data to its SPX partner.

TCP is the connection-oriented protocol portion of the TCP/IP protocol stack. Connection-oriented protocols are used when you want to ensure that each packet is received by the other side without requiring a higher-layer protocol to track the communications. For example, when you do an IPX-based file read, the IPX protocol itself does not track and acknowledge data packets. If, however, you are using an SPX-based file read application, each data packet sent from the server to the client may be acknowledged with an SPX acknowledgment packet.

**For detailed information on SPX, refer to Chapter 8.**

**X-REF**

### What Applications Use SPX?

SPX is typically used by backup programs, print server programs, remote control software, and gateway software. Some example programs that use SPX include:

- ▸ Remote Console programs (Novell's RCONSOLE.EXE and PC Anywhere)

- ▸ NetWare Print Server (Novell's and most third-party print servers)

- ▸ NetWare for SAA

- ▸ Backup solutions (such as Cheyenne's ARCserve and Seagate's Backup Exec)

- ▸ Some paranoid games (such as Spectre)

When would you want to use IPX when SPX offers guaranteed connection-oriented delivery? When you don't want to put up with the extra overhead caused by the handshake process, a longer packet header (it now includes a 12-byte SPX portion), and the acknowledgment packets.

### How Much Slower Is SPX Than IPX?

SPX has overhead and limitations that do not plague IPX. The additional overhead is caused by a larger header structure (thereby reducing the actual data portion of the packet). The biggest limitation on SPX is its inability to do large bursty data exchanges (like IPX's Burst Mode communications). These inherent faults cause SPX-based applications to perform slower than IPX-based applications.

Let's compare the communication sequence of IPX to that of standard SPX.

In Figure 6.3, we can see an IPX-based Burst Mode file read process on a Token Ring network. The reply burst transmits 17 packets (averaging around 4,100 bytes each).

FIGURE 6.3

*An example of an IPX-based Burst Mode read on a 4 Mbps Token Ring network*

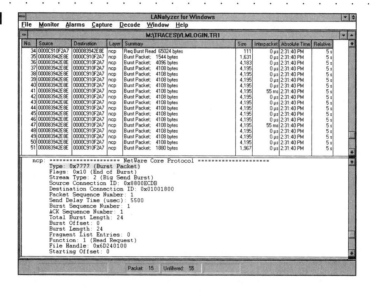

**On an Ethernet network, the maximum packet size is 1,518 bytes.**

NOTE

In Figure 6.4, however, we can see how an SPX-based file read process works. Standard SPX requires that the handshake process be performed up front, and it does not support windowing (and thus is limited to one outstanding packet at a time, requiring an acknowledgment for each data packet sent). Also, it can only support a 576-byte packet size (512 bytes for data and up to 64 bytes for header).

**The 576-byte limitation can be seen in a number of areas of NetWare communications. It is a throwback to the days when ARCnet networks were one of the top three network types. ARCnet networks only support 576-byte packet sizes. When you wanted to program a protocol to use the lowest common denominator in networking, you'd choose ARCnet defaults. Newer protocol versions communicate with the LAN driver to find out the current packet size used.**

NOTE

F I G U R E   6.4

An example of an SPX-
based communication

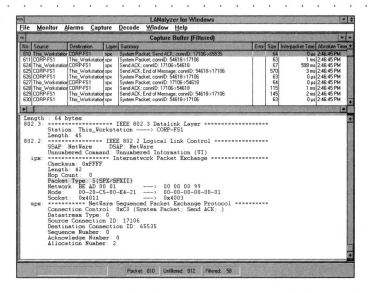

The SPX partners must handshake first. After that process, SPX data packets can be sent one at a time, requiring an acknowledgment for each packet sent before the next packet can be transmitted. Each packet can be a maximum of 576 bytes in length and requires an additional 12 bytes in the header for SPX information.

When you compare the two protocols, you can see that IPX-based communications are much faster for standard file transfers. SPX, however, offers the connection-oriented, guaranteed delivery needed for some applications. In order to provide this connection-oriented, guaranteed delivery and increase the efficiency of file transfers, Novell developed a second iteration of SPX (called SPX II).

### What Is the Difference Between SPX and SPX II?

Realizing the limitations that SPX imposed on the development community, Novell developed and released a new version of SPX called SPX II. SPX II has the following advantages over SPX:

- ▶ *Windowing.* SPX II headers use fields for sequencing, acknowledgment, and window sizing.

- ▶ *Large packets.* SPX II can use the full packet size that is determined as the connection is established—it is not limited to 576 bytes.

▸ *Renegotiation on route failure.* SPX II will renegotiate the packet sizes used for communication upon failure. (This takes into account the fact that different packet sizes may be used for send and receive paths as a result of parallel routes between two points.)

### A Glimpse at SPX Headers

An SPX header contains sequencing information and acknowledgment requests (Return Receipt Requested) whenever necessary. Communications that use SPX have an IPX header and a 12-byte SPX header. These headers immediately follow the datalink layer header. For example, Figure 6.5 shows a packet that contains an SPX header. This packet is an acknowledgment packet for data received.

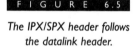

F I G U R E   6.5

*The IPX/SPX header follows the datalink header.*

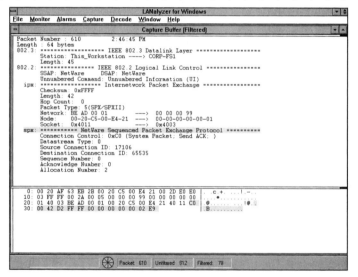

An SPX II header can be more extensive. Typically, SPX II headers have additional information that is exchanged during the connection setup routine. Figure 6.6 shows an SPX II packet. In the Connection Control field, a bit is set to indicate that this client wants to use SPX II.

FIGURE 6.6

The SPX II bit (SPX II) in the Connection Control field is set to indicate that SPX II is the desired connection-oriented protocol.

**Detailed information on SPX and SPX II can be found in Chapter 8.**

X-REF

## SERVICE ADVERTISING PROTOCOL (SAP)

Novell's SAP is used for two purposes: to locate a single service (perform a lookup) and to exchange information about services between servers/routers on the network. SAP is one of the protocols that has come under attack in the NetWare protocol stack because of its "broadcasty" nature. Ideally, in the future, clients and devices will use NDS to look up services and NLSP to exchange routing information.

### Looking Up Services

When a client is looking up a service on the network, there are two ways to perform the lookup—send out a SAP query for a specific service type or "walk" the NDS tree structure to locate the service. Currently, many vendors still use SAP to look up a service, but the future clearly defines NDS lookups as taking over this role.

When a client performs a SAP lookup, as shown in Figure 6.7, it broadcasts a SAP query packet that defines the type of service it is looking for. For example, type 0x0004 (hexadecimal number) is a NetWare bindery-based file service; type 0x0278 is a NetWare NDS server.

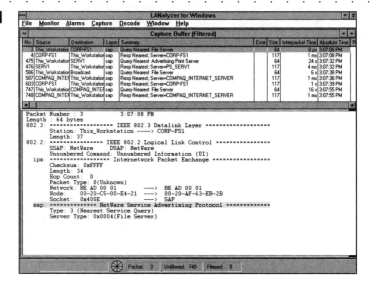

F I G U R E   6.7

*Clients include the server type information inside the SAP request.*

**X-REF**

**Refer to Appendix E, "SAP Number List," for a complete listing of assigned SAP numbers. Servers and routers maintain a Server Information Table (SIT) that lists all known network services. They respond directly to the client with the service's internetwork address. The client can then use the Routing Information Protocol (RIP) to find a route to the service. For more information on IPX internetwork addressing, refer to Chapter 7.**

### Exchanging Service Information

By default, every NetWare server uses SAP to broadcast its Server Information Table onto the network—it broadcasts its table every 60 seconds. In fact, any product that sits on top of run-time NetWare, such as the Multiprotocol Router or NetWare for SAA, also broadcasts its Service Information Table onto the network every 60 seconds. Most third-party IPX/SPX routers are also configured by default to broadcast their Service Information Table onto the network every 60 seconds.

As your network grows and the number of services offered increases, this type of broadcast-based information exchange can cause a bandwidth bottleneck. In Figure 6.8, for example, we see a network that supports an FDDI backbone with

NetWare Multiprotocol Routers (MPRs) that connect the various networks to the backbone. Every 60 seconds the MPRs broadcast information about all 700 backbone services onto each of the connected networks.

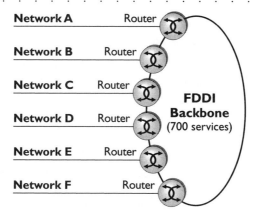

F I G U R E   6.8

*A sample network that*
*supports 700 services*

**Network A**  Router

**Network B**  Router

**Network C**  Router

**Network D**  Router

**FDDI Backbone**
**(700 services)**

**Network E**  Router

**Network F**  Router

Not only is this SAP information exchange dumping ugly broadcast packets onto the network, but SAP uses itty-bitty stinkin' packet sizes (576 bytes) by default—that's what limits you to seven services in each packet. Not very efficient.

You have a number of ways to enhance SAP performance on your network now. Newer versions of the NetWare routing specification enable you to alter the packet size to use the appropriate media access control size. You can also filter unnecessary SAP traffic on the network and change the update interval.

**For details on SAP packet size limitations, reconfiguring the update interval, filtering techniques, and performance issues, refer to Chapter 9.**

X-REF

### The Future for SAP

Because of its inherent limitations, SAP does not have a very bright future as the service lookup/information exchange protocol for NetWare. NDS can be used to look up services, and NetWare Link Services Protocol (NLSP) can be used to exchange service information more efficiently.

Later in this chapter we'll cover NDS and NLSP functionality in general.

**X-REF**

For details on **NDS** and **NLSP** communications, refer to Chapters 13 and 11, respectively.

## ROUTING INFORMATION PROTOCOL (RIP)

Novell's RIP protocol also has two functions—it is used to look up routes to networks, and it is used to exchange network information between NetWare servers/routers. Just like SAP, NetWare's RIP is a very "broadcasty" protocol. Routers send RIP broadcasts to send out their routing tables every 60 seconds by default.

### Lookup Routes

RIP route lookups typically occur immediately following SAP lookups. Once a client learns the internetwork address of a service (using SAP), the client sends a RIP broadcast packet onto the network to see what device can get to that network.

A NetWare server or router answers this query directly and tells the client how far away the service is based on the number of routers that must be crossed (hops) to get to the destination, as shown in Figure 6.9. NetWare servers and routers maintain a Routing Information Table (RIT) that lists all known network numbers and their distances away from the local router.

F I G U R E   6.9

*RIP replies inform the client of the number of hops and ticks to the destination.*

### Exchanging Network Information

By default, every NetWare operating system (including run-time NetWare) uses RIP to broadcast its Routing Information Table onto the network every 60 seconds. Once again, any product that sits on top of run-time NetWare, such as the Multiprotocol Router or NetWare for SAA, also broadcasts its Routing Information Table onto the network every 60 seconds. Most third-party IPX/SPX routers also are configured by default to broadcast their Routing Information Table onto the network every 60 seconds, as well.

**NOTE**

**The TCP/IP protocol stack also has a RIP protocol. NetWare's RIP and TCP/IP's RIP are entirely different protocols.**

Unlike SAP, these RIP updates are unlikely to cause a tremendous bandwidth bottleneck because more information can be carried in each RIP packet—up to 50 networks can be listed in a single RIP update packet. Each RIP entry takes up only 8 bytes, as shown in Figure 6.10. The packets are still itty-bitty stinkin' packets (576 bytes maximum) by default, however. Newer versions of the NetWare routing specification enable you to alter the packet size to use the appropriate media access control size. You can also filter unnecessary RIP traffic on the network and change the update interval.

▶ . . . . . . . . . . . . . . . . . . . . . . . . . . . . ◀

F I G U R E   6.10

*RIP packets can contain up to 50 network numbers and their associated distance in hops and ticks from the local network.*

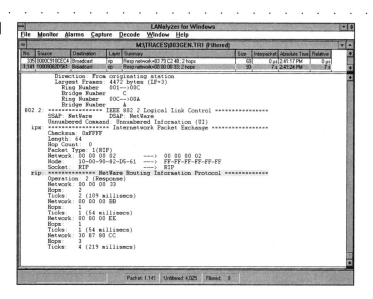

**For details on RIP packet size limitations, reconfiguring the update interval, filtering techniques, and performance issues, refer to Chapter 10.**

X-REF

### The Future for RIP

NetWare's RIP protocol has several problems. First, RIP has a slow convergence time. *Convergence* is the process that a routing protocol undergoes to learn of a topology or service change and make the information known to all active routers on the network. Second, RIP has a distance limitation of 15 hops, making it unsuitable for larger internetworks. Third, RIP makes assumptions on how long it takes to traverse a network—regardless of actual throughput times. Finally, the current implementations of RIP do not have the ability to load-balance. All these factors should be considered when you are looking at RIP's replacement, NLSP.

**NLSP is covered next in this chapter and in Chapter 11.**

X-REF

The limitations of RIP are due to its nature as a distance vector–based routing protocol. Distance vector routing protocols only keep track of the distance to the destination network address; they do not have the ability to load-balance—they cannot "see" the entire picture of the network. Some folks have described distance vector routers as "street signs" that just point you in the general direction of your destination. You follow the signs one at a time, never consulting a map to see if you are taking the best route. You could end up driving along side streets instead of hopping on a freeway. You could also hop on the freeway when it is a commute-hour parking lot.

A newer and more efficient link state routing protocol is available for NetWare—NetWare Link Services Protocol (NLSP).

## NETWARE LINK SERVICES PROTOCOL (NLSP)

As mentioned earlier, the limitations of RIP are due to its nature as a distance vector–based routing protocol. Distance vector routing protocols only keep track of the distance to the destination network address; they do not have the ability to load balance—they cannot "see" the entire picture of the network.

To combat this problem, Novell developed NLSP, a link state routing protocol, back around 1992. NLSP is derived from the IS-IS (Intermediate System to Intermediate System) routing protocol developed by the ISO (International Standards Organization). Link state routing protocols track the entire network layout based on the links between routers and networks. A diagram of the entire network is built upon this link information and used as the basis for making forwarding decisions.

NLSP can now be added to NetWare 3.11, NetWare 3.12, and NetWare 4.02 servers. NLSP is included in NetWare 4.10 and IntranetWare 4.11, as shown in Table 6.1.

| **T A B L E   6.1**  _Enabling NLSP for Various NetWare Versions_ | **NETWARE 3.11 AND NETWARE 4.02** |
|---|---|
| | IPXRT3.EXE file (available at www.support.novell.com) |
| | Release 1.0c is an update to the 1.0 release that upgrades NetWare 3.11 and NetWare 4.02 servers with the latest IPX router software. NOTE: This release does not support servers running NetWare MultiProtocol Router(TM), NetWare WAN Links(TM), or NetWare 3.x SFT III(TM). A revision to SFT III supporting NLSP is available with NetWare 4.1. |
| | **NETWARE 3.12** |
| | IPXRT4.EXE is only for NetWare 3.12 servers. It enhances the IPX routing capabilities of NetWare 3.12 servers by upgrading to version 1.1 of the IPX router software and by providing NLSP functionality. (Remember, IPXRT3.EXE is available for NetWare 3.11 and 4.0x servers). NOTE: IPXRT4.EXE does not support servers running NetWare MultiProtocol Router, NetWare WAN Links, NetWare Connect, or NetWare 3.12 SFT III. Provides all of the features and fixes provided by IPXRT3.EXE, and in addition provides routeless services. |
| | **NETWARE 4.1X** |
| | NLSP is included with NetWare 4.10 and IntranetWare 4.11. |
| | IPXRTR.NLM is the module that supports the NetWare NLSP routing protocol stack. IntranetWare 4.11 ships with IPXRTR.NLM version 5.07c. To check your IPXRTR version, type MODULES at the console prompt. If you are running a server that does not support NLSP, you will not see the IPXRTR.NLM listed in MODULES. |

**NOTE**

**There is no NLSP support for NetWare 4.01.**

### NLSP Overview

In a link state routing environment, such as NLSP, routers connected to the same segment are considered "neighbors," as shown in Figure 6.11.

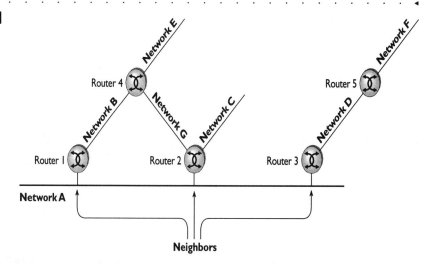

F I G U R E   6.11

*Routers connected to the same network segment are considered "neighbors."*

These neighbor routers transmit "hello" messages among themselves to build a database known as the *adjacencies database*. The adjacencies database simply lists all the other routers that are connected to the same segment. This database depicts the routers' immediate neighborhood.

Next, link state packets (LSPs) are shared among neighbors and flooded to all other routers. By sharing the adjacencies database across neighborhoods, NLSP routers can build a picture of the entire network, as shown in Figure 6.12. This picture of the entire network is called the *link state database*.

F I G U R E   6.12

*Putting together all the information learned from the adjacencies database helps build the link state database.*

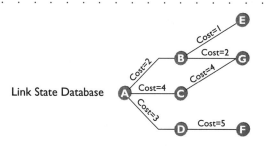

Link State Database

This logical picture of the network is just one step in the process of routing packets through the network using NLSP.

When the link state database has been built, NLSP routers use a decision process (Dijkstra's algorithm) to build a forwarding database. When a packet arrives destined to a network somewhere on the internetwork, the NLSP router looks up the network address in its forwarding database to determine which way to send the packet.

In some instances, however, NLSP and RIP/SAP must coexist on the same network. This may be a temporary situation to support migration to NLSP, or it may exist because the company wants to maintain a RIP/SAP area of their internetwork. This coexistence brings up some very important compatibility issues between NLSP and SAP/RIP.

### NLSP Compatibility Issues with RIP/SAP

NLSP was designed to seamlessly and transparently integrate with RIP/SAP. When you bring up the NetWare server, the configuration "mode" is set to use NLSP as the primary routing protocol. RIP/SAP backward compatibility and client RIP/SAP support is enabled by default, however. There are only two modes of IPX routing operation for NetWare servers: RIP/SAP only and NLSP with RIP/SAP compatibility (the default). The routing parameters are defined on a per-server basis but can be changed on a per-bindings basis if necessary.

 **This configuration is discussed further in Chapter 11.**

X-REF

**RIP/SAP Only**    In the RIP/SAP only mode, your NetWare server does not support NLSP communications with other routers. Your server broadcasts RIP and SAP update packets, not LSP packets. This is the default mode for all versions of NetWare up to version 4.1x. The new default is NLSP with RIP/SAP compatibility.

**NLSP with RIP/SAP Compatibility**    In NLSP with RIP/SAP compatibility mode, your NetWare server transmits LSP packets to build and share the link state database. Your NetWare server still answers RIP and SAP queries from client stations and can automatically detect non-NLSP devices on the network. Upon detection, the NLSP router periodically broadcasts RIP and SAP information on the required interface. This ensures seamless integration with older RIP-based routers. When an NLSP router detects only NLSP routers on the attached networks, the router stops transmitting RIP and SAP broadcasts automatically.

**Why Migrate to NLSP?**   The key reasons for moving over to NLSP include faster convergence, a larger possible number of IPX networks, load balancing between multiple paths, manageability through Management Information Bases (MIBs) and configurable link-cost assignment. Of course, if you have older versions of NetWare, you must update them to support NLSP.

**Faster Network Convergence**   *Convergence* is the process by which a routing protocol learns of a topology or service change and makes that change known to each of the active routers on the network. A network is said to have converged when all routers once again share the same view of the network. Link state routing protocols are much faster at convergence than distance vector routing protocols because network information is flooded throughout the network without being altered by routers. In a RIP environment, RIP routers receive routing information, process it, and then build and transmit a new RIP packet.

**Larger IPX Networks Possible**   Whereas packets relayed by RIP routers can travel no more than 15 hops between their source and destination, packets relayed by NLSP routers can travel up to 127 hops.

**Load Balancing**   NLSP can be configured to automatically distribute forwarded traffic across network interfaces. That is, given two or more equal-cost routes between two network nodes, NLSP distributes the traffic evenly among them.

**Configurable Link-Cost Assignment**   NLSP routers know the cost of every link and use this information to choose the most efficient route for each outgoing packet. This link cost can be configured to force data to travel a certain path, if desired.

**NLSP communications details can be found in Chapter 11.**

X-REF

## IPXWAN2

IPXWAN2, as its name implies, is the protocol used to support NetWare's IPX over various WAN media. Once the underlying medium, such as PPP, X.25, or frame relay, completes successful link establishment (as shown in Figure 6.13), IPXWAN2 begins a negotiation process between WAN routers to exchange identities and determine operational characteristics of the link. For example,

IPXWAN2 is used to time the WAN link to determine the name of the other router and the link delay.

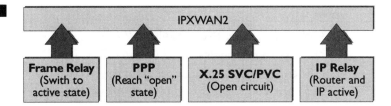

FIGURE 6.13

*IPXWAN2 can be used over a variety of WAN media link types.*

IPXWAN2 is the current version of the protocol and supports the following routing protocols across WAN media:

▸ *RIP.* A RIP WAN link supports standard RIP distance vector communications between each WAN router.

▸ *Unnumbered RIP.* Unnumbered RIP links are not assigned an IPX network number; they are seen most often on large networks that have a lot of WAN circuits.

▸ *On-demand static routes.* These routes are only initialized when there is data to be transmitted ("on-demand"). No actual routing information is exchanged—static routing and service tables are maintained by the routers at each end of the link.

▸ *Client-router connections.* These connections do not connect routers but connect a client system to a router system. No routing information is exchanged across the link other than client RIP or SAP information requests and the subsequent replies.

▸ *NLSP.* The NetWare Link Services protocol is a link state routing protocol that exchanges routing information using link state packets.

**The earlier version of IPXWAN (version 1) did not provide support for NLSP communications between WAN routers.**

**NOTE**

## NETWARE CORE PROTOCOL (NCP)

For many years I have described Novell's NCP as the "family jewels" to Novell. Most of the communications that occur on the NetWare network are NCP requests and replies for all types of network services, including file reads/writes, file searches, and the like.

NCP is a connection-based protocol that resides on top of a connectionless transport (IPX). Most often, you'll find that the NCP communications on your network consist of requests from clients and replies from servers, as shown in Figure 6.14.

**F I G U R E   6.14**

*A client makes an NCP request for a file called ~$DETAIL.DOC.*

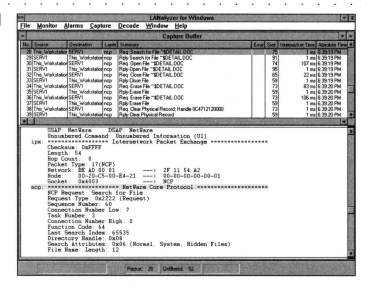

In order to receive NCP services, a client must have established an NCP connection with the server.

### What Is an NCP Connection?

An *NCP connection* is simply a logical connection between two systems. Two types of NCP connections are possible in NetWare: a *licensed connection* and an *unlicensed connection* (general service connection).

During the startup process, however, a client requests only an unlicensed NCP connection to establish communications. During the login or authentication process, the client changes its connection status to that of a licensed connection.

When you purchase NetWare, the operating system is stratified to support up to 1,000 unique NCP licensed connections, enabling up to 1,000 clients to access NetWare services on that single server at one time. All NetWare clients request and must obtain an NCP licensed connection in order to receive NCP-based services from the server or network they are working on.

Server-based NLMs can also use NCP connections. They can request and use unlicensed NCP connections above and beyond the licensed NCP connection limitation. The server-based NLMs use unlicensed connections to ensure that these NLMs do not take up NCP connections that are required by users to access network file and print services. The number of connections allowed varies depending on the version of the operating system and the number of connections licensed by that particular server, as shown in Figure 6.15.

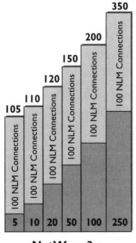

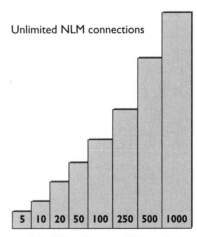

**F I G U R E   6.15**

*NetWare 3.x has only 100 NLM connections above the user-number connections, whereas NetWare and IntranetWare 4.x NLM connections are unlimited.*

**NetWare 3.x**

**NetWare/IntranetWare 4.x**

To view the number of NCP connections granted to NLMs and users, check the Connection Information area in MONITOR, as shown in Figure 6.16, which shows the Connection Information for a five-user version of NetWare 4.10. As you can see by the numbering assigned, we can assign more than five NCPs because of unlicensed NCP connections. Unlicensed connections show up as "not-logged-in" in the Connection Information screen.

F I G U R E   6.16

*NCP connection numbers assigned are not limited to licensed connections.*

Once your client has created a general service, or unlicensed connection, it can begin to use NCP calls to request services from the NetWare server.

### NCP Communications

Currently, you'll see only six different types of NCP communications on your network. They consist of the following:

▸ **1111 Create Service Connection/Echo Test Packet:** This NCP type is used for two purposes—first, a client sends this packet to request a connection ID number from the server. If the client already has a connection ID number and they are simply reestablishing a connection, the server gives the client the same number they held before disruption of service. This NCP type is also used by the NetWare VLMs to perform a Burst Mode and Big Packet test on the connection. This is called the LIP echo test.

**Refer to Chapter 13 for more details on Burst Mode and Big Packet.**

**X-REF**

▸ **2222 Standard Request:** This NCP type is used to request services such as accounting, bindery, file, messaging, server statistics, queue, and transaction tracking services. The type of request is defined by a function, subfunction (optional), and verb (optional) code field in the packet, as shown in Figure 6.17.

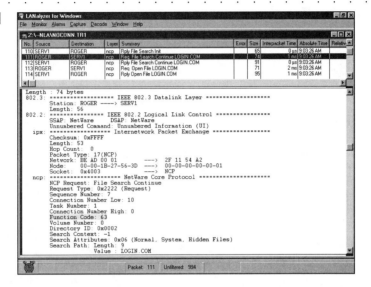

▸ **3333 Standard Reply:** This NCP type is used to respond to an NCP request. Reply packets vary in length depending on the information contained therein.

▸ **5555 Destroy Connection:** This NCP type is used to release an NCP connection. The NCP connection number can be reissued to another user or NLM that makes an NCP login request.

▸ **7777 Burst Mode Read/Write:** This NCP type is the newest of the NCP type numbers and is used to exchange files with a server using packet bursting technology.

▸ **9999 Request Being Processed:** This NCP packet type is sometimes referred to as a "Server Delay" or "Server Overload" communication. Servers transmit this packet to requesting clients to inform those clients that their request was received but the server was unable to process the request at that time. Clients will reset their timeout counters and eventually retransmit a request if no reply is forthcoming before the timeout counter value is reached.

**Refer to Chapter 13 for more information on Burst Mode technology.**

X-REF

Typically, when you are analyzing NetWare communications, the first time you'll encounter an NCP packet is during the client connection process.

**For details on NCP communications, refer to Chapter 13.**

X-REF

## NETWARE DIRECTORY SERVICES (NDS)

Many people feel that NDS is the hottest technology to be added to NetWare since drive duplexing and mirroring came around. In fact, NDS has revolutionized the way NetWare networks are structured, administered, and analyzed.

NDS is a database that is distributed across the entire network. Before NDS came along, we used bindery services and had to go from server to server to locate and access objects on the network. Those objects were created, modified, and managed on a per-server basis as well, making administration of a larger network quite tedious and time consuming.

How much traffic overhead does NDS cause? This is a common question that I receive in my lectures. Let's first look at the three primary types of NDS traffic that you'll see on the network:

- Authentication traffic

- NDS database replication traffic

- Time synchronization traffic

### Authentication Traffic

With NDS services, an authentication process verifies a user's rights and provides the user with access network servers, printers, and volumes. When you enter your username and password, the authentication process begins, as shown in Figure 6.18. Authentication is performed in the background for additional

NetWare 4.1x server connections. These additional authentications are performed transparently.

**FIGURE   6.18**

*The authentication process for user Admin.TC*

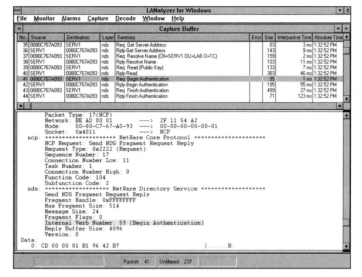

### NDS Database Replication Traffic

One of the key design factors of the NDS architecture includes redundancy of the NDS database. Branches of the NDS tree are "partitioned" and replicated across the network to other servers, as shown in Figure 6.19. You can use an analyzer to track the effect of this replication traffic on your network. There is no set formula to figure out the traffic overhead based on the size of the tree.

### Time Synchronization Traffic

Any changes to the NDS database must be time-stamped to ensure proper ordering of events that have taken place, such as object creation, modification, and deletion from the NDS database. Time synchronization is a process that is used to ensure that all servers in a directory tree report the same time.

The authentication, replication, and time synchronization processes can be seen on an analyzer, as shown in Figure 6.20. Their effect on the network is typically minimal—of course, it is dependent on the size of your tree and the number of partitions being replicated.

F I G U R E   6.19

*Replicas of NDS partitions
are copied across the wire.*

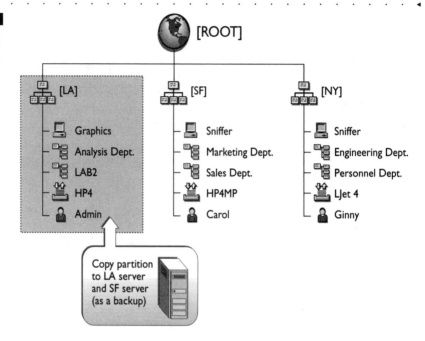

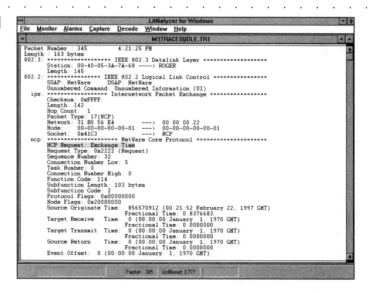

F I G U R E   6.20

*NetWare's time
synchronization process can
be tracked on an analyzer.*

**X-REF**

**For details on NDS traffic and communication sequences, refer to Chapter 13.**

## NOVELL REPLICATION SERVICES (NRS)

Cool stuff! Novell Replication Services (NRS) is a file replication system that can be used to maintain and manage identical copies of files on geographically separate NetWare 4.*x* networks. NRS can be scheduled to distribute files across a slow WAN link when no other traffic is taking up valuable bandwidth. NRS can also be designed to replicate files from a master server to a single remote server that, in turn, replicates files to its local peer servers, as shown in Figure 6.21.

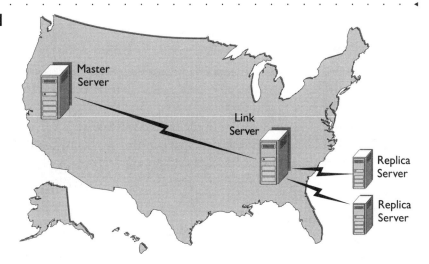

**FIGURE 6.21**

*NRS uses master, link, and replica servers to maintain replicated files across an internetwork.*

NRS can be connected with any transport protocol but must be located in the same NDS tree — file replication cannot span directory trees at this time. Depending on your network design and your company focus, you may wish to replicate a single file or a whole set of files across your internetwork.

### What Files Can You Replicate?

You can replicate documents such as word processor files, spreadsheets, and presentations, as well as system files such as applications, tools, and client/server operating system files.

You can also replicate intranet files, such as HTML files. Imagine that you have an office in San Francisco and another office in London. Each office maintains a NetWare Web server. Use NRS to replicate HTML files between locations to keep each office up to date on the international information. You can set the replication time to the end of the local day to ensure that the replication process does not interfere with workday communications across the WAN link.

In order to support this type of functionality, some special steps must be defined to ensure that the replicated file is always in sync.

### Handling a Clash

A synchronization "clash" occurs when a change made to a file on a Replica server conflicts with a change made to a file on the Master server. When two or more users make changes to the same file (located on different servers of the network), a clash will occur. Attempting to replicate a database that is accessed by multiple users may cause a clash.

When a clash occurs, an error message displays on the server console. The error is also logged in a diagnostics log on the replica server. The file updates are saved in the recovery directory—if a clash occurred because updates were being made to the Master and Replica servers, the Master updates are performed while the Replica update is stored in the recovery directory.

Use the information contained in the log to manually copy, move, or delete recovered updates as desired.

## MOBILE IPX

Mobile IPX is a technology, not a product. This technology alters the client communication process to enable a NetWare client station to move from network to network while maintaining a virtual internetwork address and keeping its connection as it moves about.

Typically, when a client station connects to a network service, it obtains its IPX internetwork address during the startup sequence. This address is used as the source address on all communications it sends from that point on. When a server replies to the client's request, the reply is sent to the client's IPX internetwork address, as shown in Figure 6.22.

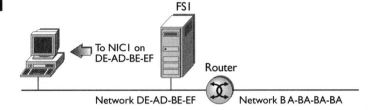

F I G U R E   6.22

*The server sends the response back to the client's IPX internetwork address.*

If the client moves from one location to another without reloading the client software, the client does not dynamically discover a new IPX internetwork address, but replies go to the client's original location, as shown in Figure 6.23.

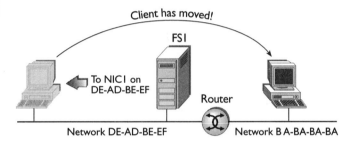

F I G U R E   6.23

*If the client moves without reloading the client software, it will use its old address and the server will respond to the wrong address.*

When a Mobile IPX client comes onto the network, it looks for a Home Router. The client tells the Home Router what its IPX internetwork address is, and the Home Router provides the Mobile IPX client with a constant, or virtual, address to use for its source address. Interestingly, the constant address makes the Mobile IPX client appear as if it is located on the Home Router's Internal IPX network, as shown in Figure 6.24.

▶ . . . . . . . . . . . . . . . . . . . . . . . . . . . . . . . . . . . . ◀

*The Mobile IPX client's
constant address makes the
client appear to be located
on the Home Router's
Internal IPX network.*

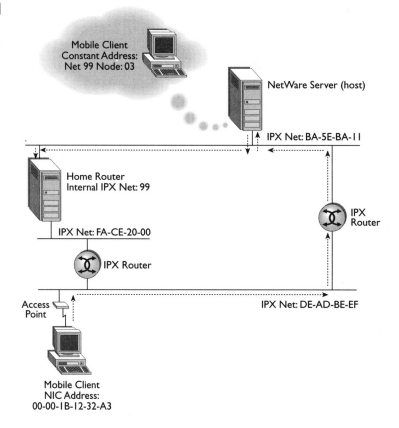

When the mobile client communicates with a server on the network, it uses its constant address as its source IPX internetwork address. The server responds to this address, which is actually at the Home Router. The Home Router changes the reply's destination address to the Mobile IPX client's true physical address and forwards the packet accordingly, as shown in Figure 6.25.

FIGURE  6.25

*The Home Router changes the destination address to forward the packet to the Mobile IPX client's true location.*

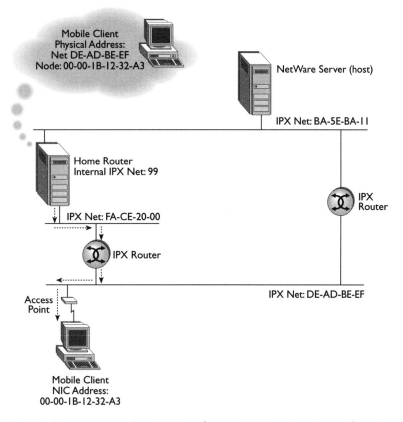

If the Mobile IPX client moves, the NESL software "kicks in" and notifies the Home Router of the new physical address. The Home Router now uses the new address for forwarding communications to the Mobile IPX client.

Mobile IPX requires special software at the client and a Home Router process. These two elements make Mobile IPX work.

### The Mobile IPX Client

You must add NESL (NetWare Event Service Layer) software and a Mobile IPX–aware LAN driver to the client in order for the Mobile IPX to know about changes in the client's location or address. Your IPXODI layer must also be loaded with an "/M" parameter to enable Mobile IPX.

**IntranetWare 4.11 and the Multiprotocol Router v3.1 software include the Mobile IPX–required software.**

**NOTE**

After you have changed your client over to Mobile IPX, your STARTNET.BAT file may look like this:

```
@ECHO OFF

SET NWLANGUAGE=ENGLISH

CD NWCLIENT

LSL

NESL

NE2000

IPXODI /M

VLM /ps=FS1

CD \
```

### The Home Router

The Home Router process can be enabled through INETCFG at the MPR or IntranetWare 4.11 server, as shown in Figure 6.26.

▶ · · · · · · · · · · · · · · · · · · · · · · · · · · · · · · · · · · ◀

| FIGURE 6.26 |
|---|

*Use INETCFG to designate a server as a Home Router.*

## DIAGNOSTIC RESPONDER

We come to the good ol' Diagnostic Responder—rarely talked about, but still a useful tool in NetWare. If you've ever used the old COMCHECK utility, you've used the Diagnostic Responder. The Diagnostic Responder is a service that is included in all versions of Novell operating system and client software.

By building a Diagnostic Responder query packet and transmitting it onto the network, you can effectively "ping" all these Novell clients and servers in one shot. You can use the Diagnostic Responder to:

▸ Determine if a client is up and running

▸ Measure round-trip delay time from various network devices

▸ Find out the internal and external addressing scheme used on a remote server

The Diagnostic Responder socket is enabled by default on all clients, but users can disable it. To see the IPXODI load options, type **IPXODI /?** at the client's DOS prompt, as shown in Figure 6.27. NetWare's Diagnostic Responder is a property of the IPX 32-bit protocol for NetWare Client 32, whose values are set through the dialog box shown in Figure 6.28.

FIGURE   6.27

*Type **IPXODI /?** to view loading options for IPXODI.*

**I personally recommend that you do not teach the general end user the /? parameter for fear they will start playing around with the default settings and ruin your networking life.**

TIP

F I G U R E   6.28

*NetWare's Diagnostic Responder is a property of the IPX 32-bit protocol for NetWare Client 32.*

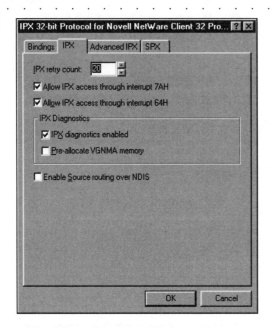

The successor to the Diagnostic Responder is IPX Ping—but IPX Ping is not enabled in older NetWare clients and servers, so you may still want to use the Diagnostic Responder to query them.

### IPX PING

IPX Ping is simply an IPX packet with the word "PING" in ASCII following an IPX header and a Request/Reply field. Although similar to the Diagnostic Responder, IPX Ping comes with a server-based NLM (PING.NLM) that is used to transmit the Ping packets and listen for responses, as shown in Figure 6.29.

**FIGURE 6.29**

*Type LOAD IPXPING at the server console to access the IPX Ping utility.*

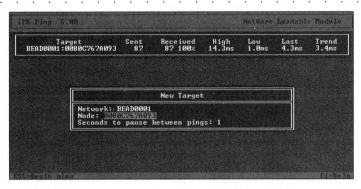

Devices that support IPX Ping reply with the same packet, except that they denote "reply" in the Request/Reply field. IPX PING.NLM provides you with the completion ratio, the slowest and fastest response times, and the average response time. Table 6.2 lists devices that will and will not respond to the IPX Ping packets.

**TABLE 6.2**

*Who Answers IPX Ping?*

| NO IPX PING SUPPORT | IPX PING SUPPORT |
| --- | --- |
| NetWare 3.x Servers | NetWare 4.1x Servers |
| NetWare 4.0x Servers | IntranetWare 4.1x Servers |
| NETX Clients | NetWare MPR v3.x |
| VLM Clients (v1.20a) | Client 32 |
| MS Client for NetWare | |

## NETWARE/IP AND NATIVE IP

With the battle of IP versus IPX raging on these days, Novell has provided solutions that enable you to mix and match transport mechanisms if you want a "TCP/IP only" network design. Since TCP/IP is a de facto, tried and tested networking protocol, many shops are trying to standardize on the TCP/IP protocol stack for all their communications. These solutions include NetWare/IP and Native IP.

**Novell currently uses the terms *Pure IP* and *Native IP* interchangeably to describe NCP over IP communications.**

**NOTE**

### NetWare/IP

The first option (available in NetWare 4) is NetWare/IP. NetWare/IP was designed to support NetWare services over the TCP/IP transport and remove the dependency on RIP and SAP for locating services and networks.

NetWare/IP requires the following components:

▸ Domain Name Server (DNS)

▸ Domain SAP Server (DSS)

▸ NetWare/IP servers

▸ NetWare/IP clients

Figure 6.30 shows these four NetWare/IP elements. Note that a DSS server can also be a NetWare/IP server.

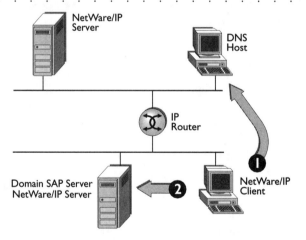

**FIGURE 6.30**

*All four components are required to support NetWare/IP.*

**Domain Name Server (DNS)**  DNS provides a name-to-IP address mapping scheme that enables users to locate a computer when they only know a name, such as "imagitech.com." As shown in Figure 6.30, this is the first communications step of a NetWare/IP client.

NetWare/IP uses this technology to help NetWare/IP clients and servers locate a specific type of service—the Domain SAP Server (DSS) within the NetWare/IP network.

**Domain SAP Server (DSS)**   DSS maintain the SAP and RIP information for NetWare/IP clients. When a NetWare/IP server comes up, it uses DNS to look up the nearest DSS. The NetWare/IP server then sends its SAP and RIP records to the DSS. As shown in Figure 6.30, this is the second communications step of a NetWare/IP client.

Whenever a client performs a lookup of services (such as NLIST), it relies on the DSS servers. DSS uses a replication scheme similar to NDS—there is a primary DSS server that maintains the master database of SAP and RIP information. Secondary DSS server(s) can provide redundancy and load balancing for busy NetWare/IP networks.

**NetWare/IP Servers**   The NetWare/IP server is a NetWare 4.*x* server that supports the TCP/IP and NWIP NLMs. By default, NetWare/IP servers provide services to TCP/IP nodes only. You can, however, configure the NetWare/IP server to act as a gateway between IP and IPX networks.

**NetWare/IP Clients**   NetWare/IP comes with 16-bit, VLM-based NetWare/IP client software; however, the following NetWare clients can access a NetWare/IP network when properly configured:

▶ NetWare Client 32 for Windows 95

▶ NetWare Client 32 for DOS and Windows

▶ NetWare Client 32 for Windows NT

▶ NetWare Client for Mac OS

NetWare/IP client packets may not be what you think they are—NetWare/IP packets are simply the NetWare NCP/IPX communication encapsulated within a UDP/IP header structure, as shown in Figure 6.31.

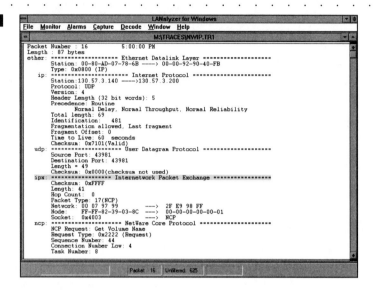

**FIGURE 6.31**

*NetWare/IP packet structures include an IPX header portion.*

## Native IP

The development of Native IP has been long awaited by Novell clients. Native IP is part of Novell's Open Communications project and provides NCP services directly over the TCP/IP stack.

Unlike NetWare/IP communications that still require an IPX header, as shown in Figure 6.32, Native IP packets place the NCP header and data directly after a UDP or TCP header. UDP transport is typically used for smaller packet exchanges, whereas TCP is used for the larger read/write NCPs.

**FIGURE 6.32**

*Unlike NetWare/IP, Native IP does not require an IPX header in the packet.*

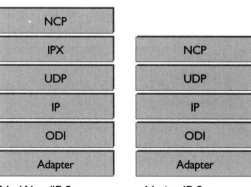

NetWare/IP Structure          Native IP Structure

Just as NetWare IP uses DNS and DSS for naming and discovery services, Native IP uses DNS and Service Location Protocol (SLP) for naming and discovery. Dynamic Host Configuration Protocol (DHCP) is used to automatically assign dynamic IP addresses to Native IP clients.

Figure 6.33 shows the basic communication steps that a Native IP client takes to locate an NDS server using Native IP.

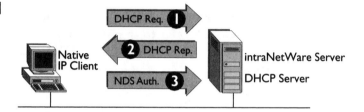

FIGURE 6.33

*A Native IP client can use DHCP to obtain an IP address before it can authenticate to NDS.*

Native IP is a significant advancement for NetWare LANs and WANs because it allows true IP-based communications from client to server. When IntranetWare ships with Native IP, it will be the first time a version of the NetWare operating system is not dependent upon IPX for transport.

Let's take a look at how DNS, DHCP, and SLP are used to create a TCP/IP-based NetWare network using Native IP.

**DNS (Domain Name System)**   In a typical DNS environment, a client makes a request to contact a host by its name (such as "ftp imagitech.com"). The client software sends a DNS lookup request to the DNS server. The reply contains the IP address of the desired host ("imagitech.com").

Novell's DNS enables IP clients to look up service IP addresses. Novell is extending the NDS schema to support DNS and enable DNS servers to read data from NDS and respond to queries.

**DHCP (Dynamic Host Configuration Program)**   DHCP enables dynamic assignment of IP addresses. DHCP clients request an IP address from a DHCP host. Once the client is finished using that IP address, it is "returned" to the DHCP server's address list to be assigned to another client upon request.

Novell's implementation of DHCP enables assignment of IP addresses based on configuration from NDS. This is accomplished by extending the NDS schema to include DHCP support. Clients request and receive an IP address from a DHCP host (implemented as an NLM on a NetWare server).

DHCP support includes client files and server files to extend the NDS schema and provide DHCP services.

**SLP (Service Location Protocol)**   SLP enables TCP/IP nodes to discover services using a service discovery mechanism. SLP is similar to SAP lookup services. Just as we typically use SAP in the IPX environment to request a certain type of service ("Get Nearest Server," for example), you can use SLP in the IP environment to request a service based on a descriptor.

**Novell's implementation of SLP is RFC-compliant. For more information on SLP refer to the RFCs at** `ftp://ietf.org/ internet-drafts`. **The name of the RFC for SLP begins with** *draft-ietf-svrloc.*

**TIP**

## NETWARE IPX-IP GATEWAY

One function of the Novell Internet Access Server (NIAS) that is included in IntranetWare 4.11 is an IPX-IP gateway. This feature was developed to enable IPX-based clients to use TCP-based Winsock applications without requiring an IP stack at the client. Novell followed other companies, such as Quarterdeck (Iware Connect) and Firefox (NOV*IX for Internet) in making such a product, but Novell's gateway is the first one that is truly NDS-enabled. IPXIPGW.NLM provides the server IPX-IP gateway functionality.

### How Does the IPX-IP Gateway Work?

The IPX-IP gateway product requires two essential components—the gateway server (a set of NLMs loaded on a NetWare 4.*x* server) and the gateway client (that includes a special WINSOCK.DLL file). Any WINSOCK v1.1 application will work with the client software.

The Winsock DLL receives all the calls made by the Winsock application and sends the appropriate messages to the gateway. The gateway executes the actions over a TCP/IP stack on behalf of the client, as shown in Figure 6.34.

Upon receipt of the packet, the IPX-IP gateway makes the TCP/IP socket connection requested by the client on its behalf. Once the remote communication channel is open, the gateway can forward IP requests and replies through the channel as quickly as they are received and allowed by client buffers.

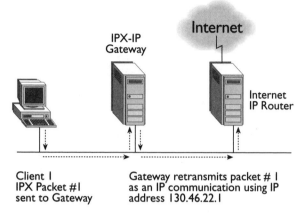

F I G U R E   6.34

*Clients transmit IPX packets directly to the IPX-IP gateway server.*

### What Is the Advantage of Being NDS-Enabled?

Although some IPX-IP gateway manufacturers claimed to have an NDS-enabled solution, Novell is the first vendor to come out with a truly NDS-enabled version of the IPX-IP gateway.

By extending the NDS schema (database structure) to include the IPX-IP gateway object, gateway clients authenticate to NDS to determine their rights regardless of which IPX-IP gateway they are going through to access the Internet/intranet. With other IPX-IP gateway solutions, all management and access is provided on a "per-gateway" basis. In a large company that supports many gateways, user accounts and management profiles must be created several times— once for each gateway the company has installed.

## NETWARE IPX ADDRESS MAPPING GATEWAY (IAMG)

IAMG, included in NetWare 4.11 and later and in Novell's Border Manager, provides IPX-to-IPX network address translation (NAT) services for connecting multiple IPX networks that have duplicate or incorrect IPX network addresses and route summarization services.

As NetWare LANs and WANs grow, you may have to connect two or more IPX-based networks that have incompatible IPX network addresses. For example, in Figure 6.35 we have our lab network that uses IPX address BE-AD-00-001 and we have our company network that uses the same address. If we connect our lab

network onto the backbone without network address translation, we will receive
Router Configuration errors that alert us to the duplicate network addresses.

*If we connect the two
BE-AD-00-01 networks
together, we will receive
configuration error
messages.*

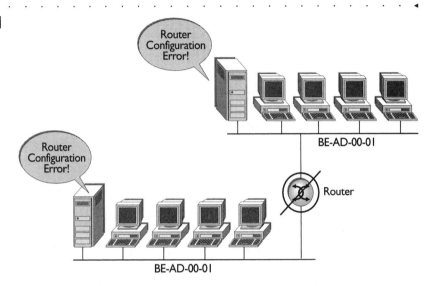

By installing an IPX Address Mapping gateway between the two networks, we
can overcome this problem. As shown in Figure 6.36, the gateway converts the
client's IPX network address to 01-02-03-8D.

*The gateway coverts the
client's IPX network address
to a legal IPX address when
it forwards the packet to
the other network.*

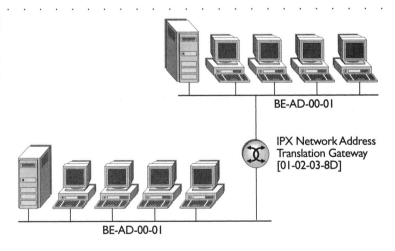

IAMG also includes a route aggregation component. *Route aggregation* (also referred to as route summarization) enables a router to summarize information about many routes into a single summary. For example, route aggregation enables a router to advertise that it can get to networks numbered 572\* (where the asterisk acts as a wildcard).

Route aggregation greatly reduces the amount of route information that must traverse the entire network.

## NCP WATCHDOG AND SERIALIZATION

NCP Watchdog and Serialization provide NCP connection and server copyright checking on the network. These are two processes that are seen on all NetWare LANs and often cause quite a bit of concern and dismay on NetWare WANs. They are notorious for bringing up dial-on-demand WAN links continuously and can cause quite a high WAN bill if allowed to go unchecked.

### NCP Watchdog

NCP Watchdog is a process that the operating system uses to determine if a client's connection is still valid. For example, if you get up from your machine and go to lunch, your connection is valid although you are no longer transmitting NCP requests to the server. If, however, you just turned off your machine (not properly unloading and sending an NCP Destroy Connection request to the server) and left for lunch, your connection is no longer valid. The NetWare server will use the NCP Watchdog process to find out that your connection is no longer valid.

By default, NCP Watchdog will wait five minutes after a client has stopped transmitting NCP requests before checking a connection's validity. If the client software (shell or requester) is still active on the station, it will send an NCP Watchdog reply to the server, as shown in Figure 6.37. If the client software is not active (in the case of the turned-off system), no reply is received and the server retransmits another watchdog one minute later (default). The server transmits another nine watchdog packets (for a total of 10 packets) before giving up and clearing the connection. Watchdog enables the operating system to differentiate between inactive valid connections (just taking a break from your workstation) and inactive invalid connections (when you just turned off your machine without shutting down properly).

*Watchdog packets are sent to each client after five minutes of inactivity.*

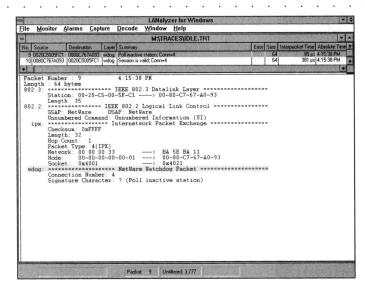

```
                                LANalyzer for Windows
 File  Monitor  Alarms  Capture  Decode  Window  Help
                            M:\TRACES\IDLE.TR1
 No. Source        Destination   Layer  Summary                              Error  Size  Interpacket Time  Absolute Time
   9 0020C5005FC1  0080C767A093  wdog   Poll inactive station; Conn=4                64    95 µs 4:15:38 PM
  10 0080C767A093  0020C5005FC1  wdog   Session is valid; Conn=4                     64   381 µs 4:15:38 PM

 Packet Number : 9              4:15:38 PM
 Length : 64 bytes
 802.3: ==================== IEEE 802.3 Datalink Layer ====================
        Station: 00-20-C5-00-5F-C1 ----> 00-80-C7-67-A0-93
        Length: 35
 802.2: ==================== IEEE 802.2 Logical Link Control ================
        SSAP: NetWare    DSAP: NetWare
        Unnumbered Command: Unnumbered Information (UI)
    ipx: ================== Internetwork Packet Exchange ==================
        Checksum: 0xFFFF
        Length: 32
        Hop Count: 1
        Packet Type: 4(IPX)
        Network: 00 00 00 33        ---> BA 5E BA 11
        Node:    00-00-00-00-00-01  ---> 00-80-C7-67-A0-93
        Socket:  0x4001             ---> 0x4021
   wdog: ==================== NetWare Watchdog Packet ====================
        Connection Number: 4
        Signature Character: ? (Poll inactive station)



                        Packet   9    Unfiltered 3,777
```

**X-REF**

**For more details on the NCP Watchdog process, packet structures, and WAN considerations, refer to Chapter 13.**

### The NetWare Serialization Process

NetWare servers exchange serialization information to ensure that the same copy of the operating system has not been loaded on more than one system. Serialization packets are transmitted onto the network addressed to a special serialization socket number, as shown in Figure 6.38. This enables Novell to check to see if a single copy of the operating system has been installed on multiple servers, thereby violating the software copyright.

Interestingly, on a NetWare 4.1x server, the serialization process will actually "rectify" the situation by reducing the license count to 1 on one of the servers that has the duplicate serial number.

**X-REF**

**For more information on the NetWare serialization process, packet structures, and WAN considerations, refer to Chapter 13.**

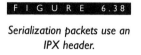

Serialization packets use an
IPX header.

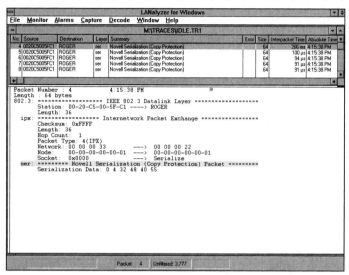

## Summary

In this chapter, we've examined the basic IPX/SPX protocol stack. Chapters 7 through 14 of this book show how the protocols work together. For example, when you look at the client connection processes for VLMs, you'll see the RIP request/reply process follow the SAP request/reply process. The RIP process is dependent upon the SAP process to obtain the network address for its request. The NCP process is used to perform the actual bindery-based login, but it may be accompanied by the NDS authentication process for NDS attachment.

In the next chapter we will take an in-depth look at NetWare's IPX protocol.

# CHAPTER 7

# NetWare IPX

It's true—NetWare's IPX/SPX protocol suite was developed based on Xerox's Xerox Network Systems (XNS) protocol suite. IPX, in fact, is almost a mirror of Xerox's Internetwork Datagram Protocol (IDP ). Over the past years, however, IPX has overcome many of the limitations imposed by the Xerox communications model. In this chapter we'll examine NetWare's connectionless protocol, IPX, in depth. We'll look at the functionality of IPX, how IPX-based applications work, and how the IPX header structure is formed and used on the network.

## Purpose of IPX

The primary purpose of IPX is to get packets through the entire internetwork. As stations transmit data across the internetwork, IPX appends a header to the beginning of the data. The header contains the source and destination internetwork addresses. A MAC header (Ethernet, Token Ring, etc.) is then placed in front of the IPX header. The MAC header can only be used to get the packet from one device on a network to another device on the same network.

Figure 7.1 shows how the MAC header and IPX headers are used to get a packet through the internetwork.

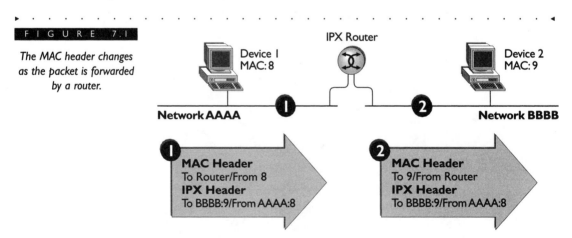

FIGURE   7.1

*The MAC header changes as the packet is forwarded by a router.*

In Figure 7.1, the device on network 0xAAAA transmits the packet to the router. The MAC address indicates local addresses only—from Device 1's local MAC address to the router's MAC address. The router receives the packet addressed to it and strips off the MAC header. It then looks at the IPX header information to determine what to do with the packet. If the router knows how to get to network address 0xBBBB, it will build a new MAC header and forward the packet. Notice that the IPX header addressing information is not changed by the router. Only the MAC header is rebuilt by the router.

Simple, eh? Of course, there are a few other aspects to IPX that you should know. Let's take a look at the applications that use IPX.

## What Applications Use IPX Instead of SPX

Applications that do not require the connection-oriented nature of SPX can use IPX. That means that most applications can use IPX for control information and file transfer. Your entire connection and login sequence is most likely an IPX-only operation.

When programmers write NetWare applications, they can write their applications to several different APIs (application programming interfaces) or stacks.

- Winsock 2 API

- NCP API level

- SPX API level

- SPX II API level

- IPX API level

Figure 7.2 shows the logical "flow" of the development levels. If a programmer writes to the Winsock 2 API level, their application can run on either an IPX/SPX stack or a TCP/IP stack. If a programmer writes to the SPX II level, the programmer will not be using NCP but will be using IPX.

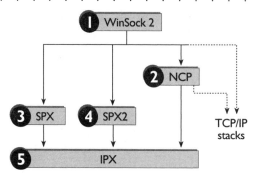

FIGURE 7.2

*IPX is at the bottom of the logical flow of development levels.*

If a programmer writes directly to the IPX level, the packet does not contain any NCP or SPX header information—the application "sits" directly on top of IPX. This type of IPX application is easy to spot on an analyzer, as shown in Figure 7.3.

FIGURE 7.3

*It is easy to spot an application that has been written directly to IPX.*

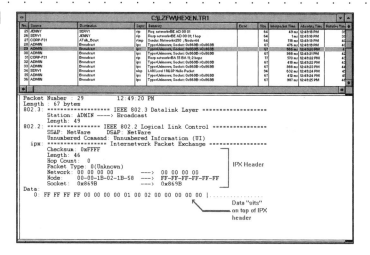

Although IPX communications can be configured to perform better in some circumstances, there's a bit of confusion about the configuration parameters. In this next section, we'll examine the timeout and retry counter mechanisms in IPX.

## IPX Timeouts and Retries

SPX provides for connection-oriented services—IPX does not. In fact, IPX doesn't care whether a packet has gotten through or not. It is the responsibility of the protocol running above IPX (such as NCP) to track the responses and signal a timeout and retry.

When an NCP-based communication using IPX does not get an answer within a certain amount of time (the Time-to-Net value), the client will retransmit the previous packet. Timeouts and retries typically signal network problems due to corrupted packets, misconfigurations, long/slow data paths, or excessive load.

**X-REF**

**We've included the information in this section simply because many people refer to the IPX Retry Count, which is in fact supposed to deal with route retries and an SPX retry setting. Refer to Chapter 8 for more information on SPX retry.**

When will an IPX-based application time out? Two settings affect timeout parameters at the IPX level:

- Minimum Time-to-Net

- IPX Retry Count (VLMs only)

### MINIMUM TIME-TO-NET

Time-to-Net is the amount of time it takes to get to another network—based on the initial RIP reply the client receives when connecting. For example, if a client RIPs for network 0x99-99-99-99 and finds out that the network is four ticks away (approximately **4/18** second), the client has a Time-to-Net value based on **4/18** second.

Time-to-Net is used to determine how long a client should wait between its first request and the first retry. Client 32 will gather more accurate round-trip statistics as the connection gets older. If you are working on a very slow link, you can set the Time-to-Net parameter higher to make the client more patient.

### IPX RETRY COUNT

The IPX Retry Count is used by the VLMs only. This value is used to indicate how many times the VLM will retry RIP requests when trying to locate a network. For example, if the network connection failed in the middle of an NCP request, the VLM client will begin to RIP for the network to see if there is another route. The default setting is 20 attempts (OS/2 Requester defaults to 15).

Upon failure, Client 32 issues only a single route retry request, as you can see in Figure 7.4. The VLM client will issue the RIP request 20 times by default (IPX Retry Count) before continuing.

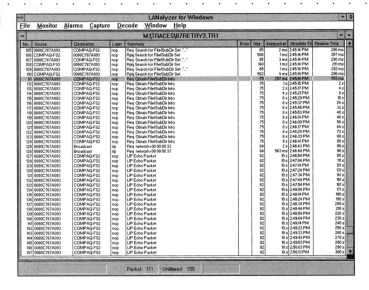

F I G U R E   7 . 4

*Client 32 issues RIP requests after a failure.*

**X-REF**
**We'll examine the issue of timeouts and retries further in Chapter 8.**

Now that you have reviewed all the basic performance characteristics of IPX, let's take a look at the IPX addressing scheme.

## IPX Internetwork Addresses

One of the great characteristics about IPX is the "plug-and-play" addressing system. When you bring up a NetWare client, you do not have to configure its internetwork address as you do with an IP client. IPX clients learn their addresses and assign themselves unique host IDs without user intervention.

The IPX internetwork address consists of two parts: the four-byte network portion and the six-byte node address portion, as shown in Figure 7.5.

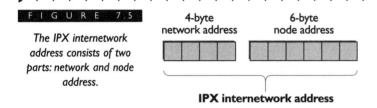

4-byte
network address

6-byte
node address

**IPX internetwork address**

Some people also include a two-byte socket field as part of the internetwork address, but that's not actually correct. The socket process is not a network layer function and does not actually deal with an internetwork location. We'll discuss socket numbers later in this chapter.

**NOTE**

**Often, you'll see the IPX internetwork address shown with colons separating the network and node portions. For example, 0xDE-AD-BE-EF:00-00-00-00-00-01.**

Let's look at each part of the IPX internetwork address, define how the address parts are assigned, and differentiate between internal and external network addresses.

### NETWORK ADDRESSES

You can think of the network address as your street address—all houses on your block use the same street address, but the house numbers differentiate them. All devices that reside within the same network (on the same side of a router) have the same network address.

The network address is 4 bytes in length and contains hexadecimal values (0–9 and A–F). The address is often written with dashes between the bytes for easier reading. For example, here are several network addresses:

0xDE-AD-BE-EF

0xBA-BE-BA-BE

0x01-00-01-2B

0xFF-FF-FF-FF

0x00-00-00-00

**NOTE**

**Hexadecimal numbers are often written with a "0x" preceding them to indicate their hexadecimal format. Dashes are used to separate bytes when the hexadecimal number is longer than 6 bytes.**

NetWare clients dynamically learn their network addresses when they first boot up and communicate on the network. NetWare servers are assigned a network addresses (either automatically or manually) when the operating system is installed.

Every server maintains a list of known networks. When you type **DISPLAY NETWORKS** at the server console, you access the list of known network addresses for that server, as shown in Figure 7.6.

**FIGURE 7.6**

*DISPLAY NETWORKS lists all the network addresses this server is aware of.*

```
COMPAQ_INTERNET_SERVER:display networks
  00000079  1/2      000EFEED  0/11    2000BACE  1/2      2F1154A2  1/2
  31D02C04  0/1      BEAD0001  0/1
There are 6 known networks.
COMPAQ_INTERNET_SERVER:
```

Six networks are listed in the display shown in Figure 7.6. These are all 4-byte IPX network addresses.

There are some special network addresses that you should be aware of:

0x00-00-00-00

0xFF-FF-FF-FF

0xFF-FF-FF-FE

### Network Address 0x00-00-00-00

This network address indicates "this network" and is often used by clients and devices that are transmitting packets for local processing only. For example, when a client boots up and sends a "Get Nearest Server" request, it addresses the packet to network 0x00-00-00-00. This ensures that routers do not forward the packets onto other networks. A decent router knows not to forward these packets.

**Refer to Chapter 9 for more details on the Get Nearest Server process.**

X-REF

### Network Address 0xFF-FF-FF-FF

Although IPX does not have a "broadcast network" address, this address has special meaning in some circumstances — it means "all networks" when contained in an RIP packet. It should never be assigned at the server, and current versions of the operating system disallow assigning 0xFF-FF-FF-FF. What would happen if you used 0xFF-FF-FF-FF? Things might work, things might not — depending on your network topology. If a client sends out a Get Nearest Server request and learns of a server at 0xFF-FF-FF-FF, the client would next send out an RIP packet looking for network 0xFF-FF-FF-FF. Servers would process this packet as a request to find out about *all* networks, and they would reply with all their known networks. The client would regard the first response as the device that could get it to 0xFF-FF-FF-FF. If the first response came from another server (other than the improperly configured one), the client would send connection attempts to that server's MAC address, but it would use 0xFF-FF-FF-FF as the destination IPX address. It just doesn't work.

### Network Address 0xFF-FF-FF-FE

This address has been assigned for the RIP default route network. If you don't know where to send a packet, you can send it to anyone advertising a route to 0xFF-FF-FF-FE, rather than dropping it.

**At Novell, there's also been talk about using 0xFF-FF-FF-FD for interdomain routing, so we'd recommend you stay away from those really high addresses starting with 0xFF-FF-FF — just in case Novell wants to use those numbers for some added functionality at a later date.**

NOTE

Clients "learn" the network address portion of their internetwork address immediately after they start up. When they first send out a Get Nearest Server (GNS) packet to locate a file server, they put all 0's in the IPX header as their source address. This indicates to the local routers that the packet should not be forwarded—it is for this network only. The local server or router replies to the GNS request with the local network address in the IPX header. When the client looks at the reply, it knows its network address!

### Internal Versus External IPX Addresses

NetWare has two distinct types of IPX addresses—the internal IPX address and the external IPX address. The external IPX address is assigned to the cabling system that the server and clients are attached to. The internal IPX address corresponds to the internal virtual network that resides in the server. Figure 7.7 is a rough diagram of the location of internal and external networks.

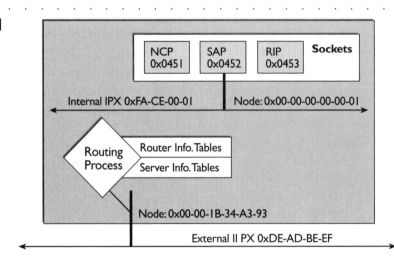

FIGURE 7.7

*NetWare 3.x and 4.x servers have a virtual network inside them—the internal IPX network.*

Inside NetWare 3.x and 4.x servers there is a "fake little network" with a "fake little network interface card hooked to it with node address 1." That "fake little network" is the internal IPX network. It's really not fake, it's just a virtual network. The "fake little network interface card" always has an address of 0x00-00-00-00-00-01.

**To get from the external network address to the internal network address, you must cross the routing process inside the server.**

NOTE

These networks, the internal ones and the external ones, must always have unique addresses throughout the internetwork. You can run into a number of very strange network communications issues when you have duplicate network addresses on one internetwork.

### THE NODE ADDRESS

In the IPX internetwork address, the 6-byte node address portion can denote a single station (unicast), a group of stations (multicast), or all stations (broadcast).

Unicast addresses must be unique, distinct from any other device on that network. One way of ensuring uniqueness is to "borrow" the client's MAC address and use that as the node address portion of the IPX internetwork address. NetWare clients do just that. When you want to address something to all devices on an internetwork or to a specific group of devices, the node address portion of the IPX internetwork address can be filled with a multicast or broadcast address.

In the case of a MAC address that is not 6 bytes long, as shown in Figure 7.8, the address will be padded with 0's to fill out the node address.

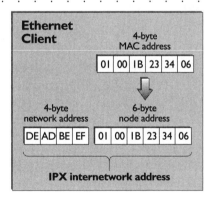 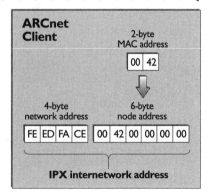

**FIGURE 7.8**

*The node address portion of the address is "borrowed" directly from the client's MAC address.*

## Detecting Addressing Problems

The most common address problem is caused by using the same network address at two locations in the network. Duplicate address problems can be very difficult to detect without an analyzer. Some users have no problem working on the servers; others can't see the servers at all. Three of the most common results of duplicate address problems are that a client can't create a connection, a client can't maintain a connection, or a client can't see servers in one direction only.

## CAN'T CREATE CONNECTIONS

Duplicate addresses can work for some clients, but not others. Figure 7.9 depicts a network that has duplicate addresses—network address 0xAAAA has been used on one Ethernet network and the Internal IPX address of a server. When the client on network 0xBBBB wants to communicate with FS2, it sends an RIP packet to learn how to get to network address 0xAAAA. The best path is through IPX router 1. Unfortunately, however, FS2 is not located over on that segment. The client will send out Create Service Connection packets to the wrong address—no one will answer.

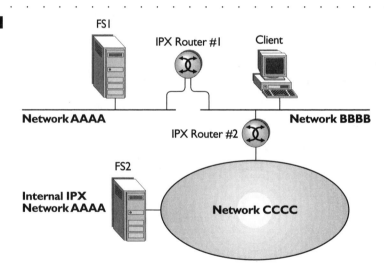

*The client cannot connect to FS2 because Network 0xAAAA is closer through IPX router 1.*

FS1

IPX Router #1

Client

**Network AAAA**

**Network BBBB**

IPX Router #2

FS2

**Internal IPX Network AAAA**

**Network CCCC**

## TIMEOUTS/DISCONNECTIONS

In another scenario, clients can sporadically disconnect from the network or lose SPX connections. This is often another indication of addressing problems. For example, in Figure 7.10, the client can successfully make a connection to FS2. As the client communicates with the server, the server simply reverses the direction of the client requests and sends packets back the way they came. NetWare's

Watchdog process, however, will send "keep alive" packets to the client after 10 minutes of inactivity (default setting). FS2 will consult its routing tables before transmitting the packets and learn that the fastest way to get to network 0xAAAA is through its locally attached Port 1.

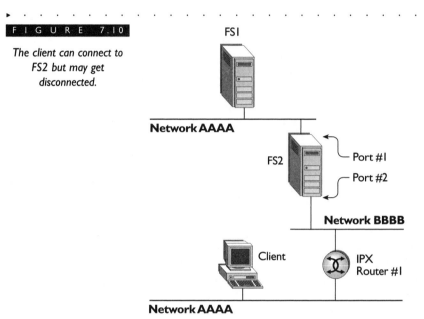

**FIGURE 7.10**

*The client can connect to FS2 but may get disconnected.*

## ONE-WAY VISION

If you have two servers with the same internal IPX address, as shown in Figure 7.11, you will see some very strange behavior indeed! Typically, you'll find that you have "one-way vision," where clients on one side of a network can see servers but clients on the other side cannot see the servers in an SLIST or NLIST—even though they can "ping" a device on the other network.

This can be a tough one to troubleshoot. You'll need to look at the DISPLAY SERVERS information on each server that seems to be "ghosting" on the network. Each server with the identical internal IPX address will keep only its own address— it will discard the entry for the other server. When you type **DISPLAY SERVERS** at the console, you'll see only the local server's name listed—the other server is nowhere in sight. Go to the other server and see the same problem.

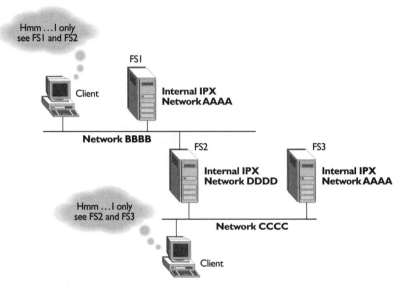

**FIGURE 7.11**

*The clients can't see both servers at the same time, and the servers ignore each other.*

**TIP**

For some of the latest and greatest scenarios on addressing issues, including translational bridged addresses and locally administered Ethernet addressing problems, refer to our Web site at www.imagitech.com.

## The IPX Header Structure

IPX is a very simple connectionless protocol that requires only a short 30-byte header in front of the data or upper-layer protocol. The 30-byte IPX header follows directly after the MAC header, as shown in Figure 7.12. Let's examine the IPX header fields and define possible values/functions of each.

**NOTE**

Some analyzers display the source address information before the destination address information. Some usability study somewhere once showed that people prefer the source information first and, if possible, on the left side of the screen with the destination information second and, if possible, on the right side of the screen.

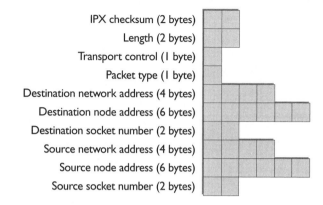

FIGURE 7.12

*The 30-byte IPX header always follows the MAC header.*

IPX checksum (2 bytes)
Length (2 bytes)
Transport control (1 byte)
Packet type (1 byte)
Destination network address (4 bytes)
Destination node address (6 bytes)
Destination socket number (2 bytes)
Source network address (4 bytes)
Source node address (6 bytes)
Source socket number (2 bytes)

## THE IPX CHECKSUM FIELD

The checksum field is 2 bytes. By default, IPX checksumming is disabled and this field contains the value 0xFFFF. A checksum is an error detection process to check the integrity of a packet from end to end. The sender calculates a checksum value based on the contents of the IPX header plus valid data and places the checksum value into the checksum field. Upon receipt of the checksummed packet, the receiver performs the same calculation and compares the results. Matching checksum values indicate that the packet has not been corrupted anywhere between the two ends.

**You cannot use the checksum feature with the Ethernet_802.3 header. That means that the IPX data cannot even cross a network where it is temporarily encapsulated in that frame format. That frame type uses the checksum field to indicate that NetWare is the upper layer protocol.**

NOTE

Do you need to enable IPX checksum? Probably not. All types of MAC frames contain some error detection mechanism (such as a cyclical redundancy check, or CRC), so checksumming may seem like a redundant process. In two instances, however, IPX checksums can help spot problems in communications.

▶ **Errors introduced in memory between the LAN driver and IPX stack processes:** There is a very short time when the IPX packet is in memory being handed off from the LAN driver to the IPX stack. At this time there is no MAC layer error detection mechanism in place.

▸ **Errors introduced by routers as packets are forwarded:** When a router forwards a packet, it strips off the MAC header upon receipt, increments the hop count (transport control) field, places a new MAC header on the frame, and sends it out the destination port. Errors can be introduced when no MAC error-detection processes are in place. Figure 7.13 illustrates the process and highlights the time when a packet can become corrupt.

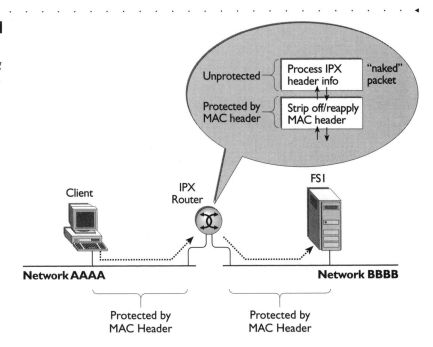

### FIGURE 7.13

*A "naked" IPX packet can become corrupt when being forwarded through a router.*

**NOTE**

**The nature of checksumming indicates that it will degrade performance in your communications. Only enable checksumming if you absolutely must.**

Let's take a look at the checksum process and enabling checksum.

### The Checksum Process (geek alert!)

Ok, ok...here's the IPX checksum process in a nutshell. First, perform the checksum on the IPX data (including the IPX header) with the assumption that the checksum field and transport control field contain 0. When the packet crosses a router, the transport control value will be incremented, and therefore the actual value of this field cannot be included in the checksum process. Next, increment the range of bytes to 16-bit "words" (we like everything in 2-byte increments here). If the packet falls short of the word boundary, pad the packet with a 0-filled byte. Now step through from byte to byte and perform an arithmetic process (two's complement arithmetic). Place the sum in the checksum field. Easy, eh?

### Enabling IPX Checksums

IPX checksums are configured at both ends of the communications (client and server). If the two sides do not agree on the checksum scheme, they cannot communicate.

#### Server Checksums

IPX checksums can be enabled using the SET parameters (SET > NCP > Enable IPX Checksums=n), as shown in Figure 7.14. The supported values are

0 = For no checksums

1 = To checksum if enabled at the client

2 = To require checksums

The default value is 1. This parameter can be set in the STARTUP.NCF file, if desired.

**FIGURE 7.14**

*Select SET > NCP to view and configure IPX Checksums settings.*

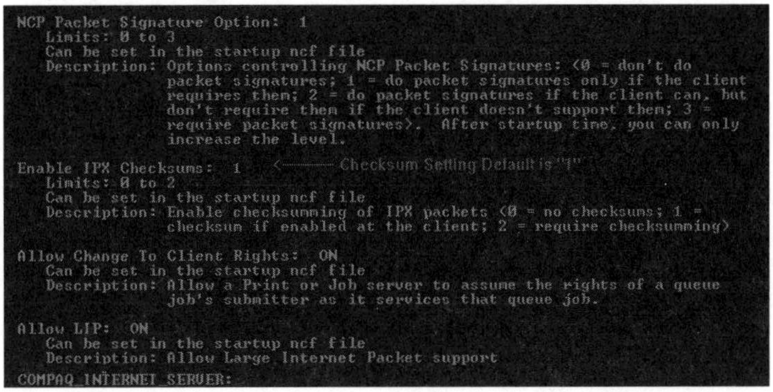

### Client Checksums

At the client, the checksum values are the following:

0 = Disabled (I never checksum packets.)

1 = Enabled but not preferred (I'll checksum only if the server checksums.)

2 = Enabled and preferred (I prefer to checksum and want the server to do so also.)

3 = Required (I always checksum packets.)

Setting the value for this parameter to 2 or 3 increases data integrity but decreases performance.

**Here's an interesting little quirk to the checksum issue—clients do not use checksums on SAP or RIP broadcast packets. They must be sure that all servers understand the packet contents.**

NOTE

## THE IPX LENGTH FIELD

The length field indicates the length of the IPX header (30 bytes) plus the valid data. The reason we specify "valid" data is because some MAC types (such as Ethernet) have a minimum data size requirement. If the actual data does not meet that minimum size, it is padded.

You may see something called "evenizing" on the network. Some network devices have had problems processing packets that are not an even number of bytes in length. Therefore, Novell requested that industry LAN drivers "evenize" IPX packets. If the IPX length field contains an uneven value (73 bytes, for example), the LAN driver should add 1 byte to the end of the data and call it a 74-byte data portion. Ethernet_802.3 and Ethernet_II frames should be evenized, whereas Ethernet_802.2 and Ethernet_SNAP frames do not need to be evenized.

## THE HOP COUNT (A.K.A. TRANSPORT CONTROL) FIELD

The hop count field (also referred to as the transport control field) indicates the number of routers or routing processes the packet has crossed. When an IPX packet is transmitted, the hop count field is initialized to 0. This is the only field in the IPX header that a router is allowed to touch—routers increment this value by 1 when they forward the packet. Maximum hop counts differ depending on whether you are using RIP or NLSP.

### RIP Hop Maximum

On an RIP network, the maximum hop count is 15. A service that is 16 hops away is considered "too far away to reach." When a router receives a packet that has an IPX hop count of 15, it discards the packet. You can use the IPXCON utility (**LOAD IPXCON** at the server console) to see if any packets are being discarded by the server because their hop count is too high.

### NLSP Hop Maximum

NLSP enables us to have a hop count up to 126. A service that is 127 hops away is considered "too far away to reach." When an NLSP router receives a packet that has an IPX hop count of 126, it discards the packet. You can mix and match RIP and NLSP routers on a network and place NLSP routers on the outer edges of the network. When you reach your 15-count maximum, NLSP routers can allow the packet to travel further without being discarded.

## THE PACKET TYPE FIELD

The packet type field was intended to define the type of communication (IPX, SPX, NCP, SAP, RIP, and so on). This field, however, has really been messed up over the years—don't rely too heavily on this field's contents. The only values that we've found are reliable are "5" for SPX and "20" for NetBIOS over IPX. Most of the time you'll see this field set to 0x00 for "unknown."

The following packet type numbers have been defined:

0x00 Unknown or NLSP packet

Type 0x01 (1d): RIP packet

Type 0x04 (4d): SAP packet

Type 0x05 (5d): SPX/SPX II packet

Type 0x11 (17d): NCP packet

Type 0x14 (20d): Propagated packet (such as NetBIOS)—a.k.a. Type 20 packet (decimal representation)

Type 0x7B (123d): Experimental (serialization)

Type 0xC7 (199d): Experimental (serialization)

The best way to identify a packet is by the source and destination socket numbers. Those fields are your definitive guide to the purpose of this packet.

## THE DESTINATION NETWORK FIELD

This field indicates the final destination network for the packet. The packet could be destined for an internal IPX address or an external IPX address. Allowable values in this field are 0x00-00-00-01 to 0xFF-FF-FF-FD, inclusive.

## THE DESTINATION NODE FIELD

This field indicates the 6-byte node address or host ID number of the destination device. Allowable destination node addresses include

▸ Broadcast address (for example, 0xFF-FF-FF-FF-FF-FF)

▸ Multicast addresses (for example, NLSP's multicast address is 0x09-00-1B-FF-FF-FF on Ethernet and FDDI and 0xC0-00-01-FF-FF-FF on token ring)

▸ Unicast address (for example, a single station's MAC address of 0x00-00-1B-34-23-3B)

▸ Internal IPX node address (defined as 0x00-00-00-00-00-01)

If the destination node address is a unicast address that is borrowed from a client's hardware address, the first three bytes of the address indicate the card manufacturer. These numbers were assigned by the IEEE (Institute of Electrical and Electronics Engineers). The following is an example of vendor IDs:

| | |
|---|---|
| 0x00-00-1B | Anthem/Eagle (formerly Novell's Ethernet card line) |
| 0x00-80-C7 | Xircom |
| 0x08-00-5A | IBM |
| 0x-00-AA-00 | Intel |

**TIP**

**Node addresses can also be manually assigned and may not have a valid manufacturer ID area to look at. For a complete listing of Ethernet manufacturer IDs, check out** `www.cavebear.com/CaveBear/Ethernet` **on the Web. For more information on the IEEE, check out** `www.ieee.org`**.**

## THE DESTINATION SOCKET FIELD

Socket numbers indicate the end process that the packet is destined for or the source process that created the packet. A socket is somewhat like an ear hooked to a mouth—ugly things, aren't they? IPX opens a socket to send data and posts listening sockets to hear the responses.

For example, when you request a connection to a NetWare server, you send a Create Service Connection request to the NCP (NetWare Core Protocol) socket number 0x0451. NCP is the process that should handle your request, as shown in the IPX header in Figure 7.15. The client's socket number 0x4007 is opened to transmit the request to the server and receive the reply.

▶ . . . . . . . . . . . . . . . . . . . . . . . . . . . . . . . ◀

F I G U R E   7.15

The destination socket number indicates the process that should handle the packet.

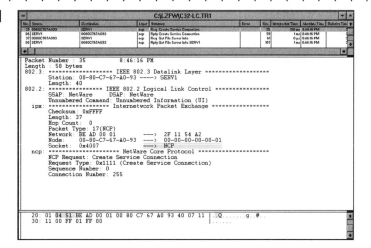

**NOTE**

In Figure 7.15, LANalyzer for Windows has decoded the destination socket number 0x0451 as NCP. By highlighting the field and looking at the hexadecimal window at the bottom, we can see the value underlying the "NCP" designation. Some analyzers, such as Network General's Sniffer, show you both the decoded value and the hexadecimal value side by side.

Some people consider the socket number part of the internetwork address, but it refers to an upper-layer process, not a network-layer addressing system. Therefore, we do not lump sockets together with the internetwork addressing system.

Many socket numbers have been assigned by Novell to the most common types of NetWare communications, and there are other sockets that are assigned to third parties for other applications. In this next section, we'll look at the well-known socket list, and then we'll look at some of the assigned/unassigned sockets, as well.

### The Well-Known Socket List

Well-known sockets are assigned by Novell to their most common NetWare communications processes. The following is a list of the well-known socket numbers that NetWare network uses:

| | |
|---|---|
| 0x0451 | NCP |
| 0x0452 | SAP |
| 0x0453 | RIP |
| 0x0455 | NetBIOS |
| 0x0456 | Diagnostic Responder |
| 0x0457 | Serialization |
| 0x4000–0x8000 | Dynamic Socket (Clients/NDS use) |
| 0x9001 | NLSP |
| 0x9004 | IPXWAN |
| 0x9086 | IPX Ping |
| 0x9088 | Mobile IPX Socket |

Sockets 0x4000–0x8000 are the dynamic sockets. Typically, you'll see clients assign a random number in the range of 0x4000–0x5000 (but usually closer to the 0x4000 side), as shown in Figure 7.15. The server replies back to this dynamic socket number. Clients can have multiple sockets open at one time.

**X-REF**

**NDS communications can also use dynamic socket numbers. For more information on NDS's use of these sockets, refer to Chapter 14.**

### Third-Party Assigned Sockets

Sockets between 0x8000 and 0x9000 are available to third parties. Many third-party developers approach Novell to have a socket number assigned for their communications—indicating that they are not relying on NCP to provide all their socket posting and services. The following is a list of the sample third-party assigned sockets. The complete list can be found in Appendix F, "Socket Number List."

8023  MCAFEE ASSOCIATES

8024  BLUE LANCE NETWORK INFO SYS

8027 GATEWAY COMMUNICATIONS INC

807F ORACLE CORP

8080 ORACLE CORP

8081 ORACLE CORP

8139 PC CHALKBOARD INTEL - AMERICAN FORK

82D8 LEGATO SYSTEMS

**NOTE** **Not all sockets listed include the product name used by the socket—many include only the company that registered the socket with Novell.**

### Game Sockets

Games on your network? Yes, they typically do affect performance. Many game manufacturers use socket numbers outside of the typical 0x4000 to 0x8000 dynamic socket range. If you need to locate these games on the network, look for the following socket numbers in the IPX headers:

| | |
|---|---|
| 869C | DOOM 1* [uses socket assigned to someone else] |
| 869B | DOOM 2*, Heretic*, Hexen* [assigned to id Software] |
| 5100 | Descent |
| 8813 | Command and Conquer* [assigned to Virgin Interactive Software] |
| ABCD | Rise of the Triad* [not in dynamic assignment range] |
| 4545 | Mortal Kombat 3 |
| 750x | NetWars |

*Configurable socket numbers

Three main problems can occur with these network games:

▶ They increase the traffic to an unacceptable level. Better players cause more traffic, and some of these games (such as DOOM 1) use broadcasting as their communications method.

▶ They can "step on" someone else's socket number—as in the case of DOOM 1.

▶ They can be configured to use a well-known socket number. Some of the manufacturers allow game players to assign their own socket numbers, thereby allowing multiple simultaneous games on the network. Although some (such as DOOM, Heretic, and Hexen) do not allow you to choose 0x0451, others might. If a user selects the NCP socket, the server will try to process the packet and finally discard it.

### The Dynamic Echo Socket

When clients are starting up, they may need to do some testing of the data path or timing to and from the server (as in the case of VLM's Burst Mode/Big Packet negotiations). In this case, the server may provide the client with a number for a temporary "echo socket," as shown in Figure 7.16.

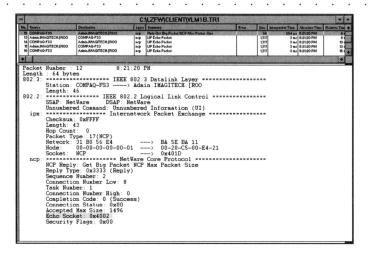

*The server tells the client what socket number to use for echo testing.*

When a packet is sent to the echo socket, the server does not process the packet. The server simply flips the source and destination information around in the IPX header and retransmits the packet back to the client the same way it arrived. Typically, the number assigned for echo testing is in the very low 0x4000 range. This is a range typically used by clients for their dynamic socket numbers.

### Unusual Socket Use

You may see some applications perform an unusual use of sockets—MS Client for NetWare Networks and MS NDS, for example, send packets to the null socket number 0x0000. There really isn't any process residing at that socket number anywhere, so the packet is not answered. Interestingly, the MS NDS and MS CFNN address the packets to themselves in the MAC header anyway—somewhat like that crazy person talking to himself at the end of the bar, eh?

**X-REF**

**For more information on client performance, refer to Chapter 13 where we examine Novell's Client 32 connection process.**

## THE SOURCE NETWORK FIELD

The source network address field indicates the network that the packet is being sent from. In the case of clients, they will use the network that they are physically attached to. Clients learn their network address after they send the first SAP packet onto the network and receive a reply.

In Figure 7.17, we see a SAP packet from a client that has just booted up. In the IPX header the source network address is 0x00-00-00-00 because the client does not know what network it is on. The destination address is also 0x-00-00-00-00.

▶ . . . . . . . . . . . . . . . . . . . . . . . . ◀

**F I G U R E    7.17**

*The client uses 0x-00-00-00-00 as its network address until it learns where it is.*

```
                                    C:\LZFW\C32-LC.TR1
No.  Source           Destination         Layer  Summary                    Error    Size  Interpacket Time  Absolute Time  Relative Time
  2  0080C767A093     Broadcast           sap    Query Nearest File Server            55    6.06 ms  0:46:13 PM    620
Packet Number : 2              8:46:13 PM
Length : 55 bytes
802.3: ================= IEEE 802.3 Datalink Layer ==================
       Station: 00-80-C7-67-A0-93 ----> Broadcast
       Length: 37
802.2: ================= IEEE 802.2 Logical Link Control =============
       SSAP: NetWare    DSAP: NetWare
       Unnumbered Command: Unnumbered Information (UI)
   ipx: ================= Internetwork Packet Exchange ==============
       Checksum: 0xFFFF
       Length: 34
       Hop Count:  0
       Packet Type: 4(IPX)
       Network: 00 00 00 00       ---> 00 00 00 00
       Node:    00-80-C7-67-A0-93 ---> FF-FF-FF-FF-FF-FF
       Socket:  0x4002            ---> SAP
   sap: ============= NetWare Service Advertising Protocol ============
       Type: 3 (Nearest Service Query)
       Server Type: 0x0004(File Server)
```

## THE SOURCE NODE FIELD

This is the host ID number of the sending station. The address is pulled directly from the MAC layer address, as discussed earlier in the "Destination Node Field" section. You cannot have a broadcast (0xFF-FF-FF-FF-FF-FF) source node address, however.

## THE SOURCE SOCKET FIELD

This number indicates the process that is sending the packet. Refer to the "Destination Socket Field" section above for more details on socket numbers and socket number assignment.

**Refer to Appendix F for a list of assigned third-party socket numbers.**

**X-REF**

# Troubleshooting at the IPX Layer

Now that you know the purpose of the various fields in an IPX header, you can use this information to troubleshoot communications that cross your network. Remember that you can isolate the source of any network packet by looking in the IPX header—don't look in the MAC header, since that changes as the packet crosses routers.

In Figure 7.18, we see the IPX header of a packet that has crossed a router. We can see that the packet is addressed to NetWare's NCP process (socket 0x0451). We can see that the packet has crossed one router (transport control is set to 1), and we know that the client is not using IPX checksums.

Take a look at the packet arriving at a server shown in Figure 7.19 and see if you can determine why this client might be timing out on the network.

If you guessed the path distance—you're correct. The transport control field value is 0x0D, which is equal to 13 decimal. The client is 13 hops away from this server. Due to queuing delays and heavy traffic, the client may not get requests to the server and reply quickly enough to stop it from timing out.

As you can see, knowing how to decipher the contents of an IPX header can dramatically increase your troubleshooting efficiency.

FIGURE 7.18

*The IPX header always reveals the true source of the packet.*

| | | |
|---|---|---|
| IPX checksum (2 bytes) | FF | FF |
| Length (2 bytes) | 00 | 24 |
| Transport control (1 byte) | 01 | |
| Packet type (1 byte) | 00 | |
| Destination network address (4 bytes) | 00 00 00 99 | |
| Destination node address (6 bytes) | 00 00 00 00 00 01 | |
| Destination socket number (2 bytes) | 04 51 | |
| Source network address (4 bytes) | DE AD BE EF | |
| Source node address (6 bytes) | 00 00 1B 2A 23 22 | |
| Source socket number (2 bytes) | 40 04 | |

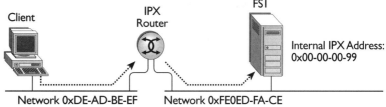

Client    IPX Router    FS1

Internal IPX Address:
0x00-00-00-99

Network 0xDE-AD-BE-EF    Network 0xFE0ED-FA-CE

FIGURE 7.19

*An IPX header can tell you the cause of client timeouts.*

| | | |
|---|---|---|
| IPX checksum (2 bytes) | FF | FF |
| Length (2 bytes) | 00 | 24 |
| Transport control (1 byte) | 0D | |
| Packet type (1 byte) | 04 | |
| Destination network address (4 bytes) | 00 00 00 88 | |
| Destination node address (6 bytes) | 00 00 00 00 00 01 | |
| Destination socket number (2 bytes) | 04 51 | |
| Source network address (4 bytes) | BE EF 00 01 | |
| Source node address (6 bytes) | 00 00 1B 23 22 EE | |
| Source socket number (2 bytes) | 40 02 | |

You can also use IPXCON to troubleshoot IPX-based communications. Figure 7.20 shows the IPXCON screen after we selected IPX Information > Detailed IPX Information. As you can see from this screen, you can isolate errors due to too many hops in a packet, header errors, unknown sockets, compression/decompression errors, filtered packets, packets sent to nonexistent routes, malformed packets, and packets discarded for other reasons.

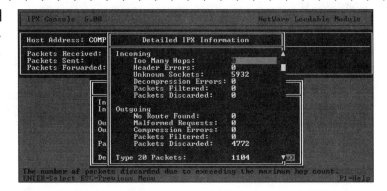

F I G U R E   7.20

*Load IPXCON at the server to view IPX statistics/errors.*

On the server shown in Figure 7.20, the server has discarded 4,772 packets because the server had been configured to support a WAN circuit (ISDN) that was not currently set up. The ISDN card was removed from the server, but the configuration remained. Our server also indicates that it has been sent 1,104 type 20 packets for forwarding. These are NetBIOS packets that are transmitted as a result of bringing up some Windows 95 stations on our network. Watch this counter to ensure you do not have excessive and unnecessary NetBIOS traffic on your network.

## Summary

In this chapter we've covered NetWare's IPX protocol functionality, addressing, and header structure. In the next chapter, we'll examine SPX and SPX II, Novell's connection-oriented protocols.

# CHAPTER 8

# NetWare SPX and SPX II

Novell's SPX was designed based on Xerox's SPP (Sequenced Packet Protocol). SPX offers connection-oriented guaranteed delivery of packets. This chapter provides in-depth coverage of Novell's SPX protocol including the benefits and drawbacks of SPX, SPX/SPX II functionality, header structures, and troubleshooting.

SPX is similar to Federal Express—when something absolutely, positively has to be there, use SPX. When an application uses SPX, the sides make a connection first and ensure they are using the same functionality. Acknowledgments guarantee delivery of the data and require immediate error recovery for any lost packets.

**NOTE**

**In the TCP/IP environment, the protocol most similar to NetWare's SPX protocol is TCP.**

As shown in Figure 8.1, SPX communications rely on IPX for the network layer functionality. In every SPX packet, you'll see an IPX header that is used by routers to get the SPX packet through the network.

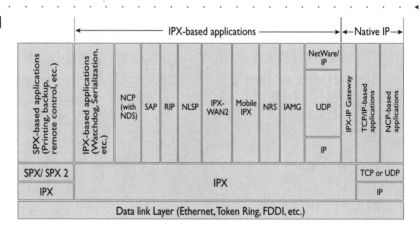

**FIGURE 8.1**

*SPX relies on the IPX stack for network layer functionality.*

When developers build applications, they must decide whether to use IPX or SPX. IPX is faster, with less overhead in packets/second and buffer space required. SPX, however, offers guaranteed delivery of packets. If the application programmers feel that they must be certain every packet makes it to the destination, they will use SPX.

Some applications that are SPX-based include

- ▸ Novell print server

- ▸ NetWare for SAA

- ▸ Lotus Notes

- ▸ ManageWise/NetExplorer

- ▸ Rconsole

- ▸ NASI applications

- ▸ Most backup solutions

- ▸ Many IPX-IP gateways

- ▸ Many remote control programs

- ▸ Some database applications

There are some definite drawbacks to using SPX, however. Following the Xerox SPP protocol, SPX uses a maximum packet size of 576 bytes, allowing 512 bytes for data and 64 bytes for headers. SPX also allows only one packet at a time to be outstanding. Finally, SPX connections provide for very slow data transfer.

People always wonder why their backup takes so long. Easy answer: SPX. When you back up 5GB of data using SPX, you are backing up 512 bytes of data at a time. And each 512-byte packet must receive an acknowledgment before you can continue.

Novell developed SPX II to get past some of the drawbacks of SPX. This chapter will first examine SPX functionality and then look at SPX II.

## SPX Functionality

SPX functionality is enabled when you load IPXODI.COM at the client. If you are using Client 32, SPX functionality is enabled through NWSIPX.NLM.

There are four basic functions of SPX communications:

▶ SPX handshake (connection establishment)

▶ SPX data transfer

▶ SPX Watchdog

▶ SPX connection termination

This section will examine each of these functions.

### THE SPX HANDSHAKE

In order to successfully transfer data using SPX, both sides of the SPX communication must participate in a "two-way handshake," as shown in Figure 8.2.

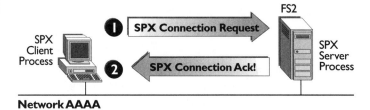

**FIGURE 8.2**

*Both sides must participate in a handshake before starting SPX data transfer.*

**NOTE**

**TCP requires a three-way handshake: request connection synchronization (SYN); ACK (acknowledge) and request connection synchronization (ACK SYN); and finally, an acknowledgment (ACK).**

When the SPX client application is launched, the SPX handshake process starts. The client side opens an SPX socket to communicate through. The server side, upon receipt of the first handshake packet, opens an SPX socket. If the server side is out of SPX sockets, it will refuse the SPX connection.

During the handshake process, the client side assigns itself a connection ID number. The client sends a connection request packet and its connection ID number to the server. Since the client has not communicated with the server yet and therefore does not know the server's connection ID number, the client states that the server's connection ID number is 65535 (0xFFFF).

This connection request packet is an ACK packet with an acknowledgment request. The server responds with an acknowledgment packet, as shown in Figure 8.3. When the server responds, it includes its own connection ID number.

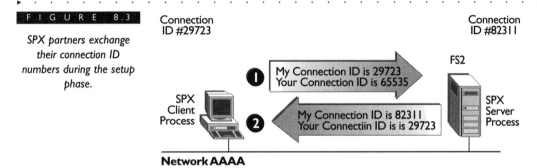

**FIGURE 8.3**

*SPX partners exchange their connection ID numbers during the setup phase.*

Connection ID #29723

Connection ID #82311

FS2

**①** My Connection ID is 29723
Your Connection ID is 65535

SPX Client Process

**②** My Connection ID is 82311
Your Connectiin ID is is 29723

SPX Server Process

**Network AAAA**

Throughout their communications, these two devices will use the connection ID numbers they learned during this initial setup process. Later in this chapter you'll see the packet structure of the setup routine.

## SPX DATA TRANSFER

During data transfer, an SPX client tracks the sequence of packets sent on the network. The first data packet sent starts with sequence number 0, as shown in Figure 8.4. This data packet contains an acknowledgment request (send ACK). In our example, FS2 returns an acknowledgment packet to the client.

When an acknowledgment is received, the client can increment the sequence number by 1. The next data packet sent by the client will have sequence number 1.

FIGURE 8.4

*The sender's sequence number increments upon acknowledgment receipt.*

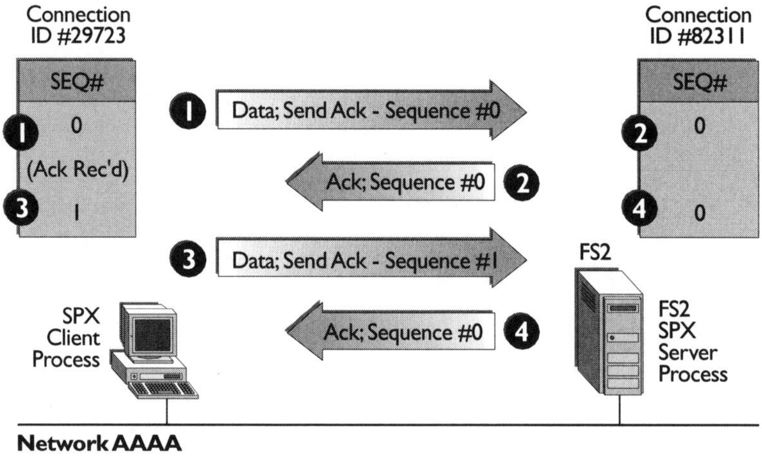

Both sides of the connection actually maintain a sequence number table. On the server side, the sequence number table maintains sequence number 0 because the server has not sent any data that has been acknowledged. The server cannot increment the sequence number until it receives acknowledgments for data sent. Figure 8.4 shows that the server's sequence number table still contains a sequence of 0.

This sequence number cannot get out of order. For example, a station cannot send sequence number 1 unless it has received an acknowledgment for sequence number 0. Next, we'll look at how we maintain the sequenced order.

### Maintaining the Data Packet Order

In order to maintain a perfect sequence, each side includes a sequence number that indicates which data packet it is sending and also sends an acknowledgment number. The acknowledgment number indicates the other side's next sequence number, as shown in Figure 8.5.

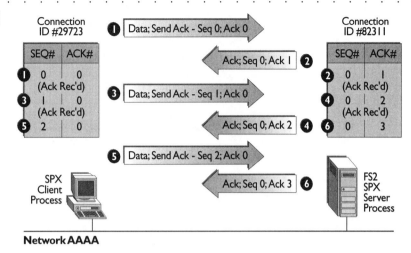

FIGURE 8.5

*The acknowledgment value indicates the other side's next sequence number.*

## Two-Way Data Transfer Sequences

Up to this point, the examples seem to show a nice even "ping-pong" type of communication. That is not how most data transfer looks on the wire, however. Since both sides are sending data and command sequences across the wire, you can observe communications similar to those shown in Figure 8.6.

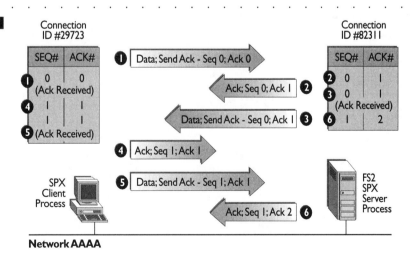

FIGURE 8.6

*The flow of data is not necessarily one-sided.*

This information can be very useful in determining which direction data is flowing on an SPX connection. When you capture an SPX packet, look at the sequence number and the acknowledgment number. If the sequence number is higher than the acknowledgment number, the source station is sending most of the data. If the acknowledgment number is higher than the sequence number, the destination has been sending most of the data.

**SPX does not allow you to piggyback data on an acknowledgment packet.**

NOTE

### Error Recovery

An SPX error can occur when an acknowledgment packet is not received after data is transmitted with an acknowledgment request. In standard SPX, only one packet of data can be outstanding on the connection at any time. No windowing is allowed.

The SPX abort timeout value (discussed later in this chapter) specifies how long (in ticks) the SPX protocol should wait for a response from the other side of the connection before it terminates the session. Figure 8.7 shows the typical communications that occur when an error is detected.

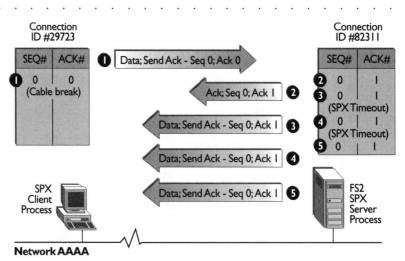

F I G U R E   8 . 7

*The SPX retry count is set at 20 by default.*

By default, an SPX connection (Client32 and VLMS) will retransmit the same packet 20 times before giving up (OS/2 Requester is set at 15 attempts by default). SPX actually uses the IPX retry count value. If all 20 attempts are unsuccessful, the SPX device considers the connection closed. The device does not need to send any "end-of-connection" packets to close the connection.

We'll cover the SPX configuration options later in this chapter.

### SPX WATCHDOG

When an SPX application has completed its task, it can either disconnect from its SPX partner or maintain an SPX connection using the SPX Watchdog feature.

The SPX Watchdog process starts where no communication has occurred between the SPX partners for a specified length of time. The default time before Watchdog starts is 60 seconds. The Watchdog process is similar to the "keep alive" process used in other protocols and is used to ensure that connections are maintained even though data is not exchanged.

Application programmers can define SPX Watchdog processes, if desired. The SPX client observes the application's desires. The Watchdog process is covered in greater detail later in this chapter.

### SPX CONNECTION TERMINATION

When an SPX application terminates, the terminating partner sends an end-of-connection request to the other partner. Upon receipt of an acknowledgment, the connection is considered terminated, as shown in Figure 8.8. If the client wants to use SPX to transmit more data, it must establish a new SPX connection.

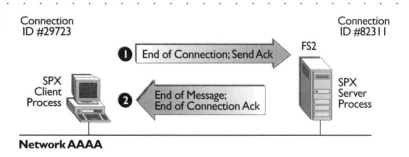

**FIGURE 8.8**

*The sender uses an end-of-connection request to terminate the SPX connection.*

Connection ID #29723

Connection ID #82311

FS2

❶ End of Connection; Send Ack

SPX Client Process

❷ End of Message; End of Connection Ack

SPX Server Process

**Network AAAA**

If the client application needs to transfer more data using SPX, it must establish a new SPX connection using the handshake process.

## SPX II (SPX 2) Functionality

Because SPX is based on the original XNS specification, it was designed with a maximum 576-byte packet size. SPX II, however, can go to the maximum packet size defined by the media access method. On an Ethernet network, for example, SPX II can use up to 1,518-byte packet sizes.

SPX II was originally designed in 1992, but it still has not surfaced as a mainstream communications protocol. I believe this is mostly because application programmers must revise their code to take advantage of the SPX II options.

The SPX II advantages include the ability to support big packets and burst mode communications.

SPX II is supported in the VLMs and Client 32. SPX II is not supported by NETX or the Windows 95 IPX/SPX Compatible Protocol for Windows from Microsoft. You can add SPX II functionality to a Windows 95 client by getting the TLI.DLL file from Novell's support site (`support.novell.com`). Any application that calls and uses TLI.DLL will get SPX II support under Windows 95.

### THE SPX II HANDSHAKE PROCESS

The SPX II bit in the SPX setup packet indicates that the sender wants an SPX II connection. If the other side supports SPX II, it will also toggle that bit in its return packet. If the other side, however, does not understand SPX II (an older version of NetWare, for example), it does not toggle that bit when responding. The SPX client, in that case, will not begin negotiating any SPX II options. The SPX client will assume that packets support only 512 bytes of data and one outstanding packet at a time, as shown in Figure 8.9.

*If one of the sides does not support SPX II, the two sides will start a standard SPX connection.*

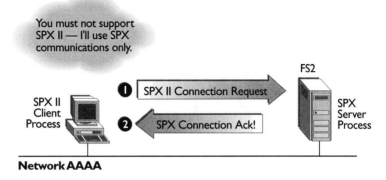

## SPX II PACKET BURSTING

SPX II has the ability to support between three and eight packets outstanding at one time. As you can imagine, this can dramatically increase the performance of data transfer. Novell file servers start off with a receive window size of eight. Clients start with a receive window size of three. As the connection gets older, it "learns" what window size it can successfully support and adjusts itself automatically. Applications can also define a static window size, if desired.

## THE SPX II BIG PACKET

During the initial SPX connection setup routine, each side of the connection defines its packet size. (See the negotiate size field definition later in this chapter.) The maximum physical packet length that SPX II supports is 64KB.

In the next section, we'll examine the SPX and SPX II packet structures.

# SPX Packet Structure

SPX packets contain an additional 12-byte SPX-specific section after the IPX header, as shown in Figure 8.10.

*Some references define both the IPX and SPX portions collectively as the SPX header.*

SPX Header {

| MAC Header |
| IPX Portion |
| SPX Portion |
| Data |
| . |
| . |
| Pad (Optional) |
| MAC Trailer |

Since the IPX portion is always 30 bytes and the SPX portion is at least 12 bytes, the minimum SPX packet size is 42 bytes plus the MAC header.

## THE SPX HEADER

In this section, we'll examine the standard SPX header first and then take a look at additions made by SPX II. Figure 8.11 shows the structure of a standard 42-byte SPX header.

### THE IPX HEADER PORTION

The "Packet Type" 0x05 in the IPX portion indicates that it is an SPX packet. Other than that one indicator, the IPX header has all the functionality and field definitions defined in Chapter 7.

### THE CONNECTION CONTROL FIELD

The connection control field defines the purpose of the SPX transaction (such as an ACK request) and controls the bidirectional flow of data across an SPX connection. Figure 8.12 shows the bit ordering in the connection control field.

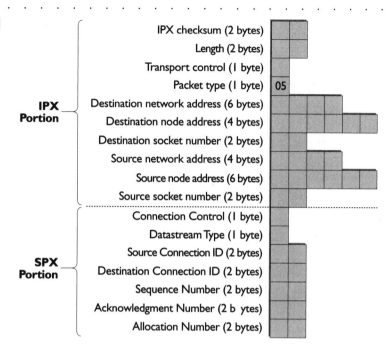

FIGURE 8.11

*SPX headers include a 30-byte IPX portion.*

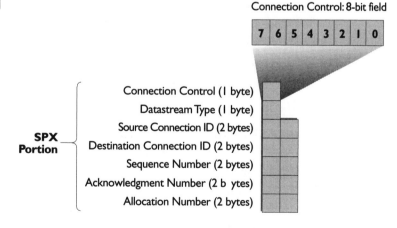

FIGURE 8.12

*The eight-bit connection control field controls the bidirectional flow of data.*

The following table lists the connection control field bit values and their definitions:

| | |
|---|---|
| Bit 0 | XHD. Reserved for SPX II to denote that the packet uses an SPX II extended header. |
| Bit 1 | RES1. Reserved. Must be 0. |
| Bit 2 | NEG. Negotiate for SPX II request/response. Must be set at 0 for standard SPX. |
| Bit 3 | SPX II. Indicates that this is an SPX II packet. Must be set at 0 for standard SPX. |
| Bit 4 | EOM. End of message. |
| Bit 5 | ATN. Reserved for attention indication. Must be set at 0 for standard SPX. |
| Bit 6 | ACK. Acknowledgment request. |
| Bit 7 | SYS. System packet. Used as an ACK. |

Some of the common connection control field values are indicated next:

| | |
|---|---|
| 0xC0 | Connection request packet: This packet is an ACK and a request for an ACK. (binary 11000000) |
| 0x80 | System packet/ACK packet: This packet is sent as a response to a packet that has Bit 6 = 1 (acknowledgment request). (binary 10000000) |
| 0x10 | End of message: This packet is used to signal the end of a data exchange, but not the end of the connection. (binary 00010000) |
| 0x50 | Send ACK/End of message: This packet is used to send data, request data, acknowledge the data enclosed, and indicate that this is the end of that data exchange. (binary 01010000) |

## THE DATASTREAM TYPE FIELD

This field indicates the type of data that is included in the packet. The following field values are defined:

| | |
|---|---|
| 0xFE (254 decimal) | End of connection; request to terminate the SPX connection |
| 0xFF (255 decimal) | End of connection acknowledgment |
| 0x80-0xFD (128-251 decimal) | Reserved for SPX II |
| 0x00-0x7F (0-127 decimal) | Application-defined values |

Figure 8.13 shows an SPX packet that is requesting termination of the connection. This request was generated when "quit Rconsole" was selected. The connection control field is set to 0x40 (Send ACK), requesting an acknowledgment from the SPX partner. The end-of-connection request is defined by the value 0xFE (254 decimal) in the datastream type field.

FIGURE 8.13

The datastream type field value 254 (or 0xFE) indicates that the application wants to terminate the SPX connection.

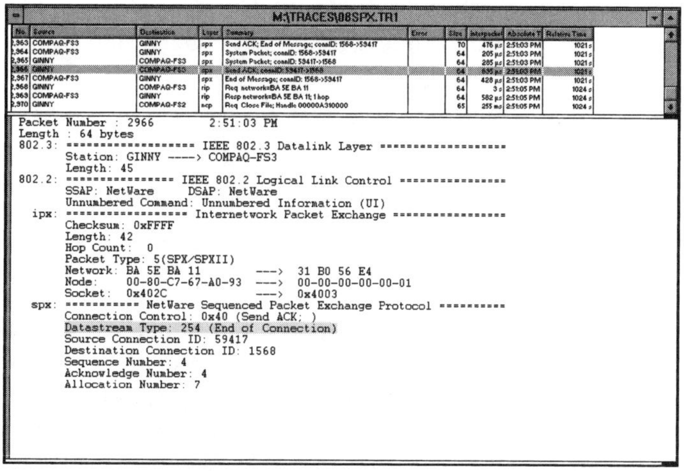

In Figure 8.14, we see the reply packet. This packet contains the end-of-packet acknowledgment indicator (0xFF or 255 decimal).

FIGURE 8.14

The datastream type field value 255 (or 0xFF) indicates acceptance of the termination request.

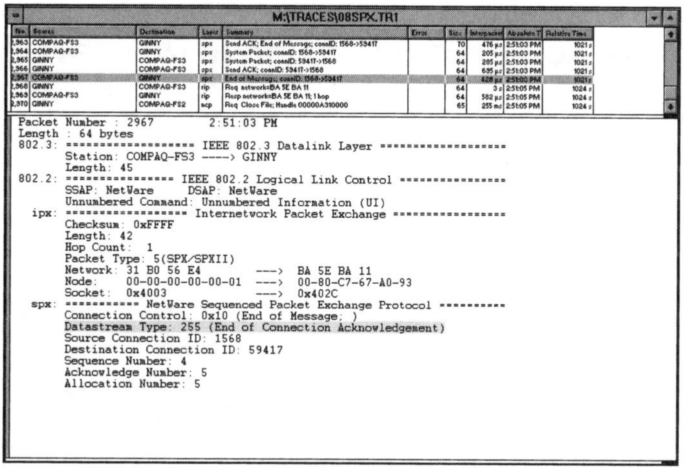

The application-defined datastream type field values can be used for control sequences and the like. For example, the following datastream type values are used by Novell's printing services:

0x00    Data portion of packet contains information to print.

0x01    Stop printing; clear buffers.

0x02    Stop printing; keep current data; wait for new instructions.

0x03    Restart printing from the data buffers.

0x04    Stop printing from data buffers; start printing data registered in the sideband.

0x05    Start new print job packet.

0x06    Hand control of remote printer to process other than print server (local mode or DOS).

0x07    Reclaim remote printer back for the print server to use.

0x08    End of job; all data has been transmitted.

**TIP** An excellent Application Note (AppNote) written by Virgil Telford, product support engineer, and Ed Leibing, research engineer, defines the process of SPX-based printing. The AppNote title is *An Inside Look at SPX Communications between RPRINTER/NPRINTER and the NetWare Print Server (December 1995).*

Some SPX applications, such as Rconsole, however, do not use the datastream field. Their control sequences are defined in the data portion of the packet.

## THE SOURCE CONNECTION ID NUMBER FIELD

The source connection ID field contains a 2-byte identification number that is assigned by the sender. The number is used to keep track of multiple SPX connections that can be supported at one time. This field will wrap to 0 after reaching 65535 (0xFFFF).

## THE DESTINATION CONNECTION ID NUMBER FIELD

This indicates the connection ID number assigned by the destination SPX partner. The first packet in an SPX connection handshake contains a destination connection ID number of 65535, making it relatively easy to spot a connection start-up packet in a trace summary, as shown in Figure 8.15. This number wraps to 0 from 65535 (0xFFFF).

FIGURE 8.15

*The destination connection ID number 65535 is used on the first handshake packet.*

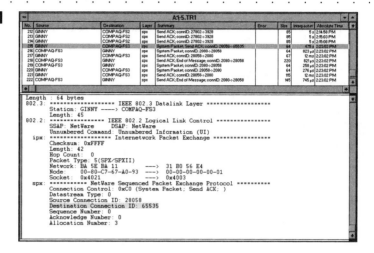

THE SEQUENCE NUMBER FIELD

The sequence number field contains a value that indicates the number of the current data packet being transmitted. This number increments for each acknowledged data packet. The sequence number field starts counting at 0. The sequence number wraps to 0 after reaching 65535 (0xFFFF).

THE ACKNOWLEDGMENT NUMBER FIELD

This field indicates the next sequence number expected from the other side of the SPX connection. Refer to Figures 8-5 and 8-6 for an example of the sequence-acknowledgment relationship. This number wraps to 0 after reaching 65535 (0xFFFF).

THE ALLOCATION NUMBER FIELD

The allocation number field is used to implement flow control. In standard SPX, it can only be used to stop communications (when the value 0 is in the allocation number field). In SPX II, this field indicates the current size of the receive window.

## THE NEGOTIATION SIZE FIELD (SPX II ONLY)

SPX II applications can use the maximum packet size by negotiating the packet size during the connection setup process. Figure 8.16 shows an SPX II header structure.

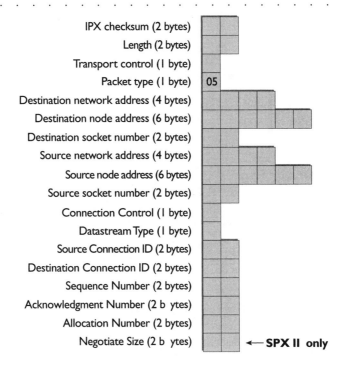

**FIGURE 8.16**

*The negotiate size field is only used in SPX II packets.*

IPX checksum (2 bytes)
Length (2 bytes)
Transport control (1 byte)
Packet type (1 byte)   05
Destination network address (4 bytes)
Destination node address (6 bytes)
Destination socket number (2 bytes)
Source network address (4 bytes)
Source node address (6 bytes)
Source socket number (2 bytes)
Connection Control (1 byte)
Datastream Type (1 byte)
Source Connection ID (2 bytes)
Destination Connection ID (2 bytes)
Sequence Number (2 bytes)
Acknowledgment Number (2 bytes)
Allocation Number (2 bytes)
Negotiate Size (2 bytes)   ← **SPX II only**

In SPX II packets, all the common SPX/SPX II fields act the same as in just SPX packets, with the exception of the allocation number field, as noted earlier. The negotiate size field is new to SPX II and is used to determine the maximum packet size that can be used by each SPX partner.

The listening SPX side places its maximum packet size in this field in its response packet. The client selects the lesser of this size and its own maximum packet size. A test packet is sent to ensure that the data path can support that packet size. If the test packet fails, the client backs off until the packet size used can go though the entire data path.

**NOTE**

**This field is not used on connection setup packets, in order to maintain backward compatibility with standard SPX applications.**

## Typical SPX Data Transfer

We'll now take a look at some typical SPX communications, including an Rconsole session and a printing session (using Novell's Pserver).

### THE RCONSOLE SESSION

The following Rconsole session used Rconsole v4.10, dated 2/16/96. This is the version of Rconsole that shipped with IntranetWare 4.11.

The Rconsole SPX session follows these basic four steps:

**1** • Locate servers that support Rconsole.

**2** • Make connection request to Rconsole server.

**3** • Request and receive server screen content.

**4** • Terminate the Rconsole session.

We'll look at the trace information for each of these steps and see how the typical Rconsole session works.

#### Step 1: Locate Servers that Support Rconsole

When you type **RCONSOLE** at the command line, you are launching RCONSOLE.EXE (located in the PUBLIC directory). This version (v4.10) of Rconsole is an SPX-based application—it does not use SPX II. Before the client makes an SPX connection to the Rconsole server, it must locate the servers that support Rconsole services. (Rconsole servers are server type 0x0107.)

As shown in Figure 8.17, the client, Ginny, broadcasts an SAP packet looking for a server (packet 417). The client will always send a server lookup SAP request even though it is currently logged into a server.

FIGURE 8.17

*The client starts an Rconsole session by locating a server.*

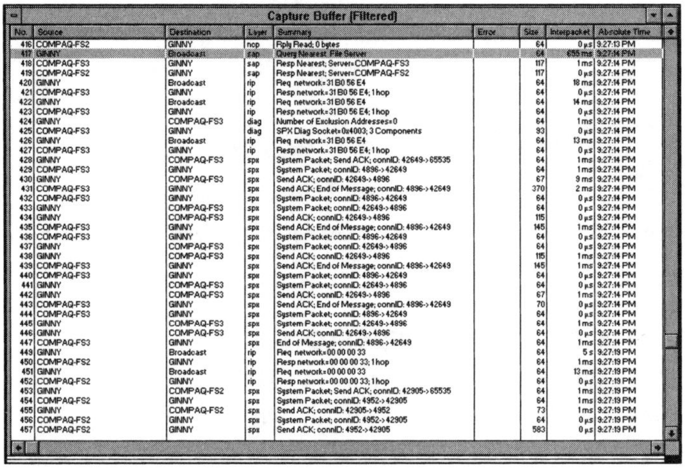

Capture Buffer [Filtered]

| No. | Source | Destination | Layer | Summary | Error | Size | Interpacket | Absolute Time |
|---|---|---|---|---|---|---|---|---|
| 416 | COMPAQ-FS2 | GINNY | ncp | Rply Read; 0 bytes | | 64 | 0 µs | 9:27:13 PM |
| 417 | GINNY | Broadcast | sap | Query Nearest File Server | | 64 | 655 ms | 9:27:14 PM |
| 418 | COMPAQ-FS3 | GINNY | sap | Resp Nearest; Server=COMPAQ-FS3 | | 117 | 1 ms | 9:27:14 PM |
| 419 | COMPAQ-FS2 | GINNY | sap | Resp Nearest; Server=COMPAQ-FS2 | | 117 | 0 µs | 9:27:14 PM |
| 420 | GINNY | Broadcast | rip | Req network=31 B0 56 E4 | | 64 | 18 ms | 9:27:14 PM |
| 421 | COMPAQ-FS3 | GINNY | rip | Resp network=31 B0 56 E4; 1 hop | | 64 | 0 µs | 9:27:14 PM |
| 422 | GINNY | Broadcast | rip | Req network=31 B0 56 E4 | | 64 | 14 ms | 9:27:14 PM |
| 423 | COMPAQ-FS3 | GINNY | rip | Resp network=31 B0 56 E4; 1 hop | | 64 | 0 µs | 9:27:14 PM |
| 424 | GINNY | COMPAQ-FS3 | diag | Number of Exclusion Addresses=0 | | 64 | 1 ms | 9:27:14 PM |
| 425 | COMPAQ-FS3 | GINNY | diag | SPX Diag Socket=0x4003; 3 Components | | 93 | 0 µs | 9:27:14 PM |
| 426 | GINNY | Broadcast | rip | Req network=31 B0 56 E4 | | 64 | 13 ms | 9:27:14 PM |
| 427 | COMPAQ-FS3 | GINNY | rip | Resp network=31 B0 56 E4; 1 hop | | 64 | 0 µs | 9:27:14 PM |
| 428 | GINNY | COMPAQ-FS3 | spx | System Packet; Send ACK; connID: 42649->65535 | | 64 | 1 ms | 9:27:14 PM |
| 429 | COMPAQ-FS3 | GINNY | spx | System Packet; connID: 4896->42649 | | 64 | 1 ms | 9:27:14 PM |
| 430 | GINNY | COMPAQ-FS3 | spx | Send ACK; connID: 42649->4896 | | 67 | 9 ms | 9:27:14 PM |
| 431 | COMPAQ-FS3 | GINNY | spx | Send ACK; End of Message; connID: 4896->42649 | | 370 | 2 ms | 9:27:14 PM |
| 432 | COMPAQ-FS3 | GINNY | spx | System Packet; connID: 4896->42649 | | 64 | 0 µs | 9:27:14 PM |
| 433 | GINNY | COMPAQ-FS3 | spx | System Packet; connID: 42649->4896 | | 64 | 0 µs | 9:27:14 PM |
| 434 | GINNY | COMPAQ-FS3 | spx | Send ACK; connID: 42649->4896 | | 115 | 0 µs | 9:27:14 PM |
| 435 | COMPAQ-FS3 | GINNY | spx | Send ACK; End of Message; connID: 4896->42649 | | 145 | 1 ms | 9:27:14 PM |
| 436 | COMPAQ-FS3 | GINNY | spx | System Packet; connID: 4896->42649 | | 64 | 0 µs | 9:27:14 PM |
| 437 | GINNY | COMPAQ-FS3 | spx | System Packet; connID: 42649->4896 | | 64 | 0 µs | 9:27:14 PM |
| 438 | GINNY | COMPAQ-FS3 | spx | Send ACK; connID: 42649->4896 | | 115 | 1 ms | 9:27:14 PM |
| 439 | COMPAQ-FS3 | GINNY | spx | Send ACK; End of Message; connID: 4896->42649 | | 145 | 1 ms | 9:27:14 PM |
| 440 | COMPAQ-FS3 | GINNY | spx | System Packet; connID: 4896->42649 | | 64 | 0 µs | 9:27:14 PM |
| 441 | GINNY | COMPAQ-FS3 | spx | System Packet; connID: 42649->4896 | | 64 | 0 µs | 9:27:14 PM |
| 442 | GINNY | COMPAQ-FS3 | spx | Send ACK; connID: 42649->4896 | | 67 | 1 ms | 9:27:14 PM |
| 443 | COMPAQ-FS3 | GINNY | spx | Send ACK; End of Message; connID: 4896->42649 | | 70 | 0 µs | 9:27:14 PM |
| 444 | COMPAQ-FS3 | GINNY | spx | System Packet; connID: 4896->42649 | | 64 | 0 µs | 9:27:14 PM |
| 445 | GINNY | COMPAQ-FS3 | spx | System Packet; connID: 42649->4896 | | 64 | 1 ms | 9:27:14 PM |
| 446 | GINNY | COMPAQ-FS3 | spx | Send ACK; connID: 42649->4896 | | 64 | 0 µs | 9:27:14 PM |
| 447 | COMPAQ-FS3 | GINNY | spx | End of Message; connID: 4896->42649 | | 64 | 1 ms | 9:27:14 PM |
| 449 | GINNY | Broadcast | rip | Req network=00 00 00 33 | | 64 | 5 s | 9:27:19 PM |
| 450 | COMPAQ-FS2 | GINNY | rip | Resp network=00 00 00 33; 1 hop | | 64 | 1 ms | 9:27:19 PM |
| 451 | GINNY | Broadcast | rip | Req network=00 00 00 33 | | 64 | 13 ms | 9:27:19 PM |
| 452 | COMPAQ-FS2 | GINNY | rip | Resp network=00 00 00 33; 1 hop | | 64 | 0 µs | 9:27:19 PM |
| 453 | GINNY | COMPAQ-FS2 | spx | System Packet; Send ACK; connID: 42905->65535 | | 64 | 1 ms | 9:27:19 PM |
| 454 | COMPAQ-FS2 | GINNY | spx | System Packet; connID: 4952->42905 | | 64 | 1 ms | 9:27:19 PM |
| 455 | GINNY | COMPAQ-FS2 | spx | Send ACK; connID: 42905->4952 | | 73 | 1 ms | 9:27:19 PM |
| 456 | COMPAQ-FS2 | GINNY | spx | System Packet; connID: 4952->42905 | | 64 | 0 µs | 9:27:19 PM |
| 457 | COMPAQ-FS2 | GINNY | spx | Send ACK; connID: 4952->42905 | | 583 | 0 µs | 9:27:19 PM |

In our example, two servers on the local network answer back (packets 418 and 419). The client sends a RIP request for the internal IPX address (0x31-B0-56-E4) of the first server that responded (COMPAQ-FS3). Once the client learns the fastest way to get to the server, it sends an SPX connection request packet to it. Figure 8.18 and Figure 8.19 show the fully decoded handshake packets.

FIGURE 8.18

*The destination connection ID of 65535 indicates that this is a handshake packet.*

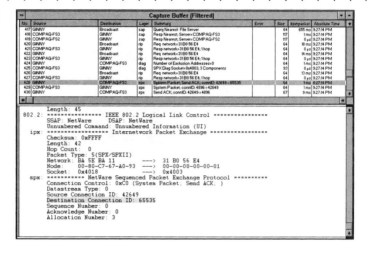

FIGURE 8.19

*In the response, the server indicates that it will use connection ID number 4896.*

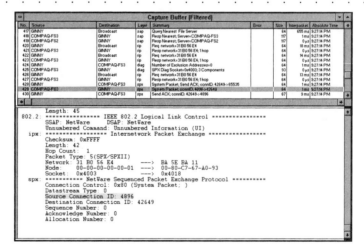

This first server that the client connects to will be used to simply build the Rconsole menu that lists Rconsole servers, as shown in Figure 8.20.

FIGURE 8.20

*The menu consists of two servers that are known to support Rconsole services.*

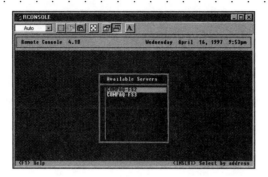

In order to build the list shown in the Rconsole menu, the client sends an Rconsole query packet to COMPAQ-FS3 (the server it just made an SPX connection to). The client makes a request for the server information table, indicating that it wants a list of all the file servers in that server's server information tables.

The server, COMPAQ-FS3, replies with its server list in packet 431, shown in Figure 8.21. Most analyzers won't decode application-layer communications that reside above SPX. In order to understand the conversation taking place, we must either contact the engineer who developed the application or do some very tedious reverse-engineering to figure it out. In this case, I simply study the values in the packets to define the conversation taking place. The findings are highlighted in the following packets.

FIGURE 8.21

*Hand-decoding shows the server supplying its server information table to the client.*

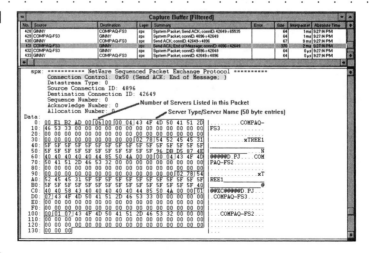

Packet 431 indicates that the server is reporting about six servers (0x06). From our studies, we have determined that the server will report only up to 10 servers (0x0A) at one time. The server will stop sending server information once it has reported all the 0x0004 (file server) entries. Once the client has learned about the servers, it must query COMPAQ-FS3 for the internal IPX addresses of those servers.

**TIP**

**If you have problems with Rconsole not displaying all the Rconsole servers you know you have, take a look at the trace to see which server is supplying the list of Rconsole servers and what addresses that server is giving the client.**

In Packet 434, shown in Figure 8.22, the client is requesting further information about the first Rconsole server, COMPAQ-FS3. This seems like a strange thing to do, because the client is already talking to the server. But since it might take longer to sort out information about the particular server the client is already attached to, you may as well go ahead and get some redundant information.

**FIGURE 8.22**

*The client is requesting information about the Rconsole server named COMPAQ-FS3.*

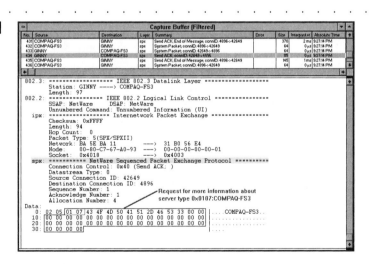

In packet 435, shown in Figure 8.23, the server provides the internal IPX address, node address, and socket number of the Rconsole service that it has in its tables. The Rconsole static socket number is 0x8104. This lookup sequence can be very helpful when you are troubleshooting Rconsole sessions—you can determine what server address you were given during the setup phase.

FIGURE    8.23

*The server supplies the internetwork address of the Rconsole server.*

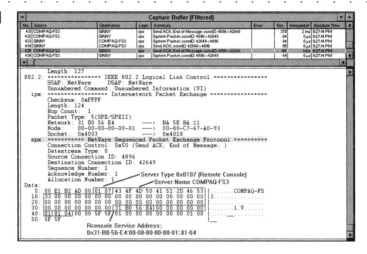

The client requests the information for COMPAQ-FS2 in packet 438 and gets its internal IPX address, the node address for Rconsole services, in packet 439 (as shown in Figure 8.17).

The client then terminates the SPX connection with the lookup server (packets 446 and 447) and sends an SPX connection setup packet to the desired Rconsole server. In this case, Ginny selected COMPAQ-FS3 from the Rconsole menu. That is the same server we performed the lookup on. The client will always tear down and restart an SPX connection after looking up the Rconsole servers available.

### Step 2: Make Connection Request to Rconsole Server

In packet 453, Ginny sends a connection request packet to COMPAQ-FS3, her desired Rconsole server. During the lookup process (packets 428 to 447), Ginny was addressing packets to a dynamic socket, but as you can see in Figure 8.24, these packets are addressed directly to the Rconsole socket, 0x8104.

**Note: Socket 0x8104 is decoded as NW386 by LANalyzer for Windows. For more socket information, refer to Appendix F.**

NOTE

*The SPX connection request packet is addressed directly to socket 0x8104, the Rconsole static socket.*

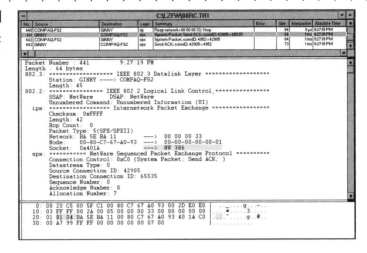

The server replies in Figure 8.25, indicating that its SPX Connection ID number is 4952.

*The server responds with an acknowledgment packet (SYS packet).*

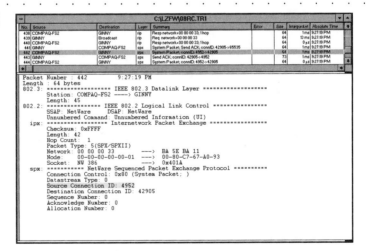

## Step 3: Request and Receive Server Screen Content

In Figure 8.26, we can see the actual screen content being downloaded to the client. This information is not encrypted and can be read in plain text off the wire. In this case, we can tell by the text contained in the packet that the server console has a message stating "Remote Console connection granted for BA5EBA11:0080C767A093" on its screen.

FIGURE 8.26

*The Rconsole screen can be read off the wire in plain text.*

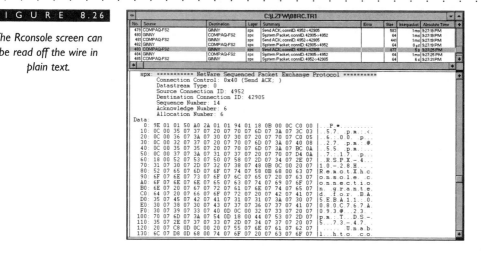

### Step 4: Terminate the Rconsole Session

Finally, when Ginny decides to exit out of Rconsole, she sends an end-of-connection packet with an acknowledgment request in the connection control field to the server, as shown in Figure 8.27. The server replies with an end-of-connection acknowledgment, as shown in Figure 8.28.

FIGURE 8.27

*The end-of-connection is accompanied by an acknowledgment request (Send ACK).*

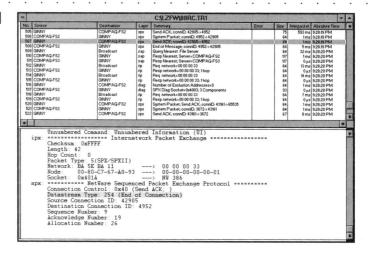

FIGURE 8.28

*The server grants the termination by sending an end-of-connection acknowledgment.*

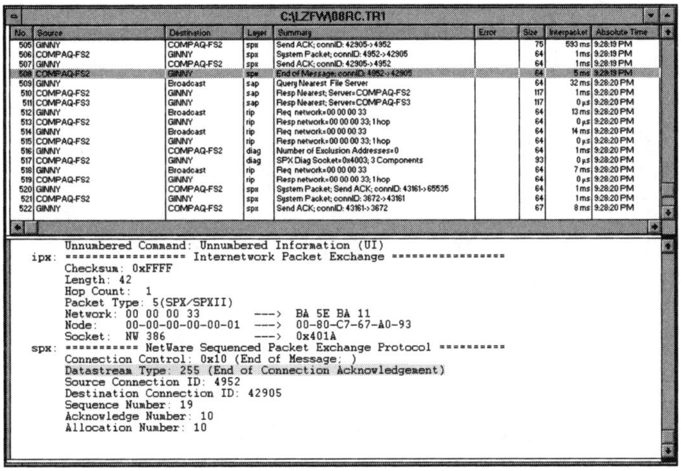

Interestingly, after terminating the SPX connection, the client must put the Rconsole menu back up on the screen. You would think that the client would just put up the same information that it had before it started the SPX Rconsole session. Unfortunately, as shown in Figure 8.29, the client does not use the same Rconsole information it had before.

FIGURE 8.29

*The client rebuilds the Rconsole list after terminating the Rconsole session with COMPAQ-FS3.*

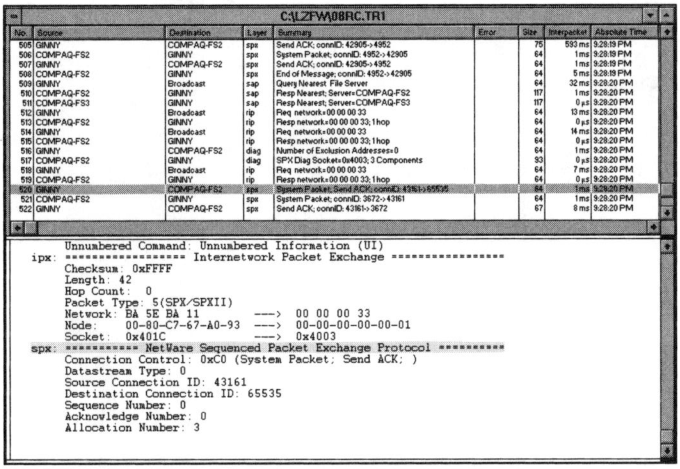

The client actually rebuilds a new Rconsole menu by sending out an SAP request to find a server, creating an SPX connection to the first server that answers, querying that server for all the servers it knows about, and looking up the internetwork address and socket number of SPX services on each of those servers.

Although this really sounds like a long and drawn-out process, the lookup process shown in our example took less than one second—86 milliseconds, to be exact.

Understanding how a typical SPX communication occurs can greatly help you in the troubleshooting process.

## The Error Recovery Process

What if things don't go as planned during the SPX session? When does the SPX client time out? How about retries? As you can see in Figure 8.30, something has gone wrong with Ginny's SPX session to COMPAQ-FS2. The server is not responding to Ginny's request for an acknowledgment (Send ACK) in packet 195.

FIGURE 8.30

*The client cannot continue sending information to the server unless it gets the requested acknowledgment.*

| No. | Source | Destination | Layer | Summary | Error | Size | Interpacket | Absolute Time |
|-----|--------|-------------|-------|---------|-------|------|-------------|---------------|
| 179 | GINNY | COMPAQ-FS2 | spx | Send ACK; connID: 27802->3928 | | 85 | 166 ms | 2:13:40 PM |
| 180 | COMPAQ-FS2 | GINNY | spx | System Packet; connID: 3928->27802 | | 64 | 588 μs | 2:13:40 PM |
| 181 | COMPAQ-FS2 | GINNY | spx | Send ACK; connID: 3928->27802 | | 93 | 2 ms | 2:13:40 PM |
| 182 | GINNY | COMPAQ-FS2 | spx | System Packet; connID: 27802->3928 | | 64 | 3 ms | 2:13:40 PM |
| 183 | GINNY | COMPAQ-FS2 | spx | Send ACK; connID: 27802->3928 | | 85 | 4 s | 2:13:44 PM |
| 184 | COMPAQ-FS2 | GINNY | spx | System Packet; connID: 3928->27802 | | 64 | 628 μs | 2:13:44 PM |
| 185 | COMPAQ-FS2 | GINNY | spx | Send ACK; connID: 3928->27802 | | 583 | 30 ms | 2:13:44 PM |
| 186 | GINNY | COMPAQ-FS2 | spx | System Packet; connID: 27802->3928 | | 64 | 604 μs | 2:13:44 PM |
| 187 | COMPAQ-FS2 | GINNY | spx | Send ACK; connID: 3928->27802 | | 583 | 2 ms | 2:13:44 PM |
| 188 | GINNY | COMPAQ-FS2 | spx | System Packet; connID: 27802->3928 | | 64 | 986 μs | 2:13:44 PM |
| 189 | COMPAQ-FS2 | GINNY | spx | Send ACK; connID: 3928->27802 | | 583 | 1 ms | 2:13:44 PM |
| 190 | GINNY | COMPAQ-FS2 | spx | System Packet; connID: 27802->3928 | | 64 | 591 μs | 2:13:44 PM |
| 191 | COMPAQ-FS2 | GINNY | spx | Send ACK; connID: 3928->27802 | | 583 | 1 ms | 2:13:44 PM |
| 192 | GINNY | COMPAQ-FS2 | spx | System Packet; connID: 27802->3928 | | 64 | 577 μs | 2:13:44 PM |
| 193 | COMPAQ-FS2 | GINNY | spx | Send ACK; connID: 3928->27802 | | 281 | 867 μs | 2:13:44 PM |
| 194 | GINNY | COMPAQ-FS2 | spx | System Packet; connID: 27802->3928 | | 64 | 1 ms | 2:13:44 PM |
| 195 | GINNY | COMPAQ-FS2 | spx | Send ACK; connID: 27802->3928 | | 85 | 6 s | 2:13:50 PM |
| 196 | GINNY | COMPAQ-FS2 | spx | Send ACK; connID: 27802->3928 | | 85 | 692 ms | 2:13:51 PM |
| 197 | GINNY | COMPAQ-FS2 | spx | Send ACK; connID: 27802->3928 | | 85 | 1 s | 2:13:52 PM |
| 198 | GINNY | COMPAQ-FS2 | spx | Send ACK; connID: 27802->3928 | | 85 | 2 s | 2:13:53 PM |
| 199 | GINNY | COMPAQ-FS2 | spx | Send ACK; connID: 27802->3928 | | 85 | 2 s | 2:13:56 PM |
| 200 | GINNY | COMPAQ-FS2 | spx | Send ACK; connID: 27802->3928 | | 85 | 3 s | 2:13:59 PM |
| 201 | GINNY | COMPAQ-FS2 | spx | Send ACK; connID: 27802->3928 | | 85 | 5 s | 2:14:04 PM |
| 202 | GINNY | COMPAQ-FS2 | spx | Send ACK; connID: 27802->3928 | | 85 | 5 s | 2:14:09 PM |
| 203 | GINNY | COMPAQ-FS2 | spx | Send ACK; connID: 27802->3928 | | 85 | 5 s | 2:14:14 PM |
| 204 | GINNY | COMPAQ-FS2 | spx | Send ACK; connID: 27802->3928 | | 85 | 5 s | 2:14:19 PM |
| 205 | GINNY | COMPAQ-FS2 | spx | Send ACK; connID: 27802->3928 | | 85 | 5 s | 2:14:23 PM |
| 206 | GINNY | COMPAQ-FS2 | spx | Send ACK; connID: 27802->3928 | | 85 | 5 s | 2:14:28 PM |
| 207 | GINNY | COMPAQ-FS2 | spx | Send ACK; connID: 27802->3928 | | 85 | 5 s | 2:14:33 PM |
| 208 | GINNY | COMPAQ-FS2 | spx | Send ACK; connID: 27802->3928 | | 85 | 5 s | 2:14:38 PM |
| 209 | GINNY | COMPAQ-FS2 | spx | Send ACK; connID: 27802->3928 | | 85 | 5 s | 2:14:43 PM |
| 210 | GINNY | COMPAQ-FS2 | spx | Send ACK; connID: 27802->3928 | | 85 | 5 s | 2:14:48 PM |
| 211 | GINNY | COMPAQ-FS2 | spx | Send ACK; connID: 27802->3928 | | 85 | 5 s | 2:14:53 PM |
| 212 | GINNY | COMPAQ-FS2 | spx | Send ACK; connID: 27802->3928 | | 85 | 5 s | 2:14:58 PM |
| 213 | GINNY | COMPAQ-FS2 | spx | Send ACK; connID: 27802->3928 | | 85 | 5 s | 2:15:03 PM |
| 214 | GINNY | COMPAQ-FS2 | spx | Send ACK; connID: 27802->3928 | | 85 | 5 s | 2:15:08 PM |
| 215 | GINNY | COMPAQ-FS3 | spx | System Packet; Send ACK; connID: 28058->65535 | | 64 | 475 s | 2:23:02 PM |
| 216 | COMPAQ-FS3 | GINNY | spx | System Packet; connID: 2080->28058 | | 64 | 823 μs | 2:23:02 PM |
| 217 | GINNY | COMPAQ-FS3 | spx | Send ACK; connID: 28058->2080 | | 67 | 12 ms | 2:23:02 PM |
| 218 | COMPAQ-FS3 | GINNY | spx | Send ACK; End of Message; connID: 2080->28058 | | 220 | 821 μs | 2:23:02 PM |
| 219 | COMPAQ-FS3 | GINNY | spx | System Packet; connID: 2080->28058 | | 64 | 258 μs | 2:23:02 PM |

In this case, the client retries 20 times (a number set by the application) before giving up on the SPX connection to COMPAQ-FS2. We can see that the request interval is changing: It started at less than one second, then went to one second, then two seconds, then three seconds, and finally, it topped out at five-second intervals between retries. This timing can be set by the application, or a programmer can let SPX handle the retry intervals.

In this case, Ginny had an Rconsole session going to the server when the server's cable broke. Just as before, Ginny's station rebuilt its Rconsole menu, but it did not SAP for the servers. It used the server it was connected to.

If you see an SPX client or server performing one or more retries, check the cabling system to see if there is an intermittent short or open. If you believe the cabling system is fine, check the timing on the replies. One side could be timing out waiting for a response. This could indicate a slow device or a long data path to reach the device. In that case, you may have to change some of the SPX settings to allow the client to function without excessive retries or timeouts.

## SPX/SPX II Settings

Fortunately, SPX can be configured to work properly regardless of the underlying network problems or configurations. There are three types of SPX settings:

SPX connections

SPX Watchdog

SPX retries/timeouts (data transfer)

Figure 8.31 shows the various timers that affect SPX-based communications. In the next section, we'll examine each of these settings and provide examples of situations in which you should change the settings on the clients and the server.

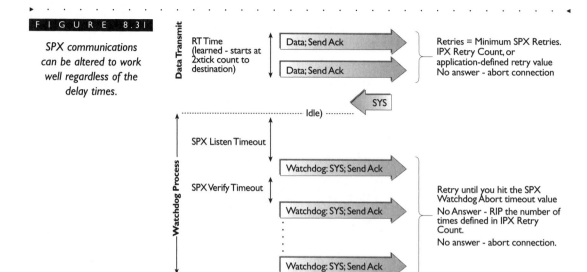

▸ · · · · · · · · · · · · · · · · · · · · · · · · · · · · · · · · · · · · ◂

F I G U R E   8.31

*SPX communications can be altered to work well regardless of the delay times.*

## SPX CONNECTIONS

The SPX connections setting specifies the "number of connections" value that is given to applications that query this information. If you load multiple SPX applications on a client, you can run out of SPX connection slots. Likewise, if you have lots of SPX connections requested of a server, it may run out of connections. Some applications may frankly state that you need to increase the SPX connections count. Others should state it but don't.

If your SPX clients receive a message indicating that the SPX connection was not granted, increase the number of SPX connections to see if that helps.

## SPX WATCHDOG

There are two Watchdog processes in NetWare. One is an NCP Watchdog (covered in detail in Chapter 13).

SPX Watchdog is used to check the validity of an SPX connection after it has gone idle for a certain amount of time. Each side of the SPX connection maintains a watchdog timer and periodically sends "keep alive" SPX packets to the other side to see if it is still there (the SPX socket is still open). You can change the way SPX Watchdog works by adjusting three SPX parameters:

- ▸ SPX Listen Timeout

- ▸ SPX Verify Timeout

- ▸ SPX Abort Timeout

### SPX Listen Timeout

The SPX Listen Timeout counter specifies how long (in ticks) the SPX protocol waits without receiving any packet from the other side of the connection before it requests the other side to send a packet to confirm that the connection is valid. For example, if a connection is idle for six seconds (the default value), an SPX partner will send an SPX Watchdog packet to the other side. This packet requests an acknowledgment. Once the acknowledgment is received, the SPX Listen Timeout timer is reset to 0.

### SPX Verify Timeout

The SPX Verify Timeout counter specifies how often (in ticks) the SPX protocol sends an SPX Watchdog packet to the other side of a connection to indicate that it exists. If no answer is received from the SPX Watchdog within the SPX Verify Timeout interval, another SPX Watchdog packet is sent.

These two timers work together to adjust the way SPX Watchdog performs, as shown in Figure 8.32. For more information on how and where to set each of these timers, see the section titled "Configuring SPX" later in this chapter.

Figure 8.33 provides an example of an Rconsole session that has been terminated because of the SPX watchdog timers. In this example, the server is not responding within the SPX Verify Timeout interval, so the client watchdog abruptly aborts the connection after looking for a new route.

As you can see in Figure 8.33, Jill sends SPX Watchdog packets to COMPAQ-FS3 (packets 757 to 762), but it never gets an answer. After six attempts at three-second intervals, Jill aborts the connection to the server. On the screen, the Rconsole session is simply halted and Jill is shown the Rconsole menu again without COMPAQ-FS3 listed.

**NOTE**

**Applications can override the Watchdog parameters you set, so you may not always see SPX Watchdog communications that match your settings.**

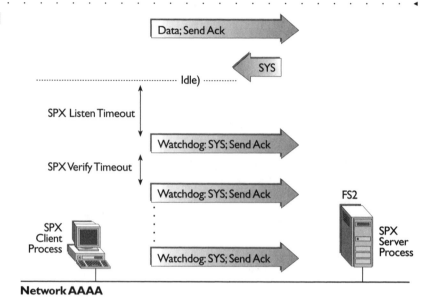

FIGURE 8.32

*Listen Timeout and Verify Timeout work together to define the Watchdog process.*

FIGURE 8.33

*If the SPX Watchdog process fails, the client must look for a new route using RIP.*

A:\08WDOG.TR1

| No. | Source | Destination | Layer | Summary | Error | Size | Interpacket | Absolute Ti |
|---|---|---|---|---|---|---|---|---|
| 756 | JILL | COMPAQ-FS3 | spx | System Packet; connID: 5476->5408 | | 64 | 3 s | 9:29:07 AM |
| 757 | JILL | COMPAQ-FS3 | spx | System Packet; Send ACK; connID: 5476->5408 | | 64 | 3 s | 9:29:11 AM |
| 758 | JILL | COMPAQ-FS3 | spx | System Packet; Send ACK; connID: 5476->5408 | | 64 | 3 s | 9:29:14 AM |
| 759 | JILL | COMPAQ-FS3 | spx | System Packet; Send ACK; connID: 5476->5408 | | 64 | 3 s | 9:29:18 AM |
| 760 | JILL | COMPAQ-FS3 | spx | System Packet; Send ACK; connID: 5476->5408 | | 64 | 3 s | 9:29:21 AM |
| 761 | JILL | COMPAQ-FS3 | spx | System Packet; Send ACK; connID: 5476->5408 | | 64 | 3 s | 9:29:24 AM |
| 762 | JILL | COMPAQ-FS3 | spx | System Packet; Send ACK; connID: 5476->5408 | | 64 | 3 s | 9:29:28 AM |
| 763 | JILL | Broadcast | rip | Req network=31 B0 56 E4 | | 64 | 3 s | 9:29:31 AM |
| 764 | JILL | Broadcast | rip | Req network=31 B0 56 E4 | | 64 | 11 s | 9:29:42 AM |
| 765 | JILL | Broadcast | rip | Req network=31 B0 56 E4 | | 64 | 717 ms | 9:29:43 AM |
| 766 | JILL | Broadcast | rip | Req network=31 B0 56 E4 | | 64 | 795 ms | 9:29:43 AM |
| 767 | JILL | Broadcast | rip | Req network=31 B0 56 E4 | | 64 | 736 ms | 9:29:44 AM |
| 768 | JILL | Broadcast | rip | Req network=31 B0 56 E4 | | 64 | 776 ms | 9:29:45 AM |
| 769 | JILL | Broadcast | rip | Req network=31 B0 56 E4 | | 64 | 737 ms | 9:29:46 AM |
| 770 | JILL | Broadcast | rip | Req network=31 B0 56 E4 | | 64 | 794 ms | 9:29:46 AM |
| 771 | JILL | Broadcast | rip | Req network=31 B0 56 E4 | | 64 | 794 ms | 9:29:47 AM |
| 772 | JILL | Broadcast | rip | Req network=31 B0 56 E4 | | 64 | 756 ms | 9:29:48 AM |
| 773 | JILL | Broadcast | rip | Req network=31 B0 56 E4 | | 64 | 718 ms | 9:29:49 AM |
| 774 | JILL | Broadcast | rip | Req network=31 B0 56 E4 | | 64 | 794 ms | 9:29:50 AM |
| 775 | JILL | Broadcast | rip | Req network=31 B0 56 E4 | | 64 | 814 ms | 9:29:50 AM |
| 776 | JILL | Broadcast | rip | Req network=31 B0 56 E4 | | 64 | 795 ms | 9:29:51 AM |
| 777 | JILL | Broadcast | rip | Req network=31 B0 56 E4 | | 64 | 813 ms | 9:29:52 AM |
| 778 | JILL | Broadcast | rip | Req network=31 B0 56 E4 | | 64 | 775 ms | 9:29:53 AM |
| 779 | JILL | Broadcast | rip | Req network=31 B0 56 E4 | | 64 | 834 ms | 9:29:54 AM |
| 780 | JILL | Broadcast | rip | Req network=31 B0 56 E4 | | 64 | 755 ms | 9:29:54 AM |
| 781 | JILL | Broadcast | rip | Req network=31 B0 56 E4 | | 64 | 717 ms | 9:29:55 AM |
| 782 | JILL | Broadcast | rip | Req network=31 B0 56 E4 | | 64 | 737 ms | 9:29:56 AM |
| 783 | JILL | Broadcast | rip | Req network=31 B0 56 E4 | | 64 | 795 ms | 9:29:57 AM |
| 784 | JILL | COMPAQ-FS2 | ncp | Req Read; Handle 0100F10D0000; 4 bytes | | 71 | 817 ms | 9:29:57 AM |
| 785 | COMPAQ-FS2 | JILL | ncp | Rply Read; 4 bytes | | 65 | 232 µs | 9:29:57 AM |
| 786 | JILL | COMPAQ-FS2 | ncp | Req Read; Handle 0100F10D0000; 256 bytes | | 71 | 2 ms | 9:29:57 AM |
| 787 | COMPAQ-FS2 | JILL | ncp | Rply Read; 256 bytes | | 318 | 778 µs | 9:29:57 AM |
| 788 | JILL | COMPAQ-FS2 | ncp | Req Read; Handle 0100F10D0000; 4 bytes | | 71 | 3 ms | 9:29:57 AM |
| 789 | COMPAQ-FS2 | JILL | ncp | Rply Read; 4 bytes | | 65 | 219 µs | 9:29:57 AM |
| 790 | JILL | COMPAQ-FS2 | ncp | Req Read; Handle 0100F10D0000; 256 bytes | | 71 | 2 ms | 9:29:57 AM |
| 791 | COMPAQ-FS2 | JILL | ncp | Rply Read; 256 bytes | | 318 | 726 µs | 9:29:57 AM |
| 792 | JILL | Broadcast | sap | Query Nearest File Server | | 64 | 36 ms | 9:29:57 AM |
| 793 | COMPAQ-FS2 | JILL | sap | Resp Nearest; Server=COMPAQ-FS2 | | 117 | 454 µs | 9:29:57 AM |
| 794 | JILL | Broadcast | rip | Req network=00 00 00 33 | | 64 | 2 ms | 9:29:57 AM |
| 795 | COMPAQ-FS2 | JILL | rip | Resp network=00 00 00 33; 1 hop | | 64 | 307 µs | 9:29:57 AM |
| 796 | JILL | Broadcast | rip | Req network=00 00 00 33 | | 64 | 866 µs | 9:29:57 AM |

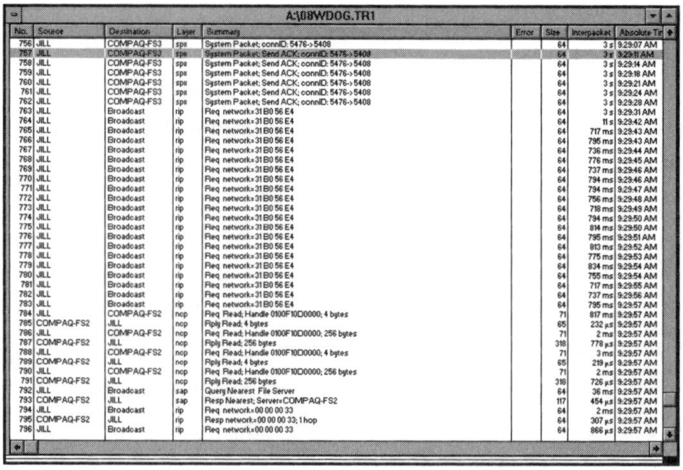

### SPX Abort Timeout

The SPX Abort Timeout value indicates how long the SPX Watchdog process continues without a response before terminating the connection. Add the round-trip time value to this setting to be exact.

At the server, however, the number of SPX Watchdog retries is manually set by the SPX Default Retry Count parameter.

If you find that your SPX application is disconnecting during idle time, but you'd like it to stay connected, you can adjust your SPX Verify Timeout and SPX Listen Timeout settings. Refer to the next section to deal with data retries and timeouts.

## SPX DATA RETRIES AND TIMEOUTS

The timeout value between SPX data transmissions can sometimes be a problem in NetWare, especially when you are communicating across a slower WAN link or high number of routers. You can even experience timeouts if the SPX partners are communicating across very busy links. There are two timers that you can adjust to help reduce retries and timeouts. They are

▸ SPX Ack Wait Timeout (adjustable at the server only)

▸ SPX Minimum Retry Count

Remember that these timers can be overridden by the application that is making calls to SPX.

### SPX Ack Wait Timeout

The amount of time that an SPX connection will wait for an acknowledgment is learned at the client and set manually at the server.

The client bases its Ack Wait Timer on the round-trip time to the target. By using a calculation based on the Van Jacobsen algorithm, the client ensures it is using a proper timeout value.

When the client made a connection to the SPX partner, it used RIP to determine how far away the partner's network was in ticks (1/18 second). For example, perhaps the client learned that the server was three ticks away. The client doubles this time (to find the approximate round-trip value) to six ticks. As the connection gets older, the client revises this round-trip estimate to double the round-trip time plus two mean deviations (average time differences between responses). This allows extra wait time for delays caused during peak utilization periods.

### SPX Retry Count

At the VLM client you can configure a Minimum SPX Retry Count minimum. Client 32, however, uses the IPX Retry Count value as the default SPX retry count.

The Minimum SPX Retries parameter became available with VLM v1.20. This entry can be added to the NET.CFG file to override the SPX retry value set by an application. The parameter is MINIMUM SPX RETRIES=*n*. The minimum value is 1, and the maximum is 255. If the value of the Minimum SPX Retries is greater than the value set by the application or the IPX Retry Count, it will override these values. This ensures that at least the specified number of retries can occur before a session is destroyed for lack of acknowledgment by the SPX partner.

The following is a NET.CFG example that includes a Minimum SPX Retries entry:

```
Link Driver NE2000

   PORT 360

   INT 5

   FRAME Ethernet_802.2


Protocol SPX

   MINIMUM SPX RETRIES = 30


NetWare DOS Requester

   VLM = AUTO.VLM

   VLM = RSA.VLM

   BIND RECONNECT = ON

   AUTO RETRY = 10

   FIRST NETWORK DRIVE = G

   PREFERRED SERVER = COMPAQ-FS2
```

```
SIGNATURE LEVEL = 0

MESSAGE LEVEL = 4

MESSAGE TIMEOUT = 183

PRINT BUFFER SIZE = 256

CACHE BUFFERS = 20

CHECKSUM = 0
```

Unfortunately, as of this writing, this parameter is not available with Client 32. Client 32 uses the value of the IPX Retry Count for SPX retries.

To adjust the IPX Retry Count in Windows 95, select Network⇨IPX/SPX Protocol for Novell NetWare Client 32⇨IPX, and adjust the value as shown in Figure 8.34.

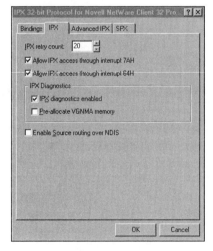

F I G U R E   8.34

*The IPX Retry Count is a configurable parameter of the IPX/SPX Protocol for Novell NetWare Client 32.*

**TIP**

**If you want a handy reference to the settings available for the VLM and Client 32, pick up a copy of Kelly Lindberg's** *IntranetWare Administrator's Handbook* **or her** *NetWare 3.12 Administrator's Handbook.* **They are an excellent quick reference guide to the settings and properties of the NetWare products. In particular, check out Appendixes A and B.**

SPX applications can, however, specify a different maximum retry number when setting up connections. For example, RCONSOLE.EXE v4.10 will always do 20 retries, as shown in Figure 8.35, regardless of whether you set the IPX Retry Count to 5 or 50.

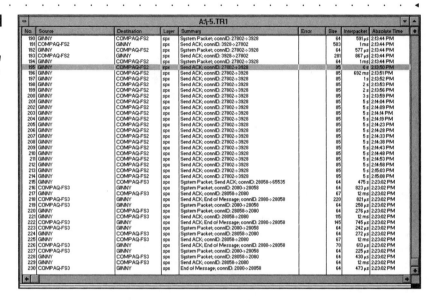

FIGURE 8.35

Rconsole makes 20 attempts to deliver the data regardless of the IPX Retry Count.

The server's retry count is set using SPXCONFG or INETCFG. The default retry count for IntranetWare v4.11 is 10. As you can see in Figure 8.36, the server attempts to deliver a 583-byte packet to the client, but it receives no acknowledgment. The server sends the same packet ten times and then aborts the SPX connection. At this time, the client receives the following message: "General failure reading device NETWORK. Abort, Retry, Fail?"

FIGURE 8.36

*The server attempts 10 times, based on the value of the SPX Default Retry Count.*

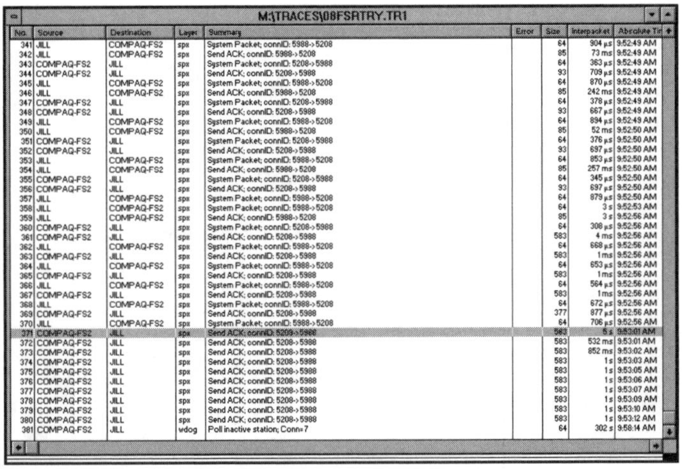

M:\TRACES\08FSRTRY.TR1

| No. | Source | Destination | Layer | Summary | Error | Size | Interpacket | Absolute Tir |
|---|---|---|---|---|---|---|---|---|
| 341 | JILL | COMPAQ-FS2 | spx | System Packet; connID: 5988->5208 | | 64 | 904 µs | 9:52:49 AM |
| 342 | JILL | COMPAQ-FS2 | spx | Send ACK; connID: 5988->5208 | | 85 | 73 ms | 9:52:49 AM |
| 343 | COMPAQ-FS2 | JILL | spx | System Packet; connID: 5208->5988 | | 64 | 363 µs | 9:52:49 AM |
| 344 | COMPAQ-FS2 | JILL | spx | Send ACK; connID: 5208->5988 | | 93 | 709 µs | 9:52:49 AM |
| 345 | JILL | COMPAQ-FS2 | spx | System Packet; connID: 5988->5208 | | 64 | 870 µs | 9:52:49 AM |
| 346 | JILL | COMPAQ-FS2 | spx | Send ACK; connID: 5988->5208 | | 85 | 242 ms | 9:52:49 AM |
| 347 | COMPAQ-FS2 | JILL | spx | System Packet; connID: 5208->5988 | | 64 | 378 µs | 9:52:49 AM |
| 348 | COMPAQ-FS2 | JILL | spx | Send ACK; connID: 5208->5988 | | 93 | 667 µs | 9:52:49 AM |
| 349 | JILL | COMPAQ-FS2 | spx | System Packet; connID: 5988->5208 | | 64 | 894 µs | 9:52:49 AM |
| 350 | JILL | COMPAQ-FS2 | spx | Send ACK; connID: 5988->5208 | | 85 | 52 ms | 9:52:50 AM |
| 351 | COMPAQ-FS2 | JILL | spx | System Packet; connID: 5208->5988 | | 64 | 376 µs | 9:52:50 AM |
| 352 | COMPAQ-FS2 | JILL | spx | Send ACK; connID: 5208->5988 | | 93 | 697 µs | 9:52:50 AM |
| 353 | JILL | COMPAQ-FS2 | spx | System Packet; connID: 5988->5208 | | 64 | 853 µs | 9:52:50 AM |
| 354 | JILL | COMPAQ-FS2 | spx | Send ACK; connID: 5988->5208 | | 85 | 257 ms | 9:52:50 AM |
| 355 | COMPAQ-FS2 | JILL | spx | System Packet; connID: 5208->5988 | | 64 | 345 µs | 9:52:50 AM |
| 356 | COMPAQ-FS2 | JILL | spx | Send ACK; connID: 5208->5988 | | 93 | 697 µs | 9:52:50 AM |
| 357 | JILL | COMPAQ-FS2 | spx | System Packet; connID: 5988->5208 | | 64 | 879 µs | 9:52:50 AM |
| 358 | JILL | COMPAQ-FS2 | spx | System Packet; connID: 5988->5208 | | 64 | 3 s | 9:52:53 AM |
| 359 | JILL | COMPAQ-FS2 | spx | Send ACK; connID: 5988->5208 | | 85 | 3 s | 9:52:56 AM |
| 360 | COMPAQ-FS2 | JILL | spx | System Packet; connID: 5208->5988 | | 64 | 308 µs | 9:52:56 AM |
| 361 | COMPAQ-FS2 | JILL | spx | Send ACK; connID: 5208->5988 | | 583 | 4 ms | 9:52:56 AM |
| 362 | JILL | COMPAQ-FS2 | spx | System Packet; connID: 5988->5208 | | 64 | 668 µs | 9:52:56 AM |
| 363 | COMPAQ-FS2 | JILL | spx | Send ACK; connID: 5208->5988 | | 583 | 1 ms | 9:52:56 AM |
| 364 | JILL | COMPAQ-FS2 | spx | System Packet; connID: 5988->5208 | | 64 | 653 µs | 9:52:56 AM |
| 365 | COMPAQ-FS2 | JILL | spx | Send ACK; connID: 5208->5988 | | 583 | 1 ms | 9:52:56 AM |
| 366 | JILL | COMPAQ-FS2 | spx | System Packet; connID: 5988->5208 | | 64 | 564 µs | 9:52:56 AM |
| 367 | COMPAQ-FS2 | JILL | spx | Send ACK; connID: 5208->5988 | | 583 | 1 ms | 9:52:56 AM |
| 368 | JILL | COMPAQ-FS2 | spx | System Packet; connID: 5988->5208 | | 64 | 672 µs | 9:52:56 AM |
| 369 | COMPAQ-FS2 | JILL | spx | Send ACK; connID: 5208->5988 | | 377 | 877 µs | 9:52:56 AM |
| 370 | JILL | COMPAQ-FS2 | spx | System Packet; connID: 5988->5208 | | 64 | 706 µs | 9:52:56 AM |
| 371 | COMPAQ-FS2 | JILL | spx | Send ACK; connID: 5208->5988 | | 583 | 5 s | 9:53:01 AM |
| 372 | COMPAQ-FS2 | JILL | spx | Send ACK; connID: 5208->5988 | | 583 | 532 ms | 9:53:01 AM |
| 373 | COMPAQ-FS2 | JILL | spx | Send ACK; connID: 5208->5988 | | 583 | 852 ms | 9:53:02 AM |
| 374 | COMPAQ-FS2 | JILL | spx | Send ACK; connID: 5208->5988 | | 583 | 1 s | 9:53:03 AM |
| 375 | COMPAQ-FS2 | JILL | spx | Send ACK; connID: 5208->5988 | | 583 | 1 s | 9:53:05 AM |
| 376 | COMPAQ-FS2 | JILL | spx | Send ACK; connID: 5208->5988 | | 583 | 1 s | 9:53:06 AM |
| 377 | COMPAQ-FS2 | JILL | spx | Send ACK; connID: 5208->5988 | | 583 | 1 s | 9:53:07 AM |
| 378 | COMPAQ-FS2 | JILL | spx | Send ACK; connID: 5208->5988 | | 583 | 1 s | 9:53:09 AM |
| 379 | COMPAQ-FS2 | JILL | spx | Send ACK; connID: 5208->5988 | | 583 | 1 s | 9:53:10 AM |
| 380 | COMPAQ-FS2 | JILL | spx | Send ACK; connID: 5208->5988 | | 583 | 1 s | 9:53:12 AM |
| 381 | COMPAQ-FS2 | JILL | wdog | Poll inactive station; Conn=7 | | 64 | 302 s | 9:58:14 AM |

## WAN Link Issues

There are two problems with SPX across a WAN link. First, SPX has a tendency to time out across slower WAN links. Second, SPX Watchdog can bring up a dial-on-demand WAN link and become very costly.

In order to deal with the timeout issue, you can configure the SPX partners to be more patient when waiting for a response. The following settings provide an example of how to allow for WAN link delay.

### FILE SERVER SETTINGS

At the server, SPX configurations can be changed through SERVMAN or by typing **LOAD SPXCFG**. These settings are appropriate for a 56Kbps WAN link:

SPX Watchdog Abort Timeout: 1080 ticks (60 seconds)

SPX Ack Wait Timeout: 108 ticks (6 seconds)

SPX Watchdog Verify Timeout: 54 ticks (3 seconds)

## CLIENT SETTINGS

Depending on the client version, the client SPX settings can be made by editing NET.CFG for the VLMs or through the SPX tab in the Control Panel ⇨ Network ⇨ IPX 32-bit Protocol for Novell NetWare Client 32:

SPX Abort Timeout: 1080 ticks (60 seconds)

SPX Listen Timeout: 108 ticks (6 seconds)

SPX Verify Timeout: 54 ticks (3 seconds)

The SPX Watchdog issue can be a bit tricky, however. Some routers perform "SPX Watchdog spoofing" on the WAN link. Spoofing techniques are used when you want a device to answer on behalf of another device by creating a false response (spoof). A router that does SPX Watchdog spoofing will answer on behalf of the SPX partner that is on the other side of a WAN link, as shown in Figure 8.37. The router will not bring up an inactive link just to route SPX Watchdog packets. When the link does become active for a data transfer, the router will stop spoofing and allow the Watchdog packets to go across the WAN link.

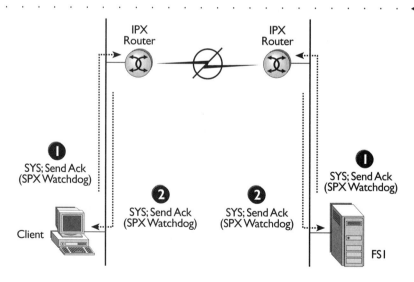

**F I G U R E   8.37**

*The spoofing routers won't bring up the link for SPX Watchdog traffic.*

You can also turn off the SPX Watchdog feature by using the SPXWDOG.NLM patch. Once you load the patch, use the command **set spx watchdogs=OFF**. To enable SPX Watchdog again, type **set spx watchdogs=ON**. Client 32 and IPXODI v3.02 and later also enable you to disable SPX Watchdog at the client.

Next, let's take a look at where you can set the SPX parameters for the VLM client, Client 32, and NetWare server.

## Configuring SPX

This next section provides more examples of how SPX can be set at the clients (VLMs and Client 32) and server. If you are making changes to improve performance or resolve timeout issues, check your SPX communications after you change these settings to verify problem resolution.

### CONFIGURING VLM SPX SETTINGS

The VLM SPX settings are configured in the NET.CFG file under the Protocol SPX heading:

```
Link Driver NE2000

    PORT 360

    INT 5

    FRAME Ethernet_802.2


Protocol SPX

    Minimum SPX Retries = 30 (default 20)

    SPX Abort Timeout = 1080 (default 540)

    SPX Connections Number = 20 (default 15)

    SPX Listen Timeout Number = 108 (default 108)

    SPX Verify Timeout Number = 108 (default 54)


NetWare DOS Requester
```

```
VLM = AUTO.VLM

VLM = RSA.VLM

BIND RECONNECT = ON

AUTO RETRY = 10

FIRST NETWORK DRIVE = G

PREFERRED SERVER = COMPAQ-FS2

SIGNATURE LEVEL = 0

MESSAGE LEVEL = 4

MESSAGE TIMEOUT = 183

PRINT BUFFER SIZE = 256

CACHE BUFFERS = 20

CHECKSUM = 0
```

## CONFIGURING CLIENT 32 SPX SETTINGS

On Client 32, configure SPX by selecting Control Panel ➪ Network ➪ IPX 32-bit Protocol for Novell NetWare Client 32 and clicking on the SPX tab, as shown in Figure 8.38.

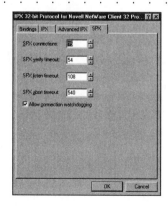

F I G U R E   8.38

*Select the SPX tab to configure SPX parameters.*

## CONFIGURING NETWARE 3.1X AND 4.X SPX SETTINGS

You can use SPXCONFG.NLM to configure SPX options at the NetWare 3.x and 4.x servers, as shown in Figures 8.39 and 8.40.

**FIGURE 8.39**

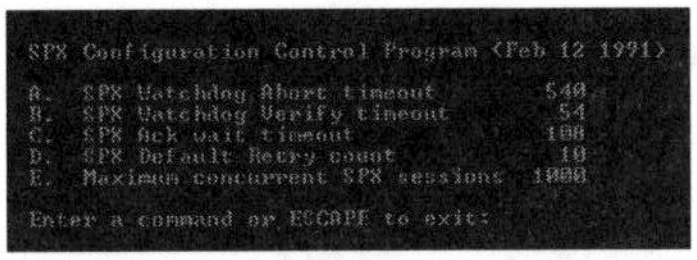

*NetWare 3.12 SPXCONFG.NLM provides five SPX configuration options.*

**FIGURE 8.40**

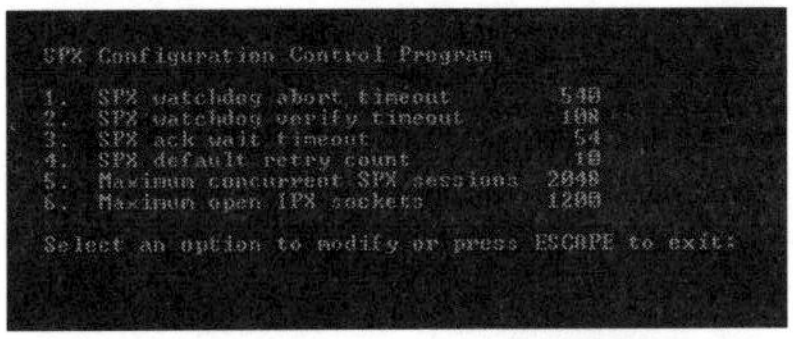

`SPXCONFG.NLM` *provides six configuration options for NetWare 4.1x/IntranetWare 4.x.*

You can also use INETCFG to configure SPX options by selecting Protocols ⇨ IPX ⇨ Expert Configuration Options ⇨ IPX/SPX Parameters, as shown in Figure 8.41.

**FIGURE 8.41**

*The settings available through SPXCONFG are also available in INETCFG.*

**In some INETCFG versions, you can get to the IPX/SPX parameters directly from the IPX window.**

NOTE

## Summary

In this chapter, you've seen more SPX information than you probably ever thought you would—more than you ever wanted, eh? SPX, however, can be one of the stickier areas in NetWare communications. In fact, about 9 out of 10 client sites that I visit have some sort of SPX problem on their network. In the next chapter, we'll take a look at how devices locate, and we'll learn about services using Novell's Service Advertising Protocol (SAP).

**CHAPTER 9**

# NetWare SAP

This chapter provides detailed information on NetWare's Service Advertising Protocol (SAP), with details on the four primary types of SAP packets and their default capabilities/limitations. This chapter also defines SAP filtering and customization options and addresses serverless segments, turning SAP off, changing SAP frequency, and SAP number listings. *Best horizon* (a.k.a. the *best information algorithm*) is also defined in this chapter, in terms of its relevance to SAP communications. Finally, we also define the SAP extension/specific SAP technology that fixes the inherent problems of Novell's Preferred Server/Preferred Tree operation.

## Why SAP?

The Service Advertising Protocol (SAP) is primarily used to look up services on the internetwork and share information about known services. Service information is maintained by all servers and routers in their server information tables.

Software vendors are being encouraged to move away from their reliance on SAP-based information exchange and write Novell Directory Services–aware applications. Since Novell Directory Services (NDS) is a distributed database of network objects and registered services, it seems a natural replacement for SAP service lookups and information exchange. NDS can be used to exchange service information in a unicast manner (directly addressed to other servers) rather than in a broadcast manner like SAP.

Although the NetWare IPX protocol stack often gets "slammed" by TCP/IP advocates, it's really not IPX's fault that NetWare has problems on larger internetworks. IPX just hangs out with some very ugly protocols, such as SAP. SAP information exchanges are broadcasts; they can cause network overload and do not scale well on larger internetworks. With the more recent versions of Novell's router mechanism (IPXRTR), we can customize SAP to perform a bit better on larger networks, but there are still some problems. We'll cover all these problems in this chapter.

We'll cover each of the three types of SAP uses:

▶ Server information table (SIT) lookups

▸ Server information table (SIT) information exchanges

▸ Auto frame type detection (Windows 95)

The server information tables can be read by typing **DISPLAY SERVERS** at the NetWare/IntranetWare console, as shown in Figure 9.1.

F I G U R E   9 . 1

*Type **DISPLAY SERVERS** to view the server information tables.*

The DISPLAY SERVERS command shows more than just file servers; it displays all registered services, such as print servers, fax servers, and directory servers.

Figure 9.2 shows the standard SAP architectural diagram. All SAP requests and replies use the destination/source socket number 0x0452. The SAP process is responsible for the periodic broadcasts used for the information exchanges and service lookups, as discussed earlier. SAP is also responsible for maintaining an aging timer on all entries in the server information table. By default, a NetWare 3.*x* server must hear about a network service at least every three minutes to avoid timing out of the tables. NetWare servers hear about these services through SAP update broadcasts that are sent every 60 seconds by NetWare servers and routers. NetWare/IntranetWare 4.*x* devices timeout entries after four minutes.

F I G U R E   9 . 2

*The SAP process is linked to the server information tables.*

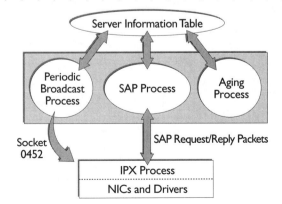

Later in this chapter, we'll examine the SIT and its aging timer in greater detail. First, we'll examine SAP's lookup process.

## The SAP Lookup Process

The SAP lookup process is used by all NetWare clients to locate a file server (if the client is configured for a bindery connection) or a directory server (if the client is configured for an NDS connection). This lookup process is often referred to as the GNS, or *Get Nearest Server*, process.

### THE STARTUP GNS PROCESS

Figure 9.3 is a LANalyzer for Windows summary screen that details the client bootup sequence. As you'll notice, the first packet sent by the NetWare client is a SAP broadcast. The client defines the type of server it is looking for (a directory server—server type 0x0278) inside the SAP packet.

FIGURE 9.3

*The GNS request indicates the type of server (0x0278) that the client is looking for.*

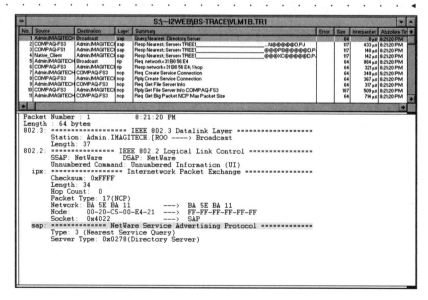

**For more information on the server type field, refer to the section titled "SAP Packet Formats" later in this chapter.**

**X-REF**

As shown in Figure 9.3, the client transmits the broadcast request onto the local network. The SAP request will be answered by all local NetWare/IntranetWare servers that support directory services by default.

If the client uses source and destination network address 0x00-00-00-00 in the IPX header of the SAP packet, the client has just booted up. If, however, the IPX header includes the actual source and destination network address (as shown in Figure 9.3), the client has simply unloaded and reloaded the client software without rebooting. In order to dynamically move around your network without rebooting, your client must use Mobile IPX.

If there is a router on the local network that also supports servers, the router will not reply to the GNS request, even though it maintains a server information table. The router does not reply because it knows that there are local servers, and the GNS should be handled by those servers, as shown in Figure 9.4.

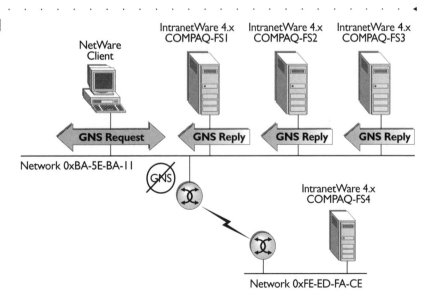

FIGURE 9.4

*The local router will not answer GNS replies if there are servers on the segment.*

In the example shown in Figure 9.4, three servers respond to the client. The router does not respond because there are servers on the client's network.

Figure 9.5 shows the GNS reply packet to the lookup for a directory server.

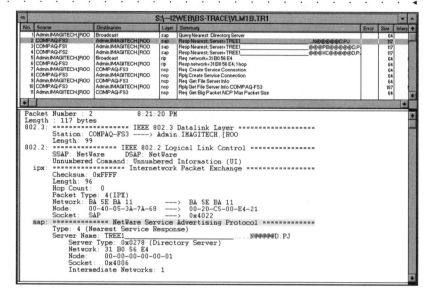

*The reply contains the network node and socket number of the desired service.*

In Figure 9.5, the summary window shows that three servers (COMPAQ-FS1, COMPAQ-FS2, and COMPAQ-FS3) replied to the requesting client's (Admin's) SAP request. The reply contains the internal IPX address, node address, and socket number of the desired server process. NetWare 3.*x* servers that do not support directory services would not answer a directory services SAP request.

Routers do not respond to SAP GNS requests unless no servers are attached locally. Routers know whether there are servers locally attached based on SAP information exchanges (discussed later in this chapter).

**Since all directory servers on the local network must reply by default, this is a quick way to get a list of directory servers attached to a network segment.**

TIP

## GNS LOOKUP ISSUES

There are a few exceptions to this simple request/reply scenario, however. What if there isn't a server on the local segment? What if the server is out of connections?

What if all the servers have GNS reply turned off? Let's take a look at each of these scenarios to understand how SAP lookup works in unusual circumstances.

### GNS on a Serverless Segment

Figure 9.6 shows a network segment that does not have a local server — a *serverless segment*. Since there aren't any servers locally attached, the router answers the GNS request by providing the name, internetwork address, and distance of the server determined to be "closest."

**FIGURE 9.6**

*Routers reply to GNS only if there are no local servers.*

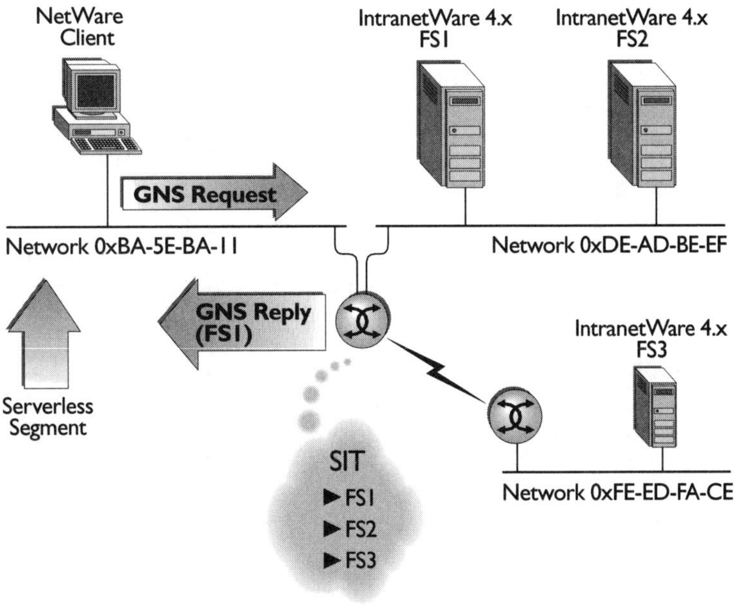

The routers know what servers are available because they keep a server information table (SIT) in memory. In Figure 9.6, the router's SIT should indicate that FS1 and FS2 are the closest servers to network 0xBA-5E-BA-11. Since FS1 and FS2 are equal distances from network 0xBA-5E-BA-11, the router can use either SIT entry for its reply.

### GNS on a Serverless Segment—Tiebreaking

When a router replies to a GNS request and it has two or more servers that are seen as equal distances in ticks from the client, the router manufacturer decides what the tiebreaker will be.

Novell has used the internal IPX address as the tiebreaker. The server with the highest internal IPX address is considered "closest."

Cisco products use the order in which the entry appeared in their tables as the tiebreaker. The oldest entry is considered "closest." Cisco products (v9.21 or later) can also use a "round-robin" process, giving each successive GNS request a different server.

Other manufacturers have used the alphanumerical order of the server names as the tiebreaker. The server listed first alphanumerically is considered "closest."

In Figure 9.6, the router is a Cisco, and FS1 was the first server up. Since FS1 was placed in the SIT first, the router would reply that FS1, not FS2, was the nearest server. Likewise, if FS2 was up first and therefore was placed in the SIT first, the router would reply that FS2, not FS1, was the nearest server.

### Connecting to a Server Even Though GNS Is Off

You can turn off the GNS reply on NetWare/IntranetWare 3.x and 4.x servers. In Figure 9.6, what if you've turned off GNS reply on FS1? Would the router now answer with FS2's address?

No. The router would still respond with FS1's address. The routers have no way of knowing that the GNS reply feature of the server has been disabled—they only look in their local SIT to locate the nearest entry and reply on behalf of the server.

In order to disable FS1, you'd have to have some sort of configuration ability at the router that allows you to select which servers you would not reply to GNS on behalf of.

### GNS Connecting to a Distant Server

Some strange things can happen in the client connection sequence. What if you have a local server (and therefore the router won't answer the GNS request) and someone has turned off GNS replies on that server? Since that server won't answer your GNS requests and the router won't answer your GNS requests, the client gets a bit panicky: After two unanswered GNS requests, the client transmits a Get General Service SAP request packet. The client indicates that it is looking for "any directory server," not necessarily the nearest.

Figure 9.7 illustrates the network design that could cause this problem.

*The Get General Service reply (Get Any Service) can yield unpredictable connections.*

Is the router at fault in this scenario? No. The router is simply replying to the client's request for any service (not the nearest) of a certain type. Using an analyzer, you can easily spot the cause for an unusual default server connection.

### Unable to Connect: Out of Connection Slots

If a server has all of its licensed connections used (for instance, five users logged into a five-user version of NetWare 4.*x*), the server should stop replying to GNS requests. If, however, this server is on the other side of a router and your client performs a GNS request, the router does not know that the server is not replying to GNS requests. The router may respond to GNS on behalf of the server. When the client sends the General Service Connection request packet to the server, the client receives the message "No free connection slots."

To fix this problem, you'll have to look at whether your router allows you to filter GNS replies (as the NetWare/IntranetWare 4.*x* server does) to reply to GNS requests with a specific server.

On the NetWare/IntranetWare server, use INETCFG to select a specific GNS server name to use in GNS replies, as shown in Figure 9.8.

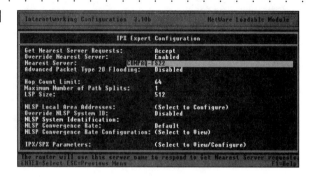

Now let's take a look at the server information tables maintained at the NetWare/IntranetWare server. Remember that all versions of NetWare maintain server information tables.

## The SAP Information Exchange Process

SAP information exchanges ensure that all devices that have a server information table maintain the same service entries. By default, SAP information exchanges occur in the following five instances:

▸ **A service announces itself.** When a file server is brought up, it sends out a SAP broadcast that includes its name, internetwork address, socket number, and distance to the local network in hops.

▸ **A service changes its state.** When you gracefully "down" a NetWare/IntranetWare server, it issues a SAP broadcast announcing that the services it offered are too far away to reach (16 hops). Fifteen hops is the maximum hop distance allowed to access SAP-based services. When a device learns that a service is 16 hops away, it is understood that the device is unreachable.

▸ **Changes occur to a SIT.** When a device that maintains a SIT learns that a device has changed its distance (it's now 16 hops away, for example), the device must propagate that information change immediately.

▸ **A manual SIT update is forced.** When you type **RESET ROUTER** on a NetWare/IntranetWare server, you force the server to broadcast its SIT to other devices on the network.

▸ **Periodic SIT update.** By default, a SAP-enabled device must broadcast its entire SIT onto the network every 60 seconds. Later in this chapter, we'll discuss how to reconfigure this timer.

Let's examine each of these processes in detail.

## A SERVICE ANNOUNCES ITSELF

When a file server comes up, it announces its presence by broadcasting its SIT onto the local network. This information is processed by other servers and routers on the local segment when they add the service entries into their SIT. The other servers and routers will propagate this information immediately.

Figure 9.9 depicts a server's broadcast announcing its presence on the network. We can see that this server supports file services (type 0x0004), remote console services (type 0x0107, decoded as "NetWare 386"), and directory services (type 0x0278).

 **NOTE** The "intermediate networks" field denotes the hop count to the specified service. As mentioned in Chapter 7, services residing on the internal IPX network are one hop away from the external network.

If the server supported other services, such as Btrieve databases, or Pserver, it would include those services in the SAP broadcast.

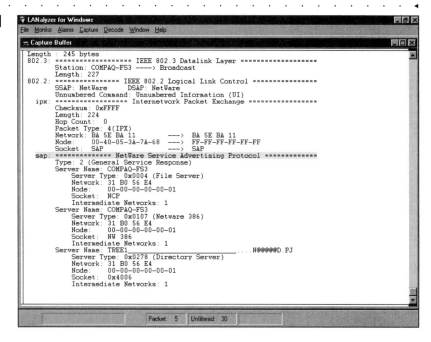

*When the server boots up, it broadcasts its local services only.*

## A SERVICE CHANGES ITS STATE

When a service is brought down gracefully (as opposed to a violent or abend-type downing), it must issue a SAP broadcast announcing that it is too far away to reach (16 hops). Figure 9.10 shows the packet the server must issue when it is brought down.

If you want to generate this type of a packet on your network without bringing down the file server, simply load REMOTE.NLM and RSPX.NLM to enable remote console to the server and then unload the NLMs in reverse order. When you unload RSPX.NLM, the server issues a SAP broadcast that indicates server type 0x0107 is unreachable (16 hops away).

*When a server is brought down, it indicates that its services are unreachable (16 hops away).*

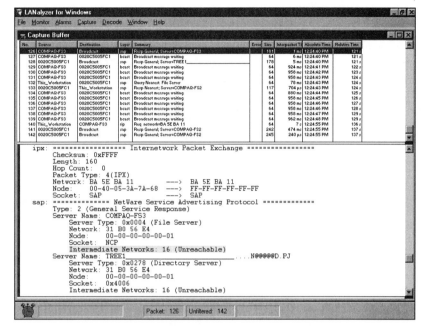

## CHANGES OCCUR TO A SIT

When a device that maintains a SIT hears of a change (such as a device becoming unreachable), that information must be propagated immediately, as shown in Figure 9.11. Once again, keep in mind that if you see the update information spit back onto the network, there's a very good chance that you have multiple frame types bound to IPX on the transmitting device.

## MANUAL SIT UPDATE FORCED

You can manually force the SIT broadcasts to occur by typing **RESET ROUTER** at a NetWare/IntranetWare server or router.

**This is a useful trick to perform if you think your SIT may be corrupt or out-of-date.**

TIP

*When changes occur to the SIT, they must be propagated immediately.*

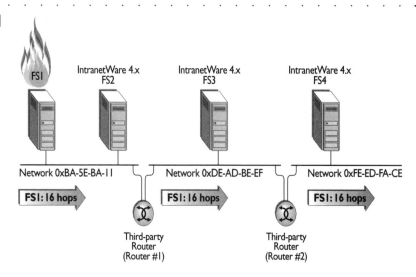

## PERIODIC SIT UPDATE

This is the ugly part of SAP. By default, a SAP-enabled device must broadcast its entire SIT onto the network every 60 seconds. Of course, it must follow the rules of split horizon (covered next in this chapter) and not send information back the way it came in.

This 60-second update process can cause quite a strain on a large NetWare intranetwork. For example, consider a network with an FDDI backbone that supports approximately 700 services on that backbone. These include file services, directory services, remote console services, printing services, fax services, Btrieve services, and the like. Every 60 seconds, the routers attached to that backbone must broadcast this information to the other networks, as shown in Figure 9.12.

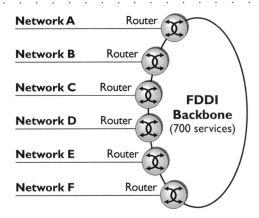

FIGURE 9.12

The SAP broadcasts can become quite extensive on a large network.

To add insult to injury, consider that the default SAP packet size is only 576 bytes—large enough to handle only seven service entries per packet. It will take 100 packets to send out the entire SITs of the routers attached to the backbone. Heaven forbid you have more than one frame type–bound IPX on those routers. If you did have all four Ethernet frame types on one of the routers, it would transmit 400 broadcast packets per minute to the connected network. Ugly!

Fortunately, you can change the default settings for SAP broadcast frequency and packet size. We'll discuss how to configure SAP for better performance later in this chapter.

## UNDERSTANDING SPLIT HORIZON

When a device transmits its SIT information onto a network, it must use a rule called *split horizon*. The split horizon rule dictates that a device cannot broadcast information about a service back onto the link that it learned about the service from. Devices can broadcast information they have learned from the other side of the "horizon" or routing process. For example, in Figure 9.13, router 1 can talk only about FS3 and FS4 onto the segment that contains FS1 and FS2. That is because router 1 learned about FS1 and FS2 from that interface and cannot send that information back the same direction it has learned about.

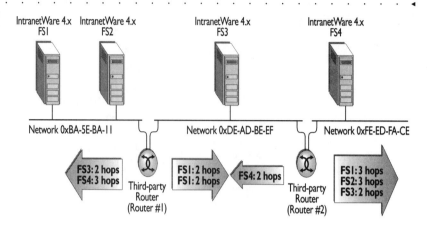

F I G U R E   9.13

*Split horizon must be used when transmitting any SAP packet.*

**Split horizon is used in SAP and RIP and will be covered again later in this chapter and in Chapter 10.**

X-REF

**Until IntranetWare 4.11, all servers came up with the standard SAP process for exchanging the server information table information. IntranetWare 4.11, however, uses NetWare Link Services Protocol (NLSP) by default and can combine service information in link state packets. The NLSP router, however, still answers specific SAP lookup requests.**

NOTE

If you ever see a device talking about a service that it learned about on that interface, it may appear that split horizon is "broken." Chances are, however, the device may support multiple frame types for IPX. For example, if router 1 supported Ethernet_802.2 and Ethernet_802.3 on network interface 0xBA-5E-BA-11, it would send back-to-back SAP packets for all information exchanges, as shown in Figure 9.14.

**The server's internal IPX network is 1 hop away from the external network.**

NOTE

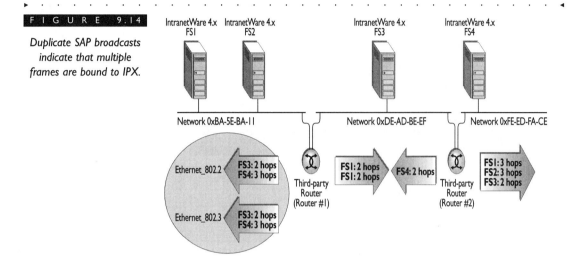

I cannot stress enough that you should use one—just one—frame type for IPX. There is rarely a need to bind IPX to multiple frames. Each frame type you bind IPX to adds traffic.

## Auto Frame Type Detection (Windows 95)

You may have noticed that when you install Novell's Client 32 or the Microsoft Client for NetWare Networks, you don't have to define the frame type you are going to use. That is because of a stinky little "enhancement" called auto frame type detection.

In order to determine which frame type it should use, Novell's Client 32 sends out a series of SAP broadcasts in all possible frame types. For example, on an Ethernet network, the client sends out a SAP GNS broadcast in Ethernet_802.2, Ethernet_802.3, Ethernet_II, and finally Ethernet_SNAP format. The client uses the replies to determine which frame type the client should use.

As you can tell, I personally do not like auto frame type detection. There are a number of instances now where network communications are being fouled up by this process. For example, if a print server boots up and passively listens to network traffic to define its frame type, it could "hear" a client sending out the

Ethernet_SNAP SAP broadcast as just defined. Although the client may eventually settle on the Ethernet_802.2 frame, the print server may decide that Ethernet_SNAP must be the frame to use since it was seen on the network.

A SAP for the nearest file server is used for the automatic frame type detection process used by Client 32, as shown in Figure 9.15.

FIGURE 9.15

*When Client 32 does auto frame typing, it sends out multiple SAP broadcasts.*

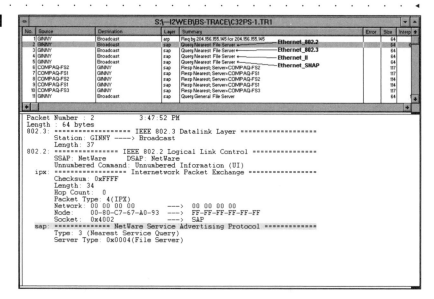

The current version of Client 32 bases its frame type on the most common frame type in use on the network.

**NOTE**

**Microsoft's Client for NetWare Networks and NDS uses RIP to perform its frame typing. The Microsoft auto frame typing process has the same potentially disastrous effect on network communications.**

## Customizing SAP for Better Performance

What is holding SAP back from being a nice internetwork protocol? Well, there are a number of things:

- GNS replies are not always reliable.

- SAP periodic broadcasts occur too often (every 60 seconds).

- Entries can be timed out of the tables too quickly.

- SAP broadcasts can overload routing devices.

- SAP packet sizes are too small (576 bytes).

- Too much unnecessary SAP information is being broadcast around the internetwork.

NetWare/IntranetWare 4.x allows you to configure SAP to perform better on larger networks. Some of the SAP characteristics that can be changed include

- Changing GNS Performance to force the proper attachment

- Setting the SAP periodic broadcast interval to reduce overall broadcast bursts

- Setting the SIT timer mechanism (aging interval) to allow less SAP update traffic

- Throttling SAP broadcasts to reduce the rate of SAP transmissions and avoid overloading network devices

- Increasing SAP packet sizes to make better use of the packet payload space

- Filtering unnecessary SAP traffic to reduce overall SAP traffic

Let's examine how each of these changes can be configured to help optimize network traffic. We'll also take a look at SAP concerns and configurations in a multivendor environment.

## CHANGING GNS PERFORMANCE

Since NetWare 3.*x*, you have been able to disable GNS replies on the server. This has always been a recommendation for products that are installed on runtime NetWare. For example, you would set GNS off on a NetWare for SAA server and a NetWare Connect server. These servers shouldn't answer the GNS request; since they are installed on top of runtime NetWare, they don't offer file and print services.

It is always important to remember to allow one local server to reply to GNS requests. If you set all local servers to GNS Off, the local clients will transmit two GNS requests, time out, and then transmit a Get General Service request, as shown in Figure 9.16.

▸ · · · · · · · · · · · · · · · · · · · · · · · · · · · · ◂

| F I G U R E   9.16 |
| :--- |
| *If no servers are enabled to reply to a GNS request, the client attempts a Get General Service request.* |

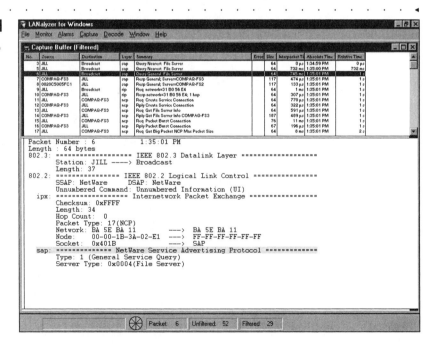

If there is a router on the network, it can reply to the client's request with a server name as well.

There are several ways to change GNS performance. You can type **SET** and select "1. Communications at the server console." Or type **SET REPLY TO GET NEAREST-SERVER = OFF/ON** directly at the server console prompt. You can also load INETCFG and select Protocols ➪ IPX ➪ Expert Configuration Options.

You can also set GNS differently on individual bindings if you have enabled Advanced IPX in INETCFG. Figure 9.17 shows the bindings-specific GNS settings.

▶ · · · · · · · · · · · · · · · · · · · · · · · · · · · · · · · · · · · · · ◀

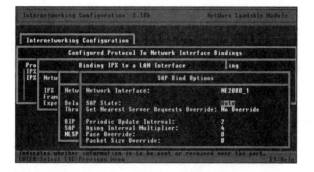

F I G U R E   9.17

*You can configure GNS override for a particular interface.*

In Figure 9.17, the Get Nearest Server Requests Override option enables you to configure GNS performance on a per-bindings basis. For example, perhaps you set the server to GNS = off, but you want it to reply on a single interface. You can set this field to Accept for that interface. There are three options on this field: No Override, Accept, and Ignore. No Override indicates that this interface should use the global GNS settings on the server. Accept indicates that interface is forced to reply to GNS requests. Ignore forces the interface to ignore GNS requests.

## SETTING THE SAP PERIODIC BROADCAST INTERVAL

On a relatively static network, you can change the frequency of the SAP periodic broadcast to reduce the overall SAP broadcast traffic. This setting is configured individually for each binding.

**NOTE**

**Some early manuals and marketing literature referred to this as "SAP on Update Only." This is a misnomer since you cannot disable SAP periodic broadcasts and enable only update packets. The most you can do is decrease the interval to about 500 minutes.**

Figure 9.18 shows the SAP Bind options. The option titled Periodic Update Interval specifies the number of 30-second increments between SAP table broadcasts. The default setting is 2 (60 seconds).

**WARNING**

**If you change this parameter on one server or router on the network, you must change it on all servers or routers that share that common network address. For example, in Figure 9.18, the third-party router and both NetWare servers are set to an update interval of 60 minutes. This ensures that none of them will time out waiting for updates every 60 seconds.**

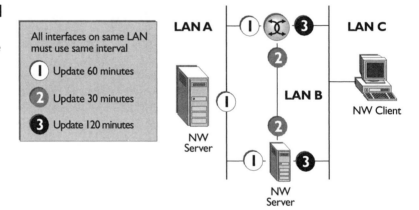

F I G U R E   9.18

*All interfaces on the same network must use the same update interval.*

**TIP**

**If you are going to change the update interval on your NetWare devices, check with your router manufacturer to ensure the router can support interval changes.**

## SETTING THE SIT TIMER MECHANISM (AGING INTERVAL)

You can increase the amount of time entries are left in the SIT without verification. This ensures that entries are not timed out too quickly. This timer is defined as a multiple of the update setting, as shown in Figure 9.19. For example, you can set an update interval at 30 (15 minutes) and then set the aging interval multiplier at 4 to hold down entries in the SIT for one hour.

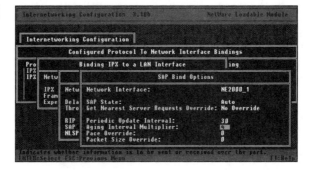

*The aging interval is a multiplier of the periodic update interval.*

## THROTTLING SAP BROADCASTS

SAP packets can be sent at a maximum rate of nine SAP packets per second. If this rate is overloading a routing device's buffer, you can increase the interpacket gap of SAP transmits. As shown in Figure 9.19, you can also set the pace override for SAP communications on a per-bindings basis. An entry of 0 indicates that the default of 9 SAP packets per second is used.

## INCREASING SAP PACKET SIZES

You can override the SAP packet size to enable a SAP broadcast to contain more entries. Each SAP entry requires 64 bytes. You can set this field to the maximum physical packet receive size of the local server to fit more entries in each packet. For example, on an Ethernet network that supports 1,500 bytes in the data portion of the packet (not including the Ethernet header), you can fit up to 22 SAP entries.

It is recommended that you configure all server and router devices that share the common network to the same packet size.

**Make certain all your router manufacturers support the larger SAP packet sizes. Some older routers stop listening after seven entries have been received in each packet.**

## FILTERING UNNECESSARY SAP TRAFFIC

Years ago at Novell, the SAP traffic became so excessive that clients were timing out. One of the local IS folks came up with a nice little NLM called RESTRICT.NLM that enabled us to filter out some of the SAP entries that were broadcast onto the network. Filtering has come a long way since those days. You can now use the FILTCFG.NLM utility to define incoming/outgoing filters based on service name, service type, or interface.

When would you use SAP filtering? Let's take the example of the FDDI backbone with 700 services loaded on it. Perhaps you want to restrict Network A from receiving SAP information about the Engineering Department servers (ENG*), Human Resources servers (HR*), remote print servers (server type 0x0047), and remote console servers (server type 0x0107). You can enable filtering through INETCFG and then use the FILTCFG utility to assign the filters shown in Figure 9.20.

▶ . . . . . . . . . . . . . . . . . . . . . . . . . . . . . . ◀

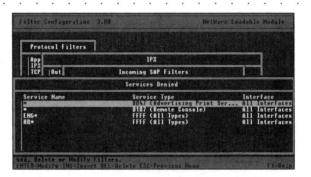

**FIGURE 9.20**

*Use FILTCFG to configure SAP incoming filters.*

**One thing to keep in mind with filtering is that you may set up SAP filtering and then move to NLSP. At the time this book was written, NLSP did not support any service filtering, so you would lose your filters once NLSP was configured.**

. . . . .

**For more information on NLSP, refer to Chapter 11.**

**X-REF**

## CUSTOMIZING SAP IN A MULTIVENDOR ENVIRONMENT

A number of SAP enhancements have been added by third-party vendors, specifically the routing and switching vendors. For example, Hewlett-Packard offers a switch that enables you to throttle the SAP broadcasts. If 100 identical SAP broadcasts are received on a switch port, the switch will forward only one broadcast to all active switch ports.

Keep in mind, however, that the one area of concern on multivendor internetworks is compatibility. Before you set the NetWare server's SAP update interval, make certain the other third-party routers on the network can support that interval.

## Server Information Tables

The server information table (SIT) is a dynamic table maintained by all NetWare/IntranetWare servers and routers. The table maintains information about network services and their internetwork addresses. This table is implicitly linked to the router information table (RIT), which maintains information about network locations on the internetwork.

The following are some sample SIT entries:

| | |
|---|---|
| Name: | ENG-SERV1 |
| Type: | 0x0004 |
| Address: | 0x00-00-00-99:00-00-00-00-00-01:0451 |
| Distance: | 3 hops away |
| Circuit: | NE2000_1 |
| Entry age: | 2 minutes |

| | |
|---|---|
| Name: | HR-SERV1 |
| Type: | 0x0004 |
| Address: | 0x00-00-00-21:00-00-00-00-00-01:0451 |
| Distance: | 2 hops away |

| | |
|---|---|
| Circuit: | NE2000_1 |
| Entry age: | 2 minutes |

| | |
|---|---|
| Name: | HR-SERV1 |
| Type: | 0x0107 |
| Address: | 0x00-00-00-99:00-00-00-00-00-01:8104 |
| Distance: | 2 hops away |
| Circuit: | NE2000_1 |
| Entry age: | 2 minutes |

| | |
|---|---|
| Name: | MFG-SERV1 |
| Type: | 0x0004 |
| Address: | 0x00-00-00-22:00-00-00-00-00-01:0451 |
| Distance: | 0 hops away |
| Interface: | Internal |
| Entry age: | N/A |

## READING SIT ENTRIES

You can see by the sample entries that it is possible to have two services use the same name (HR-SERV1 file service and HR-SERV1 Rconsole service) as long as the type number is different. This can cause quite a bit of confusion when you view the Display Servers screen by entering the DISPLAY SERVERS command. Figure 9.21 shows a screen shot from a lab network that has two servers active— COMPAQ-FS2 and COMPAQ-FS3. You can see two entries for COMPAQ-FS2, and you can see that they are zero hops away (local to this server), but you cannot decipher their server type. This screen can seem almost worthless sometimes.

**F I G U R E   9.21**

*Duplicate listings indicate multiple server types using a single name in the SIT.*

To view a more complete listing of the SIT entries, load IPXCON and select Services from the main menu, as shown in Figure 9.22. IPXCON provides the service name, the circuit, type, the network number, the node, the socket number, the tick and hop count, and the next hop information.

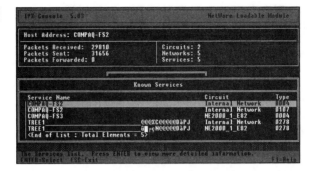

F I G U R E   9.22

IPXCON provides more details on server entries. Highlight an entry and hit Enter to get more information on an entry.

Directory service names are always easy to spot in the Display Servers screen, IPXCON, and packets on the wire because they have underscores following the tree names. In Figures 9.21 and 9.22, you can see the services named TREE1 listed. That is the tree name used in our lab.

### REBUILDING THE SIT

If you believe that your SIT is inaccurate or corrupt, type **RESET ROUTER** at the server console to automatically rebuild the table. The server will transmit a broadcast request for all known services (service type 0xFFFF) and all known networks (0xFF-FF-FF-FF), as shown in Figure 9.23, in the next section.

## GNS Preferred Server Issues

The Preferred Server process has a single major fault. When you issue a preferred server request from your client, you transmit a GNS broadcast onto the network. The servers reply with their internal IPX addresses and their server name/tree name.

Depending on the version of the client that you are running, the client may wait up to seven seconds to hear from the defined preferred server directly before proceeding. If the client does not hear from the preferred server, the client makes a general service connection to the first server that answered. The client then queries the server's SIT for the preferred server. If the server does not know about the preferred server, it responds to the client with a "No such object" response. The client cannot make a connection to the preferred server and receives an "Unknown Preferred Server" response.

The problem is that the client did not make a direct request for a specific server; it made a generic Get Nearest Server request. In order to allow a client to ask for a specific server, a technology called specific SAP/SAP extensions was designed.

## SAP EXTENSIONS/SPECIFIC SAP

Typical SAP queries include Get Nearest Service and Get General Service queries. Specific SAP adds two new queries that can include a specific service name, service type, and/or network number.

 **The term *SAP extensions* refers to the server/router side of the technology; the term *specific SAP* refers to the client side of the technology. A server or router that supports SAP extensions can**
**NOTE** **reply to a client's specific SAP query.**

SAP extensions/specific SAP (hereinafter referred to as *specific SAP*) must be enabled in the client software and at the server. IntranetWare 4.11 is enabled for specific SAP, and the client that went into open beta in May 1997 included specific SAP capabilities.

The specific SAP queries are

▸ Get nearest service matching this definition

▸ Get general service matching this definition

A device can send a specific GNS SAP that includes multiple requests. For example, a client can issue a specific GNS looking for FS1 and FS3, as shown in Figure 9.23.

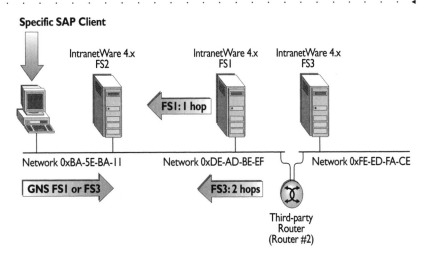

**FIGURE 9.23**

*A specific SAP client can issue a request for multiple preferred servers.*

**Specific SAP Client**

Let's examine what can be defined in a specific SAP packet.

## SPECIFIC SAP DEFINITIONS AND WILDCARDS

You can define a specific service type, service name, or network number in the specific SAP query packets. The following describes valid elements that can be used in defining a specific SAP request.

### Defining a Service Type

Standard Get Nearest Service and Get General Service queries include this field to define the type of service that you are attempting to locate. An entry of 0xFFFF indicates that you are looking for any service.

**X-REF**

> **For a comprehensive list of service types, refer to Appendix E, "SAP Number List."**

### Defining a Service Name

With specific SAP, you can define a specific service name using a case-sensitive null-terminated string with wildcards question mark (?) and asterisk (*). The wildcard character "?" matches exactly one character, whereas the wildcard character "*" matches any string length. For example, SERV* matches any service name starting with the letters SERV. FS?-ENG matches any service name that includes those letters in those exact locations with any character in the "?" position. FS2-ENG would match that search, whereas FS2A-ENG would not.

### Defining a Network Number

You can also define a specific network address or wildcard the address using all 0s in the network address field (0xFF-FF-FF-FF).

## CLIENT CONNECTION USING SPECIFIC SAP TECHNOLOGY

When a client issues a specific SAP query that includes a server name, such as FS1, local servers and routers that support SAP extensions will look up the service name in their SITs and respond if they know of a service with that name. Clients can issue multiple requests in a single packet, as well. For example, the client can issue a specific GNS SAP looking for FS1 or FS2. This is like having a Preferred Server feature that can look up multiple servers in case the preferred server is not available.

Refer to Figure 9.23 for an example of specific SAP.

**NOTE**

**If a server does not support SAP Extensions, it should not answer the specific SAP request.**

**X-REF**

**For more information on specific SAP, refer to the sections titled "Specific SAP Request Packets" and "Specific SAP Reply Packets," in the next section.**

# SAP Packet Formats

Standard SAP packets are 576 bytes or smaller, based on the limitations defined by following the XNS specifications. In this section, we'll look at the standard SAP and specific SAP packet structures.

There are two standard SAP packet formats—request packets and reply packets.

## SAP REQUEST PACKETS

Figure 9.24 shows the standard SAP request packet format.

▸ · · · · · · · · · · · · · · · · · · · · · · · · · · · · ◂

**FIGURE 9.24**

*The standard SAP request packet format*

**IPX Header:**
Destination Socket 0x0452
Source Socket 0x0452

Type/Operation (2 bytes)
Service type (2 bytes)

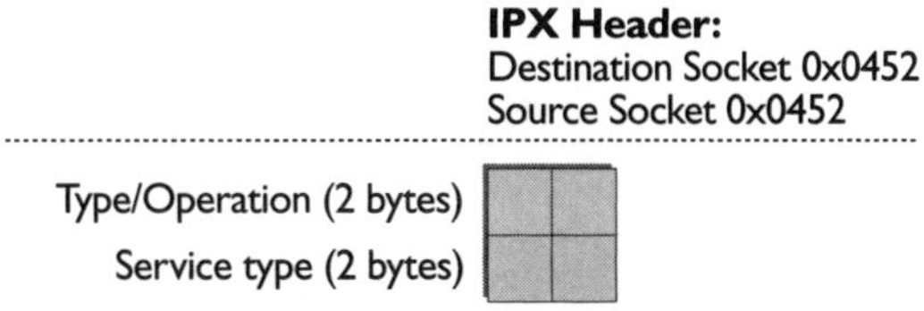

### Type/Operation Field

The type/operation field values on a request packet define whether this is a General Service query (0x0001) or a Nearest Service query (0x0003).

### Service Type Field

The service type field indicates the type of service that the sender is looking for. A value of 0xFFFF indicates that the sender is looking for any service type.

**X-REF**

**For a comprehensive listing of SAP type numbers, refer to Appendix E, "SAP Number List."**

Figure 9.25 is a sample SAP request packet from a server that has just booted up and is looking for all services to build its server information tables. This is a General Service query packet.

FIGURE 9.25

Servers and routers build
their SITs by sending
General Service query
broadcasts with a server
type 0xFFFF.

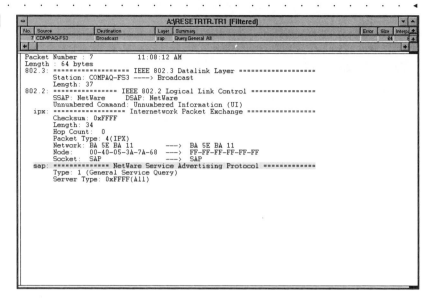

Figure 9.26 is a sample Get Nearest Service SAP request packet from a Client 32 station that is looking for the nearest directory server.

FIGURE 9.26

The client, Jessica, sends a
Nearest Service query
looking for a directory
server.

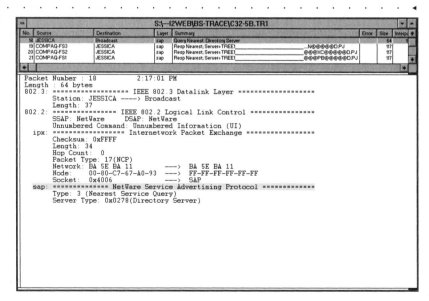

## SAP REPLY PACKETS

SAP replies are either in direct response to SAP requests or unsolicited (in the case of the periodic SAP update, which is a SAP reply packet).

Figure 9.27 shows the standard SAP reply packet format.

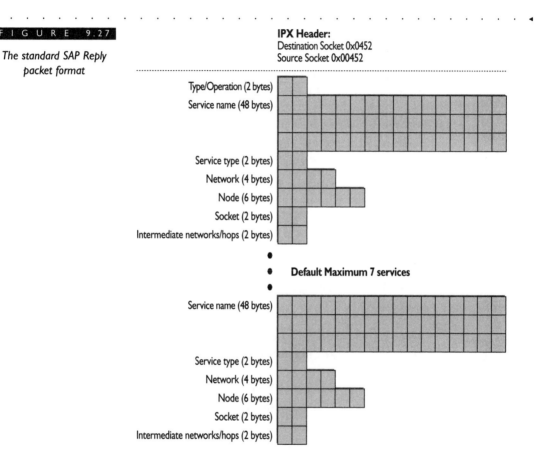

**FIGURE 9.27**

*The standard SAP Reply packet format*

### Type/Operation Field

The type/operation field values on a request packet define whether this is a General Service reply (0x0002) or a Nearest Service reply (0x0004).

### Service Name Field

This field identifies the name of the service. If the name is shorter than 48 bytes (which we hope it is), the name is padded with 0s following it.

### Service Type Field

The service type field indicates the type of service that the sender is reporting about. The value 0xFFFF is invalid in a SAP response packet.

**For a comprehensive listing of SAP type numbers, refer to Appendix E, "SAP Number List."**

X-REF

### Network Field

This is the network number of the service defined in this section of the SAP reply.

### Node Field

This is the node address of the service defined in this section of the SAP reply. For NetWare 3.x and NetWare/IntranetWare 4.x NCP-based services, the node address will be 0x00-00-00-00-00-01.

### Socket Field

This indicates the static or dynamic socket number assigned to the service.

**Refer to Appendix F, "Socket Number List," for a comprehensive list of assigned socket numbers.**

X-REF

### Intermediate Networks/Hops Field

This field indicates the distance from the service in hops. If the response packet indicates the service is 16 hops away, it is considered unreachable.

Figure 9.28 is a sample SAP periodic broadcast packet.

FIGURE 9.28

SAP periodic broadcasts are
addressed to the broadcast
address 0xFF-FF-FF-FF-FF-FF.

```
                                    A:\RESETRTR.TR1 [Filtered]
No. Source              Destination         Layer  Summary                              Error  Size  Interp.
 30 COMPAQ-FS3          Broadcast           sap    Resp General;Server=COMPAQ-FS3             245

      Length: 227
802.2: =============== IEEE 802.2 Logical Link Control ===============
       SSAP: NetWare      DSAP: NetWare
       Unnumbered Command: Unnumbered Information (UI)
  ipx: ================ Internetwork Packet Exchange =================
       Checksum: 0xFFFF
       Length: 224
       Hop Count:  0
       Packet Type: 4(IPX)
       Network: BA 5E BA 11      --->  BA 5E BA 11
       Node:    00-40-05-3A-7A-68 --->  FF-FF-FF-FF-FF-FF
       Socket:  SAP              --->  SAP
  sap: ============= NetWare Service Advertising Protocol =============
       Type: 2 (General Service Response)
       Server Name: COMPAQ-FS3
           Server Type: 0x0004 (File Server)
           Network: 31 B0 56 E4
           Node:    00-00-00-00-00-01
           Socket:  NCP
           Intermediate Networks: 1
       Server Name: COMPAQ-FS3
           Server Type: 0x0107 (Netware 386)
           Network: 31 B0 56 E4
           Node:    00-00-00-00-00-01
           Socket:  NW 386
           Intermediate Networks: 1
       Server Name: TREE1_____....N@@@@@D.PJ
           Server Type: 0x0278 (Directory Server)
           Network: 31 B0 56 E4
           Node:    00-00-00-00-00-01
           Socket:  0x4006
           Intermediate Networks: 1
```

If a server is going down gracefully, it will transmit the SAP general response and indicate that all the services are unreachable (16 hops away) as shown in Figure 9.29.

FIGURE 9.29

When a server or router is
brought down, it does a
"last dying gasp" SAP
General Service response
indicating that all services
are unreachable.

```
                                    A:\RESETRTR.TR1 [Filtered]
No Source               Destination         Layer  Summary                              Error  Size  Interp.
 3 COMPAQ-FS3           Broadcast           sap    Resp General;Server=COMPAQ-FS2             245

      Length: 227
802.2: =============== IEEE 802.2 Logical Link Control ===============
       SSAP: NetWare      DSAP: NetWare
       Unnumbered Command: Unnumbered Information (UI)
  ipx: ================ Internetwork Packet Exchange =================
       Checksum: 0xFFFF
       Length: 224
       Hop Count:  0
       Packet Type: 4(IPX)
       Network: BA 5E BA 11      --->  BA 5E BA 11
       Node:    00-40-05-3A-7A-68 --->  FF-FF-FF-FF-FF-FF
       Socket:  SAP              --->  SAP
  sap: ============= NetWare Service Advertising Protocol =============
       Type: 2 (General Service Response)
       Server Name: COMPAQ-FS2
           Server Type: 0x0107 (Netware 386)
           Network: 00 00 00 33
           Node:    00-00-00-00-00-01
           Socket:  NW 386
           Intermediate Networks: 16 (Unreachable)
       Server Name: COMPAQ-FS2
           Server Type: 0x0004 (File Server)
           Network: 00 00 00 33
           Node:    00-00-00-00-00-01
           Socket:  NCP
           Intermediate Networks: 16 (Unreachable)
       Server Name: TREE1_____@@@XC@@@@@D.PJ
           Server Type: 0x0278 (Directory Server)
           Network: 00 00 00 33
           Node:    00-00-00-00-00-01
           Socket:  0x4006
           Intermediate Networks: 16 (Unreachable)
```

Figure 9.30 is a SAP-specific reply to the packet shown in Figure 9.25. Directory service replies include the tree name that the local server is in as well as the local server's internal IPX address. File service replies include the server name and the server's internal IPX address.

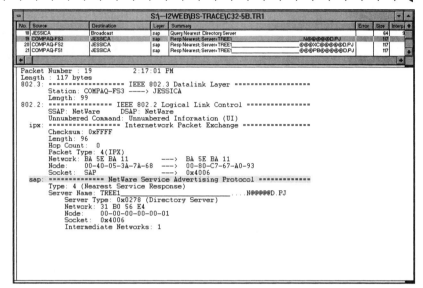

F I G U R E    9.30

*The Nearest Service response packet includes the name of the directory services tree that the replying server is in.*

## SPECIFIC SAP REQUEST PACKETS

Specific SAP request packets contain extra fields that are used to define the specific type of service being sought, as well as the service name and possibly the service address.

Figure 9.31 shows the specific SAP query packet format. You'll notice that a specific SAP query can have multiple entries, unlike the standard SAP query packet.

### Service Type Field

This field denotes whether the packet is a Get General Specific Service (0x000C or 12 decimal) or a Get Nearest Specific Service (0x000E or 14 decimal) request.

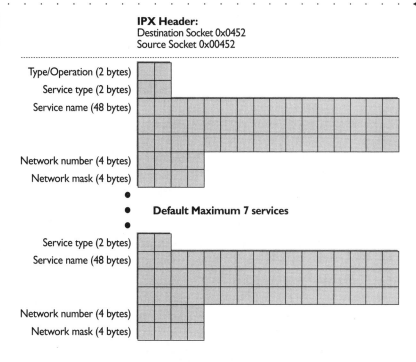

*Specific SAP packets enable you to look up a service based on its type, name, or network number.*

**IPX Header:**
Destination Socket 0x0452
Source Socket 0x00452

Type/Operation (2 bytes)
Service type (2 bytes)
Service name (48 bytes)

Network number (4 bytes)
Network mask (4 bytes)

**Default Maximum 7 services**

Service type (2 bytes)
Service name (48 bytes)

Network number (4 bytes)
Network mask (4 bytes)

### Service Name Field

This field indicates the service that the sender is looking for. This field supports wildcards "?" and "*"; the "*" is used to match any string length, whereas the "?" is used to match a single character. To look up a service without regard to its name, the value "*" should be placed in this field. Although this field can support all 0s or all Fs, no service should match those names and therefore no answer would be received.

### Network Number and Network Mask Field

These two fields work together to define a specific network address. In IPX network addressing, larger IPX-based networks can have routing areas defined (as referred to in the NLSP specification and in Chapter 11. To enable the definition of routing areas, NetWare IPX addresses can be defined by a network number and a mask. For example, network number 01234500 with a mask of FFFFFF00 is identifying an area labeled 012345. IPX networks within that area should use IPX addresses that start with those 3 bytes. As identified by the mask, the first 3 bytes indicate the area, whereas the remaining byte identifies an individual network within that routing area.

You can wildcard the network number by placing the value 0x00-00-00-00 in both the network number and the mask fields or placing the value −1 (0xFF-FF-FF-FF) in both the network number and the mask fields.

## SPECIFIC SAP REPLY PACKETS

The specific SAP reply packets are sent only in response to specific SAP request packets. They are not used for the periodic update process.

Figure 9.32 shows the standard SAP packet format.

### Type/Operation Field

The type/operation field values on a request packet define whether this is a Specific General Service reply (0x000D or 13 decimal) or a Specific Nearest Service reply (0x000F or 15 decimal).

Specific General Service replies will return as many entries as match the request and may consist of multipacket responses. Specific Nearest Service replies will return a single reply for each request in the query.

Both replies use the same packet format as the standard SAP response packets.

### Service Name Field

This field identifies the name of the service. If the name is shorter than 48 bytes (which we hope it is), the name is padded with 0s following it.

### Service Type Field

The service type field indicates the type of service that the sender is reporting about. The value 0xFFFF is invalid in a SAP response packet. For a comprehensive listing of SAP type numbers, refer to Appendix E, "SAP Number List."

### Network Field

This is the network number of the service defined in this section of the SAP reply.

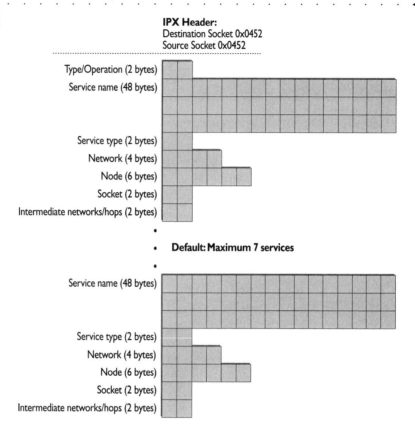

FIGURE 9.32

*The specific SAP reply packet uses the same format as the general SAP reply packet.*

### Node Field

This is the node address of the service defined in this section of the SAP reply. For NetWare 3.x and NetWare/IntranetWare 4.x NCP-based services, the node address will be 0x00-00-00-00-00-01.

### Socket Field

This indicates the static or dynamic socket number assigned to the service.

**Refer to Appendix F, "Socket Number List," for a comprehensive list of assigned socket numbers.**

X-REF

### Intermediate Networks/Hops Field

This field indicates the distance from the service in hops. If the response packet indicates that the service is 16 hops away, it is considered unreachable.

## Summary

As software developers build new products, they are moving away from the SAP technology and toward NDS. The beauty of NDS-based technology is that the information is exchanged in a unicast, not broadcast, manner, thereby reducing the overall network traffic and processing requirements.

NDS traffic is discussed in Chapter 13.

NLSP can reduce the amount of SAP traffic overhead by incorporating service information in its link state packets, as discussed in Chapter 11.

# CHAPTER 10

# NetWare RIP

This chapter focuses on NetWare's Routing Information Protocol (RIP), including the client's lookup procedure, router table information exchange, and auto-detection of frame types for the Microsoft Client for NetWare Networks with NetWare Directory Services support (MS CFNN/NDS). This chapter also covers RIP advanced features, such as turning RIP off, RIP filtering, and RIP packet enhancements (size/content changes). This chapter defines the steps performed by various client versions when a route to a service is no longer available and covers various third-party RIP issues including parallel routing/redundant routing. Finally, this chapter includes the rules of split horizon as it affects RIP communications.

## Why RIP?

NetWare RIP is the default routing mechanism for all versions of NetWare released before IntranetWare 4.11. The default routing mechanism for IntranetWare 4.11 is NetWare Link Services Protocol (NLSP) with RIP compatibility. RIP is typically used after SAP to locate a network that you have just learned about. RIP is also used to exchange network information among servers and routers. Microsoft also selected the RIP protocol as a method for determining the frame type the MS Client for NetWare Networks/NDS would use. Finally, RIP is a routing mechanism that is used to get a packet to the next hop along its path or directly to a destination if the destination is local to the router.

 **NOTE** **The TCP/IP protocol stack also defines a distance-vector routing protocol called RIP. The TCP/IP RIP protocol, although similar to NetWare's RIP, is a different protocol and is not used to route IPX-based communications.**

RIP is a *distance vector–based routing* protocol. Distance-vector protocols maintain a routing information table (RIT) based on information received from other routers. Later in this chapter we'll compare distance-vector routing protocols (like NetWare RIP) to link state routing protocols (like NLSP).

In this chapter, we'll cover the four types of RIP uses:

▶ Routing information table (RIT) lookups

▸ Routing information table (RIT) information exchanges

▸ Auto frame detection (Microsoft's NetWare clients)

▸ Routing information to the appropriate direction

The routing information tables can be read by typing **DISPLAY NETWORKS** at the NetWare/IntranetWare console, as shown in Figure 10.1.

*Type **DISPLAY NETWORKS** to view the routing information tables.*

Internal and external networks are listed when you type **DISPLAY NETWORKS** at the console. The distance to the network is also defined in hops/ticks. For example, Figure 10.1 shows that network 33 is zero hops and one tick away from COMPAQ-FS2. This is the internal IPX network of COMPAQ-FS2. The two other entries that list a zero-hop/one-tick count are the locally attached network.

**Typically, when you see multiple entries with a zero hop count on a NetWare/IntranetWare server or router, the first entry with a zero hop count is the internal IPX network.**

NOTE

Figure 10.2 illustrates the standard RIP architecture. As you can see, the RIP architecture is similar to the SAP architecture, but it carries network information instead of service information. The RIP process is also responsible for routing incoming packets in the appropriate direction.

The RIP process is responsible for the periodic broadcasts used for the information exchanges and network lookups, as discussed earlier. RIP is also responsible for maintaining an aging timer on all entries in the routing information table. By default, a NetWare 3.*x* or NetWare 2.*x* server must hear about a network at least every three minutes to avoid timing out the tables. NetWare/IntranetWare 4.*x* devices time entries out after four minutes. All RIP requests are addressed to and from the RIP socket number 0x0453.

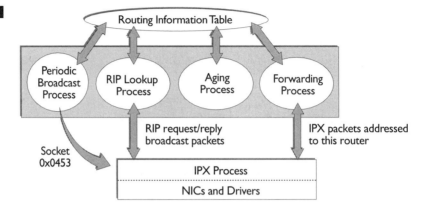

F I G U R E   10.2

*The RIP architecture is
similar to the SAP
architecture.*

Later in this chapter we'll examine the RIT and its aging timer in greater detail. First, we'll examine RIP's lookup process.

## The RIT Lookup Process

The RIT lookup process is used by all NetWare clients to locate a network. This lookup process often occurs immediately following a SAP lookup or when a communication has failed.

Figure 10.3 is a LANalyzer for Windows summary screen that details the client bootup sequence. As you'll notice, the first packet sent by the NetWare client is a SAP broadcast to locate a directory server. The SAP reply packets contain the internal IPX address of the servers that offer directory services. The client then transmits a RIP broadcast to locate the internal IPX address it just heard about. The RIP reply comes from the device that contains the internal IPX address in its RIT.

FIGURE 10.3

*The GNS request is followed by a RIT lookup request for the internal IPX address of the directory server.*

```
                        S:\—I2WEB\BS-TRACE\VLM1B.TR1
No. Source              Destination       Layer  Summary                                                      Error  Size  Interpr
  1 Admin.IMAGITECH.[ROO Broadcast         sap    Query Nearest Directory Server                                      64
  2 COMPAQ-FS3           Admin.IMAGITECH.[ROO sap  Resp Nearest: Server=TREE1                      N@@@@@@D.PJ          117
  3 COMPAQ-FS1           Admin.IMAGITECH.[ROO sap  Resp Nearest: Server=TREE1                      @@@PB@@@@@@D.PJ      117
  4 COMPAQ-FS2           Admin.IMAGITECH.[ROO sap  Resp Nearest: Server=TREE1                      @@@XC@@@@@@D.PJ      117
  5 Admin.IMAGITECH.[ROO Broadcast         rip    Req network=31 B0 56 E4                                             64
  6 COMPAQ-FS3           Admin.IMAGITECH.[ROO rip  Resp network=31 B0 56 E4; 1 hop                                     64
  7 Admin.IMAGITECH.[ROO COMPAQ-FS3        nop    Req Create Service Connection                                       64

Packet Number : 5                8:21:20 PM
Length : 64 bytes
802.3: ================== IEEE 802.3 Datalink Layer ==================
       Station: Admin.IMAGITECH.[ROO ----> Broadcast
       Length: 43
802.2: ================ IEEE 802.2 Logical Link Control ================
       SSAP: NetWare      DSAP: NetWare
       Unnumbered Command: Unnumbered Information (UI)
  ipx: ================ Internetwork Packet Exchange ==================
       Checksum: 0xFFFF
       Length: 40
       Hop Count:  0
       Packet Type: 1(RIP)
       Network: BA 5E BA 11    ---> 00 00 00 00
       Node:   00-20-C5-00-E4-21  ---> FF-FF-FF-FF-FF-FF
       Socket:  RIP            ---> RIP
  rip: =============== NetWare Routing Information Protocol =============
       Operation: 1 (Request)
       Network: 31 B0 56 E4
       Hops:    65535
       Ticks:   65535 (65482 millisecs)
```

As shown in Figure 10.3, the client transmits the RIP broadcast onto the local network after it receives an answer to its SAP request. The RIP request can be answered by either NetWare servers or RIP routers on the local network. Unlike with SAP, the client should typically receive only one reply to its RIP request. If there are multiple paths from the local network to the service, each of the local routers will have already exchanged their tables to determine which one is the closest, and only the router with the best route should reply to such requests.

**NOTE**  **In the RIP request, the hops and ticks fields are padded with 0xFFFF (65535 decimal) because they have no use in a request packet.**

If the client is trying to locate the internal IPX network of a local server, routers on the local network will not reply to the RIP lookup packet, as shown in Figure 10.4.

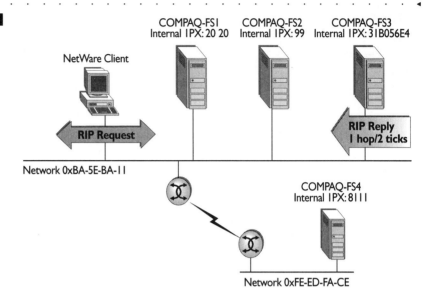

*The RIP request is answered directly by the local server.*

In the example shown in Figure 10.4, the local router does not reply to the RIP lookup for network 99. The router is not the best way to get to network 99.

Remember that NetWare servers have an internal routing process that forwards packets from the external IPX network to the internal IPX network of NetWare 3.*x* and NetWare/IntranetWare 4.*x* servers, as shown in Figure 10.5. Although NetWare 2.*x* servers do not have an internal IPX network, they do support the routing process to forward packets between external IPX networks.

If the client uses the source or destination network address 0x00-00-00-00 in the IPX header of the RIP packet, as shown in previous Figure 10.3, the client has just booted up. Even though the client may have sent a SAP packet just one moment ago and it should know its network address based on the SAP response, it can use 0x00-00-00-00 to indicate "this network only." If, however, the RIP IPX header includes the actual source and destination network addresses, the client may have simply unloaded and reloaded the client software without rebooting. In order to dynamically move around your network without rebooting, your client must use Mobile IPX.

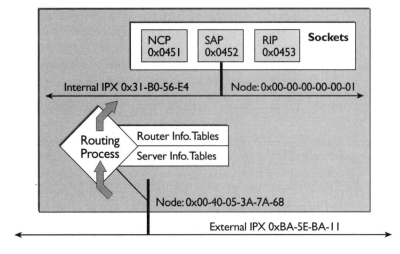

**FIGURE 10.5**

*The server's internal routing process forwards packets from the external IPX network to the internal IPX network.*

**X-REF**

In Figure 10.6, the summary window shows that the server COMPAQ-FS3 has responded to the RIP query. In the decoded window, we can see that this reply actually came from the server's routing process (hence the IPX hop count of 0, indicating that this packet has not crossed a router or routing process).

**FIGURE 10.6**

*The RIP reply is sent from the RIP socket (0x453).*

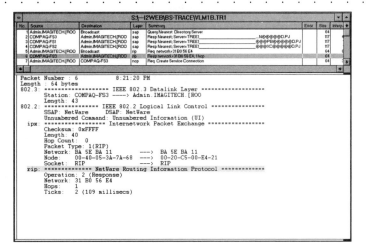

Now let's take a look at the routing information tables maintained at the NetWare/IntranetWare server or RIP routing device. Remember that all versions of NetWare maintain routing information tables.

## The RIP Information Exchange Process

RIP information exchanges ensure that all devices that have a RIT maintain the same network entries. By default, RIP information exchanges occur in the following five instances:

1 • A new network is announced. When a NetWare file server is brought up, it sends out a RIP broadcast that includes its internal IPX address (for NetWare/IntranetWare 3.*x*/4.*x* servers) and any external networks to which it can route packets. This RIP broadcast includes the network address and distance to the local network in hops and ticks.

2 • A route state changes. When you gracefully "down" a NetWare/IntranetWare server, it issues a RIP broadcast announcing that the networks it offered are too far away to reach (16 hops). (NetWare clients can only access services that are within 15 hops distance.)

3 • Changes occur to the RIT. When a device that maintains a RIT learns that a network route has changed its distance because of a rerouting somewhere along the path (it's now six hops away, for example), the device must propagate that information change immediately.

4 • Manual RIT update forced. When you type **RESET ROUTER** on a NetWare/IntranetWare server, you force the server to broadcast its RIT to other devices on the network.

5 • Periodic RIT update. By default, a RIP-enabled device must broadcast its entire RIT onto the network every 60 seconds for every frame type that IPX is bound to. Later in this chapter, we'll discuss how to reconfigure this timer.

When a device transmits its RIT information onto a network, it must use a set of rules called *split horizon*. The split horizon rules for RIP are

**1** • A device cannot broadcast information about a network back onto the link that it learned about the network (or route) from. Devices can broadcast only information that they have learned from the other side of the "horizon" or routing process. For example, in Figure 10.7, Router 1 can only talk about networks 0xDE-AD-BE-EF, 0x00-00-00-99, 0xFE-ED-FA-CE, and 0x00-00-00-AA onto network 0xBA-5E-BA-11. Router 1 cannot talk about networks 0x00-00-00-BB or 0x00-00-00-CC on that network because Router 1 learned about those networks through that interface.

**2** • The device cannot broadcast information about a network over that network. As shown in Figure 10.8, each router cannot broadcast information about networks directly attached to them over those same networks. If this rule is broken, a local client may think that the best way to locate a device on a local network is to send the packet to the local router.

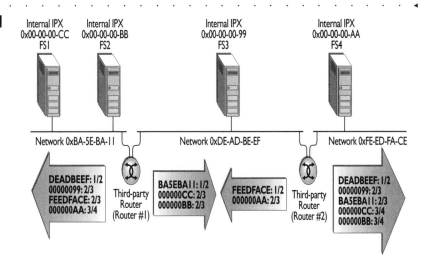

**FIGURE 10.7**

*Based on the rules of split horizon, a router cannot broadcast information back the same way it was received.*

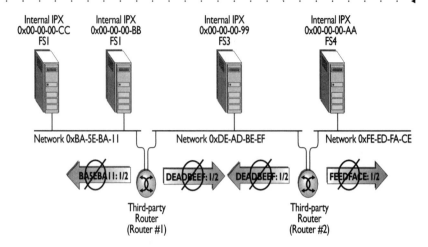

*Routers cannot broadcast RIP information about a network over that same network.*

If you ever see a device talking about a network that it learned about on that interface, chances are the device supports multiple frame types for IPX. For example, if Router 1 supports Ethernet_802.2 and Ethernet_802.3 on network interface 0xBA-5E-BA-11, it would send back-to-back SAP packets for all information exchanges, as shown in Figure 10.9.

I cannot stress enough that you should use one — just one — frame type for IPX. There is rarely a need to bind IPX to multiple frames. Each frame type you bind IPX to adds traffic.

Let's examine each of these RIP information exchange processes in detail.

## A NEW NETWORK IS ANNOUNCED

When a file server comes up, it announces its presence by broadcasting its RIT onto the local network. Of course, it must use the rules of split horizon. This information is processed by other servers and routers on the local segment when they add the network entries into their RIT. The other servers and routers will propagate this RIP information immediately.

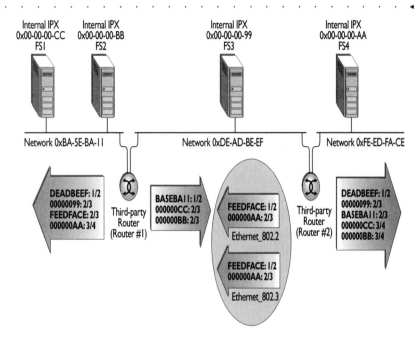

FIGURE 10.9

*Duplicate RIP broadcasts
indicate that multiple
frames are bound to IPX.*

Figure 10.10 depicts a server's broadcast announcing its presence on the network. We can see that this server contains entries for networks 0x31-B0-56-E4 and 0xDE-AD-BE-EF. We know the server also knows about the network it is broadcasting onto (network 0xBA-5E-BA-11 as shown in the IPX header), but due to the rules of split horizon, it cannot talk about this network onto the same network.

The hops and ticks fields indicate how far it is to the specified device. Upon receipt of this packet, a router or server will place the entries in its RIT, increment the hops and ticks value by one, and transmit a new RIP broadcast onto any attached networks. This is how the routing information gets propagated throughout the entire network.

There is no way to distinguish between internal IPX network addresses and external network address in the RIP broadcast packets.

*When the server boots up, it broadcasts its RIT using the split horizon rules.*

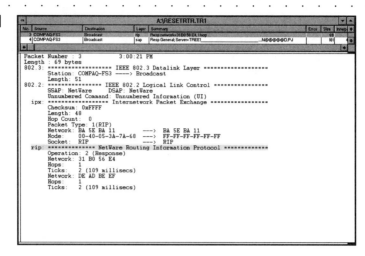

## A NETWORK STATE CHANGES

If a reconfiguration of a network or a loss of a router causes a network state to change, this information is propagated immediately onto the network. For example, if a server that supports internal IPX address 0xAA-AA-AA-AA is brought down gracefully (as opposed to a violent or abend-type downing), it must issue a RIP broadcast announcing that its networks are too far away to reach (16 hops).

Figure 10.11 shows the packet a server named COMPAQ-FS1 issues when it is brought down.

In Figure 10.11, we can assume that this server was not attached to multiple networks, since it only announced that one network was unavailable. We can also assume that the server was talking about its internal IPX network.

## CHANGES OCCUR TO THE RIT

When a device that maintains a RIT hears of a change (such as a network becoming unreachable), that information must be propagated immediately, as shown in Figure 10.12. Once again, keep in mind that if you see the update information spit back onto the network, there's a very good chance that you have multiple frame types bound to IPX on the transmitting device.

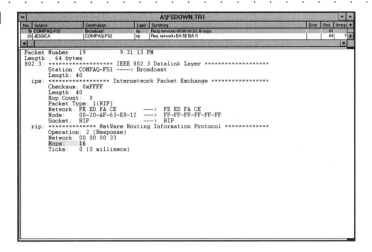

FIGURE 10.11

*When a server is brought down, it indicates that its known networks are unreachable (16 hops away).*

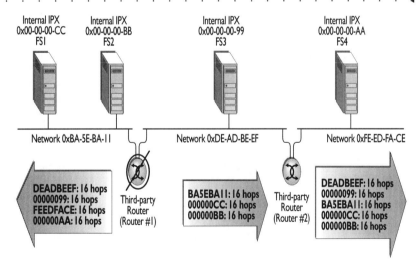

FIGURE 10.12

*When changes occur to the RIT, they must be propagated immediately.*

## MANUAL RIT UPDATE FORCED

You can manually force the RIT broadcasts to occur by typing **RESET ROUTER** at a NetWare/IntranetWare server or router.

**This is a useful trick to perform if you think your RIT may be corrupt or out-of-date.**

TIP

## PERIODIC RIT UPDATE

The periodic update process for routing information is the same as the periodic update process for server information. By default, a RIP-enabled device must broadcast its entire RIT onto the network every 60 seconds. Of course, it must follow the rules of split horizon (covered earlier in this chapter) and not send information back the way it came in or talk about a network over that network.

Fortunately, you can get information about up to 50 networks in a single RIP broadcast (based on the default maximum packet size of 576 bytes). Unfortunately, these packets are broadcast packets and must be buffered and examined by all stations on the network. Every 60 seconds, the routers attached to that backbone must broadcast this information onto the other networks, as shown in Figure 10.13.

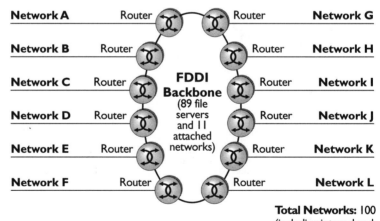

FIGURE 10.13

*Each RIP broadcast packet can contain up to 50 networks by default.*

Because each RIP packet contains 50 networks by default, the periodic update process transmits only two packets per minute onto the local network. Of course you would see more RIP broadcasts if you had more than one frame type–bound IPX on those routers. If you did have all four Ethernet frame types on one of the routers, the router would transmit eight broadcast packets per minute to the connected network.

You can change the default settings for RIP broadcast frequency and packet size. We'll discuss how to configure RIP for better performance later in this chapter.

## AUTO-DETECTION OF FRAME TYPES (MS CFNN/NDS)

Microsoft's MS CFNN/NDS uses RIP packets to determine which frame type to use when the client is configured for auto frame type detection.

FIGURE 10.14

*The Microsoft client determines the most popular frame type by generating several RIP packets the minute it boots up.*

```
                              S:\--12WEB\DS-TRACE\CFNN-1A.TR1
No. Source           Destination      Layer  Summary                              Error  Size Relative
 29 SCOTTY           Broadcast        rip    Req network=FF FF FF FF                     64
 30 COMPAQ-FS1       SCOTTY           rip    Resp network=BA 5E BA 11; 1 hop             90
 31 SCOTTY           Broadcast        rip    Req network=FF FF FF FF                     64
 32 COMPAQ-FS1       SCOTTY           rip    Resp network=00 00 00 22; 1 hop             69
 33 COMPAQ-FS3       SCOTTY           rip    Resp network=00 00 00 33; 2 hops            77
 34 SCOTTY           Broadcast        rip    Req network=FF FF FF FF                     64
 35 SCOTTY           Broadcast        rip    Req network=FF FF FF FF                     64
 36 SCOTTY           Broadcast        rip    Req network=FF FF FF FF                     64
 37 SCOTTY           Broadcast        rip    Req network=FF FF FF FF                     64

Packet Number : 29                10:39:08 PM
Length : 64 bytes
802.3: ==================== IEEE 802.3 Datalink Layer ==================
       Station: SCOTTY ----> Broadcast
       Length: 40
  ipx: ================== Internetwork Packet Exchange ================
       Checksum: 0xFFFF
       Length: 40
       Hop Count: 0
       Packet Type: 1(RIP)
       Network: 00 00 00 00      ---> 00 00 00 00
       Node:    00-20-78-10-2E-C3 ---> FF-FF-FF-FF-FF-FF
       Socket:  0x4000           ---> RIP
  rip: ============= NetWare Routing Information Protocol =============
       Operation: 1 (Request)
       Network: FF FF FF FF
       Hops:    4608
       Ticks:   240 (13179 millisecs)
```

As shown in Figure 10.14, the Microsoft client generates several RIP packets when it boots up. The client is not looking for a network, however, it is trying to determine the most popular frame type on the network. The MS CFNN/NDS client sends out RIP packets using each of the available frame types. On an Ethernet network, for example, the MS CFNN/NDS client transmits a RIP broadcast using Ethernet_802.3, another using Ethernet_802.2, another using Ethernet_II, and (a bit redundant here) another using Ethernet_802.2.

**The Microsoft CFNN/NDS does not support Ethernet_SNAP frame typing.**

NOTE

# The RIP Routing Process

As mentioned earlier, RIP is a distance vector routing protocol. Distance vector routing protocols make forwarding decisions based on their routing tables. The routing tables are built based on information learned from other routers. In order to see how an intervening RIP router handles the forwarding process, we can follow a packet that is transmitted from a client on one network to a server on another network. The following five steps illustrate this process:

1 • From Client to router

2 • MAC header verification

3 • Hop count verification

4 • Router table lookup

5 • From router to server

## FROM CLIENT TO ROUTER

The client station uses the RIP lookup process to learn the MAC address (a.k.a. node address, hardware address, or data link address) of the router to use to get to a service. The client uses that router's datalink address as the destination in the datalink header of its packet to the service, as shown in Figure 10.15.

In Figure 10.15, the client affixes an Ethernet header defining the router's MAC address as the destination. The client places its own MAC address in the source field of the Ethernet header. This is enough information to get the packet to the router on the local network, but the router must use the information in the IPX header to get the packet to another network.

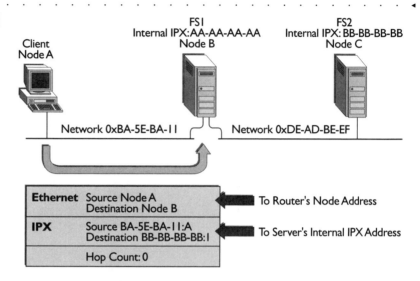

*The client addresses the packet to the router's datalink address in the Ethernet header.*

## MAC HEADER VERIFICATION

Upon receipt of the packet, the router verifies that it is a good Ethernet packet, strips off the Ethernet header, and then checks out the hop count field. The error detection process identifies packets that are too short, are too long, contain an invalid frame check sequence (FCS) value as computed by the cyclical redundancy check (CRC) process, or end on an invalid boundary (bit instead of byte).

## HOP COUNT VERIFICATION

This packet has a hop count of 0—the packet has not crossed a router or routing process yet. The router goes through the processes shown in Figure 10.16 to forward or discard the packet.

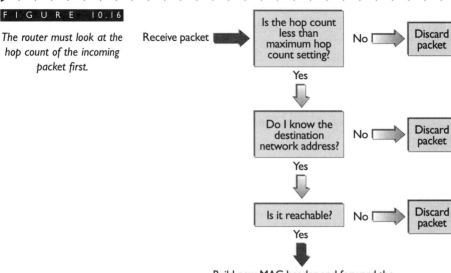

F I G U R E   10.16

*The router must look at the hop count of the incoming packet first.*

Receive packet → Is the hop count less than maximum hop count setting? → No → Discard packet

Yes ↓

Do I know the destination network address? → No → Discard packet

Yes ↓

Is it reachable? → No → Discard packet

Yes ↓

Build new MAC header and forward the packet out the appropriate interface

If the hop count is greater than the configured maximum hop count limit, the router must discard the packet. You can see the number of discarded packets due to excessive hop count in the IPXCON detailed IPX information screen, as shown in Figure 10.17.

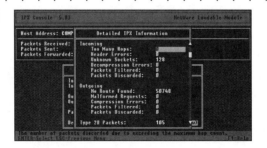

F I G U R E   10.17

*Use IPXCON to determine if your NetWare server/router has discarded packets that have exceeded the allowable hop count.*

IntranetWare v4.11 increased the default maximum hop count for IPX packets to 64. RIP and SAP packets, however, are still limited to a 16-hop maximum for reachability. NetBIOS packets are limited to 8 hops. In order to take advantage of a larger maximum hop count, consider using NLSP as your routing protocol.

Some discovery and query communications may need a higher hop count to locate devices throughout your network. For example, the NetWare Diagnostic Responder (covered in detail in Chapter 14) can be used to query a device on the other side of an internetwork. If the hop count limit is 16, that limits the discovery scope to a 15-hop radius from the transmitting station.

**Refer to Chapter 11 for details on NLSP connectivity.**

X-REF

Figure 10.18 shows a Diagnostic Responder packet that has been routed though 22 RIP routers before reaching the local network. Although this may look strange, it is the default setting on IntranetWare 4.11.

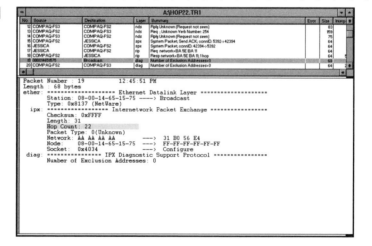

F I G U R E   10.18

*IntranetWare 4.11 has a default hop count setting of 64.*

**Some analyzer manufacturers set the hop count field decode to allow 1 through 15 only. They start counting at 1 again for any multiple of 16. For example, in Figure 10.18, the hop count field shows a value of 22. Some analyzers, however, will display the hop count as 6.**

NOTE

## ROUTER TABLE LOOKUP

Once the router determines that the hop count field contains an allowable value, the router looks up the destination network in its routing tables. If the destination network is in the tables and is considered reachable (within the allowable hop count limitation), the router can forward the packet.

**NOTE**

**If an entry for the route doesn't exist in the tables, the router looks for a Default Route entry (discussed later in this chapter). If no Default Route entry exists, the router will not respond to the request.**

If the router knows multiple paths to get to the destination address, the IPX router specifications define that the router must

▶ Consider the tick count first. Send the packet the direction that requires the lowest tick count.

▶ Use hops as a "tiebreaker." If the tick counts are equal between the different paths, use the hop count as a tiebreaker and send the packet the direction with the lowest hop count.

▶ If both ticks and hops are equal, use its own decision mechanism. This is left open for router manufacturers to determine the best route when two or more routes are equal in cost. Some manufacturers select the first entry they received in their tables. Others may use the address as a tiebreaker.

## FROM ROUTER TO SERVER

Once the router has determined the best route, it increments the hop count field of the IPX header, builds a new MAC header, and forwards the packet the appropriate direction, as shown in Figure 10.19.

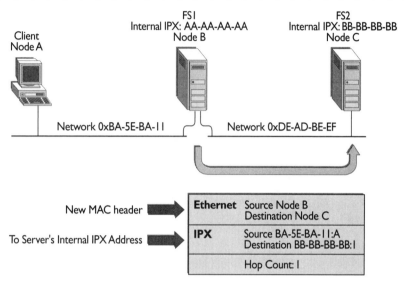

*The router builds a new MAC header and increases the hop count of the packet.*

As you can see, the router is allowed to change the hop count field in the IPX header only when it forwards the packet.

**NOTE**

During the time the router was looking up the destination address in its routing tables, the packet was sitting in a naked, unprotected state without any error checking mechanism (such as the MAC-layer CRC mechanism) surrounding the packet. If the router corrupts the data during this transition time, the corrupt packet with the new MAC header (and the new CRC value) can be sent to the server. If you suspect that a router is corrupting data along the network, enable IPX checksum on one of the clients. IPX checksum provides an end-to-end validation of the contents of the entire IPX header and data.

**NOTE**

The IPX Router Specification for RIP routers is available from Novell: part number 107-000029-001 (Document version 1.20, October 14, 1993).

One of the problems with the "best route calculation" used by RIP routers is due to the fact that the tick value is considered the primary method of selecting a path. Let's examine the problem and look at a sample LAN design scenario.

## Hops and Ticks in RIP Routing

Unfortunately, RIP routers do not actually measure the amount of time it takes to cross a network segment. RIP routers use a default crossing time of one tick — it takes one tick to cross a network.

When a router learns that a service is one hop away from a device, it makes an assumption that there is a router between two separate networks. One hop = two networks = two ticks.

 **On WAN links, the IPXWAN protocol is used to actually measure the amount of time it takes to cross the link. IPXWAN is covered in Chapter 12.**

NOTE

Figure 10.20 shows how the tick counter builds as services are determined to be more hops away from the source.

When the packet is sent to Router D, the router believes that it takes six ticks to reach network 99.

## Using Redundant Paths

When you have redundant paths, the RIP router must follow the IPX router specifications in making its forwarding decisions. The router must choose the route that has the lowest tick count.

Consider the expanded scenario in Figure 10.21.

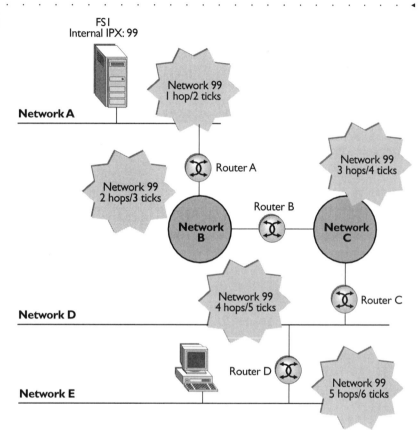

FIGURE 10.20

*Network 99 is five hops and six ticks away from a client that must communicate through Routers A, B, C, and D as well as the server's internal routing process.*

Using ticks (which are an assumed value) can be a problem on some networks that have redundant paths. What if the path that is considered to offer the lowest tick count is actually the fastest way to go? Since it is assumed that it takes one tick to cross *any* network, that means ARCnet networks (2.5 Mbps) are considered to be the same speed to cross as 100 Mbps FDDI networks.

▶ · · · · · · · · · · · · · · · · · · · · · · · · · · · · · · · · · · ◀

FIGURE 10.21

*Router D will send the packet through Path 1 because it has a lower tick count.*

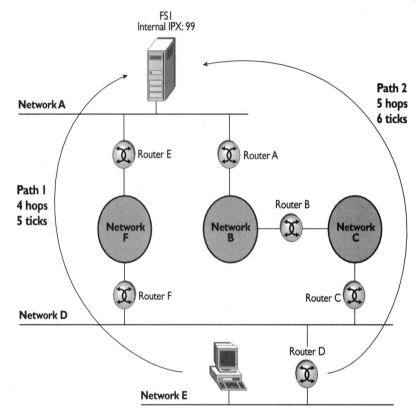

Figure 10.22 illustrates the point using the previous example. What if network F is a 4 Mbps Token Ring network and networks B and C are 100 Mbps FDDI? All traffic from network E to FS1 will travel through the slower Token Ring network because of the ticks assumption.

FIGURE 10.22

*Unfortunately, the RIP path selected is not always the fastest path.*

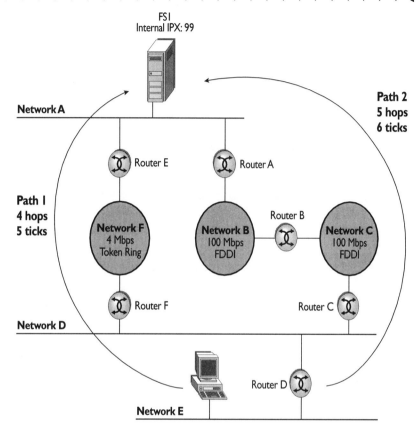

FS1
Internal IPX: 99

Network A

Path 2
5 hops
6 ticks

Router E    Router A

Path 1
4 hops
5 ticks

Router B

Network F
4 Mbps
Token Ring

Network B
100 Mbps
FDDI

Network C
100 Mbps
FDDI

Router F    Router C

Network D

Router D

Network E

## Customizing RIP for Better Performance

A number of issues arise when you use the RIP protocol. These issues are

- ▸ RIP is broadcast-based.

- ▸ RIP periodic broadcasts occur frequently (every 60 seconds).

- ▸ Entries can be timed out of the RIP tables too quickly.

- ▸ RIP broadcast rates can overload routing devices on a large network.

▸ RIP packet sizes are too small (576 bytes).

▸ Too much unnecessary RIP information is being broadcast around the internetwork.

▸ RIP is a distance vector–based protocol.

▸ RIP routers make assumptions about the amount of time it takes (ticks) to cross a network.

NetWare/IntranetWare 4.x (and products based on those OS versions) and many third-party routers allow you to configure RIP to perform better on larger networks. The following steps can be taken to optimize RIP performance and reduce overall RIP broadcast traffic:

1 • Turn off IPX packet forwarding.

2 • Set the RIP periodic broadcast interval.

3 • Set the RIT timer mechanism (aging interval).

4 • Throttle RIP broadcasts.

5 • Increase RIP packet sizes.

6 • Filter unnecessary RIP traffic.

## TURNING OFF IPX PACKET FORWARDING

You can place a NetWare server/router between two networks and turn off the ability for that server to route IPX packets between the networks. The server will still send out RIP broadcasts, but it will only talk about its internal IPX network, not any other attached networks. This type of server is often called a multihomed server.

Figure 10.23 shows a sample configuration using this technique.

*A multihomed server only talks about its internal IPX network in its RIP broadcasts.*

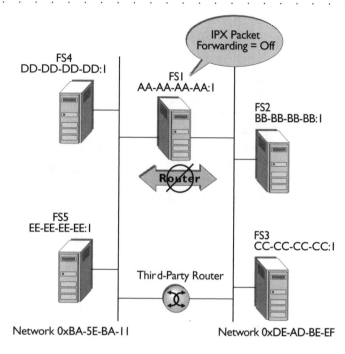

On the network shown in Figure 10.23, clients located on the 0xBA-5E-BA-11 network would send their packets through the third-party router rather than through the NetWare server. Even if the third-party router was not connecting the two LANs, the NetWare server set to IPX Packet Forwarding = Off would not advertise any attached networks.

The multihomed server sends out minimal RIP packets, advertising only a single network (the server's internal IPX network) every 60 seconds. Multihomed server configurations enable you to have a NetWare server act as a backup link between two networks. If the third-party router fails, you can turn on packet forwarding on the NetWare server to make it route packets between the external networks.

## SET THE RIP PERIODIC BROADCAST INTERVAL

On a relatively static network, you can change the frequency of the RIP periodic broadcast to reduce the overall RIP broadcast traffic. This setting is configured individually for each binding.

Figure 10.24 shows the RIP bind options. The option entitled Periodic Update Interval specifies the number of 30-second increments between RIP table broadcasts. The default setting is 2 (60 seconds).

F I G U R E   10.24

*You can configure the RIP update interval using INETCFG.*

**WARNING**

**If you change this RIP update interval parameter on one server or router on the network, you must change it on all servers or routers that share that common network address. For example, in Figure 10.25, the third-party router and both NetWare servers are set to an update interval of 60 minutes on LAN A. This ensures that none of them will time out waiting for updates every 60 seconds.**

If you are going to change the update interval on your NetWare devices, check with your router manufacturer to ensure they can support interval changes.

## SETTING THE RIT TIMER MECHANISM (AGING INTERVAL)

You can increase the amount of time entries are left in the RIT without verification. This ensures that entries are not timed out too quickly. This timer is defined as a multiple of the update setting, as shown in Figure 10.26. For example, you can set an update interval to 30 (15 minutes) and then set the Aging Interval Multiplier to 4 to hold down entries in the RIT for one hour.

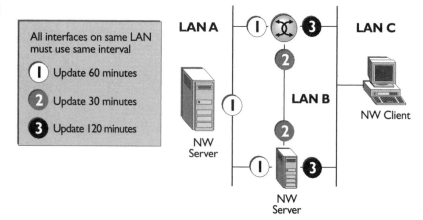

**FIGURE 10.25**

*All interfaces on the same network must use the same RIP update interval.*

All interfaces on same LAN must use same interval

① Update 60 minutes

② Update 30 minutes

③ Update 120 minutes

**FIGURE 10.26**

*The aging interval is a multiplier of the periodic RIP update interval.*

## THROTTLING RIP BROADCASTS

RIP packets can be sent with an interpacket gap of two ticks, which equates to a maximum rate of nine RIP packets per second. If this rate is overloading a routing device's buffer, you can increase the interpacket gap of RIP transmits. As shown in Figure 10.26, you can set the pace override for RIP communications on a per-bindings basis. An entry of 0 indicates that the default of nine RIP packets per second is used.

## INCREASING RIP PACKET SIZES

You can override the RIP packet size default to enable a RIP broadcast to contain more entries. Each RIP entry requires only eight bytes. You can set this field to the maximum physical packet receive size of the local server to fit more entries into each packet. For example, on an Ethernet network that supports 1,500 bytes in the data portion of the packet (not including the Ethernet header), you can fit up to 187 RIP entries.

It is recommended that you configure all devices that share the common network to the same packet size.

**WARNING**

**Make certain all your router manufacturers support the larger RIP packet sizes. Some older routers stop listening after 50 entries have been received in each packet, thereby discarding entries 51 through 187.**

## FILTERING UNNECESSARY RIP TRAFFIC

RIP traffic can be filtered in the same manner as SAP traffic. First, you must enable filtering through INETCFG under the IPX Protocol options. You can then use the FILTCFG.NLM utility to define incoming/outgoing filters based on network number, network mask, or interface.

When would you use RIP filtering? Let's take the example of the FDDI backbone that connects to 300 networks internationally. Perhaps you want to restrict local folks from receiving RIP information about the networks located in Hong Kong, since the local folks never use the Hong Kong resources. If, for example, all the Hong Kong IPX network addresses start with the designation 0xA103, you can configure a network/mask filter to stop any RIP information about "A103*" (where the asterisk is considered a wildcard) from coming onto the local network.

To define this filter, you would filter network address 0xA1-03-00-00 with a mask of 0xFF-FF-00-00. This indicates that the filter should be placed on the first 2 bytes of the network address, as shown in Figure 10.27.

**NOTE**

**One thing to keep in mind with filtering is that you may set up RIP filtering and then move to NLSP. RIP filters do not work with NLSP and should be used with caution, since they can possibly partition a network into two or more separate internetworks.**

FIGURE 10.27

*Use FILTCFG to configure
RIP filters.*

# The Routing Information Table (RIT)

The routing information table (RIT) is a dynamic table maintained by all NetWare/IntranetWare servers and routers. The table maintains information about networks and their proximity (in hops and ticks) to the local device. This table is implicitly linked to the server information table (SIT), which maintains information about services on the internetwork.

The following are some sample RIT entries:

| Network: | 0x00-00-00-99 |
|---|---|
| Hops: | 0 |
| Ticks: | 1 |
| Circuit: | Internal |
| Neighbor: | N/A |
| Entry age: | N/A |

| Network: | 0xAA-AA-AA-AA |
|---|---|
| Hops: | 0 |
| Ticks: | 1 |
| Circuit: | NE2000_1 |
| Neighbor: | N/A |
| Entry age: | 1 minute |

| Network: | 0xBB-BB-BB-BB |
|---|---|
| Hops: | 0 |

Ticks:        1
Circuit:      NE2000_2
Neighbor:     N/A
Entry age:    2 minutes

Network:      0xCC-CC-CC-CC
Hops:         1
Ticks:        2
Circuit:      NE2000_1
Neighbor:     0x00-00-1B-33-23-11
Entry age:    1 minute

Network:      0xDD-DD-DD-DD
Hops:          1
Ticks:         2
Circuit:      NE2000_2
Neighbor:     0x00-00-80-23-A3-88
Entry age:    2 minutes

These table entries imply that a RIP update packet was received on the NE2000_1 interface about one minute ago. It also implies that networks 0xAA-AA-AA-AA and 0xBB-BB-BB-BB are directly connected to a server that has an internal IPX address of 0x00-00-00-99.

The neighbor information is used by the router to determine what the MAC header should have as a destination address when packets are forwarded onto another router.

## READING RIT ENTRIES

You can use the Display Servers command to view the RIT, as shown in Figure 10.1, earlier in this chapter, but the IPXCON forwarding table is much more informative, as shown in Figure 10.28.

**Hit the F2 key while viewing the forwarding table to sort the table by network number, protocol type, or circuit name.**

NOTE

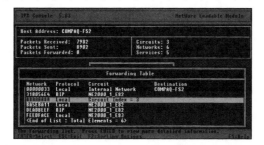

FIGURE 10.28

*The IPXCON forwarding table details how a network was learned.*

As shown in Figure 10.28, this server knows of six networks. The protocol column lists how the server learned of the network. "Local" indicates that the network is directly attached (either an internal IPX or external IPX network). "RIP" indicates that the server learned about the service through the standard RIP packets. On an NLSP network the entry NLSP indicates that the network was learned through NLSP link state packets.

NOTE

**The entry listed as circuit "Circuit Index = 3" was loaded at the server's command line, not through AUTOEXEC.NCF or INETCFG. Watch for these entries because they should typically be placed into AUTOEXEC.NCF or INETCFG.**

Figure 10.29 shows additional detail on the table entry for network "0xDE-AD-BE-EF."

FIGURE 10.29

*The Next Hop information indicates the MAC address to be used when forwarding packets to this network.*

### REBUILDING THE RIT

If you believe that your RIT is inaccurate or corrupt, type **RESET ROUTER** at the server console to automatically rebuild the table. The server will transmit a broadcast request for all known networks (network address 0xFF-FF-FF-FF).

## The RIP Default Route

RIP has a default route mechanism that can be used to forward packets even though a router does not know where the actual network is. The default route is assigned network address 0xFF-FF-FF-FE (also referred to as –2).

 **NOTE**  The network designations 1, –2, –3, and so on can be deciphered by counting backward by that amount from 0x00-00-00-00. For example, –1 would actually be –0xFF-FF-FF-FF (a negative hexadecimal number), –2 would actually be –0xFF-FF-FF-FE, –3 would actually be –0xFF-FF-FF-FD.

If a packet is sent to a router with an unknown network address, the router will forward it toward the device advertising the default RIP route (0xFF-FF-FF-FE).

## Network Error Recovery (Route Down)

What happens when a client loses connectivity through the network because a route went down? Well...that's not so easy to answer because each client behaves differently in this situation.

The NetWare Client 32 (CLIENT32.NLM, dated 8/21/96) will transmit a RIP packet after timing out on a communication, as shown in Figure 10.30.

Based on the trace shown in Figure 10.30, it is apparent that Router 2 is no longer functioning. After timing out, Jessica sends a RIP broadcast looking for network 0x00-00-00-33. If another router can get Jessica's packets to network 0x00-00-00-33, it will answer her RIP broadcast and Jessica will start using the new router.

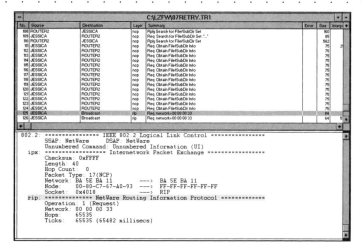

F I G U R E   10.30

*The client turns to the RIP protocol for help after a route has failed.*

## Routing Loops/Parallel Networks

In some instances, NetWare servers/routers do not work in agreement when they are placed in parallel. See, for example, Figure 10.31.

The NetWare RIP routing specifications define that if a router hears about a network on more than one interface and each of the entries has an identical hop/tick count, the router should not advertise that it knows how to get there. For example, in Figure 10.31, the server advertises network 99 as being one hop and two ticks through the server's routing process. The server sends these RIP broadcasts onto LAN A and LAN B. The router hears both advertisements and realizes it is in parallel with another routing device (in this case, the router is in parallel with the server's routing process), and therefore the router does not advertise that it is the fastest way to get there.

Be aware of some third-party routers that handle this situation in a different way. These routers may keep only the first entry when they detect duplicates. In that case, the router believes there is only one way of getting to the server.

If the router heard of network 99 through LAN A's interface first and it discards the information about network 99 received through LAN B's interface, the router believes it can talk about network 99 onto LAN B.

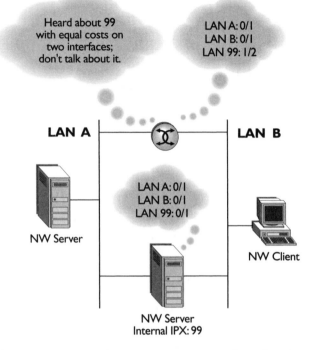

FIGURE 10.31

*If a router hears about a network with equal costs on more than one interface, the router knows it is in parallel with another routing device.*

This can really mess up network communications. When the client on LAN B boots up, it sends out a SAP broadcast looking for a file/directory server. The local server answers and announces that its internal IPX address is 99. The client then sends out a RIP broadcast looking for network 99. The local router believes it can get the client there, so it answers the request. The client believes that the router is the best way to get to network 99 and begins sending its NetWare Core Protocol (NCP) requests through the router, onto LAN A, to the server.

**In the case of Cisco routers, this problem can be stopped by increasing the Maximum Paths parameter to 2.**

TIP

## Duplicate Network Address Problems

A NetWare server sends packets to clients in either of two ways. The server can either use the client's request packet addressing information and send the packet back the way it came or look up the client's network address in the RIT and respond accordingly.

If you have a duplicate address somewhere on your network, as shown in Figure 10.32, you may experience some very odd timeouts on the network.

FIGURE 10.32

The client is located on network 0x00-00-AA-AA, and another network has been assigned that address.

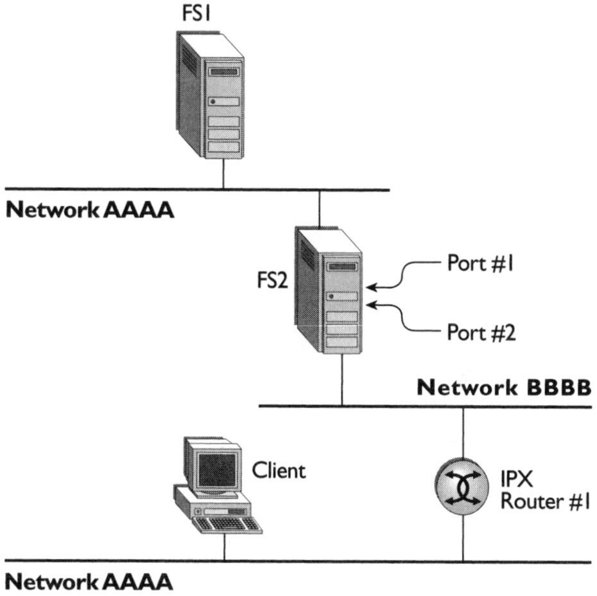

When the client sends requests to the server FS2, the server can simply use the packet addressing information to send the requests back the way they came. All operations can function normally for a while. Unfortunately, however, some NetWare communications do not rely on the solicited requests. For example, the NCP Watchdog process and the SPX Watchdog process do not require the client to send any communication to the server before the watchdog packets are sent to the clients. In order to transmit NCP or SPX watchdog packets to the client, the server looks up the client's internetwork address and consults its routing tables to find out how to get to network 0x00-00-AA-AA. The shortest path is through Port

1. The server sends the watchdog packets the wrong way. Since the client never receives the watchdog requests, it never answers the packets. Eventually, the server clears the client's connection.

## Router Configuration Errors

Router configuration errors are displayed on RIP-based routers to indicate that there is a discrepancy between a server's RIT and the RIP information the server or router is receiving through packets on the network.

For example, suppose you have two servers connected to an Ethernet network using NE2000 cards. On one server you bind IPX to NE2000 with a network address of 0xAA-AA-AA-AA. On the other server, you bind IPX to NE2000 with a network address of 0xBB-BB-BB-BB. Both cards are using the Ethernet 802.2 frame type, but they do not agree on the network addressing scheme.

Each server displays an error message on the console. The message states "Router Configuration Error: Node *xxxxx* [name] claims network address BBBBBBBB should be AAAAAAAA." In order to correct this error, you must configure both servers to use the same network address on the common frame type that IPX is bound to.

## Distance Vector versus Link State Routing

When IntranetWare 4.11 was introduced to the market, Novell changed its default routing architecture from RIP, a distance vector routing protocol, to NLSP, a link state routing protocol.

Link state routing protocols typically make better routing decisions because they know about the layout of the entire network, not just the next hop.

**X-REF**  **For details on link state routing, refer to Chapter 11.**

## RIP Packet Formats

Standard RIP packets are small packets (based on the XNS specifications) and can contain information about a maximum of 50 networks in each packet by default. In this section, we'll look at the standard RIP packet structures.

There are two standard RIP packet formats—request packets and reply packets.

### RIP REQUEST PACKETS

RIP request packets can be sent by clients (doing a service lookup) or servers that are trying to build their RIT.

Figure 10.33 shows the standard RIP request packet format.

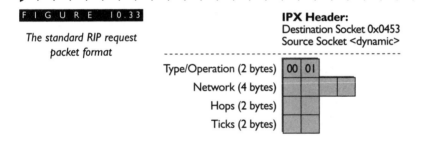

F I G U R E   10.33

*The standard RIP request packet format*

### Type/Operation Field

The type/operation field value is always 0x0001 on a RIP request packet and 0x0002 on a RIP reply packet.

### Network Field

The network field indicates the network that is being requested. This field can contain a specific network address (such as 0xBA-5E-BA-11) or an address indicating that the sender is looking for all networks (0xFF-FF-FF-FF).

### Hops Field

This field is not used on a RIP request packet and may be padded with either 0xFFFF (65535 decimal) or random values.

### Ticks Field

This field is not used on a RIP Request packet and may be padded with either 0xFFFF (65535 decimal) or random values.

Figure 10.34 is a sample RIP request packet from a client logged in as Admin that is looking for a specific network (0x31-B0-56-E4). This is a specific RIP query packet.

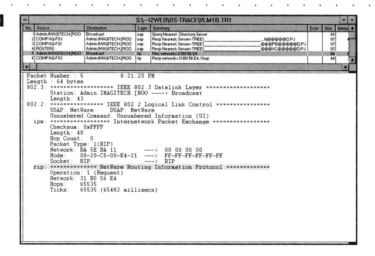

FIGURE 10.34

*The client sends out a specific RIP query packet looking for a network.*

Figure 10.35 is a RIP query looking for all networks (0xFF-FF-FF-FF). This packet was generated when we typed **RESET ROUTER** on the COMPAQ-FS3 console.

## RIP REPLY PACKETS

RIP reply packets use a format similar to that of RIP request packets, as shown in Figure 10.36. RIP reply packets, however, can have up to 50 network entries, and the operation/type field value is always 0x0002 in a RIP reply.

*In order to rebuild its RIT, the server sends a RIP broadcast request for all networks.*

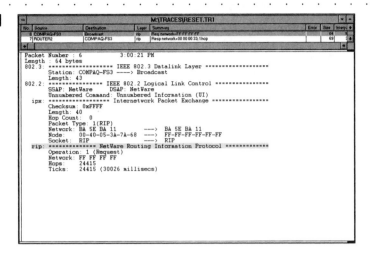

```
M:\TRACES\RESET.TRI
No. Source          Destination       Layer  Summary                                    Error  Size  Interp.
  6 COMPAQ-FS3      Broadcast         rip    Req network=FF FF FF FF                            64
  7 ROUTER2         COMPAQ-FS3        rip    Resp network=00 00 00 33, 1 hop                   69

Packet Number : 6                     3:00:21 PM
Length : 64 bytes
802.3: ===================== IEEE 802.3 Datalink Layer ====================
       Station: COMPAQ-FS3 ----> Broadcast
       Length: 43
802.2: ================== IEEE 802.2 Logical Link Control ================
       SSAP: NetWare    DSAP: NetWare
       Unnumbered Command: Unnumbered Information (UI)
  ipx: ================== Internetwork Packet Exchange ==================
       Checksum: 0xFFFF
       Length: 40
       Hop Count:  0
       Packet Type: 1(RIP)
       Network: BA 5E BA 11      --->  BA 5E BA 11
       Node:    00-40-05-3A-7A-68 --->  FF-FF-FF-FF-FF-FF
       Socket:  RIP               --->  RIP
  rip: ============== NetWare Routing Information Protocol ==============
       Operation: 1 (Request)
       Network: FF FF FF FF
       Hops:    24415
       Ticks:   24415 (30026 millisecs)
```

*Standard RIP reply packet format*

**IPX Header:**
Destination Socket <dynamic>
Source Socket 0x453

Type/Operation (2 bytes)  `00` `02`
Network (4 bytes)
Hops (2 bytes)
Ticks (2 bytes)

•

• **Default: Maximum 50 networks**

•

Network (4 bytes)
Hops (2 bytes)
Ticks (2 bytes)

### Type/Operation Field

The type/operation field value is always 0x0002 on a RIP reply packet and 0x0001 on a RIP request packet.

### Network Field

The network field lists the requested network(s).

### Hops Field

This field indicates how far away the network is located in hops. A hop is counted any time a packet crosses a router or router process. A hop count of 16 indicates that the network is unreachable.

### Ticks Field

This field indicates an assumption of how far away the network is in ticks (approximately 1/18 second) from the requesting device.

Figure 10.37 is a sample RIP reply packet to the client, Admin, who was looking for network 0x31-B0-56-E4. This is a specific RIP reply packet.

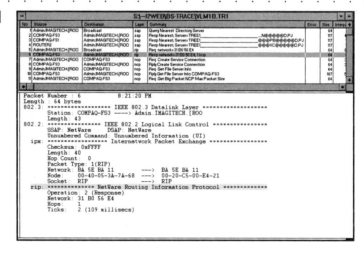

**FIGURE 10.37**

*The server sends out a specific RIP reply packet to the client.*

Figure 10.38 is a RIP response to a query looking for all networks (0xFF-FF-FF-FF), which was generated when we typed RESET ROUTER on the COMPAQ-FS3 console.

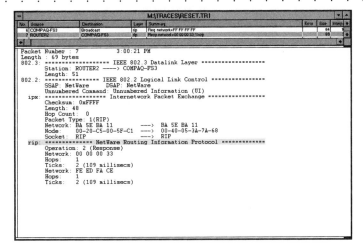

FIGURE 10.38

*A specific RIP reply listing
multiple networks is in
response to a device's
request for all networks
(0xFF-FF-FF-FF).*

Figure 10.39 is a RIP broadcast packet. This packet (sent to the broadcast address) is an unsolicited periodic RIP update packet.

FIGURE 10.39

*Any RIP reply packets sent
to the broadcast address
(0xFF-FF-FF-FF-FF-FF) are
RIP update packets.*

```
                                    A:\FSDOWN.TR1
No.  Source         Destination      Layer  Summary                                    Error  Size  Interp
 12  ROUTER2        Broadcast        rip    Resp network=BA 5E BA 11; 16 hops                  66

Packet Number : 12          9:31:13 PM
Length : 66 bytes
802.3: ================== IEEE 802.3 Datalink Layer ==================
        Station: ROUTER2 -----> Broadcast
        Length: 48
  ipx: ================ Internetwork Packet Exchange ================
        Checksum: 0xFFFF
        Length: 48
        Hop Count:  0
        Packet Type: 1(RIP)
        Network: FE ED FA CE        --->  FE ED FA CE
        Node:    00-20-C5-00-5F-C1  --->  FF-FF-FF-FF-FF-FF
        Socket:  RIP                --->  RIP
  rip: ============= NetWare Routing Information Protocol =============
        Operation: 2 (Response)
        Network: BA 5E BA 11
        Hops:     16
        Ticks:    2 (109 millisecs)
        Network: 00 00 00 33
        Hops:     16
        Ticks:    2 (109 millisecs)
```

When a router is brought down gracefully (not with a sledgehammer), it broadcasts a RIP reply packet indicating that all the networks it knows about are 16 hops away (unreachable), as shown in Figure 10.40.

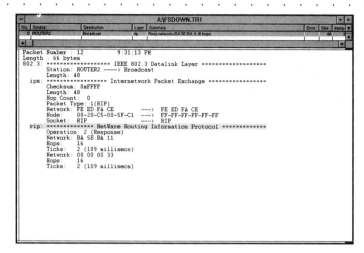

FIGURE 10.40

The "last dying gasp" packet indicates that all known networks are unreachable.

## Summary

RIP uses an older routing technology called *distance vector–based routing*. With the growth of networks came the need to find a routing technology that allowed NetWare LANs and WANs to span greater distances and exchange infrastructure information more efficiently.

NetWare Link Services Protocol (NLSP) provides a new method for routing NetWare's IPX-based communications through internetworks. It overcomes many of RIPs limiting factors, as defined in this chapter.

In the next chapter, we'll examine NLSP, the successor to RIP.

# NetWare NLSP

Chapter 11 focuses on NetWare's link state routing protocol—NLSP (NetWare Link Services Protocol). After providing a detailed look at how the NLSP link state process occurs and how the tables are created, this chapter details NLSP communications information including the LSP, CSNP, and PSNP packet structures and route propagation techniques.

## RIP Versus NLSP

NetWare 3.x and 4.x operating systems shipped with RIP configured as the default routing mechanism. IntranetWare 4.11, however, uses NLSP as the default routing protocol. NLSP offers greater flexibility and better performance for growing internetworks.

Novell's RIP routing protocol is a distance vector routing protocol. Distance vector routing protocols only know the number of hops and ticks to a destination and the next router (next hop) in the path. They do not know actual time to get to a destination, however, since RIP makes an assumption that it takes one tick to cross any LAN (ARCnet, Ethernet, FDDI, what have you—they're all the same). RIP routers do not know the complete path, either—they only know the next hop in the path.

Link state routers maintain a "map" of the internetwork and know the entire data path from one network to the distant network. Link state routers can alert each other if they are congested, enabling other routers to send data through a different path, ensuring the best end-to-end transmission time possible.

**NOTE**

**OSPF (Open Shortest Path First) is the link state routing protocol used in the TCP/IP environment.**

RIP and NLSP differ in the following ways:

- Manageability

- Network overhead

- Convergence

> ▸ Reliability

> ▸ Large internetwork support

> ▸ Load balancing

Let's examine each of these differentiating factors to get a better comparison between RIP and NLSP.

## MANAGEABILITY

In a NetWare RIP environment you can use such tools as DISPLAY NETWORKS and IPXCON to see only the next hop to get to a destination. NLSP enables you to trace an entire route from end network to end network. NLSP also enables you to force a path by manually configuring a link cost. NLSP can also show routers that are overloaded, duplicate network numbers, and other common network errors and problems.

## NETWORK OVERHEAD

NetWare RIP routers broadcast SAP and RIP information onto the network every 60 seconds using minimal packet sizes (576 bytes maximum) that can hold only 7 services or 50 network entries in each packet. NLSP defaults to sending update information only every 5 to 30 seconds and can hold up to 89 entries in every 1,518-byte packet (of course, more entries can be held in a 4K token ring packet). NLSP can also take advantage of IPX header compression techniques to reduce overall packet size.

## CONVERGENCE

Convergence is the process of propagating information throughout a network. When a RIP router learns of a change in the network layout, it records the change in its routing information tables, builds a RIP broadcast packet, and forwards it to all attached networks. NLSP routers, on the other hand, build a link state packet (LSP) announcing the change, and all NLSP routers forward the original packet throughout the internetwork. NLSP routers do not build a new information packet for all information they exchange. This "flooding" behavior increases convergence speed drastically.

### RELIABILITY

As mentioned earlier, RIP routers know only the next hop or directly attached network. They do not know if distant RIP routers are overloaded. NLSP routers maintain an accurate network map. They constantly check route integrity and will choose alternate routes if the primary path becomes unstable.

### LARGE INTERNETWORK SUPPORT

RIP communications default to a maximum hop count of 15—services and networks that are 16 hops away are advertised as too far to get to. RIP routers discard packets once they reach a hop count of 15, thereby reducing the overall size of the network to 15 hops from end to end. NLSP routers can support communications up to 127 hops. In the case of internetwork discovery (as used in management products), the larger hop count enables a larger communications radius.

### LOAD BALANCING

If the NLSP router finds that there are two or more equal-cost routes, the router can load-balance between the routes. RIP, on the other hand, chooses one of the two routes only—RIP cannot load-balance between them.

## RIP Versus NLSP Scenarios

In order to appreciate the difference between RIP and NLSP, consider the following scenario, using RIP routers. Your network, shown in Figure 11.1, uses many different types of media. RIP routers make an assumption that it takes one tick (approximately $\frac{1}{18}$ second) to cross any LAN. Router 1 believes that FS1's internal IPX network is six ticks away from Fred's station through Path 1 (LAN E, LAN D, LAN C, LAN B, LAN A, and the Internal IPX network). Router 1 believes that FS1's internal IPX network is five ticks away from Fred's station through Path 2 (LAN E, LAN D, LAN F, LAN A, and the Internal IPX network).

When Fred sends packets addressed to FS1's internal IPX address, which path will Router 1 use when routing the packets?

FIGURE  11.1

The RIP routers make an assumption that it takes one tick to cross any LAN.

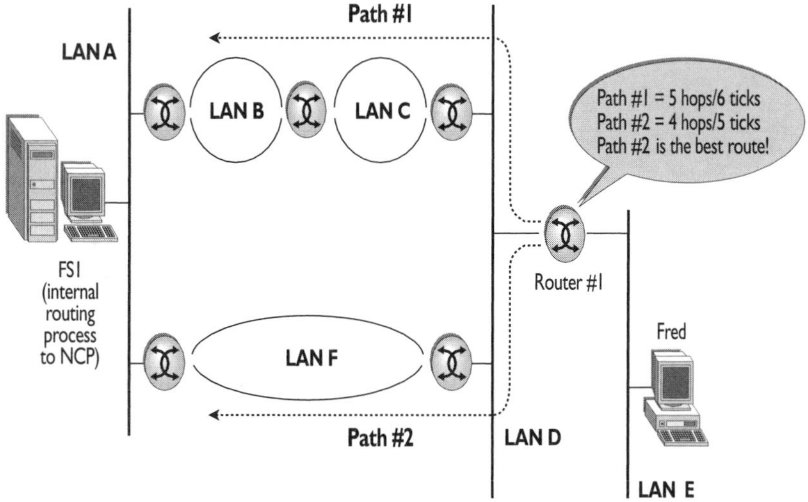

Path #1 = 5 hops/6 ticks
Path #2 = 4 hops/5 ticks
Path #2 is the best route!

Router 1 would send Fred's traffic through Path 2 because it is assumed to be faster. The RIP-based routers have defined Path 2 as only five ticks away.

Let's complete the picture now to identify the problem: LAN B is a 100-Mbps FDDI ring, LAN C is a 155-Mbps ATM network, and LAN F is a 4-Mbps Token Ring network, as shown in Figure 11.2. Which path is probably faster? Path 1 that includes a 100-Mbps network and a 150-Mbps network is probably much faster than crossing the single 4-Mbps network.

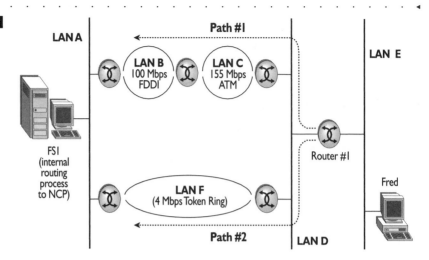

*Path 1 includes FDDI and ATM networks and is probably the fastest route.*

Now let's look at how NLSP routers would handle the same scenario. NLSP routers have default costs assigned to networks based on their throughput. Table 11.1 lists the default costs for typical network media.

T A B L E   11.1

*Default NLSP link costs are based on throughput.*

| AT LEAST | BUT LESS THAN | DEFAULT COSTS | TYPICAL MEDIA |
|---|---|---|---|
| 0K | 16K | 61 | |
| 16K | 48K | 55 | |
| 48K | 128K | 45 | ISDN (United States); ISDN (European) |
| 128K | 256K | 40 | |
| 256K | 512K | 35 | |
| 512K | 1M | 30 | |
| 1M | 2M | 27 | T1 (1.5M), Corvus Omninet (1M) |
| 2M | 3M | 26 | E1 (2M), ARCnet (2.5M) |
| 3M | 4M | 25 | Token Ring (4M) |
| 4M | 8M | 23 | |

| | AT LEAST | BUT LESS THAN | DEFAULT COSTS | TYPICAL MEDIA |
|---|---|---|---|---|
| **TABLE 11.1** | 10M | 16M | 20 | Ethernet (10M) |
| *Default NLSP link costs are based on throughput (continued).* | 16M | 32M | 19 | Token Ring (16M) |
| | 32M | 64M | 15 | |
| | 64M | 128M | 14 | FDDI (100M), CDDI (100M) |
| | 128M | 512M | 9 | ATM (155M) |
| | 512M | 4G | 6 | |
| | 4G | 32G | 3 | |

Based on the default costs just listed, we can see that the NLSP routed environment would ensure that packets were routed through Path 1 because it is the best route, as shown in Figure 11.3.

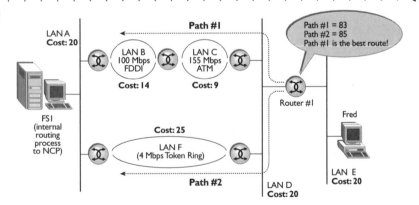

**FIGURE 11.3**

*Based on NLSP's default costs, path 1 is the best route.*

Let's examine NLSP's link state routing operation thoroughly to see how routing decisions are made and how route information is propagated through an internetwork.

## NLSP Operation

As we discuss NLSP operation, we'll use a very simple network design, as shown in Figure 11.4. The figure shows a network that supports a 10-Mbps Ethernet backbone (network 0xBA-5E-BA-11) with two attached NLSP routing devices (MPR1 and CORP-FS). MPR1 is connected to another 10-Mbps Ethernet network. CORP-FS is connected to network 0xBA-5E-BA-11 only.

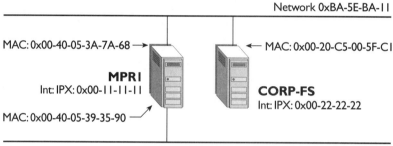

FIGURE 11.4

*This simple NLSP-based internetwork is referenced throughout this chapter.*

Network 0xBA-5E-BA-11

MAC: 0x00-40-05-3A-7A-68 →

← MAC: 0x00-20-C5-00-5F-C1

**MPR1**
Int: IPX: 0x00-11-11-11

**CORP-FS**
Int: IPX: 0x00-22-22-22

MAC: 0x00-40-05-39-35-90 —↗

Network 0xDE-AD-BE-EF

**CORP-FS is an IntranetWare 4.11 server that uses the NLSP routing protocol by default.**

NOTE

NLSP networks go through a series of processes to locate other local NLSP routers, assign network ID numbers, flood device information throughout the internetwork, and maintain a common "view" of the network. Figure 11.5 shows the architectural diagram for basic NLSP functionality.

As you can see from Figure 11.5, NLSP functionality requires three types of databases—the Adjacencies database, the Link State database, and the Forwarding database.

To build these databases, NLSP routers perform a series of functions including:

▸ Participate in the hello neighbor exchange ("neighbor notification") to build the Adjacencies database

▸ Flood LSP Information to build the Link State database

▸ Run the Decision Process to build the Forwarding Database

Each of these processes is run by all NLSP routers. In this next section, we'll examine these three processes and the results that each process provides to the NLSP routers and the link state network, in general.

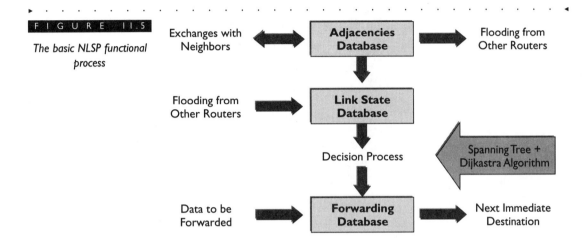

FIGURE 11.5

*The basic NLSP functional process*

Exchanges with Neighbors ⟷ **Adjacencies Database** ➡ Flooding from Other Routers

Flooding from Other Routers ➡ **Link State Database**

Decision Process ⬅ Spanning Tree + Dijkastra Algorithm

Data to be Forwarded ➡ **Forwarding Database** ➡ Next Immediate Destination

## THE LAN HELLO NEIGHBOR EXCHANGES

Each LAN NLSP router transmits NLSP hello packets onto its locally attached networks when the router is brought up. The router with the highest priority (a settable parameter) wins and becomes the "designated router" for that network. Figure 11.6 shows a hello packet from CORP-FS.

**The socket number used for all NLSP communications is 0x9001.**

NOTE

The first NLSP router that comes up on a network has a priority of 44. If the router has not heard from another router within approximately 20 seconds, the router assumes that it is the first router and therefore it must also be the designated router. The router dynamically increases its priority by 20. The router now has a priority of 64.

► · · · · · · · · · · · · · · · · · · · · · · · · · · · · · · · · · · · · · ◄

F I G U R E   11.6

*A "hello" packet indicates the router's priority setting.*

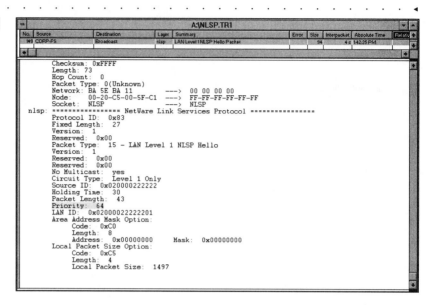

When another NLSP router comes up on the same network, it must broadcast an NLSP hello packet using the default priority of 44. The new router will not be the designated router, because an existing router has a higher priority. For example, when MPR comes up, it sends the NLSP hello seen in Figure 11.7. Since MPR's priority is set at only 44, it will not become the designated router for network 0xBA-5E-BA-11.

If two routers have the same priority, the MAC address is used as a tiebreaker. The highest MAC address becomes the designated router.

In some cases an NLSP router may be a designated router on one network, but not the designated router on another network. For example, as shown in Figure 11.8, MPR is the designated router for network 0xDE-AD-BE-EF, but it is not the designated router for network 0xBA-5E-BA-11.

The designated router makes certain that it has adequate memory to handle its responsibilities. If you have a server that is already overloaded with work, you may want to set its priority lower to ensure that it does not become the designated router.

FIGURE 11.7

FIGURE 11.7

*MPR indicates that its priority setting is only 44, a lower priority than CORP-FS.*

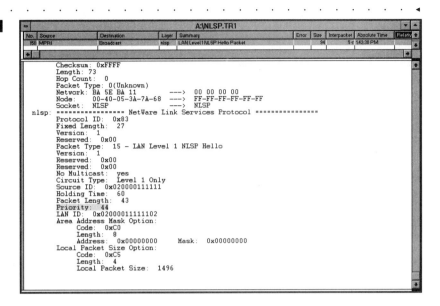

FIGURE 11.8

*A router can be the designated router for one attached network but not the other.*

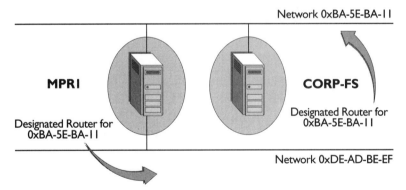

Hello packets are sent every 10 seconds by the designated router and every 20 seconds by other routers connected to the network. When a router sees another router's hello packet, the router knows that it has a neighboring router. It will include the neighboring router's MAC address in its next hello packet, as shown in Figure 11.9.

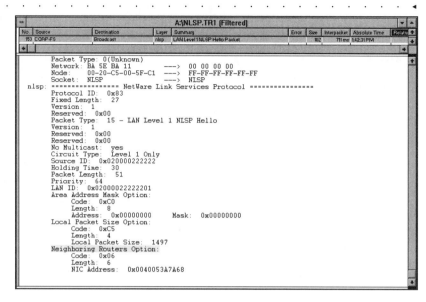

*CORP-FS includes its neighboring router's MAC address in its hello packets.*

In Figure 11.9, we can see that CORP-FS knows that it has a neighbor with MAC address 0x00-40-05-3A-7A-68—MPR's NIC that is connected to the same network as CORP-FS. MPR knows that its hello packet was received successfully by CORP-FS because CORP-FS is talking about MPR's NIC address in its hello packets.

This "learning" hello sequence is illustrated in Figure 11.10. CORP-FS is already up and running when MPR comes online. CORP-FS sees MPR's hello packet, but it is unsure whether MPR can also process information, since the neighboring routers field of MPR's hello packet is empty. CORP-FS believes that MPR is in the initializing state.

In its next hello packet, CORP-FS includes MPR's NIC address, as shown earlier in Figure 11.9. Upon receiving this packet, MPR records an adjacency to CORP-FS and notes that CORP-FS is in the "up" state because it has processed information about MPR already.

Finally, each side includes the other's NIC address in the neighboring routers field within the hello packets. If additional routers come up, they go though the same initialization process, are added to the Adjacency database, and are listed inside future hello packets from their neighboring routers.

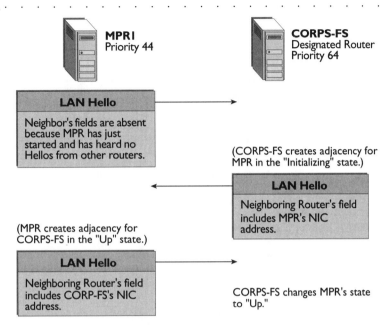

FIGURE 11.10

*The contents of hello packets are examined to determine when a new NLSP router is in the "up" state.*

How many entries can fit in a single hello packet? That depends upon the maximum packet size used on the network over which the hello packets are being sent. Each neighboring routers entry requires only 6 bytes (plus 2 bytes to define the field name and length); thus a 1,518-byte Ethernet packet can contain over 230 neighboring routers entries.

**If you have more NLSP routers connected to a single network than will fit in the LAN hello packet format, the NLSP routers register a "tooManyAdjacencies" NLSP event.**

**NOTE**

The hello process across a WAN link is slightly different. Before the neighboring WAN routers can exchange WAN hello packets, they must bring up the underlying medium (such as an X.25 or T1 link) and use the IPXWAN protocol to define operational characteristics.

**IPXWAN is covered in detail in Chapter 12.**

**X-REF**

During the WAN hello process, each WAN router sends a WAN circuit ID number to the other WAN router. This number is assigned to the router's own circuit when it is created. The routers also exchange their state information ("up," "down," or "initializing") and the maximum packet size (excluding data link header) supported by their circuits.

For more details on WAN hello packets, refer to the packet structures defined at the end of this chapter.

The moment the first NLSP router comes up on a network, a very organized numbering scheme begins to form. The designated router assigns a unique ID number to the network that it is the designated router for, and every network device assigns a unique number to each circuit (or port) that it has connected to any networks. We'll examine this numbering process now to make sense out of the numbers displayed in the packets in the remainder of this section.

## ASSIGNING ID NUMBERS (SOURCE ID AND CIRCUIT ID, LAN ID)

NLSP hello packets contain three identification numbers, as shown in Figure 11.11. These numbers are used to uniquely identify NLSP devices, their attached networks, and even their point of attachment to a network (circuits). These identification numbers are:

- ▶  Source ID

- ▶  Circuit ID

- ▶  LAN ID

### Source ID

The source ID (also referred to as the system ID) is used to uniquely identify the local device. The source ID number is derived from the NLSP router's internal IPX address. For example, if an IntranetWare server's internal IPX address is 0x00-11-11-11 (as in the case of MPR), the server's source ID is 0x02-00-00-11-11-11.

### Circuit ID

The circuit ID is a number assigned to each logical IPX attachment to a physical network. For example, if a server had a LAN driver loaded twice, once with the Ethernet_802.3 frame type and once with the Ethernet_802.2 frame type, and IPX were bound to both, that server would have two logical IPX connections to a single physical network. Each logical connection would have a separate and unique circuit ID.

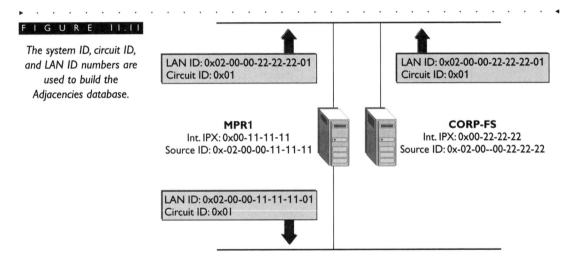

**FIGURE 11.11**

*The system ID, circuit ID, and LAN ID numbers are used to build the Adjacencies database.*

### LAN ID

The LAN ID is a combination of the designated router's system ID and the router's own circuit ID, as shown in Figure 11.12. For example, in Figure 11.9, CORP-FS advertises a source ID of 0x02-00-00-22-22-22. The starting value 0x02-00 is common throughout NLSP ID numbers. CORP-FS derives the next 4 bytes from its Internal IPX address (0x00-22-22-22). The last byte of the LAN ID is router's circuit ID (0x01).

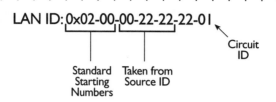

F I G U R E   11.12

The LAN ID is a combination of the designated router's source ID and the local router's circuit ID.

## ADJACENCIES DATABASE

The hello process is used to build the Adjacencies database. The Adjacencies database is just a small picture of the entire internetwork from the perspective of each router, as shown in Figure 11.13.

F I G U R E   11.13

Each NLSP router's Adjacencies database contains a small picture of the entire internetwork.

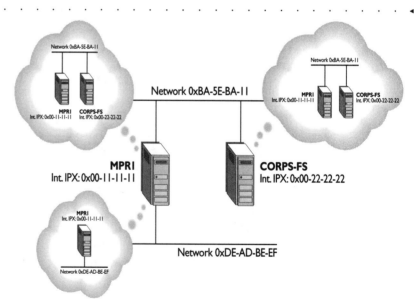

During the process of building the Adjacencies database, the network that all these neighboring routers are connected to is defined as a fictitious pseudonode. Information about the pseudonode can be distributed only by the designated router—none of the other neighboring routers offer information about the pseudonode. Figure 11.14 depicts an adjacency model in which our network has been defined as devices connecting off the pseudonode.

F I G U R E   11.14

*The LAN is collapsed into a pseudonode, and all neighbor routers are considered to be attached to the pseudonode.*

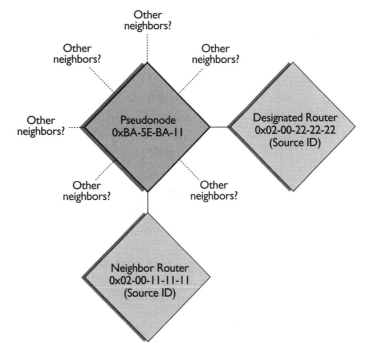

It is the responsibility of the designated router to generate link state packets (LSPs) on behalf of the pseudonode. (Later in this chapter we'll cover link state packet transmission.)

This picture of the local neighborhood is the foundation of the entire Link State database and must be current at all times. Each piece of information maintained in this Adjacencies database has a finite lifetime. The lifetime of each entry is defined in the neighbor's hello packet. For example, in Figure 11.9, the holding time indicated in CORP-FS's hello packet is 30 (seconds). The holding timer is three times the hello broadcast interval (10 seconds for designated routers), so the holding timer is 30 seconds. The hello broadcast interval is 20 seconds for the nondesignated router, so the holding timer is 60 seconds, as shown in Figure 11.7 earlier in this chapter.

If a neighbor is not heard from again within the holding timer value, the neighbor is assumed to be gone. The shorter holding timer for the designated router information ensures that a failed designated router is detected quickly (within 30 seconds).

## THE DESIGNATED ROUTER

As mentioned earlier in this chapter, the designated router is responsible for generating link state packets on behalf of the pseudonode. These link state packets are used by other routers throughout the NLSP network to build their Link State database. The Link State database contains the master list of all links and NLSP routers on the entire network, along with their associated properties (such as cost and link speed).

Remember that the designated router election process is based on the priority level set at the router. The highest-priority router becomes the designated router. Once a router determines that it is the designated router (through the hello exchange on the local circuit), the router must allocate memory and other resources necessary to generate the pseudonode LSPs.

If your designated router system is out of resources and cannot perform this duty, the router must:

1 • Enter LSP database overload state. When the router cannot store an LSP, it must discard the LSP.

2 • Lower its priority (hopefully causing it not to be the designated router). This ensures that the overloaded router does not get elected as the designated router on any other circuits to which it is attached.

Once the Adjacencies database is created, each router must announce its presence on the network by sending out a link state packet with its own characteristics and unique ID number. In this next section, we'll examine how a device announces its presence to the entire network.

## LSP FLOODING AND THE LSP DATABASE

Now that each local router knows its neighbors and has a picture of their local network, it is time to distribute this picture throughout the internetwork.

Link state packets (LSPs) include information about the local environment. Only the designated router can send LSPs that identify the pseudonode. LSPs can be sent using either the broadcast address (0xFF-FF-FF-FF) or a multicast address. The NLSP multicast addresses are:

| | |
|---|---|
| IEEE 802.3 | 0x09-00-1B-FF-FF-FF |
| IEEE 802.5 | 0xC0-00-10-00-00-00 |
| FDDI | 0X09-00-1B-FF-FF-FF |

Figure 11.15 depicts the first LSP packet transmitted by CORP-FS after the local hello packet process is completed.

▶ · · · · · · · · · · · · · · · · · · · · · · · · · · · · · · · · · · · · · · · · ◀

F I G U R E    1 1 . 1 5
*A link state packet*
*providing server information.*

```
Packet Number : 4                1:27:31 PM

Length : 133 bytes

802.3: ==================== IEEE 802.3 Datalink Layer
====================

        Station: CORP-FS ——> Broadcast

        Length: 115

802.2: ================ IEEE 802.2 Logical Link Control
================

        SSAP: NetWare        DSAP: NetWare

        Unnumbered Command: Unnumbered Information (UI)

  ipx: ================== Internetwork Packet Exchange
================

        Checksum: 0xFFFF

        Length: 112

        Hop Count:  0
```

*(continued)*

▸ • • • • • • • • • • • • • • • • • • • • • • • • • • • ◂

**F I G U R E   11.15**
*(continued)*

```
        Packet Type: 0(Unknown)

        Network: BA 5E BA 11         --> 00 00 00 00

        Node:    00-20-C5-00-5F-C1  --> FF-FF-FF-FF-FF-FF

        Socket:  NLSP                --> NLSP

   nlsp: ================= NetWare Link Services Protocol
================

        Protocol ID:  0x83

        Fixed Length:  27

        Version:  1

        Reserved:  0x00

        Packet Type:  18 - Level 1 Link State Packet

        Version:  1

        Reserved:  0x00

        Reserved:  0x00

        Packet Length:  82

        Lifetime:  7496

        LSP ID:  0x0200002222220000

        Sequence Number:  2

        Checksum:  0xD420

        Partition Repair:  Not supported

        Default Metric:  Not supported

        Delay Metric:  Not supported
```

```
Expense Metric:  Not supported

Error Metric:  Not supported

Overload:  No

Router Type:  Level 1

Area Address Mask Option:

     Code:  0xC0

     Length:  8

     Address:  0x00000000     Mask:  0x00000000

Management Information Option:

     Code:  0xC1

     Length:  19

     Internal Network Number:  0x00222222

     Internal Node Number:  0x000000000001

     IPX Version: 1

     Server Name Length: 7

     Server Name:  CORP-FS

Services Information Option:

     Code:  0xC3

     Length:  22

     Hop Count:  0 (internal)

     Network Number:  0x00222222

     Node ID:  0x000000000001
```

*(continued)*

F I G U R E    II.15

*(continued)*

```
        Socket:  0x0451

        Type:  0x0004

        Service Name:  CORP-FS
```

The LSP shown in Figure 11.15 is the first link state packet that CORP-FS has transmitted. There are no other neighboring routers on the network at this time. We can see that the packet is broadcast to the NLSP socket (0x9001).

This LSP has LSP ID 0x02-00-00-22-22-22-00-00 and contains information about the local file server and NCP services located at socket 0x0451. After learning that there are no other neighboring routers on the same network, CORP-FS transmits an updated LSP, 0x02-00-00-22-22-22-00-00. Figure 11.16 shows that the sequence number field of the new LSP is 3. The previous sequence number for this LSP ID was 2. Higher sequence numbers indicate a newer LSP.

F I G U R E    II.16

*The newer LSP has a higher sequence number — sequence number 3.*

```
    Packet Number : 7              1:27:39 PM

    Length : 160 bytes

    802.3: ==================== IEEE 802.3 Datalink Layer
    ====================

            Station: CORP-FS ——> Broadcast

            Length: 142

    802.2: ================= IEEE 802.2 Logical Link Control
    =================
```

```
        SSAP: NetWare      DSAP: NetWare

        Unnumbered Command: Unnumbered Information (UI)

   ipx: =================== Internetwork Packet Exchange
=================

        Checksum: 0xFFFF

        Length: 139

        Hop Count:  0

        Packet Type: 0(Unknown)

        Network: BA 5E BA 11        --> 00 00 00 00

        Node:    00-20-C5-00-5F-C1  --> FF-FF-FF-FF-FF-FF

        Socket:  NLSP               -->  NLSP

   nlsp: ================= NetWare Link Services Protocol
================

        Protocol ID:  0x83

        Fixed Length:  27

        Version:  1

        Reserved:  0x00

        Packet Type:  18 - Level 1 Link State Packet

        Version:  1

        Reserved:  0x00

        Packet Length:  109

        Lifetime:  7499

        LSP ID:  0x0200002222220000

        Reserved:  0x00
```

*(continued)*

```
          Sequence Number:  3

          Checksum:  0x8737

          Partition Repair:  Not supported

          Default Metric:  Not supported

          Delay Metric:  Not supported

          Expense Metric:  Not supported

          Error Metric:  Not supported

          Overload:  No

          Router Type:  Level 1

          Area Address Mask Option:

               Code:  0xC0

               Length:  8

               Address:  0x00000000    Mask:  0x00000000

          Management Information Option:

               Code:  0xC1

               Length:  19

               Internal Network Number:  0x00222222

               Internal Node Number:  0x000000000001

               IPX Version: 1

               Server Name Length: 7

               Server Name:  CORP-FS

          Link Option:

               Code:  0xC2
```

```
             Length:  25

             Default Metric:  20 (internal)

             Delay Metric:  (not supported)

             External Metric:  (not supported)

             Error Metric:  (not supported)

             Neighbor ID:  0x02000022222201

             Packet Size:  1497

             Delay:  200

             Throughput:  10000000

             Media Type:  0x0003 - Ethernet

        Services Information Option:

             Code:  0xC3

             Length:  22

             Hop Count:  0 (internal)

             Network Number:  0x00222222

             Node ID:  0x000000000001

             Socket:  0x0451

             Type:  0x0004

             Service Name:  CORP-FS
```

CORP-FS sends a third revision of LSP 0x02-00-00-22-22-22-00-00 that includes the name of the NDS tree that CORP-FS is in. The latest edition of this LSP has sequence number 4, as shown in Figure 11.17.

▶ · · · · · · · · · · · · · · · · · · · · · · · · · · · · · · · · · · · ◀

F I G U R E   11.17

*Sequence number 4 of this
LSP includes the NDS tree
information (TREE1).*

```
Packet Number : 15                    1:28:18 PM

Length : 223 bytes

802.3: =================== IEEE 802.3 Datalink Layer
===================

        Station: CORP-FS —> Broadcast

        Length: 205

802.2: ================ IEEE 802.2 Logical Link Control
================

        SSAP: NetWare      DSAP: NetWare

        Unnumbered Command: Unnumbered Information (UI)

  ipx: ================== Internetwork Packet Exchange
==================

        Checksum: 0xFFFF

        Length: 202

        Hop Count:  0

        Packet Type: 0(Unknown)

        Network: BA 5E BA 11          —>  00 00 00 00

        Node:    00-20-C5-00-5F-C1   —>  FF-FF-FF-FF-FF-FF

        Socket:  NLSP                 —>  NLSP

  nlsp: ================= NetWare Link Services Protocol
================

        Protocol ID:  0x83
```

Fixed Length:   27

Version:   1

Reserved:   0x00

Packet Type:   18 - Level 1 Link State Packet

Version:   1

Reserved:   0x00

Reserved:   0x00

Packet Length:   172

Lifetime:   7497

LSP ID:   0x0200002222220000

Sequence Number:   4

Checksum:   0x8F28

Partition Repair:   Not supported

Default Metric:   Not supported

Delay Metric:   Not supported

Expense Metric:   Not supported

Error Metric:   Not supported

Overload:   No

Router Type:   Level 1

Area Address Mask Option:

    Code:   0xC0

    Length:   8

    Address:   0x00000000     Mask:   0x00000000

*(continued)*

▶ · · · · · · · · · · · · · · · · · · · · · · · · · · · · · · · ◀

**F I G U R E  11.17**

*(continued)*

```
        Management Information Option:

                Code:  0xC1

                Length:  19

                Internal Network Number:  0x00222222

                Internal Node Number:  0x000000000001

                IPX Version: 1

                Server Name Length: 7

                Server Name:  CORP-FS

        Link Option:

                Code:  0xC2

                Length:  25

                Default Metric:  20 (internal)

                Delay Metric:  (not supported)

                External Metric:  (not supported)

                Error Metric:  (not supported)

                Neighbor ID:  0x02000022222201

                Packet Size:  1497

                Delay:  200

                Throughput:  10000000

                Media Type:  0x0003 - Ethernet

        Services Information Option:

                Code:  0xC3
```

```
          Length:  22

          Hop Count:  0 (internal)

          Network Number:  0x00222222

          Node ID:  0x000000000001

          Socket:  0x0451

          Type:  0x0004

          Service Name:  CORP-FS
     Services Information Option:

          Code:  0xC3

          Length:  61

          Hop Count:  0 (internal)

          Network Number:  0x00222222

          Node ID:  0x000000000001

          Socket:  0x4006

          Type:  0x0278

          Service Name:
TREE1_____@©HQB@@@@@D…PJ
```

Sequence number 4 of this LSP indicates the following:

▶ The LAN has ID 0x02-00-00-22-22-22-01.

▶ The LAN is a 10-Mbps Ethernet network (throughput 10,000,000 million bits/second).

▶ The maximum packet size (excluding Ethernet header) is 1,497 bytes.

▸ The delay to transmit 1 byte of data to a destination on this network is approximately 200 microseconds.

▸ The metric cost of this route is 20 (assigned by default).

▸ The NCP server is called CORP-FS, and it supports file services (type 0x0004).

▸ The NDS tree name is TREE1 and is located where the file server is.

Since this is the newest version of this LSP, all listening devices must override their existing information for LSP ID 0x02-00-00-22-22-22-00-00 with the information contained in this packet.

The next LSP that CORP-FS transmits is the pseudonode LSP—a link state packet sent on behalf of the pseudonode, as shown in Figure 11.18. The designated router sends LSPs on behalf of the pseudonode since the pseudonode —the common network—cannot send its own LSP.

▸ · · · · · · · · · · · · · · · · · · · · · · · · · · · · · · · · ◂

**FIGURE 11.18**

*The pseudonode LSP
provides information about
the network*

```
Packet Number : 8                    1:27:39 PM

Length : 119 bytes

802.3: ==================== IEEE 802.3 Datalink Layer
====================

        Station: CORP-FS —> Broadcast

        Length: 101

802.2: ================= IEEE 802.2 Logical Link Control
=================

        SSAP: NetWare       DSAP: NetWare

        Unnumbered Command: Unnumbered Information (UI)
```

```
ipx: ================== Internetwork Packet Exchange
==================

        Checksum: 0xFFFF

        Length: 98

        Hop Count:  0

        Packet Type: 0(Unknown)

        Network: BA 5E BA 11        --> 00 00 00 00

        Node:    00-20-C5-00-5F-C1  --> FF-FF-FF-FF-FF-FF

        Socket:  NLSP               --> NLSP

nlsp: ================= NetWare Link Services Protocol
================

        Protocol ID:  0x83

        Fixed Length:  27

        Version:  1

        Reserved:  0x00

        Packet Type:  18 - Level 1 Link State Packet

        Version:  1

        Reserved:  0x00

        Reserved:  0x00

        Packet Length:  68

        Lifetime:  7499

        LSP ID:  0x0200002222220100 - Pseudonode LSP

        Sequence Number:  1

        Checksum:  0xC44C
```

*(continued)*

▶ · · · · · · · · · · · · · · · · · · · · · · · · · · · · ◀

**FIGURE  11.18**

*(continued)*

```
        Partition Repair:  Not supported

        Default Metric:  Not supported

        Delay Metric:  Not supported

        Expense Metric:  Not supported

        Error Metric:  Not supported

        Overload:  No

        Router Type:  Level 1

        Management Information Option:

              Code:  0xC1

              Length:  12

              Internal Network Number:  0xBA5EBA11

              Internal Node Number:  0x0020C5005FC1

              IPX Version: 1

              Server Name Length: 0

              Server Name:  (not present)

        Link Option:

              Code:  0xC2

              Length:  25

              Default Metric:  0 (internal)

              Delay Metric:  (not supported)

              External Metric:  (not supported)

              Error Metric:  (not supported)
```

```
          Neighbor ID:   0x02000022222200

          Packet Size:   0

          Delay:  0

          Throughput:   0

          Media Type:   0x0003 - Ethernet
```

The pseudonode LSP (LSP ID 0x02-00-00-22-22-22-01-00) indicates that the network has the address 0xBA-5E-BA-11.

Remember that NLSP considers the network just another device, as shown back in Figure 11.12. That is why this LSP does not include any cost information for crossing the network. The actual cost of crossing the network is provided in the LSP that reports about a neighbor numbered 0x02-00-00-22-22-22-01 (the network connection).

From these two link state packets, we can begin to build our link state picture, as shown in Figure 11.19.

When MPR is brought online, it must announce that it knows of services that no one has "talked" about yet. Figure 11.20 contains the packet that is transmitted from MPR.

*The Link State database
information helps build a
picture of the network.*

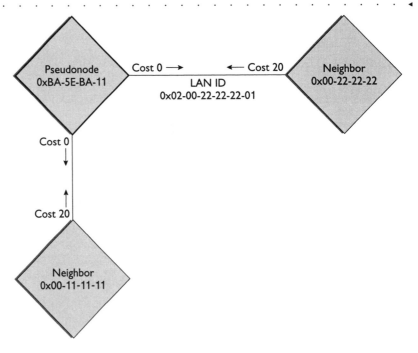

F I G U R E    11.20

*When another NLSP router
comes up, it must send out
any link information that
it has.*

```
Packet Number : 158              1:42:35 PM

Length : 154 bytes

802.3: ==================== IEEE 802.3 Datalink Layer
====================

        Station: MPR1 —> Broadcast

        Length: 136
```

```
802.2: =============== IEEE 802.2 Logical Link Control
===============

        SSAP: NetWare      DSAP: NetWare

        Unnumbered Command: Unnumbered Information (UI)

  ipx: ================== Internetwork Packet Exchange
=================

        Checksum: 0xFFFF

        Length: 133

        Hop Count:  0

        Packet Type: 0(Unknown)

        Network: BA 5E BA 11        --> 00 00 00 00

        Node:    00-40-05-3A-7A-68  --> FF-FF-FF-FF-FF-FF

        Socket:  NLSP               --> NLSP

  nlsp: ================ NetWare Link Services Protocol
================

        Protocol ID:  0x83

        Fixed Length:  27

        Version:  1

        Reserved:  0x00

        Packet Type:  18 - Level 1 Link State Packet

        Version:  1

        Reserved:  0x00

        Reserved:  0x00

        Packet Length:  103
```

*(continued)*

▶ · · · · · · · · · · · · · · · · · · · · · · · · · · · · · · · · ◀

F I G U R E    I I . 2 0

*(continued)*

```
Lifetime:  7499

LSP ID:  0x0200001111110000

Sequence Number:  2

Checksum:  0xC355

Partition Repair:  Not supported

Default Metric:  Not supported

Delay Metric:  Not supported

Expense Metric:  Not supported

Error Metric:  Not supported

Overload:  No

Router Type:  Level 1

Area Address Mask Option:

     Code:  0xC0

     Length:  8

     Address:  0x00000000     Mask:  0x00000000

Management Information Option:

     Code:  0xC1

     Length:  16

     Internal Network Number:  0x00111111

     Internal Node Number:  0x000000000001

     IPX Version: 1

     Server Name Length: 4
```

```
        Server Name:  MPR1
Link Option:
        Code:  0xC2
        Length:  25
        Default Metric:  20 (internal)
        Delay Metric:  (not supported)
        External Metric:  (not supported)
        Error Metric:  (not supported)
        Neighbor ID:  0x02000022222201
        Packet Size:  1496
        Delay:  200
        Throughput:  10000000
        Media Type:  0x0003 - Ethernet
Services Information Option:
        Code:  0xC3
        Length:  19
        Hop Count:  0 (internal)
        Network Number:  0x00111111
        Node ID:  0x000000000001
        Socket:  0x0451
        Type:  0x0004
        Service Name:  MPR1
```

In Figure 11.20, MPR is providing information about its connection to LAN 0x02-00-00-22-22-22-01. MPR indicates that its network number is 0x00-11-11-11, that it offers NCP services (socket 0x0451), and that it is a file server (type 0x0004).

MPR will update this LSP with information about its other network, 0xDE-AD-BE-EF (LSP sequence number 3), and the NDS tree called TREE1 (sequence number 4), as shown in Figure 11.21.

▶ · · · · · · · · · · · · · · · · · · · · · · · · · · · · · · · ◀

**FIGURE 11.21**

*MPR1 sends the pseudonode LSP for network 0xDE-AD-BE-EF because it is the designated router on network 0xDE-AD-BE-EF.*

```
Packet Number : 169              1:42:48 PM

Length : 119 bytes

802.3: ==================== IEEE 802.3 Datalink Layer
====================

        Station: MPR1 ──> Broadcast

        Length: 101

802.2: ================ IEEE 802.2 Logical Link Control
================

        SSAP: NetWare      DSAP: NetWare

        Unnumbered Command: Unnumbered Information (UI)

  ipx: ================== Internetwork Packet Exchange
================

        Checksum: 0xFFFF

        Length: 98

        Hop Count: 0
```

```
          Packet Type: 0(Unknown)

          Network: BA 5E BA 11        --> 00 00 00 00

          Node:    00-40-05-3A-7A-68  --> FF-FF-FF-FF-FF-FF

          Socket:  NLSP               --> NLSP

  nlsp: ================= NetWare Link Services Protocol
=================

          Protocol ID:  0x83

          Fixed Length:  27

          Version:  1

          Reserved:  0x00

          Packet Type:  18 - Level 1 Link State Packet

          Version:  1

          Reserved:  0x00

          Reserved:  0x00

          Packet Length:  68

          Lifetime:  7498

          LSP ID:  0x0200001111110100 - Pseudonode LSP

          Sequence Number:  1

          Checksum:  0x41A2

          Partition Repair:  Not supported

          Default Metric:  Not supported

          Delay Metric:  Not supported

          Expense Metric:  Not supported

          Error Metric:  Not supported
```

*(continued)*

▶ · · · · · · · · · · · · · · · · · · · · · · · · · · · · · · · · · · · · ◀

**F I G U R E   I I . 2 I**

*(continued)*

```
        Overload:  No

        Router Type:  Level 1

        Management Information Option:

                Code:  0xC1

                Length:  12

                Internal Network Number:  0xDEADBEEF

                Internal Node Number:  0x004005393590

                IPX Version: 1

                Server Name Length: 0

                Server Name:  (not present)

        Link Option:

                Code:  0xC2

                Length:  25

                Default Metric:  0 (internal)

                Delay Metric:  (not supported)

                External Metric:  (not supported)

                Error Metric:  (not supported)

                Neighbor ID:  0x02000011111100

                Packet Size:  0

                Delay:  0

                Throughput:  0

                Media Type:  0x0003 - Ethernet
```

LSP 0x02-00-00-11-11-11-01-00 is the pseudonode LSP that provides information about another network.

A new pseudonode LSP must be generated for network 0xBA-5E-BA-11, since there is a new neighbor, MPR1, connected to the pseudonode. Figure 11.22 shows the new pseudonode LSP that indicates that a new neighbor (0x00-11-11-11) is connected to this pseudonode.

▶ · · · · · · · · · · · · · · · · · · · · · · · · · · · · · · · · · · · ◀

**FIGURE 11.22**

*The revised (sequence number 2) pseudonode LSP indicates that there are two neighbors connected to this pseudonode.*

```
Packet Number : 165          1:42:35 PM

Length : 146 bytes

802.3: ==================== IEEE 802.3 Datalink Layer
====================

        Station: CORP-FS —> Broadcast

        Length: 128

802.2: ================ IEEE 802.2 Logical Link Control
================

        SSAP: NetWare      DSAP: NetWare

        Unnumbered Command: Unnumbered Information (UI)

  ipx: ================== Internetwork Packet Exchange
================

        Checksum: 0xFFFF

        Length: 125

        Hop Count:  0
```

*(continued)*

▶ . . . . . . . . . . . . . . . . . . . . . . . . . . . . . . . . ◀

## F I G U R E   11.22

*(continued)*

```
            Packet Type: 0(Unknown)

            Network: BA 5E BA 11        --> 00 00 00 00

            Node:    00-20-C5-00-5F-C1  --> FF-FF-FF-FF-FF-FF

            Socket:  NLSP               --> NLSP

      nlsp: ================= NetWare Link Services Protocol
================

            Protocol ID:  0x83

            Fixed Length:  27

            Version:  1

            Reserved:  0x00

            Packet Type:  18 - Level 1 Link State Packet

            Version:  1

            Reserved:  0x00

            Reserved:  0x00

            Packet Length:  95

            Lifetime:  7496

            LSP ID:   0x0200002222220100 - Pseudonode LSP

            Sequence Number:  2

            Checksum:  0x5C1E

            Partition Repair:  Not supported

            Default Metric:  Not supported

            Delay Metric:  Not supported
```

Expense Metric:  Not supported

Error Metric:  Not supported

Overload:  No

Router Type:  Level 1

Management Information Option:

     Code:  0xC1

     Length:  12

     Internal Network Number:  0xBA5EBA11

     Internal Node Number:  0x0020C5005FC1

     IPX Version: 1

     Server Name Length: 0

     Server Name:  (not present)

Link Option:

     Code:  0xC2

     Length:  25

     Default Metric:  0 (internal)

     Delay Metric:  (not supported)

     External Metric:  (not supported)

     Error Metric:  (not supported)

     Neighbor ID:  0x02000022222200

     Packet Size:  0

     Delay:  0

     Throughput:  0

*(continued)*

▶ . . . . . . . . . . . . . . . . . . . . . . . . . . . . . . ◀

F I G U R E   11.22

*(continued)*

```
                    Media Type:  0x0003 - Ethernet
            Link Option:

                    Code:  0xC2

                    Length:  25

                    Default Metric:  0 (internal)

                    Delay Metric:  (not supported)

                    External Metric:  (not supported)

                    Error Metric:  (not supported)

                    Neighbor ID:  0x02000011111100

                    Packet Size:  0

                    Delay:  0

                    Throughput:  0

                    Media Type:  0x0003 - Ethernet
```

These link state packets can be used to create a conceptual diagram of the network and the costs to travel in each direction, as shown in Figure 11.23.

Notice that the pseudonodes have been illustrated as nodes on the network. This is in preparation for the next step in link state routing—building the Forwarding database.

▶ · · · · · · · · · · · · · · · · · · · · · · · · · ◀

FIGURE 11.23

*The Link State database maintains node and link information and can be used to draw out the conceptual network layout.*

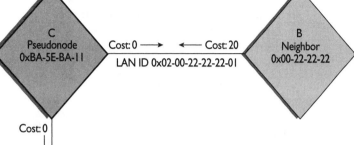

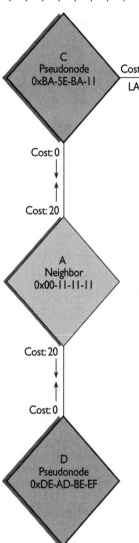

**Link State Database: Links**

| Link | Cost |
|------|------|
| A-B  | 20   |
| A-C  | 20   |
| A-D  | 20   |
| B-A  | 20   |
| B-C  | 20   |
| B-D  | 40   |

| Link | Cost |
|------|------|
| C-A  | 0    |
| C-B  | 0    |
| C-D  | 20   |
| D-A  | 0    |
| D-B  | 20   |
| D-C  | 20   |

**Link State Database: Nodes**

| Node | Type |
|------|------|
| A: 0x00-11-11-11 | Router CORP-FS |
| B: 0X00-22-22-22 | Router MPR1 |
| C: 0x02-00-00-22-22-22-01 | Pseudonode 0xBA-5E-BA-11 |
| D: 0x02-00-00-11-11-11-01 | Pseudonode 0xDE-AD-BE-EF |

**LSPs are not acknowledged on a LAN. A router receiving an LSP on a LAN simply checks to see if it has a more current version than the sender. If the packet just received is newer, the router updates its Link State database and rebuilds the Forwarding database. On a WAN, however, a router that receives an LSP replies with a partial sequence number packet (PSNP). This serves as an acknowledgment for the LSP. PSNP packets are covered in greater detail later in this chapter.**

The Link State database is not organized for quick access for decision-making processes. Imagine trying to look at a map of Switzerland to make a decision on whether to go left or right at a stoplight to take the best path somewhere. It would be much better if you had step-by-step instructions that stated "Go left at the first light — that is the best way to go." In order to make the Link State database usable, NLSP routers go through a decision process to build a database they can reference quickly for forwarding decisions. This database is called the Forwarding database.

## MAKING ROUTING DECISIONS

Since the link and node tables are not in an ideal form to make routing decisions from, a decision process is run to build a Forwarding database. This Forwarding database is consulted for all routing processes.

The decision process is called Dijkstra's algorithm after Edger W. Dijkstra, the man who defined the basic methodology. This decision process is run each time a change occurs in the Link State database.

Based on the node and link information, we can now begin the decision process. First, we must lay out the network properly. Dijkstra's algorithm treats each router and pseudonode as a node in a graph, and each link is a line connecting two nodes, as shown in Figure 11.24.

**F I G U R E   11.24**

*The Forwarding database and forwarding table*

Forwarding Graph

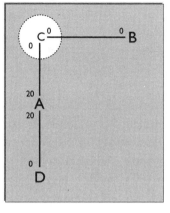

Forwarding Database: From C

| DESTINATION | Cost | Next Hop |
|---|---|---|
| 0x00-22-22-22 (B) | 0 | B |
| 0x00-11-11-11 (A) | 0 | A |
| 0xDE-AD-BE-EF (D) | 20 | A |

What if the network expands and there are multiple paths to get from one network to another? Let's expand our network to add a second path from MPR1 (C) to a new network number 0x00-00-00-99 (L), as shown in Figure 11.25.

**F I G U R E   11.25**

*The Forwarding database includes only the best route entries.*

Forwarding Graph

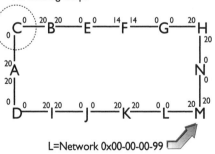

L=Network 0x00-00-00-99

Forwarding Database: From C

| Node | Cost | Next Hop |
|---|---|---|
| C | 0 | - |
| B | 0 | B |
| E | 20 | B |
| F | 20 | B |
| G | 34 | B |
| H | 34 | B |
| N | 54 | B |
| M | 54 | A |
| A | 0 | B |
| D | 20 | A |
| I | 20 | A |
| J | 40 | A |
| K | 40 | A |
| L | 60 | A |

There are two paths to get to L. One path is through B, E, F, G, H, N, and M and has a cost of 74 (20 + 14 + 20 + 20). The second path is through A, D, I, J, and K and has a cost of 60 (20 + 20 + 20). Dijkstra's algorithm uses the cost as a method for identifying the better path.

If you know how a spanning tree works, this may seem very familiar to you. Completion of Dijkstra's algorithm does create a spanning tree design with a single path through the network.

You can change the nature of the decision process by altering the way duplicate paths and multiple paths are handled. For example, in some situations you may want to use duplicate paths to provide additional functionality by load splitting across equal paths. You may also want to force data to travel a certain path in one direction and another path in another direction (asymmetric routing). Let's examine each of these functions to determine how they can be used.

### Load Splitting

If two paths have equal costs, NLSP can split the communications up among the two or more paths. This is a settable parameter in INETCFG. The default is 1 (only send data over a single path when equal-cost routes exist). A very deterministic method determines which path should be used when they are considered "equal cost." The router will use the paths in order of preference, which is based on the best cost, best throughput, lowest delay, and highest maximum transmission unit (MTU).

Do not manually assign costs to links that are not equal in throughput (such as a 4-Mbps Token Ring and a 10-Mbps Ethernet) in order to force load splitting. This can cause problems in some Novell communications implementations that are order-dependent, such as burst mode data reads and writes.

### Asymmetric/Symmetric Routes

You can change the cost system to indicate that it costs more to cross a link in one direction than another direction. This can make two separate paths—one for each direction. This is called *asymmetrical routing*. Although asymmetrical routing is possible, it can be difficult to troubleshoot any communications that are of the request/reply type. Ideally you want to see both requests and the corresponding replies when analyzing network communications.

## KEEPING THE LINK STATE DATABASE UP TO DATE

The Link State database must be kept up to date to ensure that the proper routing decisions are being made. If a link becomes unavailable, a service moves to another location, or a new high-speed link has been set up, it is imperative that all the NLSP routers know the new state, location, and links. Imagine if our roadmaps were not kept up to date and we were unaware that a freeway now exists through town!

Periodically (at least every 5 seconds, but not more than every 30 seconds) the designated router broadcasts a listing of the internetwork LSP list in a complete sequence number packet (CSNP).

CSNPs contain a list of all the LSP ID numbers and their associated sequence numbers and checksum values, as shown in Figure 11.26.

▶ . . . . . . . . . . . . . . . . . . . . . . . . . . . . . . . . . ◀

F I G U R E     I I . 2 6

*This complete sequence
number packet lists the
entire Link State database.*

```
Packet Number : 165              1:42:35 PM

Length : 146 bytes

802.3: ==================== IEEE 802.3 Datalink Layer
====================

        Station: CORP-FS ——> Broadcast

        Length: 128

802.2: ================ IEEE 802.2 Logical Link Control
================

        SSAP: NetWare      DSAP: NetWare

        Unnumbered Command: Unnumbered Information (UI)

   ipx: ================== Internetwork Packet Exchange
================
```

*(continued)*

▶ · · · · · · · · · · · · · · · · · · · · · · · · · · ◀

F I G U R E   11.26

*(continued)*

```
            Checksum: 0xFFFF

            Length: 125

            Hop Count:  0

            Packet Type: 0(Unknown)

            Network: BA 5E BA 11        --> 00 00 00 00

            Node:   00-20-C5-00-5F-C1   --> FF-FF-FF-FF-FF-FF

            Socket: NLSP                --> NLSP

    nlsp: ================= NetWare Link Services Protocol
================

            Protocol ID:  0x83

            Fixed Length:  27

            Version:  1

            Reserved:  0x00

            Packet Type:  18 - Level 1 Link State Packet

            Version:  1

            Reserved:  0x00

            Reserved:  0x00

            Packet Length:  95

            Lifetime:  7496

            LSP ID:  0x0200002222220100 - Pseudonode LSP

            Sequence Number:  2

            Checksum:  0x5C1E
```

Partition Repair:  Not supported

Default Metric:  Not supported

Delay Metric:  Not supported

Expense Metric:  Not supported

Error Metric:  Not supported

Overload:  No

Router Type:  Level 1

Management Information Option:

        Code:  0xC1

        Length:  12

        Internal Network Number:  0xBA5EBA11

        Internal Node Number:  0x0020C5005FC1

        IPX Version: 1

        Server Name Length: 0

        Server Name:  (not present)

Link Option:

        Code:  0xC2

        Length:  25

        Default Metric:  0 (internal)

        Delay Metric:  (not supported)

        External Metric:  (not supported)

        Error Metric:  (not supported)

        Neighbor ID:  0x02000022222200

        Packet Size:  0

*(continued)*

▶ • • • • • • • • • • • • • • • • • • • • • • • • • • • • ◀

F I G U R E  11.26

*(continued)*

```
                    Delay:  0

                    Throughput:  0

                    Media Type:  0x0003 - Ethernet

            Link Option:

                    Code:  0xC2

                    Length:  25

                    Default Metric:  0 (internal)

                    Delay Metric:  (not supported)

                    External Metric:  (not supported)

                    Error Metric:  (not supported)

                    Neighbor ID:  0x02000011111100

                    Packet Size:  0

                    Delay:  0

                    Throughput:  0

                    Media Type:  0x0003 - Ethernet
```

The CSNP packet also indicates the remaining lifetime of each LSP. This information is typically defined in seconds, but it can be indicated in hours, if desired. For more information on the format of this information, refer to the section entitled "CSNP (complete sequence number packet) structure" later in this chapter.

NLSP routers do not forward the CSNP packet upon receipt. They compare the contents of the packet to their Link State database to see if there are any inconsistencies. In this next section, we'll examine how inconsistencies and expired LSPs affect this process.

### LSP Mismatch: Sender (Designated Router) Has the Latest Information

If the sender (designated router) has the latest information, the receiver transmits a partial sequence number packet (PSNP) to the sender. This PSNP includes the LSP ID number of the information that is required. For example, when MPR1 came up on our network, it did not have all the LSP entries that CORP-FS had. Upon receipt of the CSNP from CORP-FS (shown in Figure 11.27), MPR1 generated a PSNP (shown in Figure 11.28) requesting more information about two LSP entries.

► · · · · · · · · · · · · · · · · · · · · · · · · · · · · · · · · · · · · · · ◄

F I G U R E   I I . 2 7

*The CSNP indicates that there are only two entries in the Link State database.*

```
Packet Number : 151          1:42:32 PM

Length : 118 bytes

802.3: =================== IEEE 802.3 Datalink Layer
===================

        Station: CORP-FS —> Broadcast

        Length: 100

802.2: ================ IEEE 802.2 Logical Link Control
================

        SSAP: NetWare      DSAP: NetWare

        Unnumbered Command: Unnumbered Information (UI)

   ipx: ================== Internetwork Packet Exchange
================

        Checksum: 0xFFFF

        Length: 97

        Hop Count:  0
                                                  (continued)
```

▶ · · · · · · · · · · · · · · · · · · · · · · · · · · · · · · · · ◀

FIGURE  11.27

*(continued)*

```
        Packet Type: 0(Unknown)

        Network: BA 5E BA 11        --> 00 00 00 00

        Node:    00-20-C5-00-5F-C1  --> FF-FF-FF-FF-FF-FF

        Socket:  NLSP               --> NLSP

   nlsp: ================= NetWare Link Services Protocol
================

        Protocol ID:  0x83

        Fixed Length:  33

        Version:  1

        Reserved:  0x00

        Packet Type:  24 - Level 1 Complete Sequence Numbers
   Packet

        Version:  1

        Reserved:  0x00

        Reserved:  0x00

        Packet Length:  67

        Source ID:  0x02000022222200

        Start LSP ID:  0x0000000000000000

        End LSP ID:  0xFFFFFFFFFFFFFFFF

        LSP Entries Option:

            Code:  0x09

            Length:  32
            _____
```

```
          Remaining Lifetime:  6634

          LSP ID:  0x0200002222220000

          Sequence Number:  4

          Checksum:  0x8F28

          _____


          Remaining Lifetime:  7499

          LSP ID:  0x0200002222220100

          Sequence Number:  2

          Checksum:  0x5C1E
```

◄ · · · · · · · · · · · · · · · · · · · · · · · · · · · · · · · · ◄

### F I G U R E   11.28

*MPR1 indicates that it
needs two entire LSP
entries.*

```
     Packet Number : 152              1:42:32 PM

     Length : 102 bytes

     802.3: ==================== IEEE 802.3 Datalink Layer
     ====================

             Station: MPR1 ──> Broadcast

             Length: 84

     802.2: ================ IEEE 802.2 Logical Link Control
     ================

             SSAP: NetWare     DSAP: NetWare

             Unnumbered Command: Unnumbered Information (UI)
```

*(continued)*

▶ · · · · · · · · · · · · · · · · · · · · · · · · · · · · · · · · ◀

F I G U R E    11.28

*(continued)*

```
    ipx: ================= Internetwork Packet Exchange
=================

        Checksum: 0xFFFF

        Length: 81

        Hop Count:  0

        Packet Type: 0(Unknown)

        Network: BA 5E BA 11        --> 00 00 00 00

        Node:    00-40-05-3A-7A-68  --> FF-FF-FF-FF-FF-FF

        Socket:  NLSP               --> NLSP

   nlsp: ================= NetWare Link Services Protocol
================

        Protocol ID:  0x83

        Fixed Length:  17

        Version:  1

        Reserved:  0x00

        Packet Type:  26 - Level 1 Partial Sequence Numbers
Packet

        Version:  1

        Reserved:  0x00

        Reserved:  0x00

        Packet Length:  51

        Source ID:  0x02000011111100

        LSP Entries Option:
```

```
                    Code:   0x09

                    Length:   32
                    _____

                    Remaining Lifetime:   59

                    LSP ID:   0x0200002222220000

                    Sequence Number:   0

                    Checksum:   0x8F28
                    _____

                    Remaining Lifetime:   59

                    LSP ID:   0x0200002222220100

                    Sequence Number:   0

                    Checksum:   0x5C1E
```

### LSP Mismatch: Receiver Has the Latest Information

If the receiver has the latest information, it does not transmit a PSNP. The receiver transmits the LSP packet with the latest information in it. Upon receipt, the designated router updates its Link State database and includes the new information in its next CSNP transmission.

### Dealing with Duplicate LSPs

At times, a router may have a copy of an LSP in its database and receive another copy of the same LSP from another router. For example, if a sequence number packet arrives from a router's neighbor, it must be examined to see if it has newer LSP entry information. Figure 11.29 illustrates the process of determining which is a newer LSP.

*Determining which of two
LSPs is newer*

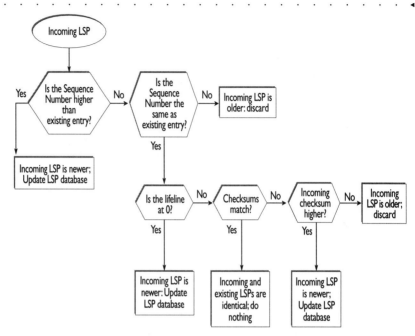

There is a preference-of-checksums rule that is used to determine which LSP is newer if they match in all other respects.

### Expired LSPs

By default, an LSP is regenerated and flooded once every 7,200 seconds (two hours). Each LSP contains a remaining lifetime field that indicates how long this particular LSP should be retained (in seconds) before timing out. For example, in the LSP shown in Figure 11.30, the remaining lifetime of this LSP is 7,499 seconds.

▶ · · · · · · · · · · · · · · · · · · · · · · · · · · · · · · · · ◀

F I G U R E   11.30

*The remaining lifetime of
this LSP is 7,499 seconds.*

```
Packet Number : 158              1:42:35 PM

Length : 154 bytes

802.3: ==================== IEEE 802.3 Datalink Layer
====================

        Station: MPR1 ——> Broadcast

        Length: 136

802.2: ================ IEEE 802.2 Logical Link Control
================

        SSAP: NetWare      DSAP: NetWare

        Unnumbered Command: Unnumbered Information (UI)

  ipx: =================== Internetwork Packet Exchange
=================

        Checksum: 0xFFFF

        Length: 133

        Hop Count:  0

        Packet Type: 0(Unknown)

        Network: BA 5E BA 11          --> 00 00 00 00

        Node:    00-40-05-3A-7A-68   --> FF-FF-FF-FF-FF-FF

        Socket:  NLSP                 --> NLSP

 nlsp: ================= NetWare Link Services Protocol
================

        Protocol ID:  0x83
```

*(continued)*

▶ · · · · · · · · · · · · · · · · · · · · · · · · · · · · · · · ◀

F I G U R E    11.30

*(continued)*

```
Fixed Length:  27

Version:  1

Reserved:  0x00

Packet Type:  18 - Level 1 Link State Packet

Version:  1

Reserved:  0x00

Reserved:  0x00

Packet Length:  103

Lifetime:  7499

LSP ID:  0x0200001111110000

Sequence Number:  2

Checksum:  0xC355

Partition Repair:  Not supported

Default Metric:  Not supported

Delay Metric:  Not supported

Expense Metric:  Not supported

Error Metric:  Not supported

Overload:  No

Router Type:  Level 1

Area Address Mask Option:

     Code:  0xC0

     Length:  8
```

```
        Address:  0x00000000    Mask:  0x00000000
Management Information Option:

        Code:  0xC1

        Length:  16

        Internal Network Number:  0x00111111

        Internal Node Number:  0x000000000001

        IPX Version: 1

        Server Name Length: 4

        Server Name:  MPR1

Link Option:

        Code:  0xC2

        Length:  25

        Default Metric:  20 (internal)

        Delay Metric:  (not supported)

        External Metric:  (not supported)

        Error Metric:  (not supported)

        Neighbor ID:  0x02000022222201

        Packet Size:  1496

        Delay:  200

        Throughput:  10000000

        Media Type:  0x0003 - Ethernet

Services Information Option:

        Code:  0xC3
```

*(continued)*

▶ · · · · · · · · · · · · · · · · · · · · · · · · · · · · · · · · · · ◀

**FIGURE   11.30**

*(continued)*

```
                    Length:   19

                    Hop Count:  0 (internal)

                    Network Number:  0x00111111

                    Node ID:  0x000000000001

                    Socket:  0x0451

                    Type:  0x0004

                    Service Name:  MPR1
```

As LSPs are flooded through the network, the remaining lifetime field is decremented by the holding time (or at least one).

Once an LSP has expired (the remaining lifetime of the LSP in memory reaches zero), the router must:

**1** •   Retain only the LSP header (fixed-length fields) and change the lifetime field to zero.

**2** •   Update the packet length and checksum fields to reflect changes previously listed.

**3** •   Record the time when the lifetime became zero.

**4** •   Purge the LSP header from the database when *zeroAgeLifetime* has been reached after the lifetime had expired. The zeroAgeLifetime default value is 60 seconds.

To easily see the lifetime values counting down, check out the CSNP packets on the wire. The remaining lifetime field decrements by the exact interval between CSNP transmissions. For example, Table 11.2 lists the remaining lifetime values detected on five sequential CSNP packets that reported our lab network LSP entries.

| TABLE 11.2 | REMAINING LIFETIME FIELD VALUES (IN SECONDS) | | | |
| --- | --- | --- | --- | --- |
| | | LSP A | LSP B | LSP C | LSP D |
| *The remaining lifetime field values decrease by the interval between CSNP packets.* | CSNP 1 at 1:48:16 P.M. | 7199 | 7166 | 6285 | 7151 |
| | CSNP 2 at 1:48:44 P.M. | 7171 | 7138 | 6257 | 7123 |
| | CSNP 3 at 1:49:11 P.M. | 7144 | 7111 | 6230 | 7096 |
| | CSNP 4 at 1:49:37 P.M. | 7117 | 7084 | 6203 | 7069 |
| | CSNP 5 at 1:50:04 P.M. | 7090 | 7057 | 6176 | 7042 |

When a newer version of an LSP is sent by the originator (every two hours by default), the sequence number is incremented by one to indicate that this is a new LSP. By looking at the sequence number field of an LSP, you can get the approximate age of a network.

## AGGREGATED ROUTES

Now that we've seen the normal operation of NLSP, let's examine *aggregated routes,* a process of combining a group of networks into a single grouping or area to speed up routing process and reduce NLSP overhead on larger internetworks. To define a group of networks in a single area, simply indicate the area mask for a group of addresses.

For example, consider an internetwork that supports five networks with the following addresses:

        0xCC-39-01-01
        0xCC-39-02-02
        0xCC-39-03-03
        0xCC-45-11-12
        0xCC-45-11-13

Three of the networks (0xCC-39-01-01, 0xCC-39-02-02, and 0xCC-39-03-03) reside in the same building, as shown in Figure 11.31.

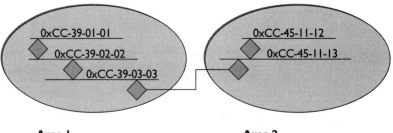

*A network mask enables you to specify a group of addresses.*

**Area 1**
Address 0xCC-39-00-00
Netmask: 0xFF-FF-00-00

**Area 2**
Address 0xCC-45-11-00
Netmask: 0xFF-FF-FF-00

Aggregated routes can be defined as a combination of network mask and network address, or by a single leading byte that indicates the length of the network mask in leading bits. For example, "16, 0xCC-39-00-00" indicates that the network mask is 16 bits (two bytes) long (0xFF-FF-00-00).

**For more information on aggregated routes, refer to the NLSP specification (NLSP.EXE) located on Novell's Web site,** www.novell.com.

**TIP**

## Changing NLSP Operating Parameters

You can adjust the way that NLSP operates through INETCFG, the Internetwork Configuration screen for the console (LOAD INETCFG). Some of the parameters are global for the NLSP router. Other settings are applied to a particular interface individually. The following subsections provide a brief description of each configuration option.

### HOP COUNT LIMIT

NLSP defaults to a maximum hop count of 64. This hop count can be increased to 127, if desired. If RIP routers exist anywhere along the path, however, they allow a maximum hop count of 15 to all services and networks.

## MAXIMUM NUMBER OF PATH SPLITS

In the case of two or more equal cost routes, this setting defines how many routes should be considered in load balancing. The default is 1, and possible parameters are 1 to 8.

## LSP SIZE

This parameter defines the size of LSP packets in bytes. The default is 512 bytes, but the possible values for this setting range from 128 bytes to 4,096 bytes.

## NLSP LOCAL AREA ADDRESS

This setting allows you to specify up to three local area addresses (IPX network number and mask), enabling you to filter out RIP routes that do not match the address-mask pairs.

## OVERRIDE NLSP SYSTEM ID

The NLSP system ID is automatically assigned. You can change the NLSP system ID to another number, but keep in mind that it must be a unique system ID internetwork-wide.

## NLSP CONVERGENCE RATE

The *convergence rate* determines how fast NLSP information is processed. The default parameters are shown in Figure 11.32. You can set this to fast or manually configure individual parameters to change the convergence rates automatically, but it is recommended that you keep the NLSP convergence rate at the default setting. Figure 11.33 shows the settings for fast convergence.

## NLSP STATE <PER BINDING>

You can change the way NLSP is handled on individual bindings, or circuits, on a server or router. For example, perhaps your server is connected to two networks, and it should only communicate using NLSP on one interface and use only RIP on the other interface.

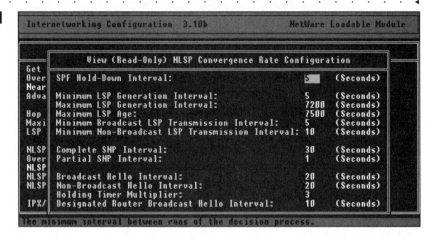

**FIGURE 11.32**

*Typical networks can operate well at the default convergence rate.*

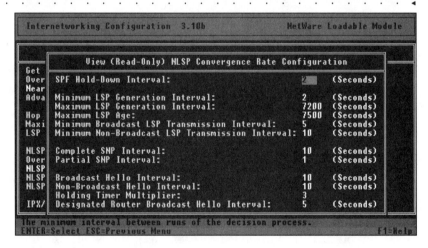

**FIGURE 11.33**

*The fast convergence rate increases the number of packets and processing requirements on the network.*

There are three NLSP states possible, "on," "off," and "auto." The default is "auto." The states have the following functions:

▸ **On:** Absorb and generate RIP packets on that link.

▸ **Off:** Do not absorb or generate RIP packets on a link.

▶ **Auto:** If a RIP router is detected on a link, generate and absorb RIP packets; otherwise, do not absorb or generate RIP packets on the link.

## MAC CHANNEL <PER BINDING>

Link state packets can be sent to either the broadcast address (0xFF-FF-FF-FF-FF-FF) or the NLSP multicast address, if desired. By default, NLSP uses multicast addressing for its communications, but it can automatically switch to broadcast if another NLSP router comes up using broadcast. The NLSP multicast addresses are:

| | |
|---|---|
| IEEE 802.3 | 0x09-00-1B-FF-FF-FF |
| IEEE 802.5 | 0xC0-00-10-00-00-00 |
| FDDI | 0X09-00-1B-FF-FF-FF |

## MTU OVERRIDE <PER BINDING>

The default for the maximum transmission unit (or packet size) override setting is not to override the maximum packet size of a LAN board. This parameter can be adjusted from 576 to 65,535 bytes.

You can adjust this parameter if you have a bridge or other device on your LAN or if you want to send smaller packets across a WAN.

## PRIORITY <PER BINDING>

This is the priority for becoming the designated router. The default value is 44, and possible values are 0 to 127. Increase this value to force a system to become the designated router.

## COST OVERRIDE <PER BINDING>

NLSP routers can determine a cost based on the link throughput. You can override the value to force a specific route if desired. The possible values for this parameter are 0–63.

## PACE OVERRIDE <PER BINDING>

This pace indicates how many routing packets can be sent in a single second from a specific port. This parameter can be changed from 1 to 1,000. The default value is based on the circuit's throughput in bits per second with a minimum of 1.

For example, on a 19,200 bps link, the following calculation determines the pace:

```
paceRate =  MAX [ 1, (19,200/10,000) ]
```

The "paceRate" equals 1.92.

A minimum gap of $1/18$ second between LSPs keeps the flooding process from overloading other devices on the network. This rule indicates that the pacing on a faster network (such as 10 Mbps Ethernet) is actually 18 packets per second.

Next, we'll look at how NLSP backward compatibility and RIP/SAP interoperability work.

# NLSP and RIP/SAP Interoperability

Even in the current implementation of NLSP, routers must still understand RIP and SAP communications to provide client interoperability and backward compatibility. In this section, we'll examine how NLSP routers use RIP/SAP to communicate with clients and to coexist with older RIP/SAP-based routers.

When your server/router is brought up as an NLSP router, "'RIP/SAP compatibility" is on. This means that the NLSP routers still use Novell's RIP and SAP protocols in the following instances:

▸ To reply to client RIP or SAP lookups

▸ To absorb SAP information for services available on the local router itself

▸ To automatically send RIP/SAP information to other RIP/SAP-only routers

**At this time, NetWare clients do not use NLSP to look up services on a network. Therefore, NLSP routers must reply to specific RIP requests if they know how to get to a network and consider themselves part of the best route.**

NOTE

## SENDING AND RECEIVING RIP INFORMATION

What if your NLSP router exists on a network that also supports one or more RIP routers? NLSP routers are very intelligent and incredibly flexible when it comes to mixing and matching routing protocols.

If an NLSP router notices that a RIP router is broadcasting RIP information on the local circuit, the NLSP router automatically begins sending RIP information to the RIP router in order to maintain backward compatibility. For example, in Figure 11.34, we have changed MPR1 into a RIP-only router.

▶ . . . . . . . . . . . . . . . . . . . . . . . . . . . . . . . . . . ◀

F I G U R E    11.34

*RIP and NLSP routers can coexist on the same network.*

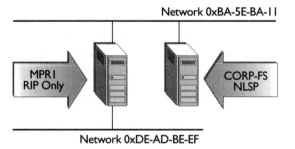

Network 0xBA-5E-BA-11

MPR1
RIP Only

CORP-FS
NLSP

Network 0xDE-AD-BE-EF

When an NLSP router learns of a network through RIP, the router absorbs the RIP information as an "Xroute" or external route. An Xroute indicates the distance to a particular network in hops and ticks.

This Xroute information is stored in the NLSP router's Link State database. Only the designated router includes Xroute information in its LSPs sent on a network. For example, Figure 11.35 is an LSP sent from CORP-FS that includes Xroute information for networks 0x00-11-11-11 and 0xDE-AD-BE-EF.

*Xroute LSPs are only sent
by the designated routers.*

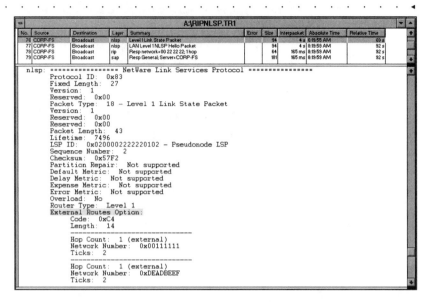

NLSP routers automatically start sending RIP and SAP periodic update packets when they detect a RIP router on a common network. By default, they send update packets every 60 seconds, but this can be configured through INETCFG.

Figure 11.36 illustrates the Xroutes as leaf nodes off the pseudonode LSP in our link state graph.

*Xroutes are considered
leaves off existing LSP
nodes.*

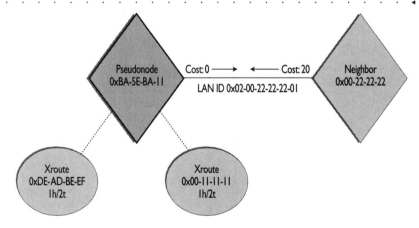

## FORWARDING PACKETS ON A MIXED NETWORK

When forwarding packets through a network that consists of NLSP and RIP routes, the NLSP router must follow these rules:

▸ Use an NLSP route to a destination if one exists.

▸ Use the RIP portion of the route only; if more than one route exists, use the lowest tick route.

▸ If more than one route exists and the tick count is equal, use the lowest hop route.

▸ If ticks and hops are equal, either route can be used.

For example, in Figure 11.37, two routes exist from network A to network F. NLSP Router 1 sees that both pseudonodes E and G are connected to network F. The NLSP router first considers the tick count between the two pseudonodes— both tick counts are equal. Then NLSP Router 1 considers the hop count—again they are equal. Finally, it considers the NLSP paths from A to G and A to E as the tiebreaker.

The NLSP path through NLSP routers 1 and 7 costs 20. This is the lowest NLSP path cost and the best way to go.

## SENDING AND RECEIVING SAP INFORMATION

When an NLSP router hears SAP information, it absorbs the data into its Link State database and begins sending periodic SAP update packets (every 60 seconds by default).

NLSP routers also propagate SAP information through LSP packets, as shown in Figure 11.38. LSP 0x02-00-00-11-11-11-01-01 indicates that two services are available on network 0x00-11-11-11, a directory server in TREE1 and a file server named MPR1.

FIGURE 11.37

*An internetwork that consists of NLSP and RIP routers*

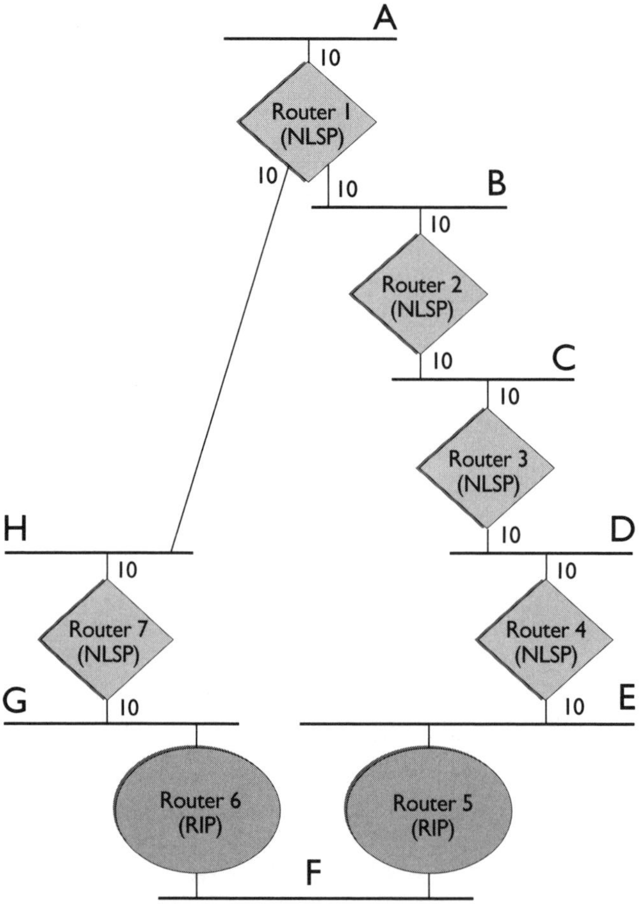

As you can see by the LSP in Figure 11.38, SAP information is linked to the network that it resides on. If the LSP router does not know a route to a network, it will not send SAP information for any services on that network. In Figure 11.39, we can see how SAP information for MPR1 and CORP-FS is linked to the route information.

*SAP information is propagated in SAP and LSP packets.*

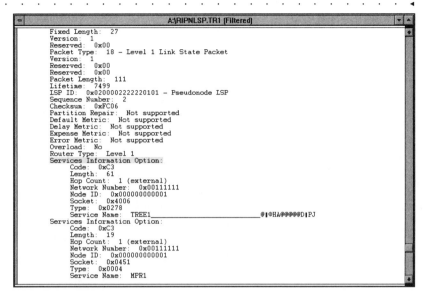

```
┌──────────────────────── A:\RIPNLSP.TR1 [Filtered] ──────────────────────────┐
     Fixed Length:   27
     Version:  1
     Reserved:  0x00
     Packet Type:  18 - Level 1 Link State Packet
     Version:  1
     Reserved:  0x00
     Reserved:  0x00
     Packet Length:  111
     Lifetime:  7499
     LSP ID:  0x0200002222220101 - Pseudonode LSP
     Sequence Number:  2
     Checksum:  0xFC06
     Partition Repair:  Not supported
     Default Metric:  Not supported
     Delay Metric:  Not supported
     Expense Metric:  Not supported
     Error Metric:  Not supported
     Overload:  No
     Router Type:  Level 1
     Services Information Option:
          Code:  0xC3
          Length:  61
          Hop Count:  1 (external)
          Network Number:  0x00111111
          Node ID:  0x000000000001
          Socket:  0x4006
          Type:  0x0278
          Service Name:  TREE1_____@¦@HA@@@@D¦PJ
     Services Information Option:
          Code:  0xC3
          Length:  19
          Hop Count:  1 (external)
          Network Number:  0x00111111
          Node ID:  0x000000000001
          Socket:  0x0451
          Type:  0x0004
          Service Name:  MPR1
```

*Service information is linked to the network it resides on.*

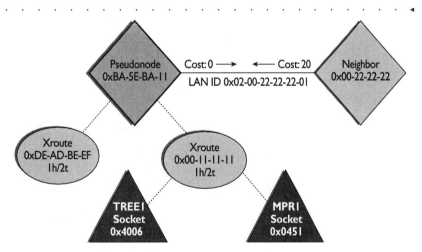

## BUILDING AND MANAGING A RIP ROUTE THROUGH LINK STATE INFORMATION

When an NLSP router detects a RIP network on one side and an NLSP network on the other side, it must convert the Link State database entries into a form usable in its RIP broadcast packets. In order to make this translation, the NLSP router must assign a hop and tick count to the LSP entry. You can disable the RIP participation on a circuit to completely disable this feature, if desired, but you cannot filter specific information from passing through a link state network inside of link state packets. Let's examine how RIP/LSP integration is performed and managed.

### Attaching a Hop Count to an LSP Entry

The hop count is determined as part of the decision process. Each time the decision process is run, NLSP routers determine the number of hops to a destination network. This information will be used as the hop count in the RIP and SAP packets sent onto the RIP-based network.

### Attaching a Tick Count to an LSP Entry

The tick count is a bit more tricky. Each time an LSP is received by an NLSP router, a tick count is automatically determined based on the NLSP delay and throughput values in the LSP packet.

The following calculation is used for a LAN:

```
MAX [ 1, (576 x 8 x 18 / Throughput) + (delay x 18 / 1,000,000) ]
```

The following calculation is used for a WAN:

```
MAX [ 1, (576 x 64 x 18 / Throughput) + (2 x delay x 18 / 1,000,000) ]
```

The tick and hop counts are calculated for and associated with each link.

Let's take an LSP packet and figure out the tick count based on the delay and throughput values provided. Consider Figure 11.40.

*The delay and throughput values will be used to determine the tick count for the LAN.*

```
                                        A:\NLSP.TR1
No.  Source      Destination   Layer  Summary                    Error  Size  Interpacket  Absolute Time  Relative Time
  7  CORP-FS     Broadcast     nlsp   Level 1 Link State Packet           160   440 ms      1:27:39 PM         18 s
        Lifetime:  7499
        LSP ID:  0x0200002222220000
        Sequence Number:  3
        Checksum:  0x8737
        Partition Repair:  Not supported
        Default Metric:  Not supported
        Delay Metric:  Not supported
        Expense Metric:  Not supported
        Error Metric:  Not supported
        Overload:  No
        Router Type:  Level 1
        Area Address Mask Option:
             Code:  0xC0
             Length:  8
             Address:  0x00000000    Mask:  0x00000000
        Management Information Option:
             Code:  0xC1
             Length:  19
             Internal Network Number:  0x00222222
             Internal Node Number:  0x000000000001
             IPX Version:  1
             Server Name Length:  7
             Server Name:  CORP-FS
        Link Option:
             Code:  0xC2
             Length:  25
             Default Metric:  20 (internal)
             Delay Metric:  (not supported)
             External Metric:  (not supported)
             Error Metric:  (not supported)
             Neighbor ID:  0x02000022222201
             Packet Size:  1497
             Delay:  200
             Throughput:  10000000
             Media Type:  0x0003 - Ethernet
```

The following calculation can be used now:

```
MAX [ 1, (576 x 8 x 18 / 10,000,000) + (200 x 18 / 10,000,000) ]
```

The result of this calculation is the higher of 1 or 0 (0.0 + 0.0). We must use the tick value of 1 for this LAN. Of course, lower-throughput networks may have a higher tick count (and lower throughput) to ensure that the best route is based on actual performance.

### Filtering Issues

As you may know, you can configure RIP and SAP filtering to cut down on broadcast traffic on RIP-based networks. You cannot, however, filter out this information through NLSP. If a RIP network or SAP service is learned from an NLSP network, the RIP/SAP information is propagated through LSPs.

### Disabling RIP and SAP on a Link

By default, an NLSP router will stop sending RIP and SAP information on a link after it stops hearing RIP and SAP broadcasts from other routers. The NLSP router waits until the RIP and SAP entries have timed out of its tables and then disables the RIP and SAP state.

If desired, you can manually force RIP and SAP participation to stop by changing the RIP and SAP state of the NLSP router to "off."

◄ · · · · · · · · · · · · · · · · · · · · · · · · · · · · · · · · · ◄

# NLSP Packet Structures

NLSP uses four basic packet structures: hello, LSP, CSNP, and PSNP, as discussed earlier in this chapter. The most complex packet structures are the hello packets and the LSP packets. (CSNP and PSNP are just summary packets, as seen earlier in this chapter.)

**Many analyzers still do not decode NLSP communications properly. Use this section as a reference for doing your own decodes and interpretations of NLSP communications.**

NOTE

### LAN HELLO PACKET STRUCTURE

LAN hello packets include a fixed-length portion and a variable-length portion. The fixed-length fields of the LAN hello packet structure are shown in Figure 11.41.

#### Fixed-Length Fields

The fixed-length fields cover the protocol ID field through the LAN ID field. This portion of the NLSP header is 27 bytes long.

#### Protocol ID (1 Byte)

The value 0x83 indicates the NLSP routing layer.

#### Length Indicator (1 Byte)

The length indicator is the byte count in the fixed-length portion of the header (up to and including the LAN ID field).

#### Minor Version (1 Byte)

The value 0x01 indicates a Level-1 NLSP router. The value 0x02 indicates that this router supports aggregated routes.

FIGURE 11.41

*The fixed-length fields of the LAN hello packet*

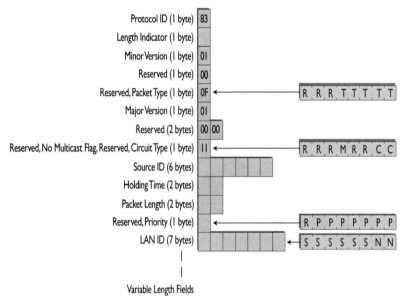

Variable Length Fields

### Reserved (1 Byte)
Set to 0x00; ignored.

### Reserved (3 Bits)
Set to 000 (binary); ignored. Denoted "R" in Figure 11.42.

### Packet Type (5 Bits)
The value 0x0F (15 decimal) indicates a LAN hello packet. The value of this field is 01111 (binary). When combined with the three-bit reserved field preceding it, the entire byte value is 0x0F or 00001111 (binary). Denoted "T" in Figure 11.42.

**Refer to the hex-decimal-binary conversion chart in Appendix A.**

**X-REF**

### Major Version (1 Byte)

NLSP is currently at version 1.1. The major version identifier indicates the number before the decimal point. 0x01 indicates that this router supports NLSP v1.*x* (with *x* denoting the minor version number specified later in this NLSP header).

### Reserved (2 Bytes)

Set to 0x00-00; ignored.

### Reserved (3 Bits)

Set to 000 (binary); ignored. Denoted "R" in Figure 11.41.

### No Multicast Flag (1 Bit)

The value 1 (binary) indicates that the sender cannot receive traffic addressed to a multicast address; future NLSP packets on this LAN must be sent to the broadcast address. The value 0 (binary) indicates that the sender can accept and transmit NLSP multicast packets. Denoted "M" in Figure 11.41.

### Reserved (2 Bits)

Set to 00 (binary); ignored.

### Circuit Type (2 Bits)

This field indicates the sending NLSP router type. The following values are valid:

| | |
|---|---|
| 0 | Reserved; ignore entire packet (00 binary) |
| 1 | Level-1 routing only (01 binary) |
| 2 | Level-2 routing only—link used for Level-2 routing only (10 binary) |
| 3 | Level 1 and Level 2—link used for Level-1 and Level-2 routing (11 binary) |

Denoted "C" in Figure 11.41.

### Source ID (6 Bytes)

The system ID of the sending router.

### Holding Time (2 Bytes)

The holding timer (in seconds) for the sending router. This value indicates the amount of time that the sending router information should be kept before timing out the entry. Designated routers send a holding time of 30 seconds (defined by a broadcast interval of 10 seconds and a holding timer multiplier of 3). Other neighboring routers indicate a holding time of 60 by default (defined by a broadcast interval of 20 seconds and a holding timer multiplier of 3).

### Packet Length (2 Bytes)

The entire length of this NLSP data including the NLSP header fixed fields and the NLSP variable-length fields. Add the IPX header (fixed 30 bytes) and data link header to determine the entire packet length.

### Reserved (1 Bit)

Set to 0 (binary); ignored. Denoted "R" in Figure 11.41.

### Priority (7 Bits)

The priority for being the designated router. The value 0x2C in this field, 010-1100 binary, converts to the decimal value 44. The value 100-0000 binary converts to the decimal value 64. The highest possible priority is 127 decimal or 111-1111 binary. Denoted "P" in Figure 11.41.

### LAN ID (7 Bytes)

A field that is composed of the system ID (6 bytes) of the designated router followed by a pseudonode ID bytes assigned by that designated router. This field is copied directly from the designated router's hello packet.

The system ID portion is denoted "S" in Figure 11.41. The pseudonode ID portion is denoted "N" in Figure 11.41.

### Variable-Length Fields

As shown in Figure 11.42, variable-length fields follow the LAN ID field and have a common three-part form that includes:

- Code

- Length

- Value

*Variable-length fields of the LAN hello packet*

Fixed-Length Fields

Code (1 byte)
Length (1 byte)
Value (length)

The code field indicates whether this packet includes an area address, neighbors, or the local packet size (MTU) information. The length and value fields are dependent on the code field value. The following code field values are defined:

| | |
|---|---|
| 0xC0 | Area addresses |
| 0x06 | Neighbors |
| 0xC5 | Local MTU |

### Area Addresses

This field is required and contains up to three manual area addresses of the sending router. The manual area addresses consist of a 4-byte network address and a 4-byte network mask, as shown in Figure 11.43.

*The area address field set is required in all LAN hello packets.*

Fixed-Length Fields

Code (1 byte)     C0
Length (1 byte)   18  ◄──────── 0x08, 0x10 or 0x18
Address (4 bytes)
Mask (4 bytes)    } Set 1
Address (4 bytes)
Mask (4 bytes)    } Set 2
Address (4 bytes)
Mask (4 bytes)    } Set 3

The length of the area address field set is 8, 16, or 24 (0x08, 0x10, or 0x18, respectively, in hexadecimal).

### Neighbors

This in an optional field and only contains entries if this router has seen LAN hello packets from NLSP neighboring routers on this circuit. The entries include the network interface card (NIC) address of the neighboring router, as shown in Figure 11.44.

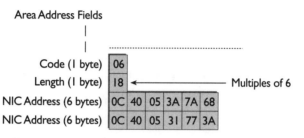

**FIGURE 11.44**

*The neighbors field contains the NIC addresses of all adjacent NLSP routers on this circuit.*

The length of the neighbors field set is a multiple of six. If there are too many neighboring routers to fit in the LAN hello packet, the router sends as many as will fit and logs an NLSP event called "tooManyAdjacencies." On an Ethernet network that supports 1,518-byte packets, a LAN hello packet can contain up to 233 entries.

### Local MTU

This is a required field and defines how large a packet the sender can transmit, as shown in Figure 11.45. The value includes the IPX header, but not the data link header.

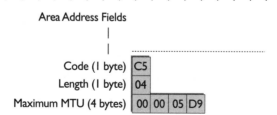

**FIGURE 11.45**

*The local MTU field is required in all LAN hello packets.*

## WAN HELLO PACKET STRUCTURE

WAN hello packets also include a fixed-length portion and a variable-length portion. The fixed-length fields of the WAN hello packet structure are shown in Figure 11.46.

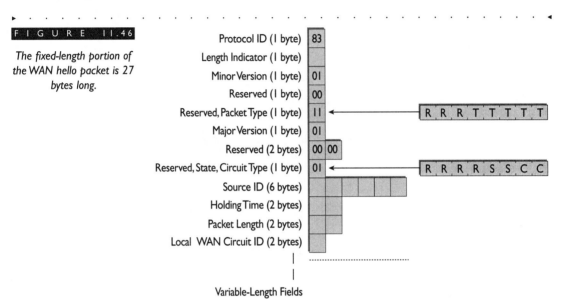

**FIGURE 11.46**

*The fixed-length portion of the WAN hello packet is 27 bytes long.*

| Protocol ID (1 byte) | 83 |
| Length Indicator (1 byte) | |
| Minor Version (1 byte) | 01 |
| Reserved (1 byte) | 00 |
| Reserved, Packet Type (1 byte) | 11 |
| Major Version (1 byte) | 01 |
| Reserved (2 bytes) | 00 00 |
| Reserved, State, Circuit Type (1 byte) | 01 |
| Source ID (6 bytes) | |
| Holding Time (2 bytes) | |
| Packet Length (2 bytes) | |
| Local WAN Circuit ID (2 bytes) | |

R R R T T T T T

R R R R S S C C

Variable-Length Fields

### Fixed-Length Fields

The fixed-length fields cover the protocol ID field through the local WAN circuit ID field. This portion of the NLSP header is 27 bytes long.

### Protocol ID (1 Byte)

The value 0x83 indicates the NLSP routing layer.

### Length Indicator (1 Byte)

This is the byte count in the fixed-length portion of the header (up to and including the WAN circuit ID field).

### Minor Version (1 Byte)

The value 0x01 indicates a Level-1 NLSP router. The value 0x02 indicates that this router supports aggregated routes.

### Reserved (I Byte)

Set to 0x00; ignored.

### Reserved (3 Bits)

Set to 000 (binary); ignored. Denoted "R" in Figure 11.46.

### Packet Type (5 Bits)

The value 0x11 (17 decimal) indicates a WAN hello packet. The value of this field is 01001 (binary). When it is combined with the three-bit reserved field preceding it, the entire byte value is 0x11 or 00010001 (binary). Denoted "T" in Figure 11.46.

**X-REF**     **Refer to the hex-decimal-binary conversion chart in Appendix A.**

### Major Version (I Byte)

NLSP is currently at version 1.1. The major version identifier indicates the number before the decimal point. 0x01 indicates that this router supports NLSP v1.*x* (with *x* denoting the minor version number specified later in this NLSP header).

### Reserved (2 Bytes)

Set to 0x00-00; ignored.

### Reserved (4 Bits)

Set to 0000 (binary); ignored. Denoted "R" in Figure 11.46.

### State (2 Bits)

This field indicates the sending router's state on this link:

| | |
|---|---|
| 0 | Up (00 binary) |
| 1 | Initializing (01 binary) |
| 2 | Down (10 binary) |

### Circuit Type (2 Bits)

This field indicates the sending NLSP router type. The following values are valid:

| | |
|---|---|
| 0 | Reserved; ignore entire packet (00 binary) |
| 1 | Level-1 routing only (01 binary) |

2      Level-2 routing only—link used for Level-2 routing only (10 binary)

3      Level 1 and Level 2—link used for Level-1 and Level-2 routing (11 binary)

Denoted "C" in Figure 11.46.

### Source ID (6 Bytes)

This is the system ID of the sending router.

### Holding Time (2 Bytes)

This is the holding timer (in seconds) for the sending router. This value indicates the amount of time that the sending router information should be kept before timing out the entry. Designated routers send a holding time of 30 seconds (defined by a broadcast interval of 10 seconds and a holding timer multiplier of 3). Other neighboring routers indicate a holding time of 60 by default (defined by a broadcast interval of 20 seconds and a holding timer multiplier of 3).

### Packet Length (2 Bytes)

The entire length of this NLSP data including the NLSP header fixed fields and the NLSP variable-length fields. Add the IPX header (fixed 30 bytes) and data link header to determine the entire packet length.

### Local WAN Circuit ID (1 Byte)

This is a unique identifier assigned to this circuit when it is created by the router.

### Variable-Length Fields

The variable-length fields follow the local WAN circuit ID field (Figure 11.47) and have a common three-part form that includes:

▸ Code

▸ Length

▸ Value

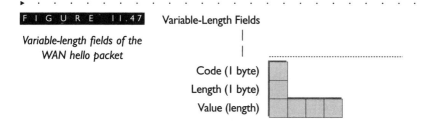

**FIGURE 11.47**

*Variable-length fields of the WAN hello packet*

Variable-Length Fields

Code (1 byte)
Length (1 byte)
Value (length)

The code field indicates whether this packet includes an area address, neighbors, or the local packet size (MTU) information. The length and value fields are dependent on the code field value. The following code field values are defined:

0xC0    Area addresses
0xC5    Local MTU

### Area Addresses

This field is required and contains up to three manual area addresses of the sending router. The manual area addresses consist of a 4-byte network address and a four-byte network mask, as shown in Figure 11.48.

**FIGURE 11.48**

*The area address field set is required in all WAN hello packets.*

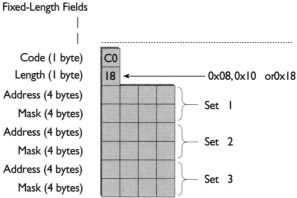

Fixed-Length Fields

Code (1 byte)        C0
Length (1 byte)      18    ← 0x08, 0x10  or 0x18
Address (4 bytes)
Mask (4 bytes)              Set 1
Address (4 bytes)
Mask (4 bytes)              Set 2
Address (4 bytes)
Mask (4 bytes)              Set 3

The length of the area address field set is either 8, 16, or 24 (0x08, 0x10, or 0x18, respectively, in hexadecimal).

### Local MTU

This is a required field and defines how large a packet the sender can transmit, as shown in Figure 11.49. The value includes the IPX header, but not the data link header.

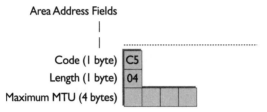

*The local MTU field is required in all WAN hello packets.*

Area Address Fields

Code (I byte)  C5
Length (I byte)  04
Maximum MTU (4 bytes)

## LSP PACKET STRUCTURE

Link state packets consist of fixed-length fields, as shown in Figure 11.50, and variable-length fields.

### Fixed-Length Fields

The fixed-length fields begin with the protocol ID field and continue to the router type bits.

### Protocol ID (I Byte)

The value 0x83 indicates the NLSP routing layer.

### Length Indicator (I Byte)

This is the byte count in the fixed-length portion of the header (up to and including the router type field).

### Minor Version (I Byte)

The value 0x01 indicates a Level-1 NLSP router. The value 0x02 indicates that this router supports aggregated routes.

### Reserved (I Byte)

Set to 0x00; ignored.

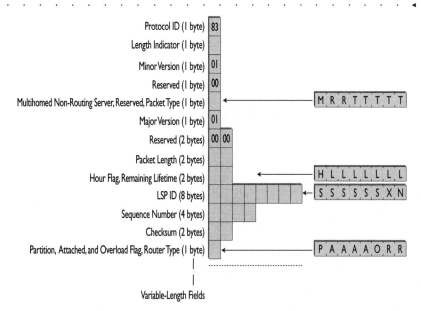

FIGURE 11.50

*LSP packets consist of fixed-length fields and variable-length fields.*

### Multihomed Non-routing Server (1 Bit)

A "1" in this bit position indicates that this server contains more than one interface but does not forward traffic from one network to another. Denoted "M" in Figure 11.50.

### Reserved (2 Bits)

Set to 0; ignored.

### Packet Type (5 Bits)

The value 0x12 (18 decimal) indicates that this is an LSP packet. The value of this field is 01010 (binary). When it is combined with the three-bit reserved field preceding it, the entire byte value is 0x12 or 00010010 (binary). Denoted "T" in Figure 11.50.

**Refer to the hex-decimal-binary conversion chart in Appendix A.**

X-REF

### Major Version (1 Byte)

NLSP is currently at version 1.1. The major version identifier indicates the number before the decimal point. 0x01 indicates that this router supports NLSP v1.*x* (with *x* denoting the minor version number specified later in this NLSP header).

### Reserved (2 Bytes)

Set to 0x00-00; ignored.

### Packet Length (2 Bytes)

The entire length of this NLSP data including the NLSP header fixed fields and the NLSP variable-length fields. Add the IPX header (fixed 30 bytes) and data link header to determine the entire packet length.

### Hour Flag (1 Bit)

When this bit is set to 1, the remaining lifetime field indicates the number of hours before this LSP expires. If this field is set to 0, the value in the remaining lifetime field indicates the number of seconds before this LSP expires.

### Remaining Lifetime (1 Byte 7 Bits)

This is the number of seconds (or hours, if the hour flag is set to 1) until this LSP expires.

### LSP ID (8 Bytes)

This is a three-part field that contains a source ID, a pseudonode ID, and an LSP number.

**Source ID (6 Bytes)**   The source ID is the system ID of the router that originated the LSP. Designated "S" in Figure 11.50.

**Pseudonode ID (1 Byte)**   If this is a pseudonode LSP, this 1-byte field is a unique number for this system ID. If this is not a pseudonode LSP, this field must contain the value 0x00. Designated "X" in Figure 11.50.

**LSP Number (1 Byte)**   If an LSP is too large to send, the source breaks it up into fragments. This field indicates the number of the LSP fragment. Designated "N" in Figure 11.50.

### Sequence Number (4 Bytes)

This number indicates the sequence of the LSP. A higher sequence number indicates a more recent version of an LSP.

### Checksum (2 Bytes)

This is the checksum of this LSP from the source ID field to the end of the LSP data.

### Partition Flag (1 Bit)

Set at 0, this bit indicates that the router does not support partition repair. Designated "P" in Figure 11.50.

### Attached Flag (4 Bits)

This indicates if this router can reach other routing areas. 0 indicates that this router cannot reach other areas; 1 indicates that this router can reach other areas. Designated "A" in Figure 11.50.

### LSP Database Overload Flag (1 Bit)

This bit, when set to 1, indicates that the local router's LSP database is overloaded. When this condition occurs, the local router floods its own LSP with the overload flag set to 1. Designated "O" in Figure 11.50.

### Router Type (2 Bits)

This field indicates whether this is a Level-1 router or a Level-2 router. A Level-2 router is typically an "exit" router that connects to other network areas. Designated "R" in Figure 11.50.

### Variable-Length Fields

The variable-length fields include options that have a three-part form that includes code, length, and value. The possible options include:

| | |
|---|---|
| Code 0xC0 | Area addresses |
| Code 0xC1 | Management information |
| Code 0xC2 | Link information |
| Code 0xC3 | Services information |
| Code 0xC4 | External routes |

These variable-length fields follow the fixed-length fields, as shown in Figure 11.51.

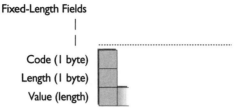

**FIGURE 11.51**

*The variable-length fields include code, length, and value fields.*

Fixed-Length Fields

Code (1 byte)
Length (1 byte)
Value (length)

## Area Addresses

This field is seen in all LSPs except the pseudonode LSP; it contains up to three manual area addresses of the sending router. The manual area addresses consist of a 4-byte network address and a 4-byte network mask, as shown in Figure 11.52.

**FIGURE 11.52**

*The area address field set is seen in all LSPs except the pseudonode LSP.*

Fixed-Length Fields

Code (1 byte) — C0
Length (1 byte) — 18 ← 0x08, 0x10 or 0x18
Address (4 bytes)
Mask (4 bytes) — Set 1
Address (4 bytes)
Mask (4 bytes) — Set 2
Address (4 bytes)
Mask (4 bytes) — Set 3

The length of the area address field set is either 8, 16, or 24 (0x08, 0x10, or 0x18, respectively, in hexadecimal).

## Management Information

This field contains information about the router that is sending the LSP. The Management Information option, shown in Figure 11.53, contains the following fields:

▸ Network number

▸ Node number

▸ IPX version number

▸ Name length

▸ Router/server name

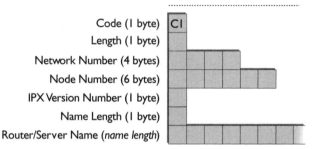

**FIGURE 11.53**

*The management information fields contain information about the sending router.*

Code (1 byte)
Length (1 byte)
Network Number (4 bytes)
Node Number (6 bytes)
IPX Version Number (1 byte)
Name Length (1 byte)
Router/Server Name (*name length*)

**Network Number (4 Bytes)**    This 4-byte field contains the internal IPX network number of the router sending the LSP. For a LAN pseudonode or a numbered WAN pseudonode LSP, this is the network number of the network segment that the pseudonode represents. For example, in the pseudonode LSP that contains information about external network 0xBA-5E-BA-11, the network number field contains the value 0xBA-5E-BA-11. On an unnumbered WAN link this value is 0x00-00-00-00.

**Node Number (6 Bytes)**    This field contains the value 0x00-00-00-00-00-01 for a nonpseudonode LSP. On a pseudonode LSP, this field indicates the NIC address of the card attaching to this network on this circuit. On a WAN pseudonode LSP, this field contains the value 0x00-00-00-00-00-01.

**IPX Version Number (1 Byte)**    The current version number 1; this field contains 0x01.

**Name Length (1 Byte)**    This field indicates the length of the router/server field. This field contains 0x00 if no name is present, as in the case of a pseudonode LSP.

**Router/Server Name (Name Length Field Value)**    The name of the router or server that originated this LSP. This field can be between 1 and 47 bytes. One byte is required for each ASCII character in the server/router name.

### Link Information

The link information option fields, shown in Figure 11.54, are used to provide information on adjacencies. The adjacencies listed in the link information fields are adjacent to the sending router.

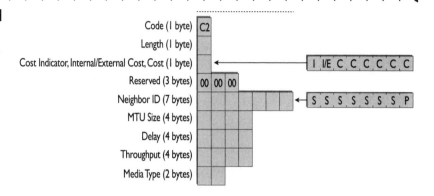

*The link information option provides information on the source router's adjacencies.*

**Cost Indicator (I Bit)**    This bit is set to 1 and indicates that a cost value is present within this byte. Designated "I" in Figure 11.54.

**Internal/External Cost (I Bit)**    If this field's value is 0, the cost is an internal metric. If the field contains the value 1, it is an external metric. Designated "I/E" in Figure 11.54.

**Cost (6 Bits)**    This is the cost for this link to the listed neighbor. See Table 11.1 for a complete list of the NLSP default costs.

**Reserved (3 Bytes)**    Set to 0x00-00-00; ignored upon receipt.

**Neighbor ID (7 Bytes)**    The neighbor ID field contains the system ID (or source ID) of the neighboring router learned from hello packets and 1 byte containing a nonzero value if this is a pseudonode neighbor. The system ID bytes are designated "S" in Figure 11.54. The pseudonode indicator byte is designated "P" in Figure 11.54.

**MTU size (4 Bytes)**    This is the maximum number of bytes (maximum transmission units) that can be sent on this link by the originating router. This includes the IPX header, but not the datalink header. This field contains the value 0x00-00-00-00 for pseudonode LSPs.

**Delay (4 Bytes)**    This is the time, in microseconds, that it takes to transmit a single byte of data to a destination if the medium is free of all other traffic. This field contains the value 0x00-00-00-00 for pseudonode LSPs.

**Throughput (4 Bytes)**   The amount of data (in bits) that can flow through the link within one second (providing there is no other traffic on the medium). The following throughput values can be assumed:

| | |
|---|---|
| 2,500,000 | ARCnet (2.5M) |
| 4,000,000 | 4M Token Ring |
| 10,000,000 | 10M Ethernet |
| 16,000,000 | 16M Token Ring |

This field contains the value 0x00-00-00-00 for pseudonode LSPs.

**Media Type (2 Bytes)**   This field contains a code identifying the type of circuit where the first bit (the most significant bit) is 1 for WAN media. Table 11.3 lists some of the common NLSP media codes.

| T A B L E  11.3 |  |  |
|---|---|---|
| *Some of the Common Media Codes Defined by the NLSP Specification.* | **CODE** | **DEFINITION** |
| | 0x0000 | Generic LAN; no applicable media defined |
| | 0x8000 | Generic WAN; no applicable media defined |
| | 0x0001 | LocalTalk |
| | 0x0002 | Ethernet using Novell's Ethernet_II frame |
| | 0x0003 | Ethernet using Novell's Ethernet_802.2 frame |
| | 0x0005 | Ethernet using Novell's Ethernet_802.3 frame |
| | 0x000A | Ethernet using Novell's Ethernet_SNAP frame |
| | 0x0004 | Token Ring using Novell's Token-Ring frame |
| | 0x000B | Token Ring using Novell's Token-Ring_SNAP frame |
| | 0x800D | ISDN |
| | 0x000E | ARCnet |
| | 0x0013 | IP Tunnel |
| | 0x8013 | IP Relay |
| | 0x0014 | FDDI using Novell's FDDI frame |
| | 0x0017 | FDDI using Novell's FDDI_SNAP frame |
| | 0x801C | PPP (Point-to-Point Protocol) |
| | 0x801E | X.25 |
| | 0x801F | Frame Relay |

**NOTE**

**A complete listing of the media codes is included in the NLSP specification.**

### Services Information

This option defines services that use the SAP protocol to describe themselves (as shown in Figure 11.55).

F I G U R E   11.55

*The service information field contains the internetwork address of services that use SAP.*

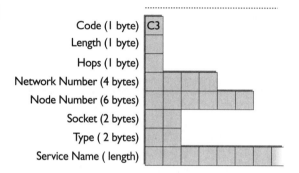

Code (1 byte)  C3
Length (1 byte)
Hops (1 byte)
Network Number (4 bytes)
Node Number (6 bytes)
Socket (2 bytes)
Type ( 2 bytes)
Service Name ( length)

**Hops (1 Byte)**   This field defines the number of hops to the listed service.

**Network Number (4 Bytes)**   This field contains the network address of the listed service.

**Node Number (6 Bytes)**   This field contains the node address of the listed service. In the case of services that are available on the internal IPX network, the node address is 0x00-00-00-00-00-01.

**Socket (2 Bytes)**   This field contains the socket number (or process identifier) where the service resides.

**X-REF**

**Refer to Appendix F for a list of assigned socket numbers.**

**Type (2 Bytes)**   This field contains the service type identifier.

**X-REF**

**Refer to Appendix E for a complete SAP number listing.**

**Service Name (Length)**   This field contains the name of the service listed. The length of this field is based on the option length value and can range from 1 to 47 bytes.

### External Routes

The external routes option, shown in Figure 11.56, lists routes that are learned through a different routing protocol than NLSP. For example, if a network has a RIP router on it, routes can be learned through the RIP periodic broadcast. Those routes are considered external routes.

▶ · · · · · · · · · · · · · · · · · · · · · · · · · · · · · · · · · · · · · ◀

F I G U R E    11.56

*The external routes option is used when non-NLSP routing devices exist on the network.*

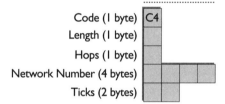

Code (1 byte) C4
Length (1 byte)
Hops (1 byte)
Network Number (4 bytes)
Ticks (2 bytes)

## CSNP (COMPLETE SEQUENCE NUMBER PACKET) STRUCTURE

The complete sequence number packet (CSNP) consists of fixed-length fields, as shown in Figure 11.57, and variable-length fields.

### Fixed-Length Fields

The fixed-length fields begin with the protocol ID field and continue to the end LSP ID field.

### Protocol ID (1 Byte)

The value 0x83 indicates the NLSP routing layer.

### Length Indicator (1 Byte)

This is the byte count in the fixed-length portion of the header (up to and including the end LSP ID field).

### Minor Version (1 Byte)

The value 0x01 indicates a Level-1 NLSP router. The value 0x02 indicates that this router supports aggregated routes.

· · · · ·

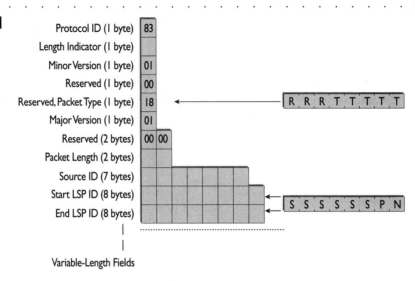

F I G U R E    11.57

*CNSP packets consist of fixed-length fields and variable-length fields.*

### Reserved (1 Byte)
Set to 0x00; ignored.

### Reserved (3 Bits)
Set to 000; ignored. Designated "R" in Figure 11.57.

### Packet Type (5 Bits)
The value 0x18 (24 decimal) indicates that this is an LSP packet. The value of this field is 11000 (binary). When it is combined with the three-bit reserved field preceding it, the entire byte value is 0x18 or 00011000 (binary). Designated "T" in Figure 11.57.

**X-REF**

**Refer to the hex-decimal-binary conversion chart in Appendix A.**

### Major Version (1 Byte)
NLSP is currently at version 1.1. The major version identifier indicates the number before the decimal point. 0x01 indicates that this router supports NLSP v1.*x* (with *x* denoting the minor version number specified later in this NLSP header).

### Reserved (2 Bytes)
Set to 0x0000; ignored.

### Packet Length (2 Bytes)
This is the entire length of this NLSP data including the NLSP header fixed fields and the NLSP variable-length fields. Add the IPX header (fixed 30 bytes) and data link header to determine the entire packet length.

### Source ID (7 Bytes)
This is the 6-byte system ID of the router that sent this packet followed by one byte with the value 0x00.

### Start LSP ID (8 Bytes)
In case the entire LSP list cannot fit in a single CSNP, the start LSP ID and end LSP ID fields identify which LSPs did fit in each CSNP transmitted. The start LSP ID field indicates the first LSP ID number covered in this CSNP. This field consists of the system ID, pseudonode ID, and LSP number fields, as denoted in Figure 11.57. An LSP number value greater than 0x00 indicates that this LSP has been fragmented because it is too large to fit in a single packet. The LSP number field provides the order information for fragmented LSPs.

### End LSP IP (8 Bytes)
This field indicates the final LSP ID number that is contained in the CSNP. If all LSP IDs can fit in a single CSNP, this field contains the value 0xFF-FF-FF-FF-FF-FF-FF-FF.

### Variable-Length Fields
The variable-length fields include options that have a three-part form that includes code, length, and value. Currently, there is only one option: LSP entries.

The variable-length fields follow the fixed-length fields, as shown in Figure 11.58.

F I G U R E     11.58

*The variable-length fields include code, length, and value fields.*

Fixed-Length Fields

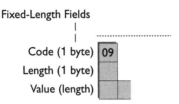

Code (1 byte)  09
Length (1 byte)
Value (length)

### LSP Entries

LSP entries are sorted and listed in ascending order with the lowest number LSP ID listed first. Each LSP entry has five fields (shown in Figure 11.59): hour flag, remaining lifetime, LSP ID, sequence number, and checksum.

**Hour Flag (1 Bit)**   If this one-bit field contains the value 0, the remaining lifetime field is denoted in hours. Designated "H" in Figure 11.59.

**Remaining Lifetime (1 Byte, 7 Bits)**   This field denotes the amount of time until the LSP expires. If the hour flag is set to 0 (the default), the remaining lifetime field is defining the number of seconds until the LSP expires. Designated "L" in Figure 11.59.

**LSP ID (8 Bytes)**   This field indicates the LSP ID number referred to by this entry. This entry uses the same source ID, pseudonode ID, and LSP number form described earlier.

**Sequence Number (4 Bytes)**   This field indicates the sequence number of this LSP. This field is referenced by receiving stations to figure out whether their own LSP database contains out-of-date entries.

**Checksum (2 Bytes)**   This field contains the checksum on the particular LSP it is listed with. This field is used to verify the integrity of the LSP database entry and as a tiebreaker when two identical LSPs are reported on the network.

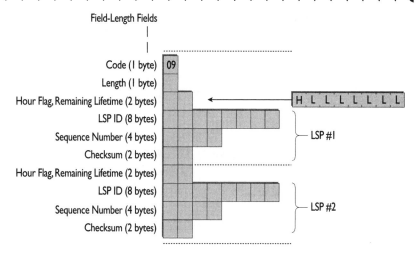

*LSP entries are sorted and listed in ascending LSP ID order.*

## PSNP (PARTIAL SEQUENCE NUMBER PACKET) STRUCTURE

The partial sequence number packet (PSNP) consists of fixed-length fields, as shown in Figure 11.60, and variable-length fields, discussed later in this section.

### Fixed-Length Fields

The fixed-length fields begin with the protocol ID field and continue to the end LSP ID field.

### Protocol ID (1 Byte)

The value 0x83 indicates the NLSP routing layer.

### Length Indicator (1 Byte)

This is the byte count in the fixed-length portion of the header (up to and including the source ID field).

### Minor Version (1 Byte)

The value 0x01 indicates a Level-1 NLSP router. The value 0x02 indicates that this router supports aggregated routes.

### Reserved (1 Byte)

Set to 0x00; ignored.

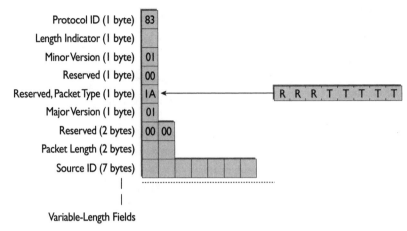

**FIGURE 11.60**

*PNSP packets consist of fixed-length fields and variable-length fields.*

Variable-Length Fields

### Reserved (3 Bits)
Set to 000; ignored. Designated "R" in Figure 11.60.

### Packet Type (5 Bits)
The value 0x1A (26 decimal) indicates that this is an LSP packet. The value of this field is 11010 (binary). When it is combined with the three-bit reserved field preceding it, the entire byte value is 0x1A or 00011010 (binary). Designated "T" in Figure 11.60.

**X-REF**

**Refer to the hex-decimal-binary conversion chart in Appendix A.**

### Major Version (1 Byte)
NLSP is currently at version 1.1. The major version identifier indicates the number before the decimal point. 0x01 indicates that this router supports NLSP v1.*x* (with *x* denoting the minor version number specified later in this NLSP header).

### Reserved (2 Bytes)
Set to 0x0000; ignored.

### Packet Length (2 Bytes)

This is the entire length of this NLSP data including the NLSP header fixed fields and the NLSP variable-length fields. Add the IPX header (fixed 30 bytes) and data link header to determine the entire packet length.

### Source ID (7 Bytes)

This is the 6-byte system ID of the router that sent this packet followed by 1 byte with the value 0x00.

### Variable-Length Fields

The variable-length fields include options that have a three-part form that includes code, length, and value. Currently, there is only one option: LSP entries.

The variable-length fields follow the fixed-length fields, as shown in Figure 11.61.

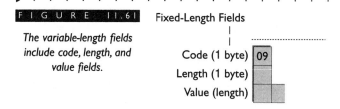

**FIGURE 11.61**

*The variable-length fields include code, length, and value fields.*

Fixed-Length Fields

Code (1 byte) 09
Length (1 byte)
Value (length)

### LSP Entries

LSP entries are sorted and listed in ascending order with the lowest-number LSP ID listed first. Each LSP entry has five fields (shown in Figure 11.62): hour flag, remaining lifetime, LSP ID, sequence number, and checksum.

**Hour Flag (1 Bit)**   If this 1-bit field contains the value 0, the remaining lifetime field is denoted in hours. Designated "H" in Figure 11.63.

**Remaining Lifetime (1 Byte, 7 Bits)**   This field denotes the amount of time until the LSP expires. If the hour flag is set to 0 (the default), the remaining lifetime field is defining the number of seconds until the LSP expires. Designated "L" in Figure 11.62.

**LSP ID (8 Bytes)**   This field indicates the LSP ID number referred to by this entry. This entry uses the same source ID, pseudonode ID, and LSP number form described earlier.

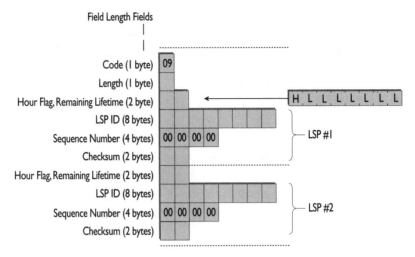

*PSNP packets contain the value 0x00-00-00-00 in the sequence number field.*

**Sequence Number (4 Bytes)**    In PSNPs this field contains the value 0x00-00-00-00 as an indication that the sender does not feel that it has the latest version of this LSP.

**Checksum (2 Bytes)**    This field contains the checksum on the particular LSP it is listed with. This field is used to verify the integrity of the LSP database entry and as a tiebreaker when two identical LSPs are reported on the network.

## Summary

Phew! That's all there is to know about analyzing NLSP communications. Actually, the NLSP specification contains additional information on NLSP operating parameters and communications processes. In the next chapter, we'll delve into how WAN routers set up their IPX-based communications circuits using IPXWAN version 2.

# CHAPTER 12

# NetWare IPXWAN2

**T**his chapter defines Novell's Internetwork Packet Exchange for Wide Area Networks (IPXWAN) protocol for establishing IPX-based links between remote NetWare LANs via Frame Relay, PPP (Point-to-Point Protocol), X.25 Switched Virtual Circuits (SVCs), and Permanent Virtual Circuits (PVCs). After examining the link establishment process and the IPXWAN operation procedures, we'll view the structure of the nine different IPXWAN packets and define how they are used to set up WAN communications.

## What Is IPXWAN?

IPXWAN is a protocol used to establish an IPX-based link between two WAN routers, as shown in Figure 12.1. The IPXWAN-based link supports IPX-based communications such as SAP (Service Advertising Protocol), RIP (Router Information Protocol), and NLSP (NetWare Link Services Protocol) communications. IPXWAN is a protocol that is used immediately following the link establishment, but before any upper-layer protocol negotiation (such as RIP or NLSP information exchanges).

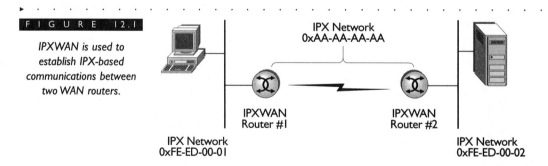

FIGURE 12.1

*IPXWAN is used to establish IPX-based communications between two WAN routers.*

There are two versions of IPXWAN — IPXWAN 1 and IPXWAN 2.

- ▶ **IPXWAN 1:** This is the original version of IPXWAN. IPXWAN 1 supports RIP-based routing across the WAN link. IPXWAN 1 also provides PPP, x.25, and Frame Relay support.

- ▶ **IPXWAN 2**: This version of IPXWAN includes all the functionality of IPXWAN 1 and adds NLSP compatibility. If you intend on supporting

NLSP across a WAN link, both WAN routers must be IPXWAN 2–compliant.

## LINK ESTABLISHMENT

The first step in setting up an IPXWAN connection is to establish the underlying data link. The following lists the common media links that can support IPXWAN.

### PPP (Point-To-Point Protocol) Link Up/Down

Link establishment is defined as both sides reaching the "open" state. Link termination is caused when one side sends a termination request packet. PPP frame encapsulation is used across the link.

### X.25 SVC Link Up/Down

The SVC link is considered "up" when one side sends (and the other side successfully receives) a Call Request frame indicating that the protocol is NetWare IPX. The protocol identifier 0x80-00-00-00-81-37 is used in the X.25 call user data field to indicate that the link is being established to support NetWare IPX. X.25 frame encapsulation is used across the link.

### X.25 PVC Link Up/Down

The X.25 PVC link does not require a setup call. The link is considered up when the X.25 layer 2 (data link) is up. X.25 frame encapsulation is used across the link.

### Frame Relay Link Up/Down

A Frame Relay PVC is considered up or down based on periodic interactions with a private Frame Relay switch or a public Frame Relay network. Frame Relay frame encapsulation is defined in RFC 1294, "Multiprotocol Interconnect over Frame Relay."

### IP Relay Link Up/Down

An IP Relay link (that encapsulates IPX within UDP/IP headers) is considered up when the IP stack is successfully loaded on either routing device. IP Relay links use the UDP/IP header structure.

## IPXWAN2 OPERATION

Regardless of the underlying link (PPP, X.25, Frame Relay, and so on), IPXWAN follows the same communications process once the link is considered up. The following three functions define IPXWAN's responsibility:

▸ Identify master/slave router

▸ Determine link characteristics

▸ Exchange router configurations

Let's examine each of these processes to see how they are used in NetWare communications.

### Identify Master/Slave Router

The two routers connected via the link must determine which one is a *master* and which one is a *slave*. The designation of master or slave is only a temporary designation used during the IPXWAN 2 communication process. Although it sounds like a great privilege and responsibility to be the master router, the role is relatively dull: The master router is simply responsible for keeping all the communications going in a neat, orderly fashion during the IPXWAN 2 exchange.

Each IPXWAN router sends a timer request packet to the other router across the WAN. This packet includes the router's internal IPX address in either the WNode ID field or the extended node ID field, depending on how the router is configured. The router with the highest internal IPX address becomes the master router.

**NOTE**

**All IPXWAN routers must have a unique internal IPX address assigned in order to complete the master/slave determination process. Some routing manufacturers have different names for this number. For example, Cisco calls this number the *primary network number* for the router.**

In the case of numbered links, a router that is prepared to assign a network number must place its internal IPX address in the Wnode ID field of the IPXWAN timer request packet, as shown in Figure 12.2. If the router is not prepared to assign a number (as in the case of an unnumbered link), the router places the value 0x00-00-00-00 in the Wnode ID field and places its internal IPX address in the extended node ID field, as shown in Figure 12.3.

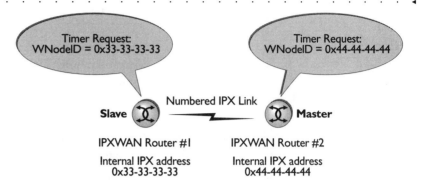

**FIGURE 12.2**

*If both routers are able to assign an address to a numbered link, they send their internal IPX addresses in the WNode ID field.*

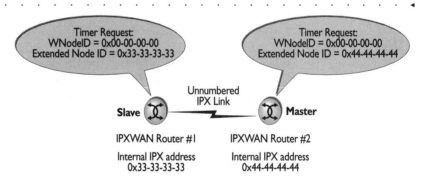

**FIGURE 12.3**

*If both routers are unable to assign an address because they are configured for an unnumbered link, they send their internal IPX addresses in the extended node ID field.*

Although it may seem straightforward, there are instances when the determination of a master may not be typical. The following scenarios indicate how the master router is defined in four different configurations.

▸ **Both timer request packets contain WNode ID field values:** If both timer requests contain a Wnode ID field value, the sender with the higher value (and therefore the router with the highest internal IPX address) becomes the master router. The extended node ID field is not used to determine the master router in this instance.

▸ **Both timer request packets contain extended node ID field values and no WNode ID field value:** If neither timer request contains a

Wnode ID field value but they both contain an extended node ID value (as shown in Figure 12.3), the sender with the higher extended node ID value (and therefore the router with the highest internal IPX address) becomes the master router.

▸ **Only one timer request packet contains a WNode ID field value:** If only one timer request packet contains Wnode ID information, it automatically becomes the master router regardless of the extended node ID field value.

▸ **Neither timer request packet contains a WNode ID field value, and only one timer request packet contains an extended WNode ID field value:** If neither timer request packet contains Wnode ID information and only one timer request contains an extended node ID value, the router that included an extended node ID value becomes the master router.

▸ **If both timer request packets contain the same Wnode ID value:** If both timer request packets have the same Wnode ID field value, a configuration error has occurred and the underlying media connection is disconnected. The Wnode ID field value is based on the internal IPX address, and all network addresses must be unique throughout the internetwork.

▸ **If both timer request packets contain the same extended node ID value:** If both timer request packets have the same extended node ID field value, a configuration error has occurred, and the underlying media connection is disconnected. The extended node ID field value is also based on the internal IPX address, and all network addresses must be unique throughout the internetwork.

Once the master and slave roles have been determined, the slave router must respond to the timer request with a timer response packet. This request/response process is used to define link characteristics.

### Determine Link Characteristics

Chapter 10 and Chapter 11 explained how the throughput value was defined on LANs. On a RIP-based network, an assumption is made: It takes one tick (1/18 second) to cross a LAN. On an NLSP-based network, the time it takes to cross a network is based on the network throughput. On a WAN link, however, IPXWAN can actually measure the delay and throughput of the link.

The type of link supported determines how link characteristics are measured. For example, on a RIP link, the time between the timer request transmission and timer response receipt defines the round-trip link delay. If, however, the link can support NLSP routing, the master router sends throughput request and delay request packets to the slave router. The time between requests and responses helps define NLSP link costs. We'll examine the link types later in this chapter.

### Exchange Router Configurations

Finally, IPXWAN permits an exchange process for router configuration information. This process enables both routers to agree upon a routing protocol and link cost. For example, after an NLSP master router has determined the link delay and throughput characteristics, it sends this information to the slave. This provides the same link cost in both directions (symmetrical routing) by default.

During the IPXWAN process, the WAN routers indicate the type of routing service or services they can support. A router can indicate that it supports multiple routing services (such as RIP and NLSP). The routing protocol selected is based on the highest common denominator between the two routers. If one router supports RIP and unnumbered RIP and the other router supports NLSP and RIP, they will agree upon and use RIP routing across the link.

## IPXWAN CONFIGURATION ROUTINES

Let's examine the configuration routine for the five different IPXWAN links:

- ▸ RIP

- ▸ Unnumbered RIP

- ▸ On-demand, static routing

> ▸ NLSP

> ▸ Client-router connection

### Setting Up a RIP Numbered Link

On a standard, numbered RIP link, the link delay is measured from the time the timer request packet is transmitted to the time the response is received by the master router. The master router calculates this information based on the following rules:

y=start_time − end_time (in ticks)

y must be at least 1

y x 6 = link delay

y x 55 = link delay in milliseconds

Once the master router determines the link delay, it sends this information to the slave, along with the link number and the master router's name.

Figure 12.4 illustrates the process and includes the basic information sent with each packet.

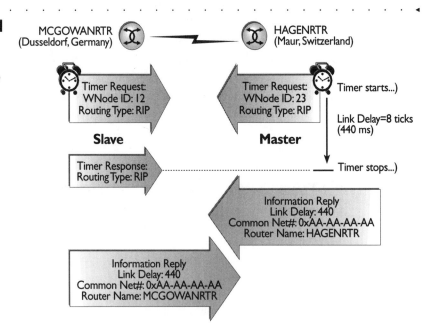

**FIGURE 12.4**

*The master router calculates the link delay in milliseconds and sends it to the slave router.*

The common network number is the WAN link's IPX network address and must be unique throughout the internetwork.

### Setting Up a RIP Unnumbered Link

On an unnumbered link, the actual WAN link is not assigned an IPX network address. This provides an easier administration process, since you do not have to guarantee a unique IPX address on the WAN link. As shown in Figure 12.5, the timer request and timer response packets indicate that the link is an unnumbered RIP link and the routers' internal IPX addresses are located in the extended node ID field of the packets.

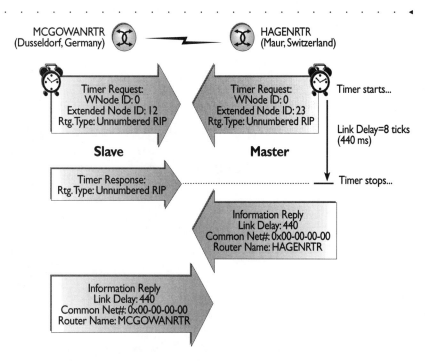

FIGURE 12.5

Network address 0x00-00-00-00 indicates that this is an unnumbered link.

The information request and reply packets indicate that the link has no IPX network address (0x00-00-00-00).

### Setting Up On-Demand, Static Routing

On-demand links are not "up" consistently. The link between on-demand routers is brought up only when there is data or command information to exchange across the link. Their routing information is static, meaning that each router is configured with the routes and services that are available across the link. No RIP, SAP, or NLSP information is exchanged across the link.

These types of routers perform a setup routing that is similar to the unnumbered RIP setup routine. Each on-demand, static router maintains a unique identifier for the other connecting routers. This unique identifier is called the remote system identifier (RSI). The RSI value can be derived through the calling DTE address (in X.25), the remote IP address (for IP relay), or similar means.

During the setup routine, the two routers start up without using a Wnode ID, as shown in Figure 12.6. Their internal IPX address is placed in the extended node ID field. The routing type in the timer request packet indicates that this is an on-demand, static connection.

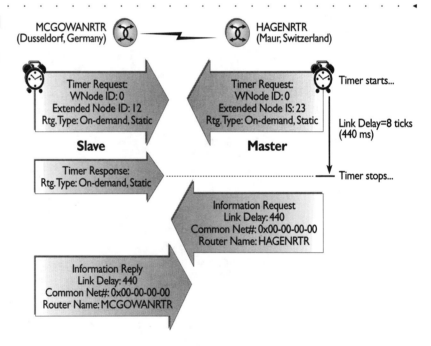

FIGURE 12.6

*On-demand, static links are configured like unnumbered RIP links.*

**If a router is attempting to establish an on-demand, static route, it will only indicate that value as a routing type option.**

NOTE

The on-demand, static link is not assigned a network number, as in unnumbered RIP.

### Setting Up an NLSP Link

As shown in Figure 12.7, the NLSP setup routine is more complex than the RIP setup routines. The additional process that occurs measures throughput and delay on the link. This information is used later in NLSP information exchanges throughout the internetwork.

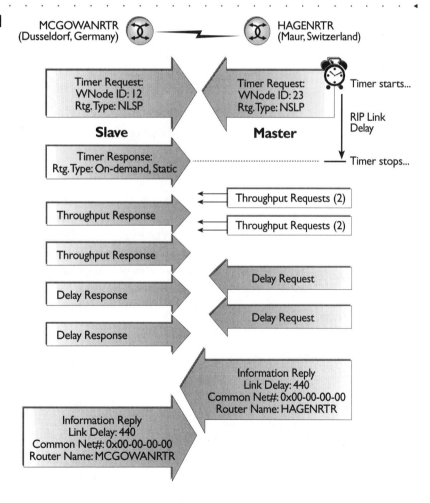

FIGURE 12.7

*The NLSP connection setup routine is more complex than RIP setup routines.*

The NLSP WAN connection setup routine starts just like the RIP setup routine. Both routers send timer request packets across the link. The timer request packets indicate that the router is using the NLSP routing protocol.

After the master router has been designated, the slave sends a timer response packet back to the master. Unlike in RIP and unnumbered RIP, however, the NLSP master router does not use just the simplistic timing between timer request transmission and reply as a measurement of link delay. Rather, the NLSP router uses special throughput and delay tests to determine the number of bits per second that the link supports (*throughput*) and the time to cross the link (*delay*).

The NLSP master router sends two throughput request packets back to back across the link. The same size packets are used for each throughput request and are based on the link data link characteristics.

The receiver (the slave router) measures the time between each of the packets in microseconds (the *delta time*) and sends this information and the throughput response packet size back to the master router.

The NLSP router also calculates the delay to get to the destination. The master router sends a delay request packet to the slave. The slave responds with a delay response—this is a simple echo test routine.

**You can find this type of echo test routine in the NetWare client connection when the client needs to measure delay to the server. For example, when the VLM sets up burst mode communication, the client sends LIP echo test packets to the server. The response time is measured and divided by 2 to get an average one-way time to the server. This information is used to determine the starting and maximum interpacket gap time used for burst mode communications.**

NOTE

The delay equation is echo_time / 2 = delay + (1 / throughput), where throughput is defined as it was earlier in this section.

**For more information on the delay and throughput testing routine, refer to the NLSP specification.**

NOTE

Finally, the master router sends the link throughput, delay, and RIP/SAP link delay information to the slave router. This information is used to define the cost to networks and services on the other side of the WAN link.

### Setting Up a Client/Router Link

In some configurations, a remote client can dial in and access the IPXWAN router. For example, NetWare Connect enables clients to dial directly into the NetWare Connect server/router. When the client-router link is established, the client and router send timer request packets to each other. The client indicates that it can support a *client-router connection*. The router, on the other hand, must indicate that it supports at least two routing types: client-router and one other routing type, such as RIP or NLSP. This differentiates the router from the client.

**Client Network Number**   If the client is making a new connection, it sets its Wnode ID to 0 and excludes the extended node ID field, indicating that the router should become the master and assign a network number to the client-router link, as shown in Figure 12.8.

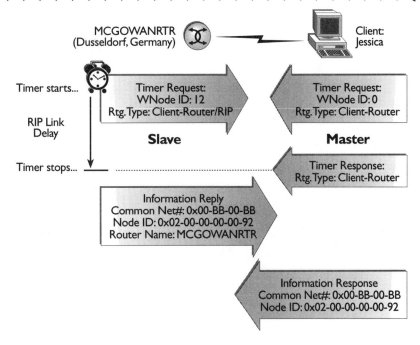

*The client indicates that the router should become the master.*

MCGOWANRTR
(Dusseldorf, Germany)

Client:
Jessica

Timer starts...

Timer Request:
WNode ID: 12
Rtg. Type: Client-Router/RIP

Timer Request:
WNode ID: 0
Rtg. Type: Client-Router

RIP Link
Delay

**Slave**

**Master**

Timer stops...

Timer Response:
Rtg. Type: Client-Router

Information Reply
Common Net#: 0x00-BB-00-BB
Node ID: 0x02-00-00-00-00-92
Router Name: MCGOWANRTR

Information Response
Common Net#: 0x00-BB-00-BB
Node ID: 0x02-00-00-00-00-92

If the client is reconnecting, however, the client sets the Wnode ID field to 0xFF-FF-FF-FF. This indicates that the client should become the master on the link. The client uses the previously assigned network address in its communications. If required, the router can reassign a network number to a reconnecting client.

Interestingly, in a client-router communication, the router can assign different network addresses to each attached client or a single network address to all attached clients. This is an implementation issue. Figure 12.9 shows a client-router addressing system where all remote clients share a single network address. When a router needs to broadcast information out to the clients, it sends the broadcast out each circuit to all clients that share the same network.

FIGURE 12.9

Although all remote nodes may share a single network address, the node address of each must be unique.

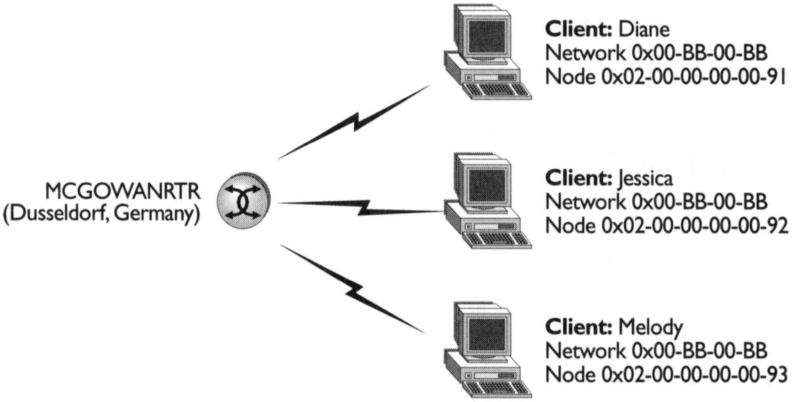

**Client Node Number**    The clients must also be assigned a node address by the master router. The master router assigns the unique node address in the information request packet. The node address always starts with 0x02. This value (in bits) represents 00000010, where the last two bit values indicate this is a nonmulticast, locally assigned address. A complete network and node client addressing system is shown in Figure 12.9.

Now that we've looked at the various types of IPXWAN connections, let's look at the packet structures for communicating over the WAN links.

## IPXWAN Packet Structures

The IPXWAN packets use an IPX header with the source and destination socket number set at 0x9004 (denoting IPXWAN protocol), as shown in Figure 12.10.

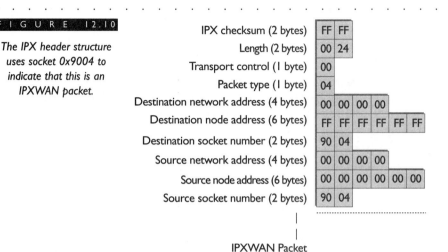

**F I G U R E    12.10**

*The IPX header structure uses socket 0x9004 to indicate that this is an IPXWAN packet.*

| | | | | | | |
|---|---|---|---|---|---|---|
| IPX checksum (2 bytes) | FF | FF | | | | |
| Length (2 bytes) | 00 | 24 | | | | |
| Transport control (1 byte) | 00 | | | | | |
| Packet type (1 byte) | 04 | | | | | |
| Destination network address (4 bytes) | 00 | 00 | 00 | 00 | | |
| Destination node address (6 bytes) | FF | FF | FF | FF | FF | FF |
| Destination socket number (2 bytes) | 90 | 04 | | | | |
| Source network address (4 bytes) | 00 | 00 | 00 | 00 | | |
| Source node address (6 bytes) | 00 | 00 | 00 | 00 | 00 | 00 |
| Source socket number (2 bytes) | 90 | 04 | | | | |

IPXWAN Packet

IPXWAN packets consist of fixed-length fields and variable-length fields. The fixed-length portion of the IPXWAN packet is detailed next.

## FIXED-LENGTH FIELDS
The fixed-length fields begin with the Widentifier field and continue through the Wnum options.

### Widentifier (4 Bytes)
This field always contains the value 0x57-41-53-4D, which is ASCII for WASM (or Wide Area Support Module). All IPXWAN communications must contain this value in each packet sent across the WAN link.

### Wpacket Type (1 Byte)
There are nine packets used for control types of processes on the IPXWAN link. The possible values are:

| | |
|---|---|
| 0x00 | Timer request |
| 0x01 | Timer response |
| 0x02 | Information request |
| 0x03 | Information response |
| 0x04 | Throughput request |
| 0x05 | Throughput response |

0x06      Delay request
0x07      Delay response
0xFF      Negative acknowledgment

**NOTE**

**Although you probably have a good idea of how each of these packets are used from reading this chapter, at the end of this chapter we break down the packet type structures and further define the uses of each.**

Packet types 0x00 through 0x04 can be used for RIP-based links. Types 0x05 through 0x07 are used only on NLSP-based links.

### Wnode ID (6 Bytes)

If a router is sending the packet, this field contains the internal IPX address of the sending router, if the sending router can assign an address to the link. If the packet contains 0, the router cannot assign a number to the link and the router places its internal IPX address in the extended node ID field.

If a client is sending the packet (on a client-router connection) and the field contains the value 0, the client is making a new connection. If the client places the value 0xFF-FF-FF-FF in this field, the client is reconnecting to the router.

### Wsequence Number (1 Byte)

This field increments by 1 for each request sent. The response packets echo the sequence number used in the corresponding request packet. This ensures that the appropriate requests and responses are matched up.

### Wnum Options (1 Byte)

This field indicates the number of options that are used in this packet. The options are contained in the variable-length fields that follow.

## VARIABLE-LENGTH FIELDS

The variable-length fields follow the fixed-length fields and use a four-part form.

### Woption Number (1 Byte)

This field indicates the option that follows. The options are:

| | |
|---|---|
| 0x00 | Routing type |
| 0x01 | RIP/SAP information exchange |
| 0x02 | NLSP information |
| 0x03 | NLSP raw throughput data |
| 0x04 | Extended node ID |
| 0x05 | Node number |
| 0x06 | MTU size |
| 0x80 | Compression |
| 0xFF | Pad |

**Each of the options just listed is detailed later in this chapter.**

NOTE

### Waccept Option (1 Byte)

This field is used to negotiate options between two routers. The field can contain the following values:

| | |
|---|---|
| 0x00 | No |
| 0x01 | Yes |
| 0x02 | Not applicable |

Let's take a look at how this field is used. If a client makes a client-router connection, it sets the routing type to client-router. In the case of client-router connections, the router must support client-router as a routing type and one additional routing type (such as RIP or NLSP). If the rRouter does not support the additional routing type, it sends the value 0x00 in the Waccept option field (No) and 0x00 (RIP) in the routing type field. This indicates that the router does not support RIP on that link and therefore the link cannot be established. One side of the link must support routing protocol functionality.

### Woption Data Length (2 Bytes)

This field indicates the length (in bytes) of the Woption data that follows the Waccept option field.

**Woption Data (Woption Data Length)**

This field layout is unique to each particular option. In this next section, we'll take a look at the format of each of the options listed next:

**Routing Type Option**    This option defines the type of routing that the sending device supports. The routing type values are listed next:

| | |
|---|---|
| 0x00 | RIP |
| 0x01 | NLSP |
| 0x02 | Unnumbered RIP |
| 0x03 | On-demand, static routing |
| 0x04 | Client-router connection |

Figure 12.11 provides the routing type option structure.

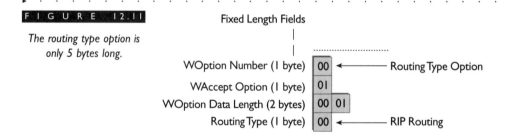

**FIGURE 12.11**

*The routing type option is only 5 bytes long.*

**RIP/SAP Information Exchange Option**

The RIP/SAP information exchange is used to provide the link delay defined by the master router as a result of subtracting the timer response receipt from the timer request transmission. Figure 12.12 details the structure of this option.

The WAN link delay field indicates the delay calculated by the time between the timer request packet transmission and receipt of the timer response by the master router. The common network number field indicates the IPX network address assigned to the link (a RIP-numbered link). The router name is a unique value for the WAN router.

**NLSP Information Option**    This option provides the delay and throughput values calculated from the NLSP link setup routine.

The delay and throughput values will be used by the receiving router to determine a link cost.

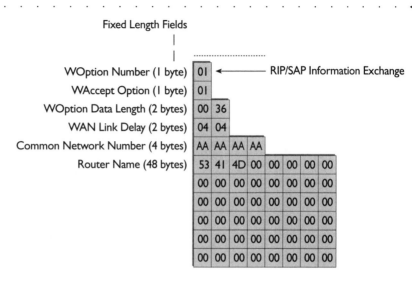

*The RIP/SAP information exchange option provides the link delay information.*

Fixed Length Fields

WOption Number (1 byte)    ←———— RIP/SAP Information Exchange
WAccept Option (1 byte)
WOption Data Length (2 bytes)
WAN Link Delay (2 bytes)
Common Network Number (4 bytes)
Router Name (48 bytes)

**NLSP Raw Throughput Data Option**   This option is used in the throughput response packets to provide the master router with the information necessary to calculate throughput. Figure 12.13 illustrates the fields of the NLSP raw throughput data option.

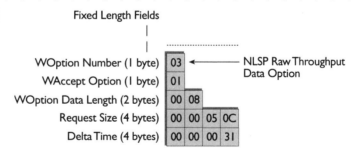

*The delta time and throughput request packet size are in this option.*

Fixed Length Fields

WOption Number (1 byte)    ←———— NLSP Raw Throughput Data Option
WAccept Option (1 byte)
WOption Data Length (2 bytes)
Request Size (4 bytes)
Delta Time (4 bytes)

The request size field indicates the throughput request packet size. The delta time field indicates the time between the two throughput request packets sent during NLSP connection setup.

**Extended Node ID Option**   The extended node ID option (Figure 12.14) is used in timer request packets to indicate that a router cannot number a link but it can provide its internal IPX address.

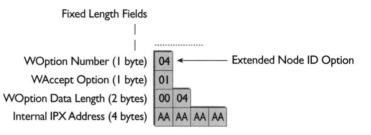

*The extended node ID option includes the sender's Internal IPX address.*

**Node Number Option**    This option (Figure 12.15) is used by a router in the client-router connections. The value contained in this field is the node address that the router is assigning the client.

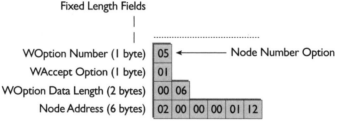

*The assigned node address must always start with 0x02.*

### MTU Size Option

This option (Figure 12.16) indicates the maximum packet size that the sender can support. The term "MTU" stands for maximum transmission unit.

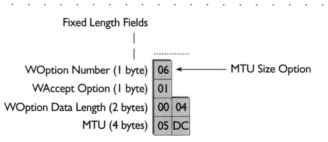

*The MTU value does not include the datalink headers.*

The acceptable range for this field is between 576 and 65535.

**Compression Option**    This option (see Figure 12.17) indicates the style of compression used across the link.

FIGURE 12.17

*The compression option field values are dependent upon the type of compression used.*

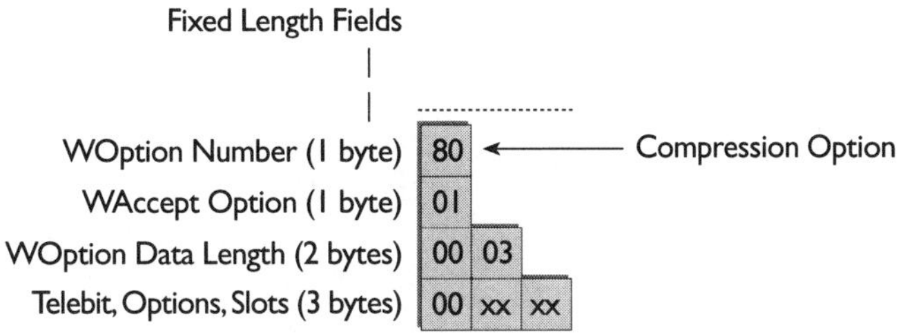


The current version of IPXWAN supports only Telebit compression. The following fields are located within the data portion:

Byte 0: Set to 0x00, this field indicates that Telebit compression is supported by the sender.

Byte 1: Compression options

Byte 2: Number of compression slots

**Pad Option** Padding (Figure 12.18) is used to make the packet reach the required minimum size. The bytes are random.

FIGURE 12.18

*The padding value has no meaning.*

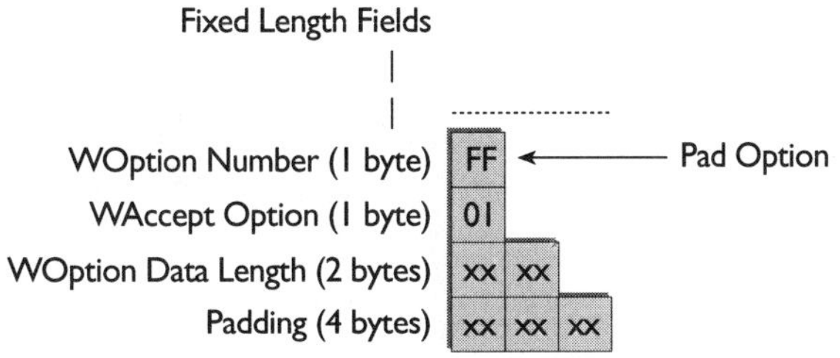


### Option Layouts

The following list indicates which options are used in the various packet types:

| *Request/Response* | *Fixed Fields* |
|---|---|
| Timer request | 0x00 routing type option |
| | 0x04 extended node ID option |
| | 0x80 compression option |
| Timer response | 0x00 routing type option |
| | 0x80 compression option |
| | 0xFF pad |

*(continued)*

| Request/Response | Fixed Fields |
|---|---|
| Throughput request | 0xFF pad option |
| Throughput response | 0x03 NLSP raw throughput data option |
| Delay request | 0xFF pad option |
| Delay response | 0xFF pad option |
| Information request | 0x01 RIP/SAP information exchange option |
| | 0x02 NLSP information option |
| | 0x05 node number |
| Information response | 0x01 RIP/SAP information exchange option |
| | 0x02 NLSP information option |
| | 0x05 node number |

**NOTE** **For more details on IPXWAN, refer to the NLSP Specification (NLSP.EXE) that can be found on Novell's Web site, www.novell.com, or read RFC 1634, "Novell IPX over Various WAN Media (IPXWAN)," dated May 1994.**

## Summary

In this chapter, we've examined Novell's IPXWAN2 protocol and packet structures. As mentioned before, IPXWAN2 supersedes IPXWAN by including NLSP support. In the next chapter, we'll look at Novell's NetWare Core Protocol, (NCP).

# CHAPTER 13

# NetWare NCP

This chapter defines NetWare Core Protocol (NCP), Novell's method for requesting and supplying services to the NetWare clients on the network. This chapter focuses on NCP functionality and communication processes, as well as the typical NCP sequences that are used to attach to a NetWare server, log in to the network, locate and download network files, and disconnect from the network. This chapter provides a detailed listing of the NCP function, subfunction, and verb numbers used to perform the many functions on NCP.

## NCP Functionality

NCP is the heart of NetWare communications. NCP defines the commands and IPX-based commands and data exchanges that flow from the clients to the server. When an application is written to use the NetWare API calls, the client's shell or requester (depending on the version of client software) translates the call into an NCP request. This request is sent to IPX, which in turn sends the request to the LAN driver and finally to the NIC, as shown in Figure 13.1.

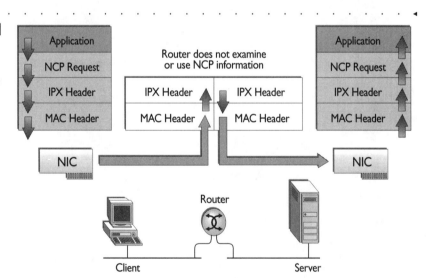

FIGURE 13.1

*NCP requests are built by the NetWare shell or requester and handed down to IPX and then on to the LAN driver.*

NCP, by its request/reply nature, is a connection-oriented type of protocol. A client makes an NCP request and waits for an NCP reply. If the client does not receive an NCP reply, it reissues the request.

There are only six basic types of NCP packets:

- ▸ 0x1111  NCP connection requests

- ▸ 0x2222  NCP requests

- ▸ 0x3333  NCP replies

- ▸ 0x5555  NCP destroy connection

- ▸ 0x7777  NCP burst mode file read/writes

- ▸ 0x9999  NCP request being processed

Let's examine each of these NCP packet types and see how they are used in typical communications.

## NCP CONNECTION REQUESTS (TYPE 0X1111)

When a NetWare client boots up, it uses the NCP connection request packet (NCP type 1111) to obtain a general service connection. This type of connection is not a licensed or authenticated connection. It does not give the client any privileges other than access to the LOGIN directory contents to look up network services.

Figure 13.2 shows an NCP connection request packet that was sent from Admin to a server called COMPAQ-FS3 (an IntranetWare v4.11 server that supports NetWare Multiprotocol Router functions).

In Figure 13.2 you can see that the NCP header follows directly after the IPX header and defines the request type as 0x1111 (create service connection). This packet is sent to the NetWare NCP socket (0x0451) from a dynamic client socket. The connection number value 255 is invalid and only indicates that the client does not know his connection number yet.

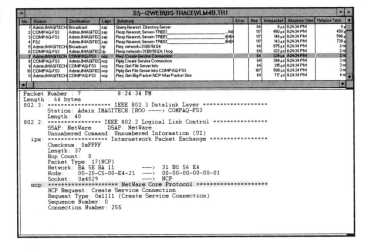

FIGURE 13.2

*A client requests a general service connection by sending a create service connection NCP request to the NCP socket (0x0451).*

The create service connection NCP packet is used for three purposes. It is primarily used to request an actual NCP connection ID number. It is also used to test round-trip latency times for the VLM burst mode communications and to determine the data path's maximum packet size.

When the create service connection packet is used as a testing packet, it is called a LIP echo test packet. Figure 13.3 shows a LIP echo test packet.

FIGURE 13.3

*The LIP echo test packet is NCP type 0x1111, but this packet is sent to an echo socket.*

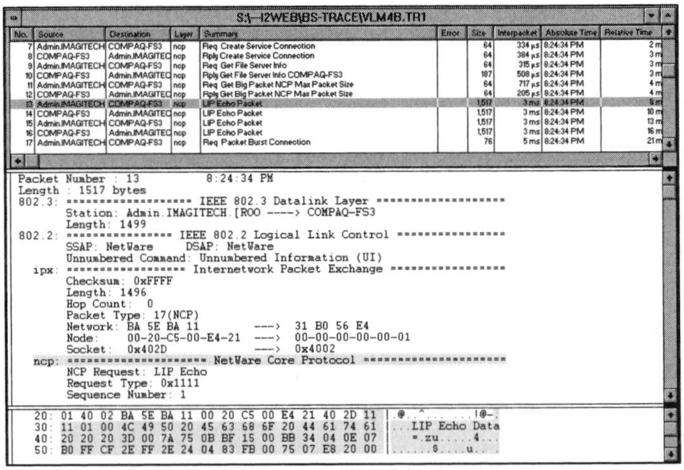

These LIP echo test packets are typically the largest packet size that the data path will support. In the data portion, you can see that the ASCII text "LIP Echo Data" is being sent to the server. The echo socket number is defined in the server in packet 12 in Figure 13.3. A packet sent to the echo socket is not processed by the NetWare server—it is simply returned to the sender the same way the packet arrived.

NetWare clients have used the LIP echo test packets in a variety of ways. The next two sections give an example of how these echo packets are used to set up burst mode communications and determine the maximum packet size for a VLM client.

### LIP Echo Test: Maximum Data Path

A LIP echo test packet can be used to determine maximum packet size for a VLM client. We are using VLM 1.22 as an example, although the performance is typical of Client 32 software, as well.

In Figure 13.4, the VLM client sends a "Get Big Packet NCP Maximum Packet Size" request to the NetWare server. This packet is used to inform the server of the maximum transmission unit (MTU) the client can use. This only defines the data portion of the packet; it does not include the MAC header. In this case, the client can support up to 1,496 bytes of data. This allows for the longest 802.2 frame size possible (in case the command field ever uses supervisory/informational format, adding a single byte).

FIGURE 13.4

*The Client uses LIP echo packets to test the MTU and determine burst mode operating parameters.*

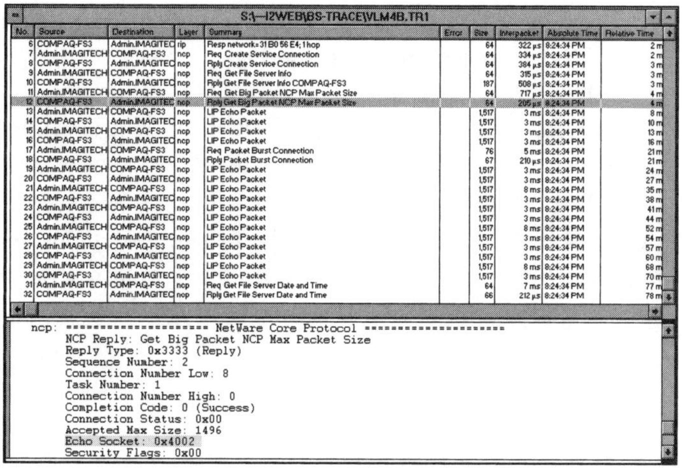

The server responds and supplies its echo socket (0x4002) as shown in Figure 13.4. The server indicates that it can accept 1,496 MTU size. The client next tests the data path to see if it can actually support this packet size. There may be a route between the client and server that uses a smaller data path, as in the case of token ring to Ethernet to token–ring–routed packets.

The LIP echo packets used to test the path in Figure 13.4 are 1,517 bytes long (1,496 bytes MTU plus 21 bytes MAC header, including the LLC layer). The test packets include the following fields to create a 1,517-byte packet:

| | |
|---|---|
| Destination address field: | 6 bytes |
| Source address field: | 6 bytes |
| Length field: | 2 bytes |
| DSAP field: | 1 byte |
| SSAP field: | 1 byte |
| Unnumbered command field: | 1 byte |
| Random data portion: | 1,496 bytes |
| Frame check sequence field: | 4 bytes (at the end of data) |
| Total: | 1,517 bytes |

**NOTE** **Although Ethernet networks support 1,518-byte packets, you may notice the LIP echo test using 1,517-byte packets when Ethernet_802.2 frames are used. This allows for an alteration in the Ethernet_802.2 frame. NetWare uses the Unnumbered 802.2 format frame. An information/supervisory 802.2 format is available as well; it increases the frame size by one byte. In case Novell ever uses the larger 802.2 frame format, the data must allow for the extra 1 byte that may be needed someday.**

When the server receives the LIP echo packet, it echoes it back to the client. The client sends a second echo test packet in case there is a second route to the server. The server echoes the packet back.

If the server did not echo back the packet, the client assumes the MTU size is too large. The client backs off the MTU size until it reaches a size supported by the data path.

**Some versions of Client 32 did not test the data path during connection establishment. This turned out to be a problem over some bridged token ring networks, so the functionality was replaced in CLIENT32.NLM files dated later than 1/1/97.**

### LIP Echo Test: Burst Mode Startup Sequence

The NetWare VLMs use the LIP echo test packets to dynamically configure burst mode data flow speeds. Client 32, however, has default flow parameters; it does not need to use a round-trip timing mechanism to obtain starting parameters. As shown in Figure 13.4, the client requests a packet burst connection (packet 17) during the connection establishment phase. The server answers back with a Completion Code 0x00, indicating that the server supports burst mode.

**NetWare 3.12 and later versions of the operating system have burst mode functionality built in. To enable burst mode for NetWare 3.11 servers, you must download PBURST.NLM from Novell's Web site, www.novell.com, or from CompuServe (GO NOVFILES).**

The client begins a process of timing the round-trip latency between the client and the server. The client starts a timer and sends the LIP echo test packet, as shown in Figure 13.5.

The client versions perform this test between two and six times, depending on their version. They use a percentage of the best round-trip time as the starting gap time between packets in a burst set. Depending on the client version you are running, the percentage may be as low as 25 percent or as high as 50 percent. The maximum round-trip time is used as a maximum allowable gap time between packets in a burst set. These gap times are called the *interpacket gap time* or IPG.

Client 32's starting IPG is set at 0. The dynamic nature of Client 32 enables it to tune its performance based on the current congestion and throughput rate on the network.

Burst mode is covered in greater detail later in this chapter.

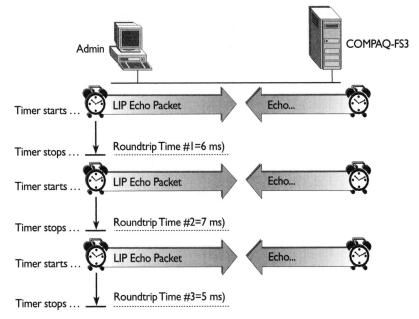

*The client measures the round-trip latency time using NCP LIP echo packets.*

## NCP REQUESTS (TYPE 0X2222)

Most of your NCP communications are standard NCP requests and replies. These packets are used for command sequences and for non-burst data transfer. Figure 13.6 shows a typical exchange of NCP packets on a network.

In the NCP packet, we can see the destination socket is NCP (0x453). This client is requesting a continued File Search for LOGIN.MSG. The server reply is shown in Figure 13.7.

When making NCP requests, NetWare clients can use dynamic socket numbers in the source socket number field. NCP sockets are covered in greater detail later in this chapter.

Each NCP request is identified with a unique sequence number. The sequence number starts at 0 (0x0000) and continues to 0xFFFF. The number wraps back to 0x0000 after hitting 0xFFFF.

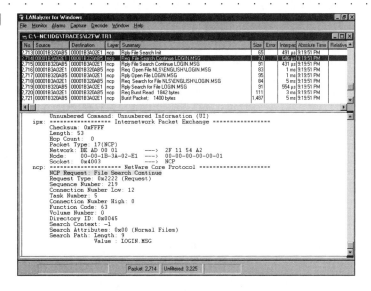

## NCP REPLIES (TYPE 0X3333)

NCP replies are linked with their associated requests through the user connection ID number and sequence number identified in the NCP portion of the packet. Figure 13.7 shows the reply to the packet in Figure 13.6.

The reply packets contain a completion code field that indicates whether the request was processed successfully (0x00) or there was an error (any nonzero number). In Figure 13.7, we can see that the requested file (LOGIN.MSG) has been located and the server is supplying the basic file information such as size, creation date, last accessed date, and attributes.

Later in this chapter, we'll examine an NCP failure.

## NCP DESTROY CONNECTION (TYPE 0X5555)

The NCP connection termination packet is sent to terminate a general service connection. This packet is sent from the client to the server when you unload the client software or when you "hop" from one server to another (as in the Preferred Server process). Figure 13.8 shows a destroy connection packet. As you can see, this is a very simple packet that contains only the type code (0x5555), the sequence number (5), and the connection number (8). The reply is a standard 0x3333 reply packet with (hopefully) a completion code 0x00.

FIGURE 13.8

*This destroy connection request will be answered with a standard reply (0x3333) packet.*

```
No.  Source        Destination    Layer  Summary                                      Error  Size  Interpacket  Absolute Time  Relative Ti
27   Admin.IMAGITECH COMPAQ-FS3   ncp    LIP Echo Packet                                     1,517    3 ms   8:27:20 PM
28   COMPAQ-FS3    Admin.IMAGITEC ncp    LIP Echo Packet                                     1,517    3 ms   8:27:20 PM
29   Admin.IMAGITECH COMPAQ-FS3   ncp    LIP Echo Packet                                     1,517    8 ms   8:27:20 PM
30   COMPAQ-FS3    Admin.IMAGITEC ncp    LIP Echo Packet                                     1,517    3 ms   8:27:20 PM
31   Admin.IMAGITECH COMPAQ-FS3   ncp    Req Read Property Value SERVINET_ADDRESS             133      2 ms   8:27:20 PM
32   COMPAQ-FS3    Admin.IMAGITEC ncp    Rply Read Property Value; No Such Object              64     764 µs  8:27:20 PM
33   Admin.IMAGITECH COMPAQ-FS3   ncp    Req Destroy Service Connection                        64     303 µs  8:27:20 PM
34   COMPAQ-FS3    Admin.IMAGITEC ncp    Rply Destroy Service Connection                       64      3 ms   8:27:20 PM
35   Admin.IMAGITECH Broadcast    sap    Query Nearest Directory Server                        64     11 ms   8:27:20 PM
36   COMPAQ-FS3    Admin.IMAGITEC sap    Resp Nearest; Server=TREE1_____N@@@       117    483 µs  8:27:20 PM
37   FS2           Admin.IMAGITEC sap    Resp Nearest; Server=TREE1_____@@@PB      117    148 µs  8:27:20 PM
```

```
Packet Number : 33              8:27:20 PM
Length : 64 bytes
802.3: ================== IEEE 802.3 Datalink Layer ==================
        Station: Admin.IMAGITECH.[ROO ----> COMPAQ-FS3
        Length: 40
802.2: ================== IEEE 802.2 Logical Link Control ==============
        SSAP: NetWare     DSAP: NetWare
        Unnumbered Command: Unnumbered Information (UI)
  ipx: ================== Internetwork Packet Exchange ==================
        Checksum: 0xFFFF
        Length: 37
        Hop Count:  0
        Packet Type: 17(NCP)
        Network: BA 5E BA 11     --->  31 B0 56 E4
        Node:    00-20-C5-00-E4-21  --->  00-00-00-00-00-01
        Socket:  0x4038           --->  NCP
  ncp: ================== NetWare Core Protocol ==================
        NCP Request: Destroy Service Connection
        Request Type: 0x5555 (Destroy Service Connection)
        Sequence Number: 5
        Connection Number: 8
```

## NCP BURST MODE FILE READ/WRITES (TYPE 0X7777)

NetWare's burst mode communications enable greater throughput for file reads and writes. Although burst mode has been implemented in a number of ways over the years, we can look at the typical Client 32 implementation to get a feel for how burst mode traffic flows.

In burst mode file read communications, the client requests a set of data (the burst window size) in a single burst read packet. The client includes the IPG (interpacket gap time) setting in the request packet, as well. The server sends the set to the client in order, starting with byte 0 of the file. In the first burst, the window size is based on the client's settings. The default setting is 3 x [frame size]. For example, on an Ethernet network, the first set size would be approximately 4,554 bytes (3 x 1518 bytes).

In Figure 13.9, we are looking at a burst read request from a client that has just booted up and connected to a server. The client is launching the NETADMIN.EXE file in the PUBLIC directory. The client first requests a small burst—just 4,104 bytes (packet 9). We can see in the decode portion of packet 9 that the client has defined the sending interpacket gap time as 0 (send delay time = 0 microseconds). This is the default for Client 32, since it does not perform the round-trip timing mechanism up front in the connection sequence.

▶ · · · · · · · · · · · · · · · · · · · · · · · · · · · · ◀

*The client requests the first 4,104 bytes of a file.*

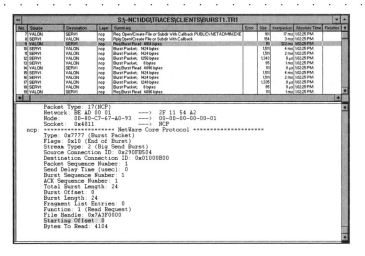

If the burst was successfully received, the window size will increase, as shown in the packet summary screen in Figure 13.10. The window size increase is very gradual and often includes some smaller burst set sizes in between (due to congestion detection mechanisms).

**FIGURE 13.10**

*The Burst Mode window sizes gradually increase upon successful completion.*

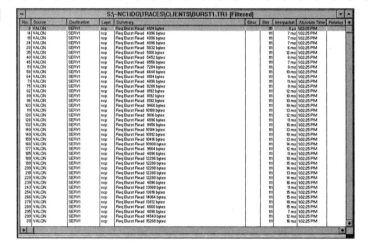

**NOTE**

**The trace summary shown in Figure 13.10 has been filtered to display only burst read requests.**

If the sender notices congestion that is affecting timing on the cabling system, the sender can drop the packet size slightly to help reduce the possible congestion.

If a burst set packet is lost during the transmission, the receiving station sends a burst mode system packet that includes a fragment list entry. The fragment list entry details the number and location of missing data bytes. When a failure like this occurs, the next burst window size request is immediately reduced to 50 percent of its previous size.

If there is a severe failure—where the receiver sends multiple duplicate system packets listing a missing fragment—the sender may also drop the packet size down to a minimum size (444 bytes, in many instances). Upon completion of the current burst set, the sender reinitializes the packet burst connection and starts building up the set size again.

Microsoft's Client for NetWare Networks (CFNN/NDS) burst mode implementation allows for a maximum window size of approximately 21K. The Microsoft burst mode implementation does not back off the window size when an error occurs. This can be devastating to the network if traffic congestion is the cause of errors and lost packets. The Microsoft clients do not throttle back their network loads during peak traffic times.

**NOTE**

Burst mode communications are covered in greater detail later in this chapter in the section "Typical NCP Sequences" and in the section "NCP Header Structure."

**X-REF**

## NCP REQUEST BEING PROCESSED (TYPE 0X9999)

Every version of the NetWare operating system and every version of the NetWare client software includes an NCP congestion control mechanism. When a client sends an NCP request to a server that is busy and cannot answer the request immediately, the client may time out waiting for the reply. In this case, the client resends the same request to the server (a reexecuted request). The server sends back a request-being-processed packet to the client to indicate that the request has been received and the client should reset its timer mechanism to zero.

The request-being-processed packet is sometimes referred to as a "server delay" or "server overload" packet.

**NOTE**

Figure 13.11 shows a request-being-processed packet. This packet uses packet type 0x9999 and simply defines the connection number and task number of the client that must wait. Upon receipt of this packet, the client should reset its timeout clock to 0 and begin counting up again as if it had just sent the request.

*The request-being-processed packet indicates that the client must wait because the server is busy.*

```
                                        M:\TRACES\DELLVLM.TR1
No.  Source          Destination       Layer  Summary                                    Error  Size  Interpacket  Absolute Time  Relative
168  Admin.IMAGITECH SERV1             ncp    Req Ping for NDS                                  64        3 s       3:37:18 PM
169  SERV1           Admin.IMAGITECH   ncp    Rply Ping for NDS                                159      793 µs     3:37:18 PM
170  Admin.IMAGITECH SERV1             nds    Req Resolve Name (CN= ADMIN.O= TC)               143        4 ms     3:37:19 PM
171  Admin.IMAGITECH SERV1             nds    Req Resolve Name (CN= ADMIN.O= TC)               143      146 ms     3:37:19 PM
172  SERV1           Admin.IMAGITECH   ncp    Rply Rqst Being Processed, Conn= 7                64      383 µs     3:37:19 PM
173  Admin.IMAGITECH SERV1             nds    Req Resolve Name (CN= ADMIN.O= TC)               143      418 ms     3:37:19 PM
174  SERV1           Admin.IMAGITECH   ncp    Rply Rqst Being Processed, Conn= 7                64      406 µs     3:37:19 PM
175  Admin.IMAGITECH SERV1             nds    Req Resolve Name (CN= ADMIN.O= TC)               143        1 s       3:37:19 PM
176  SERV1           Admin.IMAGITECH   ncp    Rply Rqst Being Processed, Conn= 7                64      348 µs     3:37:19 PM
177  Admin.IMAGITECH SERV1             nds    Req Resolve Name (CN= ADMIN.O= TC)               143        2 s       3:37:22 PM
178  Admin.IMAGITECH SERV1             ncp    Rply Rqst Being Processed, Conn= 7                64      311 µs     3:37:22 PM
179  Admin.IMAGITECH SERV1             nds    Req Resolve Name (CN= ADMIN.O= TC)               143        5 s       3:37:27 PM
180  SERV1           Admin.IMAGITECH   ncp    Rply Rqst Being Processed, Conn= 7                64      300 µs     3:37:27 PM
```

```
Length : 64 bytes
802.3: ================= IEEE 802.3 Datalink Layer ==================
       Station: SERV1 ----> Admin.IMAGITECH.[ROO
       Length: 41
802.2: ================ IEEE 802.2 Logical Link Control ================
       SSAP: NetWare      DSAP: NetWare
       Unnumbered Command: Unnumbered Information (UI)
   ipx: ================= Internetwork Packet Exchange ================
       Checksum: 0xFFFF
       Length: 38
       Hop Count:  0
       Packet Type: 17(NCP)
       Network: 2F 11 54 A2          --->  BE AD 00 01
       Node:    00-00-00-00-00-01    --->  00-20-C5-00-E4-21
       Socket:  NCP                  --->  0x4003
   ncp: ===================== NetWare Core Protocol =====================
       NCP Message: Request Being Processed
       Reply Type: 0x9999 (Request Being Processed)
       Connection Number Low: 7
       Task Number: 3
       Connection Number High: 0
```

The request-being-processed packets help avoid duplicate requests during busy server times. It is still possible, however, for a server to be too busy to service a request after the client has reset its timer. In this case, the client may reexecute the request, and the server can either answer the request or send another request-being-processed packet. Clients will not time out or lose connections when they receive request-being-processed packets from the server, but they may notice delays in their network communications.

**NOTE**

**Many times, the Windows hourglass that we dread is due to server response delays. Check your network to see how many request-being-processed packets are on your network.**

If your network experiences 15 or more request-being-processed packets every minute, you should start looking at the cause. The server could be low on memory or CPU power. The server could also be choking under the weight of too many NLMs. Check the monitor statistics for memory and processor utilization to see what tasks the server is performing. The request being processed packets could also indicate a problem with the server's file I/O, as well. Check server statistics to ensure the error counters are within reasonable range.

Now that we've examined the six NCP packet types, we can examine some typical NCP communications to see how clients use NCP to attach to a server, log in to a network, download files, and disconnect from the network.

## Typical NCP Sequences

NCP is used for a wide variety of communications between NetWare clients and servers. NCP is considered connection-oriented even though it uses IPX, not SPX, as its transport mechanism. This is because of the request/reply nature of NCP. A client's shell or requester makes an NCP request and waits for the reply. If the client does not receive a reply, it resends the request.

The following NCP sequences are typical communications processes that you will see on NetWare networks. We are not documenting every packet in detail, but we will highlight some of the more interesting exchanges between the clients and servers. These exchanges include:

- ▸ Client attachment

- ▸ Login process

- ▸ Copying a file at the server

- ▸ Launching a server-based application

- ▸ Logout process

- ▸ File reads and writes with burst mode

- ▸ NDS communications

By examining these communications one at a time, you should get a good feel for how important and pervasive NCP communications are in a typical client/server communication.

**X-REF**

**More typical communication trace files are on the CD-ROM. See Appendix H.**

## CLIENT ATTACHMENT SEQUENCE

Once the NetWare client has located a server (using SAP) and a route (using RIP), the client executes a number of NCP calls to set up the general service connection, as shown in Figure 13.12.

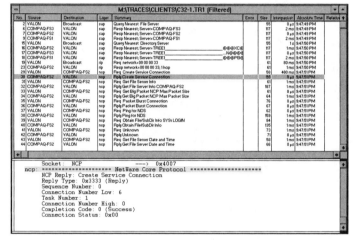

**FIGURE    13.12**

*The client is given general service connection 6 during the attachment process.*

In packet number 30 shown in Figure 13.12, we can see the connection number 6 was given to Valon. She will use this connection number in all her NCP communications to that server until a time when she destroys her connection or loses it due to some malfunction. Each user is allowed a single connection ID number for each general service connection.

Typically, the connection establishment process precedes the login process. In this next section, we'll examine a typical login process.

## LOGIN PROCESS (NDS ENVIRONMENT)

The login process can be very simple or complex, depending on the login scripts that are executed during this process. We'll use a relatively simple scenario to get you started in interpreting the login session. When you see different procedures in your network environment, examine your login scripts and user environments to see what has affected the login process.

In our example, we have a Client 32 station (running the CLIENT32.NLM file dated August 1996) that is logging in to an IntranetWare 4.11 server named

BLDG1. This login process was done through the Windows 95 NetWare Login window.

The summary shown in Figure 13.13 shows that our login process required 168 packets and a total of seven seconds. Although you may look at this and think that the login process is "dog-slow," this is an improved login process for the NetWare/IntranetWare 4.*x* environment — the original login process that is used with NetWare 3.*x* requires hundreds more packets because you must download the entire LOGIN.EXE file from the server's SYS:LOGIN directory.

Take a look at the summary shown in Figure 13.13 and then refer to the notes following the summary screen. The notes provide a brief description of the key processes that occur during the login procedure. Of course, your login process may look different if you have login scripts to process and other special circumstances.

▶ . . . . . . . . . . . . . . . . . . . . . . . . . . . . . . . . . . . . . ◀

FIGURE 13.13

*A summary of the Client32*
*to IntranetWare 4.11 login*
*process*

| No. | Source | Destination | Layer | Size | Summary |
|---|---|---|---|---|---|
| 1 | GINNY | BLDG1 | ncp | 0078 | Req Get Full Path String |
| 2 | BLDG1 | GINNY | ncp | 0083 | Rply Get Full Path String LOGIN\ |
| 3 | GINNY | BLDG1 | ncp | 0064 | Req Deallocate Directory Handle |
| 4 | BLDG1 | GINNY | ncp | 0064 | Rply Deallocate Directory Handle |
| 5 | GINNY | BLDG1 | nds | 0147 | Req Resolve Name (admin.imagitech) |
| 6 | BLDG1 | GINNY | nds | 0103 | Rply Resolve Name |
| 7 | GINNY | BLDG1 | nds | 0099 | Req Read Entry Info |
| 8 | BLDG1 | GINNY | nds | 0139 | Rply Read Entry Info |
| 9 | GINNY | BLDG1 | nds | 0147 | Req Resolve Name (admin.imagitech) |
| 10 | BLDG1 | GINNY | nds | 0103 | Rply Resolve Name |

*(continued)*

▶ · · · · · · · · · · · · · · · · · · · · · · · · · · · · · · · ◀

F I G U R E   13.13

*(continued)*

| 11 | GINNY | Broadcast | rip | 0064 | Req  network=CC CC CC 01 |
|----|-------|-----------|-----|------|--------------------------|
| 12 | BLDG1 | GINNY | rip | 0064 | Resp network=CC CC CC 01; 1 hop |
| 13 | GINNY | BLDG1 | ncp | 0064 | Req  Create Service Connection |
| 14 | BLDG1 | GINNY | ncp | 0064 | Rply Create Service Connection |
| 15 | GINNY | BLDG1 | ncp | 0064 | Req  Get File Server Info |
| 16 | BLDG1 | GINNY | ncp | 0187 | Rply Get File Server Info BLDG1 |
| 17 | GINNY | BLDG1 | ncp | 0064 | Req  Get Big Packet NCP Max Packet Size |
| 18 | BLDG1 | GINNY | ncp | 0064 | Rply Get Big Packet NCP Max Packet Size |
| 19 | GINNY | BLDG1 | ncp | 0076 | Req  Packet Burst Connection |
| 20 | BLDG1 | GINNY | ncp | 0067 | Rply Packet Burst Connection |
| 21 | GINNY | BLDG1 | ncp | 0064 | Req  Ping for NDS |
| 22 | BLDG1 | GINNY | ncp | 0159 | Rply Ping for NDS |
| 23 | GINNY | BLDG1 | nds | 0091 | Req  Begin Login |
| 24 | BLDG1 | GINNY | nds | 0079 | Rply Begin Login |
| 25 | GINNY | BLDG1 | nds | 0083 | Req  Get Server Address |
| 26 | BLDG1 | GINNY | nds | 0155 | Rply Get Server Address |
| 27 | GINNY | BLDG1 | nds | 0175 | Req  Resolve Name (CN=BLDG1.OU=LAB.O=IMA... |
| 28 | BLDG1 | GINNY | nds | 0103 | Rply Resolve Name |
| 29 | GINNY | BLDG1 | nds | 0133 | Req  Read (Public Key) |
| 30 | BLDG1 | GINNY | nds | 0497 | Rply Read |
| 31 | GINNY | BLDG1 | nds | 0099 | Req  Read Entry Info |
| 32 | BLDG1 | GINNY | nds | 0145 | Rply Read Entry Info |

| 33 | GINNY | BLDG1 | nds | 0580 | Req | Finish Login |
|----|-------|-------|-----|------|-----|--------------|
| 34 | BLDG1 | GINNY | nds | 0067 | Rply | Finish Login |
| 35 | GINNY | BLDG1 | nds | 0580 | Req | Continued Fragment (Finish Login) |
| 36 | BLDG1 | GINNY | nds | 0067 | Rply | Continued Fragment |
| 37 | GINNY | BLDG1 | nds | 0237 | Req | Continued Fragment (Finish Login) |
| 38 | BLDG1 | GINNY | nds | 0415 | Rply | Continued Fragment (Finish Login) |
| 39 | GINNY | BLDG1 | nds | 0133 | Req | Read (Public Key) |
| 40 | BLDG1 | GINNY | nds | 0469 | Rply | Read |
| 41 | GINNY | BLDG1 | ncp | 0065 | Req | Get Internet Address |
| 42 | BLDG1 | GINNY | ncp | 0072 | Rply | Get Internet Address |
| 43 | GINNY | BLDG1 | nds | 0147 | Req | Resolve Name (Admin.imagitech) |
| 44 | BLDG1 | GINNY | nds | 0103 | Rply | Resolve Name |
| 45 | GINNY | BLDG1 | nds | 0147 | Req | Resolve Name (admin.imagitech) |
| 46 | BLDG1 | GINNY | nds | 0103 | Rply | Resolve Name |
| 47 | GINNY | BLDG1 | nds | 0159 | Req | Resolve Name (CN=Admin.O=IMAGITECH) |
| 48 | BLDG1 | GINNY | nds | 0103 | Rply | Resolve Name |
| 49 | GINNY | BLDG1 | nds | 0083 | Req | Get Server Address |
| 50 | BLDG1 | GINNY | nds | 0155 | Rply | Get Server Address |
| 51 | GINNY | BLDG1 | nds | 0175 | Req | Resolve Name (CN=BLDG1.OU=LAB.O=IMA...) |
| 52 | BLDG1 | GINNY | nds | 0103 | Rply | Resolve Name |
| 53 | GINNY | BLDG1 | nds | 0133 | Req | Read (Public Key) |
| 54 | BLDG1 | GINNY | nds | 0497 | Rply | Read |
| 55 | GINNY | BLDG1 | nds | 0095 | Req | Begin Authentication |
| 56 | BLDG1 | GINNY | nds | 0195 | Rply | Begin Authentication |

*(continued)*

*(continued)*

| 57 | GINNY | BLDG1 | nds | 0511 | Req  | Finish Authentication |
| 58 | BLDG1 | GINNY | nds | 0071 | Rply | Finish Authentication |
| 59 | GINNY | BLDG1 | nds | 0135 | Req  | Read (full name) |
| 60 | BLDG1 | GINNY | nds | 0071 | Rply | Read; No Such Attribute |
| 61 | GINNY | BLDG1 | nds | 0147 | Req  | Resolve Name (admin.imagitech) |
| 62 | BLDG1 | GINNY | nds | 0103 | Rply | Resolve Name |
| 63 | GINNY | BLDG1 | nds | 0131 | Req  | Read (Surname) |
| 64 | BLDG1 | GINNY | nds | 0119 | Rply | Read |
| 65 | GINNY | BLDG1 | nds | 0147 | Req  | Resolve Name (admin.imagitech) |
| 66 | BLDG1 | GINNY | nds | 0103 | Rply | Resolve Name |
| 67 | GINNY | BLDG1 | nds | 0147 | Req  | Read (Message Server) |
| 68 | BLDG1 | GINNY | nds | 0171 | Rply | Read |
| 69 | GINNY | BLDG1 | nds | 0155 | Req  | Resolve Name (BLDG1.LAB.imagitech) |
| 70 | BLDG1 | GINNY | nds | 0103 | Rply | Resolve Name |
| 71 | GINNY | BLDG1 | nds | 0147 | Req  | Read (Network Address) |
| 72 | BLDG1 | GINNY | nds | 0151 | Rply | Read |
| 73 | GINNY | BLDG1 | nds | 0147 | Req  | Resolve Name (admin.imagitech) |
| 74 | BLDG1 | GINNY | nds | 0103 | Rply | Resolve Name |
| 75 | GINNY | BLDG1 | nds | 0135 | Req  | Read (Language) |
| 76 | BLDG1 | GINNY | nds | 0071 | Rply | Read; No Such Attribute |
| 77 | GINNY | BLDG1 | nds | 0147 | Req  | Resolve Name (admin.imagitech) |
| 78 | BLDG1 | GINNY | nds | 0103 | Rply | Resolve Name |

| 79 | GINNY | BLDG1 | nds | 0147 | Req | Read (Last Login Time) |
|----|-------|-------|-----|------|-----|------------------------|
| 80 | BLDG1 | GINNY | nds | 0135 | Rply | Read |
| 81 | GINNY | BLDG1 | ncp | 0064 | Req | Unknown |
| 82 | BLDG1 | GINNY | ncp | 0087 | Rply | Unknown |
| 83 | GINNY | BLDG1 | nds | 0135 | Req | Resolve Name (imagitech) |
| 84 | BLDG1 | GINNY | nds | 0103 | Rply | Resolve Name |
| 85 | GINNY | BLDG1 | nds | 0127 | Req | Open Stream (Login Script) |
| 86 | BLDG1 | GINNY | nds | 0071 | Rply | Open Stream; No Such Value |
| 87 | GINNY | BLDG1 | nds | 0147 | Req | Resolve Name (admin.imagitech) |
| 88 | BLDG1 | GINNY | nds | 0103 | Rply | Resolve Name |
| 89 | GINNY | BLDG1 | nds | 0131 | Req | Read (Profile) |
| 90 | BLDG1 | GINNY | nds | 0071 | Rply | Read; No Such Attribute |
| 91 | GINNY | BLDG1 | nds | 0147 | Req | Resolve Name (admin.imagitech) |
| 92 | BLDG1 | GINNY | nds | 0103 | Rply | Resolve Name |
| 93 | GINNY | BLDG1 | nds | 0127 | Req | Open Stream (Login Script) |
| 94 | BLDG1 | GINNY | nds | 0071 | Rply | Open Stream; No Such Value |
| 95 | GINNY | BLDG1 | ncp | 0064 | Req | Change Conn Authentication State |
| 96 | BLDG1 | GINNY | ncp | 0064 | Rply | Change Conn Authentication State |
| 97 | GINNY | BLDG1 | ncp | 0078 | Req | Obtain File/SubDir Info SYS |
| 98 | BLDG1 | GINNY | ncp | 0135 | Rply | Obtain File/SubDir Info |
| 99 | GINNY | BLDG1 | ncp | 0070 | Req | Allocate Short Dir Handle |
| 100 | BLDG1 | GINNY | ncp | 0065 | Rply | Allocate Short Dir Handle |
| 101 | GINNY | BLDG1 | ncp | 0074 | Req | Obtain File/SubDir Info |
| 102 | BLDG1 | GINNY | ncp | 0064 | Rply | Obtain File/SubDir Info |

*(continued)*

▶ · · · · · · · · · · · · · · · · · · · · · · · · · · · · · · ◀

F I G U R E   13.13

*(continued)*

| 103 | GINNY | BLDG1 | ncp | 0064 | Req  Deallocate Directory Handle |
| 104 | BLDG1 | GINNY | ncp | 0064 | Rply Deallocate Directory Handle |
| 105 | GINNY | BLDG1 | ncp | 0078 | Req  Obtain File/SubDir Info SYS |
| 106 | BLDG1 | GINNY | ncp | 0135 | Rply Obtain File/SubDir Info |
| 107 | GINNY | BLDG1 | ncp | 0070 | Req  Allocate Short Dir Handle |
| 108 | BLDG1 | GINNY | ncp | 0065 | Rply Allocate Short Dir Handle |
| 109 | GINNY | BLDG1 | ncp | 0074 | Req  Obtain File/SubDir Info |
| 110 | BLDG1 | GINNY | ncp | 0064 | Rply Obtain File/SubDir Info |
| 111 | GINNY | BLDG1 | ncp | 0080 | Req  Obtain File/SubDir Info ADMIN |
| 112 | BLDG1 | GINNY | ncp | 0064 | Rply Obtain File/SubDir Info; Failure |
| 113 | GINNY | BLDG1 | ncp | 0080 | Req  Obtain File/SubDir Info ADMIN |
| 114 | BLDG1 | GINNY | ncp | 0064 | Rply Obtain File/SubDir Info; Failure |
| 115 | GINNY | BLDG1 | ncp | 0064 | Req  Deallocate Directory Handle |
| 116 | BLDG1 | GINNY | ncp | 0064 | Rply Deallocate Directory Handle |
| 117 | GINNY | BLDG1 | ncp | 0078 | Req  Obtain File/SubDir Info SYS |
| 118 | BLDG1 | GINNY | ncp | 0135 | Rply Obtain File/SubDir Info |
| 119 | GINNY | BLDG1 | ncp | 0070 | Req  Allocate Short Dir Handle |
| 120 | BLDG1 | GINNY | ncp | 0065 | Rply Allocate Short Dir Handle |
| 121 | GINNY | BLDG1 | ncp | 0074 | Req  Obtain File/SubDir Info |
| 122 | BLDG1 | GINNY | ncp | 0064 | Rply Obtain File/SubDir Info |
| 123 | GINNY | BLDG1 | ncp | 0081 | Req  Obtain File/SubDir Info SYSTEM |
| 124 | BLDG1 | GINNY | ncp | 0142 | Rply Obtain File/SubDir Info |

| 125 | GINNY | BLDG1 | ncp | 0081 | Req  | Obtain File/SubDir Info SYSTEM |
|-----|-------|-------|-----|------|------|--------------------------------|
| 126 | BLDG1 | GINNY | ncp | 0135 | Rply | Obtain File/SubDir Info |
| 127 | GINNY | BLDG1 | ncp | 0070 | Req  | Set Short Dir Handle |
| 128 | BLDG1 | GINNY | ncp | 0064 | Rply | Set Short Dir Handle |
| 129 | GINNY | BLDG1 | ncp | 0078 | Req  | Get Full Path String |
| 130 | BLDG1 | GINNY | ncp | 0084 | Rply | Get Full Path String SYSTEM\SYS |
| 131 | GINNY | BLDG1 | ncp | 0078 | Req  | Obtain File/SubDir Info SYS |
| 132 | BLDG1 | GINNY | ncp | 0135 | Rply | Obtain File/SubDir Info |
| 133 | GINNY | BLDG1 | ncp | 0070 | Req  | Allocate Short Dir Handle |
| 134 | BLDG1 | GINNY | ncp | 0065 | Rply | Allocate Short Dir Handle |
| 135 | GINNY | BLDG1 | ncp | 0074 | Req  | Obtain File/SubDir Info |
| 136 | BLDG1 | GINNY | ncp | 0064 | Rply | Obtain File/SubDir Info |
| 137 | GINNY | BLDG1 | ncp | 0081 | Req  | Obtain File/SubDir Info PUBLIC |
| 138 | BLDG1 | GINNY | ncp | 0142 | Rply | Obtain File/SubDir Info |
| 139 | GINNY | BLDG1 | ncp | 0081 | Req  | Obtain File/SubDir Info PUBLIC |
| 140 | BLDG1 | GINNY | ncp | 0135 | Rply | Obtain File/SubDir Info |
| 141 | GINNY | BLDG1 | ncp | 0070 | Req  | Set Short Dir Handle |
| 142 | BLDG1 | GINNY | ncp | 0064 | Rply | Set Short Dir Handle |
| 143 | GINNY | BLDG1 | ncp | 0078 | Req  | Get Full Path String |
| 144 | BLDG1 | GINNY | ncp | 0084 | Rply | Get Full Path String PUBLIC\SYS |
| 145 | GINNY | BLDG1 | ncp | 0078 | Req  | Obtain File/SubDir Info SYS |
| 146 | BLDG1 | GINNY | ncp | 0135 | Rply | Obtain File/SubDir Info |
| 147 | GINNY | BLDG1 | ncp | 0070 | Req  | Allocate Short Dir Handle |
| 148 | BLDG1 | GINNY | ncp | 0065 | Rply | Allocate Short Dir Handle |

*(continued)*

▶ · · · · · · · · · · · · · · · · · · · · · · · · · · · · ◀

**F I G U R E   13.13**

*(continued)*

| | | | | | | |
|---|---|---|---|---|---|---|
| 149 | GINNY | BLDG1 | ncp | 0074 | Req | Obtain File/SubDir Info |
| 150 | BLDG1 | GINNY | ncp | 0064 | Rply | Obtain File/SubDir Info |
| 151 | GINNY | BLDG1 | ncp | 0100 | Req | Obtain File/SubDir Info |
| | | | | | | PUBLIC\IBM_PC\WIN95\V4.00 |
| 152 | BLDG1 | GINNY | ncp | 0064 | Rply | Obtain File/SubDir Info; Invalid Path |
| 153 | GINNY | BLDG1 | ncp | 0064 | Req | Deallocate Directory Handle |
| 154 | BLDG1 | GINNY | ncp | 0064 | Rply | Deallocate Directory Handle |
| 155 | GINNY | BLDG1 | ncp | 0078 | Req | Get Volume Number SYS |
| 156 | BLDG1 | GINNY | ncp | 0064 | Rply | Get Volume Number |
| 157 | GINNY | BLDG1 | ncp | 0065 | Req | Get Extended Vol Info |
| 158 | BLDG1 | GINNY | ncp | 0197 | Rply | Get Extended Vol Info |
| 159 | GINNY | BLDG1 | nds | 0099 | Req | Read Entry Info |
| 160 | BLDG1 | GINNY | nds | 0159 | Rply | Read Entry Info |
| 161 | GINNY | BLDG1 | ncp | 0078 | Req | Get Volume Number SYS |
| 162 | BLDG1 | GINNY | ncp | 0064 | Rply | Get Volume Number |
| 163 | GINNY | BLDG1 | ncp | 0065 | Req | Get Extended Vol Info |
| 164 | BLDG1 | GINNY | ncp | 0197 | Rply | Get Extended Vol Info |
| 165 | GINNY | BLDG1 | nds | 0099 | Req | Read Entry Info |
| 166 | BLDG1 | GINNY | nds | 0159 | Rply | Read Entry Info |
| 167 | GINNY | BLDG1 | ncp | 0064 | Req | Get File Server Date and Time |
| 168 | BLDG1 | GINNY | ncp | 0066 | Rply | Get File Server Date and Time |

The client goes through ten basic steps to log in to an IntranetWare 4.11 server using NDS. These steps are:

1 • Conduct user object resolution (tree walking) and general connection establishment.

2 • Launch login process (keyed process).

3 • Resolve name within context (keyed process).

4 • Authenticate to NDS (keyed process).

5 • Check user object attributes.

6 • Check for container, profile, and user login scripts.

7 • Change connection authentication state.

8 • Run default login script.

9 • Get volume information.

10 • Get the file server date and time.

Let's look at each of these steps a bit more closely and see how the NCP requests and replies are used during the client login process.

**TIP**

**As you can imagine, it would take another 500 pages to go through each of the NCP requests and replies that we're examining in this chapter. Therefore, I am only picking out the most interesting/relevant NCP sets to display in detail. For more information, check on our Web site, www.imagitech.com, where I typically pop newer trace files and supplemental information on IPX/SPX and TCP/IP communications.**

### Step 1. Conduct User Object Resolution (Tree Walking) and General Connection Establishment

First, the user must obtain a general services connection to a server that maintains a writeable replica of the partition. You can see in packets 5 and 9 that Ginny is attempting to connect to the network as admin.imagitech. At this point, Ginny is simply looking for a general service connection — she is not requesting authentication to NDS. The general service connection is the first connection type that any NetWare client station requests (including VLMs and the old NETX clients).

 **If you have a more sophisticated analyzer, such as Network General Sniffer or NCC LAN Network Probe, you can set up a filter to identify anyone attempting to connect as admin.**

NOTE

The object resolution process is also called *tree walking*. At this point in the login process, a client is attempting to locate a writable replica of the user's object.

If Ginny is interested in using NCP Packet Signing, she sets the Packet Security Level bit to a nonzero value in the "Get Big Packet ncp Max Packet Size" request.

Packet signing is covered in greater detail later in this chapter.

### Step 2. Launch Login Process (Keyed Process)

The second step is to launch the login process. This process can be performed in two separate ways because Client 32 changed the way we log into the network. With the VLM, we used to download the entire LOGIN.EXE file to the client to execute in memory. Now, we execute the login process as an NCP call, as you can see in packets 23 and 24.

The login process is a protected process — the client requests an encryption key from the server in packet 29. In fact, the login process has three protected processes: launching the login process itself, resolving the login name, and authenticating to the NDS environment.

In Figure 13.14, we can see the key being sent to the client.

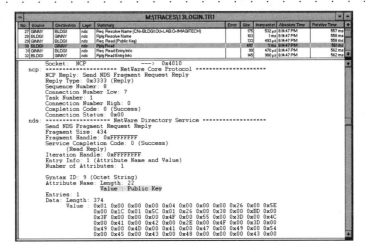

**FIGURE 13.14**

*The public key is sent to the client for use during the login sequence.*

## Step 3. Resolve Name Within Context (Keyed Process)

In the third step, the user resolves its name to the NDS context that the user object is located in. Of course, when you log in, you supply your user name and password (if used). In packet 43, shown in Figure 13.13, the client is trying to resolve its login name as Admin.imagitech. The client then tries to resolve its name using lowercase "a" in admin.imagitech in packet 45, as shown in Figure 13.15.

**FIGURE 13.15**

*The client tries to resolve its name using lowercase letters next.*

```
                          S:\-NC1IDG\TRACES\13LOGIN.TR1
No. Source      Destination    Layer  Summary                          Error    Size  Interpacket  Absolute Tim  Relative Ti
45  GINNY       BLDG1          nds    Req Resolve Name (admin.imagitech)        147   2 ms  8:14:48 PM    1 s
46  BLDG1       GINNY          nds    Rply Resolve Name                          103   1 ms  8:14:48 PM    1 s

        Length: 126
        Hop Count: 0
        Packet Type: 17(NCP)
        Network: 00 00 11 11       ---> CC CC CC 01
        Node:   00-80-5F-5C-7A-24  ---> 00-00-00-00-00-01
        Socket: 0x400C             ---> NCP
    ncp: ================== NetWare Core Protocol ==================
        NCP Request: Send NDS Fragment Request Reply
        Request Type: 0x2222 (Request)
        Sequence Number: 14
        Connection Number Low: 6
        Task Number: 53
        Connection Number High: 0
        Function Code: 104
        Subfunction Code: 2
    nds: ================== NetWare Directory Service ==================
        Send NDS Fragment Request Reply
        Fragment Handle: 0xFFFFFFFF
        Max Fragment Size: 514
        Message Size: 76
        Fragment Flags: 0
        Internal Verb Number: 1 (Resolve Name)
        Reply Buffer Size: 4096
        Version: 0
        Flags: 0x00002062 (Prefer Referrals, Dereference Aliases, Walk Tree,
               Readable)
        Scope of Referral: 0 (Any Server)
        Target Entry Name: Length: 32
                           Value : admin.imagitech
        Transport: Length: 1
                   Value : 0x00000000
        Tree Walker Type: Length: 1
                          Value : 0x00000000
```

### Step 4. Authenticate to NDS (Keyed Process)

In the fourth step, the user must authenticate to NDS to be allowed access to network services. In packets 55 and 57, the client begins authenticating to NDS. The authentication process occurs after the client is granted a general service connection, as shown in Figure 13.16. The NetWare License Manager is responsible for granting or denying licenses based on the license count available on the server. If no licenses are available — for instance, if five users are logged into a five-user version of NetWare — the License Manager will deny the license and the user remains authenticated, but not licensed/logged in.

**The License Manager function also manages general service connections.**

NOTE

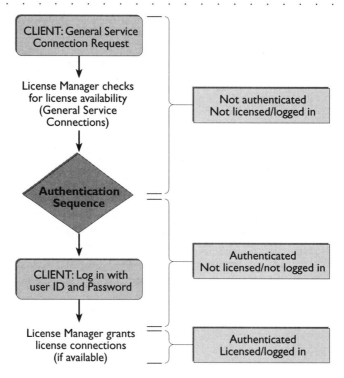

F I G U R E    13.16

*The authentication process occurs after the general service connection is granted.*

### Step 5. Check user object attributes

In the fifth step, the user reads its own object information that is contained in the NDS database. The next group of packets (packets 59 through 82) sent between the client and server provides the client with its user attributes. As we can see in the packet summary screen displayed earlier in Figure 13.13, the client reads the following attributes:

▸ Full name

▸ Surname

▸ Message server

▸ Network address

▸ Language

▸ Last login time

### Step 6. Check for Container, Profile, and User Login Scripts

In the sixth step, the client locates and executes any login scripts that have been defined, including container, profile, and user login scripts. If no user login script exists, the user executes the default login script. As you can see in packet 83, the client is looking at its container, "imagitech." The client requests to open the container's login script in packet 85. Since there is no container login script, the server returns the value –602, no such value in the reply, as show in Figure 13.17.

In packet number 89, the client checks for a profile script. No profile script exists, so the server returns a code –603 (no such attribute). Finally, in packet number 93, the client requests to open the login script for admin.imagitech (the user login script). Since there is no user login script, the server replies with –602 (no such value).

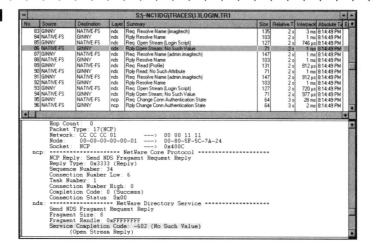

FIGURE 13.17

*The reply code indicates that there is no container script for imagitech.*

## Step 7. Change Connection Authentication State to Logged In

Now that the client has successfully logged into the server, the client can change its authentication state to logged in. As we can see in Figure 13.18, the client includes a request code in this NCP call to indicate the state change. The following request codes are possible:

01: Change logged in to temporarily authenticated.

02: Change temporarily authenticated to logged in.

Any other values are invalid and considered errors.

FIGURE 13.18

*The client requests to change its connection state to logged in.*

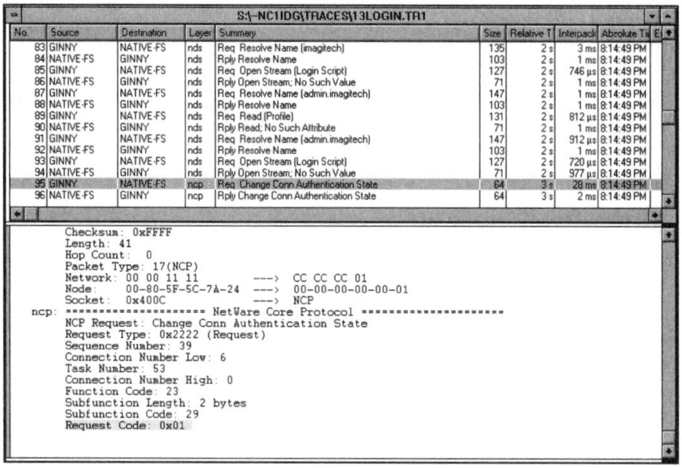

### Step 8. Run the Default Login Script

If there is no user login script, the client runs the default login script. The NetWare 4.11 default login script looks like this:

```
MAP DISPLAY OFF

MAP ERRORS OFF

MAP *1:=SYS:

MAP *1:=SYS:%LOGIN_NAME

IF "%1"="ADMIN" THEN MAP *1:=SYS:SYSTEM

MAP P:=SYS:PUBLIC (OS/2 clients only)

MAP INS S1:=SYS:PUBLIC

MAP INS S2:=SYS:PUBLIC\%MACHINE\%OS\%OS_VERSION (DOS/Windows
clients only)

MAP DISPLAY ON

MAP
```

As we examine the trace of the login sequence, we can clearly see where the default login script follows the lookup sequence for the container, profile, and user scripts.

▸ In packet 105, Ginny is mapping a drive to SYS (MAP *1:=SYS).

▸ In packet 111, Ginny is attempting to map a drive to a directory based on the login name (MAP *1:=SYS:%LOGIN_NAME). The reply packet contains completion code 255 (failure), indicating that no such directory exists.

▸ In packets 117 and 123, Ginny sets up her mapping to SYS:SYSTEM (IF "%1"="ADMIN" THEN MAP *1:=SYS:SYSTEM)—she is actually logging in using the Admin account.

**NOTE**

**The MAP P:=SYS:PUBLIC default login script command is not executed because Ginny is logging in from a Windows 95 station. This command is only executed for OS/2 clients.**

▶ In packet 151, Ginny then attempts to map a search drive to a directory that contains the OS files on the server (MAP INS S2:=SYS:PUBLIC\%MACHINE\%OS\%OS_VERSION). This is based on the client's configuration. In packet 152, shown in Figure 13.19, we can see the answer is "invalid path," which indicates that the DOS directory does not exist on the server. This is good—the client should look for COMMAND.COM in its local environment. You should only look for DOS COMMAND.COM on the NetWare server when the client is a diskless workstation.

**This default login mapping is executed only on DOS/Windows clients, not on OS/2 clients.**

NOTE

The MAP commands (MAP DISPLAY ON and MAP) are executed locally by the client after all mappings have been made or attempted.

**If you want to disable the default login script altogether, include the NO_DEFAULT command in the container or profile login script.**

NOTE

**F I G U R E   13.19**

*The default login script contains a statement to map a drive to an OS directory on the server.*

```
                                    S:\-NC1IDG\TRACES\13LOGIN.TR1
No.  Source      Destination   Layer  Summary                                           Size  Relative T  Interpack  Absolute T  E
151  GINNY       NATIVE-FS     ncp    Req Obtain File/SubDir Info PUBLIC\ IBM_PC\ WIN95\ V4.00  100   3 s    748 µs  8:14:50 PM
152  NATIVE-FS   GINNY         ncp    Rply Obtain File/SubDir Info; Invalid Path         64    3 s    432 µs  8:14:50 PM
153  GINNY       NATIVE-FS     ncp    Req Deallocate Directory Handle                    64    3 s      1 ms  8:14:50 PM
154  NATIVE-FS   GINNY         ncp    Rply Deallocate Directory Handle                   64    3 s    318 µs  8:14:50 PM
155  GINNY       NATIVE-FS     ncp    Req Get Volume Number SYS                          78    3 s     52 µs  8:14:50 PM
156  NATIVE-FS   GINNY         ncp    Rply Get Volume Number                             64    3 s    400 µs  8:14:50 PM
157  GINNY       NATIVE-FS     ncp    Req Get Extended Vol Info                          65    3 s      7 ms  8:14:50 PM
158  NATIVE-FS   GINNY         ncp    Rply Get Extended Vol Info                        197    3 s    900 µs  8:14:50 PM
159  GINNY       NATIVE-FS     nds    Req Read Entry Info                                99    3 s    592 µs  8:14:50 PM

Length : 64 bytes
802.3: ================= IEEE 802.3 Datalink Layer ==================
        Station: NATIVE-FS ----> GINNY
        Length: 41
802.2: ================= IEEE 802.2 Logical Link Control ===============
        SSAP: NetWare      DSAP: NetWare
        Unnumbered Command: Unnumbered Information (UI)
  ipx: ================= Internetwork Packet Exchange ================
        Checksum: 0xFFFF
        Length: 38
        Hop Count: 0
        Packet Type: 17(NCP)
        Network: CC CC CC 01      ---> 00 00 11 11
        Node:    00-00-00-00-00-01 ---> 00-80-5F-5C-7A-24
        Socket:  NCP              ---> 0x400C
  ncp: ================= NetWare Core Protocol =================
        NCP Reply: Obtain File/SubDir Info
        Reply Type: 0x3333 (Reply)
        Sequence Number: 67
        Connection Number Low: 6
        Task Number: 1
        Connection Number High: 0
        Completion Code: 156 (Invalid Path)
        Connection Status: 0x00
```

### Step 9. Get Volume Information

In packets 155 through 166, the client gets additional volume information. Figure 13.20 shows the content of packet 158, where the client receives extended volume information.

```
                                    S:\-NC1\DG\TRACES\13LOGIN.TR1
        Connection Status: 0x00
        Volume Info Length: 132
        Volume Type: 0
        Status Flag Bits: 0x00000003
        Sector Size: 512
        Sectors Per Cluster: 64
        Volume Size In Clusters: 9180
        Freed Clusters: 4399
        Sub Alloc Freeable Clusters: 116
        Freeable Limbo Sectors: 6305
        Non Freeable Limbo Sectors: 353
        Non Freeable Avail Sub Alloc Sectors: 60112
        Not Useable Sub Alloc Sectors: 764
        Sub Alloc Clusters: 1198
        Data Streams Count: 3336
        Limbo Data Streams Count: 214
        Oldest Deleted File Age In Tricks: 2147483648
        Compressed Data Streams Count: 1378
        Compressed Limbo Data Streams Count: 279
        Uncompressable Data Streams Count: 511
        Pre Compressed Sectors: 112153
        Compressed Sectors: 41445
        Migrated Files: 0
        Migrated Sectors: 0
        Clusters Used By FAT: 6
        Clusters Used By Directories: 650
        Clusters Used By Extended Directories: 0
        Total Directory Entries: 83200
        Unused Directory Entries: 77408
        Total Extended Directory Extants: 0
        Unused Extended Directory Extants: 0
        Extended Attributes Defined: 0
        Extended Attribute Extants Used: 0
        Directory Services Object ID: 16777455
        Volume Last Modified Date And Time:  577319712 (22:35:12 April 17, 1988 GMT)
        Volume Name: Length: 3
                     Value : SYS
```

### Step 10. Get the File Server Date and Time

Finally, the client requests the server's date and time (packet 167), allowing the client to synchronize its clock with the server.

It is always a good idea to capture and keep a copy of your clients' typical login sequence. In some instances, this is the only way to identify unusual login sequences caused by local software "hooking" onto the client immediately upon login. Your login sequence may differ if you are using another version of the NetWare client or have defined container, profile, or user login scripts.

## COPY A FILE AT THE SERVER

There are two basic ways to copy a file from one network directory to another network directory: standard copy and NCOPY. NCOPY is the network copy utility that Novell developed to allow you to copy a file at the network level without downloading the file to the workstation in the process.

As shown in Figure 13.21, standard copy utilities such as COPY.EXE read the file from the server and then write the copy back to the server. On large file duplications, this process can cause quite a load on the network communications system.

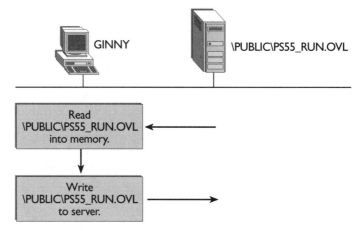

**FIGURE 13.21**

*Standard copy utilities read the file to the local client and then write the file back up to the server as a separate process.*

NCOPY, however, uses an NCP call to duplicate the file. This NCP call is shown later in Figure 13.27 (function code 74). This is a great way to reduce the amount of communications traffic caused by file copying. Unfortunately, however, additional overhead is caused in the NCOPY process.

In order to differentiate between the efficiency of COPY.EXE and NCOPY.EXE, we can look at the trace summaries of two copying operations. In Figure 13.22, we have the trace summary from a session where a client uses COPY.EXE to duplicate the file PS55_RUN.OVL (an overlay file used for this exercise only) from network directory PUBLIC to the user directory GINNY.

F I G U R E   1 3 . 2 2

The COPY command uses
burst reads and writes to
bring a file to the local
system before duplicating.

Now let's take a look at the steps involved in each of these processes. The following steps are used to duplicate the file using COPY.EXE:

**1** • Get the path to the source directory.

**2** • Get source and destination directory information.

**3** • Locate the file in the source directory.

**4** • Determine if the file (or a file with the same name) already exists in the destination directory.

**5** • Get source file information.

**6** • Recheck your facts.

**7** • Open the source file and create and open a zero-byte file in the destination directory.

**8** • Read the source file into the client memory.

**9** • Write the new file to the server.

**10** • Set the file date/time stamp and close the file.

**11** • Check to see if the file exists in the new location.

This process required 72 packets—only 8 of those packets (packets 47 through 54) are from the actual copy process.

Now let's examine how NCOPY performs a file duplication. NCOPY.EXE is a utility that, in the typical configuration, is kept in the PUBLIC directory. The client must download the NCOPY utility (and all supporting files) before the copy execution can take place. Figure 13.23 shows the basic steps of performing an NCOPY routine.

FIGURE 13.23

NCOPY is copied from the PUBLIC directory to the server's memory.

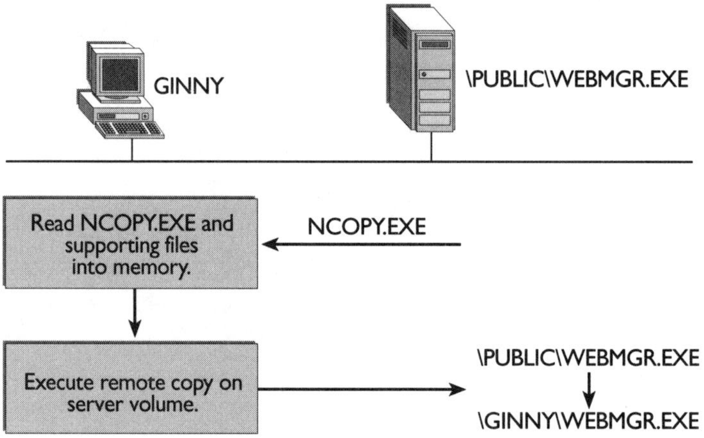

In Figure 13.24, Figure 13.25, and Figure 13.26, we see the trace summaries from an NCOPY process that was used to copy the WEBMGR.EXE file from the PUBLIC directory to Ginny's home directory.

The entire NCOPY.EXE file must be copied locally before file copying can be performed.

Supplemental files, such as UNI_MON.DOS, must also be copied locally before file copying can be performed.

Finally, NCOPY executes a single NCP call (Function 74) to execute the remote copy.

The NCOPY duplication steps are listed here:

**1** • Locate NCOPY (look in the local directory and then use the search path).

**2** • Read NCOPY.EXE into the client workstation (using burst mode).

**3** • Open supporting files (such as NCOPY.MSG, UNI_437.DOS, and UNI_MON.DOS).

**4** • Check client, server, and volume information.

**5** • Get the source file information.

**6** • Determine if the file (or a file with the same name) already exists in the destination directory.

**7** • Open, read, and close the source file.

**8** • Open the source file and create and open the destination file.

**9** • Copy from source to destination file.

**10** • Close both files.

**11** • Check to see if the new file exists.

Now, although both the COPY.EXE and NCOPY.EXE utilities use the same number of steps, the NCOPY process used 420 packets. This increase in packet number is due to the fact that you must read the NCOPY.EXE file to the local workstation before actually executing the copy process. The actual copy process used two packets—packets 393 and 394, as shown in Figures 13.27 and 13.28, respectively.

F I G U R E    13.27

*NCOPY executes a request to "Copy from One File to Another."*

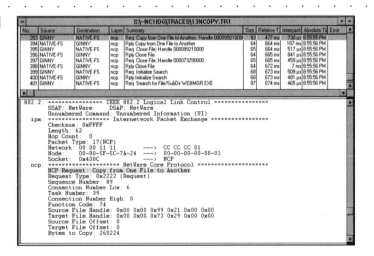

If the file that is being copied is large, NCOPY generates less overall traffic than COPY because it uses the "Copy from One File to Another" NCP call instead of copying the entire file to the client and then writing the file back to the server. If, however, the file is a relatively small file, COPY is a better utility to use. The best solution overall, of course, is to run NCOPY from a local drive. Unfortunately, in a large installation, distributed utilities can be a nightmare to standardize, manage, and troubleshoot. (NetWare Application Launcher can be used to manage these distributed application files.)

F I G U R E   13.28

*The server replies indicating the copy was successful.*

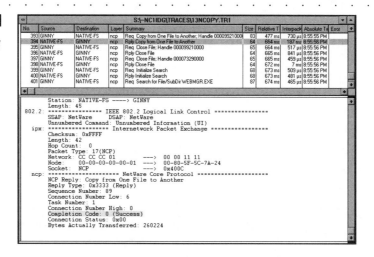

**NOTE**

**Sometimes you'll find the strangest behavior happening when you analyze network communications. Take a look at packet 329 in Figure 13.25. The client sends a request to resolve the name CN=webmgr.OU=exe.O=imagitech. It has interpreted Webmgr.Exe as an NDS object name, probably a misinterpretation of the "." between the filename and the file extension.**

Next, we'll look at the typical NCP communications used to launch an application that resides on a NetWare server.

## LAUNCHING A SERVER-BASED APPLICATION

When applications are stored on a workstation's local hard driver, they are executed locally and do not send NCP calls across the cabling system. When the applications are kept on the Novell server, however, NCP requests are made to launch the file (typically by downloading the entire application file first). Although each application has its own unique behavior, we can look at a sample application to see the typical steps required to open and execute an application that resides on the NetWare server. In this example, we are launching PCONSOLE.EXE from the SYS:PUBLIC directory. Our client is running Windows 95 with the Client 32 software.

It is always interesting to analyze the launch behavior of network applications. It gives us an insight into the file's dependencies on supplemental files and other programs. In our example, PCONSOLE.EXE must allocate and assign 18 file handles to open 11 files that PCONSOLE is dependent on. These file handles provide us with a numerical value to use when calling up various files on the server.

Table 13.1 lists the file handle numbers assigned to the files and provides a reference to the packet numbers in which these handles were assigned.

| T A B L E   13.1 | FILE HANDLE | FILE NAME | PACKET REFERENCE |
|---|---|---|---|
| *PCONSOLE.EXE Requires* | 000029640000 | PCONSOLE.EXE | 14 |
| *18 File Handles to Launch* | 000029650000 | PCONSOLE.EXE | 26 |
| *Supplemental Files as well* | 000029660000 | PCONSOLE.EXE | 82 |
| *as PCONSOLE.EXE.* | 000029670000 | PCONSOLE.EXE | 88 |
| | 000029680000 | PCONSOLE.EXE | 285 |
| | 000024A90000 | PCONSOLE.MSG | 390 |
| | 00001F620000 | TEXTUTIL.MSG | 418 |
| | 0000218E0000 | IBM_RUN.OVL | 437 |
| | 0000218F0000 | TEXTUTIL.IDX | 474 |
| | 000035550000 | PCONSOLE.HEP | 546 |
| | 00002D960000 | TEXTUTIL.HEP | 567 |
| | 0000015E0000 | UNI_437.DOS | 621 |
| | 0000015F0000 | UNI_437.DOS | 630 |
| | 000001600000 | UNI_MON.DOS | 641 |
| | 000001610000 | UNI_MON.DOS | 649 |
| | 00003A4A0000 | NWDSBRWS.MSG | 663 |
| | 0000160D0000 | SCHEMA.XLT | 687 |
| | 0000160E0000 | SCHEMA.XLT | 697 |

The summary screen shown in Figure 13.29 shows that PCONSOLE has a number of dependencies. We have filtered out traffic based on NCP function code 87, which deals primarily with file location/opening processes.

**For more information on the NCP function codes, refer to the section titled "NCP Function/Subfunction/Verb List" later in this chapter.**

X-REF

FIGURE 13.29

*PCONSOLE uses NCP function code 87 to request supplemental files.*

| No. | Source | Destination | Layer | Summary | Size | Relative T | Interpack | A |
|-----|--------|-------------|-------|---------|------|-----------|-----------|---|
| 471 | GINNY | NATIVE-FS | ncp | Req Search for File/SubDir Set TEXTUTIL.IDX | 91 | 3 s | 2 s | 8: |
| 473 | GINNY | NATIVE-FS | ncp | Req Open/Create File/SubDir TEXTUTIL.IDX | 93 | 3 s | 2 ms | 8: |
| 479 | GINNY | NATIVE-FS | ncp | Req Obtain File/SubDir Info TEXTUTIL.IDX | 87 | 3 s | 29 ms | 8: |
| 539 | GINNY | NATIVE-FS | ncp | Req Search for File/SubDir Set PCONSOLE.HEP | 91 | 4 s | 187 ms | 8: |
| 541 | GINNY | NATIVE-FS | ncp | Req Open/Create File/SubDir PCONSOLE.HEP | 94 | 4 s | 1 ms | 8: |
| 543 | GINNY | NATIVE-FS | ncp | Req Search for File/SubDir Set PCONSOLE.HEP | 91 | 4 s | 1 ms | 8: |
| 545 | GINNY | NATIVE-FS | ncp | Req Open/Create File/SubDir PUBLIC\ NLS\ ENGLISH\ PCONSOLE.HEP | 113 | 4 s | 2 ms | 8: |
| 551 | GINNY | NATIVE-FS | ncp | Req Obtain File/SubDir Info PUBLIC\ NLS\ ENGLISH\ PCONSOLE.HEP | 107 | 4 s | 98 ms | 8: |
| 560 | GINNY | NATIVE-FS | ncp | Req Search for File/SubDir Set TEXTUTIL.HEP | 91 | 4 s | 110 ms | 8: |
| 562 | GINNY | NATIVE-FS | ncp | Req Obtain File/SubDir Info PUBLIC\ NLS\ ENGLISH | 94 | 4 s | 2 ms | 8: |
| 564 | GINNY | NATIVE-FS | ncp | Req Search for File/SubDir Set TEXTUTIL.HEP | 91 | 4 s | 1 ms | 8: |
| 566 | GINNY | NATIVE-FS | ncp | Req Open/Create File/SubDir PUBLIC\ NLS\ ENGLISH\ TEXTUTIL.HEP | 113 | 4 s | 2 ms | 8: |
| 576 | GINNY | NATIVE-FS | ncp | Req Obtain File/SubDir Info PUBLIC\ NLS\ ENGLISH\ TEXTUTIL.HEP | 107 | 4 s | 104 ms | 8: |
| 618 | GINNY | NATIVE-FS | ncp | Req Open/Create File/SubDir PUBLIC\ UNI_437.DOS | 100 | 4 s | 126 ms | 8: |
| 620 | GINNY | NATIVE-FS | ncp | Req Open/Create File/SubDir SYS\ LOGIN\ NLS\ UNI_437.DOS | 106 | 4 s | 2 ms | 8: |
| 625 | GINNY | NATIVE-FS | ncp | Req Obtain File/SubDir Info SYS\ LOGIN\ NLS\ UNI_437.DOS | 100 | 4 s | 84 ms | 8: |
| 629 | GINNY | NATIVE-FS | ncp | Req Open/Create File/SubDir SYS\ LOGIN\ NLS\ UNI_437.DOS | 106 | 4 s | 3 ms | 8: |
| 634 | GINNY | NATIVE-FS | ncp | Req Obtain File/SubDir Info SYS\ LOGIN\ NLS\ UNI_437.DOS | 100 | 4 s | 5 ms | 8: |
| 638 | GINNY | NATIVE-FS | ncp | Req Open/Create File/SubDir PUBLIC\ UNI_MON.DOS | 100 | 4 s | 3 ms | 8: |
| 640 | GINNY | NATIVE-FS | ncp | Req Open/Create File/SubDir SYS\ LOGIN\ NLS\ UNI_MON.DOS | 106 | 4 s | 1 ms | 8: |
| 644 | GINNY | NATIVE-FS | ncp | Req Obtain File/SubDir Info SYS\ LOGIN\ NLS\ UNI_MON.DOS | 100 | 4 s | 45 ms | 8: |
| 648 | GINNY | NATIVE-FS | ncp | Req Open/Create File/SubDir SYS\ LOGIN\ NLS\ UNI_MON.DOS | 106 | 4 s | 3 ms | 8: |
| 652 | GINNY | NATIVE-FS | ncp | Req Obtain File/SubDir Info SYS\ LOGIN\ NLS\ UNI_MON.DOS | 100 | 4 s | 4 ms | 8: |
| 656 | GINNY | NATIVE-FS | ncp | Req Search for File/SubDir Set NWDSBRWS.MSG | 91 | 4 s | 3 ms | 8: |
| 658 | GINNY | NATIVE-FS | ncp | Req Obtain File/SubDir Info PUBLIC\ NLS\ ENGLISH | 94 | 4 s | 1 ms | 8: |
| 660 | GINNY | NATIVE-FS | ncp | Req Search for File/SubDir Set NWDSBRWS.MSG | 91 | 4 s | 1 ms | 8: |
| 662 | GINNY | NATIVE-FS | ncp | Req Open/Create File/SubDir PUBLIC\ NLS\ ENGLISH\ NWDSBRWS.MSG | 113 | 4 s | 2 ms | 8: |
| 668 | GINNY | NATIVE-FS | ncp | Req Obtain File/SubDir Info PUBLIC\ NLS\ ENGLISH\ NWDSBRWS.MSG | 107 | 4 s | 42 ms | 8: |
| 680 | GINNY | NATIVE-FS | ncp | Req Search for File/SubDir Set SCHEMA.XLT | 89 | 4 s | 80 ms | 8: |
| 682 | GINNY | NATIVE-FS | ncp | Req Obtain File/SubDir Info PUBLIC\ NLS\ ENGLISH | 94 | 4 s | 1 ms | 8: |
| 684 | GINNY | NATIVE-FS | ncp | Req Search for File/SubDir Set SCHEMA.XLT | 89 | 4 s | 1 ms | 8: |
| 686 | GINNY | NATIVE-FS | ncp | Req Open/Create File/SubDir PUBLIC\ NLS\ ENGLISH\ SCHEMA.XLT | 111 | 4 s | 1 ms | 8: |
| 692 | GINNY | NATIVE-FS | ncp | Req Obtain File/SubDir Info PUBLIC\ NLS\ ENGLISH\ SCHEMA.XLT | 105 | 4 s | 71 ms | 8: |
| 696 | GINNY | NATIVE-FS | ncp | Req Open/Create File/SubDir PUBLIC\ NLS\ ENGLISH\ SCHEMA.XLT | 111 | 4 s | 4 ms | 8: |
| 702 | GINNY | NATIVE-FS | ncp | Req Obtain File/SubDir Info PUBLIC\ NLS\ ENGLISH\ SCHEMA.XLT | 105 | 4 s | 8 ms | 8: |

Launching PCONSOLE.EXE requires approximately six steps. These steps are listed here:

**1** • Get information on PCONSOLE.EXE.

**2** • Open PCONSOLE; read the first portion of the file.

**3** • Look for supplemental files.

**4** • Get source directory information.

**5** • Read PCONSOLE.EXE and associated files (as listed in Table 13-1) using burst mode.

**6** • Close all files and deallocate the directory handles.

Typically, when you execute applications that reside on a server, you must download the executable into your local system memory. Depending on the executable, you may also download numerous supplemental files during the launch process. If you want to increase the launch time for an application, consider copying the application to a local directory. Be certain to look for any supplemental files that the application needs to call in order to work. In the case of remote clients that have to dial in to the network, moving applications out to their local drives can drastically improve performance.

**NOTE**

**Be aware, however, that there is a negative side to copying files onto users' local drives. When you update the application, you must update it at all the remote locations as well as on the server. Weigh the benefits of faster communications with the hassles of keeping multiple copies of the file up to date.**

Next, we'll look at what happens when a user logs out of the NetWare server and releases the assigned resources.

## LOGGING OUT OF A SERVER

NCP calls are used to execute the procedure, as well. The Destroy Connection NCP type (0x5555) is the NCP call used to release the assigned general services connection. When you log out of a NetWare server, you must deallocate related directory handles and notify the server that you no longer need the general service connection ID number that you were assigned upon connection. Figure 13.30 shows the summary screen for a logout process using Windows 95 Explorer to highlight a network drive and select logout.

The logout steps are:

1 • Get the path string.

2 • Deallocate the directory handle assigned to that path.

3 • Log out from your NCP connection.

4 • Destroy your general service connection.

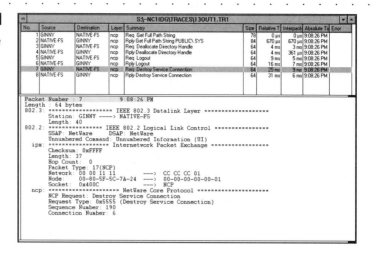

F I G U R E   13.30

*The logout process is simple and quick, requiring very little traffic overhead.*

If the client had any file handles assigned before executing the logout function, the file handles would be deallocated before the final logout procedure was completed.

Now that we've looked at a typical day in the life of a NetWare client (login through logout), let's take a look at the most common NCP processes that occur on NetWare networks—file reads and file writes.

## BURST MODE FILE READS AND WRITES

Burst mode's 0x7777 NCP type was the last to be added to the core set of six NCP types. Burst mode enables a client to read or write data to the server in a set, as opposed to one single packet at a time (ping-pong style). NetWare 4 servers and Client 32 have burst mode enabled by default.

When a client connects to the server, the client makes a burst mode connection request packet, as shown in Figure 13.31.

As shown in Figure 13.31, the client indicates its local connection ID (self-assigned) and the maximum size of the burst mode read and write windows (65,535 bytes). The client also indicates that the maximum payload (data) size for each packet is 1,490 bytes.

When the server responds, it uses the completion code field to indicate if the burst mode request was successful as well as the maximum packet size that will be used for burst mode communications.

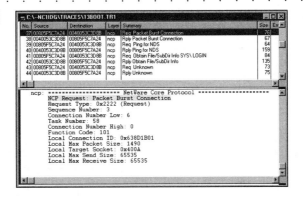

*A burst mode connection setup packet.*

The burst set size starts at approximately three times the maximum packet size. When burst mode reads or writes are successful, the set size increases incrementally. For example, in Figure 13.32, we have filtered on the burst read requests to see the gradual increase in set sizes.

The burst mode window sizing in Client 32 is quite intelligent. As burst communications are successfully completed, the client increases the window size. When an error occurs, the window size drops back by exactly 50 percent. This is called the "rapid window backoff."

*The burst set sizes gradually increase when sets are successful.*

Since network congestion is a likely cause of packet loss, it is imperative that a bursting client reduce its load on a network when packets begin to "drop." Figure 13.33 depicts a client communication sequence during a rapid window backoff. The previous burst request in this trace (off the screen) was for 35K. We temporarily disconnected the server from the network to cause this error. The next burst set request (seen in packet 716) is for 18,216 bytes, approximately half the last set request size.

FIGURE 13.33

*The rapid backoff process reduces the burst mode window by 50 percent.*

| No. | Source | Destination | Layer | Summary | Size | Relative T | Interpack | Absolute T | Error |
|-----|--------|-------------|-------|---------|------|-----------|-----------|-----------|-------|
| 686 | RTR4X-C1 | VALON | ncp | Burst Packet; 1424 bytes | 1,511 | 951 ms | 2 ms | 3:04:24 PM | |
| 687 | RTR4X-C1 | VALON | ncp | Burst Packet; 1424 bytes | 1,511 | 952 ms | 1 ms | 3:04:24 PM | |
| 688 | RTR4X-C1 | VALON | ncp | Burst Packet; 1424 bytes | 1,511 | 953 ms | 1 ms | 3:04:24 PM | |
| 689 | RTR4X-C1 | VALON | ncp | Burst Packet; 1424 bytes | 1,511 | 955 ms | 2 ms | 3:04:24 PM | |
| 690 | RTR4X-C1 | VALON | ncp | Burst Packet; 1424 bytes | 1,511 | 955 ms | 0 µs | 3:04:24 PM | |
| 691 | RTR4X-C1 | VALON | ncp | Burst Packet; 1424 bytes | 1,511 | 957 ms | 2 ms | 3:04:24 PM | |
| 692 | RTR4X-C1 | VALON | ncp | Burst Packet; 1424 bytes | 1,511 | 958 ms | 1 ms | 3:04:24 PM | |
| 693 | RTR4X-C1 | VALON | ncp | Burst Packet; 1424 bytes | 1,511 | 960 ms | 2 ms | 3:04:24 PM | |
| 694 | RTR4X-C1 | VALON | ncp | Burst Packet; 1424 bytes | 1,511 | 961 ms | 1 ms | 3:04:24 PM | |
| 695 | RTR4X-C1 | VALON | ncp | Burst Packet; 1424 bytes | 1,511 | 962 ms | 1 ms | 3:04:24 PM | |
| 696 | RTR4X-C1 | VALON | ncp | Burst Packet; 1424 bytes | 1,511 | 964 ms | 2 ms | 3:04:24 PM | |
| 697 | RTR4X-C1 | VALON | ncp | Burst Packet; 1040 bytes | 1,127 | 964 ms | 0 µs | 3:04:24 PM | |
| 698 | VALON | RTR4X-C1 | ncp | Burst System Packet; 23624 bytes missing | 93 | 2 s | 863 ms | 3:04:25 PM | |
| 699 | RTR4X-C1 | VALON | ncp | Burst Packet; 1072 bytes | 1,159 | 2 s | 2 ms | 3:04:25 PM | |
| 700 | RTR4X-C1 | VALON | ncp | Burst Packet; 1424 bytes | 1,511 | 2 s | 1 ms | 3:04:25 PM | |
| 701 | RTR4X-C1 | VALON | ncp | Burst Packet; 1424 bytes | 1,511 | 2 s | 1 ms | 3:04:25 PM | |
| 702 | RTR4X-C1 | VALON | ncp | Burst Packet; 1424 bytes | 1,511 | 2 s | 1 ms | 3:04:25 PM | |
| 703 | RTR4X-C1 | VALON | ncp | Burst Packet; 1424 bytes | 1,511 | 2 s | 1 ms | 3:04:25 PM | |
| 704 | RTR4X-C1 | VALON | ncp | Burst Packet; 1424 bytes | 1,511 | 2 s | 2 ms | 3:04:25 PM | |
| 705 | RTR4X-C1 | VALON | ncp | Burst Packet; 1424 bytes | 1,511 | 2 s | 1 ms | 3:04:25 PM | |
| 706 | RTR4X-C1 | VALON | ncp | Burst Packet; 1424 bytes | 1,511 | 2 s | 2 ms | 3:04:25 PM | |
| 707 | RTR4X-C1 | VALON | ncp | Burst Packet; 1424 bytes | 1,511 | 2 s | 0 µs | 3:04:25 PM | |
| 708 | RTR4X-C1 | VALON | ncp | Burst Packet; 1424 bytes | 1,511 | 2 s | 1 ms | 3:04:25 PM | |
| 709 | RTR4X-C1 | VALON | ncp | Burst Packet; 1424 bytes | 1,511 | 2 s | 1 ms | 3:04:25 PM | |
| 710 | RTR4X-C1 | VALON | ncp | Burst Packet; 1424 bytes | 1,511 | 2 s | 1 ms | 3:04:25 PM | |
| 711 | RTR4X-C1 | VALON | ncp | Burst Packet; 1424 bytes | 1,511 | 2 s | 2 ms | 3:04:25 PM | |
| 712 | RTR4X-C1 | VALON | ncp | Burst Packet; 1424 bytes | 1,511 | 2 s | 1 ms | 3:04:25 PM | |
| 713 | RTR4X-C1 | VALON | ncp | Burst Packet; 1424 bytes | 1,511 | 2 s | 0 µs | 3:04:25 PM | |
| 714 | RTR4X-C1 | VALON | ncp | Burst Packet; 1424 bytes | 1,511 | 2 s | 2 ms | 3:04:25 PM | |
| 715 | RTR4X-C1 | VALON | ncp | Burst Packet; 1392 bytes | 1,479 | 2 s | 1 ms | 3:04:25 PM | |
| 716 | VALON | RTR4X-C1 | ncp | Req Burst Read 18216 bytes | 111 | 2 s | 2 ms | 3:04:25 PM | |
| 717 | RTR4X-C1 | VALON | ncp | Burst Packet; 1424 bytes | 1,511 | 2 s | 3 ms | 3:04:25 PM | |
| 718 | RTR4X-C1 | VALON | ncp | Burst Packet; 408 bytes | 495 | 2 s | 1 ms | 3:04:25 PM | |
| 719 | RTR4X-C1 | VALON | ncp | Burst Packet; 1424 bytes | 1,511 | 2 s | 1 ms | 3:04:25 PM | |
| 720 | RTR4X-C1 | VALON | ncp | Burst Packet; 1424 bytes | 1,511 | 2 s | 2 ms | 3:04:25 PM | |

C:\LZFW\CLIENT\BURSTER2.TR1

**WARNING**

**The Microsoft Client for NetWare Networks does not support this rapid backoff process and may not be a suitable burst mode client for busy networks. Beware!**

Now that you know the basic performance features and functionality of burst mode communications, let's examine how a typical burst file read and burst file write should look.

### The Burst Mode Read Process

When an application makes a read request for a data size greater than 512 bytes, packet burst is automatically implemented. If a client requests a small file (one that is smaller than 512 bytes), a regular NCP read is executed, not a burst mode read.

Multiple packets, or fragments, make up a burst set, as shown in Figure 13.34.

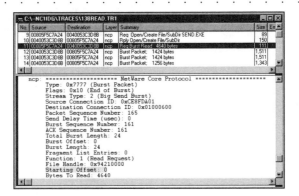

FIGURE 13.34

*There are 11 packets in this burst set.*

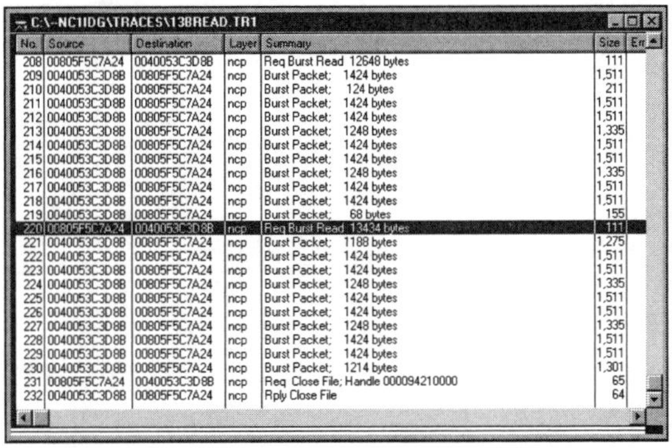

The set size changes when an error occurs. For example, if a server sends 10 packets to a client but only 9 are received, the next burst set will be only 50 percent as large as the last set. This is the "fallback" rate defined for Client 32.

The initial read of a burst set indicates the location, or offset, of the desired data in the file. The first packet typically indicates an offset of 0, as shown in Figure 13.35.

FIGURE 13.35

*The first packet of the burst file read indicates that the file should be read from the beginning (starting at offset 0).*

The burst replies contain the data and indicate a starting offset and number of bytes read for each packet of data. For example, in Figure 13.35, the client requested 4,640 bytes of the file (SEND.EXE). The reply packets contain the values shown in Table 13.2.

| T A B L E  13.2 | BURST SEQUENCE NUMBER | PACKET SEQUENCE NUMBER | BURST OFFSET | BURST LENGTH |
|---|---|---|---|---|
| *The Packet Sequence Number, Burst Offset, and Burst Length Fields Are Used to Identify Individual Fragments of Data.* | 161 | 673 | 0 | 1424 |
| | 161 | 674 | 1424 | 1424 |
| | 161 | 675 | 2848 | 1256 |
| | 161 | 676 | 4104 | 544 |

Each packet within a burst set contains a burst packet sequence number. As you may notice from Table 13-2, the burst sequence number remains the same for all the burst packets within a set. The next set would use burst sequence number 162 and continue incrementing the packet sequence number (starting at 677).

If the receiver determines that one or more burst packet is missing from a set, the receiver sends a burst system packet to the sender. The burst system packet indicates the missing fragment or fragments, as shown in Figure 13.36. In this example, the client, Valon, is notifying the server, RTR4X-C1, that part of a burst (23,824 bytes) was missing at offset 11,224. The offset indicates the fragment's starting point in number of bytes from the start of the burst set.

FIGURE 13.36

*A burst system packet indicates that a packet was missing from the last set.*

```
                                    C:\LZFW\CLIENT\BURSTER2.TR1
No.  Source     Destination  Layer  Summary                                      Size   Relative T  Interpack  Absolute T  Error
699  VALON      RTR4X-C1     ncp    Burst System Packet; 23824 bytes missing      93    2 s         363 ms     3:04:25 PM
699  RTR4X-C1   VALON        ncp    Burst Packet; 1072 bytes                   1,159    2 s           3 ms     3:04:25 PM

Length : 93 bytes
802.3: ================ IEEE 802.3 Datalink Layer ================
         Station: VALON ----> RTR4X-C1
         Length: 75
802.2: ================ IEEE 802.2 Logical Link Control ================
         SSAP: NetWare      DSAP: NetWare
         Unnumbered Command: Unnumbered Information (UI)
  ipx: ================ Internetwork Packet Exchange ================
         Checksum: 0xFFFF
         Length: 72
         Hop Count:  0
         Packet Type: 17(NCP)
         Network: BA 5E BA 11       ---> 31 B0 56 E4
         Node:    00-80-C7-67-A0-93 ---> 00-00-00-00-00-01
         Socket:  0x400A            ---> NCP
  ncp: ================ NetWare Core Protocol ================
         Type: 0x7777 (Burst Packet)
         Flags: 0x80 (System Packet)
         Stream Type: 2 (Big Send Burst)
         Source Connection ID: 0xE1581ED9
         Destination Connection ID: 0x03000300
         Packet Sequence Number: 291
         Send Delay Time (usec): 0
         Burst Sequence Number: 287
         ACK Sequence Number: 287
         Total Burst Length: 0
         Burst Offset: 0
         Burst Length: 0
         Fragment List Entries: 1
                          Entry1:
                                 Offset: 11224
                                 Bytes Missing: 23824
```

Burst fragments must be cleared up before any further burst sets can be exchanged.

### The Burst Mode Write Process

The burst mode write process works in the same manner as the burst mode read manner, except that you'll typically see write windows much smaller than read windows. The default window sizes are smaller (10 instead of 24 times the packet size, in the case of Client 32 for Windows 95).

When a client writes a new file on a server, the client first creates the file. Next, the client sends a burst write request to the server. This request includes the client's source connection ID number, the server's destination connection ID number, and the total burst length, which indicates the total number of data bytes in this set. This number is typically 24 bytes higher than the actual amount in the set (due to burst write operations overhead). The burst write request actually contains data in the packet, as shown in Figure 13.37.

F I G U R E   13.37

*The initial burst write request packet contains the first data of the set.*

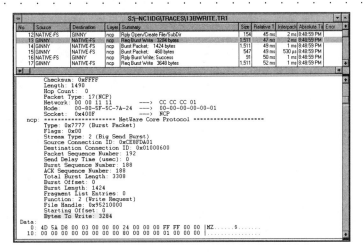

Each consecutive burst packet increments the offset value by the amount of data already sent to indicate the location of the data within the entire set. For example, in Figure 13.38, we can see that the second packet of this set contains an offset of 1,424. This indicates that this packet's data should be placed 1,424 bytes after the first set of data received.

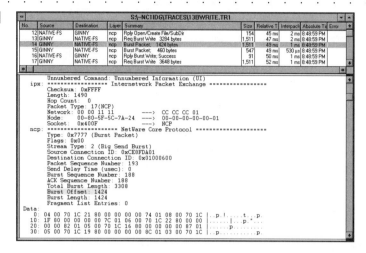

**FIGURE 13.38**

*The second burst read indicates that this packet's data resides at offset 1,424.*

When the client successfully completes a burst write to the server, the server replies with a burst reply that has the end of burst flag set. In the write reply code field, the server indicates whether the burst write was successful or any problems occurred. In Figure 13.39, we can see the burst reply that indicates that there were no missing fragments (Fragment List Entries is zero) and the burst write was successful.

**FIGURE 13.39**

*The server responds at the end of the burst write to inform the client of the status of the burst write operation.*

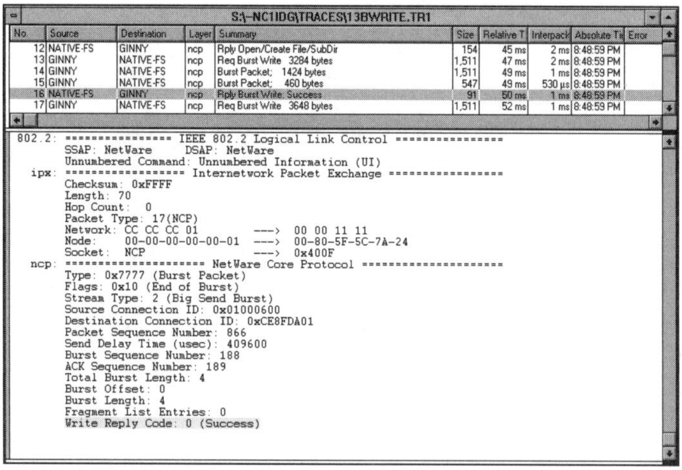

Burst mode may appear to be a very inexact science because of its dynamic nature. Many factors affect the client's performance and enable the client to adjust to network congestion and faults. The set size is one dynamic element of NetWare burst mode communications. Let's examine how the burst set sizes can change throughout the communication session to reflect the current condition of the network communications infrastructure.

In this next section, we'll focus on typical NDS communications (and their related NCP function and subfunction codes) that can be seen on the network.

## NDS COMMUNICATIONS

Although many people think NDS communications are a bit of a mystery, they are simply NCP requests and replies between servers. Figure 13.40 shows a typical NDS packet for starting the update of a replica. You'll notice that the familiar IPX and NCP header precedes an NDS header.

```
Length : 145 bytes
802.3: ================== IEEE 802.3 Datalink Layer ==================
       Station: NATIVE-FS ----> RTR4X-C1
       Length: 127
802.2: ============== IEEE 802.2 Logical Link Control ==============
       SSAP: NetWare     DSAP: NetWare
       Unnumbered Command: Unnumbered Information (UI)
  ipx: ================ Internetwork Packet Exchange ================
       Checksum: 0xFFFF
       Length: 124
       Hop Count: 1
       Packet Type: 17(NCP)
       Network: CC CC CC 01     --->  AA AA AA 01
       Node:    00-00-00-00-00-01  --->  00-00-00-00-00-01
       Socket:  0x4016           --->  NCP
  ncp: ================== NetWare Core Protocol ==================
       NCP Request: Send NDS Fragment Request Reply
       Request Type: 0x2222 (Request)
       Sequence Number: 19
       Connection Number Low: 3
       Task Number: 0
       Connection Number High: 0
       Function Code: 104
       Subfunction Code: 2
  nds: ================== NetWare Directory Service ==================
       Send NDS Fragment Request Reply
       Fragment Handle: 0xFFFFFFFF
       Max Fragment Size: 1450
       Message Size: 74
       Fragment Flags: 0
       NDS Version: 254
       CRC: 2695861945
       Internal Verb Number: 35 (Start Update Replica)
       Reply Buffer Size: 2048
       Version: 5
       Flags: 0x00000010
       Iteration Handle: 0xFFFFFFFF
```

It's relatively easy to spot NDS communications since there is only one function code for all NDS NCP calls—function code 104. There are several subfunction codes to distinguish the various NDS tasks, however.

The NDS subfunction codes supported are listed here:

| | | | |
|---|---|---|---|
| Ping for NDS NCP | 0x2222 | 104 | 01 |
| Send NDS Fragmented Request/Reply | 0x2222 | 104 | 02 |
| Return Bindery Context | 0x2222 | 104 | 04 |
| Monitor NDS Connection | 0x2222 | 104 | 05 |
| Return Statistics | 0x2222 | 104 | 06 |
| Clear Statistics | 0x2222 | 104 | 07 |
| Reload Software | 0x2222 | 104 | 08 |

Once you feel comfortable looking at and examining standard NCP calls, you should take some time to look at your network's NDS communications.

Several processes occur in NDS and affect network traffic. These processes include the NDS database synchronization that occurs between members of a replica ring. Servers that are members of a replica ring each maintain a separate replica of a common partition.

Figure 13.41 provides an example of the NDS traffic that occurs when the server that maintains the master replica of the [ROOT] partition synchronizes with a server that maintains a read-write replica of the partition.

FIGURE 13.41

The NDS synchronization process keeps partition replicas in synchronization.

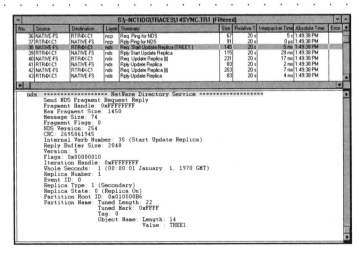

The NDS synchronization process completes with a request to End Update Replica (NDS verb 36), as shown in Figure 13.42. This packet includes the time stamp information to ensure that the replica ring partitions maintain accurate time-stamping on all partition replicas.

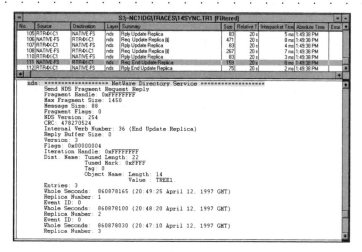

F I G U R E   13.42

*The NDS replica update process completes with time stamp information.*

The typical update process includes a series of Update Replica NDS calls after a ping for NDS request. The ping for NDS packet is sent from one server to another before all NDS update procedures. The ping for NDS packet is used to obtain a server's ping version number, the tree name, the Directory Services version, and the distance from the root of the root-most entry on that server. Figure 13.43 shows the ping for NDS reply.

F I G U R E   13.43

*The ping for NDS packet contains NDS version information.*

```
        Length: 73
802.2: ================ IEEE 802.2 Logical Link Control ================
        SSAP: NetWare        DSAP: NetWare
        Unnumbered Command: Unnumbered Information (UI)
   ipx: ================ Internetwork Packet Exchange ================
        Checksum: 0xFFFF
        Length: 70
        Hop Count:  0
        Packet Type: 17(NCP)
        Network: AA AA AA 01    ---> CC CC CC 01
        Node:    00-00-00-00-00-01  ---> 00-00-00-00-00-01
        Socket:  NCP            ---> 0x4016
   ncp: ================ NetWare Core Protocol ================
        NCP Reply: Ping for NDS
        Reply Type: 0x3333 (Reply)
        Sequence Number: 18
        Connection Number Low: 3
        Task Number: 1
        Connection Number High: 0
        Completion Code: 0 (Success)
        Connection Status: 0x00
        Version: 10
        Tree Depth: 0
        NDS Software Revision: 0x0000023D
        Reply Flags: 0x00000000
        Tree Name: Length: 12
                   Value : TREE1
```

As NDS changes over time, the schema increases in size, as does the entire database. It's a good idea to know your NDS traffic overhead by filtering on all function 104, subfunction 2 communications with a high-end analyzer.

**NOTE**

**Currently, the NDS update process is somewhat slow. When native IP communications are released with NetWare 5, NDS database updates will be performed in a data streaming method using TCP (Transmission Control Protocol). This should improve performance notably.**

## NCP Packet Signing

In the early 1990s a group based in the Netherlands showed that using sophisticated analysis techniques, they could spoof NCP packets from the Supervisor account to the server and perform Supervisor-level functions. This security breach requires a tremendous amount of knowledge about the ongoing communications from an active Supervisor account, as well as a great deal of luck to get the timing just right.

When this group proved they could break into the NetWare operating environment in this way, Novell began development of a technology called *NCP packet signing*. Packet signing uses RSA public and private key encryption methods.

Although this technology is available in the VLMs and Client 32 software, Packet signing is considered "enabled, but not preferred" by default. This means that the client will only sign packets if the server requests packet signing. On NetWare 3.12 and 4.x servers, the NCP packet signing option is set to 1, which indicates that the server is not requiring signed communications but can use signing if the client requests.

In packet-signed communications, the client includes an eight-byte "signature" with each NCP packet sent to the NetWare server. This unique signature is used as an identification method to ensure that packets are coming from the actual connection holder, not an imitator.

Keep in mind that NCP packet signing can only be used on NCP-based communications—it does not cross protocol boundaries. Since SPX communications do not use NCP, they are not affected and cannot take advantage of packet signing.

In order to prevent packet spoofing attacks, it is always a good idea to limit packet transmit utilities and tools to users who are trusted. For example, as a network analyst, I can use many different tools to transmit packets onto a network. An analyzer can be a dangerous weapon when used by an untrusted party.

Let's take a look at how you can configure NCP packet signing at the client and server.

### CLIENT CONFIGURATION

At the VLM client, NCP packet signing is enabled in the NET.CFG file. The entry should look like:

```
netware dos requester
        signature level = 1
```

In Client32, this setting is handled in Client 32 Properties, Advanced Settings. The client NCP packet signing options are:

0 = Disabled (the SECURITY.VLM file does not load). The client cannot sign the packet.

1 = Enabled but not preferred. The client will sign packets only if the server requests it (server set to 2 or higher).

2 = Preferred. The client signs packets if the server is capable of signing packets (server set to 1 or higher).

3 = Required. The client signs all packets and requests that the server sign packets.

 **Some versions of the VLMs have encountered problems when the client's packet signature level was set to 3. If you are noticing some communications problems on such a station, reduce the packet signature level to 2 or lower.**

WARNING

When the client is configured to use packet signing or has been requested by the server to use packet signing, the security flags field of the client's request NCP max packet size packet contains a nonzero value, as shown in Figure 13.44.

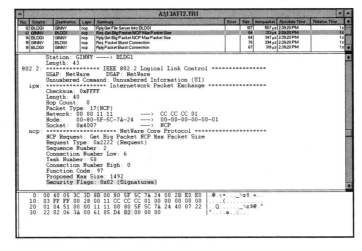

The server responds with an indication that it also supports packet signatures by placing a nonzero value in the security flags field, as shown in Figure 13.45.

Once the server and client have established a packet-signed communication, you'll notice the extra eight bytes in each NCP request sent between the two entities. Figure 13.46 is an example of a signed packet. This packet is a request to allocate a short directory handle. As we can see, after the standard NCP call fields (ending in Path Component Count), there are an extra, undecoded eight bytes, the signature.

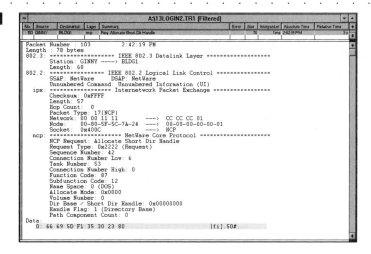

*The signature follows the last NCP call field.*

 **We know this is not padding because the packet data size was of sufficient length (over the minimum 46 bytes length) before the packet was handed to the LAN driver.**

NOTE

## SERVER CONFIGURATION

At the server, NCP packet signing can be configured using SET NCP PACKET SIGNATURE OPTION and SERVMAN > NCP.

The server settings available are:

0 = Disabled. The server cannot sign packets.

1 = Enabled but not preferred. The server will sign packets only if the client requests it.

2 = Preferred. The server signs packets if the client is capable of signing packets.

3 = Required. The server signs all packets and requests that the client sign packets.

Depending on the combined client and server configuration (shown in Table 13.3), NCP packet signing could refuse to let a client request get processed.

| TABLE 13.3 |
|:-:|
| *Setting the Client and Server to Incompatible Security Settings Can Cause Communications between the Two to Fail.* |

|  | SERVER SETTING: 0 | SERVER SETTING: 1 | SERVER SETTING: 2 | SERVER SETTING: 3 |
|---|---|---|---|---|
| **Client Setting: 0** | No packet signing | No packet signing | No packet signing | No login possible |
| **Client Setting: 1** | No packet signing | No packet signing | Packet signing | Packet signing |
| **Client Setting: 2** | No packet signing | Packet signing | Packet signing | Packet signing |
| **Client Setting: 3** | No login possible | Packet signing | Packet signing | Packet signing |

Remember that NCP packet signing does require additional processing power at the client and server side of the communications set. All the client's packets on the wire will be eight bytes longer when NCP packet signing is enabled. If you don't need NCP packet signing, don't use it.

## Identifying Upper-Layer Problems

There are several ways to identify upper-layer, or application-layer, problems. For example, you can examine the NCP communications processes to find an application that looks for supplemental files in a specific directory that does not exist. You can use Novell's own notification system to alert you to possible problems, and you can spot unusual NCP sequences.

### USING NOVELL'S NCP ALERT SYSTEM

NetWare includes a set of alerts that can notify you when strange NCP behavior is noted. Although these NCP alerts haven't been defined with examples before, they are one of the primary tools used by Novell's technical support escalation team.

Follow these steps to set up your server to notify you of unusual NCP behavior:

I • Type **SET 10** (for NCP calls) at the server console and change the following settings of the server:

  ► Set Display NCP Bad Component Warnings = ON

  ► Set Display NCP Bad Length Warnings = ON

  This reports packets the server does not like. You should be able to get some additional details from the client side (application error messages) that help define the source of the problem.

**NOTE**
**When you set these setting to "ON," you may see other error messages on the console related to unencrypted password calls being attempted. This occurs with the 5.73 DS.NLM but is fixed in the 5.73c DS.NLM in Border Manager.**

2 • If the client side does not yield enough information to identify the cause of the problem, type **SET 10** (for NCP calls) at the server console and change these settings as well:

  ► Set Reject NCP Packets with Bad Components = ON

  ► Set Reject NCP Packets with Bad Lengths = ON

  The Reject failure should give you the isolating information that points to the specific call that is causing problems.

## SEQUENCE OF NCP REQUESTS/REPLIES

In order to troubleshoot communications at the upper layers, you should be aware that there is a natural sequence to NCP communications. Likewise, there is an unnatural sequence to NCP communications. If you can differentiate between the two, you can spot upper-layer communications problems easily.

**NOTE** **The sequences are identified by the NCP type numbers. As you learned earlier in this chapter, 0x2222 indicates a request and 0x3333 indicates a reply.**

The five NCP communications sequences are:

Request/Reply

Request/Reply, Reply, Reply

Request, Request/Reply

Request, Request/Reply, Reply

Requests only

Get a sense for the NCP sequences used on your network by simply letting your analyzer capture packets for a while (get a few thousand packets). Post-filter (display filter) on a few separate significant point-to-point communications. For example, at a client site, I might gather 40,000 packets and then sort the station monitor screen on the packets/out column heading to identify the most active stations. (You'll usually get the servers and routers showing up on the top of the list this way also.) Now apply a filter to/from some of the very active stations to see the typical NCP communications sequences in use.

The following section provides some pointers on interpreting your communications sequences.

### Request/Reply Sequence

This sequence is seen when a command or request is sent to the server. For example, during the login process, the client sends a request for file server information. The server sends a single reply packet with the desired information. This simple request/reply format is seen throughout the day.

If a large file read or write uses this sequence, something may be wrong. For example, if you see a client making a file read request, a reply, another read request, another reply, and so on, a red flag should be raised in your head. It is possible that the application programmer decided not to use burst mode technology for file reads/writes. That makes NCP operate in the old "ping-pong" method. Check out the starting offset and the bytes to read, as shown in Figure 13.47, inside the NCP requests to ensure that the client is reading data in sequential order.

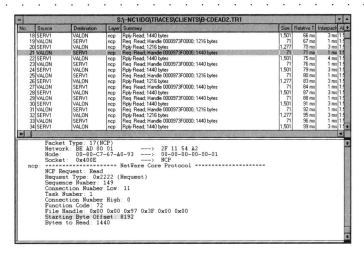

FIGURE  13.47

*Check each successive starting offset to determine if the client is reading a contiguous set of data.*

In Figure 13.47, we can see that the client is using a standard Read call (function code 72) instead of burst mode. As we examine the starting offsets of the read requests, we find that the client is reading contiguous data and should have been using burst mode communications. To troubleshoot this situation, we simply went back to the client connection sequence to see if a burst mode connection was properly established—it was not. The client setting PB Buffers = 0 disabled burst mode. We changed the setting to increase performance dramatically and reduce the ping-pong communications.

This sequence does not always indicate a problem, however. Take the example of e-mail communications. If your e-mail messages are typically rather small (which is typical of most e-mail applications), you may go through the entire mailbox making single read requests for each e-mail message. Burst mode communications are not used when less than 512 bytes of data are requested.

Also consider the sequence of the data that the client is reading. In the case of a large database, the client may not read all the data in order within the database. The client may request 1,024 bytes at offset 3094 in packet number 1, 1,024 bytes at offset 17234, and finally 1,024 bytes at 44004. In this case, it may be natural to see request/reply sequences.

### Request/Reply, Reply, Reply

This type of communication sequence is associated with burst mode file reads and writes. The client makes a burst mode read request (type 0x7777) and receives multiple reply packets from the server. During burst mode write operations, the client sends data to the server in sets, as well. For more information on burst mode operations, refer to the burst mode section earlier in this chapter.

### Request, Request/Reply

This sequence is never considered "normal." A client should require only one request packet to get a response. If you see clients making multiple requests for each reply, it is most likely that the client is timing out on the first request. In this case, you should examine the network to ensure there are no MAC-layer problems (such as excessive collisions or, in the case of token ring networks, persistent ring reconfigurations). In some instances, the latency time induced by bridges and routers may affect client performance. Novell's VLMs are much more susceptible to latency-induced timeouts than Client 32.

One setting that can cause this type of performance is the "Time to Net" setting. This setting indicates the minimum time to reach a network. If the Minimum Time to Net is small, the client believes that the network is very close and quick to get to. The client may time out waiting for a response from a server that takes longer to get to. Although the clients dynamically learn the time to get to a network during their connection time, they may have trouble during that initial period (before they've learned the true time to the destination). In this case, you can adjust the client's Minimum Time to Net value to 10,000 (milliseconds) to help.

### Request, Request/Reply, Reply

This sequence of events can look very strange on the network and always signals a problem with the network configuration. This sequence is typically seen in a network that is using "frame type translation" to get from one local device to another local device. For example, if a client is configured to use Ethernet_802.3 and its desired server uses Ethernet_802.2, they cannot communicate — they are on two separate virtual networks. If, however, another device (a router or another NetWare server) is placed on the same network and configured to use both frame types, the client can suddenly communicate with the desired server. As shown in Figure 13.48, all the client's NCP requests are sent to the frame translator

(COMPAQ-FS2), which routes the packet back onto the same physical network, but a different logical network, to the true destination (COMPAQ-FS1).

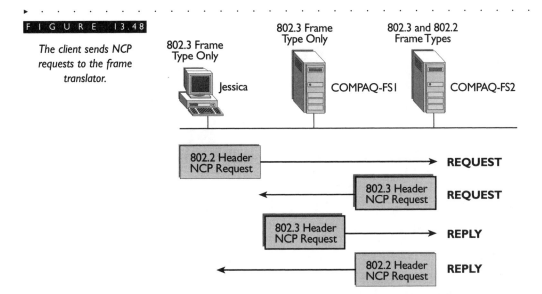

Frame translation doubles the number of packets required on a network, increases overall utilization, and places an undue burden on the device performing frame type translation. In some cases, companies have employed this design as a migration path enabling older clients (using the Ethernet_802.3 frame type) to talk to the newer server. Once all the clients are up and running the new frame type, the extra frame type should be removed to minimize traffic.

### Requests Only

A couple of years ago we encountered a client that had a very strange network trace file. The file indicated that their backup link was inundated with NCP requests. No replies — just requests. This is obviously an unnatural NCP communication flow.

We examined their network traces and found that, indeed, their backup link contained only NCP requests. All the requests had a hop count of 1, indicating that they had crossed a router. After examining the source router and the source client, we determined that their network had a configuration problem that surfaced when they put a Cisco router in parallel with a NetWare server, as shown in Figure 13.49.

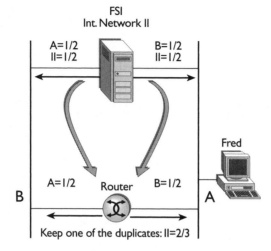

F I G U R E  13.49

*When the Cisco router was put in parallel, the client sent all requests for the server through the Cisco router.*

The server advertises internal IPX network 11 through both networks A and B. The Cisco router kept only the first entry, noting that both entries were identical. If the Cisco router received the server's announcement through the Network A side first, the following would occur:

**1** • Client Fred sends GNS SAP broadcast.

**2** • The server answers, supplying the internal IPX address 11 for services.

**3** • Client Fred sends an RIP broadcast for network 11.

**4** • The router and the server respond. The router responds more quickly than the server.

**5** • The client takes the first reply and sends all communications to the server through the router.

**6** • The server answers NCP requests by sending NCP replies directly onto network A.

In this situation, if you were on LAN A, you'd only see the NCP requests going from the client to the router and the replies from the server to the client. On LAN B, however, you'd only see the requests coming through the router to the server. You'd never see the replies on LAN B because the server is sending them directly back through LAN A to the client.

In order to fix this problem, we changed the Cisco router's Max Paths setting to 2. For more information on this problem, refer to Chapter 10.

Always give the network a little time to "settle into a pattern" before you start analyzing NCP sequences. Don't start analysis on a network that is newly installed or has just been brought up. Too many factors change during these turbulent times. You don't want to spend too much time hunting down ghost problems that resolve themselves through the network or application startup times.

In this next section, we'll look at the NCP header structure for each type of communications.

## NCP Header Structure

The header structure of NCP communications varies depending on the type of NCP call (request, reply, connection request, and so on). Some NCP calls require specific information about a file, directory, NDS object, or the like. Others are just a simple request for a specific type of service.

**X-REF**

**To see more examples of NCP communications, refer to the trace files contained in the accompanying CD-ROM. You can refer to Appendix H for more information.**

### TYPE 0X1111 PACKET STRUCTURE

The connection request packet is used primarily to obtain a general services connection. This packet is also seen to test the big packet and burst mode setup in the VLM clients, as discussed earlier in this chapter. The 0x1111 packet structure is shown in Figure 13.50.

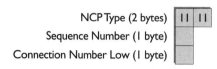

*The connection request packet contains only four bytes of information after the IPX header.*

NCP Type (2 bytes)
Sequence Number (1 byte)
Connection Number Low (1 byte)

### Type Field

This field identifies the packet as a request (0x2222).

### Sequence Number Field

The clients assign a number to all NCP requests made to the server, starting with sequence 0—used during the connection request packet only. This number wraps at 0xFF.

### Connection Number Low Field

This field is set to 255 in the initial request. Clients cannot assign themselves a connection number.

## TYPE 0X2222 (REQUEST) PACKET STRUCTURE

There are various layouts for the NCP request packets (type 0x2222), shown in Figure 13.51. Some request packets contain a function code field that specifies what the client is requesting. Other packets require function code and subfunction code fields. Let's take a look at the required fields of an NCP request packet and then look at NCP packets that use subfunctions.

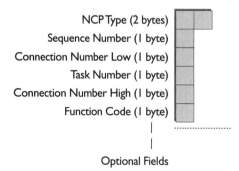

*NCP request packets must have a function code field.*

NCP Type (2 bytes)
Sequence Number (1 byte)
Connection Number Low (1 byte)
Task Number (1 byte)
Connection Number High (1 byte)
Function Code (1 byte)

Optional Fields

### Type Field

This field identifies the packet as a request (0x2222).

### Sequence Number Field

The clients assign a number to all NCP requests made to the server, starting with sequence 0 during the connection request process. This number wraps at 0xFF.

### Connection Number Low Field

This field indicates the connection number (general services connection) of the client. This number matches up with the connection ID number listed in MONITOR > Connection Status. On 500- and 1,000-user versions of NetWare, the connection number high field is also used to provide a connection ID number to the client. Clients must indicate their connection ID number in all NCP requests to the server.

### Task Number Field

Open to programmers, this enables a local application to have more than one task open at a single time. Many times you will see a client station only using Task 0 and Task 1 for communications. This field is not typically used in network analysis/troubleshooting.

### Connection Number High Field

This field is used to indicate a higher connection ID number when the operating system supports 500 or 1,000 users.

### Function Code Field

The function code defines the purpose of the NCP call. For example, Get File Server Date and Time (used during the client connection sequence) uses function code 20.

**The complete list of NetWare function codes is included at the end of this chapter. A list with accompanying descriptions can be found in Appendix G.**

X-REF

### Subfunction Code Field (Optional)

In some cases, the function codes indicate the general type of service requested and subfunction codes are used to differentiate requests. For example, the following NCP calls use function code 23 and are used for File Server Environment purposes. Each NCP call uses a different subfunction call to uniquely identify the NCP function:

| | | | |
|---|---|---|---|
| Get Disk Channel Statistics | 0x2222 | 23 | 217 |
| Get Disk Utilization | 0x2222 | 23 | 14 |
| Get Drive Mapping Table | 0x2222 | 23 | 215 |

Figure 13.52 shows the NCP request format for NCP calls that use function and subfunction calls.

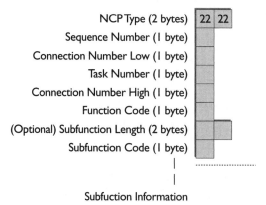

NCP Type (2 bytes)

Sequence Number (1 byte)

Connection Number Low (1 byte)

Task Number (1 byte)

Connection Number High (1 byte)

Function Code (1 byte)

(Optional) Subfunction Length (2 bytes)

Subfunction Code (1 byte)

Subfuction Information

**The complete list of NetWare subfunction codes is included at the end of this chapter. A list with accompanying descriptions can be found in Appendix G.**

X-REF

### Verb Field (NDS Only)

In the case of NDS fragmented requests, function code 104, subfunction code 02, verbs are used to differentiate the various fragmented NDS requests. Figure 13.53 depicts an NDS NCP call that uses a verb.

**These verbs are often referred to as DSVs (Directory Services verbs).**

NOTE

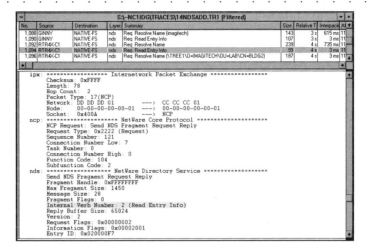

F I G U R E   13.53

*NDS fragmented requests and replies use a verb number.*

**X-REF**

**The complete list of NetWare Directory Services verbs is included at the end of this chapter. A list with accompanying descriptions can be found in Appendix G.**

The NDS fragment packet structure is longer than the standard NCP header, as shown in Figure 13.54.

F I G U R E   13.54

*NDS fragments (function 104, subfunction 2) use a Directory Services verb header.*

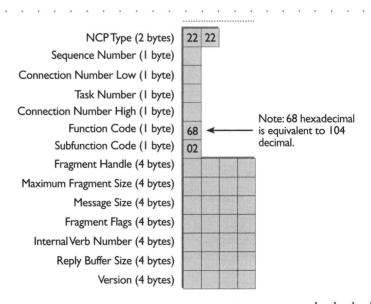

The verb includes several fields after the standard NCP request header. These fields include:

- ▶ Fragment handle

- ▶ Maximum fragment size

- ▶ Message size

- ▶ Fragment flags

- ▶ Internal verb number

- ▶ Reply buffer size

- ▶ Version

### Fragment Handle

The fragment handle is a number assigned to all fragments that are related to a single data stream. For example, if a client reads the NDS database list of object classes, all replies from the server use the same fragment handle number (0x00, for example). A fragment handle of 0xFFFFFFFF indicates that the request requires only a single reply packet to complete the operation.

### Maximum Fragment Size

The maximum fragment size is used for NDS information exchange. This is the payload size and does not include the packet header.

### Message Size

This indicates the number of bytes of NDS data expected in the reply packet.

### Fragment Flags

This field is unique for each verb and enables further functionality for the NCP call.

### Internal Verb Number

This field identifies the verb. The list of NDS verbs is located at the end of this chapter.

### Reply Buffer Size

This field contains the receiving buffer size available.

### Version

This field contains the NDS verb version number.

## TYPE 0X3333 (REPLY) PACKET STRUCTURE

The 0x3333 packets are reply packets most often sent in response to a 0x2222 request packet. They are also sent in response to a 0x1111 request for a general services connection and 0x5555 request to destroy a service connection. Figure 13.55 shows the general packet structure of 0x3333 replies.

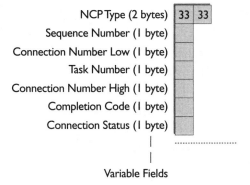

**FIGURE 13.55**

*Users obtain their connection status with each NCP reply.*

NCP Type (2 bytes)  33 33
Sequence Number (1 byte)
Connection Number Low (1 byte)
Task Number (1 byte)
Connection Number High (1 byte)
Completion Code (1 byte)
Connection Status (1 byte)

Variable Fields

### Type Field

This field identifies the packet as a reply (0x3333).

### Sequence Number Field

The clients assign a number to all NCP requests made to the server, starting with sequence 0. This number wraps at 0xFF.

### Connection Number Low Field

This field indicates the connection number (general services connection) of the client. This number matches up with the connection ID number listed in MONITOR > Connection Status. On 500- and 1,000-user versions of NetWare, the connection number high field is also used to provide a connection ID number to the client. Clients must indicate their connection ID number in all NCP requests to the server. Servers indicate the connection number in their reply packets, as well.

### Task Number Field

Open to programmers, this enables a local application to have more than one task open at a single time. Many times you will see a client station using only Task 0 and Task 1 for communications. This field is not typically used in network analysis/troubleshooting.

### Connection Number High Field

This field is used to indicate a higher connection ID number when the operating system supports 500 or 1,000 users.

### Completion Code Field

This field indicates whether the associated NCP request was handled successfully or not. NCP calls have a set of completion codes that relate to the processed request. For example, a Keyed Object Login (function code 23, subfunction code 24) reply may contain any of the following completion codes:

| | | |
|---|---|---|
| 0 | 0x00 | Successful |
| 150 | 0x96 | No Allocation Space |
| 193 | 0xC1 | No Account Balance |
| 194 | 0xC2 | Credit Limit Exceeded |
| 197 | 0xC5 | Server Login Locked |
| 217 | 0xD9 | Maximum Logins Exceeded |
| 218 | 0xDA | Bad Login Time |
| 219 | 0xDB | Node Address Violation |
| 220 | 0xDC | Account Expired |
| 222 | 0xDE | Bad Password |

Most analyzers decode the completion code field for you so that you do not have to know each NCP call's completion possibilities.

## TYPE 0X5555 PACKET STRUCTURE

The 0x5555 packet is the destroy connection request. This packet does not contain a function, subfunction, or verb designation. The type 0x5555 indicates that the client is relinquishing its connection to the server. The server uses a 0x3333 reply packet to respond to the client.

Figure 13.56 depicts the destroy connection request packet format.

FIGURE 13.56

*The destroy connection request packet does not contain any function or subfunction codes.*

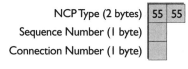

NCP Type (2 bytes) 55 55
Sequence Number (1 byte)
Connection Number (1 byte)

### Type Field

This field identifies the packet as a destroy connection request (0x5555).

### Sequence Number Field

The clients assign a number to all NCP requests made to the server, starting with sequence 0. This number wraps at 0xFF. This sequence number is the last one the client will use for this connection. When the client reestablishes a new connection, it will start at sequence number 0 again.

### Connection Number Field

This field indicates the connection number (general services connection) of the client. This number matches up with the connection ID number listed in MONITOR > Connection Status.

## PACKET 0X7777 PACKET STRUCTURES

The 0x7777 packets are used for burst mode communications. You can use this type field value to filter on all burst mode communications on the network. There are five types of burst mode packets in NetWare:

- Burst read request

- Burst read reply

- Burst write request

- Burst write reply

▸ Burst system packet

The following section defines each burst mode packet structure.

### Read Request

This packet is sent to a server that supports burst mode to request a burst mode read. As you can see in Figure 13.57, this packet indicates the file handle, Function (01 indicates Read), starting offset in the file, and the amount of data requested in this set.

F I G U R E    13.57

*The burst mode read request packets indicate the file read by its file handle.*

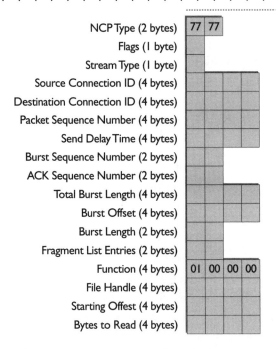

| | | | |
|---|---|---|---|
| NCP Type (2 bytes) | 77 | 77 | |
| Flags (1 byte) | | | |
| Stream Type (1 byte) | | | |
| Source Connection ID (4 bytes) | | | |
| Destination Connection ID (4 bytes) | | | |
| Packet Sequence Number (4 bytes) | | | |
| Send Delay Time (4 bytes) | | | |
| Burst Sequence Number (2 bytes) | | | |
| ACK Sequence Number (2 bytes) | | | |
| Total Burst Length (4 bytes) | | | |
| Burst Offset (4 bytes) | | | |
| Burst Length (2 bytes) | | | |
| Fragment List Entries (2 bytes) | | | |
| Function (4 bytes) | 01 | 00 | 00 | 00 |
| File Handle (4 bytes) | | | |
| Starting Offest (4 bytes) | | | |
| Bytes to Read (4 bytes) | | | |

**NCP Type**    The NCP type 0x7777 indicates that this is a burst mode transaction.

**Flags**    The following burst mode flags are available:

0x80 (SYS: System) is set for a system packet. No burst data accompanies or follows these packets.

0x10 (EOB: End of Burst) is set for end of burst. It will be set in the last packet of a burst.

0x04 (ABT: Abort) is set for an abort request. The SYS bit is set if ABT is set.

**Stream Type**    The type of burst. Only the server uses this field. 0x02 is the only valid type.

**Source Connection ID**    The source connection ID is a workstation connection identifier for burst mode communications. This number is randomly generated by the source.

**Destination Connection ID**    This field identifies the self-assigned number of the burst mode partner. For example, a client would put the server's burst mode connection ID number in the destination connection ID field when the client makes burst mode read or write requests.

**Packet Sequence Number**    This sequence number is incremented for each packet sent by a device. The other sequence number field contains sequence number information for a single burst.

**Send Delay Time**    This is the delay time between consecutive packet sends in 100 microsecond increments. On a reliable link, burst mode send delay time can reach 0.

**NOTE**    **This is a theoretical number indicating that packets are being sent back-to-back. Each media access control method interjects some sort of delay in transmission. For example, on Token Ring, you cannot send packets back-to-back—you must wait for the token to transmit. On Ethernet, a 9.6 microsecond interpacket gap is defined by the 802.3 specification.**

**Burst Sequence Number**    This is the sequence number of this packet within the burst set. The other sequence number field, packet sequence number, indicates the running sequence number of all packets sent by a device.

**ACK Sequence Number**    This field indicates the burst sequence number expected next from the burst mode partner. This field is used to determine if packets are arriving out of order on the network.

**Total Burst Length**    This field indicates the total length of data to be received in this burst set.

**Burst Offset**    This field indicates the data offset in bytes. This is used to determine where this set of data resides in the entire burst set.

**Burst Length**    This field indicates the total amount of data, in bytes, that is contained in this packet.

**Fragment List Entries** The SYS (System) bit in the flag field is set to 1 if this field is used. This field indicates the number of missing fragments (parts of a burst set) that are missing.

**Function** Function number 0x01 indicates a read request. Function 0x02 indicates a burst write request.

**File Handle** This field includes the file handle for the file being read.

**Starting Offset** This field indicates the starting offset in the file (in bytes).

**Bytes to Read** This field indicates the total number of bytes to be read in this burst set.

### Read Reply

Read reply packets actually contain the data requested by the client. These packets vary in length, of course, depending on the amount of data they contain. The first read reply packet includes read reply code and bytes read fields, as shown in Figure 13.58. Subsequent read reply packets do not contain these eight bytes.

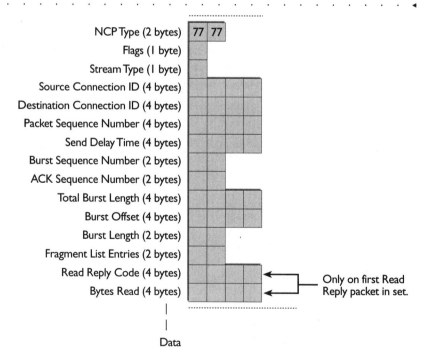

**FIGURE 13.58**

*The first read reply packet indicates the amount of data successfully read to be sent in this set.*

**Read Reply Code**   This field contains a result code for the burst read operation. The possible result codes for a read request are:

0 = No error

1 = Initial error

2 = I/O error

3 = No data read

**Bytes Read**   This field indicates the actual number of bytes read on behalf of the client.

### Write Request

Burst write requests are sent from clients to servers when the client wants to send a file to a NetWare server.

**NCP Type**   The NCP type 0x7777 indicates that this is a burst mode transaction.

**Flags**   The following burst mode flags are available:

0x80 (SYS: System) is set for a system packet. No burst data accompanies or follows these packets.

0x10 (EOB: End of Burst) is set for end of burst. It will be set in the last packet of a burst.

0x04 (ABT: Abort) is set for an abort request. The SYS bit is set if ABT is set.

**Stream Type**   The type of burst. Only the server uses this field. 0x02 is the only valid type.

**Source Connection ID**   The source connection ID is a workstation connection identifier for burst mode communications. This number is randomly generated by the source.

**Destination Connection ID**   This field identifies the self-assigned number of the burst mode partner. For example, a client would put the server's burst mode connection ID number in the destination connection ID field when the client makes burst mode write requests.

**Packet Sequence Number**   This sequence number is incremented for each packet sent by a device. The burst sequence number field listed next contains sequence number information for a single burst.

**Send Delay Time**   This is the delay time between consecutive packet sends in 100 microsecond increments. On a reliable link, burst mode send delay time can reach 0.

**NOTE**  **This is a theoretical number indicating that packets are being sent back-to-back, as fast as possible. Each media access control method interjects some sort of delay in transmission. For example, on Token Ring, you cannot send packets back-to-back—you must wait for the token to transmit. On Ethernet, a 9.6 microsecond interpacket gap is defined by the 802.3 specification.**

**Burst Sequence Number**    This is the sequence number of this packet within the burst set. The packet sequence number, listed previously, indicates the running sequence number of all burst packets sent by a device.

**ACK Sequence Number**    This field indicates the burst sequence number expected next from the burst mode partner. This field is used to determine if packets are arriving out of order on the network.

**Total Burst Length**    This field indicates the total length of data to be sent in this burst set.

**Burst Offset**    This field indicates the data offset in bytes. This is used to determine where this set of data resides in the entire burst set.

**Burst Length**    This field indicates the total amount of data, in bytes, that is contained in this packet.

**Fragment List Entries**    The SYS (System) bit in the flag field is set to 1 if this field is used. This field indicates the number of missing fragments (parts of a burst set).

**Function**    Function 0x02 indicates a burst write request. Function number 0x01 indicates a read request.

**File Handle**    This field includes the file handle for the file being read.

**Starting Offset**    This field indicates the starting offset in the file (in bytes).

**Bytes To Write**    This field indicates the total number of bytes to be written in this burst set.

**Data**    The first portion of the burst data can be contained in the Burst Write request. Data follows immediately after the bytes to write field.

### Burst Writes

After the initial burst write request packets come the standard burst writes to the server. These packets do not contain the function, file handle, starting offset, or bytes to write fields, as shown in Figure 13.59.

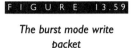

FIGURE 13.59

*The burst mode write packet*

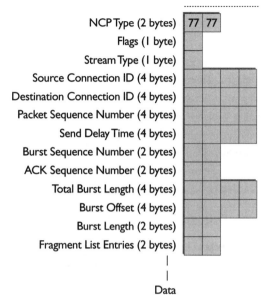

NCP Type (2 bytes)
Flags (1 byte)
Stream Type (1 byte)
Source Connection ID (4 bytes)
Destination Connection ID (4 bytes)
Packet Sequence Number (4 bytes)
Send Delay Time (4 bytes)
Burst Sequence Number (2 bytes)
ACK Sequence Number (2 bytes)
Total Burst Length (4 bytes)
Burst Offset (4 bytes)
Burst Length (2 bytes)
Fragment List Entries (2 bytes)

Data

### Burst Write Reply

When the last packet in a burst write set is received by the server, the server sends a burst write reply packet to the client. This packet contains the same fields as the standard burst write, as shown in Figure 13.60, along with a Burst Write reply code.

The burst write reply code field values can be:

0 = write successful

4 = write error

The "end of burst" flag and a null reply code indicate that the entire burst has been received successfully.

### Fragment Notification

If a packet of a burst read or write set gets lost in transmission, the intended receiver sends a fragment notification packet to the sender. The fragment notification packet contains the same burst mode header structure as burst read or write packets. The fragment notification packets end with the fragment list entries, offset, and bytes missing fields.

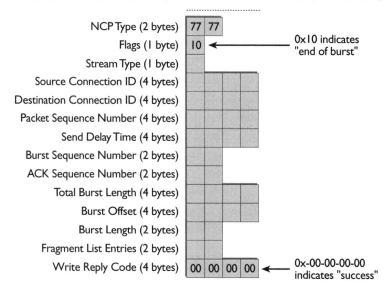

*Burst write reply packets contain a reply code.*

NCP Type (2 bytes)

Flags (1 byte) — 0x10 indicates "end of burst"

Stream Type (1 byte)

Source Connection ID (4 bytes)

Destination Connection ID (4 bytes)

Packet Sequence Number (4 bytes)

Send Delay Time (4 bytes)

Burst Sequence Number (2 bytes)

ACK Sequence Number (2 bytes)

Total Burst Length (4 bytes)

Burst Offset (4 bytes)

Burst Length (2 bytes)

Fragment List Entries (2 bytes)

Write Reply Code (4 bytes) — 0x-00-00-00-00 indicates "success"

**NOTE**

**The Microsoft Client for NetWare Networks may erroneously report missing burst mode packets when it receives packets out of order.**

### Fragment List Entries

This field indicates the number of missing fragment entries contained in the packet. The fragment entry information (offset and bytes missing) follows immediately after this field.

### Offset

This indicates the position of the missing data.

### Bytes Missing

This field indicates the number of bytes missing from the entire set.

## TYPE 0X9999 (SERVER DELAY) PACKET STRUCTURE

You should always watch for these 0x9999 server delay packets on the network —they'll always cost you money and they may be the cause of numerous headaches. Review the section in this chapter "NCP request being processed (type

0x9999)," which focuses on the server delay (also referred to as the server overload and request being processed packets) to be prepared.

### Type Field
This field identifies the packet as a server delay (0x9999).

### Sequence Number Field
The clients assign a number to all NCP requests made to the server, starting with sequence 0. This number wraps at 0xFF.

### Connection Number Low Field
This field indicates the connection number (general services connection) of the client. This number matches up with the connection ID number listed in MONITOR > Connection Status. On 500- and 1,000-user versions of NetWare, the connection number high field is also used to provide a connection ID number to the client. Clients must indicate their connection ID number in all NCP requests to the server.

### Task Number Field
The task number field is not used in this particular packet type.

### Connection Number High Field
This field is used to indicate a higher connection ID number when the operating system supports 500 or 1,000 users.

## NCP Function/Subfunction/Verb List

The following list includes NCP function, subfunction, and verb numbers. If you notice any errors or omissions, please send me an e-mail (chappell@imagitech.com). A brief definition of each NCP call follows this listing:

### ACCOUNTING SERVICE NCPS

| | | | |
|---|---|---|---|
| Get Current Account Status | 0x2222 | 23 | 150 |

*(continued)*

## ACCOUNTING SERVICE NCPS *(continued)*

| | | | |
|---|---|---|---|
| Submit Account Charge | 0x2222 | 23 | 151 |
| Submit Account Hold | 0x2222 | 23 | 152 |
| Submit Account Note | 0x2222 | 23 | 153 |

## APPLE FILE SERVICE NCPS

| | | | |
|---|---|---|---|
| AFP 2.0 Create Directory | 0x2222 | 35 | 13 |
| AFP 2.0 Create File | 0x2222 | 35 | 14 |
| AFP 2.0 Get File or Directory Information | 0x2222 | 35 | 15 |
| AFP 2.0 Scan File Information | 0x2222 | 35 | 17 |
| AFP 2.0 Set File Information | 0x2222 | 35 | 16 |
| AFP Alloc Temporary Directory Handle | 0x2222 | 35 | 11 |
| AFP Create Directory | 0x2222 | 35 | 01 |
| AFP Create File | 0x2222 | 35 | 02 |
| AFP Delete | 0x2222 | 35 | 03 |
| AFP Get DOS Name from Entry ID | 0x2222 | 35 | 18 |
| AFP Get Entry ID from NetWare Handle | 0x2222 | 35 | 06 |
| AFP Get Entry ID from Name | 0x2222 | 35 | 04 |
| AFP Get Entry ID from Path Name | 0x2222 | 35 | 12 |
| AFP Get File Information | 0x2222 | 35 | 05 |
| AFP Get Macintosh Info on Deleted File | 0x2222 | 35 | 19 |
| AFP Open File Fork | 0x2222 | 35 | 08 |
| AFP Rename | 0x2222 | 35 | 07 |
| AFP Scan File Information | 0x2222 | 35 | 10 |
| AFP Set File Information | 0x2222 | 35 | 09 |

## BINDERY NCPS

| | | | |
|---|---|---|---|
| Add Bindery Object to Set | 0x2222 | 23 | 65 |
| Change Bindery Object Password | 0x2222 | 23 | 64 |
| Change Bindery Object Security | 0x2222 | 23 | 56 |
| Change Property Security | 0x2222 | 23 | 59 |
| Change User Password (old) | 0x2222 | 23 | 01 |
| Close Bindery | 0x2222 | 23 | 68 |
| Create Bindery Object | 0x2222 | 23 | 50 |

| Create Property | 0x2222 | 23 | 57 |
|---|---|---|---|
| Delete Bindery Object | 0x2222 | 23 | 51 |
| Delete Bindery Object from Set | 0x2222 | 23 | 66 |
| Delete Property | 0x2222 | 23 | 58 |
| Get Bindery Access Level | 0x2222 | 23 | 70 |
| Get Bindery Object Access Level | 0x2222 | 23 | 72 |
| Get Bindery Object ID | 0x2222 | 23 | 53 |
| Get Bindery Object Name | 0x2222 | 23 | 54 |
| Get Group Number (old) | 0x2222 | 23 | 07 |
| Get User Number (old) | 0x2222 | 23 | 03 |
| Is Bindery Object in Set | 0x2222 | 23 | 67 |
| Is Calling Station a Manager | 0x2222 | 23 | 73 |
| Keyed Change Password | 0x2222 | 23 | 75 |
| Keyed Verify Password | 0x2222 | 23 | 74 |
| List Relations of an Object | 0x2222 | 23 | 76 |
| Open Bindery | 0x2222 | 23 | 69 |
| Read Property Value | 0x2222 | 23 | 61 |
| Rename Object | 0x2222 | 23 | 52 |
| Scan Bindery Object | 0x2222 | 23 | 55 |
| Scan Bindery Object Trustee Paths | 0x2222 | 23 | 71 |
| Scan Property | 0x2222 | 23 | 60 |
| Verify Bindery Object Password | 0x2222 | 23 | 63 |
| Write Property Value | 0x2222 | 23 | 62 |

## CONNECTION NCPS

| Change Connection State | 0x2222 | 23 | 29 |
|---|---|---|---|
| Clear Connection Number | 0x2222 | 23 | 254 |
| Create Service Connection | 0x1111 | — | — |
| Destroy Service Connection | 0x5555 | 00 | — |
| End of Job | 0x2222 | 24 | — |
| Get Big Packet NCP Max Packet Size | 0x2222 | 97 | — |
| Get Connection List from Object | 0x2222 | 23 | 31 |
| Get Internet Address | 0x2222 | 23 | 26 |
| Get Internet Address (old) | 0x2222 | 23 | 19 |

*(continued)*

## CONNECTION NCPS *(continued)*

| | | | |
|---|---|---|---|
| Get Login Key | 0x2222 | 23 | 23 |
| Get Object Connection List | 0x2222 | 23 | 27 |
| Get Object Connection List (old) | 0x2222 | 23 | 21 |
| Get Station Number | 0x2222 | 19 | |
| Get Station's Logged Info | 0x2222 | 23 | 28 |
| Get Station's Logged Info (old) | 0x2222 | 23 | 22 |
| Get Station's Logged Info (old) | 0x2222 | 23 | 05 |
| Get User Connection List (old) | 0x2222 | 23 | 02 |
| Keyed Object Login | 0x2222 | 23 | 24 |
| Login Object | 0x2222 | 23 | 20 |
| Login User (old) | 0x2222 | 23 | 00 |
| Logout | 0x2222 | 25 | — |
| Negotiate Buffer Size | 0x2222 | 33 | — |
| Packet Burst Connection Request | 0x2222 | 101 | — |
| Request Being Processed | 0x9999 | — | — |
| Request Processed | 0x3333 | — | — |
| Set Watchdog Delay Interval | 0x2222 | 23 | 30 |

## DATA MIGRATION NCPS

| | | | |
|---|---|---|---|
| DM File Information | 0x2222 | 90 | 129 |
| DM Support Module Information | 0x2222 | 90 | 132 |
| DM Support Module Capacity Request | 0x2222 | 90 | 135 |
| Get/Set Default Read-Write Support Module ID | 0x2222 | 90 | 134 |
| Migrator Status Info | 0x2222 | 90 | 131 |
| Move File Data from DM | 0x2222 | 90 | 133 |
| Move File Data to DM | 0x2222 | 90 | 128 |
| RTDM Request | 0x2222 | 90 | 136 |
| Volume DM Status | 0x2222 | 90 | 130 |

## EXTENDED ATTRIBUTE NCPS

| | | | |
|---|---|---|---|
| Close Extended Attribute Handle | 0x2222 | 86 | 01 |
| Duplicate Extended Attributes | 0x2222 | 86 | 05 |
| Enumerate Extended Attribute | 0x2222 | 86 | 04 |

| | | | |
|---|---|---|---|
| Read Extended Attribute | 0x2222 | 86 | 03 |
| Write Extended Attribute | 0x2222 | 86 | 02 |

## FILE SERVER ENVIRONMENT NCPS

| | | | |
|---|---|---|---|
| Check Console Privilege | 0x2222 | 23 | 200 |
| Clear Connection Number | 0x2222 | 23 | 254 |
| Clear Connection Number (old) | 0x2222 | 23 | 210 |
| Disable File Server Login | 0x2222 | 23 | 203 |
| Disable Transaction Tracking | 0x2222 | 23 | 207 |
| Down File Server | 0x2222 | 23 | 211 |
| Enable File Server Login | 0x2222 | 23 | 204 |
| Enable Transaction Tracking | 0x2222 | 23 | 208 |
| Get Connection's Open Files | 0x2222 | 23 | 235 |
| Get Connection's Open Files (old) | 0x2222 | 23 | 219 |
| Get Connection's Semaphores | 0x2222 | 23 | 241 |
| Get Connection's Semaphores (old) | 0x2222 | 23 | 225 |
| Get Connection's Task Information | 0x2222 | 23 | 234 |
| Get Connection Usage Statistics | 0x2222 | 23 | 229 |
| Get Connections Using a File | 0x2222 | 23 | 236 |
| Get Connections Using a File (old) | 0x2222 | 23 | 220 |
| Get Disk Channel Statistics | 0x2222 | 23 | 217 |
| Get Disk Utilization | 0x2222 | 23 | 14 |
| Get Drive Mapping Table | 0x2222 | 23 | 215 |
| Get File Server Date and Time | 0x2222 | 20 | — |
| Get File Server Description Strings | 0x2222 | 23 | 201 |
| Get File Server Information | 0x2222 | 23 | 17 |
| Get File Server LAN I/O Statistics | 0x2222 | 23 | 231 |
| Get File Server Login Status | 0x2222 | 23 | 205 |
| Get File Server Misc Information | 0x2222 | 23 | 232 |
| Get File System Statistics | 0x2222 | 23 | 212 |
| Get LAN Driver Configuration Information | 0x2222 | 23 | 227 |
| Get Logical Record Information | 0x2222 | 23 | 240 |
| Get Logical Record Information (old) | 0x2222 | 23 | 224 |
| Get Logical Records by Connection | 0x2222 | 23 | 239 |

*(continued)*

## FILE SERVER ENVIRONMENT NCPS *(continued)*

| | | | |
|---|---|---|---|
| Get Logical Records by Connection (old) | 0x2222 | 23 | 223 |
| Get Network Serial Number | 0x2222 | 23 | 18 |
| Get Object's Remaining Disk Space | 0x2222 | 23 | 230 |
| Get Physical Record Locks by Connection and File | 0x2222 | 23 | 237 |
| Get Physical Record Locks by Connection and File (old) | 0x2222 | 23 | 221 |
| Get Physical Record Locks by File | 0x2222 | 23 | 238 |
| Get Physical Record Locks by File (old) | 0x2222 | 23 | 222 |
| Get Semaphore Information | 0x2222 | 23 | 242 |
| Get Semaphore Information (old) | 0x2222 | 23 | 226 |
| Get Transaction Tracking Statistics | 0x2222 | 23 | 213 |
| Get Volume Information | 0x2222 | 23 | 233 |
| Read Disk Cache Statistics | 0x2222 | 23 | 214 |
| Read Physical Disk Statistics | 0x2222 | 23 | 216 |
| Send Console Broadcast | 0x2222 | 23 | 253 |
| Send Console Broadcast (old) | 0x2222 | 23 | 209 |
| Set File Server Date and Time | 0x2222 | 23 | 202 |
| Verify Serialization | 0x2222 | 23 | 12 |

## FILE SYSTEM NCPS

| | | | |
|---|---|---|---|
| Add Extended Trustee to Directory or File | 0x2222 | 22 | 39 |
| Add Trustee to Director | 0x2222 | 22 | 13 |
| Add Trustee Set to File or SubDirectory | 0x2222 | 87 | 10 |
| Add User Disk Space Restriction | 0x2222 | 22 | 33 |
| Alloc Permanent Directory Handle | 0x2222 | 22 | 18 |
| Allocate Short Directory Handle | 0x2222 | 87 | 12 |
| Alloc Special Temporary Directory Handle | 0x2222 | 22 | 22 |
| Alloc Temporary Directory Handle | 0x2222 | 22 | 19 |
| Close File | 0x2222 | 66 | — |
| Commit File | 0x2222 | 59 | — |
| Convert Path to Dir Entry | 0x2222 | 23 | 244 |
| Copy from One File to Another | 0x2222 | 74 | — |
| Create Directory | 0x2222 | 22 | 10 |

| | | | |
|---|---|---|---|
| Create File | 0x2222 | 67 | — |
| Create New File | 0x2222 | 77 | — |
| Deallocate Directory Handle | 0x2222 | 22 | 20 |
| Delete Directory | 0x2222 | 22 | 11 |
| Delete a File or SubDirectory | 0x2222 | 87 | 08 |
| Delete Trustee from Directory | 0x2222 | 22 | 14 |
| Delete Trustee Set from File or SubDirectory | 0x2222 | 87 | 11 |
| Erase File | 0x2222 | 68 | — |
| Extract a Base Handle | 0x2222 | 22 | 23 |
| File Migration Request | 0x2222 | 90 | 150 |
| File Search Continue | 0x2222 | 63 | — |
| File Search Initialize | 0x2222 | 62 | — |
| Generate Directory Base and Volume Number | 0x2222 | 87 | 22 |
| Get Current Size of File | 0x2222 | 71 | — |
| Get Directory Disk Space Restriction | 0x2222 | 22 | 35 |
| Get Directory Entry | 0x2222 | 22 | 31 |
| Get Directory Information | 0x2222 | 22 | 45 |
| Get Directory Path | 0x2222 | 22 | 01 |
| Get Effective Directory Rights | 0x2222 | 22 | 03 |
| Get Effective Directory Rights | 0x2222 | 87 | 29 |
| Get Effective Rights for Directory Entry | 0x2222 | 22 | 42 |
| Get Extended Volume Information | 0x2222 | 22 | 51 |
| Get File Information | 0x2222 | 87 | 31 |
| Get Full Path String | 0x2222 | 87 | 28 |
| Get Huge NS Information | 0x2222 | 87 | 26 |
| Get Mount Volume List | 0x2222 | 22 | 52 |
| Get NS Information | 0x2222 | 87 | 19 |
| Get Name Space Directory Entry | 0x2222 | 22 | 48 |
| Get Name Space Information | 0x2222 | 22 | 47 |
| Get Name Spaces Loaded List from Volume Number | 0x2222 | 87 | 24 |
| Get Object Disk Usage and Restrictions | 0x2222 | 22 | 41 |
| Get Object Effective Rights for Directory Entry | 0x2222 | 22 | 50 |
| Get Path Name of a Volume-Directory Number Pair | 0x2222 | 22 | 26 |

*(continued)*

### FILE SYSTEM NCPS *(continued)*

| | | | |
|---|---|---|---|
| Get Path String from Short Directory Handle | 0x2222 | 87 | 21 |
| Get Reference Count from Dir Entry Number | 0x2222 | 90 | 10 |
| Get Reference Count from Dir Handle | 0x2222 | 90 | 11 |
| Get Sparse File Data Block Bit Map | 0x2222 | 85 | — |
| Get Volume Info with Handle | 0x2222 | 22 | 21 |
| Get Volume Info with Number | 0x2222 | 18 | — |
| Get Volume Name | 0x2222 | 22 | 06 |
| Get Volume Number | 0x2222 | 22 | 05 |
| Get Volume and Purge Information | 0x2222 | 22 | 44 |
| Initialize Search | 0x2222 | 87 | 02 |
| Map Directory Number to Path | 0x2222 | 23 | 243 |
| Modify DOS Attributes on a File or Subdirectory | 0x2222 | 87 | 35 |
| Modify File or Subdirectory DOS Information | 0x2222 | 87 | 07 |
| Modify Maximum Rights Mask | 0x2222 | 22 | 04 |
| Obtain File or Subdirectory Information | 0x2222 | 87 | 06 |
| Open CallBack Control | 0x2222 | 87 | 34 |
| Open/Create File (old) | 0x2222 | 84 | — |
| Open/Create File or Subdirectory | 0x2222 | 87 | 01 |
| Open/Create File or Subdirectory | 0x2222 | 87 | 30 |
| Open/Create File or Subdirectory with Callback | 0x2222 | 87 | 32 |
| Open/Create File or Subdirectory II with Callback | 0x2222 | 87 | 33 |
| Open Data Stream | 0x2222 | 22 | 49 |
| Open File (old) | 0x2222 | 65 | — |
| Open File (old) | 0x2222 | 76 | — |
| Parse Tree | 0x2222 | 90 | 00 |
| Purge Erased Files (old) | 0x2222 | 22 | 16 |
| Purge Salvageable File | 0x2222 | 87 | 18 |
| Purge Salvageable File (old) | 0x2222 | 22 | 29 |
| Query NS Information Format | 0x2222 | 87 | 23 |
| Recover Erased File (old) | 0x2222 | 22 | 17 |
| Read from a File | 0x2222 | 72 | — |
| Recover Salvageable File | 0x2222 | 87 | 17 |

| | | | |
|---|---|---|---|
| Recover Salvageable File (old) | 0x2222 | 22 | 28 |
| Remove Extended Trustee from Dir or File | 0x2222 | 22 | 43 |
| Remove User Disk Space Restriction | 0x2222 | 22 | 34 |
| Rename Directory | 0x2222 | 22 | 15 |
| Rename File | 0x2222 | 69 | — |
| Rename or Move (old) | 0x2222 | 22 | 46 |
| Rename or Move a File or Subdirectory | 0x2222 | 87 | 04 |
| Restore an Extracted Base Handle | 0x2222 | 22 | 24 |
| Scan a Directory | 0x2222 | 22 | 30 |
| Scan Directory Disk Space | 0x2222 | 22 | 40 |
| Scan Directory for Trustees | 0x2222 | 22 | 12 |
| Scan Directory Information | 0x2222 | 22 | 02 |
| Scan File or Directory for Extended Trustees | 0x2222 | 22 | 38 |
| Scan File Information | 0x2222 | 23 | 15 |
| Scan File or Subdirectory for Trustees | 0x2222 | 87 | 05 |
| Scan Salvageable Files | 0x2222 | 87 | 16 |
| Scan Salvageable Files (old) | 0x2222 | 22 | 27 |
| Scan Volume's User Disk Restrictions | 0x2222 | 22 | 32 |
| Search for a File | 0x2222 | 64 | — |
| Search for File or Subdirectory | 0x2222 | 87 | 03 |
| Search for File or Subdirectory Set | 0x2222 | 87 | 20 |
| Set Compressed File Size | 0x2222 | 90 | 12 |
| Set Directory Disk Space Restriction | 0x2222 | 22 | 36 |
| Set Directory Entry Information | 0x2222 | 22 | 37 |
| Set Directory Handle | 0x2222 | 22 | 00 |
| Set Directory Information | 0x2222 | 22 | 25 |
| Set File Attributes | 0x2222 | 70 | — |
| Set File Extended Attribute | 0x2222 | 79 | — |
| Set File Information | 0x2222 | 23 | 16 |
| Set File Time Date Stamp | 0x2222 | 75 | — |
| Set Huge NS Information | 0x2222 | 87 | 27 |
| Set NS Information | 0x2222 | 87 | 25 |
| Set Short Directory Handle | 0x2222 | 87 | 09 |
| Write to a File | 0x2222 | 73 | — |

## MESSAGE NCPS

| | | | |
|---|---|---|---|
| Broadcast to Console | 0x2222 | 21 | 09 |
| Disable Broadcasts | 0x2222 | 21 | 02 |
| Enable Broadcasts | 0x2222 | 21 | 03 |
| Get Broadcast Message | 0x2222 | 21 | 11 |
| Get Broadcast Message (old) | 0x2222 | 21 | 01 |
| Log Network Message | 0x2222 | 23 | 13 |
| Send Broadcast Message | 0x2222 | 21 | 10 |
| Send Broadcast Message (old) | 0x2222 | 21 | 00 |

## NCP EXTENSION NCPS

| | | | |
|---|---|---|---|
| Execute NCP Extension | 0x2222 | 37 | — |
| Get NCP Extension Information | 0x2222 | 36 | — |

## NOVELL DIRECTORY SERVICES (NDS) NCPS

| | | | |
|---|---|---|---|
| Clear Statistics | 0x2222 | 104 | 07 |
| Monitor NDS Connection | 0x2222 | 104 | 05 |
| Ping for NDS NCP | 0x2222 | 104 | 01 |
| Reload Software | 0x2222 | 104 | 08 |
| Return Bindery Context | 0x2222 | 104 | 04 |
| Return Statistics | 0x2222 | 104 | 06 |
| Send NDS Fragmented Request/Reply | 0x2222 | 104 | 02 |

### Directory Services Verbs

| | | |
|---|---|---|
| DSV_ADD_ENTRY | 07 | (0x07) |
| DSV_ADD_PARTITION | 20 | (0x14) |
| DSV_ADD_REPLICA | 25 | (0x19) |
| DSV_BACKUP_ENTRY | 45 | (0x2D) |
| DSV_BEGIN_MOVE_ENTRY | 42 | (0x2A) |
| DSV_CHANGE_REPLICA_TYPE | 31 | (0x1F) |
| DSV_CHANGE_TREE_NAME | 70 | (0x46) |
| DSV_CLOSE_ITERATION | 50 | (0x32) |
| DSV_COMPARE | 4 | (0x04) |
| DSV_CREATE_BACK_LINK | 64 | (0x40) |

DSV_CREATE_ENTRY_DIR              67    (0x43)
DSV_CREATE_SUBORDINATE_REF        29    (0x1D)
DSV_DEFINE_ATTR                   11    (0x0B)
DSV_DEFINE_CLASS                  14    (0x0E)
DSV_DELETE_EXTERNAL_REFERENCE     65    (0x41)
DSV_DESIGNATE_NEW_MASTE           69    (0x45)
DSV_END_UPDATE_REPLICA            36    (0x24)
DSV_END_UPDATE_SCHEMA             33    (0x21)
DSV_FINISH_MOVE_ENTRY             43    (0x2B)
DSV_GET_EFFECTIVE_RIGHT           19    (0x13)
DSV_GET_REPLICA_ROOT_ID           41    (0x29)
DSV_GET_SERVER_ADDRESS            53    (0x35)
DSV_JOIN_PARTITIONS               24    (0x18)
DSV_LINK_REPLICA                  30    (0x1E)
DSV_LIST                          5     (0x05)
DSV_LIST_CONTAINABLE_CLASSES      18    (0x12)
DSV_LIST_PARTITIONS               22    (0x16)
DSV_MODIFY_CLASS_DEF              16    (0x10)
DSV_MODIFY_ENTRY                  9     (0x09)
DSV_MODIFY_RDN                    10    (0x0A)
DSV_OPEN_STREAM                   27    (0x1B)
DSV_READ                          3     (0x03)
DSV_READ_ATTR_DEF                 12    (0x0C)
DSV_READ_CLASS_DEF                15    (0x0F)
DSV_READ_ENTRY_INFO               2     (0x02)
DSV_RELEASE_MOVED_ENTRY           44    (0x2C)
DSV_REMOVE_ATTR_DEF               13    (0x0D)
DSV_REMOVE_CLASS_DEF              17    (0x11)
DSV_REMOVE_ENTRY                  8     (0x08)
DSV_REMOVE_ENTRY_DIR              68    (0x44)
DSV_REMOVE_PARTITION              21    (0x15)
DSV_REMOVE_REPLICA                26    (0x1A)
DSV_RENAME_EXTERNAL_REFERENCE     66    (0x42)
DSV_REPAIR_TIMESTAMPS             63    (0x3F)
DSV_RESOLVE_NAME                  1     (0x01)

*(continued)*

**Directory Services Verbs** *(continued)*

| | | |
|---|---|---|
| DSV_RESTORE_ENTRY | 46 | (0x2E) |
| DSV_SEARCH_ENTRIES | 6 | (0x06) |
| DSV_SPLIT_PARTITION | 23 | (0x17) |
| DSV_START_UPDATE_REPLIC | 35 | (0x23) |
| DSV_START_UPDATE_SCHEMA | 32 | (0x20) |
| DSV_SYNC_PARTITION | 38 | (0x26) |
| DSV_SYNC_SCHEMA | 39 | (0x27) |
| DSV_UPDATE_REPLICA | 37 | (0x25) |
| DSV_UPDATE_SCHEMA | 34 | (0x22) |

## PRINT SERVICES

| | | | |
|---|---|---|---|
| Close Spool File | 0x2222 | 17 | 01 |
| Create Spool File | 0x2222 | 17 | 09 |
| Get Printer's Queue | 0x2222 | 17 | 10 |
| Get Printer Status | 0x2222 | 17 | 06 |
| Set Spool File Flags | 0x2222 | 17 | 02 |
| Spool a Disk File | 0x2222 | 17 | 03 |
| Write to Spool File | 0x2222 | 17 | 00 |

## QUEUE SERVICES

| | | | |
|---|---|---|---|
| Abort Servicing Queue Job | 0x2222 | 23 | 132 |
| Abort Servicing Queue Job (old) | 0x2222 | 23 | 115 |
| Attach Queue Server to Queue | 0x2222 | 23 | 111 |
| Change Job Priority | 0x2222 | 23 | 130 |
| Change Queue Job Entry | 0x2222 | 23 | 123 |
| Change Queue Job Entry (old) | 0x2222 | 23 | 109 |
| Change Queue Job Position | 0x2222 | 23 | 110 |
| Change to Client Rights | 0x2222 | 23 | 133 |
| Change to Client Rights (old) | 0x2222 | 23 | 116 |
| Close File and Start Queue Job | 0x2222 | 23 | 127 |
| Close File and Start Queue Job (old) | 0x2222 | 23 | 105 |
| Create Queue | 0x2222 | 23 | 100 |
| Create Queue Job and File | 0x2222 | 23 | 121 |

| | | | |
|---|---|---|---|
| Create Queue Job and File (old) | 0x2222 | 23 | 104 |
| Destroy Queue | 0x2222 | 23 | 101 |
| Detach Queue Server from Queue | 0x2222 | 23 | 112 |
| Finish Servicing Queue Job | 0x2222 | 23 | 131 |
| Finish Servicing Queue Job (old) | 0x2222 | 23 | 114 |
| Get Queue Job File Size | 0x2222 | 23 | 135 |
| Get Queue Job File Size (old) | 0x2222 | 23 | 120 |
| Get Queue Job List | 0x2222 | 23 | 129 |
| Get Queue Job List (old) | 0x2222 | 23 | 107 |
| Get Queue Jobs from Form List | 0x2222 | 23 | 137 |
| Move Queue Job from Src Q to Dst Q | 0x2222 | 23 | 136 |
| Read Queue Current Status | 0x2222 | 23 | 125 |
| Read Queue Current Status (old) | 0x2222 | 23 | 102 |
| Read Queue Job Entry | 0x2222 | 23 | 122 |
| Read Queue Job Entry (old) | 0x2222 | 23 | 108 |
| Read Queue Server Current Status | 0x2222 | 23 | 134 |
| Read Queue Server Current Status (old) | 0x2222 | 23 | 118 |
| Remove Job from Queue | 0x2222 | 23 | 128 |
| Remove Job from Queue (old) | 0x2222 | 23 | 106 |
| Restore Queue Server Rights | 0x2222 | 23 | 117 |
| Service Queue Job | 0x2222 | 23 | 124 |
| Service Queue Job (old) | 0x2222 | 23 | 113 |
| Service Queue Job By Form List | 0x2222 | 23 | 138 |
| Set Queue Current Status | 0x2222 | 23 | 126 |
| Set Queue Current Status (old) | 0x2222 | 23 | 103 |
| Set Queue Server Current Status | 0x2222 | 23 | 119 |

## RPC SERVICES NCPS

| | | | |
|---|---|---|---|
| RPC Load an NLM | 0x2222 | 131 | 01 |
| RPC Unload an NLM | 0x2222 | 131 | 02 |
| RPC Mount Volume | 0x2222 | 131 | 03 |
| RPC Dismount Volume | 0x2222 | 131 | 04 |
| RPC Add Name Space to Volume | 0x2222 | 131 | 05 |
| RPC Set Command Value | 0x2222 | 131 | 06 |
| RPC Execute NCF File | 0x2222 | 131 | 07 |

## STATISTICAL NCPS

| | | | |
|---|---|---|---|
| Active LAN Board List | 0x2222 | 123 | 20 |
| Active Protocol Stacks | 0x2222 | 123 | 40 |
| CPU Information | 0x2222 | 123 | 08 |
| Garbage Collection Information | 0x2222 | 123 | 07 |
| Get Active Connection List by Type | 0x2222 | 123 | 14 |
| Get Cache Information | 0x2222 | 123 | 01 |
| Get Compression and Decompression Time and Count | 0x2222 | 123 | 72 |
| Get Current Compressing File | 0x2222 | 123 | 70 |
| Get Current Decompressing File Info List | 0x2222 | 123 | 71 |
| Get Directory Cache Information | 0x2222 | 123 | 12 |
| Get File Server Information | 0x2222 | 123 | 02 |
| Get General Router and SAP Information | 0x2222 | 123 | 50 |
| Get Known Networks Information | 0x2222 | 123 | 53 |
| Get Known Servers Information | 0x2222 | 123 | 56 |
| Get Loaded Media Number List | 0x2222 | 123 | 47 |
| Get Media Manager Object Children's List | 0x2222 | 123 | 32 |
| Get Media Manager Object Information | 0x2222 | 123 | 30 |
| Get Media Manager Objects List | 0x2222 | 123 | 31 |
| Get Media Name by Media Number | 0x2222 | 123 | 46 |
| Get Network Router Information | 0x2222 | 123 | 51 |
| Get Network Routers Information | 0x2222 | 123 | 52 |
| Get NLM Loaded List | 0x2222 | 123 | 10 |
| Get NLM Resource Tag List | 0x2222 | 123 | 15 |
| Get Operating System Version Information | 0x2222 | 123 | 13 |
| Get Protocol Stack Configuration Information | 0x2222 | 123 | 41 |
| Get Protocol Stack Custom Information | 0x2222 | 123 | 43 |
| Get Protocol Stack Numbers by LAN Board Number | 0x2222 | 123 | 45 |
| Get Protocol Stack Numbers by Media Number | 0x2222 | 123 | 44 |
| Get Protocol Stack Statistics | 0x2222 | 123 | 42 |
| Get Server Information | 0x2222 | 123 | 54 |
| Get Server Set Categories | 0x2222 | 123 | 61 |
| Get Server Set Commands Information | 0x2222 | 123 | 60 |
| Get Server Sources Information | 0x2222 | 123 | 55 |
| Get Volume Information by Level | 0x2222 | 123 | 34 |

| | | | |
|---|---|---|---|
| Get Volume Segment List | 0x2222 | 123 | 33 |
| IPX SPX Information | 0x2222 | 123 | 06 |
| LAN Common Counters Information | 0x2222 | 123 | 22 |
| LAN Configuration Information | 0x2222 | 123 | 21 |
| LAN Custom Counters Information | 0x2222 | 123 | 23 |
| LAN Name Information | 0x2222 | 123 | 24 |
| LSL Information | 0x2222 | 123 | 25 |
| LSL Logical Board Statistics | 0x2222 | 123 | 26 |
| MLID Board Information | 0x2222 | 123 | 27 |
| NetWare File Systems Information | 0x2222 | 123 | 03 |
| NLM Information | 0x2222 | 123 | 11 |
| Packet Burst Information | 0x2222 | 123 | 05 |
| User Information | 0x2222 | 123 | 04 |
| Volume Switch Information | 0x2222 | 123 | 09 |

## SYNCHRONIZATION SERVICES

| | | | |
|---|---|---|---|
| Clear File | 0x2222 | 87 | 38 |
| Clear File (old) | 0x2222 | 07 | — |
| Clear File Set | 0x2222 | 08 | — |
| Clear Lock Wait Node | 0x2222 | 112 | — |
| Clear Logical Record | 0x2222 | 11 | — |
| Clear Logical Record Set | 0x2222 | 14 | — |
| Clear Physical Record | 0x2222 | 30 | — |
| Clear Physical Record Set | 0x2222 | 31 | — |
| Close Semaphore | 0x2222 | 111 | 04 |
| Close Semaphore (old) | 0x2222 | 32 | 04 |
| Examine Semaphore | 0x2222 | 111 | 01 |
| Examine Semaphore (old) | 0x2222 | 32 | 01 |
| File Set Lock (old) | 0x2222 | 1 | |
| File Release Lock | 0x2222 | 02 | |
| Lock File Set | 0x2222 | 106 | — |
| Lock File Set (old) | 0x2222 | 04 | — |
| Lock Logical Record Set | 0x2222 | 108 | — |
| Lock Logical Record Set (old) | 0x2222 | 10 | — |
| Lock Physical Record Set | 0x2222 | 110 | — |

*(continued)*

## SYNCHRONIZATION SERVICES *(continued)*

| | | | |
|---|---|---|---|
| Lock Physical Record Set (old) | 0x2222 | 27 | — |
| Log File | 0x2222 | 87 | 36 |
| Log File (old) | 0x2222 | 105 | — |
| Log File (old) | 0x2222 | 03 | — |
| Log Logical Record | 0x2222 | 107 | — |
| Log Logical Record (old) | 0x2222 | 09 | — |
| Log Physical Record | 0x2222 | 109 | — |
| Log Physical Record (old) | 0x2222 | 26 | — |
| Open Semaphore (old) | 0x2222 | 32 | 00 |
| Open/Create a Semaphore | 0x2222 | 111 | 00 |
| Release File | 0x2222 | 87 | 37 |
| Release File (old) | 0x2222 | 05 | — |
| Release File Set | 0x2222 | 06 | — |
| Release Logical Record | 0x2222 | 12 | — |
| Release Logical Record Set | 0x2222 | 13 | — |
| Release Physical Record | 0x2222 | 28 | — |
| Release Physical Record Set | 0x2222 | 29 | — |
| Signal (V) Semaphore | 0x2222 | 111 | 03 |
| Signal Semaphore (old) | 0x2222 | 32 | 03 |
| Wait on (P) Semaphore | 0x2222 | 111 | 02 |
| Wait on Semaphore (old) | 0x2222 | 32 | 02 |

## TRANSACTION TRACKING SERVICES

| | | | |
|---|---|---|---|
| TTS Abort Transaction | 0x2222 | 34 | 03 |
| TTS Begin Transaction | 0x2222 | 34 | 01 |
| TTS End Transaction | 0x2222 | 34 | 02 |
| TTS Get Application Thresholds | 0x2222 | 34 | 05 |
| TTS Get Transaction Bit | 0x2222 | 34 | 09 |
| TTS Get Workstation Thresholds | 0x2222 | 34 | 07 |
| TTS Is Available | 0x2222 | 34 | 00 |
| TTS Set Application Thresholds | 0x2222 | 34 | 06 |
| TTS Set Transaction Bit | 0x2222 | 34 | 10 |
| TTS Set Workstation Thresholds | 0x2222 | 34 | 08 |
| TTS Transaction Status | 0x2222 | 34 | 04 |

## NCP Call Descriptions

Knowing the function/subfunction call numbers is just the starting point for NCP-layer analysis and troubleshooting. You also need an understanding of the purpose of each NCP call, as well as information on which NCP calls are out of date and the calls that replace them. Appendix G provides a description of the basic function of each NCP call listed in this chapter.

## Summary

In this chapter, we have examined NetWare's typical NCP communications. For even more information on NCP troubleshooting, refer to our Web site at www.imagitech.com. In the final chapter of this book, we'll look at two troubleshooting and connectivity tools, the Diagnostic Responder and IPX Ping.

# CHAPTER 14

# NetWare Diagnostic Responder and IPX Ping

**W**hen you need to test connectivity between NetWare LANs, WANs, or individual devices, there are two good methods you can use: IPX Ping and IPX Diagnostic Responder. These technologies enable you to determine if a client is communicating properly and measure the response time across the LAN or WAN to a single network client or server or all network devices.

In this chapter, we determine which technology should be used in various network environments. Then we will examine the IPX Diagnostic Responder and IPX Ping functionality and packet structures.

## Which Technology to Use

All versions of the NetWare server and client contain the ability to respond to a query packet for testing and network mapping purposes. If you've been involved with the NetWare environment for a long time, you may be familiar with a troubleshooting package called NetWare Care. NetWare Care used to broadcast a Diagnostic Responder query packet onto the network. The utility would then record the responses to build a map of network devices. This same technology is used to build network maps (as in the case of ManageWise and HP OpenView) and optionally, to test device response times.

Novell has updated this technology to allow you to query clients from the NetWare server using a ping utility. The term *ping* should be familiar to you if you are from the TCP/IP environment. The NetWare IPX Ping, however, is not the same thing as an IP ping. (Novell does include both ping utilities with NetWare/IntranetWare 4.*x*). Although the IPX Ping utility is easy to use and doesn't require any additional software to execute, it is not supported by every NetWare client or server operating system. In order to test every NetWare device on a network, you should be familiar with both the IPX Diagnostic Responder and IPX Ping.

Table 14.1 shows which clients and servers respond to each utility.

| | TABLE 14.1 |
| --- | --- |

*Not all versions of NetWare client and server software support IPX Ping.*

| PRODUCT | RESPONDS TO THE DIAGNOSTIC RESPONDER QUERIES | RESPONDS TO THE IPX PING QUERIES |
| --- | --- | --- |
| NetWare 2.x servers | Yes | No |
| NetWare 3.x servers | Yes | No |
| NetWare 4.0x servers | Yes | No |
| NetWare 4.1x servers | Yes | Yes |
| NetWare MPR 3.x | Yes | Yes |
| NETX Client | Yes | No |
| VLM Client (up to v1.22) | Yes | No |
| MS Client for NetWare Networks/NDSs | Yes | No |
| Novell Client 32 | Yes | Yes |

**WARNING**

**Be sure that you reference this list when selecting your testing utility. If you mistakenly use IPX Ping to determine if a MS Client for NetWare Networks system is communicating properly, your results (no response) won't be meaningful, since that client does not have the ability to reply to the IPX Ping packets.**

Let's start with the good old IPX Diagnostic Responder and then move on to the more current IPX Ping utility.

▶ · · · · · · · · · · · · · · · · · · · · · · · · · · · · · · · · · ◀

## IPX Diagnostic Responder

The IPX Diagnostic Responder runs on all NetWare clients and servers by default. Unfortunately, NetWare does not include a Diagnostic Responder transmit utility—you must rely on third-party products to build, transmit, and receive Responder packets. In our labs, we use LANQuest's NetWrx LANLoad utility, LANalyzer for Windows, Network General Sniffer, and NCC's LAN Probe to perform Diagnostic Responder tests. For example, we transmit Diagnostic

Responder packets with the LANQuest's NetWrx LANLoad utility and toggle to our LANalyzer for Windows screen to see the replies coming back. In this chapter, we'll show you LANLoad transmit screens and LANalyzer for Windows decode screens.

**Although you can disable the Responder, I don't recommend it. Many network management products use the Responder as their device discovery mechanism. They transmit the Responder query to all devices on all networks, wait, and process the results to build a network map or check device connectivity.**

NOTE

The Diagnostic Responder packet is simply an IPX header with destination socket 0x0456 and a two-byte Exclusion Address Count field, as shown in Figure 14.1.

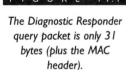

FIGURE 14.1

*The Diagnostic Responder query packet is only 31 bytes (plus the MAC header).*

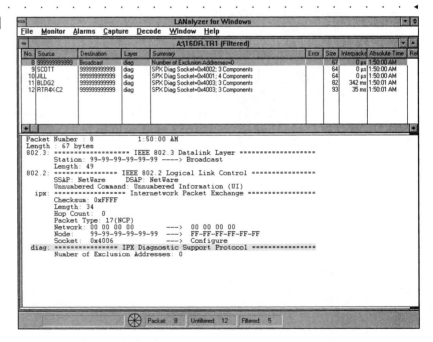

To use the Diagnostic Responder, you must know the IPX internetwork address of destination device (network and node number), and, if the device is on the other side of a router, you must know the MAC address of the router that can get your packets to the destination device. For example, suppose we have a simple two-LAN internetwork. In order to query a BLDG1 from our LANLoad product on network 00002222, we must send the packet to the local router in the Ethernet header but define BLDG1 as the ultimate destination in the IPX header.

**You can get more information about LANLoad at**
**www.lanquest.com.**

TIP

## DIAGNOSTIC RESPONDER TESTING PROCEDURES

There are several ways you can use the Diagnostic Responder:

▸ To test a single device response time

▸ To test the response time of all devices on a network

▸ To test the response time of a network link

### Testing a Single Client or Server

If you are testing a device that is located on the same network as your testing system, you can address the packet directly to the device in both the MAC header and the IPX header. In fact, you can use the destination network address 0x00-00-00-00, which means "this network only." In Figure 14.2, we have defined the addressing scheme in LANLoad to get the packet directly to RTR4X's C2 interface.

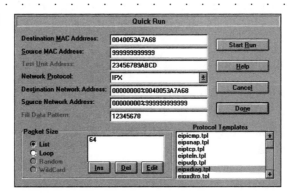

FIGURE 14.2

*In order to get to a local device, use the device's address in both the MAC header and the IPX header.*

Be certain to include your own address or an easy-to-filter address as the source so that you can trace the responses with your analyzer. The replies will be sent back to the address seen in the source network/node fields in the IPX header. The response to the packet shown in Figure 14.3 will be addressed to the local network and node 0x99-99-99-99-99-99. You can use a false node address in these tests to make the replies stand out more on the trace summary screens.

The Diagnostic Responder reply packets contain a list of the basic IPX components of the responding device, as shown in Figure 14.3.

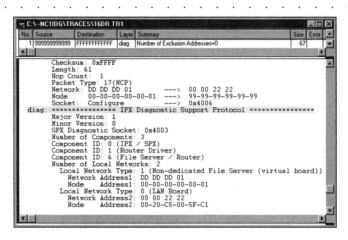

F I G U R E   14.3

*Devices reply with a list of their basic network components.*

Although the component ID listing is a bit vague, you can get the general idea of each component's functionality. The file server responses are especially useful because they supply the network addresses of each network that the server or router is attached to. This includes the server's internal IPX address, as shown in Figure 14.3.

The primary components used are listed here:

- ▶ *Component ID: 0:* IPX/SPX stack loaded

- ▶ *Component ID: 1:* Router driver (also used to get to Internal IPX network)

- ▶ *Component ID: 2:* LAN driver

- ▶ *Component ID: 3:* Shell

▶ *Component ID: 4:* VAP

▶ *Component ID: 6:* File server/router

▶ *Component ID: 9:* DOS application

You can use Table 14.2 to identify the type of device replying to Diagnostic Responder packets.

| TABLE 14.2 | RESPONDING DEVICE | COMPONENTS IN RESPONSE |
|---|---|---|
| *The component listing indicates the type of device that is responding.* | Client using VLMs | Component ID: 0 (IPX/SPX) |
| | | Component ID: 2 (LAN Driver) |
| | | Component ID: 4 (Shell) |
| | | Component ID: 9 (DOS Application) |
| | Client using Client 32 | Component ID: 0 (IPX/SPX) |
| | | Component ID: 2 (LAN Driver) |
| | | Component ID: 4 (Shell) |
| | | Component ID: 9 (DOS Application) |
| | Client using Microsoft Client for NetWare Networks/NDS | Component ID: 0 (IPX/SPX) |
| | | Component ID: 2 (LAN Driver) |
| | | Component ID: 4 (Shell) |
| | NetWare/IntranetWare File Server (2.x, 3.x, 4.x) | Component ID: 0 (IPX/SPX) |
| | | Component ID: 1 (Router Driver) |
| | | Component ID: 6 (File Server/Router) |
| | | Number of Local Networks = 2 |
| | Multiprotocol Router or NetWare server attached to multiple networks | Component ID: 0 (IPX/SPX) |
| | | Component ID: 1 (Router Driver) |
| | | Component ID: 6 (File Server/Router) |
| | | Number of Local Networks > 2 |

### Testing All NetWare Clients/Servers on a Network

When you want to test all devices on a single network, define the broadcast address in the IPX header, as shown in Figure 14.1. All devices that have the Diagnostic Responder capability built in will reply to the query packet. These replies give you a listing of all devices as well as their relative response times.

### Testing Link Speeds

In order to test a link's speed, you must perform at least two Diagnostic Responder sessions. Query each side of the link in each session. Suppose, for example, we have a WAN link between a California office and a New York office. This is the link that we want to test. Our testing equipment is located in the California office.

Using these simple steps, you can test the round-trip time across the WAN link.

**1** • Measure round-trip time to the remote router.

**2** • Measure round-trip time to local router.

**3** • Subtract the local round-trip time from the remote round-trip time. This provides you with the link round-trip time.

**4** • Divide this time in half for the approximate one-way link crossing time.

In our example, we used LANload to transmit the Diagnostic Responder packets and LANalyzer for Windows to receive and timestamp the Diagnostic Responder packets. We also used the LAN Probe because it can simultaneously transmit and receive packets.

**NOTE**

**Not all third-party routers, such as Cisco routers, support the Diagnostic Responder. In this case, you may need to use the IPX Ping utility to test connectivity and time round-trip delays to these devices.**

## IPX DIAGNOSTIC RESPONDER PACKET FORMATS

Good analyzers should include decodes for the Diagnostic Responder packets. If they don't, use this section to do your own decodes of the contents of those packets.

The two basic packet formats used by the Diagnostic Responder are:

▸ The query packet format

▸ The reply packet format

### Query Packet Format

Query packets are very simple packets that include an IPX header addressed to the intended recipient(s) and socket number 0x0456. The data portion of the packet requires only one field, exclusion address count. If you are using exclusion addresses, they will follow the exclusion address count field.

The IPX header used by Diagnostic Responder queries includes the destination socket address 0x0456, which indicates that the packet contains Diagnostic Responder information and should be handled by the Diagnostic Responder process.

The IPX header contents are important because the destination address fields indicate the device or devices that should reply to the query packet.

**Exclusion Address Count Field (1 Byte)**    The only field in the data portion of the Diagnostic Responder query packet is the exclusion address count field. This field indicates the number of MAC addresses that are defined in this packet for devices that should *not* respond to the query packet. If you do not want to exclude any device from answering the query packet, pad this field with 0x00.

**Exclusion Address(es)**    If the exclusion address count is greater than 1, the exclusion address fields contain the MAC addresses of the devices that should ignore the Diagnostic Responder query. This field must contain values in multiples of six bytes.

**We rarely use this field, because it's easier to interpret the replies and ignore the one or two stations that are not of interest to you than to obtain and input their MAC addresses in the query packets.**

NOTE

### Reply Packet Format

The Diagnostic Responder reply packets contain some information about the replying device, although you really should not count on this information to provide you with too much pertinent information about the responding device.

The IPX header used by the Diagnostic Responder response includes the source socket address 0x0456, which indicates that the packet contains the following information:

▸ *Minor Version (1 byte):* The first digit of the Diagnostic Responder version that is replying.

▸ *Major Version (1 byte):* The second digit of the Diagnostic Responder version that is replying. Version 1.1 is the current version used by clients, whereas Version 1.0 is the version used by NetWare servers.

▸ *SPX Diagnostic Socket (2 bytes):* The socket number to use for SPX diagnostic queries.

▸ *Number of Components (1 byte):* The total number of components to follow.

▸ *Component IDs (1 byte each):* The component ID information provides the basic listing of functions on the responding device. There are seven basic components, each containing one byte.

    ▸ *Component ID: 0:* IPX/SPX stack loaded

    ▸ *Component ID: 1:* Router driver (also used to get to Internal IPX network)

    ▸ *Component ID: 2:* LAN driver

    ▸ *Component ID: 3:* Shell

    ▸ *Component ID: 4:* VAP

    ▸ *Component ID: 6:* File server/router

► *Component ID: 9:* DOS application

► *Number of Local Networks (1 byte):* If the responder used Component ID 6 in its reply, this indicates that the responder is a file server/routing device. The device must provide the addresses of all attached networks (including the local MAC address used to access a particular network).

► *Local Network Type 1 (1 byte):* There are two types of local networks: the virtual network (internal IPX network) and the LAN board network (external IPX network).

► *Network Address 1 (4 bytes):* The four-byte address of the virtual (internal) or external network.

► *Node Address 1 (6 bytes):* The address of the network interface card that is attached to the network listed with the same number. Node address 0x00-00-00-00-00-01 is always assigned to the internal IPX network.

Now that we've examined the Diagnostic Responder and its capabilities, let's look at IPX Ping.

## IPX Ping

IPX Ping was initially released as a part of the Novell Multiprotocol Router. Now that InternetWare 4.11 includes the Multiprotocol Router's basic capabilities, it includes IPX Ping capability. IPX Ping is a simple ping utility similar to TCP/IP Ping. IPX Ping can be used instead of the Diagnostic Responder when you want to perform a simple "are you alive?" query to one or more devices from the NetWare 4.11 console.

Keep in mind that only the NetWare 4.1x servers, NetWare MPR 3.x routers, and Client 32–based workstations respond to IPX Ping. If you want to test other NetWare devices, use the IPX Diagnostic Responder.

**Some third-party products, such as Cisco routers (IOS v10 or later) respond to the IPX Ping packets as well.**

NOTE

The IPX Ping utility actually sends the word "Ping" to the destination address, as shown in Figure 14.4. The reply simply echoes back the data portion of the packet, as shown in Figure 14.5. Unlike with the Diagnostic Responder, no configuration information is exchanged when you use IPX Ping.

**Unfortunately, LANalyzer for Windows 2.2 does not include a complete IPX Ping decode. Refer to the section entitled "IPX Ping Packet Formats" for more details on the contents of IPX Ping packets.**

NOTE

F I G U R E  14.4

*The IPX Ping utility actually sends the ASCII characters "Ping" to the recipient.*

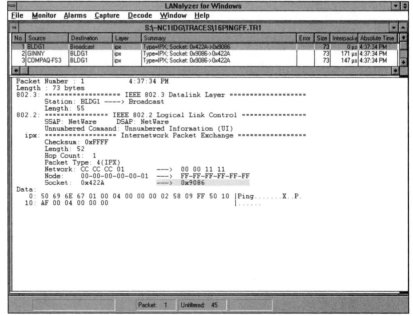

The IPX Ping respondent
simply echos back the data
portion of the IPX Ping
query.

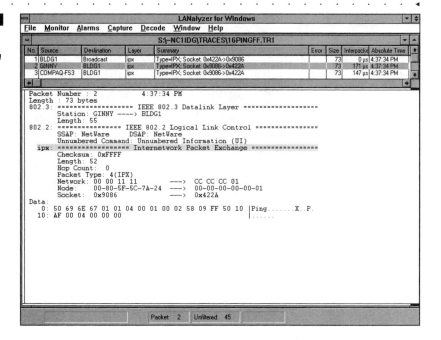

Packet Number : 2                    4:37:34 PM
Length : 73 bytes
802.3: ================== IEEE 802.3 Datalink Layer ==================
       Station: GINNY ----> BLDG1
       Length: 55
802.2: ================= IEEE 802.2 Logical Link Control ================
       SSAP: NetWare      DSAP: NetWare
       Unnumbered Command: Unnumbered Information (UI)
  ipx: ================= Internetwork Packet Exchange =================
       Checksum: 0xFFFF
       Length: 52
       Hop Count:  0
       Packet Type: 4(IPX)
       Network: 00 00 11 11      --->  CC CC CC 01
       Node:    00-80-5F-5C-7A-24 --->  00-00-00-00-00-01
       Socket:  0x9086           --->  0x422A
  Data:
      0: 50 69 6E 67 01 01 04 00 01 00 02 58 09 FF 50 10 |Ping.......X..P.
     10: AF 00 04 00 00 00                               |......

**NOTE**

**Strangely, NetWare servers that reply to the ping are often so lazy that they do not input their source node address in the IPX header. Therefore you may see a strange sight—a packet coming from the address 0xFF-FF-FF-FF-FF-FF!**

To use IPX Ping, type **LOAD IPXPING** at the NetWare console. The IPX Ping menu appears, as shown in Figure 14.6.

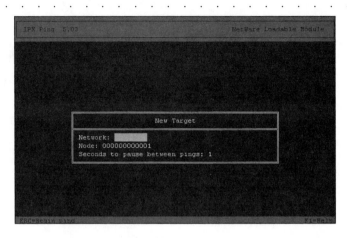

FIGURE 14.6

*The IPX Ping menu prompts you for addressing information and the frequency rate.*

## BUILDING AN IPX PING PACKET

The information you provide in the IPX Ping menu is used to build the IPX Ping packet that is sent onto the network.

### Network Address

You must know the network address of the device that you want to IPX Ping. If you type in 0xFF-FF-FF-FF, the ping utility won't transmit anything onto the cabling system. This is to ensure that you do not flood the network with ping broadcasts. (Default: none)

### Node Address

The node address of the device you want to ping. If you want to ping all devices on a network, enter FFFFFFFFFFFF (the broadcast address). (Default: 000000000001.)

### Seconds to Pause between Pings

The number of seconds to wait between each ping sent on the network. The higher you set this, the more traffic you will be generating onto the network. (Default: 1 second)

To test a single client or server, address the Ping packet directly to that server or client. To test clients/servers on a network, enter the exact network address and the broadcast node address.

To test link speeds, you can define multiple ping queries to run simultaneously. Define one ping for each router at opposite sides of the WAN link. Evaluate the difference between each router's round-trip response time. Figure 14.7 shows a ping test using multiple entries.

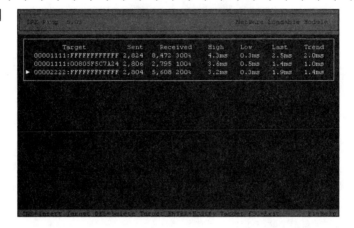

*Use the Insert key to add entries to a ping test.*

The ping console screen provides the response times for the ping tests and some trend information, as well. The following lists the information available from the ping console screen:

- *Target (network:node):* The network and node address of the target device or devices.

- *Sent:* The number of ping packets that have been sent since the IPX Ping application was launched.

- *Received (number - percentage):* The number of ping responses received since the IPX Ping application was started and the total percentage of responses to requests. On broadcast pings, you can see responses over 100 percent. If there are five stations responding to a broadcast ping, the response percentage is 500 percent. On unicast pings (pings directed to a specific node address), the highest response percentage is 100 percent. If, on a saturated network, responses are not able to arrive successfully due to congestion, you might see responses lower than 100 percent.

▸ *High (Round-trip Timestamp):* The slowest round-trip time seen since the IPXPING application was launched.

▸ *Low (Round-trip Timestamp):* The fastest round-trip time seen since the IPXPING application was launched.

▸ *Last (Round-trip Timestamp):* The last round-trip time seen.

▸ *Trend (Round-trip Timestamp):* The average round-trip time since the IPXPING application was launched.

### IPX PING PACKET FORMATS

The request and reply IPX Ping packets have the same structure. All ping requests must be sent to the IPX Ping socket number 0x9086.

Some analyzers that are out of date may not provide complete decodes of Novell's IPX Ping packets. Use the following packet information to do your own decoding, if necessary:

▸ *Ping data (4 bytes):* This field simply contains the ASCII word "Ping" in both the request and reply packets. The hex value is 0x50-69-6E-67.

▸ *Version (1 byte):* The current version of the IPX Ping utility is 1.

▸ *Type (1 byte):* The value 0x00 indicates a ping request. The value 0x01 indicates a ping reply.

▸ *Ping ID (2 bytes):* A unique identifier assigned by the requester and echoed in the response packet. This information is used to match up ping requests and replies.

▸ *Result (1 byte):* In a ping request, this field is set to 0x00. In the reply, we see 0x01 indicating a successful reply.

▸ *Reserved (1 byte):* Set at 0x00 and ignored upon receipt.

> ▸ *Data (var)*: A variable set of data inserted into the ping request by the sender and echoed back by the responding station.

Using these tools, we can do a variety of troubleshooting tests to determine connectivity between NetWare devices and even the round-trip response times. The next time a user complains that they cannot connect to the server, use the Diagnostic Responder or IPX Ping to test connectivity.

## Summary

The Diagnostic Responder and IPX Ping can be extremely useful tools in troubleshooting your network. In this chapter, we've examined the uses, compatibility, and formats of both tools. Become familiar with each tool so that you're prepared to use them when they're needed.

At this point, I'd recommend that you look through the trace files contained on the accompanying CD-ROM. The traces are listed and briefly described in Appendix H, "CD-ROM Content List/Trace Files on CD-ROM." You can get a chance to interpret the communications and compare them with the information contained in this book. In fact, as you peruse this book, you'll see many instances where the trace filename is shown at the top of a LANalyzer for Windows screenshot.

Happy analyzing!

# PART III

# Appendixes

The appendixes include a set of references that will help you analyze and manage your network.

Appendix A is a standard hexadecimal-decimal-binary conversion chart. You'll want to keep this handy as we explain the packet field values throughout this book.

Appendix B, C, and D provide the MIBs (Management Information Bases) for IPX, RIP/SAP and NLSP. If you have a MIB browser, you can browse and obtain this information from any SNMP agent that supports these MIBs.

Appendix E is the list of SAP numbers assigned by Novell to the various industry developers (and Novell departments) for their applications. You can use this list to determine which applications are being used on your network when your analyzer doesn't decipher the SAP number value.

Appendix F is the assigned socket number list from Novell. This list defines all the socket numbers assigned to developers who want to write directly to IPX or SPX without being limited to using NCP services.

Appendix G is the master list of NCP function, subfunction, and verb codes, along with a brief description of the use of each NCP call. This list can be tremendously helpful in determining the process that applications undergo to execute their functions.

Appendix H provides a description of the CD-ROM contents (LANalyzer for Windows demo and ImagiTech lab trace files).

When you complete this book, you should be proficient in reading IPX/SPX communications, and should have a keen understanding of the upper-layer processes that enable us to network using IPX/SPX.

Remember that additional information on analysis, troubleshooting, and optimization can be found on our web site, www.imagitech.com.

# Hex-Decimal-Binary
# Conversion Chart

| DECIMAL VALUE | HEXADECIMAL VALUE | BINARY VALUE |
| --- | --- | --- |
| 0 | 00 | 0000 0000 |
| 1 | 01 | 0000 0001 |
| 2 | 02 | 0000 0010 |
| 3 | 03 | 0000 0011 |
| 4 | 04 | 0000 0100 |
| 5 | 05 | 0000 0101 |
| 6 | 06 | 0000 0110 |
| 7 | 07 | 0000 0111 |
| 8 | 08 | 0000 1000 |
| 9 | 09 | 0000 1001 |
| 10 | 0A | 0000 1010 |
| 11 | 0B | 0000 1011 |
| 12 | 0C | 0000 1100 |
| 13 | 0D | 0000 1101 |
| 14 | 0E | 0000 1110 |
| 15 | 0F | 0000 1111 |
| 16 | 10 | 0001 0000 |
| 17 | 11 | 0001 0001 |
| 18 | 12 | 0001 0010 |
| 19 | 13 | 0001 0011 |
| 20 | 14 | 0001 0100 |
| 21 | 15 | 0001 0101 |
| 22 | 16 | 0001 0110 |
| 23 | 17 | 0001 0111 |
| 24 | 18 | 0001 1000 |
| 25 | 19 | 0001 1001 |
| 26 | 1A | 0001 1010 |
| 27 | 1B | 0001 1011 |

| DECIMAL VALUE | HEXADECIMAL VALUE | BINARY VALUE |
|:---:|:---:|:---:|
| 28 | IC | 0001 1100 |
| 29 | ID | 0001 1101 |
| 30 | IE | 0001 1110 |
| 31 | IF | 0001 1111 |
| 32 | 20 | 0010 0000 |
| 33 | 21 | 0010 0001 |
| 34 | 22 | 0010 0010 |
| 35 | 23 | 0010 0011 |
| 36 | 24 | 0010 0100 |
| 37 | 25 | 0010 0101 |
| 38 | 26 | 0010 0110 |
| 39 | 27 | 0010 0111 |
| 40 | 28 | 0010 1000 |
| 41 | 29 | 0010 1001 |
| 42 | 2A | 0010 1010 |
| 43 | 2B | 0010 1011 |
| 44 | 2C | 0010 1100 |
| 45 | 2D | 0010 1101 |
| 46 | 2E | 0010 1110 |
| 47 | 2F | 0010 1111 |
| 48 | 30 | 0011 0000 |
| 49 | 31 | 0011 0001 |
| 50 | 32 | 0011 0010 |
| 51 | 33 | 0011 0011 |
| 52 | 34 | 0011 0100 |
| 53 | 35 | 0011 0101 |
| 54 | 36 | 0011 0110 |

*(continued)*

| DECIMAL VALUE | HEXADECIMAL VALUE | BINARY VALUE |
|:---:|:---:|:---:|
| 55 | 37 | 0011 0111 |
| 56 | 38 | 0011 1000 |
| 57 | 39 | 0011 1001 |
| 58 | 3A | 0011 1010 |
| 59 | 3B | 0011 1011 |
| 60 | 3C | 0011 1100 |
| 61 | 3D | 0011 1101 |
| 62 | 3E | 0011 1110 |
| 63 | 3F | 0011 1111 |
| 64 | 40 | 0100 0000 |
| 65 | 41 | 0100 0001 |
| 66 | 42 | 0100 0010 |
| 67 | 43 | 0100 0011 |
| 68 | 44 | 0100 0100 |
| 69 | 45 | 0100 0101 |
| 70 | 46 | 0100 0110 |
| 71 | 47 | 0100 0111 |
| 72 | 48 | 0100 1000 |
| 73 | 49 | 0100 1001 |
| 74 | 4A | 0100 1010 |
| 75 | 4B | 0100 1011 |
| 76 | 4C | 0100 1100 |
| 77 | 4D | 0100 1101 |
| 78 | 4E | 0100 1110 |
| 79 | 4F | 0100 1111 |
| 80 | 50 | 0101 0000 |
| 81 | 51 | 0101 0001 |
| 82 | 52 | 0101 0010 |

**HEX-DECIMAL-BINARY CONVERSION CHART**

| DECIMAL VALUE | HEXADECIMAL VALUE | BINARY VALUE |
|:---:|:---:|:---:|
| 83 | 53 | 0101 0011 |
| 84 | 54 | 0101 0100 |
| 85 | 55 | 0101 0101 |
| 86 | 56 | 0101 0110 |
| 87 | 57 | 0101 0111 |
| 88 | 58 | 0101 1000 |
| 89 | 59 | 0101 1001 |
| 90 | 5A | 0101 1010 |
| 91 | 5B | 0101 1011 |
| 92 | 5C | 0101 1100 |
| 93 | 5D | 0101 1101 |
| 94 | 5E | 0101 1110 |
| 95 | 5F | 0101 1111 |
| 96 | 60 | 0110 0000 |
| 97 | 61 | 0110 0001 |
| 98 | 62 | 0110 0010 |
| 99 | 63 | 0110 0011 |
| 100 | 64 | 0110 0100 |
| 101 | 65 | 0110 0101 |
| 102 | 66 | 0110 0110 |
| 103 | 67 | 0110 0111 |
| 104 | 68 | 0110 1000 |
| 105 | 69 | 0110 1001 |
| 106 | 6A | 0110 1010 |
| 107 | 6B | 0110 1011 |
| 108 | 6C | 0110 1100 |
| 109 | 6D | 0110 1101 |

*(continued)*

| DECIMAL VALUE | HEXADECIMAL VALUE | BINARY VALUE |
|:---:|:---:|:---:|
| 110 | 6E | 0110 1110 |
| 111 | 6F | 0110 1111 |
| 112 | 70 | 0111 0000 |
| 113 | 71 | 0111 0001 |
| 114 | 72 | 0111 0010 |
| 115 | 73 | 0111 0011 |
| 116 | 74 | 0111 0100 |
| 117 | 75 | 0111 0101 |
| 118 | 76 | 0111 0110 |
| 119 | 77 | 0111 0111 |
| 120 | 78 | 0111 1000 |
| 121 | 79 | 0111 1001 |
| 122 | 7A | 0111 1010 |
| 123 | 7B | 0111 1011 |
| 124 | 7C | 0111 1100 |
| 125 | 7D | 0111 1101 |
| 126 | 7E | 0111 1110 |
| 127 | 7F | 0111 1111 |
| 128 | 80 | 1000 0000 |
| 129 | 81 | 1000 0001 |
| 130 | 82 | 1000 0010 |
| 131 | 83 | 1000 0011 |
| 132 | 84 | 1000 0100 |
| 133 | 85 | 1000 0101 |
| 134 | 86 | 1000 0110 |
| 135 | 87 | 1000 0111 |
| 136 | 88 | 1000 1000 |
| 137 | 89 | 1000 1001 |

| DECIMAL VALUE | HEXADECIMAL VALUE | BINARY VALUE |
|:---:|:---:|:---:|
| 138 | 8A | 1000 1010 |
| 139 | 8B | 1000 1011 |
| 140 | 8C | 1000 1100 |
| 141 | 8D | 1000 1101 |
| 142 | 8E | 1000 1110 |
| 143 | 8F | 1000 1111 |
| 144 | 90 | 1001 0000 |
| 145 | 91 | 1001 0001 |
| 146 | 92 | 1001 0010 |
| 147 | 93 | 1001 0011 |
| 148 | 94 | 1001 0100 |
| 149 | 95 | 1001 0101 |
| 150 | 96 | 1001 0110 |
| 151 | 97 | 1001 0111 |
| 152 | 98 | 1001 1000 |
| 153 | 99 | 1001 1001 |
| 154 | 9A | 1001 1010 |
| 155 | 9B | 1001 1011 |
| 156 | 9C | 1001 1100 |
| 157 | 9D | 1001 1101 |
| 158 | 9E | 1001 1110 |
| 159 | 9F | 1001 1111 |
| 160 | A0 | 1010 0000 |
| 161 | A1 | 1010 0001 |
| 162 | A2 | 1010 0010 |
| 163 | A3 | 1010 0011 |
| 164 | A4 | 1010 0100 |

*(continued)*

| DECIMAL VALUE | HEXADECIMAL VALUE | BINARY VALUE |
|:---:|:---:|:---:|
| 165 | A5 | 1010 0101 |
| 166 | A6 | 1010 0110 |
| 167 | A7 | 1010 0111 |
| 168 | A8 | 1010 1000 |
| 169 | A9 | 1010 1001 |
| 170 | AA | 1010 1010 |
| 171 | AB | 1010 1011 |
| 172 | AC | 1010 1100 |
| 173 | AD | 1010 1101 |
| 174 | AE | 1010 1110 |
| 175 | AF | 1010 1111 |
| 176 | B0 | 1011 0000 |
| 177 | B1 | 1011 0001 |
| 178 | B2 | 1011 0010 |
| 179 | B3 | 1011 0011 |
| 180 | B4 | 1011 0100 |
| 181 | B5 | 1011 0101 |
| 182 | B6 | 1011 0110 |
| 183 | B7 | 1011 0111 |
| 184 | B8 | 1011 1000 |
| 185 | B9 | 1011 1001 |
| 186 | BA | 1011 1010 |
| 187 | BB | 1011 1011 |
| 188 | BC | 1011 1100 |
| 189 | BD | 1011 1101 |
| 190 | BE | 1011 1110 |
| 191 | BF | 1011 1111 |
| 192 | C0 | 1100 0000 |

| DECIMAL VALUE | HEXADECIMAL VALUE | BINARY VALUE |
|---|---|---|
| 193 | C1 | 1100 0001 |
| 194 | C2 | 1100 0010 |
| 195 | C3 | 1100 0011 |
| 196 | C4 | 1100 0100 |
| 197 | C5 | 1100 0101 |
| 198 | C6 | 1100 0110 |
| 199 | C7 | 1100 0111 |
| 200 | C8 | 1100 1000 |
| 201 | C9 | 1100 1001 |
| 202 | CA | 1100 1010 |
| 203 | CB | 1100 1011 |
| 204 | CC | 1100 1100 |
| 205 | CD | 1100 1101 |
| 206 | CE | 1100 1110 |
| 207 | CF | 1100 1111 |
| 208 | D0 | 1101 0000 |
| 209 | D1 | 1101 0001 |
| 210 | D2 | 1101 0010 |
| 211 | D3 | 1101 0011 |
| 212 | D4 | 1101 0100 |
| 213 | D5 | 1101 0101 |
| 214 | D6 | 1101 0110 |
| 215 | D7 | 1101 0111 |
| 216 | D8 | 1101 1000 |
| 217 | D9 | 1101 1001 |
| 218 | DA | 1101 1010 |
| 219 | DB | 1101 1011 |

*(continued)*

| DECIMAL VALUE | HEXADECIMAL VALUE | BINARY VALUE |
|:---:|:---:|:---:|
| 220 | DC | 1101 1100 |
| 221 | DD | 1101 1101 |
| 222 | DE | 1101 1110 |
| 223 | DF | 1101 1111 |
| 224 | E0 | 1110 0000 |
| 225 | E1 | 1110 0001 |
| 226 | E2 | 1110 0010 |
| 227 | E3 | 1110 0011 |
| 228 | E4 | 1110 0100 |
| 229 | E5 | 1110 0101 |
| 230 | E6 | 1110 0110 |
| 231 | E7 | 1110 0111 |
| 232 | E8 | 1110 1000 |
| 233 | E9 | 1110 1001 |
| 234 | EA | 1110 1010 |
| 235 | EB | 1110 1011 |
| 236 | EC | 1110 1100 |
| 237 | ED | 1110 1101 |
| 238 | EE | 1110 1110 |
| 239 | EF | 1110 1111 |
| 240 | F0 | 1111 0000 |
| 241 | F1 | 1111 0001 |
| 242 | F2 | 1111 0010 |
| 243 | F3 | 1111 0011 |
| 244 | F4 | 1111 0100 |
| 245 | F5 | 1111 0101 |
| 246 | F6 | 1111 0110 |
| 247 | F7 | 1111 0111 |

| DECIMAL VALUE | HEXADECIMAL VALUE | BINARY VALUE |
|:---:|:---:|:---:|
| 248 | F8 | 1111 1000 |
| 249 | F9 | 1111 1001 |
| 250 | FA | 1111 1010 |
| 251 | FB | 1111 1011 |
| 252 | FC | 1111 1100 |
| 253 | FD | 1111 1101 |
| 254 | FE | 1111 1110 |
| 255 | FF | 1111 1111 |

# IPX MIB

```
IPX DEFINITIONS ::= BEGIN


— This MIB defines the management information for a system using the
IPX

— protocol.  The MIB consists of four groups:

—

—    1.  System Group - contains general information about all
instances

—                       of IPX on the system

—

—    2.  Circuit Group - contains information about all circuits
used by

—                       IPX on the system

—

—    3.  Forwarding Group - contains generic routing information
that

—                       must be provided by any IPX routing
protocol.

—

—    4.  Services Group - contains information about all known
services.

—

— The MIB is designed to support multiple instances of the IPX

— protocol on one system via a system instance identifier that is
the

— primary index for every table in this MIB.

—

— This MIB is designed to provide a basic framework for the
management

— of systems implementing the IPX protocol.  Additional MIBs may be

— created (especially in the area of IPX routing protocols) to
contain

— more specific information.  Whenever possible, these additional
MIBs
```

— should follow the format of this IPX MIB.  Information in these MIBs

— should be linked to this MIB via the use of the system instance

— identifier mentioned previously.

—

—

— Changes:

—

—    4/15/94:  Cleanup of some typographical errors

—

—    4/21/94:  Change ipxCircNetNumber access to read-write


```
IMPORTS

        enterprises, Counter

                FROM RFC1155-SMI

        OBJECT-TYPE

                FROM RFC-1212

        TRAP-TYPE

                FROM RFC-1215

        PhysAddress

                FROM RFC1213-MIB;


novell  OBJECT IDENTIFIER ::= { enterprises 23 }

mibDoc  OBJECT IDENTIFIER ::= { novell 2 }

ipx     OBJECT IDENTIFIER ::= { mibDoc 5 }



— Groups


ipxSystem OBJECT IDENTIFIER ::= {ipx 1}
```

```
ipxCircuit OBJECT IDENTIFIER ::= {ipx 2}

ipxForwarding OBJECT IDENTIFIER ::= {ipx 3}

ipxServices OBJECT IDENTIFIER ::= {ipx 4}

ipxTraps OBJECT IDENTIFIER ::= {ipx 5}


— Types


NetNumber ::= OCTET STRING (SIZE(4))


— System Group

—   This group contains global information about each instance of
IPX

—   running on one system.


— Basic System Table

—   This table contains one entry for each instance of IPX running
on

—   the system.  It contains the management information that should

—   be made available by all implementations of the IPX protocol.


ipxBasicSysTable OBJECT-TYPE

    SYNTAX        SEQUENCE OF IPXBasicSysEntry

    ACCESS        not-accessible

    STATUS        mandatory

    DESCRIPTION "The IPX System table - basic information."

    ::= {ipxSystem 1}


ipxBasicSysEntry OBJECT-TYPE

    SYNTAX        IPXBasicSysEntry

    ACCESS        not-accessible

    STATUS        mandatory
```

DESCRIPTION "Each entry corresponds to one instance of IPX running

on the system."

INDEX        {ipxBasicSysInstance}

::= {ipxBasicSysTable 1}


IPXBasicSysEntry ::= SEQUENCE {

        ipxBasicSysInstance

           INTEGER,

        ipxBasicSysExistState

           INTEGER,

        ipxBasicSysNetNumber

           NetNumber,

        ipxBasicSysNode

           OCTET STRING,

        ipxBasicSysName

           OCTET STRING,

        ipxBasicSysInReceives

           Counter,

        ipxBasicSysInHdrErrors

           Counter,

        ipxBasicSysInUnknownSockets

           Counter,

        ipxBasicSysInDiscards

           Counter,

        ipxBasicSysInBadChecksums

           Counter,

        ipxBasicSysInDelivers

           Counter,

        ipxBasicSysNoRoutes

           Counter,

```
                                ipxBasicSysOutRequests

                                    Counter,

                                ipxBasicSysOutMalformedRequests

                                    Counter,

                                ipxBasicSysOutDiscards

                                    Counter,

                                ipxBasicSysOutPackets

                                    Counter,

                                ipxBasicSysConfigSockets

                                    INTEGER,

                                ipxBasicSysOpenSocketFails

                                    Counter

                    }


    ipxBasicSysInstance OBJECT-TYPE

        SYNTAX        INTEGER

        ACCESS        read-write

        STATUS        mandatory

        DESCRIPTION "The unique identifier of the instance of IPX to
    which this

                    row corresponds.  This value may be written only
    when

                    creating a new entry in the table."

        ::= {ipxBasicSysEntry 1}


    ipxBasicSysExistState OBJECT-TYPE

        SYNTAX        INTEGER {

                            off(1),

                            on(2)

                            }

        ACCESS        read-write
```

STATUS          mandatory

DESCRIPTION "The validity of this entry in the IPX system table.

Setting this field to off indicates that this entry may be

deleted from the system table at the IPX implementer's

discretion."

::= {ipxBasicSysEntry 2}


ipxBasicSysNetNumber OBJECT-TYPE

SYNTAX          NetNumber

ACCESS          read-write

STATUS          mandatory

DESCRIPTION "The network number portion of the IPX address of this

system."

::= {ipxBasicSysEntry 3}


ipxBasicSysNode OBJECT-TYPE

SYNTAX          OCTET STRING (SIZE(6))

ACCESS          read-write

STATUS          mandatory

DESCRIPTION "The node number portion of the IPX address of this

system."

::= {ipxBasicSysEntry 4}


ipxBasicSysName OBJECT-TYPE

SYNTAX          OCTET STRING (SIZE(0..48))

ACCESS          read-write

STATUS          mandatory

DESCRIPTION "The readable name for this system."

```
            ::= {ipxBasicSysEntry 5}


    ipxBasicSysInReceives OBJECT-TYPE

        SYNTAX        Counter

        ACCESS        read-only

        STATUS        mandatory

        DESCRIPTION "The total number of IPX packets received, including

                        those received in error."

        ::= {ipxBasicSysEntry 6}


    ipxBasicSysInHdrErrors OBJECT-TYPE

        SYNTAX        Counter

        ACCESS        read-only

        STATUS        mandatory

        DESCRIPTION "The number of IPX packets discarded due to errors
    in

                        their headers, including any IPX packet with a
    size less

                        than the minimum of 30 bytes."

        ::= {ipxBasicSysEntry 7}


    ipxBasicSysInUnknownSockets OBJECT-TYPE

        SYNTAX        Counter

        ACCESS        read-only

        STATUS        mandatory

        DESCRIPTION "The number of IPX packets discarded because the

                        destination socket was not open."

        ::= {ipxBasicSysEntry 8}


    ipxBasicSysInDiscards OBJECT-TYPE

        SYNTAX        Counter
```

```
    ACCESS       read-only

    STATUS       mandatory

    DESCRIPTION "The number of IPX packets received but discarded
due to

                reasons other than those accounted for by

                ipxBasicSysInHdrErrors,
ipxBasicSysInUnknownSockets,

                ipxAdvSysInDiscards, and
ipxAdvSysInCompressDiscards."

    ::= {ipxBasicSysEntry 9}


ipxBasicSysInBadChecksums OBJECT-TYPE

    SYNTAX       Counter

    ACCESS       read-only

    STATUS       mandatory

    DESCRIPTION "The number of IPX packets received with incorrect
                checksums."

    ::= {ipxBasicSysEntry 10}


ipxBasicSysInDelivers OBJECT-TYPE

    SYNTAX       Counter

    ACCESS       read-only

    STATUS       mandatory

    DESCRIPTION "The total number of IPX packets delivered locally,
                including packets from local applications."

    ::= {ipxBasicSysEntry 11}


ipxBasicSysNoRoutes OBJECT-TYPE

    SYNTAX       Counter

    ACCESS       read-only

    STATUS       mandatory

    DESCRIPTION "The number of times no route to a destination was
```

```
                              found."
         ::= {ipxBasicSysEntry 12}


     ipxBasicSysOutRequests OBJECT-TYPE

         SYNTAX        Counter

         ACCESS        read-only

         STATUS        mandatory

         DESCRIPTION "The number of IPX packets supplied locally for

                        transmission, not including any packets counted in

                        ipxAdvForwPackets."

         ::= {ipxBasicSysEntry 13}


     ipxBasicSysOutMalformedRequests OBJECT-TYPE

         SYNTAX        Counter

         ACCESS        read-only

         STATUS        mandatory

         DESCRIPTION "The number of IPX packets supplied locally that
     contained

                        errors in their structure."

         ::= {ipxBasicSysEntry 14}


     ipxBasicSysOutDiscards OBJECT-TYPE

         SYNTAX        Counter

         ACCESS        read-only

         STATUS        mandatory

         DESCRIPTION "The number of outgoing IPX packets discarded due to

                        reasons other than those accounted for in

                        ipxBasicSysOutMalformedRequests,
     ipxAdvSysOutFiltered,

                        and ipxAdvSysOutCompressDiscards."

         ::= {ipxBasicSysEntry 15}
```

ipxBasicSysOutPackets OBJECT-TYPE

    SYNTAX      Counter

    ACCESS      read-only

    STATUS      mandatory

    DESCRIPTION "The total number of IPX packets transmitted."

    ::= {ipxBasicSysEntry 16}


ipxBasicSysConfigSockets OBJECT-TYPE

    SYNTAX      INTEGER

    ACCESS      read-only

    STATUS      mandatory

    DESCRIPTION "The configured maximum number of IPX sockets that may be

               open at one time."

    ::= {ipxBasicSysEntry 17}


ipxBasicSysOpenSocketFails OBJECT-TYPE

    SYNTAX      Counter

    ACCESS      read-only

    STATUS      mandatory

    DESCRIPTION "The number of IPX socket open calls that failed."

    ::= {ipxBasicSysEntry 18}


— Advanced System Table

—   This table contains one entry for each instance of IPX running on

—   the system.  It contains the advanced management information that

—   may not be available from all implementations of the IPX protocol.

```
ipxAdvSysTable OBJECT-TYPE

     SYNTAX        SEQUENCE OF IPXAdvSysEntry

     ACCESS        not-accessible

     STATUS        mandatory

     DESCRIPTION "The IPX System table - advanced information."

     ::= {ipxSystem 2}


ipxAdvSysEntry OBJECT-TYPE

     SYNTAX        IPXAdvSysEntry

     ACCESS        not-accessible

     STATUS        mandatory

     DESCRIPTION "Each entry corresponds to one instance of IPX
running

                  on the system."

     INDEX         {ipxAdvSysInstance}

     ::= {ipxAdvSysTable 1}


IPXAdvSysEntry ::= SEQUENCE {

                     ipxAdvSysInstance

                         INTEGER,

                     ipxAdvSysMaxPathSplits

                         INTEGER,

                     ipxAdvSysMaxHops

                         INTEGER,

                     ipxAdvSysInTooManyHops

                         Counter,

                     ipxAdvSysInFiltered

                         Counter,

                     ipxAdvSysInCompressDiscards

                         Counter,
```

```
                        ipxAdvSysNETBIOSPackets

                            Counter,

                        ipxAdvSysForwPackets

                            Counter,

                        ipxAdvSysOutFiltered

                            Counter,

                        ipxAdvSysOutCompressDiscards

                            Counter,

                        ipxAdvSysCircCount

                            INTEGER,

                        ipxAdvSysDestCount

                            INTEGER,

                        ipxAdvSysServCount

                            INTEGER

                    }


ipxAdvSysInstance OBJECT-TYPE

        SYNTAX          INTEGER

        ACCESS          read-write

        STATUS          mandatory

        DESCRIPTION "The unique identifier of the instance of IPX to
which this

                    row corresponds.  This value may be written only
when

                    creating a new entry in the table."

        ::= {ipxAdvSysEntry 1}


ipxAdvSysMaxPathSplits OBJECT-TYPE

        SYNTAX          INTEGER (1..32)

        ACCESS          read-write

        STATUS          mandatory
```

```
            DESCRIPTION "The maximum number of paths with equal routing
metric

                          value that this instance of the IPX may split

                          between when forwarding packets."

            DEFVAL         { 1 }

            ::= {ipxAdvSysEntry 2}


    ipxAdvSysMaxHops OBJECT-TYPE

            SYNTAX         INTEGER

            ACCESS         read-write

            STATUS         mandatory

            DESCRIPTION "The maximum number of hops a packet may take."

            DEFVAL         { 64 }

            ::= {ipxAdvSysEntry 3}


    ipxAdvSysInTooManyHops OBJECT-TYPE

            SYNTAX         Counter

            ACCESS         read-only

            STATUS         mandatory

            DESCRIPTION "The number of IPX packets discarded due to
exceeding the

                          maximum hop count."

            ::= {ipxAdvSysEntry 4}


    ipxAdvSysInFiltered OBJECT-TYPE

            SYNTAX         Counter

            ACCESS         read-only

            STATUS         mandatory

            DESCRIPTION "The number of incoming IPX packets discarded due to

                          filtering."

            ::= {ipxAdvSysEntry 5}
```

ipxAdvSysInCompressDiscards OBJECT-TYPE

    SYNTAX      Counter

    ACCESS      read-only

    STATUS      mandatory

    DESCRIPTION "The number of incoming IPX packets discarded due to decompression errors."

    ::= {ipxAdvSysEntry 6}


ipxAdvSysNETBIOSPackets OBJECT-TYPE

    SYNTAX      Counter

    ACCESS      read-only

    STATUS      mandatory

    DESCRIPTION "The number of NETBIOS packets received."

    ::= {ipxAdvSysEntry 7}


ipxAdvSysForwPackets OBJECT-TYPE

    SYNTAX      Counter

    ACCESS      read-only

    STATUS      mandatory

    DESCRIPTION "The number of IPX packets forwarded."

    ::= {ipxAdvSysEntry 8}


ipxAdvSysOutFiltered OBJECT-TYPE

    SYNTAX      Counter

    ACCESS      read-only

    STATUS      mandatory

    DESCRIPTION "The number of outgoing IPX packets discarded due to filtering."

    ::= {ipxAdvSysEntry 9}

```
ipxAdvSysOutCompressDiscards OBJECT-TYPE

    SYNTAX        Counter

    ACCESS        read-only

    STATUS        mandatory

    DESCRIPTION "The number of outgoing IPX packets discarded due to
                        compression errors."

    ::= {ipxAdvSysEntry 10}


ipxAdvSysCircCount OBJECT-TYPE

    SYNTAX        INTEGER

    ACCESS        read-only

    STATUS        mandatory

    DESCRIPTION "The number of circuits known to this instance of
IPX."

    ::= {ipxAdvSysEntry 11}


ipxAdvSysDestCount OBJECT-TYPE

    SYNTAX        INTEGER

    ACCESS        read-only

    STATUS        mandatory

    DESCRIPTION "The number of currently reachable destinations
known to

                this instance of IPX."

    ::= {ipxAdvSysEntry 12}


ipxAdvSysServCount OBJECT-TYPE

    SYNTAX        INTEGER

    ACCESS        read-only

    STATUS        mandatory

    DESCRIPTION "The number of services known to this instance of
IPX."

    ::= {ipxAdvSysEntry 13}
```

— Circuit Group

—     This group contains management information for each circuit known

—     to this system.


— Circuit Table

—     The Circuit table contains an entry for each circuit known to the

—     system.


ipxCircTable OBJECT-TYPE

    SYNTAX        SEQUENCE OF IPXCircEntry

    ACCESS        not-accessible

    STATUS        mandatory

    DESCRIPTION "The Circuit table."

    ::= {ipxCircuit 1}


ipxCircEntry OBJECT-TYPE

    SYNTAX        IPXCircEntry

    ACCESS        not-accessible

    STATUS        mandatory

    DESCRIPTION "Each entry corresponds to one circuit known to the
                         system."

    INDEX            {

               ipxCircSysInstance,

               ipxCircIndex

             }

    ::= {ipxCircTable 1}

```
IPXCircEntry ::= SEQUENCE {
                ipxCircSysInstance
                    INTEGER,
                ipxCircIndex
                    INTEGER,
                ipxCircExistState
                    INTEGER,
                ipxCircOperState
                    INTEGER,
                ipxCircIfIndex
                    INTEGER,
                ipxCircName
                    OCTET STRING,
                ipxCircType
                    INTEGER,
                ipxCircDialName
                    OCTET STRING,
                ipxCircLocalMaxPacketSize
                    INTEGER,
                ipxCircCompressState
                    INTEGER,
                ipxCircCompressSlots
                    INTEGER,
                ipxCircStaticStatus
                    INTEGER,
                ipxCircCompressedSent
                    Counter,
                ipxCircCompressedInitSent
                    Counter,
                ipxCircCompressedRejectsSent
                    Counter,
```

```
            ipxCircUncompressedSent

                Counter,

            ipxCircCompressedReceived

                Counter,

            ipxCircCompressedInitReceived

                Counter,

            ipxCircCompressedRejectsReceived

                Counter,

            ipxCircUncompressedReceived

                Counter,

            ipxCircMediaType

                OCTET STRING,

            ipxCircNetNumber

                NetNumber,

            ipxCircStateChanges

                Counter,

            ipxCircInitFails

                Counter,

            ipxCircDelay

                INTEGER,

            ipxCircThroughput

                INTEGER,

            ipxCircNeighRouterName

                OCTET STRING,

            ipxCircNeighInternalNetNum

                NetNumber
        }


    ipxCircSysInstance OBJECT-TYPE

        SYNTAX      INTEGER

        ACCESS      read-write
```

```
        STATUS      mandatory
     DESCRIPTION "The unique identifier of the instance of IPX
                  to which this entry corresponds.  This value may
be
                  written only when creating a new entry in the
table."
        ::= {ipxCircEntry 1}



ipxCircIndex OBJECT-TYPE
        SYNTAX      INTEGER
        ACCESS      read-write
        STATUS      mandatory
     DESCRIPTION "The identifier of this circuit, unique within the
                  instance of IPX.  This value may be written
                  only when creating a new entry in the table."
        ::= {ipxCircEntry 2}



ipxCircExistState OBJECT-TYPE
        SYNTAX      INTEGER {
                            off(1),
                            on(2)

                                }
        ACCESS      read-write
        STATUS      mandatory
     DESCRIPTION "The validity of this circuit entry.  A circuit
with this
                  value set to off may be deleted from the table at
the
                  IPX implementer's discretion."
        ::= {ipxCircEntry 3}



ipxCircOperState OBJECT-TYPE
```

```
SYNTAX        INTEGER {

                        down(1),

                        up(2),

                        sleeping(3)

                        }

    ACCESS     read-write

    STATUS     mandatory

    DESCRIPTION "The operational state of the circuit."

    ::= {ipxCircEntry 4}


ipxCircIfIndex OBJECT-TYPE

    SYNTAX        INTEGER

    ACCESS        read-write

    STATUS        mandatory

    DESCRIPTION "The value of ifIndex for the interface used by
this

                circuit.  This value may be written only when
creating

                a new entry in the table."

    ::= {ipxCircEntry 5}


ipxCircName OBJECT-TYPE

    SYNTAX        OCTET STRING (SIZE(0..48))

    ACCESS        read-write

    STATUS        mandatory

    DESCRIPTION "The readable name for the circuit."

    ::= {ipxCircEntry 6}


ipxCircType OBJECT-TYPE

    SYNTAX        INTEGER {

                        other(1),
```

```
                                        broadcast(2),

                                        ptToPt(3),

                                        wanRIP(4),

                                        unnumberedRIP(5),

                                        dynamic(6),

                                        wanWS(7)

                                    }

        ACCESS          read-write

        STATUS          mandatory

        DESCRIPTION "The type of the circuit."

        ::= {ipxCircEntry 7}


ipxCircDialName OBJECT-TYPE

        SYNTAX          OCTET STRING (SIZE(0..48))

        ACCESS          read-write

        STATUS          mandatory

        DESCRIPTION "The symbolic name used to reference the dialing
information

                        used to create this circuit.  This value may be
written

                        only when creating a new entry in the table."

        ::= {ipxCircEntry 8}


ipxCircLocalMaxPacketSize OBJECT-TYPE

        SYNTAX          INTEGER

        ACCESS          read-write

        STATUS          mandatory

        DESCRIPTION "The maximum size (including header), in bytes, that
the

                        system supports locally on this circuit."

        ::= {ipxCircEntry 9}
```

ipxCircCompressState OBJECT-TYPE

    SYNTAX          INTEGER {

                                   off(1),

                                   on(2)

                                 }

    ACCESS          read-write

    STATUS          mandatory

    DESCRIPTION "The compression state on this circuit.  This value may

              be written only when creating a new entry in the table."

    DEFVAL          { off }

    ::= {ipxCircEntry 10}


ipxCircCompressSlots OBJECT-TYPE

    SYNTAX          INTEGER

    ACCESS          read-write

    STATUS          mandatory

    DESCRIPTION "The number of compression slots available on this

              circuit.  This value may be written only when creating a

              new entry in the table."

    DEFVAL          { 16 }

    ::= {ipxCircEntry 11}


ipxCircStaticStatus OBJECT-TYPE

    SYNTAX          INTEGER {

                                     unknown(1),

                                     current(2),

                                     changed(3),

                                     read(4),

                                     reading(5),

```
                              write(6),

                              writing(7)

                          }
```

ACCESS          read-write

STATUS          mandatory

DESCRIPTION "Indicates whether the information about static routes

and services reached via this circuit matches that

saved in permanent storage (current).  Setting the

value to write when it had the value changed will write

the information currently in use to permanent storage,

if supported.  Setting the value to read when it had

the value changed will replace any routes and services

currently defined for the circuit with those read from

permanent storage, if supported."

```
   ::= {ipxCircEntry 12}
```

ipxCircCompressedSent OBJECT-TYPE

SYNTAX          Counter

ACCESS          read-only

STATUS          mandatory

DESCRIPTION "The number of compressed packets sent."

```
   ::= {ipxCircEntry 13}
```

ipxCircCompressedInitSent OBJECT-TYPE

SYNTAX          Counter

ACCESS          read-only

STATUS        mandatory

DESCRIPTION "The number of compression initialization packets
sent."

   ::= {ipxCircEntry 14}


ipxCircCompressedRejectsSent OBJECT-TYPE

   SYNTAX        Counter

   ACCESS        read-only

   STATUS        mandatory

DESCRIPTION "The number of compressed packet rejected packets
sent."

   ::= {ipxCircEntry 15}


ipxCircUncompressedSent OBJECT-TYPE

   SYNTAX        Counter

   ACCESS        read-only

   STATUS        mandatory

DESCRIPTION "The number of packets sent without being compressed
                even though compression was turned on for this
circuit."

   ::= {ipxCircEntry 16}


ipxCircCompressedReceived OBJECT-TYPE

   SYNTAX        Counter

   ACCESS        read-only

   STATUS        mandatory

DESCRIPTION "The number of compressed packets received."

   ::= {ipxCircEntry 17}


ipxCircCompressedInitReceived OBJECT-TYPE

   SYNTAX        Counter

   ACCESS        read-only

STATUS          mandatory

DESCRIPTION "The number of compression initialization packets
received."

::= {ipxCircEntry 18}


ipxCircCompressedRejectsReceived OBJECT-TYPE

SYNTAX          Counter

ACCESS          read-only

STATUS          mandatory

DESCRIPTION "The number of rejected compressed packets
received."

::= {ipxCircEntry 19}


ipxCircUncompressedReceived OBJECT-TYPE

SYNTAX          Counter

ACCESS          read-only

STATUS          mandatory

DESCRIPTION "The number of packets received without having been
                compressed even though compression was turned on
for
                this circuit."

::= {ipxCircEntry 20}


ipxCircMediaType OBJECT-TYPE

SYNTAX          OCTET STRING (SIZE(2))

ACCESS          read-only

STATUS          mandatory

DESCRIPTION "The media type used on this circuit."

::= {ipxCircEntry 21}


ipxCircNetNumber OBJECT-TYPE

SYNTAX          NetNumber

ACCESS      read-write

STATUS      mandatory

DESCRIPTION "The IPX network number of this circuit.   This value may

            be written only when creating a new entry in the table."

   ::= {ipxCircEntry 22}


ipxCircStateChanges OBJECT-TYPE

   SYNTAX      Counter

   ACCESS      read-only

   STATUS      mandatory

   DESCRIPTION "The number of times the circuit has changed state."

   ::= {ipxCircEntry 23}


ipxCircInitFails OBJECT-TYPE

   SYNTAX      Counter

   ACCESS      read-only

   STATUS      mandatory

   DESCRIPTION "The number of times that initialization of this
                circuit has failed."

   ::= {ipxCircEntry 24}


ipxCircDelay OBJECT-TYPE

   SYNTAX      INTEGER

   ACCESS      read-only

   STATUS      mandatory

   DESCRIPTION "The period of time, in milliseconds, that it takes to

                transmit one byte of data, excluding protocol headers,

                to a destination on the other end of the circuit,

if

the circuit is free of other traffic."

::= {ipxCircEntry 25}

ipxCircThroughput OBJECT-TYPE

SYNTAX          INTEGER

ACCESS          read-only

STATUS          mandatory

DESCRIPTION "The amount of data, in bits per second, that may flow

through the circuit if there is no other traffic."

::= {ipxCircEntry 26}

ipxCircNeighRouterName OBJECT-TYPE

SYNTAX          OCTET STRING (SIZE(0..48))

ACCESS          read-only

STATUS          mandatory

DESCRIPTION "The name of the neighboring router on a WAN circuit."

::= {ipxCircEntry 27}

ipxCircNeighInternalNetNum OBJECT-TYPE

SYNTAX          NetNumber

ACCESS          read-only

STATUS          mandatory

DESCRIPTION "The internal network number of the neighboring router

on a WAN circuit."

::= {ipxCircEntry 28}

— Forwarding Group

—    This group provides a representation of the forwarding database used

—    by all instances of IPX on the system.


— Destination Table

—    The Destination table contains information about all known

—    destinations.  The routing information shown in this table represents

—    the path currently being used to reach the destination.


ipxDestTable OBJECT-TYPE

    SYNTAX          SEQUENCE OF IPXDestEntry

    ACCESS          not-accessible

    STATUS          mandatory

    DESCRIPTION "The Destination table contains information about all

               known destinations."

    ::= {ipxForwarding 1}


ipxDestEntry OBJECT-TYPE

    SYNTAX          IPXDestEntry

    ACCESS          not-accessible

    STATUS          mandatory

    DESCRIPTION "Each entry corresponds to one destination."

    INDEX           {

               ipxDestSysInstance,

               ipxDestNetNum

               }

    ::= {ipxDestTable 1}


IPXDestEntry ::= SEQUENCE {

             ipxDestSysInstance

```
                                    INTEGER,

                            ipxDestNetNum

                                NetNumber,

                            ipxDestProtocol

                                INTEGER,

                            ipxDestTicks

                                INTEGER,

                            ipxDestHopCount

                                INTEGER,

                            ipxDestNextHopCircIndex

                                INTEGER,

                            ipxDestNextHopNICAddress

                                PhysAddress,

                            ipxDestNextHopNetNum

                                NetNumber

                        }


    ipxDestSysInstance OBJECT-TYPE

        SYNTAX      INTEGER

        ACCESS      read-only

        STATUS      mandatory

        DESCRIPTION "The unique identifier of the instance of IPX
                        to which this row corresponds."

        ::= {ipxDestEntry 1}


    ipxDestNetNum OBJECT-TYPE

        SYNTAX      NetNumber

        ACCESS      read-only

        STATUS      mandatory

        DESCRIPTION "The IPX network number of the destination."

        ::= {ipxDestEntry 2}
```

ipxDestProtocol OBJECT-TYPE

    SYNTAX       INTEGER {

                            other(1),

                            local(2),

                            rip(3),

                            nlsp(4),

                            static(5)

                            }

    ACCESS       read-only

    STATUS       mandatory

    DESCRIPTION "The routing protocol from which knowledge of this
                    destination was obtained."

    ::= {ipxDestEntry 3}


ipxDestTicks OBJECT-TYPE

    SYNTAX       INTEGER

    ACCESS       read-only

    STATUS       mandatory

    DESCRIPTION "The delay in ticks to reach this destination."

    ::= {ipxDestEntry 4}


ipxDestHopCount OBJECT-TYPE

    SYNTAX       INTEGER

    ACCESS       read-only

    STATUS       mandatory

    DESCRIPTION "The number of hops necessary to reach the
destination."

    ::= {ipxDestEntry 5}


ipxDestNextHopCircIndex OBJECT-TYPE

```
SYNTAX        INTEGER

ACCESS        read-only

STATUS        mandatory

DESCRIPTION "The unique identifier of the circuit used to reach
the

                next hop."

::= {ipxDestEntry 6}


ipxDestNextHopNICAddress OBJECT-TYPE

SYNTAX        PhysAddress

ACCESS        read-only

STATUS        mandatory

DESCRIPTION "The NIC address of the next hop."

::= {ipxDestEntry 7}


ipxDestNextHopNetNum OBJECT-TYPE

SYNTAX        NetNumber

ACCESS        read-only

STATUS        mandatory

DESCRIPTION "The IPX network number of the next hop."

::= {ipxDestEntry 8}




— Static Routes Table

—   This table contains the information about all the static routes

—   defined.  There may be more than one static route to any given

—   destination.  Only the route currently being used will also be

—   present in the Destination table defined above.


ipxStaticRouteTable OBJECT-TYPE

SYNTAX        SEQUENCE OF IPXStaticRouteEntry
```

```
    ACCESS        not-accessible

    STATUS        mandatory

    DESCRIPTION  "The Static Routes table contains information about
all
               destinations reached via statically configured
routes."

    ::= {ipxForwarding 2}


ipxStaticRouteEntry OBJECT-TYPE

    SYNTAX        IPXStaticRouteEntry

    ACCESS        not-accessible

    STATUS        mandatory

    DESCRIPTION  "Each entry corresponds to one static route."

    INDEX          {

                     ipxStaticRouteSysInstance,

                     ipxStaticRouteCircIndex,

                     ipxStaticRouteNetNum

                     }

    ::= {ipxStaticRouteTable 1}


IPXStaticRouteEntry ::= SEQUENCE {

                        ipxStaticRouteSysInstance

                            INTEGER,

                        ipxStaticRouteCircIndex

                            INTEGER,

                        ipxStaticRouteNetNum

                            NetNumber,

                        ipxStaticRouteExistState

                            INTEGER,

                        ipxStaticRouteTicks

                            INTEGER,
```

```
                              ipxStaticRouteHopCount

                                 INTEGER

                                   }


    ipxStaticRouteSysInstance OBJECT-TYPE

        SYNTAX      INTEGER

        ACCESS      read-write

        STATUS      mandatory

        DESCRIPTION "The unique identifier of the instance of IPX to
                    which this row corresponds."

        ::= {ipxStaticRouteEntry 1}


    ipxStaticRouteCircIndex OBJECT-TYPE

        SYNTAX      INTEGER

        ACCESS      read-write

        STATUS      mandatory

        DESCRIPTION "The unique identifier of the circuit used to
                    reach the first hop in the static route."

        ::= {ipxStaticRouteEntry 2}


    ipxStaticRouteNetNum OBJECT-TYPE

        SYNTAX      NetNumber

        ACCESS      read-write

        STATUS      mandatory

        DESCRIPTION "The IPX network number of the route's destination."

        ::= {ipxStaticRouteEntry 3}


    ipxStaticRouteExistState OBJECT-TYPE

        SYNTAX      INTEGER {

                        off(1),

                        on(2)
```

```
                          }
     ACCESS       read-write

     STATUS       mandatory

     DESCRIPTION  "The validity of this static route.  Entries with
the

                  value set to off may be deleted from the table at
the

                  implementer's discretion."

     ::= {ipxStaticRouteEntry 4}


ipxStaticRouteTicks OBJECT-TYPE

     SYNTAX       INTEGER

     ACCESS       read-write

     STATUS       mandatory

     DESCRIPTION  "The delay, in ticks, to reach the route's
destination."

     ::= {ipxStaticRouteEntry 5}


ipxStaticRouteHopCount OBJECT-TYPE

     SYNTAX       INTEGER

     ACCESS       read-write

     STATUS       mandatory

     DESCRIPTION  "The number of hops necessary to reach the
destination."

     ::= {ipxStaticRouteEntry 6}



— Services Group

—   The Services group contains management information for all
known

—   services.
```

— Services Table

—    This table contains the services information indexed by service

—    name and type.


ipxServTable OBJECT-TYPE

    SYNTAX        SEQUENCE OF IPXServEntry

    ACCESS        not-accessible

    STATUS        mandatory

    DESCRIPTION "The table of services, indexed by name and type."

    ::= {ipxServices 1}


ipxServEntry OBJECT-TYPE

    SYNTAX        IPXServEntry

    ACCESS        not-accessible

    STATUS        mandatory

    DESCRIPTION "Each entry corresponds to one service."

    INDEX         {

            ipxServSysInstance,

            ipxServType,

            ipxServName

            }

    ::= {ipxServTable 1}


IPXServEntry ::= SEQUENCE {

            ipxServSysInstance

              INTEGER,

            ipxServType

              OCTET STRING,

            ipxServName

              OCTET STRING,

```
ipxServProtocol

    INTEGER,

ipxServNetNum

    NetNumber,

ipxServNode

    OCTET STRING,

ipxServSocket

    OCTET STRING,

ipxServHopCount

    INTEGER

}


ipxServSysInstance OBJECT-TYPE

    SYNTAX      INTEGER

    ACCESS      read-only

    STATUS      mandatory

    DESCRIPTION "The unique identifier of the instance of IPX

                to which this entry corresponds."

    ::= {ipxServEntry 1}


ipxServType OBJECT-TYPE

    SYNTAX      OCTET STRING (SIZE(2))

    ACCESS      read-only

    STATUS      mandatory

    DESCRIPTION "The service type."

    ::= {ipxServEntry 2}


ipxServName OBJECT-TYPE

    SYNTAX      OCTET STRING (SIZE(1..48))

    ACCESS      read-only

    STATUS      mandatory
```

```
        DESCRIPTION "The service name."

        ::= {ipxServEntry 3}


ipxServProtocol OBJECT-TYPE

    SYNTAX        INTEGER {

                            other(1),

                            local(2),

                            nlsp(4),

                            static(5),

                            sap(6)

                        }

    ACCESS      read-only

    STATUS      mandatory

    DESCRIPTION "The protocol from which knowledge of this service
was

            obtained."

    ::= {ipxServEntry 4}


ipxServNetNum OBJECT-TYPE

    SYNTAX        NetNumber

    ACCESS        read-only

    STATUS        mandatory

    DESCRIPTION "The IPX network number portion of the IPX address
of the

            service."

    ::= {ipxServEntry 5}


ipxServNode OBJECT-TYPE

    SYNTAX        OCTET STRING (SIZE(6))

    ACCESS        read-only

    STATUS        mandatory
```

DESCRIPTION "The node portion of the IPX address of the service."

    ::= {ipxServEntry 6}


ipxServSocket OBJECT-TYPE

    SYNTAX       OCTET STRING (SIZE(2))

    ACCESS       read-only

    STATUS       mandatory

    DESCRIPTION "The socket portion of the IPX address of the service."

    ::= {ipxServEntry 7}


ipxServHopCount OBJECT-TYPE

    SYNTAX       INTEGER

    ACCESS       read-only

    STATUS       mandatory

    DESCRIPTION "The number of hops to the service."

    ::= {ipxServEntry 8}



— Destination Services Table

—   This table contains the services information indexed by address,

—   name, and type.


ipxDestServTable OBJECT-TYPE

    SYNTAX       SEQUENCE OF IPXDestServEntry

    ACCESS       not-accessible

    STATUS       mandatory

    DESCRIPTION "The table of services, indexed by address, name,

                and type."

    ::= {ipxServices 2}

```
ipxDestServEntry OBJECT-TYPE

    SYNTAX        IPXDestServEntry

    ACCESS        not-accessible

    STATUS        mandatory

    DESCRIPTION   "Each entry corresponds to one service."

    INDEX         {

                      ipxDestServSysInstance,

                      ipxDestServNetNum,

                      ipxDestServNode,

                      ipxDestServSocket,

                      ipxDestServName,

                      ipxDestServType

                  }

    ::= {ipxDestServTable 1}


IPXDestServEntry ::= SEQUENCE {

                      ipxDestServSysInstance

                          INTEGER,

                      ipxDestServNetNum

                          NetNumber,

                      ipxDestServNode

                          OCTET STRING,

                      ipxDestServSocket

                          OCTET STRING,

                      ipxDestServName

                          OCTET STRING,

                      ipxDestServType

                          OCTET STRING,

                      ipxDestServProtocol

                          INTEGER,
```

                    ipxDestServHopCount

                        INTEGER

                    }


ipxDestServSysInstance OBJECT-TYPE

    SYNTAX        INTEGER

    ACCESS        read-only

    STATUS        mandatory

    DESCRIPTION "The unique identifier of the instance of IPX

                    to which this entry corresponds."

    ::= {ipxDestServEntry 1}


ipxDestServNetNum OBJECT-TYPE

    SYNTAX        NetNumber

    ACCESS        read-only

    STATUS        mandatory

    DESCRIPTION "The IPX network number portion of the IPX address
of the

                    service."

    ::= {ipxDestServEntry 2}


ipxDestServNode OBJECT-TYPE

    SYNTAX        OCTET STRING (SIZE(6))

    ACCESS        read-only

    STATUS        mandatory

    DESCRIPTION "The node portion of the IPX address of the
service."

    ::= {ipxDestServEntry 3}


ipxDestServSocket OBJECT-TYPE

    SYNTAX        OCTET STRING (SIZE(2))

```
    ACCESS        read-only

    STATUS        mandatory

    DESCRIPTION "The socket portion of the IPX address of the
service."

    ::= {ipxDestServEntry 4}


ipxDestServName OBJECT-TYPE

    SYNTAX        OCTET STRING (SIZE(1..48))

    ACCESS        read-only

    STATUS        mandatory

    DESCRIPTION "The service name."

    ::= {ipxDestServEntry 5}


ipxDestServType OBJECT-TYPE

    SYNTAX        OCTET STRING (SIZE(2))

    ACCESS        read-only

    STATUS        mandatory

    DESCRIPTION "The service type."

    ::= {ipxDestServEntry 6}


ipxDestServProtocol OBJECT-TYPE

    SYNTAX        INTEGER {

                        other(1),

                        local(2),

                        nlsp(4),

                        static(5),

                        sap(6)

                    }

    ACCESS        read-only

    STATUS        mandatory

    DESCRIPTION "The protocol from which knowledge of this service
```

was

            obtained."

    ::= {ipxDestServEntry 7}


ipxDestServHopCount OBJECT-TYPE

    SYNTAX       INTEGER

    ACCESS       read-only

    STATUS       mandatory

    DESCRIPTION "The number of hops to the service."

    ::= {ipxDestServEntry 8}



— Static Services Table

—   This table contains information for all services reached via a

—   static route.


ipxStaticServTable OBJECT-TYPE

    SYNTAX       SEQUENCE OF IPXStaticServEntry

    ACCESS       not-accessible

    STATUS       mandatory

    DESCRIPTION "The Static Services table contains information about

            all services reached via statically configured routes."

    ::= {ipxServices 3}


ipxStaticServEntry OBJECT-TYPE

    SYNTAX       IPXStaticServEntry

    ACCESS       not-accessible

    STATUS       mandatory

    DESCRIPTION "Each entry corresponds to one service."

```
INDEX          {

                    ipxStaticServSysInstance,

                    ipxStaticServCircIndex,

                    ipxStaticServName,

                    ipxStaticServType

               }

     ::= {ipxStaticServTable 1}


     IPXStaticServEntry ::= SEQUENCE {

                              ipxStaticServSysInstance

                                  INTEGER,

                              ipxStaticServCircIndex

                                  INTEGER,

                              ipxStaticServName

                                  OCTET STRING,

                              ipxStaticServType

                                  OCTET STRING,

                              ipxStaticServExistState

                                  INTEGER,

                              ipxStaticServNetNum

                                  NetNumber,

                              ipxStaticServNode

                                  OCTET STRING,

                              ipxStaticServSocket

                                  OCTET STRING,

                              ipxStaticServHopCount

                                  INTEGER

                           }


     ipxStaticServSysInstance OBJECT-TYPE

          SYNTAX        INTEGER
```

```
    ACCESS       read-write

    STATUS       mandatory

    DESCRIPTION "The unique identifier of the instance of IPX to
which

                 this entry corresponds."

    ::= {ipxStaticServEntry 1}



ipxStaticServCircIndex OBJECT-TYPE

    SYNTAX       INTEGER

    ACCESS       read-write

    STATUS       mandatory

    DESCRIPTION "The circuit used to reach this service."

    ::= {ipxStaticServEntry 2}



ipxStaticServName OBJECT-TYPE

    SYNTAX       OCTET STRING (SIZE(1..48))

    ACCESS       read-write

    STATUS       mandatory

    DESCRIPTION "The service name."

    ::= {ipxStaticServEntry 3}



ipxStaticServType OBJECT-TYPE

    SYNTAX       OCTET STRING (SIZE(2))

    ACCESS       read-write

    STATUS       mandatory

    DESCRIPTION "The service type."

    ::= {ipxStaticServEntry 4}



ipxStaticServExistState OBJECT-TYPE

    SYNTAX       INTEGER {

                     off(1),
```

```
                              on(2)
                                }
        ACCESS        read-write
        STATUS        mandatory
        DESCRIPTION  "The validity of this static service.  Entries with
the
                      value set to off may be deleted from the table at
the
                      implementer's discretion."
        ::= {ipxStaticServEntry 5}


ipxStaticServNetNum OBJECT-TYPE
        SYNTAX        NetNumber
        ACCESS        read-write
        STATUS        mandatory
        DESCRIPTION  "The IPX network number portion of the IPX address
of the
                      service."
        ::= {ipxStaticServEntry 6}


ipxStaticServNode OBJECT-TYPE
        SYNTAX        OCTET STRING (SIZE(6))
        ACCESS        read-write
        STATUS        mandatory
        DESCRIPTION  "The node portion of the IPX address of the
service."
        ::= {ipxStaticServEntry 7}


ipxStaticServSocket OBJECT-TYPE
        SYNTAX        OCTET STRING (SIZE(2))
        ACCESS        read-write
        STATUS        mandatory
```

DESCRIPTION "The socket portion of the IPX address of the service."

::= {ipxStaticServEntry 8}


ipxStaticServHopCount OBJECT-TYPE

SYNTAX        INTEGER

ACCESS        read-write

STATUS        mandatory

DESCRIPTION "The number of hops to the service."

::= {ipxStaticServEntry 9}


— Traps

—    The section describes the traps defined for IPX.


ipxTrapCircuitDown TRAP-TYPE

ENTERPRISE      ipxTraps

VARIABLES       {

                    ipxCircSysInstance,

                    ipxCircIndex

                }

DESCRIPTION     "This trap signifies that the specified circuit has

                    gone down."

—#TYPE "IPXTrapCircuitDown"

—#SUMMARY "IPX Circuit has gone down at: Instance = %d, Index = %d"

—#ARGUMENTS {0, 1}

—#SEVERITY INFORMATIONAL

—#TIMEINDEX 8

—#HELP "nms.hlp"

—#HELPTAG 56025

```
    —#STATE   OPERATIONAL

    ::= 1


ipxTrapCircuitUp  TRAP-TYPE
    ENTERPRISE    ipxTraps
    VARIABLES     {
                    ipxCircSysInstance,
                    ipxCircIndex
                  }
    DESCRIPTION   "This trap signifies that the specified circuit has
                   come up."
    —#TYPE "NLM: Informational alert"
    —#SUMMARY "IPX Circuit has come up: Instance = %d, Index = %d"
    —#ARGUMENTS {0, 1}
    —#SEVERITY INFORMATIONAL
    —#TIMEINDEX 8
    —#HELP "nms.hlp"
    —#HELPTAG 56026
    —#STATE   OPERATIONAL
    ::= 2


END
```

# RIP/SAP MIB

```
RIPSAP DEFINITIONS ::= BEGIN

— This MIB defines the management information for the RIP and SAP
— protocols running in an IPX environment.  It provides information in
— addition to that contained in the IPX MIB itself.  All tables in this
— MIB are linked to an instance of IPX via the system instance
— identifier as defined in the IPX MIB.


IMPORTS
    enterprises, Counter
             FROM RFC1155-SMI
    OBJECT-TYPE
             FROM RFC-1212;

novell  OBJECT IDENTIFIER ::= {enterprises 23}
mibDoc  OBJECT IDENTIFIER ::= { novell 2 }
ripsap  OBJECT IDENTIFIER ::= {mibDoc 20}


— Groups

ripsapSystem  OBJECT IDENTIFIER ::= {ripsap 1}
ripsapCircuit OBJECT IDENTIFIER ::= {ripsap 2}


— System Group
—    This group contains global information about each instance of
—    RIP/SAP running on one system.

— RIP System Table
—    This table contains an entry for each instance of RIP
—    running on the system.

ripSysTable OBJECT-TYPE
    SYNTAX        SEQUENCE OF RIPSysEntry
    ACCESS        not-accessible
    STATUS        mandatory
    DESCRIPTION "The RIP system table."
    ::= {ripsapSystem 1}

ripSysEntry OBJECT-TYPE
    SYNTAX        RIPSysEntry
    ACCESS        not-accessible
    STATUS        mandatory
    DESCRIPTION "Each entry corresponds to one instance of RIP
                    running on the system."
```

```
        INDEX         {ripSysInstance}
        ::= {ripSysTable 1}

RIPSysEntry ::= SEQUENCE {
                        ripSysInstance
                            INTEGER,
                        ripSysState
                            INTEGER,
                        ripSysIncorrectPackets
                            Counter
                        }

ripSysInstance OBJECT-TYPE
    SYNTAX       INTEGER
    ACCESS       read-write
    STATUS       mandatory
    DESCRIPTION "The unique identifier of the instance of RIP to
                which this row corresponds.  This value links the
                instance of RIP to an instance of IPX running on the
                system  (i.e. the value of ripSysInstance should be the
                same as a value of ipxSysInstance).  This value may be
                written only when creating a new entry in the table."
    ::= {ripSysEntry 1}

ripSysState OBJECT-TYPE
    SYNTAX       INTEGER {
                        off(1),
                        on(2)
                        }
    ACCESS       read-write
    STATUS       mandatory
    DESCRIPTION "Indicates the operational state of this instance of RIP."
    ::= {ripSysEntry 2}

ripSysIncorrectPackets OBJECT-TYPE
    SYNTAX       Counter
    ACCESS       read-only
    STATUS       mandatory
    DESCRIPTION "The number of times that an incorrectly formatted RIP
                packet was received."
    ::= {ripSysEntry 3}


— SAP System Table
—   This table contains an entry for each instance of SAP
—   running on the system.

sapSysTable OBJECT-TYPE
```

```
         SYNTAX        SEQUENCE OF SAPSysEntry
         ACCESS        not-accessible
         STATUS        mandatory
         DESCRIPTION "The SAP system table."
         ::= {ripsapSystem 2}

   sapSysEntry OBJECT-TYPE
         SYNTAX        SAPSysEntry
         ACCESS        not-accessible
         STATUS        mandatory
         DESCRIPTION "Each entry corresponds to one instance of SAP
                      running on the system."
         INDEX        {sapSysInstance}
         ::= {sapSysTable 1}

   SAPSysEntry ::= SEQUENCE {
                             sapSysInstance
                                 INTEGER,
                             sapSysState
                                 INTEGER,
                             sapSysIncorrectPackets
                                 Counter
                         }

   sapSysInstance OBJECT-TYPE
         SYNTAX        INTEGER
         ACCESS        read-write
         STATUS        mandatory
         DESCRIPTION "The unique identifier of the instance of SAP to
                      which this row corresponds.  This value links the
                      instance of SAP to an instance of IPX running on the
                      system  (i.e. the value of SApSysInstance should be the
                      same as a value of ipxSysInstance).  This value may be
                      written only when creating a new entry in the table."
         ::= {sapSysEntry 1}

   sapSysState OBJECT-TYPE
         SYNTAX        INTEGER {
                             off(1),
                             on(2)
                         }
         ACCESS        read-write
         STATUS        mandatory
         DESCRIPTION "Indicates the operational state of this instance of SAP."
         ::= {sapSysEntry 2}

   sapSysIncorrectPackets OBJECT-TYPE
         SYNTAX        Counter
```

```
    ACCESS        read-only
    STATUS        mandatory
    DESCRIPTION   "The number of times that an incorrectly formatted SAP
                   packet was received."
    ::= {sapSysEntry 3}


— Circuit Group
—   This group contains RIP and SAP management information for each
—   circuit known to this system.

— RIP Circuit Table
—   The RIP Circuit table contains an entry for the RIP information for
—   each circuit known to the system.

ripCircTable OBJECT-TYPE
    SYNTAX        SEQUENCE OF RIPCircEntry
    ACCESS        not-accessible
    STATUS        mandatory
    DESCRIPTION   "The RIP Circuit table."
    ::= {ripsapCircuit 1}

ripCircEntry OBJECT-TYPE
    SYNTAX        RIPCircEntry
    ACCESS        not-accessible
    STATUS        mandatory
    DESCRIPTION   "Each entry corresponds to one circuit known to the
                   system."
    INDEX         {
                    ripCircSysInstance,
                    ripCircIndex
                  }
    ::= {ripCircTable 1}

RIPCircEntry ::= SEQUENCE {
                        ripCircSysInstance
                            INTEGER,
                        ripCircIndex
                            INTEGER,
                        ripCircState
                            INTEGER,
                        ripCircPace
                            INTEGER,
                        ripCircUpdate
                            INTEGER,
                        ripCircAgeMultiplier
                            INTEGER,
                        ripCircPacketSize
```

```
                                            INTEGER,
                                     ripCircOutPackets
                                         Counter,
                                     ripCircInPackets
                                         Counter
                                  }


    ripCircSysInstance OBJECT-TYPE
        SYNTAX      INTEGER
        ACCESS      read-write
        STATUS      mandatory
        DESCRIPTION "The unique identifier of the instance of RIP and IPX
                    (via ipxSysInstance) to which this entry corresponds.
                    This value may be written only when creating a new entry in
                    the table."
        ::= {ripCircEntry 1}


    ripCircIndex OBJECT-TYPE
        SYNTAX      INTEGER
        ACCESS      read-write
        STATUS      mandatory
        DESCRIPTION "The identifier of this circuit, unique within the
                    instance of RIP.  This value corresponds to the circuit
                    identifier found in ipxCircIndex.  This value may be
                    written only when creating a new entry in the table."
        ::= {ripCircEntry 2}


    ripCircState OBJECT-TYPE
        SYNTAX      INTEGER {
                            off(1),
                            on(2),
                            auto-on(3),
                            auto-off(4)
                            }
        ACCESS      read-write
        STATUS      mandatory
        DESCRIPTION "Indicates whether RIP information may be sent/received
                    over this circuit."
        DEFVAL      { auto-off }
        ::= {ripCircEntry 3}


    ripCircPace OBJECT-TYPE
        SYNTAX      INTEGER
        ACCESS      read-write
        STATUS      mandatory
        DESCRIPTION "The maximum pace, in packets per second, at which RIP
                    packets may be sent on this circuit."
        ::= {ripCircEntry 4}
```

```
ripCircUpdate OBJECT-TYPE
    SYNTAX       INTEGER
    ACCESS       read-write
    STATUS       mandatory
    DESCRIPTION  "The RIP periodic update interval, in seconds."
    DEFVAL       { 60 }
    ::= {ripCircEntry 5}

ripCircAgeMultiplier OBJECT-TYPE
    SYNTAX       INTEGER
    ACCESS       read-write
    STATUS       mandatory
    DESCRIPTION  "The holding multiplier for information received in RIP
                    periodic updates."
    DEFVAL       { 4 }
    ::= {ripCircEntry 6}

ripCircPacketSize OBJECT-TYPE
    SYNTAX       INTEGER
    ACCESS       read-write
    STATUS       mandatory
    DESCRIPTION  "The RIP packet size used on this circuit."
    ::= {ripCircEntry 7}

ripCircOutPackets OBJECT-TYPE
    SYNTAX       Counter
    ACCESS       read-only
    STATUS       mandatory
    DESCRIPTION  "The number of RIP packets sent on this circuit."
    ::= {ripCircEntry 8}

ripCircInPackets OBJECT-TYPE
    SYNTAX       Counter
    ACCESS       read-only
    STATUS       mandatory
    DESCRIPTION  "The number of RIP packets received on this circuit."
    ::= {ripCircEntry 9}


— SAP Circuit Table
—    The SAP Circuit table contains an entry for the SAP information for
—    each circuit known to the system.

sapCircTable OBJECT-TYPE
    SYNTAX       SEQUENCE OF SAPCircEntry
    ACCESS       not-accessible
    STATUS       mandatory
```

```
          DESCRIPTION  "The SAP Circuit table."
          ::= {ripsapCircuit 2}

     sapCircEntry OBJECT-TYPE
          SYNTAX       SAPCircEntry
          ACCESS       not-accessible
          STATUS       mandatory
          DESCRIPTION  "Each entry corresponds to one circuit known to the
                       system."
          INDEX        {
                         sapCircSysInstance,
                         sapCircIndex
                       }
          ::= {sapCircTable 1}

     SAPCircEntry ::= SEQUENCE {
                              sapCircSysInstance
                                  INTEGER,
                              sapCircIndex
                                  INTEGER,
                              sapCircState
                                  INTEGER,
                              sapCircPace
                                  INTEGER,
                              sapCircUpdate
                                  INTEGER,
                              sapCircAgeMultiplier
                                  INTEGER,
                              sapCircPacketSize
                                  INTEGER,
                              sapCircGetNearestServerReply
                                  INTEGER,
                              sapCircOutPackets
                                  Counter,
                              sapCircInPackets
                                  Counter
                         }

     sapCircSysInstance OBJECT-TYPE
          SYNTAX       INTEGER
          ACCESS       read-write
          STATUS       mandatory
          DESCRIPTION  "The unique identifier of the instance of SAP and IPX
                       (via ipxSysInstance) to which this entry corresponds.
                       This value may be written only when creating a new entry in
                       the table."
          ::= {sapCircEntry 1}
```

```
sapCircIndex OBJECT-TYPE
    SYNTAX      INTEGER
    ACCESS      read-write
    STATUS      mandatory
    DESCRIPTION "The identifier of this circuit, unique within the
                instance of SAP.  This value corresponds to the circuit
                identifier found in ipxCircIndex.  This value may be
                written only when creating a new entry in the table."
    ::= {sapCircEntry 2}


sapCircState OBJECT-TYPE
    SYNTAX      INTEGER {
                            off(1),
                            on(2),
                            auto-on(3),
                            auto-off(4)
                        }
    ACCESS      read-write
    STATUS      mandatory
    DESCRIPTION "Indicates whether SAP information may be sent/received
                over this circuit."
    DEFVAL      { auto-off }
    ::= {sapCircEntry 3}


sapCircPace OBJECT-TYPE
    SYNTAX      INTEGER
    ACCESS      read-write
    STATUS      mandatory
    DESCRIPTION "The maximum pace, in packets per second, at which SAP
                packets may be sent on this circuit."
    ::= {sapCircEntry 4}


sapCircUpdate OBJECT-TYPE
    SYNTAX      INTEGER
    ACCESS      read-write
    STATUS      mandatory
    DESCRIPTION "The SAP periodic update interval, in seconds."
    DEFVAL      { 60 }
    ::= {sapCircEntry 5}


sapCircAgeMultiplier OBJECT-TYPE
    SYNTAX      INTEGER
    ACCESS      read-write
    STATUS      mandatory
    DESCRIPTION "The holding multiplier for information received in SAP
                periodic updates."
    DEFVAL      { 4 }
    ::= {sapCircEntry 6}
```

```
sapCircPacketSize OBJECT-TYPE
    SYNTAX       INTEGER
    ACCESS       read-write
    STATUS       mandatory
    DESCRIPTION  "The SAP packet size used on this circuit."
    ::= {sapCircEntry 7}

sapCircGetNearestServerReply OBJECT-TYPE
    SYNTAX       INTEGER {
                            no(1),
                            yes(2)
                         }
    ACCESS       read-write
    STATUS       mandatory
    DESCRIPTION  "Indicates whether to respond to SAP get nearest server
                 requests received on this circuit."
    DEFVAL       { yes }
    ::= {sapCircEntry 8}

sapCircOutPackets OBJECT-TYPE

    SYNTAX       Counter

    ACCESS       read-only

    STATUS       mandatory

    DESCRIPTION  "The number of SAP packets sent on this circuit."

    ::= {sapCircEntry 9}


sapCircInPackets OBJECT-TYPE

    SYNTAX       Counter

    ACCESS       read-only

    STATUS       mandatory

    DESCRIPTION  "The number of SAP packets received on this circuit."

    ::= {sapCircEntry 10}


END
```

# NLSP MIB

```
NLSP DEFINITIONS ::= BEGIN

— This MIB defines the management information for the NLSP protocol
— running in an IPX environment.  It provides information in addition
— to that contained in the IPX MIB itself.  All tables in this MIB are
— linked to an instance of IPX via the system instance identifier as
— defined in the IPX MIB.
—
— Change History:
—
—  01/11/94
—    The following DEFVAL values were changed to match the NLSP
—    specification:
—
—       nlspSysMinNonBcastLSPTransInt   5 -> 10
—       nlspSysBcastHelloInt           10 -> 20
—       nlspSysNonBcastHelloInt        10 -> 20
—       nlspSysHoldMult                 5 ->  3
—       nlspSysPartSNPInt               5 ->  1
—       nlspCircHelloTimer             10 -> 20
—
—    The units of nlspDestEstDelay, nlspNodeEstDelay, and nlspLinkDelay
—    were changed from milliseconds to microseconds.
—

IMPORTS
    enterprises, Counter
            FROM RFC1155-SMI
    OBJECT-TYPE
            FROM RFC-1212
    PhysAddress
            FROM RFC1213-MIB;

novell  OBJECT IDENTIFIER ::= {enterprises 23}
mibDoc  OBJECT IDENTIFIER ::= { novell 2 }
nlsp    OBJECT IDENTIFIER ::= {mibDoc 19}


— Groups

nlspSystem        OBJECT IDENTIFIER ::= {nlsp 1}
nlspCircuit       OBJECT IDENTIFIER ::= {nlsp 2}
nlspForwarding    OBJECT IDENTIFIER ::= {nlsp 3}
nlspNeighbors     OBJECT IDENTIFIER ::= {nlsp 4}
nlspTranslation   OBJECT IDENTIFIER ::= {nlsp 5}
nlspGraph         OBJECT IDENTIFIER ::= {nlsp 6}
nlspLSP           OBJECT IDENTIFIER ::= {nlsp 7}
```

— Types

```
SystemID   ::= OCTET STRING (SIZE(6))
NLSPID     ::= OCTET STRING (SIZE(7))
NetNumber ::= OCTET STRING (SIZE(4))
```

— System Group
—   This group contains global information about each instance of NLSP
—   running on one system.

— System Table
—   This table contains an entry for each instance of NLSP running on
—   the system.

```
nlspSysTable OBJECT-TYPE
    SYNTAX      SEQUENCE OF NLSPSysEntry
    ACCESS      not-accessible
    STATUS      mandatory
    DESCRIPTION "The NLSP System table."
    ::= {nlspSystem 1}


nlspSysEntry OBJECT-TYPE
    SYNTAX      NLSPSysEntry
    ACCESS      not-accessible
    STATUS      mandatory
    DESCRIPTION "Each entry corresponds to one instance of NLSP running
                 on the system."
    INDEX       {nlspSysInstance}
    ::= {nlspSysTable 1}


NLSPSysEntry ::= SEQUENCE {
                    nlspSysInstance
                        INTEGER,
                    nlspSysState
                        INTEGER,
                    nlspSysID
                        SystemID,
                    nlspSysMinNonBcastLSPTransInt
                        INTEGER,
                    nlspSysMinBcastLSPTransInt
                        INTEGER,
                    nlspSysMinLSPGenInt
                        INTEGER,
                    nlspSysMaxLSPGenInt
                        INTEGER,
                    nlspSysMaxLSPAge
                        INTEGER,
```

```
                              nlspSysBcastHelloInt
                                 INTEGER,
                              nlspSysNonBcastHelloInt
                                 INTEGER,
                              nlspSysDRBcastHelloInt
                                 INTEGER,
                              nlspSysHoldTimeMultiplier
                                 INTEGER,
                              nlspSysCompSNPInt
                                 INTEGER,
                              nlspSysPartSNPInt
                                 INTEGER,
                              nlspSysWaitTime
                                 INTEGER,
                              nlspSysOrigL1LSPBufSize
                                 INTEGER,
                              nlspSysVersion
                                 INTEGER,
                              nlspSysCorrLSPs
                                 Counter,
                              nlspSysL1Overloaded
                                 INTEGER,
                              nlspSysL1DbaseOverloads
                                 Counter,
                              nlspSysMaxSeqNums
                                 Counter,
                              nlspSysSeqNumSkips
                                 Counter,
                              nlspSysTransmittedLSPs
                                 Counter,
                              nlspSysReceivedLSPs
                                 Counter,
                              nlspSysOwnLSPPurges
                                 Counter,
                              nlspSysVersionErrors
                                 Counter,
                              nlspSysIncorrectPackets
                                 Counter,
                              nlspSysNearestL2DefaultExists
                                 INTEGER,
                              nlspSysNearestL2DefaultRouter
                                 SystemID,
                              nlspSysResourceFailures
                                 Counter,
                          }


            nlspSysInstance OBJECT-TYPE
                  SYNTAX      INTEGER
```

```
ACCESS        read-write
STATUS        mandatory
DESCRIPTION   "The unique identifier of the instance of NLSP to which this
              corresponds.  This value links the instance of NLSP to an
              instance of IPX running on the system  (i.e. the value
              of nlspSysInstance should be the same as a value of
              ipxSysInstance).  This value may be written only when
              creating a new entry in the table."
::= {nlspSysEntry 1}


nlspSysState OBJECT-TYPE
    SYNTAX        INTEGER {
                        off(1),
                        nlspLevel1Router(2)
                        }
    ACCESS        read-write
    STATUS        mandatory
    DESCRIPTION   "Indicates the operational state of this instance of NLSP."
    ::= {nlspSysEntry 2}


nlspSysID OBJECT-TYPE
    SYNTAX        SystemID
    ACCESS        read-write
    STATUS        mandatory
    DESCRIPTION   "The system ID for this instance of NLSP."
    ::= {nlspSysEntry 3}


nlspSysMinNonBcastLSPTransInt OBJECT-TYPE
    SYNTAX        INTEGER (1..30)
    ACCESS        read-write
    STATUS        mandatory
    DESCRIPTION   "The minimum interval, in seconds, between transmission
                  of LSPs on a nonbroadcast circuit."
    DEFVAL        { 10 }
    ::= {nlspSysEntry 4}


nlspSysMinBcastLSPTransInt OBJECT-TYPE
    SYNTAX        INTEGER (1..30)
    ACCESS        read-write
    STATUS        mandatory
    DESCRIPTION   "The minimum interval, in seconds, between transmission
                  of LSPs on a broadcast circuit."
    DEFVAL        { 5 }
    ::= {nlspSysEntry 5}


nlspSysMinLSPGenInt OBJECT-TYPE
    SYNTAX        INTEGER (1..30)
    ACCESS        read-write
```

```
          STATUS        mandatory
          DESCRIPTION   "The minimum interval, in seconds, between the generation
                        of the same LSP."
          DEFVAL        { 5 }
          ::= {nlspSysEntry 6}


    nlspSysMaxLSPGenInt OBJECT-TYPE
          SYNTAX        INTEGER (1..50000)
          ACCESS        read-write
          STATUS        mandatory
          DESCRIPTION   "The maximum interval, in seconds, between the generation
                        of the same LSP."
          DEFVAL        { 7200 }
          ::= {nlspSysEntry 7}


    nlspSysMaxLSPAge OBJECT-TYPE
          SYNTAX        INTEGER (1..50000)
          ACCESS        read-write
          STATUS        mandatory
          DESCRIPTION   "The value, in seconds, placed in the lifetime field of
                        LSPs generated by this instance of NLSP."
          DEFVAL        { 7500 }
          ::= {nlspSysEntry 8}


    nlspSysBcastHelloInt OBJECT-TYPE
          SYNTAX        INTEGER (1..100)
          ACCESS        read-write
          STATUS        mandatory
          DESCRIPTION   "The interval, in seconds, at which NLSP Hellos will be
                        sent on a broadcast circuit, if this system is not the
                        designated router."
          DEFVAL        { 20 }
          ::= {nlspSysEntry 9}


    nlspSysNonBcastHelloInt OBJECT-TYPE
          SYNTAX        INTEGER (1..100)
          ACCESS        read-write
          STATUS        mandatory
          DESCRIPTION   "The interval, in seconds, at which NLSP Hellos will be
                        sent on a nonbroadcast circuit."
          DEFVAL        { 20 }
          ::= {nlspSysEntry 10}


    nlspSysDRBcastHelloInt OBJECT-TYPE
          SYNTAX        INTEGER (1..100)
          ACCESS        read-write
          STATUS        mandatory
```

```
    DESCRIPTION "The interval, in seconds, at which the designated
                 router sends NLSP Hellos on a broadcast circuit."
    DEFVAL      { 3 }
    ::= {nlspSysEntry 11}


nlspSysHoldTimeMultiplier OBJECT-TYPE
    SYNTAX      INTEGER (2..20)
    ACCESS      read-write
    STATUS      mandatory
    DESCRIPTION "The holding time multiplier used to specify the holding
                 time for NLSP neighbor entries as a function of the NLSP
                 Hello interval."
    DEFVAL      { 3 }
    ::= {nlspSysEntry 12}


nlspSysCompSNPInt OBJECT-TYPE
    SYNTAX      INTEGER (1..600)
    ACCESS      read-write
    STATUS      mandatory
    DESCRIPTION "The interval, in seconds, between generation of complete
                 sequence number packets by a designated router on a
                 broadcast circuit."
    DEFVAL      { 30 }
    ::= {nlspSysEntry 13}


nlspSysPartSNPInt OBJECT-TYPE
    SYNTAX      INTEGER (1..60)
    ACCESS      read-write
    STATUS      mandatory
    DESCRIPTION "The minimum interval, in seconds, between transmission of
                 partial sequence number packets."
    DEFVAL      { 1 }
    ::= {nlspSysEntry 14}


nlspSysWaitTime OBJECT-TYPE
    SYNTAX      INTEGER (1..300)
    ACCESS      read-write
    STATUS      mandatory
    DESCRIPTION "The number of seconds to delay in the waiting state
                 before entering the on state."
    DEFVAL      { 120 }
    ::= {nlspSysEntry 15}


nlspSysOrigL1LSPBufSize OBJECT-TYPE
    SYNTAX      INTEGER (512..4096)
    ACCESS      read-write
    STATUS      mandatory
```

```
            DESCRIPTION "The maximum size of Level-1 LSPs originated by
                        this instance of NLSP."
            DEFVAL      { 512 }
            ::= {nlspSysEntry 16}


    nlspSysVersion OBJECT-TYPE
            SYNTAX      INTEGER
            ACCESS      read-only
            STATUS      mandatory
            DESCRIPTION "The version number of this instance of NLSP."
            ::= {nlspSysEntry 17}


    nlspSysCorrLSPs OBJECT-TYPE
            SYNTAX      Counter
            ACCESS      read-only
            STATUS      mandatory
            DESCRIPTION "The number of corrupt LSPs detected."
            ::= {nlspSysEntry 18}


    nlspSysL1Overloaded OBJECT-TYPE
            SYNTAX      INTEGER {
                            no(1),
                            yes(2)
                        }
            ACCESS      read-only
            STATUS      mandatory
            DESCRIPTION "Indicates whether the NLSP Level-1 database is overloaded."
            ::= {nlspSysEntry 19}


    nlspSysL1DbaseOloads OBJECT-TYPE
            SYNTAX      Counter
            ACCESS      read-only
            STATUS      mandatory
            DESCRIPTION "The number of times the NLSP Level-1 LSP database has
                        become overloaded."
            ::= {nlspSysEntry 20}


    nlspSysMaxSeqNums OBJECT-TYPE
            SYNTAX      Counter
            ACCESS      read-only
            STATUS      mandatory
            DESCRIPTION "The number of times the router has attempted to exceed
                        NLSP's maximum sequence number."
            ::= {nlspSysEntry 21}


    nlspSysSeqNumSkips OBJECT-TYPE
            SYNTAX      Counter
            ACCESS      read-only
```

```
         STATUS      mandatory
         DESCRIPTION "The number of times a sequence number skip has occurred."
         ::= {nlspSysEntry 22}


nlspSysTransmittedLSPs OBJECT-TYPE
         SYNTAX      Counter
         ACCESS      read-only
         STATUS      mandatory
         DESCRIPTION "The number of LSPs transmitted by this system."
         ::= {nlspSysEntry 23}


nlspSysReceivedLSPs OBJECT-TYPE
         SYNTAX      Counter
         ACCESS      read-only
         STATUS      mandatory
         DESCRIPTION "The number of LSPs received by this system."
         ::= {nlspSysEntry 24}


nlspSysOwnLSPPurges OBJECT-TYPE
         SYNTAX      Counter
         ACCESS      read-only
         STATUS      mandatory
         DESCRIPTION "The number of times a zero-aged copy of the router's own
                     LSP has been received from some other node."
         ::= {nlspSysEntry 25}


nlspSysVersionErrors OBJECT-TYPE
         SYNTAX      Counter
         ACCESS      read-only
         STATUS      mandatory
         DESCRIPTION "The number of times that a received NLSP packet was
                     rejected because its version number was invalid."
         ::= {nlspSysEntry 26}


nlspSysIncorrectPackets OBJECT-TYPE
         SYNTAX      Counter
         ACCESS      read-only
         STATUS      mandatory
         DESCRIPTION "The number of times that an incorrectly formatted NLSP
                     packet was received."
         ::= {nlspSysEntry 27}


nlspSysNearestL2DefaultExists OBJECT-TYPE
         SYNTAX      INTEGER {
                         no(1),
                         yes(2)
                         }
         ACCESS      read-only
```

```
         STATUS      mandatory
         DESCRIPTION "Indicates whether this instance of NLSP knows
                     of an NLSP Level-2 router that currently can reach other
                     areas using the default metric."
         ::= {nlspSysEntry 28}


nlspSysNearestL2DefaultRouter OBJECT-TYPE
         SYNTAX      SystemID
         ACCESS      read-only
         STATUS      mandatory
         DESCRIPTION "The system ID of the nearest NLSP Level-2 router that
                     currently can reach other areas using the default
                     metric.  The value is undefined if the value of
                     nlspSysNearestL2DefaultExists is no."
         ::= {nlspSysEntry 29}


nlspSysResourceFailures OBJECT-TYPE
         SYNTAX      Counter
         ACCESS      read-only
         STATUS      mandatory
         DESCRIPTION "The number of times this instance of the NLSP has been
                     unable to obtain needed resources (memory, etc.)"
         ::= {nlspSysEntry 30}



-- System Area Address Table
--    The System Area Address table contains the area addresses configured
--    for NLSP.


nlspSysAreaTable OBJECT-TYPE
         SYNTAX      SEQUENCE OF NLSPSysAreaEntry
         ACCESS      not-accessible
         STATUS      mandatory
         DESCRIPTION "The System Area Address table contains the area addresses
                     configured for NLSP."
         ::= {nlspSystem 2}


nlspSysAreaEntry OBJECT-TYPE
         SYNTAX      NLSPSysAreaEntry
         ACCESS      not-accessible
         STATUS      mandatory
         DESCRIPTION "Each entry in the table corresponds to one NLSP
                     System Area Address."
         INDEX       {
                     nlspSysAreaSysInstance,
                     nlspSysAreaNet,
                     nlspSysAreaMask
                     }
```

```
          ::= {nlspSysAreaTable 1}

NLSPSysAreaEntry ::= SEQUENCE {
                          nlspSysAreaSysInstance
                             INTEGER,
                          nlspSysAreaNet
                             OCTET STRING,
                          nlspSysAreaMask
                             OCTET STRING
                          }

nlspSysAreaSysInstance OBJECT-TYPE
    SYNTAX       INTEGER
    ACCESS       read-write
    STATUS       mandatory
    DESCRIPTION "The unique identifier of the instance of NLSP and IPX
                (via ipxSysInstance) to which this row corresponds."
    ::= {nlspSysAreaEntry 1}

nlspSysAreaNet OBJECT-TYPE
    SYNTAX       OCTET STRING (SIZE(4))
    ACCESS       read-write
    STATUS       mandatory
    DESCRIPTION "The network address portion of the area address."
    ::= {nlspSysAreaEntry 2}

nlspSysAreaMask OBJECT-TYPE
    SYNTAX       OCTET STRING (SIZE(4))
    ACCESS       read-write
    STATUS       mandatory
    DESCRIPTION "The mask portion of the area address."
    ::= {nlspSysAreaEntry 3}


- Actual Area Address Table
-   The Actual Area Address table contains the area addresses actually
-   used by NLSP.

nlspActAreaTable OBJECT-TYPE
    SYNTAX       SEQUENCE OF NLSPActAreaEntry
    ACCESS       not-accessible
    STATUS       mandatory
    DESCRIPTION "The Actual Area Address table contains the area addresses
                actually used by NLSP."
    ::= {nlspSystem 3}

nlspActAreaEntry OBJECT-TYPE
    SYNTAX       NLSPActAreaEntry
```

```
              ACCESS       not-accessible
              STATUS       mandatory
              DESCRIPTION  "Each entry in the table corresponds to one NLSP
                           Actual Area Address."
              INDEX        {
                            nlspActAreaSysInstance,
                            nlspActAreaNet,
                            nlspActAreaMask
                           }
          ::= {nlspActAreaTable 1}

    NLSPActAreaEntry ::= SEQUENCE {
                                nlspActAreaSysInstance
                                    INTEGER,
                                nlspActAreaNet
                                    OCTET STRING,
                                nlspActAreaMask
                                    OCTET STRING
                                }

    nlspActAreaSysInstance OBJECT-TYPE
        SYNTAX       INTEGER
        ACCESS       read-write
        STATUS       mandatory
        DESCRIPTION  "The unique identifier of the instance of NLSP and IPX
                     (via ipxSysInstance) to which this row corresponds."
        ::= {nlspActAreaEntry 1}

    nlspActAreaNet OBJECT-TYPE
        SYNTAX       OCTET STRING (SIZE(4))
        ACCESS       read-write
        STATUS       mandatory
        DESCRIPTION  "The network address portion of the area address."
        ::= {nlspActAreaEntry 2}

    nlspActAreaMask OBJECT-TYPE
        SYNTAX       OCTET STRING (SIZE(4))
        ACCESS       read-write
        STATUS       mandatory
        DESCRIPTION  "The mask portion of the area address."
        ::= {nlspActAreaEntry 3}


    — Circuit Group
    —   This group contains the NLSP information for each circuit known
    —   to this system.

    — Circuit Table
```

— The Circuit table contains an entry containing the NLSP information
— for each circuit known to the system.

```
nlspCircTable OBJECT-TYPE
    SYNTAX      SEQUENCE OF NLSPCircEntry
    ACCESS      not-accessible
    STATUS      mandatory
    DESCRIPTION "The Circuit table."
    ::= {nlspCircuit 1}


nlspCircEntry OBJECT-TYPE
    SYNTAX      NLSPCircEntry
    ACCESS      not-accessible
    STATUS      mandatory
    DESCRIPTION "Each entry corresponds to one circuit known to the
                 system."
    INDEX       {
                 nlspCircSysInstance,
                 nlspCircIndex
                }
    ::= {nlspCircTable 1}


NLSPCircEntry ::= SEQUENCE {
                        nlspCircSysInstance
                            INTEGER,
                        nlspCircIndex
                            INTEGER,
                        nlspCircState
                            INTEGER,
                        nlspCircPace
                            INTEGER,
                        nlspCircHelloTimer
                            INTEGER,
                        nlspCircL1DefaultCost
                            INTEGER,
                        nlspCircL1DesRouterPriority
                            INTEGER,
                        nlspCircL1CircID
                            OCTET STRING,
                        nlspCircL1DesRouter
                            SystemID,
                        nlspCircLANL1DesRouterChanges
                            Counter,
                        nlspCircNeighChanges
                            Counter,
                        nlspCircRejNeighbors
                            Counter,
                        nlspCircOutPackets
```

```
                                        Counter,
                                nlspCircInPackets
                                        Counter,
                                nlspCircActualMaxPacketSize
                                        INTEGER,
                                nlspCircPSNPsSent
                                        Counter,
                                nlspCircPSNPsReceived
                                        Counter
                                }

        nlspCircSysInstance OBJECT-TYPE
            SYNTAX        INTEGER
            ACCESS        read-write
            STATUS        mandatory
            DESCRIPTION "The unique identifier of the instance of NLSP and IPX
                        (via ipxSysInstance) to which this entry corresponds.
                        This value may be written only when creating a new
                        entry in the table."
            ::= {nlspCircEntry 1}

        nlspCircIndex OBJECT-TYPE
            SYNTAX        INTEGER
            ACCESS        read-write
            STATUS        mandatory
            DESCRIPTION "The identifier of this circuit, unique within the
                        instance of NLSP.  This value may be written
                        only when creating a new entry in the table."
            ::= {nlspCircEntry 2}

        nlspCircState OBJECT-TYPE
            SYNTAX        INTEGER {
                                off(1),
                                on(2)
                                }
            ACCESS        read-write
            STATUS        mandatory
            DESCRIPTION "Indicates whether NLSP information may be sent/received
                        over this circuit."
            DEFVAL        { on }
            ::= {nlspCircEntry 3}

        nlspCircPace OBJECT-TYPE
            SYNTAX        INTEGER
            ACCESS        read-write
            STATUS        mandatory
            DESCRIPTION "The maximum pace, in packets per second, at which NLSP
                        packets may be sent on this circuit."
```

```
        ::= {nlspCircEntry 4}


nlspCircHelloTimer OBJECT-TYPE
    SYNTAX      INTEGER (1..100)
    ACCESS      read-write
    STATUS      mandatory
    DESCRIPTION "The interval, in seconds, between NLSP hello packets
                sent on this circuit."
    DEFVAL      { 20 }
    ::= {nlspCircEntry 5}


nlspCircL1DefaultCost OBJECT-TYPE
    SYNTAX      INTEGER (1..63)
    ACCESS      read-write
    STATUS      mandatory
    DESCRIPTION "The NLSP default cost of this circuit for Level-1
                traffic."
    ::= {nlspCircEntry 6}


nlspCircL1DesRouterPriority OBJECT-TYPE
    SYNTAX      INTEGER (1..127)
    ACCESS      read-write
    STATUS      mandatory
    DESCRIPTION "The priority for becoming the NLSP LAN Level-1
                designated router on a broadcast circuit."
    ::= {nlspCircEntry 7}


nlspCircL1CircID OBJECT-TYPE
    SYNTAX      OCTET STRING (SIZE(7))
    ACCESS      read-only
    STATUS      mandatory
    DESCRIPTION "The NLSP ID for this circuit."
    ::= {nlspCircEntry 8}


nlspCircL1DesRouter OBJECT-TYPE
    SYNTAX      SystemID
    ACCESS      read-only
    STATUS      mandatory
    DESCRIPTION "The system ID of the NLSP LAN Level-1 designated router
                on this circuit."
    ::= {nlspCircEntry 9}


nlspCircLANL1DesRouterChanges OBJECT-TYPE
    SYNTAX      Counter
    ACCESS      read-only
    STATUS      mandatory
    DESCRIPTION "The number of times the NLSP LAN Level-1 designated
                router has changed on this circuit."
```

```
        ::= {nlspCircEntry 10}

nlspCircNeighChanges OBJECT-TYPE
    SYNTAX      Counter
    ACCESS      read-only
    STATUS      mandatory
    DESCRIPTION "The number of times a NLSP neighbor state change has
                occurred on this circuit."
    ::= {nlspCircEntry 11}

nlspCircRejNeighbors OBJECT-TYPE
    SYNTAX      Counter
    ACCESS      read-only
    STATUS      mandatory
    DESCRIPTION "The number of times that a NLSP neighbor has been
                rejected on this circuit."
    ::= {nlspCircEntry 12}

nlspCircOutPackets OBJECT-TYPE
    SYNTAX      Counter
    ACCESS      read-only
    STATUS      mandatory
    DESCRIPTION "The number of NLSP packets sent on this circuit."
    ::= {nlspCircEntry 13}

nlspCircInPackets OBJECT-TYPE
    SYNTAX      Counter
    ACCESS      read-only
    STATUS      mandatory
    DESCRIPTION "The number of NLSP packets received on this circuit."
    ::= {nlspCircEntry 14}

nlspCircActualMaxPacketSize OBJECT-TYPE
    SYNTAX      INTEGER
    ACCESS      read-only
    STATUS      mandatory
    DESCRIPTION "The actual maximum packet size (including header),
                in bytes, that has been used on this circuit."
    ::= {nlspCircEntry 15}

nlspCircPSNPsSent OBJECT-TYPE
    SYNTAX      Counter
    ACCESS      read-only
    STATUS      mandatory
    DESCRIPTION "The number of PSNPs sent on this circuit."
    ::= {nlspCircEntry 16}
```

```
nlspCircPSNPsReceived OBJECT-TYPE
    SYNTAX        Counter
    ACCESS        read-only
    STATUS        mandatory
    DESCRIPTION "The number of PSNPs received on this circuit."
    ::= {nlspCircEntry 17}


—  Forwarding Group
—    This group contains NLSP forwarding information in addition to that
—    contained in the IPX forwarding group.

—  Destination Table
—    The Destination table contains additional NLSP forwarding
—    information about all destinations learned about via NLSP.

nlspDestTable OBJECT-TYPE
    SYNTAX        SEQUENCE OF NLSPDestEntry
    ACCESS        not-accessible
    STATUS        mandatory
    DESCRIPTION "The Destination table contains information about all
                 known destinations learned about via NLSP."
    ::= {nlspForwarding 1}


nlspDestEntry OBJECT-TYPE
    SYNTAX        NLSPDestEntry
    ACCESS        not-accessible
    STATUS        mandatory
    DESCRIPTION "Each entry corresponds to one destination."
    INDEX         {
                    nlspDestSysInstance,
                    nlspDestNetNum
                  }
    ::= {nlspDestTable 1}

NLSPDestEntry ::= SEQUENCE {
                        nlspDestSysInstance
                            INTEGER,
                        nlspDestNetNum
                            NetNumber,
                        nlspDestID
                            NLSPID,
                        nlspDestEstDelay
                            INTEGER,
                        nlspDestEstThroughput
                            INTEGER,
                        nlspDestNextHopID
                            NLSPID,
```

```
                            nlspDestCost
                              INTEGER
                    }


    nlspDestSysInstance OBJECT-TYPE
        SYNTAX      INTEGER
        ACCESS      read-only
        STATUS      mandatory
        DESCRIPTION "The unique identifier of the instance of NLSP and IPX
                    (via ipxSysInstance) to which this row corresponds."
        ::= {nlspDestEntry 1}


    nlspDestNetNum OBJECT-TYPE
        SYNTAX      NetNumber
        ACCESS      read-only
        STATUS      mandatory
        DESCRIPTION "The IPX network number of the destination."
        ::= {nlspDestEntry 2}


    nlspDestID OBJECT-TYPE
        SYNTAX      NLSPID
        ACCESS      read-only
        STATUS      mandatory
        DESCRIPTION "The destination NLSP ID (6-octet system ID plus 1-octet
                    pseudo-node ID)."
        ::= {nlspDestEntry 3}


    nlspDestEstDelay OBJECT-TYPE
        SYNTAX      INTEGER
        ACCESS      read-only
        STATUS      mandatory
        DESCRIPTION "The estimated delay, in microseconds, to reach the
                    destination."
        ::= {nlspDestEntry 4}


    nlspDestEstThroughput OBJECT-TYPE
        SYNTAX      INTEGER
        ACCESS      read-only
        STATUS      mandatory
        DESCRIPTION "The estimated throughput, in bits per second, to the
                    destination."
        ::= {nlspDestEntry 5}


    nlspDestNextHopID OBJECT-TYPE
        SYNTAX      NLSPID
        ACCESS      read-only
        STATUS      mandatory
        DESCRIPTION "The NLSP ID (6-octet system ID plus 1-octet pseudo-node
```

```
                              ID) of the next hop."
      ::= {nlspDestEntry 6}


nlspDestCost OBJECT-TYPE
      SYNTAX     INTEGER
      ACCESS     read-only
      STATUS     mandatory
      DESCRIPTION "The total path default cost to reach this destination."
      ::= {nlspDestEntry 7}



 — NLSP Neighbors Group
 —   This group contains management information for each neighboring
 —   NLSP router known to the system.


 — NLSP Neighbors Table
 —   This table contains an entry for each neighboring NLSP router
 —   known to the system.


nlspNeighTable OBJECT-TYPE
      SYNTAX     SEQUENCE OF NLSPNeighEntry
      ACCESS     not-accessible
      STATUS     mandatory
      DESCRIPTION "The NLSP Neighbors table."
      ::= {nlspNeighbors 1}


nlspNeighEntry OBJECT-TYPE
      SYNTAX     NLSPNeighEntry
      ACCESS     not-accessible
      STATUS     mandatory
      DESCRIPTION "Each entry corresponds to one neighboring NLSP router
                   known to the system."
      INDEX      {
                   nlspNeighSysInstance,
                   nlspNeighCircIndex,
                   nlspNeighIndex
                   }
      ::= {nlspNeighTable 1}


NLSPNeighEntry ::= SEQUENCE {
                              nlspNeighSysInstance
                                  INTEGER,
                              nlspNeighCircIndex
                                  INTEGER,
                              nlspNeighIndex
                                  INTEGER,
                              nlspNeighState
                                  INTEGER,
```

```
                                    nlspNeighNICAddress
                                        PhysAddress,
                                    nlspNeighSysType
                                        INTEGER,
                                    nlspNeighSysID
                                        SystemID,
                                    nlspNeighName
                                        OCTET STRING,
                                    nlspNeighUsage
                                        INTEGER,
                                    nlspNeighHoldTimer
                                        INTEGER,
                                    nlspNeighRemainingTime
                                        INTEGER,
                                    nlspNeighPriority
                                        INTEGER
                                }

        nlspNeighSysInstance OBJECT-TYPE
            SYNTAX      INTEGER
            ACCESS      read-only
            STATUS      mandatory
            DESCRIPTION "The unique identifier of the instance of NLSP and IPX
                        (via ipxSysInstance) to which this row corresponds."
            ::= {nlspNeighEntry 1}

        nlspNeighCircIndex OBJECT-TYPE
            SYNTAX      INTEGER
            ACCESS      read-only
            STATUS      mandatory
            DESCRIPTION "The identifier of the parent circuit of this neighbor
                        within this instance of the NLSP and IPX."
            ::= {nlspNeighEntry 2}

        nlspNeighIndex OBJECT-TYPE
            SYNTAX      INTEGER
            ACCESS      read-only
            STATUS      mandatory
            DESCRIPTION "The identifier for this NLSP neighbor entry, unique
                        within the parent circuit."
            ::= {nlspNeighEntry 3}

        nlspNeighState OBJECT-TYPE
            SYNTAX      INTEGER {
                            initializing(1),
                            up(2),
                            failed(3),
                            down(4)
```

```
                              }
      ACCESS       read-only
      STATUS       mandatory
      DESCRIPTION  "The state of the connection to the neighboring NLSP
                   router."
      ::= {nlspNeighEntry 4}


nlspNeighNICAddress OBJECT-TYPE
      SYNTAX       PhysAddress
      ACCESS       read-only
      STATUS       mandatory
      DESCRIPTION  "The NIC address of the neighboring NLSP router."
      ::= {nlspNeighEntry 5}


nlspNeighSysType OBJECT-TYPE
      SYNTAX       INTEGER {
                          unknown(1),
                          nlspLevel1Router(2)
                          }
      ACCESS       read-only
      STATUS       mandatory
      DESCRIPTION  "The type of the neighboring NLSP router."
      ::= {nlspNeighEntry 6}


nlspNeighSysID OBJECT-TYPE
      SYNTAX       SystemID
      ACCESS       read-only
      STATUS       mandatory
      DESCRIPTION  "The neighboring NLSP router's system ID."
      ::= {nlspNeighEntry 7}


nlspNeighName OBJECT-TYPE
      SYNTAX       OCTET STRING (SIZE(0..48))
      ACCESS       read-only
      STATUS       mandatory
      DESCRIPTION  "The readable name for the neighboring NLSP router."
      ::= {nlspNeighEntry 8}


nlspNeighUsage OBJECT-TYPE
      SYNTAX       INTEGER {
                          undefined(1),
                          level1(2)
                          }
      ACCESS       read-only
      STATUS       mandatory
      DESCRIPTION  "The usage of the connection to the neighboring NLSP
                   router."
      ::= {nlspNeighEntry 9}
```

```
nlspNeighHoldTimer OBJECT-TYPE
    SYNTAX       INTEGER (1..65535)
    ACCESS       read-only
    STATUS       mandatory
    DESCRIPTION "The initial holding time, in seconds, for this NLSP
                 neighbor entry as specified in the NLSP hello packet."
    ::= {nlspNeighEntry 10}


nlspNeighRemainingTime OBJECT-TYPE
    SYNTAX       INTEGER
    ACCESS       read-only
    STATUS       mandatory
    DESCRIPTION "The remaining time to live, in seconds, for this NLSP
                 neighbor entry."
    ::= {nlspNeighEntry 11}


nlspNeighPriority OBJECT-TYPE
    SYNTAX       INTEGER (1..127)
    ACCESS       read-only
    STATUS       mandatory
    DESCRIPTION "The priority of the neighboring NLSP router for
                 becoming the LAN Level-1 designated router if the value
                 of nlspNeighSysType is nlspLevel1Router."
    ::= {nlspNeighEntry 12}



— Translation Group
—   The translation group contains tables providing mappings between
—   network numbers, NLSP system IDs, and router names.


— NLSP ID Mapping Table
—   This table maps NLSP system IDs to router names and IPX network
—   numbers.

nlspIDMapTable OBJECT-TYPE
    SYNTAX       SEQUENCE OF NLSPIDMapEntry
    ACCESS       not-accessible
    STATUS       mandatory
    DESCRIPTION "This table maps NLSP system IDs to router names and
                 IPX network numbers."
    ::= {nlspTranslation 1}


nlspIDMapEntry OBJECT-TYPE
    SYNTAX       NLSPIDMapEntry
    ACCESS       not-accessible
    STATUS       mandatory
    DESCRIPTION "Each entry maps one NLSP system ID to its corresponding
```

```
                        router name and IPX network number."
        INDEX           {
                        nlspIDMapSysInstance,
                        nlspIDMapID
                        }
        ::= {nlspIDMapTable 1}


NLSPIDMapEntry ::= SEQUENCE {
                                nlspIDMapSysInstance
                                    INTEGER,
                                nlspIDMapID
                                    NLSPID,
                                nlspIDMapServerName
                                    OCTET STRING,
                                nlspIDMapNetNum
                                    NetNumber
                        }


nlspIDMapSysInstance OBJECT-TYPE
    SYNTAX      INTEGER
    ACCESS      read-only
    STATUS      mandatory
    DESCRIPTION "The unique identifier of the instance of NLSP and IPX
                (via ipxSysInstance) to which this row corresponds."
    ::= {nlspIDMapEntry 1}


nlspIDMapID OBJECT-TYPE
    SYNTAX      NLSPID
    ACCESS      read-only
    STATUS      mandatory
    DESCRIPTION "The NLSP ID (six-octet system ID plus the pseudonode ID)."
    ::= {nlspIDMapEntry 2}


nlspIDMapServerName OBJECT-TYPE
    SYNTAX      OCTET STRING (SIZE(0..48))
    ACCESS      read-only
    STATUS      mandatory
    DESCRIPTION "The readable name corresponding to this NLSP ID."
    ::= {nlspIDMapEntry 3}


nlspIDMapNetNum OBJECT-TYPE
    SYNTAX      NetNumber
    ACCESS      read-only
    STATUS      mandatory
    DESCRIPTION "The IPX network number corresponding to this NLSP ID."
    ::= {nlspIDMapEntry 4}
```

```
—  IPX Network Number Mapping Table
—    This table maps IPX network numbers to router names and NLSP IDs.

nlspNetMapTable OBJECT-TYPE
    SYNTAX      SEQUENCE OF NLSPNetMapEntry
    ACCESS      not-accessible
    STATUS      mandatory
    DESCRIPTION "This table maps IPX network numbers to router names
                and NLSP IDs."
    ::= {nlspTranslation 2}

nlspNetMapEntry OBJECT-TYPE
    SYNTAX      NLSPNetMapEntry
    ACCESS      not-accessible
    STATUS      mandatory
    DESCRIPTION "Each entry maps one IPX network number to its
                corresponding router name and NLSP ID."
    INDEX       {
                 nlspNetMapSysInstance,
                 nlspNetMapNetNum
                }
    ::= {nlspNetMapTable 1}

NLSPNetMapEntry ::= SEQUENCE {
                        nlspNetMapSysInstance
                            INTEGER,
                        nlspNetMapNetNum,
                            NetNumber,
                        nlspNetMapServerName
                            OCTET STRING,
                        nlspNetMapID,
                            NLSPID
                        }

nlspNetMapSysInstance OBJECT-TYPE
    SYNTAX      INTEGER
    ACCESS      read-only
    STATUS      mandatory
    DESCRIPTION "The unique identifier of the instance of NLSP and IPX
                (via ipxSysInstance) to which this row corresponds."
    ::= {nlspNetMapEntry 1}

nlspNetMapNetNum OBJECT-TYPE
    SYNTAX      NetNumber
    ACCESS      read-only
    STATUS      mandatory
    DESCRIPTION "The IPX network number."
```

```
        ::= {nlspNetMapEntry 2}

nlspNetMapServerName OBJECT-TYPE
    SYNTAX      OCTET STRING (SIZE(0..48))
    ACCESS      read-only
    STATUS      mandatory
    DESCRIPTION "The router name corresponding to the IPX network number."
    ::= {nlspNetMapEntry 3}

nlspNetMapID OBJECT-TYPE
    SYNTAX      NLSPID
    ACCESS      read-only
    STATUS      mandatory
    DESCRIPTION "The NLSP ID corresponding to the IPX network number."
    ::= {nlspNetMapEntry 4}


— Name Mapping Table
—   This table maps router names to their corresponding IPX network
—   number and NLSP ID.

nlspNameMapTable OBJECT-TYPE
    SYNTAX      SEQUENCE OF NLSPNameMapEntry
    ACCESS      not-accessible
    STATUS      mandatory
    DESCRIPTION "This table maps router names to the corresponding IPX
                network number and NLSP ID."
    ::= {nlspTranslation 3}

nlspNameMapEntry OBJECT-TYPE
    SYNTAX      NLSPNameMapEntry
    ACCESS      not-accessible
    STATUS      mandatory
    DESCRIPTION "Each entry maps one router name to its corresponding
                IPX network number and NLSP ID."
    INDEX       {
                nlspNameMapSysInstance,
                nlspNameMapServerName
                }
    ::= {nlspNameMapTable 1}

NLSPNameMapEntry ::= SEQUENCE {
                        nlspNameMapSysInstance
                            INTEGER,
                        nlspNameMapServerName
                            OCTET STRING,
                        nlspNameMapNetNum
                            NetNumber,
```

```
                                    nlspNameMapID
                                      NLSPID
                                  }


    nlspNameMapSysInstance OBJECT-TYPE
        SYNTAX       INTEGER
        ACCESS       read-only
        STATUS       mandatory
        DESCRIPTION "The unique identifier of the instance of NLSP and IPX
                     (via ipxSysInstance) to which this row corresponds."
        ::= {nlspNameMapEntry 1}


    nlspNameMapServerName OBJECT-TYPE
        SYNTAX       OCTET STRING (SIZE(0..48))
        ACCESS       read-only
        STATUS       mandatory
        DESCRIPTION "The readable name for this system."
        ::= {nlspNameMapEntry 2}


    nlspNameMapNetNum OBJECT-TYPE
        SYNTAX       NetNumber
        ACCESS       read-only
        STATUS       mandatory
        DESCRIPTION "The IPX network number corresponding to the router name."
        ::= {nlspNameMapEntry 3}


    nlspNameMapID OBJECT-TYPE
        SYNTAX       NLSPID
        ACCESS       read-only
        STATUS       mandatory
        DESCRIPTION "The NLSP ID corresponding to the router name.  This value
                     is undefined if the value of nlspSysState is off."
        ::= {nlspNameMapEntry 4}



    — Graph Group
    —   The Graph group provides a representation of the network topology.
    —   The group is optional.


    — Node Table
    —   The Node table contains an entry for each node in the graph.


    nlspNodeTable OBJECT-TYPE
        SYNTAX       SEQUENCE OF NLSPNodeEntry
        ACCESS       not-accessible
        STATUS       mandatory
        DESCRIPTION "The Node table contains an entry for each node in the
                     graph."
```

```
            ::= {nlspGraph 1}

nlspNodeEntry OBJECT-TYPE
    SYNTAX       NLSPNodeEntry
    ACCESS       not-accessible
    STATUS       mandatory
    DESCRIPTION "Each entry corresponds to one graph node."
    INDEX        {
                  nlspNodeSysInstance,
                  nlspNodeID
                 }
    ::= {nlspNodeTable 1}

NLSPNodeEntry ::= SEQUENCE {
                        nlspNodeSysInstance
                            INTEGER,
                        nlspNodeID
                            NLSPID,
                        nlspNodeNetNum
                            NetNumber,
                        nlspNodeType
                            INTEGER,
                        nlspNodeEstDelay
                            INTEGER,
                        nlspNodeEstThroughput
                            INTEGER,
                        nlspNodeMaxPacketSize
                            INTEGER,
                        nlspNodeCost
                            INTEGER,
                        nlspNodeOverload
                            INTEGER,
                        nlspNodeReachable
                            INTEGER
                        }

nlspNodeSysInstance OBJECT-TYPE
    SYNTAX      INTEGER
    ACCESS      read-only
    STATUS      mandatory
    DESCRIPTION "The unique identifier of the instance of NLSP and IPX
                (via ipxSysInstance) to which this row corresponds."
    ::= {nlspNodeEntry 1}

nlspNodeID OBJECT-TYPE
    SYNTAX      NLSPID
    ACCESS      read-only
    STATUS      mandatory
```

```
                DESCRIPTION "The NLSP ID for this node."
                ::= {nlspNodeEntry 2}

        nlspNodeNetNum OBJECT-TYPE
                SYNTAX      NetNumber
                ACCESS      read-only
                STATUS      mandatory
                DESCRIPTION "The IPX network number of this node."
                ::= {nlspNodeEntry 3}

        nlspNodeType OBJECT-TYPE
                SYNTAX      INTEGER {
                                    unknown(1),
                                    nlspLevel1Router(2),
                                    nlspLevel2Router(3),
                                    router(4),
                                    network(5)
                                    }
                ACCESS      read-only
                STATUS      mandatory
                DESCRIPTION "The type of system the node represents."
                ::= {nlspNodeEntry 4}

        nlspNodeEstDelay OBJECT-TYPE
                SYNTAX      INTEGER
                ACCESS      read-only
                STATUS      mandatory
                DESCRIPTION "The estimated delay, in microseconds, to reach the
                            destination represented by this node."
                ::= {nlspNodeEntry 5}

        nlspNodeEstThroughput OBJECT-TYPE
                SYNTAX      INTEGER
                ACCESS      read-only
                STATUS      mandatory
                DESCRIPTION "The estimated throughput, in bits per second, to the
                            destination represented by this node."
                ::= {nlspNodeEntry 6}

        nlspNodeMaxPacketSize OBJECT-TYPE
                SYNTAX      INTEGER
                ACCESS      read-only
                STATUS      mandatory
                DESCRIPTION "The maximum packet size, in bytes, that can be sent to
                            the destination represented by this node."
                ::= {nlspNodeEntry 7}

        nlspNodeCost OBJECT-TYPE
```

```
    SYNTAX       INTEGER
    ACCESS       read-only
    STATUS       mandatory
    DESCRIPTION  "The cost to reach this node."
    ::= {nlspNodeEntry 8}

nlspNodeOverload OBJECT-TYPE
    SYNTAX       INTEGER {
                      no(1),
                      yes(2)
                      }
    ACCESS       read-only
    STATUS       mandatory
    DESCRIPTION  "Indicates whether this node is overloaded."
    ::= {nlspNodeEntry 9}

nlspNodeReachable OBJECT-TYPE
    SYNTAX       INTEGER {
                      no(1),
                      yes(2)
                      }
    ACCESS       read-only
    STATUS       mandatory
    DESCRIPTION  "Indicates whether the destination represented by this
                 node is reachable."
    ::= {nlspNodeEntry 10}


— Link Table
—   This table contains the entries for all of the links in the graph.

nlspLinkTable OBJECT-TYPE
    SYNTAX       SEQUENCE OF NLSPLinkEntry
    ACCESS       not-accessible
    STATUS       mandatory
    DESCRIPTION  "The Link table contains entries for all of the links in
                 the graph."
    ::= {nlspGraph 2}

nlspLinkEntry OBJECT-TYPE
    SYNTAX       NLSPLinkEntry
    ACCESS       not-accessible
    STATUS       mandatory
    DESCRIPTION  "Each entry corresponds to one link."
    INDEX        {
                  nlspLinkSysInstance,
                  nlspLinkNLSPID,
                  nlspLinkIndex
```

```
                         }
              ::= {nlspLinkTable 1}

    NLSPLinkEntry ::= SEQUENCE {
                          nlspLinkSysInstance
                             INTEGER,
                          nlspLinkNLSPID
                             NLSPID,
                          nlspLinkIndex
                             INTEGER,
                          nlspLinkNeighNLSPID
                             NLSPID,
                          nlspLinkFromNeighCost
                             INTEGER,
                          nlspLinkMaxPacketSize
                             INTEGER,
                          nlspLinkThroughput
                             INTEGER,
                          nlspLinkDelay
                             INTEGER,
                          nlspLinkMediaType
                             OCTET STRING,
                          nlspLinkToNeighCost
                             INTEGER
                       }

    nlspLinkSysInstance OBJECT-TYPE
        SYNTAX      INTEGER
        ACCESS      read-only
        STATUS      mandatory
        DESCRIPTION "The unique identifier of the instance of NLSP and IPX
                    (via ipxSysInstance) to which this row corresponds."
        ::= {nlspLinkEntry 1}

    nlspLinkNLSPID OBJECT-TYPE
        SYNTAX      NLSPID
        ACCESS      read-only
        STATUS      mandatory
        DESCRIPTION "The NLSP ID (six-byte system ID plus one-octet pseudonode
                    ID) of the node to which this link belongs."
        ::= {nlspLinkEntry 2}

    nlspLinkIndex OBJECT-TYPE
        SYNTAX      INTEGER
        ACCESS      read-only
        STATUS      mandatory
        DESCRIPTION "The unique value identifying the link within the node."
```

```
    ::= {nlspLinkEntry 3}

nlspLinkNeighNLSPID OBJECT-TYPE
    SYNTAX      NLSPID
    ACCESS      read-only
    STATUS      mandatory
    DESCRIPTION "The NLSP ID (six-byte system ID plus one-octet pseudonode
                    ID) of the neighboring node."
    ::= {nlspLinkEntry 4}

nlspLinkFromNeighCost OBJECT-TYPE
    SYNTAX      INTEGER
    ACCESS      read-only
    STATUS      mandatory
    DESCRIPTION "The cost to use this link to reach this node from
                    the neighboring node."
    ::= {nlspLinkEntry 5}

nlspLinkMaxPacketSize OBJECT-TYPE
    SYNTAX      INTEGER
    ACCESS      read-only
    STATUS      mandatory
    DESCRIPTION "The maximum size, in bytes, of a packet that may be sent
                    over this link."
    ::= {nlspLinkEntry 6}

nlspLinkThroughput OBJECT-TYPE
    SYNTAX      INTEGER
    ACCESS      read-only
    STATUS      mandatory
    DESCRIPTION "The link's maximum throughput, in bits per second."
    ::= {nlspLinkEntry 7}

nlspLinkDelay OBJECT-TYPE
    SYNTAX      INTEGER
    ACCESS      read-only
    STATUS      mandatory
    DESCRIPTION "The delay, in microseconds, on this link."
    ::= {nlspLinkEntry 8}

nlspLinkMediaType OBJECT-TYPE
    SYNTAX      OCTET STRING (SIZE(2))
    ACCESS      read-only
    STATUS      mandatory
    DESCRIPTION "The media type of this link."
    ::= {nlspLinkEntry 9}

nlspLinkToNeighCost OBJECT-TYPE
```

```
        SYNTAX      INTEGER
        ACCESS      read-only
        STATUS      mandatory
        DESCRIPTION "The cost to use this link to reach the neighbor from
                    this node."
        ::= {nlspLinkEntry 10}


    — Path Table
    —    This table allows the path(s) that a packet may take to reach a
    —    destination to be reconstructed.  The entries in this table
    —    represent those links that are one hop closer to the source and
    —    would be used for the minimum cost path(s) to reach the
    —    destination.

    nlspPathTable OBJECT-TYPE
        SYNTAX      SEQUENCE OF NLSPPathEntry
        ACCESS      not-accessible
        STATUS      mandatory
        DESCRIPTION "The Path table."
        ::= {nlspGraph 3}


    nlspPathEntry OBJECT-TYPE
        SYNTAX      NLSPPathEntry
        ACCESS      not-accessible
        STATUS      mandatory
        DESCRIPTION "Each row in this table represents a link to a node that
                    is one hop closer to the source and would be used for
                    the minimum cost path(s) to reach the destination."
        INDEX       {
                    nlspPathSysInstance,
                    nlspPathDestNLSPID,
                    nlspPathLinkIndex
                    }
        ::= {nlspPathTable 1}


    NLSPPathEntry ::= SEQUENCE {
                        nlspPathSysInstance
                            INTEGER,
                        nlspPathDestNLSPID
                            NLSPID,
                        nlspPathLinkIndex
                            INTEGER
                        }


    nlspPathSysInstance OBJECT-TYPE
        SYNTAX      INTEGER
        ACCESS      read-only
```

```
    STATUS      mandatory
    DESCRIPTION "The unique identifier of the instance of NLSP and IPX
                 (via ipxSysInstance) to which this row corresponds."
    ::= {nlspPathEntry 1}


nlspPathDestNLSPID OBJECT-TYPE
    SYNTAX      NLSPID
    ACCESS      read-only
    STATUS      mandatory
    DESCRIPTION "The NLSP ID (six-octet system ID plus one-octet pseudonode
                 ID) of this destination."
    ::= {nlspPathEntry 2}


nlspPathLinkIndex OBJECT-TYPE
    SYNTAX      INTEGER
    ACCESS      read-only
    STATUS      mandatory
    DESCRIPTION "The unique value identifying this link within the
                 destination node."
    ::= {nlspPathEntry 3}



— Graph XRoutes Table
—   This table contains information about all of the XRoutes provided by
—   a node in the graph.

nlspGraphXRouteTable OBJECT-TYPE
    SYNTAX      SEQUENCE OF NLSPGraphXRouteEntry
    ACCESS      not-accessible
    STATUS      mandatory
    DESCRIPTION "This table contains the information about the XRoutes
                 associated with a node in the graph."
    ::= {nlspGraph 4}


nlspGraphXRouteEntry OBJECT-TYPE
    SYNTAX      NLSPGraphXRouteEntry
    ACCESS      not-accessible
    STATUS      mandatory
    DESCRIPTION "Each entry in the table contains the information for one
                 XRoute associated with the node."
    INDEX       {
                  nlspGraphXRouteSysInstance,
                  nlspGraphXRouteNLSPID,
                  nlspGraphXRouteNetNum
                }
    ::= {nlspGraphXRouteTable 1}


NLSPGraphXRouteEntry ::= SEQUENCE {
```

```
                                nlspGraphXRouteSysInstance
                                    INTEGER,
                                nlspGraphXRouteNLSPID
                                    NLSPID,
                                nlspGraphXRouteNetNum
                                    NetNumber,
                                nlspGraphXRouteCost
                                    INTEGER,
                                nlspGraphXRouteHopCount
                                    INTEGER
                            }

        nlspGraphXRouteSysInstance OBJECT-TYPE
            SYNTAX      INTEGER
            ACCESS      read-only
            STATUS      mandatory
            DESCRIPTION "The unique identifier of the instance of NLSP and IPX
                        (via ipxSysInstance) to which this entry corresponds."
            ::= {nlspGraphXRouteEntry 1}


        nlspGraphXRouteNLSPID OBJECT-TYPE
            SYNTAX      NLSPID
            ACCESS      read-only
            STATUS      mandatory
            DESCRIPTION "The NLSP ID of the node."
            ::= {nlspGraphXRouteEntry 2}


        nlspGraphXRouteNetNum OBJECT-TYPE
            SYNTAX      NetNumber
            ACCESS      read-only
            STATUS      mandatory
            DESCRIPTION "The IPX network number of the XRoute's destination."
            ::= {nlspGraphXRouteEntry 3}


        nlspGraphXRouteCost OBJECT-TYPE
            SYNTAX      INTEGER
            ACCESS      read-only
            STATUS      mandatory
            DESCRIPTION "The cost to reach the XRoute's destination."
            ::= {nlspGraphXRouteEntry 4}


        nlspGraphXRouteHopCount OBJECT-TYPE
            SYNTAX      INTEGER
            ACCESS      read-only
            STATUS      mandatory
            DESCRIPTION "The number of hops necessary to reach the XRoute's
                        destination."
            ::= {nlspGraphXRouteEntry 5}
```

— Graph Services Table
—   This table contains information about all of the services provided by
—   a node in the graph.

```
nlspGraphServTable OBJECT-TYPE
    SYNTAX      SEQUENCE OF NLSPGraphServEntry
    ACCESS      not-accessible
    STATUS      mandatory
    DESCRIPTION "This table contains the information about the services
                 associated with a node in the graph."
    ::= {nlspGraph 5}

nlspGraphServEntry OBJECT-TYPE
    SYNTAX      NLSPGraphServEntry
    ACCESS      not-accessible
    STATUS      mandatory
    DESCRIPTION "Each entry in the table contains the information for one
                 service associated with the node."
    INDEX       {
                  nlspGraphServSysInstance,
                  nlspGraphServNLSPID,
                  nlspGraphServName,
                  nlspGraphServTypeValue
                }
    ::= {nlspGraphServTable 1}

NLSPGraphServEntry ::= SEQUENCE {
                          nlspGraphServSysInstance
                              INTEGER,
                          nlspGraphServNLSPID
                              NLSPID,
                          nlspGraphServName
                              OCTET STRING,
                          nlspGraphServTypeValue
                              OCTET STRING,
                          nlspGraphServType
                              INTEGER,
                          nlspGraphServNetNum
                              NetNumber,
                          nlspGraphServNode
                              OCTET STRING,
                          nlspGraphServSocket
                              OCTET STRING
                        }

nlspGraphServSysInstance OBJECT-TYPE
```

```
SYNTAX       INTEGER
ACCESS       read-only
STATUS       mandatory
DESCRIPTION "The unique identifier of the instance of NLSP and IPX
             (via ipxSysInstance) to which this entry corresponds."
::= {nlspGraphServEntry 1}

nlspGraphServNLSPID OBJECT-TYPE
SYNTAX       NLSPID
ACCESS       read-only
STATUS       mandatory
DESCRIPTION "The NLSP ID of the node."
::= {nlspGraphServEntry 2}

nlspGraphServName OBJECT-TYPE
SYNTAX       OCTET STRING (SIZE(1..48))
ACCESS       read-only
STATUS       mandatory
DESCRIPTION "The service name."
::= {nlspGraphServEntry 3}

nlspGraphServTypeValue OBJECT-TYPE
SYNTAX       OCTET STRING (SIZE(2))
ACCESS       read-only
STATUS       mandatory
DESCRIPTION "The service type's hexadecimal value."
::= {nlspGraphServEntry 4}

nlspGraphServType OBJECT-TYPE
SYNTAX       INTEGER {
                    unknown(1)
                    }
ACCESS       read-only
STATUS       mandatory
DESCRIPTION "The service type."
::= {nlspGraphServEntry 5}

nlspGraphServNetNum OBJECT-TYPE
SYNTAX       NetNumber
ACCESS       read-only
STATUS       mandatory
DESCRIPTION "The IPX network number portion of the IPX address of
             the service."
::= {nlspGraphServEntry 6}

nlspGraphServNode OBJECT-TYPE
SYNTAX       OCTET STRING (SIZE(6))
ACCESS       read-only
```

```
    STATUS      mandatory
    DESCRIPTION "The node portion of the IPX address of the service."
    ::= {nlspGraphServEntry 7}


nlspGraphServSocket OBJECT-TYPE
    SYNTAX      OCTET STRING (SIZE(2))
    ACCESS      read-only
    STATUS      mandatory
    DESCRIPTION "The socket portion of the IPX address of the service."
    ::= {nlspGraphServEntry 8}



—  LSP Group
—    The LSP group provides a representation of NLSP's LSP database.  This
—    group is optional.


—  LSP Header Table
—    The LSP Header table contains summary information about each LSP
—    in the database as well as an OCTET STRING containing the entire
—    LSP header.


nlspLSPTable OBJECT-TYPE
    SYNTAX      SEQUENCE OF NLSPLSPEntry
    ACCESS      not-accessible
    STATUS      mandatory
    DESCRIPTION "The LSP Header table."
    ::= {nlspLSP 1}


nlspLSPEntry OBJECT-TYPE
    SYNTAX      NLSPLSPEntry
    ACCESS      not-accessible
    STATUS      mandatory
    DESCRIPTION "Each entry corresponds to one LSP's header."
    INDEX       {
                 nlspLSPSysInstance,
                 nlspLSPID
                 }
    ::= {nlspLSPTable 1}


NLSPLSPEntry ::= SEQUENCE {
                        nlspLSPSysInstance
                            INTEGER,
                        nlspLSPID
                            OCTET STRING,
                        nlspLSPLifetime
                            INTEGER,
                        nlspLSPSeqNum
                            INTEGER,
```

```
                        nlspLSPChecksum
                            INTEGER,
                        nlspLSPRouterType
                            INTEGER,
                        nlspLSPOverload
                            INTEGER,
                        nlspLSPHeader
                            OCTET STRING
                    }

    nlspLSPSysInstance OBJECT-TYPE
        SYNTAX      INTEGER
        ACCESS      read-only
        STATUS      mandatory
        DESCRIPTION "The unique identifier for the instance of NLSP and IPX
                    (via ipxSysInstance) to which this entry corresponds."
        ::= {nlspLSPEntry 1}


    nlspLSPID OBJECT-TYPE
        SYNTAX      OCTET STRING (SIZE(8))
        ACCESS      read-only
        STATUS      mandatory
        DESCRIPTION "The value that uniquely identifies this LSP."
        ::= {nlspLSPEntry 2}


    nlspLSPLifetime OBJECT-TYPE
        SYNTAX      INTEGER (0..65535)
        ACCESS      read-only
        STATUS      mandatory
        DESCRIPTION "The number of seconds prior to the expiration of the
                    LSP."
        ::= {nlspLSPEntry 3}


    nlspLSPSeqNum OBJECT-TYPE
        SYNTAX      INTEGER (0..255)
        ACCESS      read-only
        STATUS      mandatory
        DESCRIPTION "The sequence number of the LSP."
        ::= {nlspLSPEntry 4}


    nlspLSPChecksum OBJECT-TYPE
        SYNTAX      INTEGER (0..65535)
        ACCESS      read-only
        STATUS      mandatory
        DESCRIPTION "The checksum value of the LSP."
        ::= {nlspLSPEntry 5}


    nlspLSPRouterType OBJECT-TYPE
```

. . . . .

```
SYNTAX        INTEGER {
                      unknown(1),
                      nlspLevel1Router(2)
                      }
ACCESS        read-only
STATUS        mandatory
DESCRIPTION "The type of the router that sent the LSP."
::= {nlspLSPEntry 6}

nlspLSPOverload OBJECT-TYPE
SYNTAX        INTEGER {
                      no(1),
                      yes(2)
                      }
ACCESS        read-only
STATUS        mandatory
DESCRIPTION "Indicates whether the sending router's LSP database is
              overloaded."
::= {nlspLSPEntry 7}

nlspLSPHeader OBJECT-TYPE
SYNTAX        OCTET STRING (SIZE(27))
ACCESS        read-only
STATUS        mandatory
DESCRIPTION "The complete LSP header."
::= {nlspLSPEntry 8}


— LSP Options Table
—     The LSP Options table is used to obtain each option contained in
—     an LSP.

nlspLSPOptTable OBJECT-TYPE
SYNTAX        SEQUENCE OF NLSPLSPOptEntry
ACCESS        not-accessible
STATUS        mandatory
DESCRIPTION "The LSP Options table."
::= {nlspLSP 2}

nlspLSPOptEntry OBJECT-TYPE
SYNTAX        NLSPLSPOptEntry
ACCESS        not-accessible
STATUS        mandatory
DESCRIPTION "Each entry corresponds to one option from an LSP."
INDEX         {
                 nlspLSPOptSysInstance,
                 nlspLSPOptLSPID,
                 nlspLSPOptIndex
                 }
```

```
            ::= {nlspLSPOptTable 1}

    NLSPLSPOptEntry ::= SEQUENCE {
                            nlspLSPOptSysInstance
                                INTEGER,
                            nlspLSPOptLSPID
                                OCTET STRING,
                            nlspLSPOptIndex
                                INTEGER,
                            nlspLSPOptCode
                                INTEGER,
                            nlspLSPOptLength
                                INTEGER,
                            nlspLSPOptValue
                                OCTET STRING
                            }

    nlspLSPOptSysInstance OBJECT-TYPE
        SYNTAX      INTEGER
        ACCESS      read-only
        STATUS      mandatory
        DESCRIPTION "The unique identifier of the instance of NLSP and IPX
                    (via ipxSysInstance) to which this entry corresponds."
        ::= {nlspLSPOptEntry 1}

    nlspLSPOptLSPID OBJECT-TYPE
        SYNTAX      OCTET STRING (SIZE(8))
        ACCESS      read-only
        STATUS      mandatory
        DESCRIPTION "The value that uniquely identifies the LSP."
        ::= {nlspLSPOptEntry 2}

    nlspLSPOptIndex OBJECT-TYPE
        SYNTAX      INTEGER
        ACCESS      read-only
        STATUS      mandatory
        DESCRIPTION "The value that uniquely identifies this option within the
                    LSP."
        ::= {nlspLSPOptEntry 3}

    nlspLSPOptCode OBJECT-TYPE
        SYNTAX      INTEGER (0..255)
        ACCESS      read-only
        STATUS      mandatory
        DESCRIPTION "The code that identifies the type of the option."
        ::= {nlspLSPOptEntry 4}

    nlspLSPOptLength OBJECT-TYPE
```

```
    SYNTAX      INTEGER (0..255)
    ACCESS      read-only
    STATUS      mandatory
    DESCRIPTION "The length of the option's value field."
    ::= {nlspLSPOptEntry 5}

nlspLSPOptValue OBJECT-TYPE
    SYNTAX      OCTET STRING (SIZE(0..255))
    ACCESS      read-only
    STATUS      mandatory
    DESCRIPTION "The option's value field."
    ::= {nlspLSPOptEntry 6}

END
```

# SAP Number List

| 0000 | UNKNOWN | |
|------|---------|---|
| 0001 | USER | NOVELL - PROVO   CORP HQ |
| 0002 | USER GROUP | NOVELL - PROVO   CORP HQ |
| 0003 | PRINT QUEUE OR PRINT GROUP | NOVELL - PROVO CORP HQ |
| 0004 | FILE SERVER (SLIST SOURCE) | NOVELL - PROVO CORP HQ |
| 0005 | JOB SERVER | NOVELL - PROVO CORP HQ |
| 0006 | GATEWAY | NOVELL - PROVO CORP HQ |
| 0007 | PRINT SERVER OR SILENT PRINT SERVER | NOVELL - PROVO CORP HQ |
| 0008 | ARCHIVE QUEUE | NOVELL - PROVO CORP HQ |
| 0009 | ARCHIVE SERVER | NOVELL - PROVO CORP HQ |
| 000A | JOB QUEUE | NOVELL - PROVO CORP HQ |
| 000B | ADMINISTRATION | NOVELL - PROVO CORP HQ |
| 0017 | DIAGNOSTICS | |
| 0020 | NetBIOS | |
| 0021 | NAS SNA GATEWAY | |
| 0022 | | SPERRY CORP. COMPUTER SYSTEMS |
| 0023 | NACS ASYNC GATEWAY OR ASYNCHRONOUS GATEWAY | |
| 0024* | REMOTE BRIDGE SERVER | NOVELL - PROVO   CORP HQ |
| 0026* | BRIDGE SERVER OR ASYNCHRONOUS BRIDGE SERVER | |
| 0028 | POINT-POINT | EICON TECHNOLOGY |
| 0029 | MULTI-POINT | EICON TECHNOLOGY |
| 002C | | INTEL - AMERICAN FORK |
| 002E | TARGET SERVICE AGENT | NOVELL - PROVO   CORP HQ |
| 002D | TIME SYNCHRONIZATION VAP | NOVELL - PROVO   CORP HQ |
| 002A | | CHI CORP |
| 0047 | ADVERTISING PRINT SERVER | NOVELL - PROVO   CORP HQ |
| 0048 | TCP/IP GATEWAY | MICOM INTERLAN |
| 0049 | | BUSINESS RECORDS CORP |
| 004A | | PARADATA COMPUTER NETWORKS |
| 004D | XTREE-NET - MVD FRM 23539-00111-12-93 | CENTRAL POINT SOFTWARE |
| 0050 | BTRIEVE VAP 4.11 | NOVELL - PROVO   CORP HQ |
| 0053 | MAC PROJECT | NOVELL - PROVO   CORP HQ |
| 0054 | VALUE ADDED FILE SYSTEM | NOVELL - PROVO   CORP HQ |
| 0055 | TERM EMULATOR | SYSTEMS ANALYSIS INC |
| 0056 | STOCKNET BROKER SAP TYPE | NOVELL - PROVO |
| 0057 | STOCKNET EXCHANGER SAP TYPE | NOVELL - PROVO |
| 0058 | MULTI-POINT X.25 | EICON TECHNOLOGY |
| 005A | | BUSINESS RECORDS CORP |
| 005B | | BUSINESS RECORDS CORP |
| 005C | | BUSINESS RECORDS CORP |
| 005D | | BUSINESS RECORDS CORP |

| | | |
|---|---|---|
| 005E | | BUSINESS RECORDS CORP |
| 005F | | BUSINESS RECORDS CORP |
| 0060 | STOCKNET BROKER - STATIC | NOVELL - PROVO |
| 0061 | STOCKNET QUEUE TYPE | NOVELL - PROVO |
| 0062 | STOCKNET PLAYER TYPE | NOVELL - PROVO |
| 0063 | | INTERACTIVE FINANCIAL SOL INC |
| 0064 | | INTERACTIVE FINANCIAL SOL INC |
| 0065 | | INTERACTIVE FINANCIAL SOL INC |
| 0066 | | INTERACTIVE FINANCIAL SOL INC |
| 0067 | | INTERACTIVE FINANCIAL SOL INC |
| 0068 | | INTERACTIVE FINANCIAL SOL INC |
| 0069 | | INTERACTIVE FINANCIAL SOL INC |
| 006A | | INTERACTIVE FINANCIAL SOL INC |
| 006B | | INTERACTIVE FINANCIAL SOL INC |
| 006C | | INTERACTIVE FINANCIAL SOL INC |
| 006D | STOCKNET EXCHANGE - STATIC | NOVELL - PROVO  CORP HQ |
| 006E | NACS | NETPRO INC |
| 006F | MVD FRM 31137 4-19-94 | RABBIT SOFTWARE CORP |
| 0070 | MIC SNA DFV SERVER | COMPUTERLAND - BONN |
| 0071 | TAPE DRIVE SERVER | DIGI DATA CORP |
| 0072 | WANCOPY UTILITY | NOVELL - PROVO  CORP HQ |
| 0073 | | NOVELL - PROVO  CORP HQ |
| 0074 | | NOVELL - PROVO  CORP HQ |
| 0075 | NETWARE BTRIEVE | NOVELL - PROVO  CORP HQ |
| 0076 | NETWARE SQL | NOVELL - PROVO  CORP HQ |
| 0077 | | NOVELL - PROVO  CORP HQ |
| 0078 | | NOVELL - PROVO  CORP HQ |
| 0079 | | NOVELL - PROVO  CORP HQ |
| 007A | TES - NETWARE VMS | NOVELL - PROVO  CORP HQ |
| 007B | CHGD FRM #31270-901, 12-29-93 | MERGENT INTERNATIONAL |
| 007C | | INTERACTIVE FINANCIAL SOL INC |
| 007D | | INTERACTIVE FINANCIAL SOL INC |
| 007E | | INTERACTIVE FINANCIAL SOL INC |
| 007F | | INTERACTIVE FINANCIAL SOL INC |
| 0080 | | INTERACTIVE FINANCIAL SOL INC |
| 0081 | | INTERACTIVE FINANCIAL SOL INC |
| 0082 | | INTERACTIVE FINANCIAL SOL INC |
| 0083 | | INTERACTIVE FINANCIAL SOL INC |
| 0084 | | INTERACTIVE FINANCIAL SOL INC |
| 0085 | | INTERACTIVE FINANCIAL SOL INC |
| 0086 | | INTERACTIVE FINANCIAL SOL INC |
| 0087 | | INTERACTIVE FINANCIAL SOL INC |
| 0088 | | INTERACTIVE FINANCIAL SOL INC |
| 0089 | | INTERACTIVE FINANCIAL SOL INC |
| 008A | | INTERACTIVE FINANCIAL SOL INC |
| 008B | | INTERACTIVE FINANCIAL SOL INC |

| | | |
|---|---|---|
| 008C | | INTERACTIVE FINANCIAL SOL INC |
| 008D | MAIL SERVER | MCGILL UNIVERSITY |
| 008E | RATIONAL DATA SYSTEMS008F | TATE ASSOCIATES INC |
| | - QUEUE TYPES | |
| 0090 | TNET X.21 IDA BRIDGE | BRITISH TELECOM |
| 0091 | TNET X.21 BRIDGE | BRITISH TELECOM |
| 0093 | | WATCOM |
| 0094 | SILA COM SOFTWARE | NOVELL - PROVO |
| 0095 | VMS ROUTER CONTROL | INTERCONNECTIONS |
| 0096 | | MICRO DATA BASE SYSTEMS |
| 0097 | DART | COLLEGE HILL SYSTEMS |
| 0098 | NETWARE ACCESS SERVER | NOVELL - PROVO  CORP HQ |
| 0099 | NETWORK COURIER | MICROSOFT WORKGROUP CANADA |
| 009A | NAMED PIPES SERVER | NOVELL - PROVO |
| 009B | JOB SERVER | DIS INC |
| 009C | RAYLYNN KNIGHT | |
| 009D | CQ3270 LAN | CQ COMPUTER COMMUNICATIONS |
| 009E | UNIX - PORTABLE GROUP | NOVELL - PROVO  CORP HQ |
| 009F | PROGRESS DATABASE | PROGRESS SOFTWARE CORP |
| 00A0 | GUPTA SQL BASE SERVER | GUPTA TECHNOLOGIES |
| 00A1 | POWERCHUTE—VAP/NLM | AMERICAN POWER CONVERSION |
| | SERVER POWER SUPPLY | |
| 00A2 | AUDITOR PACKAGE | BLUE LANCE NETWORK INFO SYS |
| 00A3 | SECURITY | BLUE LANCE NETWORK INFO SYS |
| 00A4 | COREL DRIVER PRODUCT | COREL SYSTEMS, OPTICAL DIV |
| | UNDER NOVELL 386 | |
| 00A5 | ARCHIVE SERVER | GIGATREND INC |
| 00A6 | MENU PROGRAM | R&S DATA SYSTEMS |
| 00A7 | 386 NLM | UNISYS - CAMARILLO |
| 00A8 | LAN 1 ROUTER | ATLANTA TECHNOLOGIES |
| 00A9 | OBJECT TYPE | COREL SYSTEMS, OPTICAL DIV |
| 00AA | OBJECT | COREL SYSTEMS, OPTICAL DIV |
| 00AC | IDA STATUS UTIL - | COMPAQ COMPUTER CORP |
| | MVD FRM 31905, 5-29-92 | |
| 00AD | LANPORT VIRTUAL | MICROTEST INC |
| | EXTENSION OF PORTS | |
| 0100 | | PEER LOGIC |
| 0101 | | R21PX CROSSTALK |
| 0102 | | INTEL - AMERICAN FORK |
| 0103 | SEQUELNET | ORACLE CORP |
| 0105 | GATEWAY TO UNISYS | MARSHFIELD CLINIC |
| 0106 | GATEWAYS TO UNISYS | MARSHFIELD CLINIC |
| 0107 | 386 NETWARE | NOVELL - PROVO  CORP HQ |
| 010C | NET 3270 | MCGILL UNIVERSITY COMPUTING CT |
| 010F | SAP | NOVELL - PROVO  CORP HQ |
| 0110 | | ARTEFACT NETWORK SUPPORT |
| 0112 | PRINT SERVER | HEWLETT PACKARD - BOISE |
| 0113 | COMMUNICATION SERVER | NOVELL - PROVO  CORP HQ |

| | | |
|---|---|---|
| 0114 | COMMUNICATION SERVER | NOVELL - PROVO CORP HQ |
| 0115 | COMMUNICATION SERVER | NOVELL - PROVO CORP HQ |
| 0116 | COMMUNICATION SERVER | NOVELL - PROVO CORP HQ |
| 0117 | COMMUNICATION SERVER | NOVELL - PROVO CORP HQ |
| 0118 | COMMUNICATION SERVER | NOVELL - PROVO CORP HQ |
| 0119 | COMMUNICATION SERVER | NOVELL - PROVO CORP HQ |
| 011A | COMMUNICATION SERVER | NOVELL - PROVO CORP HQ |
| 011B | COMMUNICATION SERVER | NOVELL - PROVO CORP HQ |
| 011C | SAA DATA LINK AGENT | NOVELL - PROVO CORP HQ |
| 011D | COMMUNICATION SERVER | NOVELL - PROVO CORP HQ |
| 012C | COMMUNICATION SERVER | NOVELL - PROVO CORP HQ |
| 011E | COMMUNICATION SERVER | NOVELL - PROVO CORP HQ |
| 011F | COMMUNICATION SERVER | NOVELL - PROVO CORP HQ |
| 0120 | COMMUNICATION SERVER | NOVELL - PROVO CORP HQ |
| 0121 | COMMUNICATION SERVER | NOVELL - PROVO CORP HQ |
| 0122 | COMMUNICATION SERVER | NOVELL - PROVO CORP HQ |
| 0123 | COMMUNICATION SERVER | NOVELL - PROVO CORP HQ |
| 0124 | COMMUNICATION SERVER | NOVELL - PROVO CORP HQ |
| 0125 | COMMUNICATION SERVER | NOVELL - PROVO CORP HQ |
| 0126 | COMMUNICATION SERVER | NOVELL - PROVO CORP HQ |
| 0127 | COMMUNICATION SERVER | NOVELL - PROVO CORP HQ |
| 0128 | COMMUNICATION SERVER | NOVELL - PROVO CORP HQ |
| 0129 | COMMUNICATION SERVER | NOVELL - PROVO CORP HQ |
| 012A | COMMUNICATION SERVER | NOVELL - PROVO CORP HQ |
| 012B | SUPER SNA AGENT | NOVELL - PROVO CORP HQ |
| 012D | COMMUNICATIONS SERVER | NOVELL - PROVO CORP HQ |
| 012E | COMMUNICATIONS SERVER | NOVELL - PROVO CORP HQ |
| 012F | COMMUNICATIONS SERVER | NOVELL - PROVO CORP HQ |
| 0130 | COMMUNICATIONS SERVER | NOVELL - PROVO CORP HQ |
| 0132 | BT X.25 | BRITISH TELECOM |
| 013F | | NETWORK DESIGNERS LTD |
| 0140 | NETWORK MANAGEMENT SYSTEM | ACCUNETICS |
| 0141 | SOFTWARE GMBH | LUFTHANSA INFORMATION SERVICE |
| 0143 | CDROM | ONLINE COMPUTER SYSTEMS |
| 0144 | | NETWISE INC |
| 0145 | COMMUNICATION PROCESSOR | EVERGREEN SYSTEMS |
| 0147 | PIGGYBACK LOGIN NET_INC | MICRO ENHANCEMENT INC |
| 0149 | ADVERTISING REMOTE SERVER | ARTEFACT NETWORK SUPPORT |
| 014A | ID 5001 WEATHER STATION | ZENITH DATA SYSTEMS |
| 014B | | NOVELL - PROVO CORP HQ |
| 0151 | DCS SYSTEM SERVER | COMPUTER CONCEPTS CORPORATION |
| 0154 | FORMS CAPABILITY | ROCHESTER TELEPHONE CORP |
| 0155 | FORMS CAPABILITY | ROCHESTER TELEPHONE CORP |
| 0156 | FORMS CAPABILITY | ROCHESTER TELEPHONE CORP |
| 0157 | FORMS CAPABILITY | ROCHESTER TELEPHONE CORP |
| 0158 | FORMS CAPABILITY | ROCHESTER TELEPHONE CORP |
| 0159 | FORMS CAPABILITY | ROCHESTER TELEPHONE CORP |
| 015A | FORMS CAPABILITY | ROCHESTER TELEPHONE CORP |

| | | |
|---|---|---|
| 015B | FORMS CAPABILITY | ROCHESTER TELEPHONE CORP |
| 015C | | NETWORK COMPUTING INC - NCI |
| 015D | | NETWORK COMPUTING INC - NCI |
| 015E | | NETWORK COMPUTING INC - NCI |
| 015F | | NETWORK COMPUTING INC - NCI |
| 0160 | | NETWORK COMPUTING INC - NCI |
| 0161 | ADVERTISING REMOTE SERVER | ARTEFACT NETWORK SUPPORT |
| 0162 | SYSTEM 9 | HBF GROUP |
| 0163 | SYSTEM 9 | HBF GROUP |
| 0164 | SYSTEM 9 | HBF GROUP |
| 0165 | SYSTEM 9 | HBF GROUP |
| 0166 | NW MANAGEMENT | NOVELL - PROVO |
| 0168 | PICKIT (COMM SERVER) | INTEL |
| 0169 | | PEER LOGIC |
| 0170 | TXD | THOMAS CONRAD CORP |
| 0171 | LANFAX REDIRECTOR | ALCOM INC |
| 0172 | FILE SHARE | COMPAQ COMPUTER CORP |
| 0173 | FILE SHARE | COMPAQ COMPUTER CORP |
| 0174 | FILE SHARE | COMPAQ COMPUTER CORP |
| 0175 | FILE SHARE | COMPAQ COMPUTER CORP |
| 0176 | FILE SHARE | COMPAQ COMPUTER CORP |
| 0177 | LANWARE Mvd frm #12638-7, 1-20-92 | HORIZON TECHNOLOGY INC |
| 0178 | LANWARE Mvd frm #12638-7, 1-20-92 | HORIZON TECHNOLOGY INC |
| 0179 | LANWARE Mvd frm #12638-7, 1-20-92 | HORIZON TECHNOLOGY INC |
| 017A | LANWARE Mvd frm #12638-7, 1-20-92 | HORIZON TECHNOLOGY INC |
| 017B | LANWARE Mvd frm #12638-7, 1-20-92 | HORIZON TECHNOLOGY INC |
| 017C | LANWARE Mvd frm #12638-7, 1-20-92 | HORIZON TECHNOLOGY INC |
| 017D | LANWARE Mvd frm #12638-7, 1-20-92 | HORIZON TECHNOLOGY INC |
| 017E | LANWARE Mvd frm #12638-7, 1-20-92 | HORIZON TECHNOLOGY INC |
| 017F | LANWARE Mvd frm #12638-7, 1-20-92 | HORIZON TECHNOLOGY INC |
| 0188 | SYSM/LAN2 | H&W COMPUTER SYSTEMS |
| 0189 | XTREE SERVR - MVD FRM 23539-001 11-12-93 | CENTRAL POINT SOFTWARE |
| 018E | PC METRO | CRYSTAL POINT |
| 018F | PC METRO | CRYSTAL POINT |
| 0190 | SERVICE POINT | INTERPOINT SOFTWARE |
| 0191 | SERVICE POINT | INTERPOINT SOFTWARE |
| 0192 | NETWAY 2000 | TRI DATA SYSTEMS |

| | | |
|---|---|---|
| 0193 | NETWAY SNA | TRI DATA SYSTEMS |
| 0194 | MAXWAY 500 | TRI DATA SYSTEMS |
| 0195 | TCP/IP GATEWAY | COMPUTERVISION SERVICES |
| 0196 | | INTEGRATED TECHNOLOGIES INC |
| 0197 | SHARE MASTER | STORAGE DIMENSIONS |
| 0198 | | ZENITH DATA SYSTEMS |
| 0199 | | ZENITH DATA SYSTEMS |
| 019A | | ZENITH DATA SYSTEMS |
| 019B | APT NET REMOTE | AUTOMATED PROGRAMMING TECH |
| 019C | APT NET REMOTE | AUTOMATED PROGRAMMING TECH |
| 019D | APT NET REMOTE | AUTOMATED PROGRAMMING TECH |
| 019E | APT NET REMOTE | AUTOMATED PROGRAMMING TECH |
| 019F | MAILSLOTS (Chgd from 08840-134 10-21-91) | IBM - FRANKLIN LAKES |
| 01A1 | DB SERVER | LODGISTIX INC |
| 01A2 | SPARE | LODGISTIX INC |
| 01A3 | GATEWAY, COMPOSITE PAGE, & ETC SERVERS | TEKNOS SYSTEMS |
| 01A4 | GATEWAY, COMPOSITE PAGE, & ETC SERVERS | TEKNOS SYSTEMS |
| 01A5 | GATEWAY, COMPOSITE PAGE, & ETC SERVERS | TEKNOS SYSTEMS |
| 01A6 | GATEWAY, COMPOSITE PAGE, & ETC SERVERS | TEKNOS SYSTEMS |
| 01A7 | GATEWAY, COMPOSITE PAGE, & ETC SERVERS | TEKNOS SYSTEMS |
| 01A8 | GATEWAY, COMPOSITE PAGE, & ETC SERVERS | TEKNOS SYSTEMS |
| 01A9 | GATEWAY, COMPOSITE PAGE, & ETC SERVERS | TEKNOS SYSTEMS |
| 01AA | GATEWAY, COMPOSITE PAGE, & ETC SERVERS | TEKNOS SYSTEMS |
| 01AB | GATEWAY, COMPOSITE PAGE, & ETC SERVERS | TEKNOS SYSTEMS |
| 01AC | GATEWAY, COMPOSITE PAGE, & ETC SERVERS | TEKNOS SYSTEMS |
| 01AD | MENU PROGRAM | R&S DATA SYSTEMS |
| 01AE | MENU PROGRAM | R&S DATA SYSTEMS |
| 01B0 | OBJECT TYPE FOR GARP SERVER | NET RESEARCH PTY LTD |
| 01B1 | LICENSING RESTRICTIONS/ BINDERY TYPE | LAN SUPPORT GROUP, NETWORK RES |
| 01B2 | LICENSING RESTRICTIONS/ BINDERY TYPE | LAN SUPPORT GROUP, NETWORK RES |
| 01B3 | | MEDIA TOUCH SYSTEMS |
| 01B4 | NETWORK MANAGEMENT PRODUCT | NCR - COLUMBIA |

| | | |
|---|---|---|
| 01B5 | NETWORK MANAGEMENT PRODUCT | NCR - COLUMBIA |
| 01B6 | NETWORK MANAGEMENT PRODUCT | NCR - COLUMBIA |
| 01B7 | NETWORK MANAGEMENT PRODUCT | NCR - COLUMBIA |
| 01B8 | NETWORK MANAGEMENT PRODUCT | NCR - COLUMBIA |
| 01B9 | | BONSAI TECHNOLOGIES |
| 01BB | | BONSAI TECHNOLOGIES |
| 01BC | | BONSAI TECHNOLOGIES |
| 01BD | | BONSAI TECHNOLOGIES |
| 01BE | SERVER TYPE | KM SYSTEMS |
| 01C0 | OBJECT TYPE | LA CITE COLLEGIALE |
| 01C1 | OBJECT TYPES | J&L INFORMATION SYSTEMS |
| 01C2 | OBJECT TYPES | J&L INFORMATION SYSTEMS |
| 01C3 | OBJECT TYPES | J&L INFORMATION SYSTEMS |
| 01C4 | OBJECT TYPES | J&L INFORMATION SYSTEMS |
| 01C5 | OBJECT TYPES | J&L INFORMATION SYSTEMS |
| 01C6 | DISTRIBUTED APPLICATION | FOLIO CORPORATION |
| 01C7 | BINDERY TYPE | MICROTEST INC |
| 01C8 | OBJECT BINDERY TYPE | MADGE NETWORKS LTD |
| 01C9 | OBJECT TYPES | FUNK SOFTWARE |
| 01CA | OBJECT TYPES | FUNK SOFTWARE |
| 01CB | | SHIVA CORP |
| 01CC | | SHIVA CORP |
| 01CD | | SHIVA CORP |
| 01CE | | SHIVA CORP |
| 01CF | E-MAIL QUEUE OBJECT-TYPE | C&D DATA SERVICES |
| 01D0 | E-MAIL SERVER OBJECT-TYPE | C&D DATA SERVICES |
| 01D1 | LANLORD PRODUCT | MICROCOM CLIENT SERVER TECHNOL |
| 01D5 | | CENTERS FOR DISEASE CONTROL |
| 01D6 | ON-QUEUE TASK QUEUE | NETPLUS SOFTWARE INC |
| 01D7 | ON-QUEUE TASK SERVER | NETPLUS SOFTWARE INC |
| 01D8 | | CASTELLE INC |
| 01D9 | | CASTELLE INC |
| 01DA | | CASTELLE INC |
| 01DB | | CASTELLE INC |
| 01DC | | CASTELLE INC |
| 01DD | | CASTELLE INC |
| 01DE | | CASTELLE INC |
| 01DF | | CASTELLE INC |
| 01E0 | | CASTELLE INC |
| 01E1 | | CASTELLE INC |
| 01E2 | AREA CODE & EXCHANGE LOOK-UP SERVER | EQUINOX INFORMATION SYSTEMS |
| 01E3 | SORTING SERVER | EQUINOX INFORMATION SYSTEMS |
| 01E4 | | WALL DATA |

| | | | |
|---|---|---|---|
| 01E7 | | RATIONAL DATA SYSTEMS | |
| 01E8 | | RATIONAL DATA SYSTEMS | |
| 01E9 | | RATIONAL DATA SYSTEMS | |
| 01EA | | RATIONAL DATA SYSTEMS | |
| 01EB | | MEDIA TOUCH SYSTEMS | |
| 01ED | | INTEGRALIS LTD | |
| 01EE | | INTEGRALIS LTD | |
| 01EF | | FELSINA SOFTWARE | |
| 01F0 | | LEGATO SYSTEMS | |
| 01F1 | | LEGATO SYSTEMS | |
| 01F2 | | LEGATO SYSTEMS | |
| 01F3 | | LEGATO SYSTEMS | |
| 01F4 | | LEGATO SYSTEMS | |
| 01F5 | | LEGATO SYSTEMS | |
| 01F6 | | ANDERSEN CONSULTING - CHICAGO | |
| 01F8 | | SYTRON CORP | |
| 01F9 | FOR UNIBASE BV, BASED IN HOLLAND | INTEGRALIS LTD | |
| 01FB | | NORTHEAST BROADCAST CONSULTANT | |
| 01FC | | EXTENDED SYSTEMS | |
| 01FD | | IBM - ENDICOTT | |
| 0200 | NP/SQL SERVER | NOVELL - PROVO | |
| 0201 | THE MAKE SERVER | NOVELL - PROVO | |
| 0202 | GENERIC JOB SERVER | NOVELL - PROVO | CORP HQ |
| 0204 | | NOVELL - PROVO | CORP HQ |
| 0205 | | NOVELL - PROVO | CORP HQ |
| 0206 | | NOVELL - PROVO | CORP HQ |
| 0207 | | NOVELL - PROVO | CORP HQ |
| 0208 | | NOVELL - PROVO | CORP HQ |
| 0209 | | NOVELL - PROVO | CORP HQ |
| 020A | | NOVELL - PROVO | CORP HQ |
| 020B | | NOVELL - PROVO | CORP HQ |
| 020C | | NOVELL - PROVO | CORP HQ |
| 020D | | NOVELL - PROVO | CORP HQ |
| 020E | | NOVELL - PROVO | CORP HQ |
| 020F | | NOVELL - PROVO | CORP HQ |
| 0210 | | NOVELL - PROVO | CORP HQ |
| 0211 | | NOVELL - PROVO | CORP HQ |
| 0212 | | NOVELL - PROVO | CORP HQ |
| 0213 | | NOVELL - PROVO | CORP HQ |
| 0214 | | NOVELL - PROVO | CORP HQ |
| 0215 | | NOVELL - PROVO | CORP HQ |
| 026B | TIME SYNCHRONIZATION | NOVELL - PROVO | |
| 026D | ADVERTISING JOB SERVER | NOVELL - PROVO | |
| 0272 | DATALINK SWITCHING (DLSW) | NOVELL - SAN JOSE | |
| 0273 | NEST DEVICE | NOVELL - PROVO | |
| 0274 | GROUPWISE MESSAGE MULTIPLE SERVERS | NOVELL - OREM | |

```
0275     SAMPLE CODE FROM DEV.     NOVELL
         SUPPORT
0281     DOMAIN APPLICATION        NOVELL - SUNNYVALE
         SERVICES
0282     NDPS SERVICE REGISTRY     NOVELL - PROVO
         SERVICE
0283     DOMAIN APPLICATION        NOVELL - SUNNYVALE
         SERVICES
0284     DOMAIN APPLICATION        NOVELL - SUNNYVALE
         SERVICES
0285     DOMAIN APPLICATION        NOVELL - SUNNYVALE
         SERVICES
0286     DOMAIN APPLICATION        NOVELL - SUNNYVALE
         SERVICES
0287     DOMAIN APPLICATION        NOVELL - SUNNYVALE
         SERVICES
0288     DOMAIN APPLICATION        NOVELL - SUNNYVALE
         SERVICES
028A     MPR - IPX ADDRESS         NOVELL - SAN JOSE
          MAPPING GATEWAY
028D     SALUTATION MANAGER        NOVELL - OREM
028E     TABASCO                   NOVELL - PROVO
021A     OT_MESSAGING_SERVER       NOVELL - SAN JOSE
021D     MPR - NETWARE MOBILE IPX  NOVELL - SAN JOSE
0222                               NOVELL - PROVO
0233     NETWORK MANAGEMENT AGENT  NOVELL - PROVO
0234     NETWORK MANAGEMENT        NOVELL - PROVO
         INFO SERVER
0236                               NOVELL - SALT LAKE CITY
0237     NETWARE MANAGEMENT -      NOVELL - SAN JOSE
         LANTERN
0238     NETWARE MANAGEMENT -      NOVELL - SAN JOSE
         LANTERN
0239     NETWARE MANAGEMENT        NOVELL - SAN JOSE
023A     NETWARE MANAGEMENT        NOVELL - SAN JOSE
023B     BINDERY TYPE FOR          NOVELL - PROVO
         BROADCAST
023C     DOS TARGET SERVICE        NOVELL - PROVO
         AGENT
023D     SMS WORKSTATION           NOVELL - PROVO
         NAME OBJECT
023E     SMS TESTING & DEVELOPMENT NOVELL - PROVO
023F     SMS TESTING & DEVELOPMENT NOVELL - PROVO
0240                               NOVELL - SAN JOSE
0241                               NOVELL - SAN JOSE
0242                               NOVELL - SAN JOSE
0243     NOVELL MHS DS GATEWAY     NOVELL - WALNUT CREEK
         FOR OCE
```

| 0244 | NDS GATEWAY FOR OCE | NOVELL - WALNUT CREEK |
|------|---------------------|------------------------|
| 0245 | SUPERLAB FILE DISTRIBUTION SERVER | NOVELL - PROVO |
| 0246 | VERSION CONTROL QUEUE | NOVELL - PROVO |
| 0247 | NVT REMOTE LOGIN OVER SPX | NOVELL - SALT LAKE CITY |
| 0248 | QUEUE SERVER FOR IBM PSF/2 | NOVELL - PROVO   CORP HQ |
| 0249 | LANTERN RMON | NOVELL - SAN JOSE, NMPD |
| 024A | LAT TRANSPORT SERVICE PROVIDER | NOVELL - SUNNYVALE |
| 024B | LAT SESSION MANAGER | NOVELL - SUNNYVALE |
| 024C | LAT NETWORK FROM NETWARE | NOVELL - SUNNYVALE |
| 024D | ADDRESS SERVER | NOVELL - PROVO |
| 025E | XAPIA INTERFACE FOR NW 3.11 | NOVELL - RICHMOND HILL |
| 025F | X.400 PROTOCOL ACCESS MODULE | NOVELL - RICHMOND HILL |
| 0260 | SNADS PROTOCOL ACCESS MODULE | NOVELL - RICHMOND HILL |
| 0261 | SUPERLAB NETWORK SWITCH SERVER | NOVELL - PROVO |
| 0262 | HUB SERVICES | NOVELL - SUNNYVALE |
| 0263 | NETWARE MANAGEMENT AGENT | NOVELL - SUNNYVALE |
| 0264 | GLOBAL MHS | NOVELL - SUNNYVALE |
| 0265 | SNMP | NOVELL - SUNNYVALE |
| 0266 | VERSION CONTROL SERVER | NOVELL - PROVO |
| 0267 | APPLICATION RIGHTS PROGRAM | NOVELL - PROVO |
| 0268 | | NOVELL - SAN JOSE |
| 0269 | SUPERLAB AUTOMATION SERVER | NOVELL - PROVO |
| 026A | NETWORK MANAGEMENT SERVICES | NOVELL - SAN JOSE |
| 0277 | SAP SERVER TYPE | NOVELL - SAN JOSE |
| 0278 | DIRECTORY SERVER | NOVELL - PROVO |
| 02FF | | NOVELL - PROVO   CORP HQ |
| 0300 | VAP - ADVERTISING SERVICES | FIREFOX COMMUNICATIONS LTD |
| 0301 | VAP - ADVERTISING SERVICES | FIREFOX COMMUNICATIONS LTD |
| 0302 | VAP - ADVERTISING SERVICES | FIREFOX COMMUNICATIONS LTD |
| 0303 | VAP - ADVERTISING SERVICES | FIREFOX COMMUNICATIONS LTD |
| 0304 | VAP - ADVERTISING SERVICES | FIREFOX COMMUNICATIONS LTD |

| | | |
|---|---|---|
| 0305 | VAP - ADVERTISING SERVICES | FIREFOX COMMUNICATIONS LTD |
| 0306 | NPS (NETWARE PRINT SERVICES) | INTER CONNECTIONS INC |
| 0307 | NPS SPOOL CLIENT | INTER CONNECTIONS INC |
| 0308 | HP NS UTIL | HEWLETT PACKARD - BOISE |
| 0309 | DOCUMENT MANAGEMENT PACKAGE | PERFECT SOLUTIONS CORPORATION |
| 030A | BBS SERVER | GALACTICOMM INC |
| 030C | QUICK SILVER | HEWLETT PACKARD - BOISE |
| 0320 | | ATTACHMATE CORPORATION |
| 0321 | | CHICAGO RESEARCH & TRADING |
| 0322 | | FRYE COMPUTER SYSTEMS |
| 0323 | | WANG LABORATORIES |
| 0324 | | WANG LABORATORIES |
| 0325 | X.500 DSA SERVER | AAC SYSTEMS |
| 0326 | NOVELL REMOTE ISDN ROUTER | LANWORKS |
| 0327 | BOOTWARE/MSD | LANWORKS |
| 0328 | | WATCOM |
| 0329 | | AETNA LIFE & CASUALTY |
| 032A | | AETNA LIFE & CASUALTY |
| 032B | FAX SERVER | DIGITAL VISIONS CORP |
| 032C | VOICE SERVER | DIGITAL VISIONS CORP |
| 032D | INTERPROCESS EXCHANGE SERVER | DIGITAL VISIONS CORP |
| 032E | APPLICATION SERVER | NATIONSBANK APPL SYSTEMS SUPP |
| 0330 | SAS SHARE SERVER | SAS INSTITUTE |
| 0331 | SAS CONNECT | SAS INSTITUTE |
| 0332 | | ARCHETYPE |
| 0333 | | ARCHETYPE |
| 0334 | | AETNA LIFE & CASUALTY |
| 0335 | COMMUNICATIONS SERVER | MULTITECH |
| 0336 | COMMUNICATIONS SERVER | MULTITECH |
| 0337 | | MAGEE ENTERPRISES INC |
| 0338 | | MAGEE ENTERPRISES INC |
| 0339 | | MAGEE ENTERPRISES INC |
| 033A | | MAGEE ENTERPRISES INC |
| 033B | | MAGEE ENTERPRISES INC |
| 033C | | MAGEE ENTERPRISES INC |
| 033D | | MAGEE ENTERPRISES INC |
| 033E | | MAGEE ENTERPRISES INC |
| 033F | | MAGEE ENTERPRISES INC |
| 0340 | | MAGEE ENTERPRISES INC |
| 0341 | DATA SERVICE TO WORKSTATION/SCHOOL ADMIN | CHANCERY SOFTWARE |
| 0342 | BINDERY TYPE | MICROTEST INC |
| 0343 | BINDERY TYPE | MICROTEST INC |
| 0344 | BINDERY TYPE | MICROTEST INC |

| | | |
|---|---|---|
| 0345 | BINDERY TYPE | MICROTEST INC |
| 0346 | BINDERY TYPE | MICROTEST INC |
| 0347 | BINDERY TYPE | MICROTEST INC |
| 0348 | BINDERY TYPE | MICROTEST INC |
| 0349 | BINDERY TYPE | MICROTEST INC |
| 034A | | PREFERRED SYSTEMS INC. |
| 034B | | PREFERRED SYSTEMS INC. |
| 034C | | PREFERRED SYSTEMS INC. |
| 034D | | PREFERRED SYSTEMS INC. |
| 034E | | PREFERRED SYSTEMS INC. |
| 034F | | PREFERRED SYSTEMS INC. |
| 0350 | | PREFERRED SYSTEMS INC. |
| 0351 | | PREFERRED SYSTEMS INC. |
| 0352 | BINDERY TYPE | FUJITSU LTD |
| 0353 | BINDERY TYPE | FUJITSU LTD |
| 0354 | BINDERY TYPE | FUJITSU LTD |
| 0355 | | ARCADA SOFTWARE |
| 0356 | | LANOVATION |
| 0357 | | LANOVATION |
| 0358 | BINDERY OBJECT TYPE | CBIS INC |
| 035A | | MBAC |
| 035B | RIGHT-HAND-MAN, E-MAIL/ SCHEDULING PKG | LAN ACES INC |
| 035C | FAX SERVER | TRANSFAX CORPORATION |
| 035D | FAX PRINT SERVER | TRANSFAX CORPORATION |
| 035E | FAX MERGE SERVER | TRANSFAX CORPORATION |
| 035F | NETWORK MANAGEMENT SERVER | TRANSFAX CORPORATION |
| 0360 | OBJECT TYPE | FUNK SOFTWARE |
| 0363 | PRINT SERVER - LASER JET | EXTENDED SYSTEMS |
| 036A | | EXCALIBUR TECHNOLOGIES CORP |
| 0364 | SERVER-TYPE FOR LAN TIMES JAPAN ARTICLE | LAN TIMES JAPAN, SOFTBANK CORP |
| 0365 | QUEUE-TYPE FOR LAN TIMES JAPAN ARTICLE | LAN TIMES JAPAN, SOFTBANK CORP |
| 0366 | MGATE - COMMUNICATION GATEWAY/LANS + VAX | COEFFICIENT SYSTEMS CORP |
| 0367 | | EXCALIBUR TECHNOLOGIES CORP |
| 0368 | | EXCALIBUR TECHNOLOGIES CORP |
| 0369 | | EXCALIBUR TECHNOLOGIES CORP |
| 0372 | | DIGITAL EQUIPMENT - MERRIMACK |
| 0373 | NLM ADVERTISING FOR UPS INFO | BRAINSTORM ENGINEERING |
| 0374 | SHAREWARE COMMUNICATIONS SERVER | CHERRY TREE SOFTWARE |
| 0375 | ENTERPRISE ECS | INTEL CORP |
| 0376 | ENTERPRISE INITIALIZATION MODE | INTEL CORP |

| | | |
|---|---|---|
| 036B | BINDERY TYPE | AETNA LIFE & CASUALTY |
| 036C | IPX LAYER PEER-TO-PEER COMMUNICATIONS | SEWELL DEVELOPMENT |
| 036D | | MICRO INTEGRATION |
| 036E | NLM SERVER | PRAXIS |
| 036F | BINDERY TYPE | AVAIL SYSTEMS CORP |
| 0377 | COMM SVR - NET BIOS IPX (MVD FRM 27341-1 | US ROBOTICS SOFTWARE |
| 0378 | NLM ADVERTISING FOR UPS INFO | BRAINSTORM ENGINEERING |
| 0379 | FAX SERVER | EXTENDED SYSTEMS |
| 037A | FAX SERVER | EXTENDED SYSTEMS |
| 037B | FAX SERVER | EXTENDED SYSTEMS |
| 037C | FAX SERVER | EXTENDED SYSTEMS |
| 037D | GATEWAY MANAGEMENT | WALL DATA |
| 037E | POWERCHUTE ALERT-UPS MONITORING | AMERICAN POWER CONVERSION |
| 037F | MVD FRM 23539-001 11-12-93 | CENTRAL POINT SOFTWARE |
| 0380 | FAX SERVER | OPTUS INFORMATION SYSTEMS |
| 0383 | POWERCHUTE ADMINISTRATIVE | AMERICAN POWER CONVERSION |
| 0384 | SEQUEL LINK CLIENT- SERVER MIDDLEWARE | TECHGNOSIS INC |
| 0385 | MAIL SYSTEMS | SYNECTIC SYSTEMS LTD |
| 0386 | HEWLETT PACKARD BRIDGES | HEWLETT PACKARD - ROSEVILLE |
| 0387 | HEWLETT PACKARD HUBS | HEWLETT PACKARD - ROSEVILLE |
| 0388 | WORKSTATION PEER-TO-PEER COMMUNICATIONS | IBM - RESEARCH TRIANGLE PARK |
| 0389 | | DATANEX CORPORATION |
| 039A | HP OPEN MAIL&PORTABLE NETWARE | HEWLETT PACKARD-BERKSHIRE |
| 039B | | IRIS ASSOCIATES |
| 039C | COMMUNICATIONS SERVER BINDERY | DATOR 3 SPOL SRO |
| 039D | COMMUNICATIONS SERVER SAP | DATOR 3 SPOL SRO |
| 039E | FAX SERVER | FERRARI ELECTRONIC GMBH |
| 039F | | COMPUTERVISION SERVICES |
| 03A0 | BINDERY TYPE FOR CD SERVER | JOSTENS LEARNING CORP |
| 03A1 | | NEUMEIER & WALCH SYSTEMTECHNIK |
| 03A2 | | HYPROTECH LTD |
| 03A3 | | KYOCERA CORP, YOHAGA OFFICE |
| 03A4 | | KYOCERA CORP, YOHAGA OFFICE |
| 03A5 | | KYOCERA CORP, YOHAGA OFFICE |
| 03A6 | | KYOCERA CORP, YOHAGA OFFICE |
| 03A7 | OBJECT TYPE FOR A GROUP | STADT PFORZHEIM POA |
| 03A8 | OBJECT TYPE FOR A QUEUE | STADT PFORZHEIM POA |

| 03A9 | OBJECT TYPE FOR A SERVER | STADT PFORZHEIM POA |
| 03AA | | UDS MOTOROLA |
| 03AB | | UDS MOTOROLA |
| 03AC | | UDS MOTOROLA |
| 03AD | | UDS MOTOROLA |
| 03AE | | RAIMA CORP |
| 03AF | COPY PROTECTION SERVER | PACE SOFTWARE SYSTEMS INC |
| 03B0 | TNA COMMUNICATION WITH 2 NLM'S | PALINDROME |
| 03B1 | ETHERNET LAN CONTROLLER FOR NETWARE | BUS TECH |
| 03B2 | SERVER ID FOR NLM | NETWORK DESIGNERS |
| 03B3 | FILE MANAGEMENT SERVICES | SYSTEMS AXIS PLC |
| 03B4 | QUEUE MANAGEMENT SERVICES OBJECT TYPE IWI | SYSTEMS AXIS PLC 03B5 |
| 03B6 | LANTECH SERVICES | |
| 03B8 | MODEM PROTOCALL-SHARING SERIAL PORTS | LANSOURCE TECHNOLOGIES |
| 03B9 | GLOBAL INFO APPLICATION EXEC ENVIRONMENT | FUNK SOFTWARE |
| 03BA | MAGIX DATABASE SERVER | ADVANCED SOFTWARE TECHNOLOGIES |
| 03BB | PERFORMANCE MONITOR | AMERIDATA |
| 03BC | NETPORT ADVERTISING | INTEL PCED |
| 03BD | WAN CONNECTION SERVER | IDEASSOCIATION |
| 03BE | WICAT | JOSTENS LEARNING CORP |
| 03BF | WICAT SERVER | JOSTENS LEARNING CORP |
| 03C0 | EMBEDDED IN OEM PLOTTER PRODUCT | CAL COMP |
| 03C1 | EMBEDDED IN OEM PLOTTER PRODUCT | CAL COMP |
| 03C2 | EMBEDDED IN OEM PLOTTER PRODUCT | CAL COMP |
| 03C3 | EMBEDDED IN OEM PLOTTER PRODUCT | CAL COMP |
| 03C7 | LAN SPOOL 3.5 | INTEL - AMERICAN FORK |
| 03C8 | NETWORK MANAGEMENT | MADGE NETWORKS LTD |
| 03CA | POINT-OF-SALE SERVER | OPTICAL MARK SYSTEMS LTD |
| 03CB | SOFTWARE ACCESS CONTROL SERVER | U OF PLYMOUTH |
| 03CF | DATABASE ENGINE | BLUE LANCE NETWORK INFO SYS |
| 03D0 | REPORT ENGINE | BLUE LANCE NETWORK INFO SYS |
| 03D1 | JOB SERVER | BLUE LANCE NETWORK INFO SYS |
| 03D2 | OBJECT TYPE | BLUE LANCE NETWORK INFO SYS |
| 03D3 | OBJECT TYPE | BLUE LANCE NETWORK INFO SYS |
| 03D4 | VISINET NLM ID# | TECHNOLOGY DYNAMICS INC |
| 03D5 | PRINT SERVERS | LEXMARK INTERNATIONAL |
| 03D6 | PRINT SERVERS | LEXMARK INTERNATIONAL |
| 03D7 | PRINT SERVERS | LEXMARK INTERNATIONAL |

| 03D8 | PRINT SERVERS | LEXMARK INTERNATIONAL |
| 03D9 | SERVER MONITORING PROGRAM | TRELLIS |
| 03DA | MULTIPLE SERVICES<br>& APPLICATIONS | THINK SYSTEMS CORP |
| 03DB | MULTIPLE SERVICES<br>& APPLICATIONS | THINK SYSTEMS CORP |
| 03DC | MULTIPLE SERVICES<br>& APPLICATIONS | THINK SYSTEMS CORP |
| 03DD | DEVELOPING SERVER<br>PERFORMANCE ANALYZER | BANYAN SYSTEMS INC |
| 03DE | GUPTA SEQUEL BASE SERVER | GUPTA TECHNOLOGIES |
| 03DF | REMOTE DATABASE SERVICES | INTERACTIVE DATA |
| 03E0 | OBJECT STORE SERVER | OBJECT DESIGN |
| 03E1 | UNIVEL SERVER TYPE | UNIVEL |
| 03E2 | UNIVEL SERVER TYPE | UNIVEL |
| 03E3 | UNIVEL SERVER TYPE | UNIVEL |
| 03E4 | UNIVEL SERVER TYPE | UNIVEL |
| 03E5 | UNIVEL SERVER TYPE | UNIVEL |
| 03E6 | UNIVEL SERVER TYPE | UNIVEL |
| 03E7 | UNIVEL SERVER TYPE | UNIVEL |
| 03E8 | UNIVEL SERVER TYPE | UNIVEL |
| 03E9 | UNIVEL SERVER TYPE | UNIVEL |
| 03EA | UNIVEL SERVER TYPE | UNIVEL |
| 03EB | UNIVEL SERVER TYPE | UNIVEL |
| 03EC | UNIVEL SERVER TYPE | UNIVEL |
| 03ED | UNIVEL SERVER TYPE | UNIVEL |
| 03EE | UNIVEL SERVER TYPE | UNIVEL |
| 03EF | UNIVEL SERVER TYPE | UNIVEL |
| 03F0 | UNIVEL SERVER TYPE | UNIVEL |
| 03F1 | FIRST CALL | THOMSON FINANCIAL |
| 03F3 | VITAL SIGNS/LAN SERVER | BLUELINE SOFTWARE INC |
| 03F4 | LAA SERVER BINDERY | SABER SOFTWARE |
| 03F5 | MICROSOFT SQL SERVER<br>IPX/SPX SUPPORT | MICROSOFT |
| 03F6 | ASYNCHRONOUS SERIAL<br>COMMUNICATIONS | BLACK CREEK INTEGRATED SYSTEMS |
| 03F7 | ASYNCHRONOUS SERIAL<br>COMMUNICATIONS | BLACK CREEK INTEGRATED SYSTEMS |
| 03F8 | ASYNCHRONOUS SERIAL<br>COMMUNICATIONS | BLACK CREEK INTEGRATED SYSTEMS |
| 03F9 | ASYNCHRONOUS SERIAL<br>COMMUNICATIONS | BLACK CREEK INTEGRATED SYSTEMS |
| 03FA | WATSON - COMMUNICATIONS<br>SERVER | PRODIGY SERVICES |
| 03FB | NETPORT ADVERTISING | INTEL PCED |
| 03FC | NETPORT ADVERTISING | INTEL PCED |
| 03FD | NETPORT ADVERTISING | INTEL PCED |
| 03FE | NETPORT ADVERTISING | INTEL PCED |

| | | |
|---|---|---|
| 03FF | | MODULAR SOFTWARE CORPORATION |
| 0400 | BINDERY OBJECT TYPES | ARTEFACT NETWORK SUPPORT |
| 0401 | BINDERY OBJECT TYPES | ARTEFACT NETWORK SUPPORT |
| 0402 | BINDERY OBJECT TYPES | ARTEFACT NETWORK SUPPORT |
| 0403 | BINDERY OBJECT TYPES | ARTEFACT NETWORK SUPPORT |
| 0404 | BINDERY OBJECT TYPES | ARTEFACT NETWORK SUPPORT |
| 0405 | BINDERY OBJECT TYPES | ARTEFACT NETWORK SUPPORT |
| 0406 | BINDERY OBJECT TYPES | ARTEFACT NETWORK SUPPORT |
| 0407 | BINDERY OBJECT TYPES | ARTEFACT NETWORK SUPPORT |
| 0408 | BINDERY OBJECT TYPES | ARTEFACT NETWORK SUPPORT |
| 0409 | BINDERY OBJECT TYPES | ARTEFACT NETWORK SUPPORT |
| 040A | IMAGE APPLICATION | LASER DATA |
| 040B | IMAGE APPLICATION | LASER DATA |
| 040C | IMAGE APPLICATION | LASER DATA |
| 040D | IMAGE APPLICATION | LASER DATA |
| 040E | IMAGE APPLICATION | LASER DATA |
| 040F | IMAGE APPLICATION | LASER DATA |
| 0410 | IMAGE APPLICATION | LASER DATA |
| 0411 | IMAGE APPLICATION | LASER DATA |
| 0412 | IMAGE APPLICATION | LASER DATA |
| 0413 | IMAGE APPLICATION | LASER DATA |
| 0414 | NETSPRINT | DIGITAL PRODUCTS INC |
| 0415 | REMOTE DATABASE SERVICES-BINDERY | INTERACTIVE DATA |
| 0416 | DEALING ROOM SERVERS | TEKNOS SYSTEMS LTD |
| 0417 | DEALING ROOM SERVERS | TEKNOS SYSTEMS LTD |
| 0418 | DEALING ROOM SERVERS | TEKNOS SYSTEMS LTD |
| 0419 | DEALING ROOM SERVERS | TEKNOS SYSTEMS LTD |
| 041A | DEALING ROOM SERVERS | TEKNOS SYSTEMS LTD |
| 041B | DEALING ROOM SERVERS | TEKNOS SYSTEMS LTD |
| 041C | DEALING ROOM SERVERS | TEKNOS SYSTEMS LTD |
| 041D | DEALING ROOM SERVERS | TEKNOS SYSTEMS LTD |
| 041E | DEALING ROOM SERVERS | TEKNOS SYSTEMS LTD |
| 041F | DEALING ROOM SERVERS | TEKNOS SYSTEMS LTD |
| 0420 | DEALING ROOM SERVERS | TEKNOS SYSTEMS LTD |
| 0421 | DEALING ROOM SERVERS | TEKNOS SYSTEMS LTD |
| 0422 | DEALING ROOM SERVERS | TEKNOS SYSTEMS LTD |
| 0423 | DEALING ROOM SERVERS | TEKNOS SYSTEMS LTD |
| 0424 | DEALING ROOM SERVERS | TEKNOS SYSTEMS LTD |
| 0425 | DEALING ROOM SERVERS | TEKNOS SYSTEMS LTD |
| 0426 | DEALING ROOM SERVERS | TEKNOS SYSTEMS LTD |
| 0427 | DEALING ROOM SERVERS | TEKNOS SYSTEMS LTD |
| 0428 | DEALING ROOM SERVERS | TEKNOS SYSTEMS LTD |
| 0429 | DEALING ROOM SERVERS | TEKNOS SYSTEMS LTD |
| 042A | FULL TEXT RETRIEVAL CLIENT/SERVER DB ENG | IMPACT ITALIANA SRL |
| 042B | GATEWAY SOFTWARE | DATEV EG |
| 042C | GATEWAY SOFTWARE | DATEV EG |

| | | |
|---|---|---|
| 042D | CLIENT-SERVER DRIVER FOR IPX/SPX | REFERENCE POINT SOFTWARE |
| 042E | | INTRAK INC |
| 042F | LOADER BINDERY TYPE | NETWORK TECHNICAL SOLUTIONS |
| 0430 | FINDER BINDERY TYPE | NETWORK TECHNICAL SOLUTIONS |
| 0432 | FILEMAKER PRO | CLARIS CORP |
| 0433 | NETWORKING HUB | SYNOPTICS |
| 0434 | NETWORK TERMINAL EMULATOR | IDE ASSOCIATION |
| 0435 | ADMINISTRATION SERVER | MCGILL UNIVERSITY FAC OF ENGIN |
| 0436 | NETWORK DYNAMIC DATA EXCHANGE | NETLOGIC INC |
| 0437 | ASYNCH COMM SVR (MVD FRM 27341-1, 062294) | US ROBOTICS SOFTWARE |
| 0438 | BACK UP PRODUCT | COREL SYSTEMS, OPTICAL DIV |
| 0439 | BACK UP PRODUCT | COREL SYSTEMS, OPTICAL DIV |
| 043A | MISCELLANEOUS SOFTWARE COMMUNICATIONS | TENTERA COMPUTER SERVICES |
| 043B | ENTERPRISE IN MAINTENANCE MODE | INTEL |
| 043C | CONNECTION STATION SERVICE TYPE | COROLLARY INC |
| 043D | CONNECTION STATION SERVICE TYPE | COROLLARY INC |
| 043E | CONNECTION STATION SERVICE TYPE | COROLLARY INC |
| 043F | CONNECTION STATION SERVICE TYPE | COROLLARY INC |
| 0440 | CONNECTION STATION SERVICE TYPE | COROLLARY INC |
| 0441 | CONNECTION STATION SERVICE TYPE | COROLLARY INC |
| 0442 | CONNECTION STATION SERVICE TYPE | COROLLARY INC |
| 0443 | CONNECTION STATION SERVICE TYPE | COROLLARY INC |
| 0444 | SNA GATEWAY | MICROSOFT |
| 0445 | WORKSTATION TERMINAL ACCESS | HSD HARDWARE SOFTWARE DEVELOPMENT |
| 0446 | | DE INTERNATIONAL LTD |
| 0447 | DISTRIBUTIVE CACHE PRODUCT | RAIMA CORP |
| 044D | IBM HOST GATEWAY | IDEA COURIER |
| 044E | PROJECT ID | URBAN SCIENCE APPLICATIONS |
| 044F | COMMON COMMUNICATION INTERFACE | COMPUTER ASSOCIATES |
| 0450 | COMMUNICATIONS SERVER SDD SYNTHESIZER | SCANDINAVIAN AIRLINES DATA |

| | | |
|---|---|---|
| 0451 | TAPE BACK-UP FOR NLM APPLICATIONS | MOUNTAIN NETWORK SOLUTIONS INC |
| 0452 | TAPE BACK-UP FOR NLM APPLICATIONS | MOUNTAIN NETWORK SOLUTIONS INC |
| 0453 | TAPE BACK-UP FOR NLM APPLICATIONS | MOUNTAIN NETWORK SOLUTIONS INC |
| 0454 | TAPE BACK-UP FOR NLM APPLICATIONS | MOUNTAIN NETWORK SOLUTIONS INC |
| 0455 | TAPE BACK-UP FOR NLM APPLICATIONS | MOUNTAIN NETWORK SOLUTIONS INC |
| 0456 | TAPE BACK-UP FOR NLM APPLICATIONS | MOUNTAIN NETWORK SOLUTIONS INC |
| 0457 | CANON PERIPHERAL SERVER | CANON INFORMATION SYSTEMS |
| 0458 | NETWARE SERVER PRODUCT | INTEL CORP |
| 0459 | OBJECT ORIENTED DATABASE SYSTEM | ONTOS INC |
| 045A | QMS PRINTER - REMOTE CONFIGURATION | QMS |
| 045B | CLIENT SERVER MONITORING UTILITY | DELL COMPUTER |
| 045C | BINDERY TYPE - APPLICATION DEFINITION | LANOVATION |
| 045D | FAX SERVER | FERRARI ELECTRONIC GMBH |
| 045E | FAX SERVER | FERRARI ELECTRONIC GMBH |
| 045F | FAX SERVER | FERRARI ELECTRONIC GMBH |
| 0460 | FAX SERVER | FERRARI ELECTRONIC GMBH |
| 0461 | COMMUNICATIONS GATEWAY - OSI | EICON TECHNOLOGY |
| 0462 | COMMUNICATIONS GATEWAY - SNA | EICON TECHNOLOGY |
| 0464 | BATCHFILER APPLICATION | JOVANDI INTERNATIONAL INC |
| 0465 | NLM ON FILE SERVER | JOVANDI INTERNATIONAL INC |
| 0466 | TIME SYNCHRONIZATION SERVER | JOVANDI INTERNATIONAL INC |
| 0468 | TELEPHONE ANSWERING SYSTEM | A&M COMMUNICATIONS |
| 046A | FAX SERVER | EXTENDED SYSTEMS |
| 0470 | MEASURESERVERS AND MEASURECLIENTS | ADVANTECH BENELUX BV |
| 0471 | DISK MONITOR | STORAGE DIMENSIONS |
| 0472 | ENTERPRISE NETWORK SERVICES | BANYAN SYSTEMS INC |
| 0474 | SYBASE SQL SERVER | SYBASE INC |
| 0475 | SYBASE SQL SERVER CONSOLE | SYBASE INC |
| 0476 | SYBASE SQL SERVER MONITOR | SYBASE INC |
| 0477 | SYBASE SQL SERVER BACK-UP | SYBASE INC |
| 0478 | SYBASE OPEN SERVER | SYBASE INC |

| | | |
|---|---|---|
| 0479 | SYBASE OPEN SERVER CONSOLE | SYBASE INC |
| 047C | REMOTE PRINTER CONSOLE | PEERLESS GROUP |
| 047D | AUTO-ON/OFF CONTROL NLM | MITSUBISI DENKI COMPUTER |
| 047E | ASCOM FAX SERVER | ASCOM TELECOMMUNICATION LTD |
| 047F | ASCOM ADVERTISING FAX SERVER | ASCOM TELECOMMUNICATION LTD |
| 0480 | ASCOM FAX QUEUE | ASCOM TELECOMMUNICATION LTD |
| 0481 | JOB SERVER | HIGH ASPECT DEVELOPMENT |
| 0482 | JOB QUEUE | HIGH ASPECT DEVELOPMENT |
| 0483 | FINANCE | THINK SYSTEMS CORP |
| 0484 | FORCASTING | THINK SYSTEMS CORP |
| 0485 | SCHEMA | THINK SYSTEMS CORP |
| 0486 | FAIL SAFE ANALYSIS | THINK SYSTEMS CORP |
| 0487 | | THINK SYSTEMS CORP |
| 0488 | COMMUNICATION BETWEEN CLIENT AND SERVER | CDC - OFFICE OF PROGRAM SUPPRT |
| 0489 | STORE NAME OF SPECIAL FILE ON FILESERVER | DELTA INFORMATION SYSTEMS |
| 048A | MAIN NLM SERVER FOR CALENDAR MANAGER | RUSSELL INFORMATION SCIENCES |
| 048B | ARRAY MONITOR SERVER | CORE INTERNATIONAL |
| 048D | DOCUMENT PROCESSING SERVER NLM | BOSS LOGIC INC |
| 048E | DOCUMENT PROCESSING SERVER NLM | BOSS LOGIC INC |
| 048F | DOCUMENT PROCESSING SERVER NLM | BOSS LOGIC INC |
| 0490 | POWER PRODUCT FOR FILE SERVER | BRAINSTORM ENGINEERING |
| 0491 | NETBLAZER COMMUNICATION SERVER | TELEBIT CORPORATION |
| 0495 | REMOTE BACK-UP DEVICE | ASTORA SOFTWARE INC |
| 0496 | SQL SERVER IPX/SPX HIDDEN SERVER | MICROSOFT |
| 0497 | DATABASE LOCK SERVER | HIGH ASPECT DEVELOPMENT |
| 0498 | METER SERVER | POLYMETER RESPONSE LTD |
| 0499 | LANCORP EOMS | LANCORP PTY LTD |
| 049A | BULL HN SDM | LANCORP PTY LTD |
| 049B | NETWORK MANAGEMENT AGENT | EICON TECHNOLOGY |
| 049C | ICOT SNA GATEWAY | ICOT CORP |
| 049D | SOFTWARE NLM (MVDFRM-008 6-7-94) | INTERCONNECTIONS |
| 049E | INTERNET GATEWAY | METASCYBE SYSTEMS LTD |
| 049F | EMAIL & CALENDARING COMMUNICATION SERVER | ATTACHMATE CANADA |
| 04A1 | AUTOMATION INFORMATION ROUTER | KURT MANUFACTURING |

| | | |
|---|---|---|
| 04A2 | XBASE RECORD ENGINE | EXTENDED SYSTEMS |
| 04A3 | REMOTE PROCEDURE CALL SYSTEM | FORTUNET INC |
| 04A4 | DELVRY OF VALUABLE INFO W/USAGE TRACKING | WAVE SYSTEMS CORPORATION |
| 04A5 | REMOTE ACCESS SERVER | TRAVELING SOFTWARE |
| 04A6 | BINDERY FOR PROGRAM METERING DATABASE | PILOTT SYSTEMS |
| 04A7 | LT AUDITOR 4.00 PLUS | BLUE LANCE INC |
| 04A8 | BINDERY SERVICE | FUJITSU LTD |
| 04A9 | BINDERY SERVICE | FUJITSU LTD |
| 04AA | SAP SERVICE | FUJITSU LTD |
| 04AB | SAP SERVICE | FUJITSU LTD |
| 04AC | CALENDAR SERVER | CAMPBELL SERVICES |
| 04AE | LED SERVER | INOVA CORPORATION |
| 04B0 | CDNET SERVER | MERIDIAN DATA INC |
| 04B1 | POLICY ENGINE | EMERALD SYSTEMS |
| 04B2 | POLICY ENGINE | EMERALD SYSTEMS |
| 04B3 | POLICY ENGINE | EMERALD SYSTEMS |
| 04B4 | POLICY ENGINE | EMERALD SYSTEMS |
| 04B5 | POLICY ENGINE | EMERALD SYSTEMS |
| 04B6 | POLICY ENGINE | EMERALD SYSTEMS |
| 04B7 | LAN ASSIST PLUS REMOTE CONTROL | MICROTEST |
| 04B8 | LAN ASSIST PLUS REMOTE CONTROL | MICROTEST |
| 04B9 | LAN ASSIST PLUS REMOTE CONTROL | MICROTEST |
| 04BA | LAN ASSIST PLUS REMOTE CONTROL | MICROTEST |
| 04BB | MAP ASSIST PEER-TO-PEER | MICROTEST |
| 04BC | MAP ASSIST PEER-TO-PEER | MICROTEST |
| 04BD | MAP ASSIST PEER-TO-PEER | MICROTEST |
| 04BE | MAP ASSIST PEER-TO-PEER | MICROTEST |
| 04BF | JETNET DRIVER FOR NOVELL | JETSTREAM TECHNOLOGY LTD04C0 |
| | IPX PROTOCOLS DATABASE SERVER RUNNING AS NLM | LODESTAR DATA SYSTEMS |
| 04C1 | ASYNCHRONOUS COMMUNICATIONS SERVERS | US ROBOTICS SOFTWARE |
| 04C2 | DATABASE SERVER | FAIR COM |
| 04C3 | TAURUS DATABASE SERVER | DCI |
| 04C4 | TAURUS SERIAL SERVER | DCI |
| 04C5 | CASPER QUEUE | NETWORK TECHNICAL SOLUTIONS |
| 04C6 | CASPER GHOST | NETWORK TECHNICAL SOLUTIONS |
| 04C7 | CONFERENCING SERVICE | FUJITSU SYSTEMS BUSINESS |
| 04C8 | MAIL SYSTEM QUEUE SERVICE | MITSUBISHI ELECTRIC ENGINEERING |
| 04C9 | VIDEO SERVER | NOVELL - MULTI MEDIA |

| | | |
|---|---|---|
| 04CA | MESSAGE EXPRESS PRODUCT | HORIZON STRATEGIES INC |
| 04CB | CD ROM SERVER | CBIS INC |
| 04CC | COST RECOVERY SERVER | VINCENT LARSEN |
| 04CD | PC-BASED SNA GATEWAY | UNGERMANN BASS |
| 04CF | USER RESTRICTIONS | VAL LABORATORY CO LTD |
| 04D0 | USER RESTRICTIONS | VAL LABORATORY CO LTD |
| 04D1 | SAP ADVERTISING ON PRINT SERVER | NISSIN ELECTRIC CO LTD |
| 04D2 | OT_ELLIPSE_SERVER | BACHMAN INFORMATION SYSTEMS |
| 04D3 | ASYNCHRONOUS ACCESS SERVER | SKYLINE TECHNOLOGY |
| 04D4 | ENTERPRISE DESCRIPTION OBJECT | HANS SPATZIER |
| 04D5 | PRINT SERVER | FORESYTE TECHNOLOGIES |
| 04D7 | CUBIX QL SERVER | CUBIX CORP |
| 04D8 | CUBIX QL CLIENT | CUBIX CORP |
| 04D9 | JOB SERVER | STORAGE DIMENSIONS |
| 04DA | COMMUNICATION SERVER | FIREFOX COMMUNICATIONS LTD |
| 04DB | COMMUNICATION SERVER | FIREFOX COMMUNICATIONS LTD |
| 04DC | COMMUNICATION SERVER | FIREFOX COMMUNICATIONS LTD |
| 04DD | COMMUNICATION SERVER | FIREFOX COMMUNICATIONS LTD |
| 04DE | COMMUNICATION SERVER | FIREFOX COMMUNICATIONS LTD |
| 04DF | COMMUNICATION SERVER | FIREFOX COMMUNICATIONS LTD |
| 04E0 | COMMUNICATION SERVER | FIREFOX COMMUNICATIONS LTD |
| 04E1 | COMMUNICATION SERVER | FIREFOX COMMUNICATIONS LTD |
| 04E2 | COMMUNICATION SERVER | FIREFOX COMMUNICATIONS LTD |
| 04E3 | COMMUNICATION SERVER | FIREFOX COMMUNICATIONS LTD |
| 04E4 | COMMUNICATION SERVER | FIREFOX COMMUNICATIONS LTD |
| 04E5 | COMMUNICATION SERVER | FIREFOX COMMUNICATIONS LTD |
| 04E6 | COMMUNICATION SERVER | FIREFOX COMMUNICATIONS LTD |
| 04E7 | COMMUNICATION SERVER | FIREFOX COMMUNICATIONS LTD |
| 04E8 | COMMUNICATION SERVER | FIREFOX COMMUNICATIONS LTD |
| 04E9 | COMMUNICATION SERVER | FIREFOX COMMUNICATIONS LTD |
| 04EA | COMMUNICATION SERVER | FIREFOX COMMUNICATIONS LTD |
| 04EB | COMMUNICATION SERVER | FIREFOX COMMUNICATIONS LTD |
| 04EC | COMMUNICATION SERVER | FIREFOX COMMUNICATIONS LTD |
| 04ED | COMMUNICATION SERVER | FIREFOX COMMUNICATIONS LTD |
| 04EE | REMOTE ACCESS SERVER | DCA |
| 04EF | STATISTIC MANAGEMENT | MULTITECH |
| 04F0 | STATISTIC MANAGEMENT | MULTITECH |
| 04F1 | REMOTE CONTROL SOFTWARE | MULTITECH |
| 04F2 | REMOTE CONTROL SOFTWARE | MULTITECH |
| 04F3 | | MULTITECH |
| 04F4 | NETLYNX COMMUNICATION SERVER | ANDREW CORPORATION |
| 04F5 | NETLYNX COMMUNICATION SERVER | ANDREW CORPORATION |

| | | |
|---|---|---|
| 04F6 | NETLYNX COMMUNICATION SERVER | ANDREW CORPORATION |
| 04F7 | NETLYNX COMMUNICATION SERVER | ANDREW CORPORATION |
| 04F8 | NETLYNX COMMUNICATION SERVER | ANDREW CORPORATION |
| 04F9 | NETLYNX COMMUNICATION SERVER | ANDREW CORPORATION |
| 04FA | NETLYNX COMMUNICATION SERVER | ANDREW CORPORATION |
| 04FB | NETLYNX COMMUNICATION SERVER | ANDREW CORPORATION |
| 04FC | NETLYNX COMMUNICATION SERVER | ANDREW CORPORATION |
| 04FD | NETLYNX COMMUNICATION SERVER | ANDREW CORPORATION |
| 04FE | NETLYNX COMMUNICATION SERVER | ANDREW CORPORATION |
| 04FF | NETLYNX COMMUNICATION SERVER | ANDREW CORPORATION |
| 048C | DOCUMENT PROCESSING SERVER NLM | BOSS LOGIC INC |
| 0500 | NETLYNX COMMUNICATION SERVER | ANDREW CORPORATION |
| 0501 | NETLYNX COMMUNICATION SERVER | ANDREW CORPORATION |
| 0502 | NETLYNX COMMUNICATION SERVER | ANDREW CORPORATION |
| 0503 | NETLYNX COMMUNICATION | ANDREW CORPORATION |
| 0504 | DESKVIEW X BINDERY TYPE | QUARTERDECK OFFICE SYSTEMS |
| 0505 | PRINT SERVER ADD-ON | INTEL - AMERICAN FORK |
| 0506 | INDEX SEQUENTIAL ACCESS NLM | INFOPOINT SYSTEMS |
| 0507 | ASSOCIATIVE INDEX SERVER | INFOPOINT SYSTEMS |
| 0508 | NETSCRIBE SERVER | MERIDIAN DATA CORP |
| 0509 | PRINT SERVER FOR REMOTE WORKSTATIONS | FUJI XEROX CO LTD |
| 050A | NETMAGIC BINDERY ID | NETMAGIC SYSTEMS INC |
| 050B | FINANCIAL MARKET INFORMATION SERVER | AT FINANCIAL |
| 050C | NETWORK MODEM | NANAGRAM |
| 050D | NETWORK MODEM | NANAGRAM |
| 050E | DOCUMENT MANAGEMENT SERVICE | IMAGERY SOFTWARE INC |
| 050F | IMAGE MANAGEMENT SERVICE | IMAGERY SOFTWARE INC |
| 0510 | MASS STORAGE SERVICE | IMAGERY SOFTWARE INC |
| 0511 | DATABASE SERVER | TOBIT SOFTWARE GMBH |
| 0512 | TELI-LINK VOICE SERVER | COMPUTER & COMMUNICATIONS CO |

| | | |
|---|---|---|
| 0513 | PRINT SERVER | EMULEX CORPORATION |
| 0514 | 1012 HUB AGENT | ASANTE TECHNOLOGIES |
| 0515 | 1012 HUB AGENT | ASANTE TECHNOLOGIES |
| 0516 | 1012 HUB AGENT | ASANTE TECHNOLOGIES |
| 0517 | 1012 HUB AGENT | ASANTE TECHNOLOGIES |
| 0518 | 1012 HUB AGENT | ASANTE TECHNOLOGIES |
| 0519 | 1012 HUB AGENT | ASANTE TECHNOLOGIES |
| 051A | 1012 HUB AGENT | ASANTE TECHNOLOGIES |
| 051B | 1012 HUB AGENT | ASANTE TECHNOLOGIES |
| 051C | 1012 HUB AGENT | ASANTE TECHNOLOGIES |
| 051D | 1012 HUB AGENT | ASANTE TECHNOLOGIES |
| 051E | ADVERTISING NETWORK MODEMS | LANSOURCE TECHNOLOGIES |
| 051F | APPLICATION PROGRAMS | U OF PLYMOUTH |
| 0520 | BLOOMBERG AUDIO SERVER | BLOOMBERG LP |
| 0521 | BLOOMBERG PROCESS SERVER | BLOOMBERG LP |
| 0522 | NET MODEM SERVER | PRACTICAL PERIPHERALS INC |
| 0525 | AGENT FOR HUB MANAGEMENT | IDEA COURIER |
| 0526 | NAMED PIPE COMMUNICATIONS | |
| 0527 | PRINT SERVER/REMOTE PRINTER | PACIFIC DATA PRODUCTS |
| 0528 | PRINT SERVER | SEIKO EPSON CORP |
| 0529 | INTERSERVER FILE COPYING | BANKERS TRUST CO |
| 052A | FAX & VOICE SERVER | DCA |
| 052C | REMOTE LOGIN TERMINAL | GORDIAN |
| 052D | APPLICATION SERVER | CITRIX SYSTEMS |
| 052E | OT_BLOOMBERG | MEDIA TOUCH SYSTEMS |
| 052F | MICROCOM REMOTE ACCESS SERVER | MICROCOM INC |
| 0530 | REMARK VOICE SERVER | SIMPACT & ASSOC INC |
| 0531 | IPX COMMUNICATION SERVER | SYMANTEC PETER NORTON GROUP |
| 0532 | ACCESS SERVER FOR MODEM SHARING | BAY TECHNICAL ASSOCIATES |
| 0533 | GATEWAY BETWEEN NETWORK & VISA POS-PORT | HEMKO SYSTEMS CORP |
| 0534 | DEVICE LOCATION VIA REMOTE CONFIG TOOL | MILAN TECHNOLOGY CORP |
| 0535 | DEVICE LOCATION VIA REMOTE CONFIG TOOL | MILAN TECHNOLOGY CORP |
| 0536 | DEVICE LOCATION VIA REMOTE CONFIG TOOL | MILAN TECHNOLOGY CORP |
| 0537 | DEVICE LOCATION VIA REMOTE CONFIG TOOL | MILAN TECHNOLOGY CORP |
| 0538 | DEVICE LOCATION VIA REMOTE CONFIG TOOL | MILAN TECHNOLOGY CORP |
| 0539 | DEVICE LOCATION VIA REMOTE CONFIG TOOL | MILAN TECHNOLOGY CORP |

| 053A | DEVICE LOCATION VIA REMOTE CONFIG TOOL | MILAN TECHNOLOGY CORP |
| 053B | DEVICE LOCATION VIA REMOTE CONFIG TOOL SMS SERVER | MILAN TECHNOLOGY CORP053E NEW REMOTED ERA SYSTEMS SERVICES LTD |
| 053F | LISTENER/NETWARE | STERLING TEFEN LAB |
| 0540 | LISTENER/DOS | STERLING TEFEN LAB |
| 0541 | LISTENER/WINDOWS | STERLING TEFEN LAB |
| 0542 | LISTENER/OS2 | STERLING TEFEN LAB |
| 0543 | LISTENER/MAC | STERLING TEFEN LAB |
| 0544 | LISTENER/UNIX | STERLING TEFEN LAB |
| 0545 | TECHRA CLIENT/SERVER RDBMS | KVATRO AS |
| 0546 | DOCRA CLIENT/SERVER DOC MGMT SYSTEM | KVATRO AS |
| 0547 | VOICE/FAX RESPONDING MACHINE | SYSTEM SOPHIA |
| 0548 | I4/LS NAMING SERVICE | GRADIENT TECHNOLOGIES |
| 0549 | TNSI NETWORK UTILITIES | TOADALLY NETWORK SYSTEMS INC |
| 054A | RM3 CONFIGURATION | CAYMAN SYSTEMS INC |
| 054B | SNMP CONFIGURATION | CAYMAN SYSTEMS INC |
| 054D | IMAGESOLVE_OFS | IMAGESOLVE INTERNATIONAL |
| 054E | DISTRICT COMMUNICATION GATEWAY | CHANCERY SOFTWARE LTD |
| 054F | DISTRICT LINK | CHANCERY SOFTWARE LTD |
| 0550 | EDM CLIENT/PC | COMPUTER VISION |
| 0555 | PRINTERS, PLOTTERS & ROUTERS | SEIKO INSTRUMENTS INC |
| 0556 | FAX SERVICES | OAZ |
| 0557 | FAX SERVICES | OAZ |
| 0558 | FAX SERVICES | OAZ |
| 0559 | AT&T JOINT VENTURE TELEPHONY SERVER | NOVELL - PROVO |
| 055A | AT&T JOINT VENTURE TELEPHONY SERVER | NOVELL - PROVO |
| 055B | AT&T JOINT VENTURE TELEPHONY SERVER | NOVELL - PROVO |
| 055C | AT&T JOINT VENTURE TELEPHONY SERVER | NOVELL - PROVO |
| 055D | HOSTVIEW UTILITY | ATTACHMATE CORP |
| 055E | PRINT SERVER | LEXMARK INTERNATIONAL INC |
| 055F | PRINT SERVER | LEXMARK INTERNATIONAL INC |
| 0560 | PRINT SERVER | LEXMARK INTERNATIONAL INC |
| 0561 | PRINT SERVER | LEXMARK INTERNATIONAL INC |
| 0562 | STATISTICS GATHERING AGENT | NETCRAFT SOFTWARE DEVELOPMENT |
| 0563 | ERL DATABASE SERVER | SILVER PLATTER INFORMATION LTD |
| 0564 | ERL DIRECTORY SERVER | SILVER PLATTER INFORMATION LTD |

| 0565 | NEWSWIRE NOTIFICATION | GENERATION TECHNOLOGIES CORP |
|------|----------------------|------------------------------|
| 0568 | X-BASE DATABASE SERVER | EXTENDED SYSTEMS |
| 0569 | ADVERTISING MEDIA-DB SERVER | RAVI TECHNOLOGIES INC |
| 056A | OEM REMOTE ACCESS FOR ETHERNET | SHIVA CORP |
| 056B | OEM REMOTE ACCESS FOR TOKENRING | SHIVA CORP |
| 056C | INTEGRATED REMOTE ACCESS FOR ETHERNET | SHIVA CORP |
| 056D | INTEGRATED REMOTE ACCESS FOR TOKENRING | SHIVA CORP |
| 056F | MED STATION SERVER | PYXIS CORPORATION |
| 0570 | TELNET IPX ROUTER | TELETROL SYSTEMS INC |
| 0571 | NLM SERVER | SR ASSOCIATES/CYBERMEDIA |
| 0572 | ADVERTISING NETMODEM SERVER | PRACTICAL PERIPHERALS INC |
| 0573 | SATELLITE CONNECTIONS | ULF ZIMMERMANN |
| 0574 | LAN/CD SERVER | LOGICRAFT |
| 0576 | PEER COMMUNICATIONS TOOL | INTELEC SYSTEMS CORPORATION |
| 0577 | COMMUNICATION SERVER | NORMAN DATA DEFANSE SYSTEMS |
| 0578 | MODEM SHARING SOFTWARE | SEG |
| 0579 | HOPS DATABASE SERVER | HOPS INTERNATIONAL |
| 057A | DATAFILE ACCESS HANDLER | LMS |
| 057B | NOVUS GATEWAY PRODUCT | FIREFOX COMMUNICATIONS |
| 057C | LGS | INTERCONNECTIONS |
| 057D | LGS-PFT | INTERCONNECTIONS |
| 057E | LGS-PPS | INTERCONNECTIONS |
| 057F | TN 3270 GATEWAY | BUS TECH INC |
| 0580 | MCAFEE VIRUS PATTERN SERVER | MCAFEE ASSOCIATES |
| 0581 | OPTICAL SERVER | OPTISYS |
| 0582 | PRORIDE X.500 LDAP SUPPORT | CONTROL DATA SYSTEMS |
| 0583 | NET TRAX ALARM MONITOR | NET X CORP |
| 0584 | NET TRAX FILE SERVER AGENT | NET X CORP |
| 0585 | NET TRAX WORKSTATION AGENT | NET X CORP |
| 0586 | NET TRAX BRIDGE AGENT | NET X CORP |
| 0587 | TEAM OFFICE PRODUCT | CL PERSONAL SYSTEMS OY |
| 0589 | HYPERDESK DISTRIBUTE OBJECT MGMT SYSTEM | HYPERDESK |
| 058A | HYPERDESK DATABASE TYPE | HYPERDESK |
| 058B | TCP/SUPERLAT HOST PRINT SAP | MERIDIAN TECHNOLOGY CORP |
| 058C | OCS SAFESERVER | OMNITECH CORPORATE SOLUTIONS |
| 058D | JUKEBOX USER GROUP | TODD ENTERPRISES INC |

| | | |
|---|---|---|
| 058E | FULL SCREEN LOGIN | CONFIRM |
| 058F | MEETING SPACE SERVER | WORLD BENDERS INC |
| 0590 | LAN PRODUCT SERVER | BMC SOFTWARE INC |
| 0591 | CBT SERVER | FIRST CLASS SYSTEMS |
| 0592 | NET TUNE SERVICE | HAWKNET INC |
| 0593 | PRINT SERVER | RICOH COMPANY LTD |
| 0594 | REMOTE PRINTER | RICOH COMPANY LTD |
| 0595 | SLATHP STATUS NLM | MERIDIAN TECHNOLOGY CORP |
| 0597 | IPX NAMED PIPES COMMUNICATION SERVICE | SYMANTEC PETER NORTON GROUP |
| 0598 | APPMETER FOR SUITES | FUNK SOFTWARE |
| 059C | SERVERLOG | DIAMOND SOFTWARE INC |
| 05A0 | SERVICE LOCATION PROTOCOL | EICON TECHNOLOGY |
| 05A1 | NMS ICONS | NETWORTH INC |
| 05A2 | NMS ICONS | NETWORTH INC |
| 05A3 | NMS ICONS | NETWORTH INC |
| 05A4 | NMS ICONS | NETWORTH INC |
| 05A5 | NMS ICONS | NETWORTH INC |
| 05A6 | NMS ICONS | NETWORTH INC |
| 05A7 | NMS ICONS | NETWORTH INC |
| 05A8 | NMS ICONS | NETWORTH INC |
| 05A9 | NMS ICONS | NETWORTH INC |
| 05AA | NMS ICONS | NETWORTH INC |
| 05AB | NMS ICONS | NETWORTH INC |
| 05AC | NMS ICONS | NETWORTH INC |
| 05AD | NMS ICONS | NETWORTH INC |
| 05AE | NMS ICONS | NETWORTH INC |
| 05AF | NMS ICONS | NETWORTH INC |
| 05B0 | NMS ICONS | NETWORTH INC |
| 05B1 | NMS ICONS | NETWORTH INC |
| 05B2 | NMS ICONS | NETWORTH INC |
| 05B3 | MULTI-SYSTEM MANAGER - NETVIEW INTERFACE | IBM - RESEARCH TRIANGLE PARK |
| 05B4 | ONLINE TRANSACTION TRANSPORTATION SYSTEM | ABG TECHNOLOGY/UNITED CARD SVC |
| 05B6 | DATASTAR NLM | APERTUS TECHNOLOGIES |
| 05B7 | DS_LCC - LOGICAL LINK CONTROLLER | APERTUS TECHNOLOGIES |
| 05B8 | DATABASE MANAGEMENT SERVICES | REVELATION TECHNOLOGIES |
| 05B9 | DISTRIBUTION SERVICES DISCOVERY | IBM - ROME |
| 05BA | MANAGING HARDWARE ROUTERS | COMPATIBLE SYSTEMS CORP |
| 05C0 | CALENDAR SERVER | CAMPBELL SERVICES INC |
| 05C1 | NETWORK MANAGEMENT APPLICATION | XIRCOM |

| 05C2 | NETWORK MANAGEMENT APPLICATION | XIRCOM |
| 05C3 | NETWORK MANAGEMENT APPLICATION | XIRCOM |
| 05C4 | NETWORK MANAGEMENT APPLICATION | XIRCOM |
| 05C5 | NETWORK MANAGEMENT APPLICATION | XIRCOM |
| 05C6 | NETWORK MANAGEMENT APPLICATION | XIRCOM |
| 05D9 | ETHERNET-MANAGED STACKABLE HUB | IBM - RESEARCH TRIANGLE PARK |
| 05E4 | FILENET NETWORK CLEARINGHOUSE | FILE NET |
| 05E5 | HPCS DATA-BASED PRODUCTS | TOBIT SOFTWARE GMBH |
| 05E6 | AST SNMP INSTRUMENTED SERVER | AST RESEARCH INC |
| 05EB | OFFICE EXTEND SERVER | FRANSEN KING |
| 05EC | WINDOWS NT NAMED PIPE SERVER | OPTUS INFORMATION SYSTEMS |
| 05ED | GATEWAY SERVER | FUJITSU LTD |
| 05EE | BINDERY FILE | FUJITSU LTD |
| 05EF | FAX WORKSTATION OBJECT | SOFNET INC |
| 0C29 | LICENSE PROFILE | INTEGRITY SOFTWARE |
| 05F3 | CLIENT SERVER ARRAY MONITOR PROGRAM | ALLODYNE INC |
| 05F4 | EVERGREEN MANAGEMENT AGENT | GOODALL SOFTWARE |
| 05F5 | WINDOWS BULLETIN BOARD SYSTEM | PACER SOFTWARE |
| 05F8 | UPS SNMP MONITOR NLM | COMPUTER SITE TECHNOLOGIES INC |
| 05FA | GOODALL VIRTUAL PROTOCOL ADAPTOR | GOODALL SOFTWARE |
| 053C | DEVICE LOCATION VIA REMOTE CONFIG TOOL | MILAN TECHNOLOGY CORP |
| 053D | DEVICE LOCATION VIA REMOTE CONFIG TOOL | MILAN TECHNOLOGY CORP |
| 0566 | ZIFF PROPRIETARY SERVICES | ZIFF INFORMATION SERVICES |
| 0567 | TIME SERVER NLM | MEINBERG FUNKUHREN |
| 0603 | TIME CARD SERVER | ADVANCED MANAGEMENT SOLUTIONS |
| 0606 | IMAGE SERVER ADDRESS LOOK-UP | WATERMARK SOFTWARE |
| 0607 | ARTS RLOGIND SERVER | AMERICAN REAL TIME, REUTERS CO |
| 0608 | ARTS GENERIC SERVER | AMERICAN REAL TIME, REUTERS CO |
| 0609 | ARTS RUUPD - ARE YOU UP DAEMON | AMERICAN REAL TIME, REUTERS CO |
| 060A | MONEY CENTER DATA SERVER | KNIGHT RIDDER FINANCIAL INC |
| 060C | AXIS PRINTER SERVER | AXIS COMMUNICATIONS AB |

| 060D | UNIX MAIL SERVER | FELPAUSCH |
|------|------------------|-----------|
| 0610 | SCSI MANAGEMENT | ADAPTEC |
| 0611 | STEALTH EVENT CAPTURE ENGINE | INTELLIGENCE QUOTIENT INTL LTD |
| 0613 | UNIVERSAL DATA TRANSPORTER | CONSEIL FORMATION ET DEVELOPPE |
| 0614 | COMMUNICATION SOFTWARE (NLM) | NEC - NIPPON ELECTRIC COMPANY |
| 0615 | COMMUNICATION SOFTWARE (NLM) | NEC - NIPPON ELECTRIC COMPANY |
| 0616 | FAX GATEWAY SERVER | RUSSELL CONSULTING |
| 061C | PRINT SERVER | EMULEX CORPORATION |
| 061D | PRINT SERVER | EMULEX CORPORATION |
| 061E | PRINT SERVER | EMULEX CORPORATION |
| 061F | PRINT SERVER | EMULEX CORPORATION |
| 0620 | PRINT SERVER | EMULEX CORPORATION |
| 0625 | SETUP MANAGER ACCESS CONTROL | MAXIMIZED SOFTWARE |
| 062F | METERING PROGRAM | SECURE DESIGN |
| 0636 | COMET TERMINAL SERVER | GOODALL SOFTWARE |
| 0637 | COMET FILE SERVER | GOODALL SOFTWARE |
| 05F2 | ROUTER ADMINISTRATION SERVER | LIVINGSTON ENTERPRISES |
| 073D | CONNECT:DIRECT NLM SERVER | STERLING SOFTWARE |
| 073E | CONNECT:DIRECT NLM SERVER | STERLING SOFTWARE |
| 073F | CONNECT:DIRECT NLM SERVER | STERLING SOFTWARE |
| 0740 | CONNECT:DIRECT NLM SERVER | STERLING SOFTWARE |
| 0741 | CONNECT:DIRECT NLM SERVER | STERLING SOFTWARE |
| 0742 | CONNECT:DIRECT NLM SERVER | STERLING SOFTWARE |
| 0743 | MAXSERV 3270 | MAXSERV |
| 0744 | MAXSERV PRICE | MAXSERV |
| 0745 | MAXSERV MAIL | MAXSERV |
| 0746 | MAXSERV MACS | MAXSERV |
| 0747 | MAXSERV RESERVED | MAXSERV |
| 0748 | MAXSERV RESERVED | MAXSERV |
| 0749 | TASKING IPX/LWSI GATEWAY | TASKING SOFTWARE BV |
| 074D | NLM APPLICATIONS | KNX LTD |
| 074E | NLM APPLICATIONS | KNX LTD |
| 074F | NLM APPLICATIONS | KNX LTD |
| 0750 | NLM APPLICATIONS | KNX LTD |

| 0753 | STP PROTOCOL SERVICE AGENT (CSA_FTP) | DIGITAL TECHNOLOGIES |
|------|------|------|
| 0754 | IND$FILE FILE TRANSFER AGT (CSA_INDFILE) | DIGITAL TECHNOLOGIES |
| 0755 | ALL KALPANA SWITCHES | KALPANA |
| 0756 | CHAT SERVER | MICROSOFT |
| 0757 | TITANIUM DATABASE ENGINE | MICRO DATA BASE SYSTEMS INC |
| 0758 | TCS COMMUNICATION SERVER | MICRO TEMPUS INC |
| 0759 | PC COMMUNICATION PARTNER SAP | FUJITSU LTD |
| 075A | PC COMMUNICATION PARTNER SAP | FUJITSU LTD |
| 075B | PC COMMUNICATION PARTNER BINDERY | FUJITSU LTD |
| 075C | DPC SERVER SAP | FUJITSU LTD |
| 075D | DPC SERVER BINDERY | FUJITSU LTD |
| 075E | CAM HOST | TMD CONSULTING |
| 075F | SERVER MONITORING APPLICATION | SOFTWORK GMBH |
| 076A | ALARM MANAGER NLM | CONNER PERIPHERALS |
| 076B | EVENT MANAGER NLM | CONNER PERIPHERALS |
| 076D | DESKTOP MANAGEMENT NLM | ADVANCED MODULAR SOLUTIONS INC |
| 0770 | REAL-TIME INTEGRATION SERVICES | INDUSTRIAL PEER TO PEER |
| 0771 | LANDEEP SERVER MONITOR | DEERFIELD COMPUTER SOLUTIONS |
| 0773 | HITECSOFT API MANAGER | HITECSOFT CORP |
| 0774 | HITECSOFT PUBLIC LIBRARY | HITECSOFT CORP |
| 0775 | HITECSOFT PHONE SERVER | HITECSOFT CORP |
| 077B | ADVANTAGE X-BASE SERVER | EXTENDED SYSTEMS |
| 077F | SECURITY AUDITOR | SECURE DESIGN |
| 0780 | U OF WISCONSIN UTILITIES | U OF WISCONSIN - MADISON, CAE |
| 0781 | U OF WISCONSIN UTILITIES | U OF WISCONSIN - MADISON, CAE |
| 0782 | U OF WISCONSIN UTILITIES | U OF WISCONSIN - MADISON, CAE |
| 0783 | U OF WISCONSIN UTILITIES | U OF WISCONSIN - MADISON, CAE |
| 078B | A NON-NAME-PIPE PIPE SERVER | TEAM DEVELOPMENT CORP |
| 0798 | NETHOPPER ROUTER | ROCKWELL NETWORK SYSTEMS |
| 0799 | NETHOPPER CLIENT ROUTER | ROCKWELL NETWORK SYSTEMS |
| 079A | NETHOPPER CLIENT | ROCKWELL NETWORK SYSTEMS |
| 079F | TIMBUKTU ADDRESS RESOLUTIONS | FARALLON COMPUTING |
| 07A0 | REMOTE ACCESS SERVER | MERIDIAN TECHNOLOGY CORP |
| 07A7 | BACKUP EXEC JOB QUEUE | ARCADA SOFTWARE |
| 07A8 | BACKUP EXEC JOB MANAGER | ARCADA SOFTWARE |
| 07A9 | BACKUP EXEC JOB SERVICE | ARCADA SOFTWARE |
| 07AC | SERVICE NW_CONNECT_PW_ SERVER | FLAGSTAR |
| 07AF | SITE METER SERVER | MCAFEE ASSOCIATES |

| | | |
|---|---|---|
| 07B0 | PROXY AGENT SITE MTER | MCAFEE ASSOCIATES |
| 07B3 | DISC DISASTER RECOVERY S/W SCHEDULER | COLUMBIA DATA PRODUCTS |
| 07B4 | CUBIX COMM. SERVER | CUBIX |
| 07B8 | IDENTIFY SERVER VENDOR FOR NMS | SIEMENS-NIXDORF INFOSYSTEME |
| 07BA | FILE TRANSFER BETWEEN LAN/MAINFRAME | PROGINET CORP |
| 07BF | DATABASE SERVER | COMP SOFT PLC |
| 07C0 | APPLICATION ADVERTISEMENT | COMP SOFT PLC |
| 07C1 | INTERNET APPS ON NW PCs | MANGO SYSTEMS |
| 07CE | COMPUTER SUPPORTED TELEPHONY APPS | GLOBAL COMMUNICATIONS LTD |
| 07D3 | GENERIC NW MANAGEMENT PRODUCT | 3 COM CORPORATION |
| 07D4 | SCSI MNGMT | ADAPTEC |
| 07D9 | DISTRIBUTION JOB SERVER | EMOTION INC |
| 07DA | DISTRIBUTION QUE | EMOTION INC |
| 07DB | DISTRIBUTION FEEDBACK JOB SERVER | EMOTION INC |
| 07DC | VOICE PROCESSING SERVER | INTERNATIONAL VOICE EXCHANGE |
| 07DD | TELEPHONY SERVER MONITOR | INTERNATIONAL VOICE EXCHANGE |
| 07E0 | PRINT SERVER | CREATIVE CONTROLLERS |
| 07E1 | BOX ROUTER SUPPORTING IP, IPX & APPLE T | FURUKAWA ELECTRIC CO LTD |
| 07E2 | TEL SERVE | FUJITSU NS CENTER |
| 07E3 | TELEMARKETING LIBRARY | FUJITSU NS CENTER |
| 07E4 | MULTI-SERVER METERING | MCAFEE ASSOCIATES |
| 07E6 | STRESS MAGIC INSTALLATION UTILITY HANDLE | NETMAGIC SYSTEMS INC |
| 07EC | FINANCIAL DATA SERVER | TELEMET AMERICA INC |
| 07ED | ISDN SOFTWARE SHARING OF ISDN BOARDS | HIGH SOFT TECH |
| 07EE | COMGATE-COMM GATEWAY FOR IBM AS 400 | COMWARE INTERNATIONAL |
| 07F0 | ZIP CODE SERVER | THIRD PLANET SOFTWARE |
| 07F2 | NORTON ANTI-VIRUS CLIENT SERVER COMM | SYMANTEC PETER NORTON GROUP |
| 07F8 | SOFTWARE ENTERTAINMENT | ORIGIN SYSTEMS |
| 07F9 | REMOTE MANAGEMENT OF REMOTE ACCESS SERVER | MERIDIAN TECHNOLOGY CORP |
| 07FC | FTMANAGER-CONTROLS NETWARE SERVER | MITSUBISHI DENKI COMPUTER |
| 07FD | SAP FOR AUDITTRACK VS. 2.0 | E.G. SOFTWARE INC |
| 07FF | SOFT-TUB AGENT PROXY FOR TRI-COM ADAPTOR | 3-COM CORP |

| | | |
|---|---|---|
| 07D1 | A SYNCHRONOUS COMMUNICATION | LAN ACCESS |
| 07D2 | RM AUDITOR-MONITORING NW USAGE | RESEARCH MACHINES |
| 0801 | SAP FOR ONGUARD | E.G. SOFTWARE INC |
| 080D | IFONY FLOW FOR NETWARE | FUJITSU SOCIAL SCIENCE LAB |
| 080E | PRINT SERVER FOR NW 3.X | ISHIGAKI COMPUTER SYSTEM CORP |
| 0810 | ELAN LICENSE SERVER DEMO | ELAN COMPUTER GROUP |
| 0811 | ELAN LICENSE SERVER | ELAN COMPUTER GROUP |
| 0813 | BVNCS ENTERPRISE WAN | LAN SUPPORT GROUP |
| 0814 | EVERGREEN WINDCAP MANAGEMENT AGENT | GOODALL SOFTWARE |
| 0816 | POLICY ENGINE | EMERALD SYSTEMS |
| 0817 | POLICY ENGINE | EMERALD SYSTEMS |
| 0818 | POLICY ENGINE | EMERALD SYSTEMS |
| 081D | OFF-LINE COPYING | ON TECHNOLOGIES |
| 0827 | PALINDROME SERVICE BROKER | PALINDROME |
| 0829 | LAN LENS SERVER | DIGITAL EQUIPMENT CORP |
| 082A | LAN LENS PROBE | DIGITAL EQUIPMENT CORP |
| 082B | JOB QUEUE | ARCADA SOFTWARE |
| 082F | DB SERVER 3.X | SIMULTAN AG |
| 0830 | PIN64 | ASAHI ELECTRONICS CO LTD |
| 0832 | APPMETER 2-LICENSING PRODUCT | FUNK SOFTWARE |
| 0833 | COMMUNICATION SERVER | DIGITAL PRODUCTS INC |
| 0834 | FTANALYZER | MITSUBISHI ELECTORIC CORP |
| 0835 | INSTANT INTERNET | PERFORMANCE TECHNOLOGY |
| 0836 | HIGH SPEED COMMUNICATION SERVER | C SPEC CORP |
| 0837 | ATLANTA/3 PRINT SERVER | KELLY COMPUTER SYSTEMS |
| 083D | APPLICATION SERVER FOR NT | CITRIX SYSTEMS |
| 083E | CUSTOM AUTHENTICATION/ LOAD BALANCING | UNIVERSITY OF PITTSBURGH |
| 0840 | IP TO IPX GATEWAY | INTERNET JUNCTION |
| 0841 | RDB/7000 | FUJITSU LTD |
| 084C | BOX-TYPE HDWR ROUTER SUPPTS APPLETALK | BUG INC |
| 084D | SNAP-IN TOOL FOR NMS | NEC CORPORATION |
| 0850 | APLINKTERM | MIKASA SYSTEM ENGINEERING |
| 0853 | APLINKGATE | MIKASA SYSTEM ENGINEERING |
| 0854 | AUTOMATION PROTOCOL SERVER | ARCADA SOFTWARE |
| 0855 | TAPE ID SERVER | ARCADA SOFTWARE |
| 0858 | NETWARE TO INTERNET GATEWAY | ON TECHNOLOGY |
| 085A | RDB/7000 SERVER FOR NW | FUJITSU LIMITED |

| | | |
|---|---|---|
| 085C | DB-EXPRESS | FUJITSU KOBE ENGINEERING LTD |
| 085F | AGENT ROUTER PROXY | ARCADA SOFTWARE |
| 0860 | CATALOG SERVER | ARCADA SOFTWARE |
| 0861 | INETIX GATEWAY | MICRO COMPUTER SYSTEMS |
| 0868 | SOUNDBYTE SERVER | ENVISION TELEPHONY INC |
| 0869 | PEER TO PEER FILE REDIRECTION | ALEX LLOYD |
| 086F | VISION 20 MULTI-FUNCTIONAL PRODUCT | RICOH CORP |
| 0870 | DPS-SV | PFU LIMITED |
| 0876 | AUDIT SERVER | LAN SUPPORT GROUP |
| 0877 | ALERT SERVER | LAN SUPPORT GROUP |
| 0878 | NETSQUEEZE | LAN SUPPORT GROUP |
| 0879 | EWAM | LAN SUPPORT GROUP |
| 087A | BINDING SERVER | LAN SUPPORT GROUP |
| 087B | AUTHENTICATION SERVER | LAN SUPPORT GROUP |
| 087D | MODEM POOL SERVER | ATTACHMATE |
| 087E | FLORA MANAGER FOR NETWARE | HITACHI LTD SOFTWARE DEVT CTR |
| 0886 | MULTI-USER DOS GOLD | CONCURRENT CONTROLS INC |
| 088B | SPX TELENET AGENT | TELEBIT |
| 0892 | UPS CONTROL SOFTWARE UPSCON | AKIRA SAITO |
| 0897 | SHARED LAN CACHE | MEASUREMENT TECHNIQUES |
| 089A | "CLEAR IT" | DELL COMPUTER CORP |
| 089D | FAX SERVER - PERFECT FIT | NEWTECH SYSTEMS |
| 089F | NET TUNE PRO LICENSE | HAWKNET INC |
| 08A0 | NET TUNE PRO ALERT SERVICE | HAWKNET INC |
| 08A1 | POWERVISOR, POWER MONITOR | ALFATECH INC |
| 08A4 | INETIX GATEWAY ADMIN SERVICE | MICRO COMPUTER SYSTEMS |
| 08A8 | RAPPORT 112 | SHIVA CORP |
| 08AA | CPA "CORP PRINT ACCOUNTING" | BLUE LANCE |
| 08AC | GROUPEASE FOR WIN-NEIGHBORHOOD WATCH | ETHOSOFT, INC |
| 08AD | CS-CARE NETWORK MANAGEMENT SYSTEM | COMPU-SHACK PRAGUE |
| 08AE | FIRECALL | TEAM DEVELOPMENT CORP |
| 08B0 | NETWARE ENHANCED INTEGRATION FOR AS400 | IBM - ROCHESTER |
| 08B2 | OVERDRIVE | STAMPEDE TECHNOLOGY INC |
| 08B3 | IIR | ANSWERSOFT INC. |
| 08B4 | WANDERLINK DIALOUT | FUNK SOFTWARE |
| 08B7 | WEB MANAGEMENT | VIRTUAL MOTION INC |
| 08B8 | CNA DISTRIBUTED TRAFFIC MONITOR | CHEVIN SOFTWARE ENGINEERING LT |

| | | |
|---|---|---|
| 08B9 | DS GATE | DATASTREAM INTERNATIONAL |
| 08BA | VTD/X GATEWAY | MICRO MATIC RESEARCH |
| 08BB | SALIENT CORP | SALIENT TECHNOLOGIES INC |
| 08BC | IP ACCESS | AMERICAN INTERNET CORPORATION |
| 08BE | ELECTRONIC ARTS GAMES | ELECTRONIC ARTS INC |
| 08BF | IPX/IP GATEWAY | UKIAH SOFTWARE SOLUTIONS INC |
| 08C0 | NORTON ENTERPRISE FRAMEWORK (NEF) | SYMANTEC CORP |
| 08C1 | XYRATEX VIRTUALSCSI NLM | XYRATEX |
| 08C2 | 8235 DIALS SWITCH FOR G TOKEN RIN | IBM - RESEARCH TRIANGLE PARK |
| 08C3 | STAMPEDE OVERDRIVE | STAMPEDE TECHNOLOGY INC |
| 08C4 | INTERGATE | NETSPHERE COMMUNICATIONS CORP |
| 08C8 | SERVERTRAK | INTRAK INC |
| 08C9 | CDSERVE | M4COM LTD |
| 08CC | POWERBURST/INTEGRATED | SHIVA |
| 08CD | SURFCONTROL | WONDERWARE CORPORATION |
| 08CE | TREND TRAK | INTRAK INC |
| 08CF | SURFCONTROL | JSB COMPUTER SYSTEMS LTD |
| 08D0 | INTERNET LANBRIDGE | VIRTUAL MOTION INC |
| 08D1 | HYPERDRIVE | PAPERWISE |
| 08D2 | GOLF SCORING SYSTEM | INFORMATION AND DISPLAY SYST |
| 08D3 | SURFCONTROL | JSB COMPUTER SYSTEMS LTD |
| 08D4 | SURFCONTROL | JSB COMPUTER SYSTEMS LTD |
| 08D5 | SURFCONTROL | JSB COMPUTER SYSTEMS LTD |
| 08D6 | SURFCONTROL | JSB COMPUTER SYSTEMS LTD |
| 08D7 | SURFCONTROL | JSB COMPUTER SYSTEMS LTD |
| 08D8 | SURFCONTROL | JSB COMPUTER SYSTEMS LTD |
| 08D9 | SURFCONTROL | JSB COMPUTER SYSTEMS LTD |
| 08DA | SURFCONTROL | JSB COMPUTER SYSTEMS LTD |
| 08DB | SURFCONTROL | JSB COMPUTER SYSTEMS LTD |
| 08DC | SURFCONTROL | JSB COMPUTER SYSTEMS LTD |
| 08DD | SURFCONTROL | JSB COMPUTER SYSTEMS LTD |
| 08DE | SURFCONTROL | JSB COMPUTER SYSTEMS LTD |
| 08DF | SURFCONTROL | JSB COMPUTER SYSTEMS LTD |
| 08E0 | HTTP-WEBMAIL,EXPRESSIT!_ 2000 | INFINITE TECHNOLOGIES |
| 08E1 | SMTP-EXPRESSIT!2000, WEBMAIL, & INFINITE INTERCHANGE | INFINITE TECHNOLOGIES |
| 08E2 | POP3-EXPRESSIT!2000 & INFINITE INTERCHANGE | INFINITE TECHNOLOGIES |
| 08E3 | IMAP4-EXPRESSIT!2000& INFINITE INTERCHANGE | INFINITE TECHNOLOGIES |
| 08E4 | NNTP-EXPRESSIT!2000& INFINITE INTERCHANGE | INFINITE TECHNOLOGIES |
| 08E5 | MPR FOR ISDN | AVM GMBH |
| 0C2A | VIRUS FILE LIST | INTEGRITY SOFTWARE |

| | | |
|---|---|---|
| 0C2C | GLOBAL LICENSE SAP | INTEGRITY SOFTWARE |
| 0C31 | LICENSE REPORT DEFINITION | INTEGRITY SOFTWARE |
| 238C | MEETING MAKER XP | ON TECHNOLOGY |
| 238D | NLM | ON TECHNOLOGY |
| 238E | NLM | ON TECHNOLOGY |
| 9620 | LICENSE PROFILE ADMINISTRATOR | INTEGRITY SOFTWARE |
| FFFF | ALL TYPES | NOVELL - PROVO CORP HQ |

# Socket Number List

All values listed herein are in hexadecimal (0x) format. For more information on IPX sockets, refer to Chapter 7.

```
8000   NATIONAL ADVANCED SYSTEMS
8001   NATIONAL ADVANCED SYSTEMS
8002   NATIONAL ADVANCED SYSTEMS
8003   COMM DRIVER  SPERRY CORP. COMPUTER SYSTEMS
8004   KTA
8005   KTA
8006   KTA
8007   KTA
8008   NOVELL - PROVO
8009   SPERRY TERM EMULATOR  TURNBULL AUTOMATIONS
800A   PRINT SERVER  COMMUNICATION HORIZONS
800B   DATA LANGUAGE CORP
800F   BATRAM  SANTA CLARA SYSTEMS
8010   OFFICE WARE  CENTURY ANALYSIS
8011   UPS  ELGAR CORP
8012   UPS  ELGAR CORP
8013   CHI CORP
8014   INTEL - AMERICAN FORK
8015   COMPASS COMPUTING
8016   COMPASS COMPUTING
8017   COMPASS COMPUTING
8018   COMPASS COMPUTING
8019   COMPASS COMPUTING
801A   COMPASS COMPUTING
801B   COMPASS COMPUTING
801C   COMPASS COMPUTING
801D   COMPASS COMPUTING
801E   COMPASS COMPUTING
801F   NOVELL - SUNNYVALE LATIN AMERI
8020   NOVELL - SUNNYVALE LATIN AMERI
8021   NOVELL - SUNNYVALE LATIN AMERI
8022   NOVELL - SUNNYVALE LATIN AMERI
8023   MCAFEE ASSOCIATES
8024   BLUE LANCE NETWORK INFO SYS
8027   GATEWAY COMMUNICATIONS INC
8028   GATEWAY COMMUNICATIONS INC
8029   GATEWAY COMMUNICATIONS INC
802A   FILE SHARING  NETLINE INC
802B   FILE SHARING  NETLINE INC
802C   INTEL - AMERICAN FORK
802D   INTEL - AMERICAN FORK
802E   ICM
802F   C-TREE VAP  FAIR COM
8030   MICROMIND
```

```
8031   MICROMIND
8032   NORTH STAR COMPUTERS
8033   NORTH STAR COMPUTERS
8034   X.25 GATEWAY   RSJ SOFTWARE
8035   SANYO ICON INC
8036   DATA ACCESS CORP
8039   NET MANAGEMENT   NOVELL - AUSTIN
803A   BETA SOFT
803B   PHASER SYSTEMS
803C   PHASER SYSTEMS
803D   PHASER SYSTEMS
803E   PERFORMANCE GROUP
803F   PERFORMANCE GROUP
8040   HORIZON TECHNOLOGY INC
8041   CD-ROM SERVER   MERIDIAN DATA CORP
8042   NATIONWIDE COMPUTER SERVICES
8043   COMM SERVER   COMPUTER LANGUAGE RESEARCH INC
8047   3274 CONTROLLER EMULATORS   SOFTWARE DYNAMICS
8048   3274 CONTROLLER EMULATORS   SOFTWARE DYNAMICS
8049   3274 CONTROLLER EMULATORS   SOFTWARE DYNAMICS
804A   3274 CONTROLLER EMULATORS   SOFTWARE DYNAMICS
804B   MIC SNA DFV SERVER   COMPUTERLAND - BONN
804C   MIC SNA DFV SERVER   COMPUTERLAND - BONN
804D   DATABASE SERVER   MIGENT SOFTWARE INC
804E   SWITCH LINK SYSTEMS
804F   INTERACTIVE FINANCIAL SOL INC
8050   INTERACTIVE FINANCIAL SOL INC
8051   INTERACTIVE FINANCIAL SOL INC
8052   INTERACTIVE FINANCIAL SOL INC
8053   Unknown
8054   Unknown
8055   E-MAIL CHAT   NICHE CO
8056   MONEY TRANSFER   IPI INC
8057   E-MAIL CHAT   NICHE CO
805E   TELEBASE SYSTEMS
805F   TELEBASE SYSTEMS
8060   PRINT SERVER   NOVELL - PROVO
8061   T-NET, LAN BRIDGES   BRITISH TELECOM
8062   WOLLONGONG GROUP
8064   MICRO DATA BASE SYSTEMS
8065   MICRO DATA BASE SYSTEMS
8066   NORTON LAMBERT CORP
8067   NORTON LAMBERT CORP
8068   NORTON LAMBERT CORP
8069   NETWARE TO HP LAN GATEWAY   HEWLETT PACKARD - SUNNYVALE
806A   REMOTE PC SOFTWARE   ALM
806C   CHAT PROGRAM   DIGITAL AV INC
806D   PC DEX   MERGENT INTERNATIONAL
```

```
806E   DART   COLLEGE HILL SYSTEMS
8070   NETWORK COURIER   MICROSOFT WORKGROUP CANADA
8071   PIPES   PEER LOGIC
8072   WORDPERFECT CORP
8073   DATABASE & 4GL   PROGRESS SOFTWARE CORP
8074   RIGHT HAND MAN   FUTURESOFT
8075   RIGHT HAND MAN   FUTURESOFT
8076   LASER DISK PROGRAM   U OF WISCONSIN - SUPERIOR
8077   FAX LINK & VAX MANAGER   OPTUS INFORMATION SYSTEMS
8078   FAX LINK & VAX MANAGER   OPTUS INFORMATION SYSTEMS
8079   TELECOMMUNICATIONS   VAN AUTO PARTS
807A   TELECOMMUNICATIONS   VAN AUTO PARTS
807B   TELECOMMUNICATIONS   VAN AUTO PARTS
807C   TELECOMMUNICATIONS   VAN AUTO PARTS
807D   TELECOMMUNICATIONS   VAN AUTO PARTS
807E   R21PX   CROSSTALK
807F   ORACLE CORP
8080   ORACLE CORP
8081   ORACLE CORP
8082   ORACLE CORP
8083   ORACLE CORP
8084   ORACLE CORP
8085   ORACLE CORP
8086   ORACLE CORP
8087   ORACLE CORP
8088   ORACLE CORP
8089   REMOTE PC SOFTWARE   ALM
808A   Unknown
808B   Unknown
808C   Unknown
808D   Unknown
808E   Unknown
808F   Unknown
8090   VAP   PILLSBURY CO
8091   VAP   PILLSBURY CO
8092   VAP   PILLSBURY CO
8093   VAP   PILLSBURY CO
8094   VAP   PILLSBURY CO
8095   VAP   PILLSBURY CO
8096   VAP   PILLSBURY CO
8097   VAP   PILLSBURY CO
8098   VAP   PILLSBURY CO
8099   VAP   PILLSBURY CO
809A   MARSHFIELD CLINIC
809B   MARSHFIELD CLINIC
809C   MARSHFIELD CLINIC
809D   MARSHFIELD CLINIC
809E   MARSHFIELD CLINIC
```

```
809F   MARSHFIELD CLINIC
80AF   DSI DYNAPRO SYSTEMS INC
80B0   DSI DYNAPRO SYSTEMS INC
80B1   DSI DYNAPRO SYSTEMS INC
80B2   DSI DYNAPRO SYSTEMS INC
80B3   DSI DYNAPRO SYSTEMS INC
80B4   CHICAGO RESEARCH & TRADING
80B5   STREETWISE SYSTEMS INC
80B6   STREETWISE SYSTEMS INC
80B7   FAX SERVER  DIGITAL VISIONS CORP
80B8   VOICE SERVER
DIGITAL VISIONS CORP
80B9   DIGITAL VISIONS CORP
80BA   NETWARE MANAGEMENT APPLICATION  FRYE COMPUTER SYSTEMS
80BB   MAJOR BBS SOFTWARE   GALACTICOMM INC
80BC   MAJOR BBS SOFTWARE   GALACTICOMM INC
80BD   MAJOR BBS SOFTWARE   GALACTICOMM INC
80BE   MAJOR BBS SOFTWARE   GALACTICOMM INC
80BF   MAJOR BBS SOFTWARE   GALACTICOMM INC
80C0   MAJOR BBS SOFTWARE   GALACTICOMM INC
80C1   MAJOR BBS SOFTWARE   GALACTICOMM INC
80C2   MAJOR BBS SOFTWARE   GALACTICOMM INC
80C3   CHAT PROGRAM/IPX TALK  FELSINA SOFTWARE
80C4   IPX/SPX COMM PROTOCOL APPLICATIONS  MAGEE ENTERPRISES INC
80C5   WATCOM
80C6   NEWPORT SYSTEMS SOLUTIONS INC
80C7   NEWPORT SYSTEMS SOLUTIONS INC
80C8   NEWPORT SYSTEMS SOLUTIONS INC
80C9   NEWPORT SYSTEMS SOLUTIONS INC
80CA   NEWPORT SYSTEMS SOLUTIONS INC
80CB   NEWPORT SYSTEMS SOLUTIONS INC
80CC   NEWPORT SYSTEMS SOLUTIONS INC
80CD   NEWPORT SYSTEMS SOLUTIONS INC
80CE   SPX DRIVER/NOVA FOCUS REMOTE PC ACCESS  DRIGGS CORPORATION
80CF   APPL IPX/SPX COMMUNICATIONS   MAGEE ENTERPRISES INC
80D0   APPL IPX/SPX COMMUNICATIONS   MAGEE ENTERPRISES INC
80D1   APPL IPX/SPX COMMUNICATIONS   MAGEE ENTERPRISES INC
80D2   APPL IPX/SPX COMMUNICATIONS   MAGEE ENTERPRISES INC
80D3   APPL 1PX/SPX COMMUNICATIONS   MAGEE ENTERPRISES INC
80D5   DATABASE SERVER  GUPTA TECHNOLOGIES
80D6   DATABASE SERVER  GUPTA TECHNOLOGIES
80D7   LAN/FILE TRANSFER, COMM SERVERS, REMOTES  US ROBOTICS SOFTWARE
80D8   POWERCHUTE—VAP/NLM SERVER POWER SUPPLY  Amercian Power Conversion
80D9   COREL DRIVER PRODUCT UNDER NOVELL 386
COREL SYSTEMS, OPTICAL DIV
80DA   ARCHIVE SERVER  GIGATREND INC
80DB   GATEWAY PRODUCT  ATLANTA TECHNOLOGIES
80DC   GATEWAY PRODUCT  ATLANTA TECHNOLOGIES
```

```
80DD   OFFICE ORGANIZER NLM   UNISYS - CAMARILLO
80DE   UNIVERSAL NETWORK SYSTEMS
80DF   APPLICATION SERVER   NATIONSBANK APPL SYSTEMS SUPP
80E1   MODULAR SOFTWARE CORPORATION
80E2   CLIENT SERVER APPLICATION   SOFTWARE AG
80E4   LANPORT VIRTUAL EXTENSION OF PORTS   MICROTEST INC
80E5   WORK STATION PEER-TO-PEER   CONVEYANT SYSTEMS INC
80E6   DESKVIEW X - IPX SOCKET INTERFACE   QUARTERDECK OFFICE SYSTEMS
80E7   DESKVIEW X - IPX SOCKET INTERFACE   QUARTERDECK OFFICE SYSTEMS
80E8   DESKVIEW X - IPX SOCKET INTERFACE   QUARTERDECK OFFICE SYSTEMS
80E9   DESKVIEW X - IPX SOCKET INTERFACE   QUARTERDECK OFFICE SYSTEMS
80EA   DESKVIEW X - IPX SOCKET INTERFACE   QUARTERDECK OFFICE SYSTEMS
80EB   DESKVIEW X - IPX SOCKET INTERFACE   QUARTERDECK OFFICE SYSTEMS
80EC   MERIDIAN DATA INC
80ED   BIZTECH
80EE   RATIONAL DATA SYSTEMS
80EF   RATIONAL DATA SYSTEMS
80F0   RATIONAL DATA SYSTEMS
80F1   RATIONAL DATA SYSTEMS
80F4   GARP SERVER COMMUNICATION   NET RESEARCH PTY LTD
80F5   NETWORK MANAGEMENT PRODUCT   NCR - COLUMBIA
80F6   NETWORK MANAGEMENT PRODUCT   NCR - COLUMBIA
80F7   NETWORK MANAGEMENT PRODUCT   NCR - COLUMBIA
80F8   NETWORK MANAGEMENT PRODUCT   NCR - COLUMBIA
80F9   NETWORK MANAGEMENT PRODUCT   NCR - COLUMBIA
80FA   NETWORK MANAGEMENT PRODUCT   NCR - COLUMBIA
80FB   PROFESSIONAL PROGRAMMING SVCS
80FC   PROFESSIONAL PROGRAMMING SVCS
80FD   PEER LOGIC
80FE   WALL DATA
80FF   DISTRIBUTED APPLICATION   FOLIO CORPORATION
8100   MARSHFIELD CLINIC
8101   MARSHFIELD CLINIC
8102   MARSHFIELD CLINIC
8103   MARSHFIELD CLINIC
8105   VIA
8106
8107
8108
8109
810A
810B
810C
810D
810E
810F   NET 3270   MCGILL UNIVERSITY COMPUTING CT
8110   PROFESSIONAL PRODUCTIVITY CORP
8111   TODS   TELETRAK
```

```
8112   LUFTHANSA BS   LUFTHANSA GERMAN AIRLINES
8113   LANPORT   MICROTEST
8114   LANPORT   MICROTEST
8115   LANPORT   MICROTEST
8116   LANPORT   MICROTEST
8117   LANPORT   MICROTEST
8118   LANPORT   MICROTEST
8119   LANPORT   MICROTEST
811A   LANPORT   MICROTEST
811B   LANPORT   MICROTEST
811C   LANPORT   MICROTEST
811D   IMAGE SERVER   FILE NET CORPORATION
811F   RTK OPERATING SYSTEM   OWL MICRO SYSTEMS
8120   TXD   THOMAS CONRAD CORP
8121   SPECIAL REQUEST   SPECTRAFAX
8122   NET MONITOR   ARTEFACT NETWORK SUPPORT
8123   NET MONITOR   ARTEFACT NETWORK SUPPORT
8124   NET MONITOR   ARTEFACT NETWORK SUPPORT
8125   NET MONITOR   ARTEFACT NETWORK SUPPORT
8126   NET MONITOR   ARTEFACT NETWORK SUPPORT
8127   NET MONITOR   ARTEFACT NETWORK SUPPORT
8128   NET MONITOR   ARTEFACT NETWORK SUPPORT
8129   NET MONITOR   ARTEFACT NETWORK SUPPORT
812A   NET MONITOR   ARTEFACT NETWORK SUPPORT
812B   NET MONITOR   ARTEFACT NETWORK SUPPORT
812C   NET MONITOR   ARTEFACT NETWORK SUPPORT
812D   NET MONITOR   ARTEFACT NETWORK SUPPORT
8138   LANSIGHT   LAN SYSTEMS
8139   PC CHALKBOARD   INTEL - AMERICAN FORK
813B   REAL TIME BACK-UP   EMERALD SYSTEMS
813C   NETWORK MANAGEMENT   PURE DATA INC
813E   FILE TRANSFER   AAC SYSTEMS
813F   IMAGE SERVER   WANG LABORATORIES
8140   IMAGE SERVER   WANG LABORATORIES
8141   IMAGE SERVER   WANG LABORATORIES
8142   IMAGE SERVER   WANG LABORATORIES
8143   NETWORK DESIGNERS LTD
8144   MAYNESTREAM   ARCADA SOFTWARE
8145   MAYNESTREAM   ARCADA SOFTWARE
8146   NETWORK MANAGEMENT SYSTEM   ACCUNETICS
8147   NETWORK MANAGEMENT SYSTEM   ACCUNETICS
8148   NETWORK MANAGEMENT SYSTEM   ACCUNETICS
8149   NETWORK MANAGEMENT SYSTEM   ACCUNETICS
814A   BR COMPUTING
814B   NLM   AUTOMATED DESIGN SYSTEMS
814C   BR COMPUTING
814D   BR COMPUTING
814E   BR COMPUTING
```

```
814F   BR COMPUTING
8150   BR COMPUTING
8151   BR COMPUTING
8152   BR COMPUTING
8153   BR COMPUTING
8154   BR COMPUTING
8155   BR COMPUTING
8156   BR COMPUTING
8157   BR COMPUTING
8158   BR COMPUTING
8159   BR COMPUTING
815A   BR COMPUTING
815B   BR COMPUTING
815C   BR COMPUTING
815D   BR COMPUTING
815E   BR COMPUTING
815F   BR COMPUTING
8160   PRINTQLAN   SOFTWARE DIRECTIONS INC
8161   PRINTQLAN   SOFTWARE DIRECTIONS INC
8162   PRINTQLAN   SOFTWARE DIRECTIONS INC
8163   PRINTQLAN   SOFTWARE DIRECTIONS INC
8164   PRINTQLAN   SOFTWARE DIRECTIONS INC
8165   PRINTQLAN   SOFTWARE DIRECTIONS INC
8166   PRINTQLAN   SOFTWARE DIRECTIONS INC
8167   PRINTQLAN   SOFTWARE DIRECTIONS INC
8168   PRINTQLAN   SOFTWARE DIRECTIONS INC
8169   PRINTQLAN   SOFTWARE DIRECTIONS INC
816A   PRINTQLAN   SOFTWARE DIRECTIONS INC
816B   PRINTQLAN   SOFTWARE DIRECTIONS INC
816C   PRINTQLAN   SOFTWARE DIRECTIONS INC
816D   PRINTQLAN   SOFTWARE DIRECTIONS INC
816E   PRINTQLAN   SOFTWARE DIRECTIONS INC
816F   PRINTQLAN   SOFTWARE DIRECTIONS INC
8170   CDROM   ONLINE COMPUTER SYSTEMS
8171   CDROM   ONLINE COMPUTER SYSTEMS
8172   BENTLEY SYSTEMS
8173   AVALAN
8174   AVALAN
8175   AVALAN
8176   AVALAN
8177   AVALAN
8178   AVALAN
8179   AVALAN
817A   AVALAN
817B   ACCOUNTING APD   SUPERNET
817C   ACS
817D   SERVER DB   XDB SYSTEMS
817E   PIPES   PEER LOGIC
```

```
817F   PIPES    PEER LOGIC
8180   NETWARE SOFTWARE ASSOCIATES
8181   PEER-TO-PEER   LODGISTIX INC
8182   PEER-TO-PEER   LODGISTIX INC
8183   PEER-TO-PEER   LODGISTIX INC
8184   PEER-TO-PEER   LODGISTIX INC
8185   PEER-TO-PEER   LODGISTIX INC
8186   DANWARE
8187   DANWARE
8188   DANWARE
8189   DANWARE
818A   DANWARE
818B   NETFRAME NW 386    NETFRAME
818C   NETFRAME NW 386    NETFRAME
818D   NETFRAME NW 386    NETFRAME
818E   NETFRAME NW 386    NETFRAME
818F   MAXIBACK   SYSGEN INC
8190   MAXIBACK   SYSGEN INC
8191   MAXIBACK   SYSGEN INC
8192   MAXIBACK   SYSGEN INC
8193   DCA IPX COMM PRODUCT   DIGITAL COMMUNICATIONS ASSOC
8194   DCA IPX COMM PRODUCT   DIGITAL COMMUNICATIONS ASSOC
8195   DCA IPX COMM PRODUCT   DIGITAL COMMUNICATIONS ASSOC
8196   QUICKCHART   HEALTHWARE
8197   QUICKCHART   HEALTHWARE
8198   QUICKCHART   HEALTHWARE
8199   QUICKCHART   HEALTHWARE
819A   U OF OTAGO
819B   U OF OTAGO
819C   MINI SQL   ISICAD
81A0   DEALING ROOM SYSTEMS
81A1   DEALING ROOM SYSTEMS
81A2   DEALING ROOM SYSTEMS
81A3   DEALING ROOM SYSTEMS
81A4   DEALING ROOM SYSTEMS
81A5   DEALING ROOM SYSTEMS
81A6   DEALING ROOM SYSTEMS
81A7   DEALING ROOM SYSTEMS
81A8   DEALING ROOM SYSTEMS
81A9   DEALING ROOM SYSTEMS
81AA   DEALING ROOM SYSTEMS
81AB   DEALING ROOM SYSTEMS
81AC   DEALING ROOM SYSTEMS
81AD   DEALING ROOM SYSTEMS
81AE   DEALING ROOM SYSTEMS
81AF   DEALING ROOM SYSTEMS
81B0   DEALING ROOM SYSTEMS
81B1   DEALING ROOM SYSTEMS
```

```
81B2   DEALING ROOM SYSTEMS
81B3   DEALING ROOM SYSTEMS
81B4   DEALING ROOM SYSTEMS
81B5   DEALING ROOM SYSTEMS
81B6   DEALING ROOM SYSTEMS
81B7   DEALING ROOM SYSTEMS
81B8   DEALING ROOM SYSTEMS
81B9   DEALING ROOM SYSTEMS
81BA   DEALING ROOM SYSTEMS
81BB   DEALING ROOM SYSTEMS
81BC   DEALING ROOM SYSTEMS
81BD   DEALING ROOM SYSTEMS
81BE   DEALING ROOM SYSTEMS
81BF   DEALING ROOM SYSTEMS
81C0   DEALING ROOM SYSTEMS
81C1   DEALING ROOM SYSTEMS
81C2   DEALING ROOM SYSTEMS
81C3   DEALING ROOM SYSTEMS
81C4   DEALING ROOM SYSTEMS
81C5   DEALING ROOM SYSTEMS
81C6   DEALING ROOM SYSTEMS
81C7   DEALING ROOM SYSTEMS
81C8   DEALING ROOM SYSTEMS
81C9   DEALING ROOM SYSTEMS
81CA   DEALING ROOM SYSTEMS
81CB   DEALING ROOM SYSTEMS
81CC   DEALING ROOM SYSTEMS
81CD   DEALING ROOM SYSTEMS
81CE   DEALING ROOM SYSTEMS
81CF   DEALING ROOM SYSTEMS
81D0   DEALING ROOM SYSTEMS
81D1   DEALING ROOM SYSTEMS
81D2   DEALING ROOM SYSTEMS
81D3   DEALING ROOM SYSTEMS
81D4   DEALING ROOM SYSTEMS
81D5   DEALING ROOM SYSTEMS
81D6   DEALING ROOM SYSTEMS
81D7   DEALING ROOM SYSTEMS
81D8   DEALING ROOM SYSTEMS
81D9   DEALING ROOM SYSTEMS
81DA   DEALING ROOM SYSTEMS
81DB   DEALING ROOM SYSTEMS
81DC   DEALING ROOM SYSTEMS
81DD   DEALING ROOM SYSTEMS
81DE   DEALING ROOM SYSTEMS
81DF   DEALING ROOM SYSTEMS
81E0   DEALING ROOM SYSTEMS
81E1   DEALING ROOM SYSTEMS
```

```
81E2   DEALING ROOM SYSTEMS
81E3   DEALING ROOM SYSTEMS
81E4   DEALING ROOM SYSTEMS
81E5   DEALING ROOM SYSTEMS
81E6   DEALING ROOM SYSTEMS
81E7   DEALING ROOM SYSTEMS
81E8   DEALING ROOM SYSTEMS
81E9   DEALING ROOM SYSTEMS
81EA   DEALING ROOM SYSTEMS
81EB   DEALING ROOM SYSTEMS
81EC   DEALING ROOM SYSTEMS
81ED   DEALING ROOM SYSTEMS
81EE   DEALING ROOM SYSTEMS
81EF   DEALING ROOM SYSTEMS
81F0   DEALING ROOM SYSTEMS
81F1   DEALING ROOM SYSTEMS
81F2   DEALING ROOM SYSTEMS
81F3   DEALING ROOM SYSTEMS
81F4   DEALING ROOM SYSTEMS
81F5   DEALING ROOM SYSTEMS
81F6   DEALING ROOM SYSTEMS
81F7   DEALING ROOM SYSTEMS
81F8   DEALING ROOM SYSTEMS
81F9   DEALING ROOM SYSTEMS
81FA   DEALING ROOM SYSTEMS
81FB   DEALING ROOM SYSTEMS
81FC   NETWORK SUPPORT MGR/PC REMOTE CNTRL PRGM   PCI LTD
81FD   NETWORK SUPPORT MGR/PC REMOTE CNTRL PRGM   PCI LTD
81FE   IWI
81FF   MARTELLO & ASSOCIATES
8203   NETWORK COMPUTING INC - NCI
8204   NETWORK COMPUTING INC - NCI
8205   NETWORK COMPUTING INC - NCI
8206   NETWORK COMPUTING INC - NCI
8207   NETWORK COMPUTING INC - NCI
8208   NETWORK COMPUTING INC - NCI
8209   NETWORK COMPUTING INC - NCI
820A   NETWORK COMPUTING INC - NCI
820B   NETWORK COMPUTING INC - NCI
820C   NETWORK COMPUTING INC - NCI
820D   DATA VOICE SOLUTIONS CORP
820E   ID 5001 WEATHER STATION   ZENITH DATA SYSTEMS
820F   WRITE SERVER   ARC CALCULON
8210   WRITE SERVER   QUANTUM CONSULTING
8211   SYSTEM 9   HBF GROUP
8212   SYSTEM 9   HBF GROUP
8213   SYSTEM 9   HBF GROUP
8214   SYSTEM 9   HBF GROUP
```

```
8215   SYSTEM 9   HBF GROUP
8216   SYSTEM 9   HBF GROUP
8217   SYSTEM 9   HBF GROUP
8218   SYSTEM 9   HBF GROUP
8219   ARGUS   TRITICOM
821A   ARGUS   TRITICOM
821B   TCP/IP GATEWAY   COMPUTERVISION SERVICES
821C   PICKIT (COMM SERVER)   INTEL
821D   PEER LOGIC
821E   PEER LOGIC
821F   DATA FACE NET BATCH
8220   DATA FACE NET BATCH
8221   LUMINAR OPTICAL SERVER   COREL SYSTEMS CORP
8222   Unknown
8223   Unknown
8224   Unknown
8225   Unknown
8226   Unknown
8227   X-BRIDGE   ADVANCED POLICY COMMUNICATIONS
8228   X-BRIDGE   ADVANCED POLICY COMMUNICATIONS
8229   FLEXCOM   EVERGREEN SYSTEMS
822A   FLEXCOM   EVERGREEN SYSTEMS
822B   FLEXCOM   EVERGREEN SYSTEMS
822C   FLEXCOM   EVERGREEN SYSTEMS
822D   FLEXCOM   EVERGREEN SYSTEMS
822E   GATEWAYS & WKST PROCESSOR   TEKNOS SYSTEMS
822F   GATEWAYS & WKST PROCESSOR   TEKNOS SYSTEMS
8230   GATEWAYS & WKST PROCESSOR   TEKNOS SYSTEMS
8231   GATEWAYS & WKST PROCESSOR   TEKNOS SYSTEMS
8232   GATEWAYS & WKST PROCESSOR   TEKNOS SYSTEMS
8233   GATEWAYS & WKST PROCESSOR   TEKNOS SYSTEMS
8234   GATEWAYS & WKST PROCESSOR   TEKNOS SYSTEMS
8235   GATEWAYS & WKST PROCESSOR   TEKNOS SYSTEMS
8236   GATEWAYS & WKST PROCESSOR   TEKNOS SYSTEMS
8237   GATEWAYS & WKST PROCESSOR   TEKNOS SYSTEMS
8238   LANWARE   HORIZON TECHNOLOGY INC
8239   LANWARE   HORIZON TECHNOLOGY INC
823A   LANWARE   HORIZON TECHNOLOGY INC
823B   LANWARE   HORIZON TECHNOLOGY INC
823C   LANWARE   HORIZON TECHNOLOGY INC
823D   Unknown
823E   TEAM 286   IWI
823F   DBMS LOCK MANAGER   RAIMA CORP
8240   DBMS LOCK MANAGER   RAIMA CORP
8241   CENTRAL POINT SOFTWARE
8242   REMOTE COMPUTING   CENTRAL POINT SOFTWARE
8243   REMOTE COMPUTING   CENTRAL POINT SOFTWARE
8244   REMOTE COMPUTING   CENTRAL POINT SOFTWARE
```

```
8245   REMOTE COMPUTING   CENTRAL POINT SOFTWARE
8246   REMOTE COMPUTING   CENTRAL POINT SOFTWARE
8247   REMOTE COMPUTING   CENTRAL POINT SOFTWARE
8248   REMOTE COMPUTING   CENTRAL POINT SOFTWARE
8249   TOKEN RING RPL   NCR - DAYTON
824A   TOKEN RING RPL   NCR - DAYTON
824B   DEALING ROOM SYSTEMS
824C   DEALING ROOM SYSTEMS
824D   DEALING ROOM SYSTEMS
824E   DEALING ROOM SYSTEMS
824F   DEALING ROOM SYSTEMS
8250   DEALING ROOM SYSTEMS
8251   DEALING ROOM SYSTEMS
8252   DEALING ROOM SYSTEMS
8253   TOTAL AUTOMATION SYSTEMS   DYNATECH UTAH SCIENTIFIC
8254   TOTAL AUTOMATION SYSTEMS   DYNATECH UTAH SCIENTIFIC
8255   VANTAGE POINT   CONNECT COMPUTER
8256   NETARC SCHEDULER   EMERALD SYSTEMS
8257   DISTRIBUTED PROCESSING   BRIGHAM YOUNG UNIVERSITY
8258   XTREE NET -   CENTRAL POINT SOFTWARE
8259   XTREE NET -   CENTRAL POINT SOFTWARE
825A   SYSM/LAN2   H&W COMPUTER SYSTEMS
825B   VANTAGE POINT   CONNECT COMPUTER
825C   VANTAGE POINT   CONNECT COMPUTER
825D   VANTAGE POINT   CONNECT COMPUTER
825E   TIME OUT   NORDRA INC
825F   MULIT-PROCESSOR CONTROLLER   MBAC
8260   MULIT-PROCESSOR CONTROLLER   MBAC
8261   MULIT-PROCESSOR CONTROLLER   MBAC
8262   MULIT-PROCESSOR CONTROLLER   MBAC
8263   MULIT-PROCESSOR CONTROLLER   MBAC
8264   TIME OUT   NORDRA INC
8265   INGRES DATABASE   INGRES CORPORATION
8266   EASY STREET PREM FINANCE   STREETWISE SYSTEMS INC
8267   EASY STREET PREM FINANCE   STREETWISE SYSTEMS INC
8269   APT NET   AUTOMATED PROGRAMMING TECH
826A   APT NET   AUTOMATED PROGRAMMING TECH
826B   APT NET   AUTOMATED PROGRAMMING TECH
826C   APT NET   AUTOMATED PROGRAMMING TECH
826D   TOTAL AUTOMATION SYS ED   LUTHERAN SOCIAL SERVICES
826E   TOTAL AUTOMATION SYS MC   LUTHERAN SOCIAL SERVICES
826F   TOTAL AUTOMATION SYS ML     DYNATECH UTAH SCIENTIFIC
8270   TOTAL AUTOMATION SYS - ADI   DYNATECH UTAH SCIENTIFIC
8271   TOTAL AUTOMATION SYS - FAX   DYNATECH UTAH SCIENTIFIC
8272   SERVICE POINT   INTERPOINT SOFTWARE
8273   SERVICE POINT   INTERPOINT SOFTWARE
8274   PRODIGY GATEWAY   COMPUTEREASE SOFTWARE
8275   PRODIGY GATEWAY   COMPUTEREASE SOFTWARE
```

```
8276   NEWSMANAGER  VSS INC
8277   NEWSMANAGER  VSS INC
8278   NEWSMANAGER  VSS INC
827F   MARTELLO & ASSOCIATES
8280   MARK HURST
8281   MARK HURST
8282   MARK HURST
8283   MARK HURST
8284   BARR GATE/PC-TO-MAINFRAME COMMUNICATION  BARR SYSTEMS INC
8285   BARR GATE/PC-TO-MAINFRAME COMMUNICATION  BARR SYSTEMS INC
8286   PURE DATA RESEARCH LTD
8287   VOICE MAIL  PLAN COMMUNICATIONS
8288   CENTERS FOR DISEASE CONTROL
8289   RPC CALLS  INTEGRATED DATA SYSTEMS
828A   INTEGRATED DATA SYSTEMS
828B   FOLIO CORPORATION
828C   MULTITECH
828D   MULTITECH
828E   MULTITECH
828F   MULTITECH
8290   MULTITECH
8291   BUS TECH
8292   AMericAN AIRLINES DECISION TEC
8293   DORELOWITZ - CONSULTING  MICROCOM INC
8294   GATEWAY USA
8295   GATEWAY USA
8296   GATEWAY USA
8297   GATEWAY USA
8298   GATEWAY USA
8299   GATEWAY USA
829A   COMPUTERVISION SERVICES
829B   COMPUTERVISION SERVICES
829C   COMPUTERVISION SERVICES
829D   SHIVA CORP
829E   SHIVA CORP
829F   TODD WEISS
82A0   TODD WEISS
82A1   TODD WEISS
82A2   TAPE NLM  ARCADA SOFTWARE  - CONSULTING MATZE
82A3   LANLORD PRODUCT  MICROCOM CLIENT SERVER TECHNOL
82A4   LANLORD PRODUCT  MICROCOM CLIENT SERVER TECHNOL
82A5   X25 AUTOMATED BRIDGE MONITOR & CONTROL
82A6   DORELOWITZ - CONSULTING  MICROCOM INC
82A7   PEER-TO-PEER COMMUNICATIONS  WITNESS SYSTEMS
82A8   MICRO INTEGRATION
82A9   MICRO INTEGRATION
82AA   IBM - POUGHKEEPSIE
82AB   IBM - POUGHKEEPSIE
```

```
82AC   IBM - POUGHKEEPSIE
82AD   IBM - POUGHKEEPSIE
82AE   IBM - POUGHKEEPSIE
82AF   IBM - POUGHKEEPSIE
82B0   J&L INFORMATION SYSTEMS
82B1   J&L INFORMATION SYSTEMS
82B2   J&L INFORMATION SYSTEMS
82B3   J&L INFORMATION SYSTEMS
82B4   J&L INFORMATION SYSTEMS
82B5   J&L INFORMATION SYSTEMS
82B6   J&L INFORMATION SYSTEMS
82B7   J&L INFORMATION SYSTEMS
82B8   J&L INFORMATION SYSTEMS
82B9   J&L INFORMATION SYSTEMS
82BA   J&L INFORMATION SYSTEMS
82BB   J&L INFORMATION SYSTEMS
82BC   J&L INFORMATION SYSTEMS
82BD   J&L INFORMATION SYSTEMS
82BE   J&L INFORMATION SYSTEMS
82BF   J&L INFORMATION SYSTEMS
82C0   J&L INFORMATION SYSTEMS
82C1   J&L INFORMATION SYSTEMS
82C2   J&L INFORMATION SYSTEMS
82C3   J&L INFORMATION SYSTEMS
82C4   J&L INFORMATION SYSTEMS
82C5   J&L INFORMATION SYSTEMS
82C6   J&L INFORMATION SYSTEMS
82C7   J&L INFORMATION SYSTEMS
82C8   J&L INFORMATION SYSTEMS
82C9   J&L INFORMATION SYSTEMS
82CA   J&L INFORMATION SYSTEMS
82CB   J&L INFORMATION SYSTEMS
82CC   J&L INFORMATION SYSTEMS
82CD   J&L INFORMATION SYSTEMS
82CE   J&L INFORMATION SYSTEMS
82CF   J&L INFORMATION SYSTEMS
82D0   J&L INFORMATION SYSTEMS
82D1   J&L INFORMATION SYSTEMS
82D2   J&L INFORMATION SYSTEMS
82D3   J&L INFORMATION SYSTEMS
82D4   J&L INFORMATION SYSTEMS
82D5   J&L INFORMATION SYSTEMS
82D6   J&L INFORMATION SYSTEMS
82D7   J&L INFORMATION SYSTEMS
82D8   LEGATO SYSTEMS
82D9   LEGATO SYSTEMS
82DA   LEGATO SYSTEMS
82DB   LEGATO SYSTEMS
```

```
82DC   LEGATO SYSTEMS
82DD   LEGATO SYSTEMS
82DE   VALUE ADDED SERVER   SKYLINE TECHNOLOGY
82DF   VALUE ADDED SERVER   SKYLINE TECHNOLOGY
82E0   FCP FOR OS/2 SUPPORT (FOUNDTN COOP PROC)   Andersen Consulting - Chicago
82E1   FCP FOR OS/2 SUPPORT (FOUNDTN COOP PROC)   Andersen Consulting - Chicago
82E3   SYTRON CORP
82E4   AMERICAN AIRLINES DECISION TEC
82E5   IMAGE RETRIEVAL INC
82E6   CONNECT COMPUTER
82E7   CONNECT COMPUTER
82E8   CONNECT COMPUTER
82E9   CONNECT COMPUTER
82EA   CONNECT COMPUTER
82EB   CONNECT COMPUTER
82EC   CONNECT COMPUTER
82ED   CONNECT COMPUTER
82EE   CONNECT COMPUTER
82EF   CONNECT COMPUTER
82F0   CONNECT COMPUTER
82F1   CONNECT COMPUTER
82F2   CONNECT COMPUTER
82F3   CONNECT COMPUTER
82F4   CONNECT COMPUTER
82F5   CONNECT COMPUTER
82F6   HELLO-1   JOSHIN DENKI CO LTD J&P DIV
82F7   HELLO-1   JOSHIN DENKI CO LTD J&P DIV
82F8   HELLO-1   JOSHIN DENKI CO LTD J&P DIV
82F9   HELLO-1   JOSHIN DENKI CO LTD J&P DIV
82FA   HELLO-1   JOSHIN DENKI CO LTD J&P DIV
82FD   NETWARE JUKEBOX   COREL SYSTEMS, OPTICAL DIV
82FE   FCP FOR WINDOWS SUPPORT (FNDTN COOP PROC   Andersen Consulting - Chicago
82FF   FCP FOR WINDOWS SUPPORT (FNDTN COOP PROC   Andersen Consulting - Chicago
8300   SMITH MICRO SOFTWARE INC
8301   SMITH MICRO SOFTWARE INC
8302   SMITH MICRO SOFTWARE INC
8303   SMITH MICRO SOFTWARE INC
8304   SMITH MICRO SOFTWARE INC
8305   SMITH MICRO SOFTWARE INC
8306   SMITH MICRO SOFTWARE INC
8307   SMITH MICRO SOFTWARE INC
8308   SMITH MICRO SOFTWARE INC
8309   SMITH MICRO SOFTWARE INC
830A   SMITH MICRO SOFTWARE INC
830B   SMITH MICRO SOFTWARE INC
830C   SMITH MICRO SOFTWARE INC
830D   SMITH MICRO SOFTWARE INC
830E   SMITH MICRO SOFTWARE INC
```

```
830F   SMITH MICRO SOFTWARE INC
8310   SMITH MICRO SOFTWARE INC
8311   SMITH MICRO SOFTWARE INC
8312   SMITH MICRO SOFTWARE INC
8313   SMITH MICRO SOFTWARE INC
8314   SMITH MICRO SOFTWARE INC
8315   SMITH MICRO SOFTWARE INC
8316   SMITH MICRO SOFTWARE INC
8317   SMITH MICRO SOFTWARE INC
8318   SMITH MICRO SOFTWARE INC
8319   SMITH MICRO SOFTWARE INC
831A   SMITH MICRO SOFTWARE INC
831B   SMITH MICRO SOFTWARE INC
831C   SMITH MICRO SOFTWARE INC
831D   SMITH MICRO SOFTWARE INC
831E   SMITH MICRO SOFTWARE INC
831F   SMITH MICRO SOFTWARE INC
8320   SMITH MICRO SOFTWARE INC
8321   SMITH MICRO SOFTWARE INC
8322   SMITH MICRO SOFTWARE INC
8323   SMITH MICRO SOFTWARE INC
8324   SMITH MICRO SOFTWARE INC
8325   SMITH MICRO SOFTWARE INC
8326   SMITH MICRO SOFTWARE INC
8327   SMITH MICRO SOFTWARE INC
8328   SMITH MICRO SOFTWARE INC
8329   SMITH MICRO SOFTWARE INC
832A   SMITH MICRO SOFTWARE INC
832B   SMITH MICRO SOFTWARE INC
832C   SMITH MICRO SOFTWARE INC
832D   SMITH MICRO SOFTWARE INC
832E   SMITH MICRO SOFTWARE INC
832F   SMITH MICRO SOFTWARE INC
8330   SMITH MICRO SOFTWARE INC
8331   SMITH MICRO SOFTWARE INC
8332   SMITH MICRO SOFTWARE INC
8333   SMITH MICRO SOFTWARE INC
8334   SMITH MICRO SOFTWARE INC
8335   SMITH MICRO SOFTWARE INC
8336   SMITH MICRO SOFTWARE INC
8337   SMITH MICRO SOFTWARE INC
8338   SMITH MICRO SOFTWARE INC
8339   SMITH MICRO SOFTWARE INC
833A   SMITH MICRO SOFTWARE INC
833B   SMITH MICRO SOFTWARE INC
833C   SMITH MICRO SOFTWARE INC
833D   SMITH MICRO SOFTWARE INC
833E   SMITH MICRO SOFTWARE INC
```

```
833F   SMITH MICRO SOFTWARE INC
8340   SMITH MICRO SOFTWARE INC
8341   SMITH MICRO SOFTWARE INC
8342   SMITH MICRO SOFTWARE INC
8343   SMITH MICRO SOFTWARE INC
8344   SMITH MICRO SOFTWARE INC
8345   SMITH MICRO SOFTWARE INC
8346   SMITH MICRO SOFTWARE INC
8347   SMITH MICRO SOFTWARE INC
8348   SMITH MICRO SOFTWARE INC
8349   SMITH MICRO SOFTWARE INC
834A   SMITH MICRO SOFTWARE INC
834B   SMITH MICRO SOFTWARE INC
834C   SMITH MICRO SOFTWARE INC
834D   SMITH MICRO SOFTWARE INC
834E   SMITH MICRO SOFTWARE INC
834F   SMITH MICRO SOFTWARE INC
8350   POWER GRID SERVER  COGNOS INC
8351   DATA SERVICE TO WORKSTATION/SCHOOL ADMIN  CHANCERY SOFTWARE
8352   TRANSMITTING  UNISYNC
8353   RECEIVING     UNISYNC
8354   MULTICOM NET - MODEM SHARING SOFTWARE
8355   MULTICOM NET - MODEM SHARING SOFTWARE
8356   MULTICOM NET - MODEM SHARING SOFTWARE
8357   CD CONNECTIONS  CBIS INC
8359   RIVERVIEW SYSTEMS
835A   TOTAL AUTOMATION SYSTEMS  DYNATECH UTAH SCIENTIFIC
835B   TOTAL AUTOMATION SYSTEMS  DYNATECH UTAH SCIENTIFIC
835C   ITAC INC
835D   ASP COMPUTER PRODUCTS INC
835E   ASP COMPUTER PRODUCTS INC
835F   ASP COMPUTER PRODUCTS INC
8361   FAX SERVER               TRANSFAX CORPORATION
8362   FAX PRINT SERVER         TRANSFAX CORPORATION
8363   FAX MERGE SERVER         TRANSFAX CORPORATION
8364   NETWORK MANAGEMENT SERVER  TRANSFAX CORPORATION
8365   FUNK SOFTWARE
8366   MICRO INTEGRATION
8367   MICRO INTEGRATION
8368   MICRO INTEGRATION
8369   MICRO INTEGRATION
836A   MICRO INTEGRATION
836B   TRIPLE A MOTOR CLUB
836C   LAN TIMES JAPAN, SOFTBANK CORP
836D   WATCHTOWER
836E   CLIENT SERVER COMM SYSTEMS, SPX PROTOCOL  MICRORIM
836F   NORTON LAMBERT CORP
8370   NORTON LAMBERT CORP
```

8371 NORTON LAMBERT CORP
8372 NORTON LAMBERT CORP
8373 NORTON LAMBERT CORP
8374 CENTRAL POINT SOFTWARE
8375 DRIVERS   PRESOFT ARCHITECTS
8376 NLM FOR REMOTE VOLUME MOUNT   INTECK CORPORATION
8377 NLM FOR REMOTE VOLUME MOUNT   INTECK CORPORATION
8378 SYMANTEC PETER NORTON GROUP
8379 SYMANTEC PETER NORTON GROUP
837A DIGITAL EQUIPMENT - MERRIMACK
837B CBS FACILITIES ASSIGNMENT - REQUEST   DYNATECH UTAH SCIENTIFIC
837C CBS FACILITIES ASSIGNMENT - REPLY   DYNATECH UTAH SCIENTIFIC
837D MULTI-PROTOCOL ROUTER INSIDE IPX   RESEARCH MACHINES PLC
837E SHAREWARE   CHERRY TREE SOFTWARE
837F ENTERPRISE ECS   INTEL CORP
8380 ENTERPRISE MMT   INTEL CORP
8381 STOCK TICKER BROADCAST SERVER   NCOMPASS DEVELOPMENT INTL
8382 QUERY UNIQUE USERS   US ROBOTICS SOFTWARE
8383 CBS ADA SERVER   DYNATECH UTAH SCIENTIFIC
8384 PACE SOFTWARE SYSTEMS INC
8385 ANDERSEN CONSULTING - CHICAGO
8386 GATEWAY MANAGEMENT   WALL DATA
8387 GATEWAY MANAGEMENT   WALL DATA
838B POWERCHUTE ALERT - UPS MONITORING   AMericAN POWER CONVERSION
838D AVAIL SYSTEMS CORP
838E QA+ FOR WINDOWS/REMOTE DIAGNOSTICS   DIAGSOFT INC
838F POWERCHUTE ADMINISTRATIVE SOCKET   AMericAN POWER CONVERSION
8390 DATAMEDIC
8391 COREL DRIVER   COREL SYSTEMS, OPTICAL DIV
8392 ID FOR LASERMASTER PRINTER PRODUCTS   LASER MASTER CORP
8393 TFTP TRIVIAL FILE TRANSFER PROTOCOL   HEWLETT PACKARD - ROSEVILLE
8394 FTP FILE TRANSFER PROTOCOL   HEWLETT PACKARD - ROSEVILLE
8395 HEWLETT PACKARD - ROSEVILLE
8396 HEWLETT PACKARD - ROSEVILLE
8397 SITA
8398 SITA
8399 TECHGNOSIS INC
839A QA+ FOR WINDOWS/REMOTE DIAGNOSTICS   DIAGSOFT INC
839B MAIL SYSTEMS   SYNECTIC SYSTEMS LTD
839C MAIL SYSTEMS   SYNECTIC SYSTEMS LTD
839D NLM/VIDEO FILES ON NOVELL SERVICE   PROTOCOMM CORPORATION
839E TURNAX EMULATION GATEWAY   IDE CORPORATION
839F CNF 16000 CONNECTION STATION   COROLLARY INC
83A0 CNF 16000 CONNECTION STATION   COROLLARY INC
83A1 CNF 16000 CONNECTION STATION   COROLLARY INC
83A2 CNF 16000 CONNECTION STATION   COROLLARY INC
83A3 CNF 16000 CONNECTION STATION   COROLLARY INC
83A4 CNF 16000 CONNECTION STATION   COROLLARY INC

```
83A5   WORKSTATION PEER-TO-PEER COMMUNICATIONS   IBM - RESEARCH TRIANGLE PARK
83A6   WORKSTATION PEER-TO-PEER COMMUNICATIONS   IBM - RESEARCH TRIANGLE PARK
83A7   WORKSTATION PEER-TO-PEER COMMUNICATIONS   IBM - RESEARCH TRIANGLE PARK
83A8   WORKSTATION PEER-TO-PEER COMMUNICATIONS   IBM - RESEARCH TRIANGLE PARK
83A9   WORKSTATION PEER-TO-PEER COMMUNICATIONS   IBM - RESEARCH TRIANGLE PARK
83AA   WORKSTATION PEER-TO-PEER COMMUNICATIONS   IBM - RESEARCH TRIANGLE PARK
83AB   DATANEX CORPORATION
83AC   HP OPEN MAIL & PORTABLE NETWARE   HEWLETT PACKARD - BERKSHIRE
83AD   COMMUNICATION/MAIL SERVER SOFTWARE   DATOR 3 SPOL SRO
83AE   COMMUNICATION/MAIL SERVER SOFTWARE   DATOR 3 SPOL SRO
83AF   COMMUNICATION/MAIL SERVER SOFTWARE   DATOR 3 SPOL SRO
83B0   COMMUNICATION/MAIL SERVER SOFTWARE   DATOR 3 SPOL SRO
83B1   POWER MANAGEMENT SERVER   ELGAR CORP
83B2   POWER MANAGEMENT CLIENT   ELGAR CORP
83B3   NETWORK PERIPHERALS - PRINT SERVER   CANON INFORMATION SYSTEMS
83B4   NETWORK PERIPHERALS   CANON INFORMATION SYSTEMS
83B5   NETWORK PERIPHERALS   CANON INFORMATION SYSTEMS
83B6   NETWORK PERIPHERALS   CANON INFORMATION SYSTEMS
83B7   NETWORK PERIPHERALS   CANON INFORMATION SYSTEMS
83B8   NETWORK PERIPHERALS   CANON INFORMATION SYSTEMS
83B9   FAX SERVER   FERRARI ELECTRONIC GMBH
83BA   FAX SERVER   FERRARI ELECTRONIC GMBH
83BB   FAX SERVER   FERRARI ELECTRONIC GMBH
83BC   FAX SERVER   FERRARI ELECTRONIC GMBH
83BD   CLIENT SERVER DATABASE ENGINE/SQL FOR NW   SYBASE INC
83BE   PRINTER CONTROLLER BOARD/VAP OR NLM   DP TEK
83BF   PRINTER CONTROLLER BOARD/VAP OR NLM   DP TEK
83C0   IWI
83C1   LEXMARK INTERNATIONAL
83C2   LEXMARK INTERNATIONAL
83C3   LEXMARK INTERNATIONAL
83C4   LEXMARK INTERNATIONAL
83C5   LEXMARK INTERNATIONAL
83C6   LEXMARK INTERNATIONAL
83C7   OKNA CORP
83C8   OKNA CORP
83C9   OKNA CORP
83CA   OKNA CORP
83CB   OKNA CORP
83CC   OKNA CORP
83CD   DEVELOPMENT/COMMUNICATIONS TOOLKIT   MICHAEL RICH
83CE   RESET PRINT SERVERS   MOTOROLA
83CF   NETWORK DESIGNERS
83D0   REMOTE PRINTER SOCKET   INDUSTRIAL EXOTICA
83D1   FILE MANAGEMENT SERVICES   SYSTEMS AXIS PLC
83D2   QUEUE MANAGEMENT SERVICES   SYSTEMS AXIS PLC
83D4   Lantech Services CC MAIL GATEWAY 3.30/SPX Transport CC MAIL
83D6   REMOTE CONTROL - NODE-TO-NODE   DST - DISTRIBUTED SYSTEMS TECH
```

```
83D7  REMOTE CONTROL - BANK OF MODEMS  DST - DISTRIBUTED SYSTEMS TECH
83D9  GENERAL COMMUNICATION FORUM ON NOVELL NW  CREDIT LYONNAIS
83DA  DATABASE ENGINES  SYBASE INC
83DB  DATABASE ENGINES  SYBASE INC
83DC  DATABASE ENGINES  SYBASE INC
83DD  DATABASE ENGINES  SYBASE INC
83DE  DATABASE ENGINES  SYBASE INC
83DF  DATABASE ENGINES  SYBASE INC
83E0  DATABASE ENGINES  SYBASE INC
83E1  DATABASE ENGINES  SYBASE INC
83E2  GATEWAY SERVER PRODUCT TO SPERRY HOST  ICC
83E3  WAN CONNECTION SERVER  IDEASSOCIATION
83E4  LAN SPOOL 3.5  INTEL - AMERICAN FORK
83E6  REMOTE INTERNAL HUB DRIVER  INTEL PCED
83E7  SOFTWARE ACCESS CONTROL SERVER  U OF PLYMOUTH
83E9  COMMUNICATIONS SYSTEM  UNICABLES SA
83EA  COMMUNICATIONS SYSTEM  UNICABLES SA
83EB  COMMUNICATIONS SYSTEM  UNICABLES SA
83EC  COMMUNICATIONS SYSTEM  UNICABLES SA
83ED  COMMUNICATIONS SYSTEM  UNICABLES SA
83EE  COMMUNICATIONS SYSTEM  UNICABLES SA
83EF  COMMUNICATIONS SYSTEM  UNICABLES SA
83F0  COMMUNICATIONS SYSTEM  UNICABLES SA
83F1  COMMUNICATIONS SYSTEM  UNICABLES SA
83F2  COMMUNICATIONS SYSTEM  UNICABLES SA
83F3  COMMUNICATIONS SYSTEM  UNICABLES SA
83F4  COMMUNICATIONS SYSTEM  UNICABLES SA
83F5  COMMUNICATIONS SYSTEM  UNICABLES SA
83F6  COMMUNICATIONS SYSTEM  UNICABLES SA
83F7  COMMUNICATIONS SYSTEM  UNICABLES SA
83F8  COMMUNICATIONS SYSTEM  UNICABLES SA
83F9  COMMUNICATIONS SYSTEM  UNICABLES SA
83FA  COMMUNICATIONS SYSTEM  UNICABLES SA
83FB  COMMUNICATIONS SYSTEM  UNICABLES SA
83FC  COMMUNICATIONS SYSTEM  UNICABLES SA
83FD  COMMUNICATIONS SYSTEM  UNICABLES SA
83FE  COMMUNICATIONS SYSTEM  UNICABLES SA
83FF  COMMUNICATIONS SYSTEM  UNICABLES SA
8400  COMMUNICATIONS SYSTEM  UNICABLES SA
8401  COMMUNICATIONS SYSTEM  UNICABLES SA
8402  GEN SERVER  GREENBAUM ASSOCIATES
8403  OBJECT-STORE, DATABASE ACCESS PROTOCOL  OBJECT DESIGN
8404  OBJECT-STORE, DATABASE ACCESS PROTOCOL  OBJECT DESIGN
8405  OBJECT-STORE, DIRECTORY PROTOCOL  OBJECT DESIGN
8406  OBJECT-STORE, DIRECTORY PROTOCOL  OBJECT DESIGN
8407  OBJECT-STORE, CACHE COHERENCE PROTOCOL  OBJECT DESIGN
8408  OBJECT-STORE, CACHE COHERENCE PROTOCOL  OBJECT DESIGN
8409  VISINET NLM ID#  TECHNOLOGY DYNAMICS INC
```

```
840A   WDAGR - VAP   JOSTENS LEARNING CORP
840B   WKILL         JOSTENS LEARNING CORP
840C   INTERNET LAN CONTROLLER FOR NETWARE SAA   BUS TECH
840D   PEER-TO-PEER COMMUNICATIONS   M&M MARS INC
840E   PEER-TO-PEER COMMUNICATIONS   M&M MARS INC
840F   CONNECTION MANAGER (SOFTWARE HOUSE PROD)   TBR INTERNATIONAL CORP
8410   CONNECTION MANAGER (SOFTWARE HOUSE PROD)   TBR INTERNATIONAL CORP
8411   CONNECTION MANAGER (SOFTWARE HOUSE PROD)   TBR INTERNATIONAL CORP
8412   CONNECTION MANAGER (SOFTWARE HOUSE PROD)   TBR INTERNATIONAL CORP
8413   CONNECTION MANAGER (SOFTWARE HOUSE PROD)   TBR INTERNATIONAL CORP
8414   CONNECTION MANAGER (SOFTWARE HOUSE PROD)   TBR INTERNATIONAL CORP
8415   FOR PROXY HOST   FUNK SOFTWARE
8416   WORKSTATION 3-LAN   ADVANCED TECHNICAL SOLUTIONS
8417   DEVELOPING SERVER PERFORMANCE ANALIZER   BANYAN SYSTEMS INC
8418   DEVELOPING SERVER PERFORMANCE ANALIZER   BANYAN SYSTEMS INC
8419   DEVELOPING SERVER PERFORMANCE ANALIZER   BANYAN SYSTEMS INC
841A   DEVELOPING SERVER PERFORMANCE ANALIZER   BANYAN SYSTEMS INC
841B   DEVELOPING SERVER PERFORMANCE ANALIZER   BANYAN SYSTEMS INC
841C   DEVELOPING SERVER PERFORMANCE ANALIZER   BANYAN SYSTEMS INC
841D   REMOTE DATABASE SERVICES   INTERACTIVE DATA
841E   REMOTE DATABASE SERVICES   INTERACTIVE DATA
841F   ENVELOPE PRINTER FOR NETWORK   THURIDION SOFTWARE ENGINEERING
8420   DACS OFFICE II   DOCUNET GMBH
8421   TERMINAL EMULATOR FOR MDOS - TRANSMIT   INTELLIGENT MICRO SOFTWARE LTD
8422   TERMINAL EMULATOR FOR MDOS - RECEIVE   INTELLIGENT MICRO SOFTWARE LTD
8423   PRAXIS
8424   REFLEX COMPLIANCE   PRODIGY SERVICES
8425   REFLEX COMPLIANCE   PRODIGY SERVICES
8426   REFLEX COMPLIANCE   PRODIGY SERVICES
8427   REFLEX COMPLIANCE   PRODIGY SERVICES
8428   REFLEX COMPLIANCE   PRODIGY SERVICES
8429   REFLEX COMPLIANCE   PRODIGY SERVICES
842A   IPX REMOTE CONTROL FUNCTION   NETWORTH INC
842B   IPX REMOTE CONTROL FUNCTION   NETWORTH INC
842C   SERVER-CLIENT COMMUNICATION VIA SPX   AT&T JENS CORP
842D   TSR BROADCASTING VIA IPX   AT&T JENS CORP
842E   SITA
842F   SITA
8430   INSTANT RECALL I   DAYTIMER TECHNOLOGIES
8431   APPLICATION SERVER FC1   THOMSON FINANCIAL
8432   APPLICATION SERVER FC2   THOMSON FINANCIAL
8433   APPLICATION SERVER FC3   THOMSON FINANCIAL
8434   APPLICATION SERVER FC3   THOMSON FINANCIAL
8435   ENVELOPE MANAGER SOFTWARE   PSI ASSOCIATES
8436   ENVELOPE MANAGER SOFTWARE   PSI ASSOCIATES
8437   ENVELOPE MANAGER SOFTWARE   PSI ASSOCIATES
8438   ENVELOPE MANAGER SOFTWARE   PSI ASSOCIATES
8439   LAA SERVER BINDARY SOCKET   SABER SOFTWARE
```

```
843A  440 IPX COMMUNICATIONS   INFORMATION BUILDERS
843B  VITAL SIGNS/LAN SERVER   BLUELINE SOFTWARE INC
843C  VITAL SIGNS/LAN SERVER   BLUELINE SOFTWARE INC
843D  ENVELOPE PRINTER FOR NETWORK   THURIDION SOFTWARE ENGINEERING
843E  OS2 SEQUEL SERVER IPX/SPX SUPPORT  MICROSOFT
843F  ASYNCHRONOUS SERIAL COMMUNICATIONS   BLACK CREEK INTEGRATED SYSTEMS
8440  ASYNCHRONOUS SERIAL COMMUNICATIONS   BLACK CREEK INTEGRATED SYSTEMS
8441  ASYNCHRONOUS SERIAL COMMUNICATIONS   BLACK CREEK INTEGRATED SYSTEMS
8442  ASYNCHRONOUS SERIAL COMMUNICATIONS   BLACK CREEK INTEGRATED SYSTEMS
8443  COMMUNICATION BETWEEN SAGES   AMericAN AUTO MATRIX INC
8444  TV BROADCAST AUTOMATION STATUS   UTAH SCIENTIFIC
8445  TV BROADCAST AUTOMATION STATUS   UTAH SCIENTIFIC
8446  TV BROADCAST AUTOMATION STATUS   UTAH SCIENTIFIC
8447  CLIENT-SERVER VERSION OF CC MAIL   CC MAIL
8448  TV BROADCAST AUTOMATION STATUS   UTAH SCIENTIFIC
8449  NETSPRINT   DIGITAL PRODUCTS INC
844A  WORKSTATION REMOTE CONTROL   CALIFORNIA FEDERAL
844B  FULL TEXT RETRIEVAL CLIENT/SERVER DB ENG   IMPACT ITALIANA SRL
844C  GATEWAY IPX           ICOT
844D  GATEWAY SPX           ICOT
844E  WORKSTATION IPX       ICOT
844F  WORKSTATION SPX       ICOT
8450  NETWORK SERVICES IPX   ICOT
8451  NETWORK SERVICES SPX   ICOT
8452  NETWORK LOGGER IPX     ICOT
8453  NETWORK LOGGER SPX     ICOT
8454  GATEWAY SOFTWARE   DATEV EG
8455  GATEWAY SOFTWARE   DATEV EG
8456  NOVELL - PROVO
8457  RE:ACTION   CONCENTRIC TECHNOLOGIES
8458  RE:ACTION   CONCENTRIC TECHNOLOGIES
8459  CAD SERVER   ISICAD
845A  CAD SERVER   ISICAD
845B  ICL PORTABLE NETWARE   ICL
845C  LOCATE   ZENITH DATA SYSTEMS
845D  BOML   ZENITH DATA SYSTEMS
845E  RHOTHEOS   ZENITH DATA SYSTEMS
845F  CHAT PROGRAM   INTEL - AMericAN FORK
8460  MAILSLOTS IBM - FRANKLIN LAKES
8461  MAILSLOTS IBM - FRANKLIN LAKES
8462  FILE TALK   MOUNTAIN NETWORK SOLUTIONS INC
8463  FILE TALK   MOUNTAIN NETWORK SOLUTIONS INC
8464  FILE TALK   MOUNTAIN NETWORK SOLUTIONS INC
8465  FILE TALK   MOUNTAIN NETWORK SOLUTIONS INC
8466  FILE TALK   MOUNTAIN NETWORK SOLUTIONS INC
8467  FILE TALK   MOUNTAIN NETWORK SOLUTIONS INC
8468  MICROCOM
8469  MICROCOM
```

```
846A   MICROCOM
846B   MICROCOM
846C   MICROCOM
846D   MICROCOM
846E   MICROCOM
846F   MICROCOM
8470   MICROCOM
8471   MICROCOM
8472   MICROCOM
8473   MICROCOM
8474   MICROCOM
8475   MICROCOM
8476   MICROCOM
8478   DOCUMENT MANGEMENT PACKAGE   PERFECT SOLUTIONS CORPORATION
8479   LITIGATION SUPPORT   GIBSON OCHSNER & ADKINS
847A   MONOTREX   PRIME COMPUTER
847B   MONOTREX   PRIME COMPUTER
847C   MONOTREX   PRIME COMPUTER
847D   MONOTREX   PRIME COMPUTER
847E   MONOTREX   PRIME COMPUTER
847F   MONOTREX   PRIME COMPUTER
8480   MONOTREX   PRIME COMPUTER
8481   MONOTREX   PRIME COMPUTER
8482   MONOTREX   PRIME COMPUTER
8483   MONOTREX   PRIME COMPUTER
8484   LITIGATION SUPPORT   GIBSON OCHSNER & ADKINS
8485   LITIGATION SUPPORT   GIBSON OCHSNER & ADKINS
8486   LITIGATION SUPPORT   GIBSON OCHSNER & ADKINS
8487   ARGUS/N   TRITICOM
8488   ARGUS/N   TRITICOM
8489   ARGUS/N   TRITICOM
848A   CHANNEL SWITCHER APPLICATION   DYNATECH UTAH SCIENTIFIC
848B   CHANNEL SWITCHER APPLICATION   DYNATECH UTAH SCIENTIFIC
848C   CHANNEL SWITCHER APPLICATION   DYNATECH UTAH SCIENTIFIC
848D   CHANNEL SWITCHER APPLICATION   DYNATECH UTAH SCIENTIFIC
848E   CHANNEL SWITCHER APPLICATION   DYNATECH UTAH SCIENTIFIC
848F   CHANNEL SWITCHER APPLICATION   DYNATECH UTAH SCIENTIFIC
8490   CHANNEL SWITCHER APPLICATION   DYNATECH UTAH SCIENTIFIC
8491   CHANNEL SWITCHER APPLICATION   DYNATECH UTAH SCIENTIFIC
8492   OXFORD INFORMATION TECHNOLOGY
8493   GATEWAY INTEGRATION ARCHITECT   MORRISEY ASSOCIATES
8494   BOOTWARE/MSD   LANWORKS
8495   WORKGROUP COMPUTING TOOL   MEMOREX TELEX
8496   WORKGROUP COMPUTING TOOL   MEMOREX TELEX
8497   WORKGROUP COMPUTING TOOL   MEMOREX TELEX
8498   WORKGROUP COMPUTING TOOL   MEMOREX TELEX
8499   WORKGROUP COMPUTING TOOL   MEMOREX TELEX
849A   WORKGROUP COMPUTING TOOL   MEMOREX TELEX
```

```
849B   WORKGROUP COMPUTING TOOL   MEMOREX TELEX
84A0   IPX/SPX SOCKETS   ARTEFACT NETWORK SUPPORT
84A1   IPX/SPX SOCKETS   ARTEFACT NETWORK SUPPORT
84A2   IPX/SPX SOCKETS   ARTEFACT NETWORK SUPPORT
84A3   IPX/SPX SOCKETS   ARTEFACT NETWORK SUPPORT
84A4   IPX/SPX SOCKETS   ARTEFACT NETWORK SUPPORT
84A5   IPX/SPX SOCKETS   ARTEFACT NETWORK SUPPORT
84A6   IPX/SPX SOCKETS   ARTEFACT NETWORK SUPPORT
84A7   IPX/SPX SOCKETS   ARTEFACT NETWORK SUPPORT
84A8   IPX/SPX SOCKETS   ARTEFACT NETWORK SUPPORT
84A9   IPX/SPX SOCKETS   ARTEFACT NETWORK SUPPORT
84AA   CLIENT-SERVER DRIVER FOR IPX/SPX   REFERENCE POINT SOFTWARE
84AB   INTRAK INC
84AC   INTRAK INC
84AD   INTRAK INC
84AE   INTRAK INC
84AF   INTRAK INC
84B0   INTRAK INC
84B1   DATABASE APPLICATIONS   DIGITAL EQUIPMENT - NASHUA
84B2   DATABASE APPLICATIONS   DIGITAL EQUIPMENT - NASHUA
84B3   LOADER SOCKET   NETWORK TECHNICAL SOLUTIONS
84B4   FINDER SOCKET   NETWORK TECHNICAL SOLUTIONS
84B5   AUTOMATED CONTROL SYSTEM   AIR PRODUCTS & CHEMICALS
84B6   AUTOMATED CONTROL SYSTEM   AIR PRODUCTS & CHEMICALS
84B7   AUDIT TRAIL PACKAGE   BLUE LANCE INC
84B8   SBACKUP ENHANCEMENT PRODUCT   SYTRON CORP
84B9   TAPE BACKUP SYSTEMS   COLORADO MEMORY SYSTEMS
84BA   QA+ ATTENTION SOCKET   DIAGSOFT INC
84BB   ADMINISTRATION SERVER   MCGILL UNIVERSITY FAC OF ENGIN
84BC   ADMINISTRATION SERVER   MCGILL UNIVERSITY FAC OF ENGIN
84BD   WORKSTATION COMMUNICATIONS   SYMANTEC PETER NORTON GROUP
84BE   WORKSTATION COMMUNICATIONS   SYMANTEC PETER NORTON GROUP
84BF   NETWORK DYNAMIC DATA EXCHANGE   NETLOGIC INC
84C0   ASYNCHRONOUS COMMUNICATIONS SERVER   US ROBOTICS SOFTWARE
84C1   MISCELLANEOUS SOFTWARE COMMUNICATIONS   TENTERA COMPUTER SERVICES
84C2   FORUM SEND      TEXAS A&M UNIVERSITY
84C3   FORUM RECEIVE   TEXAS A&M UNIVERSITY
84C4   FORUM CONTROL   TEXAS A&M UNIVERSITY
84C5   REMOTE PRINTER CONFIGURATION   NEWGEN SYSTEMS CORP
84C6   AUDIT TRAIL PACKAGE   BLUE LANCE INC
84C7   PEER-TO-PEER COMMUNICATIONS   FUJITSU NETWORKS INDUSTRY
84C8   SNA GATEWAY   MICROSOFT
84C9   SNA GATEWAY   MICROSOFT
84CA   WORKSTATION TERMINAL ACCESS   HSD HARDWARE SOFTWARE DEVELOPM
84CB   SERCOMM
84CC   DE INTERNATIONAL LTD
84CD   APPLICATION TRACKING SYSTEM   HOLTEN WHITE & ASSOCIATES
84CE   IBM HOST GATEWAY   IDEA COURIER
```

```
84CF   CREDIT AUTHORIZATION GATEWAY  MERCHANTEC INTERNATIONAL
84D0   GRAPHICAL HOTEL MANAGEMENT APPLICATION  INSURE INC
84D1   GRAPHICAL HOTEL MANAGEMENT APPLICATION  INSURE INC
84D2   NETWORK BACK-UP  DIGITAL EQUIPMENT - SHREWSBURY
84D3   CLIENT SERVER APPLICATION  ALCON SYSTEMS
84D4   CLIENT SERVER APPLICATION  ALCON SYSTEMS
84D5   COMMUNICATIONS SERVER SDD SYNTHESIZER  SCANDINAVIAN AIRLINES DATA
84D6   INFORMATION SYSTEMS PRODUCT  PROSOFTIA AB
84D7   INFORMATION SYSTEMS PRODUCT  PROSOFTIA AB
84D8   INFORMATION SYSTEMS PRODUCT  PROSOFTIA AB
84D9   INFORMATION SYSTEMS PRODUCT  PROSOFTIA AB
84DA   INFORMATION SYSTEMS PRODUCT  PROSOFTIA AB
84DB   INFORMATION SYSTEMS PRODUCT  PROSOFTIA AB
84DC   INFORMATION SYSTEMS PRODUCT  PROSOFTIA AB
84DD   INFORMATION SYSTEMS PRODUCT  PROSOFTIA AB
84DE   INFORMATION SYSTEMS PRODUCT  PROSOFTIA AB
84DF   INFORMATION SYSTEMS PRODUCT  PROSOFTIA AB
84E0   OBJECT ORIENTED DATABASE SYSTEM  ONTOS INC
84E1   OBJECT ORIENTED DATABASE SYSTEM  ONTOS INC
84E2   TAPE BACK-UP FOR NLM APPLICATION  MOUNTAIN NETWORK SOLUTIONS INC
84E3   TAPE BACK-UP FOR NLM APPLICATION  MOUNTAIN NETWORK SOLUTIONS INC
84E4   TAPE BACK-UP FOR NLM APPLICATION  MOUNTAIN NETWORK SOLUTIONS INC
84E5   TAPE BACK-UP FOR NLM APPLICATION  MOUNTAIN NETWORK SOLUTIONS INC
84E6   ATTACHMATE CORPORATION
84E7   TAPE BACK-UP FOR NLM APPLICATION  MOUNTAIN NETWORK SOLUTIONS INC
84E8   TAPE BACK-UP FOR NLM APPLICATION  MOUNTAIN NETWORK SOLUTIONS INC
84E9   BRMSG NETWORK MAIL SERVER  SOFTBRIDGE INC
84EA   CLIENT SERVER MONITORING UTILITY  DELL COMPUTER
84EB   SYNECTICS FOR OS/2 VERSION 2.0  PARALLEL PCS INC
84EC   SYNECTICS FOR OS/2 VERSION 2.0  PARALLEL PCS INC
84ED   INFORMATION SYSTEMS PRODUCT  PROSOFTIA AB
84EE   INFORMATION SYSTEMS PRODUCT  PROSOFTIA AB
84EF   INFORMATION SYSTEMS PRODUCT  PROSOFTIA AB
84F0   INFORMATION SYSTEMS PRODUCT  PROSOFTIA AB
84F1   INFORMATION SYSTEMS PRODUCT  PROSOFTIA AB
84F2   INFORMATION SYSTEMS PRODUCT  PROSOFTIA AB
84F3   INFORMATION SYSTEMS PRODUCT  PROSOFTIA AB
84F4   INFORMATION SYSTEMS PRODUCT  PROSOFTIA AB
84F5   INFORMATION SYSTEMS PRODUCT  PROSOFTIA AB
84F6   INFORMATION SYSTEMS PRODUCT  PROSOFTIA AB
84F7   INFORMATION SYSTEMS PRODUCT  PROSOFTIA AB
84F8   INFORMATION SYSTEMS PRODUCT  PROSOFTIA AB
84F9   INFORMATION SYSTEMS PRODUCT  PROSOFTIA AB
84FA   INFORMATION SYSTEMS PRODUCT  PROSOFTIA AB
84FB   NETSCRIBE  MERIDIAN DATA CORP
84FC   NETSCRIBE  MERIDIAN DATA CORP
84FD   NETSCRIBE  MERIDIAN DATA CORP
84FE   NETSCRIBE  MERIDIAN DATA CORP
```

```
84FF   FAX SERVER  FERRARI ELECTRONIC GMBH
8502   FOURTH SHIFT MFG ADD-ON PACKAGE
8503
8504
8505
8506
8507
8508
8509
850A   MODEM-SHARING SOFTWARE - DOS  LANSOURCE TECHNOLOGIES
850B   MODEM-SHARING SOFTWARE - WINDOWS  LANSOURCE TECHNOLOGIES
850C   TELEPHONE ANSWERING SYSTEM  A&M COMMUNICATIONS
850D   FILE/IPX-BASED RPC SYSTEM
850E   NETWORK DISC BACK-UP SOFTWARE  FORTUNET INC
850F   ARCHIVES & MUSEUM MANAGEMENT  CACTUS SOFTWARE
8510   FAX SERVER  EXTENDED SYSTEMS
8511   TELETEXT SERVICE   U OF PLYMOUTH
8512   NETWORK ERROR LOG  U OF PLYMOUTH
8513   MEASURESERVERS AND MEASURECLIENTS  ADVANTECH BENELUX BV
8514   3270 NETWARE FOR SAA EMULATOR  FORVUS RESEARCH INC
8515   3270 NETWARE FOR SAA EMULATOR  FORVUS RESEARCH INC
8516   WORKSTATION UTILIZATION DATA COLLECTION  NETWORK SECURITY SYSTEMS
8517   WORKSTATION UTILIZATION DATABASE MGMT  NETWORK SECURITY SYSTEMS
8518   DATABASE GATEWAY  INFORMATION BUILDERS
8519   FAX SERVER  EXTENDED SYSTEMS
851A   REMOTE PRINTER CONSOLE  PEERLESS GROUP
851B   BATCHFILER IPX SOCKET          JOVANDI INTERNATIONAL INC
851C   TIME SYNCHRONIZATION IPX SOCKET  JOVANDI INTERNATIONAL INC
851D   FAX SERVER LOGIN SOCKET           ASCOM TELECOMMUNICATION LTD
851E   FAX SERVER - CAS REQUEST SOCKET         ASCOM TELECOMMUNICATION LTD
851F   FAX SERVER - WORKSTATION UTILITY REQUEST  ASCOM TELECOMMUNICATION LTD
8520   FAX SERVER - FAXBIOS REQUEST SOCKET     ASCOM TELECOMMUNICATION LTD
8521   FAX SERVER - NETWORKED ATTACHED FAX UNIT  ASCOM TELECOMMUNICATION LTD
8522   DFDSM DATA FACILITIES DATA STORAGE MGMT  IBM - SAN JOSE
8523   RELATIONAL DATABASE  GUPTA TECHNOLOGIES
8524   REPORT SERVER STATS  CENTRAL POINT SOFTWARE
8525   REPORT SERVER STATS  CENTRAL POINT SOFTWARE
8526   COMMUNICATION BETWEEN CLIENT AND SERVER  CDC - OFFICE OF PROGRAM SUPPRT
8529   DOCUMENT PROCESSING SERVER NLM  BOSS LOGIC INC
852A   DOCUMENT PROCESSING SERVER NLM  BOSS LOGIC INC
852B   DOCUMENT PROCESSING SERVER NLM  BOSS LOGIC INC
852C   DOCUMENT PROCESSING SERVER NLM  BOSS LOGIC INC
852D   DOCUMENT PROCESSING SERVER NLM  BOSS LOGIC INC
852E   DOCUMENT PROCESSING SERVER NLM  BOSS LOGIC INC
852F   FINANCIAL MARKETS INFORMATION SERVER  AT FINANCIAL
8530   EMAIL NOTIFICATION  ON TECHNOLOGY
8531   NETVIEW SUPPORT  MEMOREX TELEX
8532   LANLORD PRODUCT  MICROCOM CLIENT SERVER TECHNOL
```

```
8533   RTS TERMINAL EMULATION  DATA RESEARCH & APPLICATIONS
8534   RSCF CLIENT-SERVER API  DATA RESEARCH & APPLICATIONS
8535   CD NETWORKER IPX VERSION
8536   SQL SERVER IPX/SPX HIDDEN SERVER  MICROSOFT
853D   DATABASE LOCK SERVER  HIGH ASPECT DEVELOPMENT
853E   MESSAGE MANAGER  LANCORP PTY LTD
853F   OBJECT MANAGER    LANCORP PTY LTD
8540   OBJECT AGENT      LANCORP PTY LTD
8541   REQUEST MANAGER  LANCORP PTY LTD
8544   WORKSTATION 4-LAN  ADVANCED TECHNICAL SOLUTIONS
8545   GENESYS NETWORK PRODUCT DOS  GENESYS DATA TECHNOLOGY
8546   GENESYS NETWORK PRODUCT OS/2  GENESYS DATA TECHNOLOGY
8548   INTERNET GATEWAY  METASCYBE SYSTEMS LTD
8549   INTELLIGENT HOST GATEWAY  AMericAN AIRLINES DECISION TEC
854C   INTERNAL PROTOCOL/WIRELESS LAN PRODUCT   IBM - LA GAUDE
854D   MULTI-SYSTEM MGR - ACCESS TO SERVER INFO  IBM - RESEARCH TRIANGLE PARK
854E   NETPRINT CALLING CHANNEL  INTERLINK COMMUNICATIONS LTD
854F   NETPRINT WORKING CHANNEL  INTERLINK COMMUNICATIONS LTD
8550   REMOTE SESSION  DST - DISTRIBUTED SYSTEMS TECH
8551   REMOTE SESSION  DST - DISTRIBUTED SYSTEMS TECH
8552   REMOTE SESSION  DST - DISTRIBUTED SYSTEMS TECH
8553   REMOTE SESSION  DST - DISTRIBUTED SYSTEMS TECH
8554   PEER-TO-PEER COMMUNICATIONS - DESKTOP  FUJITSU NETWORKS INDUSTRY
8555   DIAGNOSTIC UTILITY  FUJITSU NETWORKS INDUSTRY
8556   NLM HEALTH MONITOR  PRESOFT ARCHITECTS
8557   CRISLER MCGEE  CRISLER MCKEE SOFTWARE DEVELOP
8558   CRISLER MCGEE  CRISLER MCKEE SOFTWARE DEVELOP
8559   INFORMATION SHARING BETWEEN WORKSTATIONS   INTEL
855A   POLICY ENGINE   EMERALD SYSTEMS
855B   POLICY ENGINE   EMERALD SYSTEMS
855C   POLICY ENGINE   EMERALD SYSTEMS
855D   POLICY ENGINE   EMERALD SYSTEMS
855E   POLICY ENGINE   EMERALD SYSTEMS
855F   POLICY ENGINE   EMERALD SYSTEMS
8560   STAND-ALONE PRINT SERVER  BAY TECHNICAL ASSOCIATES
8561   SERVICE DISTRIBUTION  US WEST ADVANCED TECHNOLOGIES
8562   SERVICE DISTRIBUTION  US WEST ADVANCED TECHNOLOGIES
8563   SERVICE DISTRIBUTION  US WEST ADVANCED TECHNOLOGIES
8564   SERVICE DISTRIBUTION  US WEST ADVANCED TECHNOLOGIES
8565   SERVICE DISTRIBUTION  US WEST ADVANCED TECHNOLOGIES
8566   SERVICE DISTRIBUTION  US WEST ADVANCED TECHNOLOGIES
8568   MPRST PEER-TO-PEER  US SPRINT
8569   MPRST BROADCAST      US SPRINT
856A   LAN ASSIST PLUS REMOTE CONTROL   MICROTEST
856B   LAN ASSIST PLUS REMOTE CONTROL   MICROTEST
856C   LAN ASSIST PLUS REMOTE CONTROL   MICROTEST
856D   LAN ASSIST PLUS REMOTE CONTROL   MICROTEST
856E   MAP ASSIST PEER-TO-PEER          MICROTEST
```

```
856F   MAP ASSIST PEER-TO-PEER        MICROTEST
8570   MAP ASSIST PEER-TO-PEER        MICROTEST
8571   MAP ASSIST PEER-TO-PEER        MICROTEST
8572   ASYNCHRONOUS COMMUNICATIONS SERVERS  US ROBOTICS SOFTWARE
8573   DATABASE SERVER  FAIR COM
8574   NLM-BASED DATABASE ENGINE  AUTO GRAPHICS INC
8575   TIGER QUOTE INCOMING SERVER REQUESTS  JOSHUA GROUP LTD
8576   TIGER QUOTE BROADCAST             JOSHUA GROUP LTD
8577   USER SOCKET    NETWORK TECHNICAL SOLUTIONS
8578   GHOST SOCKET   NETWORK TECHNICAL SOLUTIONS
8579   REMOTE PROCEDURE PROTOCOL  FORTUNET INC
857A   EICON INTERCONNECT SERVER  EICON TECHNOLOGY
857B   EICON SECURITY AGENT   EICON TECHNOLOGY
857C   COST RECOVERY SERVER  VINCENT LARSEN
857D   COST RECOVERY SERVER  VINCENT LARSEN
857E   PC-BASED SNA GATEWAY  UNGERMANN BASS
857F   COMMUNICATION BETWEEN PRINT SERVER & W/S  NISSIN ELECTRIC CO LTD
8580   PEER-TO-PEER MESSAGING  HANS SPATZIER  DIPL-ING
8581   BANKING DEALING ROOMS   ART & SCIENCE LTD
8582   BANKING DEALING ROOMS   ART & SCIENCE LTD
8583   BANKING DEALING ROOMS   ART & SCIENCE LTD
8584   BANKING DEALING ROOMS   ART & SCIENCE LTD
858E   CLIENT UTILITY - WS TO PRINTER COMMUNICA  TOKYO DENSHI SEKKEI KK
8590   NETWORK WORKSTATION CONTROL  WESTERN PACIFIC TECHNOLOGIES
8591   TELETEXT SERVER   TEVESCOM
8592   PRINT SERVER   FORESYTE TECHNOLOGIES
8599   WAN NETWORKS
859A   WAN NETWORKS
859B   WAN NETWORKS
859C   WAN NETWORKS
859D   WAN NETWORKS
859E   WAN NETWORKS
859F   WAN NETWORKS
85A0   WAN NETWORKS
85A1   WAN NETWORKS
85A2   WAN NETWORKS
85A7   DATABASE SERVER   SOFTWRIGHT SYSTEMS
85A8   CHANGE CONTROL PRODUCT   OCCIDENTAL PETROLEUM SVCS INC
85A9   CHANGE CONTROL PRODUCT   OCCIDENTAL PETROLEUM SVCS INC
85AA   STATISTIC MANAGEMENT      MULTITECH
85AB   STATISTIC MANAGEMENT      MULTITECH
85AC   REMOTE CONTROL SOFTWARE  MULTITECH
85AD   REMOTE CONTROL SOFTWARE  MULTITECH
85AE                             MULTITECH
85AF   REMOTE ACCESS SERVER  DCA
85B0   WINDOWS-BASED FAX SYSTEM  ICONOGRAPHIC SYSTEMS
85B1   PRINT SERVER ADD-ON   INTEL - American FORK
85B2   AGV CONTROLLER COMMUNICATIONS  CONTROL ENGINEERING
```

```
85B3   INDEX SEQUENTIAL ACCESS NLM   INFOPOINT SYSTEMS
85B4   ASSOCIATIVE INDEX SERVER      INFOPOINT SYSTEMS
85B5   STRESSMAGIC SERVER UTILITY   NETMAGIC SYSTEMS INC
85B6   NETWORK POWER TOOLS          NETMAGIC SYSTEMS INC
85B7   DOCUMENT MANAGEMENT SVC   IMAGERY SOFTWARE INC
85B8   IMAGE MANAGEMENT SVC      IMAGERY SOFTWARE INC
85B9   MASS STORAGE SVC          IMAGERY SOFTWARE INC
85BA   CITRIX APPLICATION SERVER  CITRIX SYSTEMS
85BB   CITRIX APPLICATION SERVER  CITRIX SYSTEMS
85BC   KLOS TECHNOLOGIES INC
85BD   HOSPITAL MANAGEMENT PACKAGE  SOFTWORK GMBH
85BE   ROUTER MANAGEMENT APPLICATION  CISCO SYSTEMS
85BF   NETWORK MODEM   NANAGRAM
85C0   NETWORK MODEM   NANAGRAM
85C4   5250 GATEWAY COMMUNICATIONS   MICRO INTEGRATION
85C5   SOFTWARE DISTRIBUTION SUITE   CENTERA PTY LTD
85C6   SOFTWARE DISTRIBUTION SUITE   CENTERA PTY LTD
85C7   SOFTWARE DISTRIBUTION SUITE   CENTERA PTY LTD
85C8   SOFTWARE DISTRIBUTION SUITE   CENTERA PTY LTD
85C9   TOBIT !TEAM - REMOTE CONTROLLING   TOBIT SOFTWARE GMBH
85CA   FAXWARE 3.0 - API COMMUNICATION    TOBIT SOFTWARE GMBH
85CB   TOBIT PLZ5 - DATABASE SERVER       TOBIT SOFTWARE GMBH
85CC   AVL NLM DATABASE   AETNA LIFE & CASUALTY
85CD   LU6.2 GATEWAY   AETNA LIFE & CASUALTY
85CF   TELI-LINK VOICE SERVER   COMPUTER & COMMUNICATIONS CO
85D0   REMOTE DOWNLOAD SOFTWARE   ASANTE TECHNOLOGIES
85D5   LAN EXPANDERS MANAGEMENT & DATA TRANSFER   GATEWAY COMMUNICATIONS INC
85D6   CALENDAR SERVER   CAMPBELL SERVICES
85D7   CA UNICENTER   COMPUTER ASSOCIATES
85D8   CA UNICENTER   COMPUTER ASSOCIATES
85D9   CA UNICENTER   COMPUTER ASSOCIATES
85DA   CA UNICENTER   COMPUTER ASSOCIATES
85DB   CA UNICENTER   COMPUTER ASSOCIATES
85DC   CA UNICENTER   COMPUTER ASSOCIATES
85DD   NET MODEM SPX SOCKET   PRACTICAL PERIPHERALS INC
85DE   NET MODEM IPX SOCKET   PRACTICAL PERIPHERALS INC
85DF   ALERT SERVER NLM   CENTRAL POINT SOFTWARE
85E0   MESSAGE ROUTER      CENTRAL POINT SOFTWARE
85E1   OPTICAL FILE SERVER COMMUNICATIONS   PEGASUS DISK TECHNOLOGIES INC
85E2   OPTICAL FILE SERVER LOGIN/LOGOUT     PEGASUS DISK TECHNOLOGIES INC
85E5   PRINT SERVER   RASTEROPS PRINTER TECH DIV
85E6   QUARK EXPRESS   QUARK INC
85E7   SECURITY NLM   NOVELL
85E8   ENDPOINT MAPPER FOR RPC   MICROSOFT
85E9   PC ANYWHERE/NETWARE LITE   SYMANTEC CORP
85EA   INTERSERVER FILE COPYING   BANKERS TRUST CO
85EB   CONNECTION SERVICES      RABBIT SOFTWARE CORP
85EC   DISCOVERY SERVICES       RABBIT SOFTWARE CORP
```

```
85ED   NETWORK MONITOR SERVICES  RABBIT SOFTWARE CORP
85EE   CA-DATACOM/PC  COMPUTER ASSOCIATES
85EF   CA-IDMS/PC      COMPUTER ASSOCIATES
85F1   INDUSTRIAL CONTROL AUTOMATION NETWORK  TELE DENKEN
85F2   PRINT SERVER  RINGDALE UK LTD
85F3   COMMUNICATIONS SERVER  CSB SYSTEMS GMBH
85F6   DATABASE DATAGRAM SOCKET  LYNC INC
85F7   NETPORT EXPRESS STATUS RESPONDER  INTEL - American FORK
85F8   CADENCE TIME SYNCHRONIZATION PRODUCT  POLYGON INC
85F9   CADENCE TIME SYNCHRONIZATION PRODUCT  POLYGON INC
85FA   REMOTE VIRUS SCANNING  MCAFEE ASSOCIATES
85FB   REMOTE MEMORY CONTROL  MCAFEE ASSOCIATES
85FC   NORTON BACK-UP DEVICE SHARING PROTOCOL  ASTORA SOFTWARE INC
85FD   SAMS:EXPERT       STERLING TEFEN LAB
85FE   SAMS:CONTROL      STERLING TEFEN LAB
85FF   SAMS:VANTAGE      STERLING TEFEN LAB
8600   SAMS:SAVE         STERLING TEFEN LAB
8601   SAMS:DISPATCHER  STERLING TEFEN LAB
8602   RENDEZVOUS IPX  GREYHOUSE TECHNOLOGIES
8603   RENDEZVOUS IPX  GREYHOUSE TECHNOLOGIES
8604   RENDEZVOUS SPX  GREYHOUSE TECHNOLOGIES
8605   RENDEZVOUS SPX  GREYHOUSE TECHNOLOGIES
8606   VOICE/FAX RESPONDING MACHINE  SYSTEM SOPHIA
8608   SHARE MODE BROADCAST
8609   IPX ENCAPSULATED RM3 PACKETS  CAYMAN SYSTEMS INC
860A   DATABASE SERVICE  TRIFOX INC
860B   IMAGESOLVE_OFS  IMAGESOLVE INTERNATIONAL
860C   TECHRA: CLIENT\SERVER RDBMS          KVATRO AS
860D   DOCRA: CLIENT\SERVER DOC MGMT SYSTEM  KVATRO AS
860E   NETWORK MANAGEMENT APPLICATION  WANDEL & GOLTERMANN
860F   NETWORK MANAGEMENT APPLICATION  WANDEL & GOLTERMANN
8610   NETWORK MANAGEMENT APPLICATION  WANDEL & GOLTERMANN
8611   NETWORK MANAGEMENT APPLICATION  WANDEL & GOLTERMANN
8612   NETWORK MANAGEMENT APPLICATION  WANDEL & GOLTERMANN
8613   NETWORK MANAGEMENT APPLICATION  WANDEL & GOLTERMANN
8614   CONNECTION ACCEPTANCE SOCKET  CHANCERY SOFTWARE LTD
8615   OPTIDRIVER-NET  OPTISYS
8616   EDM CLIENT/PC  COMPUTER VISION
8617   VIDEO CONFERENCING  LLOYD ALLAN CORPORATION
8618   PRINTER GATEWAY/PEER-TO-PEER COMMUNICATI  ADACOM GROUP
861C   COMMUNICATIONS UTILITY  LEXMARK INTERNATIONAL INC
861D   COMMUNICATIONS UTILITY  LEXMARK INTERNATIONAL INC
861E   PRINT SERVER  LEXMARK INTERNATIONAL INC
861F   PRINT SERVER  LEXMARK INTERNATIONAL INC
8620   PHONE SYSTEM CONTROL  DASH OPEN PHONE SYSTEMS
8621   PHONE SYSTEM CONTROL  DASH OPEN PHONE SYSTEMS
8622   PHONE SYSTEM CONTROL  DASH OPEN PHONE SYSTEMS
8623   PHONE SYSTEM CONTROL  DASH OPEN PHONE SYSTEMS
```

```
8624   OVERSIGHT AGENT   NETWORK UTILITIES SOFTWARE LTD
8625   OVERSIGHT MASTER  NETWORK UTILITIES SOFTWARE LTD
8626   ERL DATABASE SERVER   SILVER PLATTER INFORMATION LTD
8627   ERL DIRECTORY SERVER  SILVER PLATTER INFORMATION LTD
8628   IPX BROADCAST  INTERTECH IMAGING CORPORATION
8629   SPX CONNECT    INTERTECH IMAGING CORPORATION
862A   ZIFF PROPRIETARY SERVICES  ZIFF INFORMATION SERVICES
862B   GAMES   LOOKING GLASS
862C   LPT PORTS   LEXMARK INTERNATIONAL INC
862D   LPT PORTS   LEXMARK INTERNATIONAL INC
862E   LPT PORTS   LEXMARK INTERNATIONAL INC
862F   LPT PORTS   LEXMARK INTERNATIONAL INC
8630   LPT PORTS   LEXMARK INTERNATIONAL INC
8631   LPT PORTS   LEXMARK INTERNATIONAL INC
8632   LPT PORTS   LEXMARK INTERNATIONAL INC
8633   LPT PORTS   LEXMARK INTERNATIONAL INC
8634   TIME SERVER BROADCAST SOCKET  MEINBERG FUNKUHREN
8635   ACCELERATION DATA   SABLE TECHNOLOGY CORP
8636   CALLPATH   IBM - RESEARCH TRIANGLE PARK
8637   CALLPATH   IBM - RESEARCH TRIANGLE PARK
8638   COMMUNICATION INTEGRATOR - SPX  COVIA CORP
8639   COMMUNICATION INTEGRATOR - IPX  COVIA CORP
863B   NETWARE AWARE INFORMATION MGMT SYSTEM   INTUITIVE SOLUTIONS
863C   NETWARE AWARE INFORMATION MGMT SYSTEM   INTUITIVE SOLUTIONS
863D   NETWARE AWARE INFORMATION MGMT SYSTEM   INTUITIVE SOLUTIONS
863E   NETWARE AWARE INFORMATION MGMT SYSTEM   INTUITIVE SOLUTIONS
863F   ARTS RLOGIN APPLICATION  American REAL TIME, REUTERS CO
8640   ARTS GEN SERVER          American REAL TIME, REUTERS CO
8641   NETOP PROGRAM   DANWARE DATA AS
8642   NETOP PROGRAM   DANWARE DATA AS
8643   NETOP PROGRAM   DANWARE DATA AS
8644   NETOP PROGRAM   DANWARE DATA AS
8645   NETOP PROGRAM   DANWARE DATA AS
8646   DOCUMENT MANAGEMENT SYSTEM  SR ASSOCIATES/CYBERMEDIA
8647   SECURITY CHECK  MCAFEE ASSOCIATES
8648   NEWSWIRE NOTIFICATION  GENERATION TECHNOLOGIES CORP
8649   P-NET GATEWAY  PROCES DATA SILKEBORG APS
864A   VIRTUAL MANUFACTURING DEVICE  PROCES DATA SILKEBORG APS
864B   SALES APPLICATION  PROXIM INC
864C   BROADCASTS      NETWORK XCELLENCE
864D   COMMUNICATIONS  NETWORK XCELLENCE
864E   LAN/CD ROM SERVER  LOGICRAFT
8650   SERVER SOCKET             KNIGHT RIDDER FINANCIAL INC
8651   PING SOCKET              KNIGHT RIDDER FINANCIAL INC
8652   BROADCAST DATAGRAM SOCKET  KNIGHT RIDDER FINANCIAL INC
8653   EMPOWER LINK APPLICATION LOADER  NETWORK SECURITY SYSTEMS
8654   NAME RESOLUTION  INTELEC SYSTEMS CORPORATION
8655   MESSAGE LINE             NORMAN DATA DEFANSE SYSTEMS
```

```
8656   CLIENT MESSAGE LINE   NORMAN DATA DEFANSE SYSTEMS
8657   CD SHARING ON NOVELL WORKSTATION     CROSS INTERNATIONAL CORP
8658   NETTALK LAN COMMUNICATIONS SOFTWARE   CROSS INTERNATIONAL CORP
8659   TELEPHONE COMMUNICATIONS SOFTWARE     CROSS INTERNATIONAL CORP
865A   LAN CHATTING                          CROSS INTERNATIONAL CORP
865B   NETWORK MANAGEMENT SERVER   POLE POSITION SOFTWARE GMBH
865C   REMOTE ACCESS SOCKET #1   TRAVELING SOFTWARE
865D   REMOTE ACCESS SOCKET #2   TRAVELING SOFTWARE
865E   NET TRAX ADMINISTRATION   NET X CORP
865F   NET TRAX AGENT   NET X CORP
8660   NET TRAX ALARM MONITOR   NET X CORP
8661   AO CLIENT                     ICL PERSONAL SYSTEMS OY
8662   AO SERVER FOR CLIENT          ICL PERSONAL SYSTEMS OY
8663   AO DIRECTORY SERVER           ICL PERSONAL SYSTEMS OY
8664   AO SERVER ALARMER             ICL PERSONAL SYSTEMS OY
8665   AO CLIENT ALARMER             ICL PERSONAL SYSTEMS OY
8666   AO LAN RTS                    ICL PERSONAL SYSTEMS OY
8667   AO REMOTE CMD SERVER          ICL PERSONAL SYSTEMS OY
8668   AO REMOTE CMD CLIENT          ICL PERSONAL SYSTEMS OY
8669   AO DIR JOIN SERVER            ICL PERSONAL SYSTEMS OY
866A   AO STORAGE SERVER FOR CLIENT  ICL PERSONAL SYSTEMS OY
866B   SAVE UTILITY/2             IBM - CARY
866C   SAVE UTILITY/LIBRARIAN     IBM - CARY
866D   SAVE UTILITY/CURATOR       IBM - CARY
866E   SAVE UTILITY/JANITOR       IBM - CARY
866F   SAVE UTILITY/ARCHIVES I     IBM - CARY
8670   SAVE UTILITY/ARCHIVES II    IBM - CARY
8671   SAVE UTILITY/ARCHIVES III   IBM - CARY
8672   SAVE UTILITY/ARCHIVES IV    IBM - CARY
8673   SAVE UTILITY/ARCHIVES V     IBM - CARY
8674   SAVE UTILITY/ARCHIVES VI    IBM - CARY
8675   SAVE UTILITY/ARCHIVES VII   IBM - CARY
8676   SAVE UTILITY/ARCHIVES VIII  IBM - CARY
8677   SAFESERVER REQUEST SOCKET   OMNITECH CORPORATE SOLUTIONS
8678   CLIENT NLM COMMUNICATIONS   SOFTWARE SECURITY INC
8679   NLM SERVER TO SERVER        SOFTWARE SECURITY INC
867A   FILE TRANSFER APPLICATION   URS ZURBUCHEN
867B   SD ROM JUKEBOX COMMAND SERVER   TODD ENTERPRISES INC
867C   COURSEWARE SERVER   FIRST CLASS SYSTEMS
867D   UDP OVER IPX TRANSMIT   SYNOPTICS
867E   UDP OVER IPX RECEIVE   SYNOPTICS
867F   REALTIME VOICE COMMUNICATION SOFTWARE   VOCALTEC INC
8681   PERSON TO PERSON PRODUCT
8682   NET TUNE   HAWKNET INC
8683   NET TUNE   HAWKNET INC
8684   NET TUNE   HAWKNET INC
8685   NET TUNE   HAWKNET INC
868A   ACCESS CONTROL & LICENSE MANAGEMENT   DALLAS SEMICONDUCTOR
```

```
868B   STAND-ALONE PRINT SERVER   SERCOMM
868C   CD-VINE PEER-TO-PEER COMMUNICATIONS   INFO LINE
868D   FTP       CENTRAL POINT SOFTWARE
868E   TFTP      CENTRAL POINT SOFTWARE
868F   BOOT PS   CENTRAL POINT SOFTWARE
8690   BOOT PC   CENTRAL POINT SOFTWARE
8692   CLIENT TO SERVER COMMUNICATION   NBS SYSTEMS INC
8693   SERVER TO SERVER COMMUNICATION   NBS SYSTEMS INC
8694   NOTIFICATION PURPOSES            NBS SYSTEMS INC
8695   FUTURE EXPANSION                 NBS SYSTEMS INC
8696   FUTURE EXPANSION                 NBS SYSTEMS INC
8697   SNA SERVICES   NETWORK CONTROLS INTERNATIONAL
8698   SNA SERVICES   NETWORK CONTROLS INTERNATIONAL
869A   PROTOCOL IPX   OST-OUEST STANDARD TELEMATIQUE
869B   PROTOCOL IPX   OST-OUEST STANDARD TELEMATIQUE
869C   MULTI-PLAYER GAME - DOOM   ID SOFTWARE
869D   NETWORK MANAGEMENT   HEWLETT PACKARD - GRENOBLE
869E   NETWORK MANAGEMENT   HEWLETT PACKARD - GRENOBLE
869F   DISTRIBUTION SERVICES DISCOVERY   IBM - ROME
86A0   DOCUMENT MANAGEMENT PACKAGE   NOVELL
86A1   DOCUMENT MANAGEMENT PACKAGE   NOVELL
86A2   DOCUMENT MANAGEMENT PACKAGE   NOVELL
86A3   DOCUMENT MANAGEMENT PACKAGE   NOVELL
86A8   CENTRAL MONITORING SYSTEM   TALX CORP
86A9   CENTRAL MONITORING SYSTEM   TALX CORP
86AA   CENTRAL MONITORING SYSTEM   TALX CORP
86AB   CENTRAL MONITORING SYSTEM   TALX CORP
86AC   CENTRAL MONITORING SYSTEM   TALX CORP
86AD   END POINT MAPPER ID'S   MICROSOFT
86AE   END POINT MAPPER ID'S   MICROSOFT
86AF   END POINT MAPPER ID'S   MICROSOFT
86B0   CALENDAR SERVER   CAMPBELL SERVICES INC
86BA   NETWORK MANAGEMENT APPLICATION   XIRCOM
86BB   NETWORK MANAGEMENT APPLICATION   XIRCOM
86BC   NETWORK MANAGEMENT APPLICATION   XIRCOM
86BD   NETWORK MANAGEMENT APPLICATION   XIRCOM
86BE   NETWORK MANAGEMENT APPLICATION   XIRCOM
86BF   NETWORK MANAGEMENT APPLICATION   XIRCOM
86CE   SERVICE LOCATION PROTOCOL   EICON TECHNOLOGY
86CF   TWINSCOPE FOR IPX   NIPPON SYSTEM KAIHUTSU
86D0   MAJOR BBS SOFTWARE   GALACTICOMM INC
86D1   MAJOR BBS SOFTWARE   GALACTICOMM INC
86D2   MAJOR BBS SOFTWARE   GALACTICOMM INC
86D3   MAJOR BBS SOFTWARE   GALACTICOMM INC
86D4   MAJOR BBS SOFTWARE   GALACTICOMM INC
86D5   MAJOR BBS SOFTWARE   GALACTICOMM INC
86D6   MAJOR BBS SOFTWARE   GALACTICOMM INC
86D7   MAJOR BBS SOFTWARE   GALACTICOMM INC
```

```
86D8  MAJOR BBS SOFTWARE   GALACTICOMM INC
86D9  MAJOR BBS SOFTWARE   GALACTICOMM INC
86DC  FAXWARE 3.0 (C-REQ)                    TOBIT SOFTWARE GMBH
86DD  FAXWARE 3.0 (HS-COMM)                  TOBIT SOFTWARE GMBH
86DE  FAXWARE 3.0 (TLD)                      TOBIT SOFTWARE GMBH
86DF  HIGH PERFORMANCE COMMUNICATION SERVER  TOBIT SOFTWARE GMBH
86E0  HIGH PERFORMANCE COMMUNICATION SERVER  TOBIT SOFTWARE GMBH
86E1  HIGH PERFORMANCE COMMUNICATION SERVER  TOBIT SOFTWARE GMBH
86E2  HIGH PERFORMANCE COMMUNICATION SERVER  TOBIT SOFTWARE GMBH
86E3  HIGH PERFORMANCE COMMUNICATION SERVER  TOBIT SOFTWARE GMBH
86E4  HIGH PERFORMANCE COMMUNICATION SERVER  TOBIT SOFTWARE GMBH
86E5  ELECTRONIC SPELLING BOOK (SPOOK!)      TOBIT SOFTWARE GMBH
86E6  ELECTRONIC SPELLING BOOK (SPOOK!)      TOBIT SOFTWARE GMBH
86E7  ELECTRONIC SPELLING BOOK (SPOOK!)      TOBIT SOFTWARE GMBH
86E8  ELECTRONIC SPELLING BOOK (SPOOK!)      TOBIT SOFTWARE GMBH
86F1  OFFICE EXTEND SERVER   FRANSEN KING
86F2  WINDOWS NT FACSYS SERVER   OPTUS INFORMATION SYSTEMS
86F3  WINDOWS NT FACSYS SERVER   OPTUS INFORMATION SYSTEMS
86F4  WINDOWS NT FACSYS SERVER   OPTUS INFORMATION SYSTEMS
86F7  KEYFILE NAME SERVICE   KEYFILE CORP
86F8  EVERGREEN MANAGEMENT AGENT   GOODALL SOFTWARE
86F9  EVERGREEN MANAGEMENT AGENT   GOODALL SOFTWARE
86FA  EVERGREEN MANAGEMENT AGENT   GOODALL SOFTWARE
86FB  EVERGREEN MANAGEMENT AGENT   GOODALL SOFTWARE
86FC  EVERGREEN MANAGEMENT AGENT   GOODALL SOFTWARE
86FD  EVERGREEN MANAGEMENT AGENT   GOODALL SOFTWARE
86FE  FILE SYNCHRONIZATION   NOMADIC SYSTEMS
86FF  WINDOWS BULLETIN BOARD SYSTEM   PACER SOFTWARE
8702  LAN NETVIEW MANAGEMENT UTILITIES   IBM - RESEARCH TRIANGLE PARK
8703  LAN NETVIEW MANAGEMENT UTILITIES   IBM - RESEARCH TRIANGLE PARK
8704  LAN NETVIEW MANAGEMENT UTILITIES   IBM - RESEARCH TRIANGLE PARK
8705  LAN NETVIEW MANAGEMENT UTILITIES   IBM - RESEARCH TRIANGLE PARK
8706  LAN NETVIEW MANAGEMENT UTILITIES   IBM - RESEARCH TRIANGLE PARK
8707  ETHERNET-MANAGED STACKABLE HUB   IBM - RESEARCH TRIANGLE PARK
8708  DOCUMENT MANAGEMENT PACKAGE   NOVELL
8709  DOCUMENT MANAGEMENT PACKAGE   NOVELL
870A  DOCUMENT MANAGEMENT PACKAGE   NOVELL
870B  DOCUMENT MANAGEMENT PACKAGE   NOVELL
870C  DOCUMENT MANAGEMENT PACKAGE
870D  GOODALL VIRTUAL PROTOCOL ADAPTOR   GOODALL SOFTWARE
870E  GOODALL VIRTUAL PROTOCOL ADAPTOR   GOODALL SOFTWARE
870F  GOODALL VIRTUAL PROTOCOL ADAPTOR   GOODALL SOFTWARE
8710  GOODALL VIRTUAL PROTOCOL ADAPTOR   GOODALL SOFTWARE
8712  ENTERPRISE WAN BVNCS   LAN SUPPORT GROUP
871D  PINNACLE RELATIONAL ENGINE   VERMONT DATABASE CORP
871E  FAULT TOLERANCE   CLONE STAR SOFTWARE
8724  UNIX MAIL SERVER   FELPAUSCH
8727  INDUSTIRAL TEST & HANDLING EQUIPMENT   Q CORP
```

```
8728   INDUSTIRAL TEST & HANDLING EQUIPMENT   Q CORP
8729   INDUSTIRAL TEST & HANDLING EQUIPMENT   Q CORP
872A   TELI-LINK VOICE SERVER   COMPUTER & COMMUNICATIONS CO
872B   SECURE FAX CLIENT SOCKET   RUSSELL CONSULTING
8733   BRIDGE ROUTER MENU CONNECTION   NETWORKS NORTHWEST INC
8734   BRIDGE ROUTER ERROR LOG         NETWORKS NORTHWEST INC
8735   IMAGE SERVER CONNECTION   WATERMARK SOFTWARE
8737   EXSEKEY INTERFACE FOR PROTECTED PROGRAMS   CLOVER INFORMATICA SNC
8738   METERING PROGRAM   SECURE DESIGN
873C   COMET TERMINAL SERVER   GOODALL SOFTWARE
873D   COMET TERMINAL SERVER   GOODALL SOFTWARE
873E   COMET TERMINAL SERVER   GOODALL SOFTWARE
873F   COMET TERMINAL SERVER   GOODALL SOFTWARE
8740   COMET TERMINAL SERVER   GOODALL SOFTWARE
8741   COMET TERMINAL SERVER   GOODALL SOFTWARE
8742   COMET FILE SERVER       GOODALL SOFTWARE
8743   COMET FILE SERVER       GOODALL SOFTWARE
8744   COMET FILE SERVER       GOODALL SOFTWARE
8745   COMET FILE SERVER       GOODALL SOFTWARE
8746   COMET FILE SERVER       GOODALL SOFTWARE
8747   COMET FILE SERVER       GOODALL SOFTWARE
874A   MAXSERV COMMUNICATIONS   MAXSERV
874B   MAXSERV COMMUNICATIONS   MAXSERV
874C   NCP COMMUNICATION - JOB SCHEDULER & NLM   LEGENT
874E   TRACE ROUTE   3COM
874F   CLIENT COLLABORATIVE DATA SHARE PRODUCT   AT&T
875B   TVI DESKTOP SERVER   TARGET VISION
875C   MASTERSHOW            TARGET VISION
875D   USER-ACCESS SERVER    TMD CONSULTING
875E   TCP GATEWAY           TMD CONSULTING
875F   CAM SERVER            TMD CONSULTING
8760   CAM SECURE DATABASE   TMD CONSULTING
8761   CAM RESOURCE MANAGER  TMD CONSULTING
8762   CAM BACK-UP           TMD CONSULTING
8763   FIREFOX NLMS AND CLIENT SOFTWARE   FIREFOX COMMUNICATIONS LTD
8764   FIREFOX NLMS AND CLIENT SOFTWARE   FIREFOX COMMUNICATIONS LTD
8765   FIREFOX NLMS AND CLIENT SOFTWARE   FIREFOX COMMUNICATIONS LTD
8766   FIREFOX NLMS AND CLIENT SOFTWARE   FIREFOX COMMUNICATIONS LTD
8767   FIREFOX NLMS AND CLIENT SOFTWARE   FIREFOX COMMUNICATIONS LTD
8768   FIREFOX NLMS AND CLIENT SOFTWARE   FIREFOX COMMUNICATIONS LTD
8769   FIREFOX NLMS AND CLIENT SOFTWARE   FIREFOX COMMUNICATIONS LTD
876A   FIREFOX NLMS AND CLIENT SOFTWARE   FIREFOX COMMUNICATIONS LTD
876B   FIREFOX NLMS AND CLIENT SOFTWARE   FIREFOX COMMUNICATIONS LTD
876C   FIREFOX NLMS AND CLIENT SOFTWARE   FIREFOX COMMUNICATIONS LTD
876D   DATA TRANSACTIONS   TENFORE RESEARCH & DEVELOPMENT
876E   FLOW CONTROL   TENFORE RESEARCH & DEVELOPMENT
8770   REMOTE CONTROL PRODUCT   IBM - RALEIGH
8771   REMOTE CONTROL PRODUCT   IBM - RALEIGH
```

```
8772   REMOTE CONTROL PRODUCT   IBM - RALEIGH
8773   REMOTE CONTROL PRODUCT   IBM - RALEIGH
877C   HITECSOFT SEND SOCKET      HITECSOFT CORP
877D   HITECSOFT RECEIVE SOCKET  HITECSOFT CORP
877E   LAN SCHOOL FOR WINDOWS   LAN FAN TECHNOLOGIES
877F   REMOTE ACCESS PROTOCOL FOR DESKTOP MGMT   INTEL - American FORK
8787   VIDEO SERVER   COREL SYSTEMS CORP
8788   LAN PERFORMANCE MNGMT TOOL IPX/SPX   DIGITAL EQUIPMENT CORP
8789   LAN PERFORMANCE MNGMT TOOL TCP        DIGITAL EQUIPMENT CORP
878B   STATUS SOCKET      NATIONAL SOFTWARE DEVELOPMENT
878C   PRODUCTION SOCKET   NATIONAL SOFTWARE DEVELOPMENT
878E   U OF WISCONSIN UTILITIES   U OF WISCONSIN - MADISON, CAE
878F   U OF WISCONSIN UTILITIES   U OF WISCONSIN - MADISON, CAE
8790   MARC SOFTWARE SYSTEMS   QDATA
8791   TIMBUKTU APPLICATION   FARALLON COMPUTING
8792   LED DISPLAY SERVER   INOVA CORPORATION
8794   BORLAND INTERFACE SERVER FOR NW   BORLAND INTERNATIONAL
8795   NPTN SPX   IBM - RTP
8796   NPTN IPX   IBM - RTP
8797   REMOTE ACCESS SOCKET 3   TRAVELING SOFTWARE
8798   SERVERBENCH
8799   INITIAL CONNECTION TO NLM   FLAGSTAR
879B   SITE METER SECURITY      MCAFEE ASSOCIATES
879C   SITE METER COMMAND       MCAFEE ASSOCIATES
879D   PROXY AGENT SITE METER   MCAFEE ASSOCIATES
879E   DATABASE SERVER/DB2 INSTANCES   IBM - CANADA LTD.
879F   DATABASE SERVER/DB2 INSTANCES   IBM - CANADA LTD.
87A0   DATABASE SERVER/DB2 INSTANCES   IBM - CANADA LTD.
87A1   DATABASE SERVER/DB2 INSTANCES   IBM - CANADA LTD.
87A9   FILE TRANSFER BETWEEN LAN/MAINFRAME   PROGINET CORP
87AA   CONNECTION SERVICE AND SECURITY      PROGINET CORP
87AD   ENTERTAINMENT PRODUCT-BILLIARD POOL   CELERIS INC.
87AE   GAME DEVELOPMENT   GOLDSTEIN GOLLUB KESSLER & CO
87B2   NOVELL SERVER MNGMT BY MAESTROVISION   CALYPSO SOFTWARE
87BA   HEALTHCARE VALIDATIONS APP FOR DOS    OPEN VISION
87BB   HEALTHCARE VALIDATIONS APP FOR UNIX   OPEN VISION
87BD   A SYNCHRONOUS COMMUNICATION   LAN ACCESS
87BE   NETHOPPER SOCKETS   ROCKWELL NETWORK SYSTEMS
87BF   NETHOPPER SOCKETS   ROCKWELL NETWORK SYSTEMS
87C0   NETHOPPER SOCKETS   ROCKWELL NETWORK SYSTEMS
87C1   BACNET TUNNELING OVER IPX   ASHRAE
87C7   MULTIMEDIA DISTRIBUTION SERVER       EMOTION INC
87C8   MULTIMEDIA CONTENT CATALOG SERVER   EMOTION INC
87C9   VOICE PROCESSING SERVER   INTERNATIONAL VOICE EXCHANGE
87CC   MULTIPOINT CONFERENCING PRODUCT BROWSE   DATABEAM CORPORATION
87CD   X1180 POINT OF SELL TICKETING SYSTEM   GATEWAY TICKETING SYSTEMS INC
87D9   T-MEK VIDEO GAME FOR TIME-WARNER   BITS CORP
87DA   THRASH-RACE VIDEO GAME               BITS CORP
```

| | | |
|---|---|---|
| 87DB | ARCUS NETWORK COMMANDER & EXECUTOR | ARCUS COMPUTER |
| 87DC | ARCUS CLIPBOARD SYNCHRONIZER | ARCUS COMPUTER |
| 87DD | ARCUS MENU FOR NW USERS & ADMINISTRATORS | ARCUS COMPUTER |
| 87DF | MULTIPOINT DATA CONFERENCING APP ON SPX | INTEL - HILLSBORO |
| 87E0 | LAN COMMUNICATIONS  CROSS INTERNATIONAL CORP | |
| 87E1 | ZIP CODE SERVER  THIRD PLANET SOFTWARE | |
| 87E2 | WING COMMANDER VERMADA PROVING GROUNDS | ORIGIN SYSTEMS INC |
| 87E5 | SOFTWARE ENTERTAINMENT | ORIGIN SYSTEMS |
| 87E8 | OINET-120  OI ELECTRIC CO LTD | |
| 87E9 | HELP DESK TSR | HILLARD CO |
| 87EA | HELP DESK APPLICATION  HILLARD CO | |
| 87EC | MULTI-PLAYER PLATE SIMULATION  ELECTRONIC ARTS | |
| 87EE | CCTV CONTROL SYSTEM  DIMEX LTD | |
| 87F0 | PRINT SERVER FOR NW3.X  ISHIGAKI COMPUTER SYSTEM CORP | |
| 87F1 | DISTRIBUTED FILE SYSTEM FOR TALXWARE  TALX CORP | |
| 87F2 | DISTRIBUTED FILE SYSTEM FOR TALXWARE  TALX CORP | |
| 87F4 | ALERT MANAGEMENT SYSTEM  INTEL | |
| 87F5 | SERVER COMMANDS ON UXP/DS  FUJITSU LTD | |
| 87FB | PREVAIL/XP  LEGENT | |
| 87FC | OFF LINE COPYING  ON TECHNOLOGIES | |
| 87FD | INTEREGISTER COMMUNICATIONS  ARNEL LTD | |
| 87FE | EFT SERVER | ARNEL LTD |
| 87FF | SCI MULTIPLAYER GAMES SOCKET  SALES CURVE INTERACTIVE LTD | |
| 8802 | PIN64-AUTOMATED DATA TRANSMITTING  ASAHI ELECTRONICS CO LTD | |
| 8805 | INTELLECT USER AUTHENTICATION SYSTEM  INTELLECT AUSTRALIA P/L | |
| 8807 | TO BE ASSURED NO ONE WILL PROCESS PACKET  IBM - RESEARCH TRIANGLE PARK | |
| 880B | DINA GATEWAY  DENSAN SYSTEM CO LTD | |
| 8813 | INTRACTIVE MULTI-PLAYER GAMES  VIRGIN INTRACTIVE ENTERTAINMET | |
| 8814 | LAN UTILITY PROGRAMS  LAN UTILITIES, L.L.C. | |
| 8815 | ATLANTA/3 DIAGNOSTIC SOCKET  KELLY COMPUTER SYSTEMS | |
| 9000 | NP/SQL SERVER | NOVELL - PROVO |
| 9001 | WIDE AREA ROUTER | NOVELL - SUNNYVALE (CPD) |
| 9002 | WIDE AREA ROUTER | NOVELL - SUNNYVALE (CPD) |
| 9003 | WIDE AREA ROUTER | NOVELL - SUNNYVALE (CPD) |
| 9004 | WIDE AREA ROUTER | NOVELL - SUNNYVALE (CPD) |
| 9005 | WIDE AREA ROUTER | NOVELL - SUNNYVALE (CPD) |
| 9006 | WIDE AREA ROUTER | NOVELL - SUNNYVALE (CPD) |
| 9007 | WIDE AREA ROUTER | NOVELL - SUNNYVALE (CPD) |
| 9008 | WIDE AREA ROUTER | NOVELL - SUNNYVALE (CPD) |
| 9009 | WIDE AREA ROUTER | NOVELL - SUNNYVALE (CPD) |
| 900A | WIDE AREA ROUTER | NOVELL - SUNNYVALE (CPD) |
| 900B | WIDE AREA ROUTER | NOVELL - SUNNYVALE (CPD) |
| 900C | WIDE AREA ROUTER | NOVELL - SUNNYVALE (CPD) |
| 900F | SMNP OVER IPX | NOVELL - SAN JOSE |
| 9010 | SMNP OVER IPX | NOVELL - SAN JOSE |
| 9012 | SOFTWARE DISTRIBUTION  PHASER SYSTEMS | |
| 9013 | SOFTWARE DISTRIBUTION  PHASER SYSTEMS | |
| 9014 | SOFTWARE DISTRIBUTION  PHASER SYSTEMS | |

```
9015   SOFTWARE DISTRIBUTION   PHASER SYSTEMS
9016   SOFTWARE DISTRIBUTION   PHASER SYSTEMS
9017   CHAT - WINDOWS                    NOVELL - PROVO  CORP HQ
9019   RPC BIND                          NOVELL - AUSTIN
901A   RPC BIND                          NOVELL - AUSTIN
901E                                     NOVELL - PROVO
901F   NETWARE 'SLURPY'                  NOVELL - PROVO
9021   SPX CONNECTION                    NOVELL - PROVO
9022   JOB SERVER                        NOVELL - PROVO
9023   NETWARE 'SLURPY'                  NOVELL - PROVO
9024   NETWARE 'SLURPY'                  NOVELL - PROVO
9025   NETWARE 'SLURPY'                  NOVELL - PROVO
9026   NETWARE 'SLURPY'                  NOVELL - PROVO
9027                                     NOVELL - PROVO
9028   NETWORK MANAGEMENT                NOVELL - PROVO
9029                                     NOVELL - SALT LAKE CITY
902A                                     NOVELL - SALT LAKE CITY
902B                                     NOVELL - SALT LAKE CITY
902C   NETWORK MANAGEMENT CLIENT INFO  NOVELL - PROVO
902D                                     NOVELL - PROVO
902E   DOS TARGET SERVICE AGENT          NOVELL - PROVO
902F                                     NOVELL - PROVO
9030   SUPERLAB AUTOMATION SERVER  NOVELL - PROVO
9031   RPC BIND                          NOVELL
9032   IPX BIFF            UNIVEL
9033   IPX BOOTPC          UNIVEL
9034   IPX BOOTPS          UNIVEL
9035   IPX CHARGEN         UNIVEL
9036   IPX DAYTIME         UNIVEL
9037   IPX DISCARD         UNIVEL
9038   IPX ECHO            UNIVEL
9039   IPX EPRC            UNIVEL
903A   IPX MONITOR         UNIVEL
903B   IPX NAME            UNIVEL
903C   IPX NAMESERVER      UNIVEL
903D   IPX NETSTAT         UNIVEL
903E   IPX NEW-RWHO        UNIVEL
903F   IPX NFSD            UNIVEL
9040   IPX NTP             UNIVEL
9041   IPX QOTD            UNIVEL
9042   IPX RMONITOR        UNIVEL
9043   IPX ROUTE           UNIVEL
9044   IPX SYSLOG          UNIVEL
9045   IPX SYSTAT          UNIVEL
9046   IPX TALK            UNIVEL
9047   IPX TIME            UNIVEL
9048   IPX WHO             UNIVEL
9049   IPX WHOIS           UNIVEL
```

| | | | |
|---|---|---|---|
| 904A | SPX | APFS | UNIVEL |
| 904B | SPX | APTS | UNIVEL |
| 904C | SPX | AUTH | UNIVEL |
| 904D | SPX | BFTP | UNIVEL |
| 904E | SPX | CHARGEN | UNIVEL |
| 904F | SPX | CMIP-AGENT | UNIVEL |
| 9050 | SPX | CMIP-MANAGE | UNIVEL |
| 9051 | SPX | COURIER | UNIVEL |
| 9052 | SPX | CSNET-NS | UNIVEL |
| 9053 | SPX | DAYTIME | UNIVEL |
| 9054 | SPX | DISCARD | UNIVEL |
| 9055 | SPX | ECHO | UNIVEL |
| 9056 | SPX | EXEC | UNIVEL |
| 9057 | SPX | FINGER | UNIVEL |
| 9058 | SPX | FTP | UNIVEL |
| 9059 | SPX | FTP-DATA | UNIVEL |
| 905A | SPX | HOSTNAMES | UNIVEL |
| 905B | SPX | INGRESLOCK | UNIVEL |
| 905C | SPX | ISO-IP | UNIVEL |
| 905D | SPX | ISO-TP0 | UNIVEL |
| 905E | SPX | ISO-TSAP | UNIVEL |
| 905F | SPX | LINK | UNIVEL |
| 9060 | SPX | LISTEN | UNIVEL |
| 9061 | SPX | LOGIN | UNIVEL |
| 9062 | SPX | NAME | UNIVEL |
| 9063 | SPX | NAMESERVER | UNIVEL |
| 9064 | SPX | NETSTAT | UNIVEL |
| 9065 | SPX | NNTP | UNIVEL |
| 9066 | SPX | NTP | UNIVEL |
| 9067 | SPX | PCSERVER | UNIVEL |
| 9068 | SPX | POP-2 | UNIVEL |
| 9069 | SPX | PRINT-SRV | UNIVEL |
| 906A | SPX | PRINTER | UNIVEL |
| 906B | SPX | QOTD | UNIVEL |
| 906C | SPX | RJE | UNIVEL |
| 906D | SPX | SFTP | UNIVEL |
| 906E | SPX | SHELL | UNIVEL |
| 906F | SPX | SMTP | UNIVEL |
| 9070 | SPX | SUPDUP | UNIVEL |
| 9071 | SPX | SYSTAT | UNIVEL |
| 9072 | SPX | TELNET | UNIVEL |
| 9073 | SPX | TIME | UNIVEL |
| 9074 | SPX | TTYMON | UNIVEL |
| 9075 | SPX | UUCP | UNIVEL |
| 9076 | SPX | UUCP-PATH | UNIVEL |
| 9077 | SPX | WHOIS | UNIVEL |
| 9078 | SPX | X400 | UNIVEL |
| 9079 | SPX | X400-SND | UNIVEL |

```
907A  SPX XSERVER0      UNIVEL
907B  SMS                              NOVELL - PROVO
907C  SMS                              NOVELL - PROVO
907D  QUEUE SERVER FOR IBM PSF/2       NOVELL - PROVO  CORP HQ
907E  IPX SOCKET FOR BTRIEVE REQUESTER NOVELL - AUSTIN
907F  NETWARE FOR SAA                  NOVELL - SUNNYVALE
9080  ADDRESS SERVER                   NOVELL - PROVO
9081  NOVELL MHS DS GATEWAY FOR OCE    NOVELL - WALNUT CREEK
9082  NDS GATEWAY FOR OCE              NOVELL - WALNUT CREEK
9083  X.400 PROTOCOL ACCESS MODULE     NOVELL - RICHMOND HILL
9084  SNADS PROTOCOL ACCESS MODULE     NOVELL - RICHMOND HILL
9085  REMOTE PROGRAM SPAWNING          NOVELL - SAN JOSE
9086  IPX PING                         NOVELL - SAN JOSE
9087  ENHANCED NCP COMMUNICATIONS      NOVELL - PROVO
9088  ROAMING CLIENT SUPPORT           NOVELL - FORTUNE
9089  NETWARE FOR SAA - LOAD BALANCING NOVELL - SUNNYVALE
9094  DATALINK SWITCHING (DLSW)        NOVELL - SAN JOSE
9095  REMOTE CONTROL SOFTWARE PROGRAM  NOVELL - PROVO  CORP HQ
9097  NETWORK INSTALL OF UNIXWARE #2   NOVELL
9098  NEST DEVICE                      NOVELL - PROVO
9099  DATABASE SERVER DOC. MNGMT. PKG. NOVELL - Orem
909A  DATABASE SERVER DOC. MNGMT. PKG. NOVELL - Orem
909B  DATABASE SERVER DOC. MNGMT. PKG. NOVELL - Orem
909C  DATABASE SERVER DOC. MNGMT. PKG. NOVELL - Orem
909D  DATABASE SERVER DOC. MNGMT. PKG. NOVELL - Orem
909E  DATABASE SERVER DOC. MNGMT. PKG. NOVELL - Orem
909F  DATABASE SERVER DOC. MNGMT. PKG. NOVELL - Orem
90A0  DATABASE SERVER DOC. MNGMT. PKG. NOVELL - Orem
90A1  DATABASE SERVER DOC. MNGMT. PKG. NOVELL - Orem
90A2  DATABASE SERVER DOC. MNGMT. PKG. NOVELL - Orem
90B0  MPR IPX ADDRESS MAPPING GATEWAY. NOVELL
90B2  NDPS PRINTER AGENT. NOVELL
```

# NCP Descriptions

The following NCP descriptions can be used to give you a brief definition of the NCPs that you'll see crossing the wire.

These NCPs are separated into the following categories:

- ▸ Accounting Service NCPs

- ▸ Apple File Service NCPs

- ▸ Bindery NCPs

- ▸ Connection NCPs

- ▸ Data Migration NCPs

- ▸ Extended Attribute NCPs

- ▸ File Server Environment NCPs

- ▸ File System NCPs

- ▸ Message NCPs

- ▸ NCP Extension NCPs

- ▸ Novell Directory Services (NDS) NCPs

- ▸ Print Service NCPs

- ▸ Queue Service NCPs

- ▸ RPC Services NCPs

- ▸ Statistical NCPs

- ▸ Synchronization Service NCPs

- ▸ Transaction Tracking Service NCPs

## Accounting Service NCPs

These accounting system NCP calls are used by developers to create servers that charge for their services (such as records viewed, connect time, and pages printed).

Get Current Account Status     0x2222     23     150

This NCP call enables an account server to get an account status at the time of a request for service.

Submit Account Charge     0x2222     23     151

This NCP call enables an account server to submit a charge to an account.

Submit Account Hold     0x2222     23     152

This NCP call enables an account server to hold an amount in reserve for future charging to a client's account.

Submit Account Note     0x2222     23     153

This NCP enables an account server to attach a note about client account activities in the audit file.

## Apple File Service NCPs

These NCP calls provide AppleTalk Filing Protocol (AFP) services, which allow applications to create and access Macintosh-format files and directories that reside on a NetWare file server.

AFP 2.0 Create Directory     0x2222     35     13

This NCP call enables the client to create a directory with an AFP directory name.

AFP 2.0 Create File     0x2222     35     14

This NCP call enables the client to create a file with an AFP name. Note that the file is not opened when it is created.

### AFP 2.0 Get File or Directory Information     0x2222    35     15

This call enables a client to get information about an AFP file or directory. The information returned may include attributes, creation date, long name, access privileges, resource fork length, and the like.

### AFP 2.0 Scan File Information     0x2222    35     17

This NCP file enables a client to obtain information about an AFP entry (either a directory or file). This NCP call allows iterative scanning.

### AFP 2.0 Set File Information     0x2222    35     16

This NCP call enables the client to set information regarding a specific AFP file or directory. Settings include attributes, create date, access date, and such.

### AFP Alloc Temporary Directory Handle     0x2222    35     11

This NCP call maps a NetWare directory handle to an AFP directory.

### AFP Create Directory     0x2222    35     01

This call creates a directory using an AFP directory name.

### AFP Create File     0x2222    35     02

This NCP call creates a file with an AFP filename. Note that the new file is not opened with this NCP call.

### AFP Delete     0x2222    35     03

This NCP call deletes an AFP file or an AFP directory. In order for a file to be deleted, it must be closed by all users.

### AFP Get DOS Name from Entry ID     0x2222    35     18

This NCP call gets the DOS directory path that corresponds to a 32-bit Macintosh file or directory entry ID.

## AFP Get Entry ID from Name                 0x2222    35    04

This NCP call returns the AFP ID number of the specified ID number or file.

## AFP Get Entry ID from NetWare Handle       0x2222    35    06

This NCP call returns an AFP entry ID for the specified NetWare file handle.

## AFP Get Entry ID from Path Name            0x2222    35    12

This NCP call converts a NetWare-type path specification into a unique 32-bit Macintosh file or directory entry ID.

## AFP Get File Information                   0x2222    35    05

This NCP call is used to get AFP file information, such as creation date, access date, modify date and time, and AFP entry ID.

## AFP Get Macintosh Info on Deleted File     0x2222    35    19

This NCP call returns the Finder and Pro DOS info structures for a Macintosh directory entry that has been deleted.

## AFP Open File Fork                         0x2222    35    08

This NCP call opens an AFP data or resource fork.

## AFP Rename                                 0x2222    35    07

This NCP call is used to move or rename an AFP directory or file.

## AFP Scan File Information                  0x2222    35    10

This NCP call returns information about an AFP directory or file. This NCP call is used to provide iterative scanning of a directory.

## AFP Set File Information                   0x2222    35    09

This NCP call sets information pertaining to a specific AFP file or directory.

## Bindery NCPs

NetWare File Servers include a small data base called a *bindery*. Novell's bindery uses hidden files located within the SYS:system directory.

### Add Bindery Object to Set 0x2222 23 65

This NCP call enables a client to add an object to a group property.

### Change Bindery Object Password 0x2222 23 64

This NCP call enables a user to change an object's password. Typically this would enable clients to change their own password.

### Change Bindery Object Security 0x2222 23 56

This NCP call enables a supervisor to change the security level of an object in the bindery.

### Change Property Security 0x2222 23 59

This NCP call enables a client to change the security level on a property.

### Change User Password (old) 0x2222 23 01

This NCP call has been replaced with Change Bindery Object Password (function 23, subfunction 64).

### Close Bindery 0x2222 23 68

This NCP call closes down the bindery. Closing the bindery disables most network functions but can be useful for network administration functions.

### Create Bindery Object 0x2222 23 50

This NCP call is used to create a bindery object.

### Create Property 0x2222 23 57

This NCP call creates a new property and attaches the property to a specific object.

### Delete Bindery Object 0x2222 23 51

This NCP call is used to remove an object and all its related properties from the bindery.

### Delete Bindery Object from Set 0x2222 23 66

This NCP call removes a member from a set property of a specific object.

### Delete Property 0x2222 23 58

This NCP call deletes one or more properties from a specific object.

### Get Bindery Access Level 0x2222 23 70

This NCP call returns the client's current security level in the bindery.

### Get Bindery Object Access Level 0x2222 23 72

This NCP call returns the client's bindery access level to a specific object.

### Get Bindery Object ID 0x2222 23 53

This NCP call enables a client to map an object name to a unique object ID number.

### Get Bindery Object Name 0x2222 23 54

This NCP call allows a client to map an object ID number to an object name and object type.

### Get Group Number (old) 0x2222 23 07

This old NCP call was used in shells for NetWare version 2.0a and below.

### Get User Number (old) 0x2222 23 03

This NCP call has been replaced by Get Bindery Option Number (function 23, subfunction 53).

### Is Bindery Object in Set          0x2222     23     67

This NCP call enables a client to check whether an object appears as a member in a set property.

### Is Calling Station a Manager      0x2222     23     73

This NCP function checks to see if a calling station has manager privileges within the bindery.

### Keyed Change Password             0x2222     23     75

This NCP call changes the password for bindery object that requires a key log in.

### Keyed Verify Password             0x2222     23     74

This NCP verifies a password for a bindery object that requires a key log in.

### List Relations of an Object       0x2222     23     76

This NCP request returns a list of up to 32 bindery object IDs that are in a set property of the bindery object specified by name and type.

### Open Bindery                      0x2222     23     69

This NCP call reopens bindery files that have closed with the Closed Bindery NCP call.

### Read Property Value               0x2222     23     61

This NCP call enables a client to retrieve a value associated with a specific property.

### Rename Object                     0x2222     23     52

This NCP call is used to rename a bindery object.

### Scan Bindery Object               0x2222     23     55

This NCP call enables a client to scan the server's bindery to determine what objects are there.

Scan Bindery Object Trustee Paths     0x2222    23    71

This NCP call provides a path on a specified volume where a specific object ID is a trustee.

Scan Property     0x2222    23    60

This NCP call enables a client to scan the properties that are attached to a bindery object.

Verify Bindery Object Password     0x2222    23    63

This NCP call allows other servers or clients to verify the identity of an object or check the validity of a password. Any client can use this call.

Write Property Value     0x2222    23    62

This NCP call allows a client to write a value to an item property.

## Connection NCPs

These connection NCPs enable a client and a server to establish, maintain, and destroy service connections.

Change Connection State     0x2222    23    29

This NCP call is used to change the connection state of a client or server. For example, a client can request to change a logged-in state to a temporarily authenticated state.

Clear Connection Number     0x2222    23    254

This NCP call logs out a specific station. This NCP is used when a station can be used and when station numbers are greater than 256.

Create Service Connection     0x1111    —    —

This NCP call creates a general service connection between a client and a server.

| Destroy Service Connection | 0x5555 | 00 | — |

This NCP call is used to make a server destroy a specific general service connection.

| End of Job | 0x2222 | 24 | — |

This NCP call is used by a client to inform a server that one of its tasks has been executed completely. If the task number field is set to 0, all the client's tasks have been completed.

| Get Big Packet NCP Max Packet Size | 0x2222 | 97 | — |

This NCP call is used to negotiate a maximum packet size to be used between client and server. This NCP call also contains a security flag that indicates whether packet signing is enabled.

| Get Connection List from Object | 0x2222 | 23 | 31 |

This NCP call gets a list of connections by using the object ID.

| Get Internet Address | 0x2222 | 23 | 26 |

This NCP call enables the client to obtain its internetwork address, including the IPX network address and the node ID.

| Get Internet Address (old) | 0x2222 | 23 | 19 |

This NCP call has been replaced by Get Internet Address (function 23, subfunction 26).

| Get Login Key | 0x2222 | 23 | 23 |

This NCP request provides a password key for the requesting client.

| Get Object Connection List | 0x2222 | 23 | 27 |

This NCP call is used to obtain a list of connections currently granted by the server.

Get Object Connection List (old)     0x2222     23     21

This older NCP call was replaced by the Get Object Connection List call (function 23, subfunction 27).

Get Station Number                   0x2222     19

This NCP call provides the client with its 3-byte station number.

Get Station's Logged Info            0x2222     23     28

This NCP call returns basic client information, such as log-in time, user name, and user type.

Get Station's Logged Info (old)      0x2222     23     22

This NCP call is replaced by the call Get Station's Logged Info (function 23, subfunction 28).

Get Station's Logged Info (old)      0x2222     23     05

This NCP call is replaced by Get Station's Logged Info (function 23, subfunction 28).

Get User Connection List (old)       0x2222     23     02

This NCP call is the same as Get Object Connection List (function 23, subfunction 21), except that this NCP assumes an object type of User.

Keyed Object Login                   0x2222     23     24

This NCP call logs a specific bindery object using its 8-byte assigned key.

Login Object                         0x2222     23     20

This NCP call enables a client to identify itself to a file server in order to access the directory system.

Login User (old)                     0x2222     23     00

This NCP call is basically the same as Login Object (function 23, subfunction 20), except that it assumes that the object is always User.

| Logout | 0x2222 | 25 | — |

This NCP call enables a client to relinquish all server access privileges without destroying its service connection.

| Negotiate Buffer Size | 0x2222 | 33 | — |

This NCP call is used to negotiate the buffer size that would be used to send file read and write requests to a file server.

| Packet Burst Connection Request | 0x2222 | 101 | — |

This NCP call is used to obtain a burst mode connection to a server. The client indicates its desired maximum packet size in this request.

| Request Being Processed | 0x9999 | — | — |

This NCP call is sent by a server to a client when it receives a duplicate service request while the original service request is still in the processing state.

| Request Processed | 0x3333 | — | — |

This NCP call is returned by the server to the client when the server has completed handling a request.

| Set Watchdog Delay Interval | 0x2222 | 23 | 30 |

This NCP request enables a connection to specify the watchdog delay interval. The watchdog delay interval is the amount of time that a server will wait before it sends its first NCP watchdog packet to a client.

## Data Migration NCPs

These NCPs deal primarily with migrating or moving data from a NetWare volume to some online medium, such as a disk tape or CD-ROM.

| DM File Information | 0x2222 | 90 | 129 |

This NCP file is used to get information about data migration files.

## DM Support Module Information    0x2222    90    132

This NCP call is used to get information about data migration NLMs or a list of all loaded Support Module IDs.

## DM Support Module Capacity Request    0x2222    90    135

This NCP call is used to identify the server's block size in sectors, total blocks, and used blocks.

## Get/Set Default Read-Write Support Module ID    0x2222    90    134

This NCP call is used to set the default read-write support module ID.

## Migrator Status Info    0x2222    90    131

This NCP call is used to get information about the migrator, such as the migrator state (loaded and running or unloaded), major version, and minor version.

## Move File Data from DM    0x2222    90    133

This NCP call is used to move a file back to a NetWare volume.

## Move File Data to DM    0x2222    90    128

This NCP file is used to move a file's data to some long-term storage medium but leave the file visible on a NetWare volume.

## RTDM Request    0x2222    90    136

This NCP call is used to access a removable tape medium.

## Volume DM Status    0x2222    90    130

This NCP file is used to get information, such as total migrated size and space used on a specific volume.

## Extended Attribute NCPs

These NCPs provide extended attribute support for NetWare 386 version 3.11.

Close Extended Attribute Handle      0x2222      86      01

This NCP call closes the extended attribute handle that has been defined previously.

Duplicate Extended Attributes      0x2222      86      05

This NCP call is used to duplicate extended attributes.

Enumerate Extended Attributes      0x2222      86      04

This NCP call is used to find additional details on extended attributes.

Read Extended Attributes      0x2222      86      03

This NCP call is used to read extended attributes related to a file or directory.

Write Extended Attributes      0x2222      86      02

This NCP Call is used to write extended attributes to the server.

## File Server Environment NCPs

These NCPs are used to obtain information about the file servers (such as disk channel, volumes, connections, and transaction tracking systems statistics) and set certain server perimeters (enable or disable transaction tracking, enable or disable login, set the server time and date, and down the server).

Check Console Privilege      0x2222      23      200

This NCP call is used by clients to determine whether it has console privileges on a server.

Clear Connection Number              0x2222    23    254

This NCP logs out the defined station.

Clear Connection Number (old)    0x2222    23    210

This NCP call has been replaced by Clear Connection Number (function 23, subfunction 254).

Disable File Server Login            0x2222    23    203

This NCP call enables an operator to block new login requests from a server.

Disable Transaction Tracking        0x2222    23    207

This NCP is used to disable the transaction tracking system (TTS) on a server. This NCP does not affect NetWare 4.1 or higher servers—TTS is always enabled on these versions of NetWare.

Down File Server                        0x2222    23    211

This NCP call is used by a file server to take down a server using a remote console.

Enable File Server Login            0x2222    23    204

This NCP call is used to allow client logins after client logins have been disabled using Disable File Server Login (function 23, subfunction 203).

Enable Transaction Tracking        0x2222    23    208

This NCP is used to enable transaction tracking after it has been disabled using Disable Transaction Tracking (function 23, subfunction 207). Note that in NetWare 4.11 or greater, TTS is always enabled.

Get Connection's Open Files        0x2222    23    235

This NCP call provides information about files currently opened by the desired connection number.

### Get Connection's Open Files (old)   0x2222   23   219

This NCP has been replaced by Get Connection's Open File (function 23, subfunction 235).

### Get Connection's Semaphores   0x2222   23   241

This NCP call enables an operator to get a list of all semaphores that a connection is using.

### Get Connection's Semaphores (old)   0x2222   23   225

This NCP call has been replaced by Get Connection's Semaphores (function 23, subfunction 241).

### Get Connection's Task Information   0x2222   23   234

This NCP call enables an operator to receive information about the current status of a connection's active tasks.

### Get Connection Usage Statistics   0x2222   23   229

This NCP call enables a client to get its own usage statistics, such as bytes read, bytes written, and total request packets.

### Get Connections Using a File   0x2222   23   236

This NCP call is used to find all the logical connections that are using a specified file.

### Get Connections Using a File (old)   0x2222   23   220

This NCP call has been replaced by Get Connections Using a File (function 23, subfunction 236).

### Get Disk Channel Statistics   0x2222   23   217

This NCP call is used to get disk channel statistics and status, such as channel state, shared memory addresses, interrupt number used, and software driver type.

Get Disk Utilization                      0x2222    23    14

This NCP call is used by a client to find out how much physical space a certain trustee is using on a given volume.

Get Drive Mapping Table                   0x2222    23    215

This NCP call is used to read the server's drive mapping table.

Get File Server Date and Time             0x2222    20    —

This NCP call is used to obtain the current date and time that is kept by the server.

Get File Server Description Strings        0x2222    23    201

This NCP call returns descriptive information about the server, such as NetWare version.

Get File Server Information                0x2222    23    17

This NCP call is used by clients to obtain basic file server information. Clients make this request of a server to which they have just established a service connection. Information provided includes NetWare version number, maximum connections in use, and the number of mounted volumes possible.

Get File Server LAN I/O Statistics         0x2222    23    231

This NCP call is used to obtain statistical information about incoming and outgoing packets to and from a server. Information includes routing buffers configured and used, packets from invalid connections, requests being processed, notifications, and NETBIOS broadcast propagations.

Get File Server Login Status               0x2222    23    205

This NCP call enables a client to determine if login is currently enabled at a server.

Get File Server Misc Information        0x2222    23    232

This NCP call provides miscellaneous statistical information and configuration information on a server, such as processor type, number of service processes, and currently used bindery objects.

Get File System Statistics        0x2222    23    212

This NCP call is used to obtain file server statistics dealing with the file system itself, such as maximum open files, total read requests, and FAT writers.

Get LAN Driver Configuration Information    0x2222    23    227

This NCP call provides configuration information about the server's LAN drivers, such as network addresses, boards installed, and host address.

Get Logical Record Information        0x2222    23    240

This NCP call is used to obtain logical record information from the server, such as connection number, task number, and lock status of devices.

Get Logical Record Information (old)      0x2222    23    224

This NCP call has been replaced by Get Logical Record Information (function 23, subfunction 240).

Get Logical Records by Connection      0x2222    23    239

This NCP call provides logical record information that a connection has logged with a server. This includes the number and definition of records that have been locked and the lock status.

Get Logical Records by Connection (old)    0x2222    23    223

This NCP has been replaced by Get Logical Records by Connection (function 23, subfunction 239).

Get Network Serial Number        0x2222    23    18

This NCP call provides a file server's serial number and an application number.

## Get Object's Remaining Disk Space    0x2222    23    230

This NCP call provides the amount of unused disk blocks available for specific object ID.

## Get Physical Record Locks by
## Connection and File    0x2222    23    237

This NCP provides the logical connection's physical records locks within a file.

## Get Physical Record Locks by
## Connection and File (old)    0x2222    23    221

This NCP call has been replaced by Get Physical Record Locks by Connection and File (function 23 and subfunction 237).

## Get Physical Record Locks by File    0x2222    23    238

This NCP call provides a list of all records that are locked within a file.

## Get Physical Record Locks by File (old)    0x2222    23    222

This NCP call has been replaced by Get Physical Record Locks by File (function 23, subfunction 238).

## Get Semaphore Information    0x2222    23    242

This NCP provides information about a single semaphore, such as the open count, semaphore value, and number of records.

## Get Semaphore Information (old)    0x2222    23    226

This NCP call was replaced by Get Semaphore Information (function 23, subfunction 242).

## Get Transaction Tracking Statistics    0x2222    23    213

This NCP call is used to obtain the statistical information about the server's TTS.

Get Volume Information          0x2222    23    233

This NCP call is used to obtain information about a specific volume. The information includes: the volume number, block size, total blocks, free blocks, free directory entries, and volume name.

Read Disk Cache Statistics      0x2222    23    214

This NCP call is used to obtain statistical information about file server caching, such as dirty cache buffers, cache buffer size, cache read request, and cache write request.

Read Physical Disk Statistics   0x2222    23    216

This NCP call is used to obtain statistics about a server disk, such as controller type, drive size, sectors per track, and drive head.

Send Console Broadcast          0x2222    23    253

This NCP call is used to send a message to a group of logical connections.

Send Console Broadcast (old)    0x2222    23    209

This NCP call has been replaced by send console broadcast (function 23, subfunction 253).

Set File Server Date and Time   0x2222    23    202

This NCP call is used to set the file server date and time.

Verify Serialization            0x2222    23    12

This NCP call is used to identify duplicate serial numbers on the network.

## File System NCPs

This set of NCPs is used to obtain information about the NetWare file system and manipulate files and directories.

### Add Extended Trustee to Directory or File          0x2222     22      39

This function adds a trustee and sets that trustee's rights for a file or directory.

### Add Trustee Set to File or SubDirectory          0x2222     87      10

This NCP call is used to add a trustee set to a file's or directory's trustee list.

### Add Trustee to Director          0x2222     22      13y

This NCP call is used to add a new trustee to a directory trustee list.

### Add User Disk Space Restriction          0x2222     22      33

This NCP call is used to set an object volume disk space restriction—restrictions are in 4K blocks.

### Alloc Permanent Directory Handle          0x2222     22      18

This NCP call is used to create a permanent directory handle and point the handle to a specific directory.

### Allocate Short Directory Handle          0x2222     87      12

This NCP call is used to allocate a short directory handle.

### Alloc Special Temporary Directory Handle     0x2222     22      22

This NCP call is used to create a temporary directory handle. This handle cannot be mapped to another place using Set Directory Handle (function 22).

### Alloc Temporary Directory Handle          0x2222     22      19

This NCP call is used to create a new temporary directory handle for a client. This temporary directory handle will be released once the client indicates that its task is completed.

### Close File                                    0x2222       66       —

This NCP call is used to completely close a file. Once a file is closed, the file handle is no longer valid.

### Commit File                                   0x2222       59       —

This NCP call is used to ensure that any data written to a server from a client has been written to the server's disk and is not remaining in a cache at the server.

### Convert Path to Dir Entry           0x2222       23       244

This NCP call converts a path name to a directory entry.

### Copy from One File to Another     0x2222       74       —

This NCP call is used to copy from one file on a file server to another file on the same file server. This NCP call is used by the NCOPY utility.

### Create Directory                          0x2222       22       10

This NCP call is used by a client to create a new directory on the server.

### Create File                                    0x2222       67       —

This NCP call is used to create a new file on a NetWare server. This file may be replaced by the "Open Create File" or "SubDirectory NCP call" (function 87, subfunction 1).

### Create New File                           0x2222       77       —

This NCP call is the same as "Create File" (function 67), except that this request fails if a file with the specified name already exists.

### Deallocate Directory Handle        0x2222       22       20

This NCP call is used to deallocate a specific directory handle (permanent or temporary).

Delete Directory                                    0x2222        22        11

This NCP call is used to delete a specific directory.

Delete a File or SubDirectory          0x2222        87        08

This NCP call is used to delete a specific file or subdirectory.

Delete Trustee from Directory          0x2222        22        14

This NCP Call is used to remove a trustee from the trustee list of a specific directory.

Delete Trustee Set from File or SubDirectory      0x222287        11

This NCP call is used to delete a trustee set from a specific file or subdirectory.

Erase File                                          0x2222        68        —

This NCP call is used to erase a file on a NetWare server. This call supports wildcards.

Extract a Base Handle                     0x2222        22        23

This NCP call is used to obtain the server's form of directory address for a workstation.

File Migration Request                    0x2222        90        150

This NCP call is used to change or to set file migration attributes of a file.

File Search Continue                       0x2222        63        —

This NCP call is used to locate a file and to provide file or directory information to the requesting client, if available.

File Search Initialize                       0x2222        62        —

This NCP call is used to begin a search for files within a specified directory. This call is replaced by Initialized Search (function 87, subfunction 2).

## Generate Directory Base and Volume Number    0x2222    87    22

This NCP call is used to generate a directory base and a volume number.

## Get Current Size of File    0x2222    71    —

This NCP call is used by the client to define the current length of a file that the client has open.

## Get Directory Disk Space Restriction    0x2222    22    35

This NCP call is used to determine the amount of space assigned to all directories between the current directory and the root directory.

## Get Directory Entry    0x2222    22    31

This NCP call is used to get the directory information that is associated with a specific directory handle. The information includes name space support, directory name, creation date and time, and owner ID.

## Get Directory Information    0x2222    22    45

This NCP is used to provide the real size information for a NetWare 386 directory. This NCP call can handle volumes larger than 256MB.

## Get Directory Path    0x2222    22    01

This NCP call is used to obtain the full directory path of a directory based on its directory handle.

## Get Effective Directory Rights    0x2222    22    03

This NCP call is used by a client to determine its access rights for a specific directory.

## Get Effective Directory Rights    0x2222    87    29

This NCP call is used by a client to determine its current effective right in a specific directory. This NCP call enables the server to supply a directory handle in the reply.

Get Effective Rights for Directory Entry    0x2222    22    42

This NCP call is used to obtain a client's effective access rights to a directory or file.

Get Extended Volume Information    0x2222    22    51

This NCP call is used to obtain full volume information, including freed clusters, sub Alloc clusters, volume size in clusters, sector size, extended attributes defined, and volume last modified date and time.

Get File Information    0x2222    87    31

This NCP is used to obtain information about a file based on its file handle, or information about a directory based on its directory handle.

Get Full Path String    0x2222    87    28

This NCP call is used to get the full path string for a specific NetWare path that is defined by the client.

Get Huge NS Information    0x2222    87    26

This NCP call is used to obtain huge name space information.

Get Mount Volume List    0x2222    22    52

This NCP call is used to get a list of all currently mounted volumes.

Get NS Information    0x2222    87    19

This NCP call is used to obtain name space information.

Get Name Space Directory Entry    0x2222    22    48

This NCP call is used to obtain directory entry information associated with a name space supported on a volume.

Get Name Space Information    0x2222    22    47

This NCP call is used to obtain name space and data stream information for a server and its volumes.

Get Name Spaces Loaded List from
Volume Number                                          0x2222      87      24

This NCP call is used to identify the types of names spaces on a volume.

Get Object Disk Usage and Restrictions                 0x2222      22      41

This NCP call is used to obtain a client's disk restrictions for a specific volume and current usage statistics.

Get Object Effective Rights for Directory Entry        0x2222      22      50

This NCP call is used to obtain an object's effective rights for a specific file or directory.

Get Path Name of a Volume
Directory Number Pair                                  0x2222      22      26

This NCP call is used to obtain the directory path for a volume number/directory entry number pair.

Get Path String from Short Directory Handle            0x2222      87      21

This NCP call is used to obtain the complete path string from a short directory handle as defined by the client.

Get Reference Count from Dir Entry Number              0x2222      90      10

This NCP call provides a reference count for a particular directory entry number.

Get Reference Count from Dir Handle                    0x2222      90      11

This NCP call provides a reference count for a specific directory handle.

Get Sparse File Data Block Bit Map                     0x2222      85      —

This NCP call returns a bit map that indicates the used and unused blocks on the server.

### Get Volume and Purge Information                          0x2222    22    44

This NCP call returns the volume information for a NetWare 386 volume.

### Get Volume Info with Handle                               0x2222    22    21

This NCP call is used to obtain information about the physical limitations of a server volume.

### Get Volume Info with Number                              0x2222    18    —

This NCP call is used to return the same information as Get Volume Info with Handle (function 22, subfunction 21).

### Get Volume Name                                          0x2222    22    06

This NCP call uses a volume number to retrieve a specific volume name.

### Get Volume Number                                        0x2222    22    05

This NCP call is used to retrieve a volume number based on a volume name.

### Initialize Search                                        0x2222    87    02

This NCP initializes the search for a specific file or a directory.

### Map Directory Number to Path                             0x2222    23    243

This NCP call maps a specific directory number to a path, which includes a directory, subdirectory, or filename.

### Modify DOS Attributes on a File or SubDirectory          0x2222    87    35

This NCP call is used to set DOS attributes on a file or directory entry.

### Modify File or SubDirectory DOS Information              0x2222    87    07

This NCP call is used to modify DOS information while using another name space.

Modify Maximum Rights Mask        0x2222    22    04

This NCP call enables a client to change the maximum rights mask associated with a directory.

Obtain File or SubDirectory Information    0x2222    87    06

This NCP call is used to obtain information, such as file/subdirectory size, owner, or last accessed date.

Open CallBack Control          0x2222    87    34

This NCP is used to control callbacks to previously defined functions. A callback is simply a method an application can use to set up notification of task completion (successful or not).

Open/Create File (old)         0x2222    84    —

This NCP call is replaced by Open/Create File or SubDirectory (function 87, subfunction 01).

Open/Create File or SubDirectory     0x2222    87    01

This NCP call is used to open or create a file or subdirectory and enables the developer to open or create a hidden or system file or create only a subdirectory.

Open/Create File or SubDirectory     0x2222    87    30

This NCP call can be used to provide the same functionality as Open/Create File or SubDirectory (function 87, subfunction 01) while allowing SubDirectories to be created by a client but not opened by the client.

Open/Create File or SubDirectory
with Callback               0x2222    87    32

This NCP call enhances the Open/Create File or SubDirectory (function 87, subfunction 01) NCP call. This NCP, however, allows the developer to receive a callback, a notification of completion of the desired function.

| Open/Create File or SubDirectory II with Callback | 0x2222 | 87 | 33 |

This NCP call is an enhancement of the Open/Create File or SubDirectory (function 87, subfunction 30) NCP call.

| Open Data Stream | 0x2222 | 22 | 49 |

This NCP call is used to open a data stream for a name space on the server. It also provides a NetWare file handle.

| Open File (old) | 0x2222 | 65 | — |

This NCP call is very old and has been replaced by Open File (function 76) and later Open/Create File or SubDirectory (function 87, subfunction 01). The desired access rights cannot be defined using this NCP call.

| Open File (old) | 0x2222 | 76 | — |

This NCP call, used to open an existing file, has been replaced with Open/Create File or SubDirectory (function 87, subfunction 01).

| Parse Tree | 0x2222 | 90 | 00 |

This NCP call is used to parse a tree by the directory base.

| Purge Erased Files (old) | 0x2222 | 22 | 16 |

This NCP call is replaced by the Purge Salvageable File (function 22, subfunction 29) and later by Purge Salvageable File (function 87, subfunction 18) NCP calls.

| Purge Salvageable File | 0x2222 | 87 | 18 |

This NCP call is used to purge files that have been deleted by the client and have been moved into the holding area.

| Purge Salvageable File (old) | 0x2222 | 22 | 29 |

This NCP call has been replaced by the Purge Salvageable File (function 87, subfunction 18) NCP call.

Query NS Information Format      0x2222    87    23

This NCP call is used to obtain the format of name space information.

Recover Erased File (old)      0x2222    22    17

This NCP call is replaced by Recover Salvageable File (function 22, subfunction 28) and later by Recover Salvageable File (function 87, subfunction 17).

Read from a File      0x2222    72    —

This NCP call is used to do a file read from a specific file offset.

Recover Salvageable File      0x2222    87    17

This NCP call is used to recover a file or a subdirectory entry that has been located when scanning for salvageable files.

Recover Salvageable File (old)      0x2222    22    28

This NCP call has been replaced by Recover Salvageable File (function 87, subfunction 17).

Remove Extended Trustee from Dir or File      0x2222    22    43

This NCP call removes a trustee from a directory or file.

Remove User Disk Space Restriction      0x2222    22    34

This NCP call is used to remove any disk space restrictions that have been assigned to a user for a specific volume.

Rename Directory      0x2222    22    15

This NCP call is used by a client to rename a directory on the server.

Rename File      0x2222    69    —

This NCP call is used by a client to rename a file on the server. This call has been replaced by Rename or Move a File or SubDirectory (function 87, subfunction 04).

## Rename or Move (old)                    0x2222    22    46

This NCP call was used to rename or move files or directories within a single volume and has been replaced by the Rename Directory (function 22, subfunction 15) or Rename or Move a File or SubDirectory (function 87, subfunction 04) NCP call.

## Rename or Move a File or SubDirectory      0x2222    87    04

This is the current NCP call used to rename or move files or subdirectories within NetWare server volumes.

## Restore an Extracted Base Handle         0x2222    22    24

This NCP call is used to obtain a directory handle from NetWare's internal identifier.

## Scan a Directory                          0x2222    22    30

This NCP call is used to scan a directory using an 8.3 wildcard.

## Scan Directory Disk Space                 0x2222    22    40

This NCP call is used to scan a directory using the wildcard function.

## Scan Directory for Trustees               0x2222    22    12

This NCP call is used to obtain the trustee list of a specified directory.

## Scan Directory Information                0x2222    22    02

This NCP call is used to obtain information about a file server directory, such as creation date, creation time, and owner trustee ID.

## Scan File or Directory for Extended Trustees    0x2222    22    38

This NCP call is used to obtain extended trustee information for a file or directory. This call provides extended information, such as the object ID of a file or directory object being scanned or the trustee rights of that file or directory.

Scan File Information                         0x2222    23    15

This NCP call is used to obtain a file's extended status information, such as the owner trustee ID.

Scan File or SubDirectory for Trustees    0x2222    87    05

This NCP call is used to obtain the list of trustees for a file or subdirectory.

Scan Salvageable Files                       0x2222    87    16

This NCP call is used to obtain a list of files or subdirectories that are reserved in a holding area and have been deleted but not yet purged.

Scan Salvageable Files (old)              0x2222    22    27

This NCP call has been replaced by Scan Salvageable Files (function 87, subfunction 16).

Scan Volume's User Disk Restrictions    0x2222    22    32

This NCP call supplies a list of the object restrictions for a specific volume. All restrictions are placed in 4K blocks.

Search for a File                               0x2222    64    —

This NCP call is used to search for a file in a specific server directory. The searching application defines whether or not system and hidden files will be seen by setting specific bits inside this NCP request.

Search for File or SubDirectory         0x2222    87    03

This NCP call is used to search for a file or subdirectory starting with a specific sequence number returned by the NCP initialized search request.

Search for File or SubDirectory Set    0x2222    87    20

This NCP call is used to search for sets of files and subdirectories on a NetWare server.

### Set Compressed File Size                0x2222     90     12

This NCP call is used to set size on a compressed file to a size defined by the requesting NCP client.

### Set Directory Disk Space Restriction    0x2222     22     36

This NCP call is used to set a disk space restriction for a specific server directory.

### Set Directory Entry Information          0x2222     22     37

This NCP call is used to set or change directory or file entry information to values defined within this NCP call. Some of the attributes that can be changed include the create date, create time, owner ID, and last archived date.

### Set Directory Handle                     0x2222     22     00

This NCP call is used to assign a directory handle to the source directory path.

### Set Directory Information                 0x2222     22     25

This NCP call is used to change information about a directory. This information includes the directory's creation date, creation time, and possibly owner ID.

### Set File Attributes                       0x2222     70     —

This NCP call is used to set a file's attributes, such as shareable, nonshareable, and execute only. Note that once "execute only" has been set it cannot be reset.

### Set File Extended Attribute              0x2222     79     —

This NCP call is similar to the Set File Attributes (function 70) NCP call, except that it also allows you to define the search-mode Transaction Tracking System for a file and the index bit of the file.

### Set File Information                      0x2222     23     16

This NCP call allows a client to change a file's status information, such as last access date, last update time, owner ID, or file creation date.

Set File Time/Date Stamp      0x2222      75      —

This NCP call is used to change the time/date stamp on a file (provide a forged time).

Set Huge NS Information      0x2222      87      27

This NCP call is used to set huge name space information, such as huge mask and huge data links.

Set NS Information      0x2222      87      25

This NCP call is used to set specific name space information.

Set Short Directory Handle      0x2222      87      09

This NCP call is used to assign a short directory handle to a directory. A directory handle is simply a numerical identifier associated with a directory.

Write to a File      0x2222      73      —

This NCP call is used to write a block of data to a file. This is not a burst mode right.

## Message NCPs

These NCPs can be used by applications to send messages to the broadcast address or to specific target clients. These messages are not necessarily peer-to-peer messages but are actually server-based messages that are retrieved by clients attached to that server. Each NetWare server connection maintains a 58-byte message buffer where messages are placed until the client picks up the messages. The NetWare SEND utility uses message NCP services.

Broadcast to Console      0x2222      21      09

This NCP call broadcasts a message to the system console, which can be no longer than 60 bytes.

Disable Broadcasts            0x2222     21     02

This NCP call notifies the server that a client does not want to receive messages from other clients.

Enable Broadcasts             0x2222     21     03

This NCP call is used to enable message reception from other clients.

Get Broadcast Message         0x2222     21     11

This NCP call is used by a client to retrieve a message that is sitting in the client's message receive buffer.

Get Broadcast Message (old)    0x2222     21     01

This NCP call can be replaced by Send Broadcast Message (function 21). This NCP call only allows up to station number 256.

Log Network Message          0x2222     23     13

This NCP call can be used to place a message in NetWare's log file (NET$LOG.MSG).

Send Broadcast Message       0x2222     21     10

The NCP call is used to send a message from a client to another client.

Send Broadcast Message (old)   0x2222     21     00

This NCP call can be replaced by Send Broadcast Message (function 21, subfunction 10). This NCP call only supports up to station number 256.

▶ · · · · · · · · · · · · · · · · · · · · · · · · · · · ◀

## NCP Extension NCPs

These NCPs are used to extend NetWare's NCP base for applications. An NLM-based application can register itself with the operating system and have the operating system return the function number. This creates a custom-built NCP call to support the application.

### Execute NCP Extension                     0x2222    37    —

This NCP call is used to execute an NCP extension that has been registered with the NetWare operating system.

### Get NCP Extension Information              0x2222    36    —

This NCP call can be replaced by Return NCP Extension Information (function 36, subfunction 5).

### Get NCP Extension Information by Name      0x2222    36    02

This NCP call is used to retrieve information about an NCP extension based on its NCP extension name. Information includes NCP extension major version, NCP extension minor version, and NCP extension revision number.

### Get NCP Extension Maximum Data Size       0x2222    36    01

This NCP call provides the maximum amount of data that can be sent in an NCP data packet.

### Get Number of Registered NCP Extensions   0x2222    36    03

This NCP call is used to get the number of currently registered NCP extensions.

### Get NCP Extension Registered Verbs List   0x2222    36    04

This NCP call is used to obtain a list of registered NCP extension numbers.

### Return NCP Extension Information          0x2222    36    05

This NCP call is used to obtain NCP extension information based on the NCP extension number.

Return NCP Extension Maximum Data Size      0x2222    36    06

This NCP call is used to define the largest size of data that can be used in a specific NCP extension packet.

## Novell Directory Services (NDS) NCPs

These NCPs enable NDS-type communications with the server and allow a client to send or receive NDS fragments and monitor NDS statistics and connection status.

### Clear Statistics                                      0x2222    104    07

This NCP call is used to clear the statistics that may be reported by the NTPreturn statistics (function 104, subfunction 06) call.

### Monitor NDS Connection                               0x2222    104    05

This NCP call is used to obtain the current status of the NDS connection between the requesting station or server and the destination station or server.

### NDS Fragment Close                                   0x2222    104    03

This NCP call is used to indicate the end of a fragmented NDS information transmission.

### Ping for NDS NCP                                      0x2222    104    01

This NCP call is used to query a server for its ping version, tree name, and information about distance from the root.

### Reload Software                                      0x2222    104    08

This NCP call is used by a supervisor to reload and restart the NDS software on the server.

### Return Bindery Context                               0x2222    104    04

This NCP call is used to obtain the current bindery context.

Return Statistics                          0x2222 104          06

This NCP call is used to obtain statistics that relate to NDS operation.

Send NDS Fragmented Request/Reply   0x2222 104          02

This NCP call allows you to send fragmented requests to a server and receive fragmented replies. Fragmented requests and replies do not necessarily end on a specified boundary.

## Directory Services Verbs

These protocol verbs provide NDS functionality at the NCP level.

DSV_ADD_ENTRY                          07      (0x07)

This verb is used to add a leaf entry to a directory.

DSV_ADD_PARTITION                      20      (0x14)

This verb is used to create the route entry in a new partition.

DSV_ADD_REPLICA                        25      (0x19)

This verb is used to add a replica of an existing partition to a defined server.

DSV_BACKUP_ENTRY                       45      (0x2D)

This verb is used to back up an existing directory services entry.

DSV_BEGIN_MOVE_ENTRY                   42      (0x2A)

This verb is used to move a leaf object from one partition to another in the directory.

DSV_CHANGE_REPLICA_TYPE       31      (0x1F)

This verb is used to change the type of replica of a partition.

## DSV_CHANGE_TREE_NAME       70    (0x46)

This verb is used to change the directory services tree name.

## DSV_CLOSE_ITERATION       50    (0x32)

This verb is used to indicate the close of an iteration (set) of NCP information exchanges.

## DSV_COMPARE       4    (0x04)

This verb is used to compare an attribute value of one entry with an attribute value of another entry.

## DSV_CREATE_BACK_LINK       64    (0x40)

This verb is used to create a backlink to two servers holding partition replicas. A backlink is used to track external references to NDS objects and ensure that real objects exist and are in the correct location.

## DSV_CREATE_ENTRY_DIR       67    (0x43)

This verb is used to create an entry in directory services.

## DSV_CREATE_SUBORDINATE_REF       29    (0x1D)

This verb is used to add a subordinate to the parent partition.

## DSV_DEFINE_ATTR       11    (0x0B)

This verb is used to enable you to add an attribute definition to the NDS schema.

## DSV_DEFINE_CLASS       14    (0x0E)

This verb is used to create a new class definition for the schema.

## DSV_DELETE_EXTERNAL_REFERENCE       65    (0x41)

This verb is used to delete an external reference to NDS objects.

DSV_DESIGNATE_NEW_MASTER     69      (0x45)

This verb is used to define the new master replica holder.

DSV_END_UPDATE_REPLICA          36      (0x24)

This verb is used to indicate that the replica process has ended and includes the time stamp information and partition name.

DSV_END_UPDATE_SCHEMA          33      (0x21)

This verb is used to indicate the completion of the schema update process.

DSV_FINISH_MOVE_ENTRY          43      (0x2B)

This verb allows you to finish moving a leaf entry from one partition to another partition in the directory.

DSV_GET_EFFECTIVE_RIGHT        19      (0x13)

This verb enables you to get the 32-bit effective rights of an object for the operation the object wishes to perform.

DSV_GET_REPLICA_ROOT_ID        41      (0x29)

This verb gets the partition ID number of the replica.

DSV_GET_SERVER_ADDRESS         53      (0x35)

This verb gets the server internetwork address.

DSV_JOIN_PARTITIONS            24      (0x18)

This verb is used to join partitions or to join a subordinate partition with a superior partition.

DSV_LINK_REPLICA               30      (0x1E)

This verb is used to link a replica to a master replica set.

DSV_LIST                        5      (0x05)

This verb is used to list the immediate subordinates of a defined entry.

## DSV_LIST_CONTAINABLE_CLASSES 18 (0x12)

This verb is used to obtain the set of classes that can be contained in a directory subordinate.

## DSV_LIST_PARTITIONS 22 (0x16)

This verb enables you to list the partitions available on a particular server.

## DSV_MODIFY_CLASS_DEF 16 (0x10)

This verb is used to change a class definition in the domain schema.

## DSV_MODIFY_ENTRY 9 (0x09)

This verb is used to modify attributes of an entry. For example, with this NCP call, you can add a new attribute or attribute values, remove an attribute or attribute values, or replace an attribute value.

## DSV_MODIFY_RDN 10 (0x0A)

This verb is used to change the relative distinguished name of a directory entry.

## DSV_OPEN_STREAM 27 (0x1B)

This verb is used to open a stream for data exchange between a client process and the server process.

## DSV_READ 3 (0x03)

This verb is used to read attribute values of a directory entry. This verb can also be used to verify a distinguished name.

## DSV_READ_ATTR_DEF 12 (0x0C)

This verb enables you to list attribute definitions from the schema.

## DSV_READ_CLASS_DEF 15 (0x0F)

This verb is used to read class definitions from the schema.

### DSV_READ_ENTRY_INFO 2 (0x02)

This verb is used to obtain information associated with an entry.

### DSV_RELEASE_MOVED_ENTRY 44 (0x2C)

This verb is used to release a "hold" on an object entry that has been moved.

### DSV_REMOVE_ATTR_DEF 13 (0x0D)

This verb enables you to delete an attribute definition from the schema.

### DSV_REMOVE_CLASS_DEF 17 (0x11)

This verb is used to delete a class definition from the schema.

### DSV_REMOVE_ENTRY 8 (0x08)

This verb allows you to remove a leaf entry from the directory.

### DSV_REMOVE_ENTRY_DIR 68 (0x44)

This verb is used to remove an entry from the directory.

### DSV_RENAME_EXTERNAL_REFERENCE 66 (0x42)

This entry is used to rename an reference to an external object.

### DSV_REMOVE_PARTITION 21 (0x15)

This verb is used to remove a master partition in a replica.

### DSV_REMOVE_REPLICA 26 (0x1A)

This verb is used to remove a replica of a partition.

### DSV_REPAIR_TIMESTAMPS 63 (0x3F)

This verb is a request verb that is sent to the master of the partition root whose time stamps are being repaired.

## DSV_RESOLVE_NAME 1 (0x01)

This verb is used to resolve a portion of an NDS entry name and return a set of service which may be able to continue the name resolution process.

## DSV_RESTORE_ENTRY 46 (0x2E)

This verb is used to restore an entry to the directory.

## DSV_SEARCH_ENTRIES 6 (0x06)

This verb is used to search a portion of the directory for specific entries and return information from those entries.

## DSV_SPLIT_PARTITION 23 (0x17)

This verb is used to split a partition. This request goes to the master of the superior partition.

## DSV_START_UPDATE_REPLICA 35 (0x23)

This verb is used to launch the periodic replica update process.

## DSV_START_UPDATE_SCHEMA 32 (0x20)

This verb is used to start the periodic schema update process.

## DSV_SYNC_PARTITION 38 (0x26)

This verb is used to start the partition synchronization process.

## DSV_SYNC_SCHEMA 39 (0x27)

This verb is used to start the schema synchronization process.

## DSV_UPDATE_REPLICA 37 (0x25)

This verb is used to start the periodic replica of the process.

## DSV_UPDATE_SCHEMA 34 (0x22)

This verb is used to launch the periodic schema update process.

## Print Services

These NCPs are used to enable clients to submit, manage, and delete print jobs through the NetWare Print Server process.

Close Spool File          0x2222     17       01

This NCP call is used to note the end of the file that is spooling to the file server for eventual printing.

Create Spool File          0x2222     17       09

This NCP call is used to create a new spool file into which to load a print job.

Get Printer's Queue        0x2222     17       10

This NCP call is used to obtain the object ID of the queue that is servicing a defined printer.

Get Printer Status         0x2222     17       06

This NCP call enables a client to check the status of a network printer. The status may indicate that a printer has been halted, or that a printer is offline.

Set Spool File Flags       0x2222     17       02

This NCP call enables a client to set the printing environment for a job submitted to a queue.

Spool a Disk File          0x2222     17       03

This NCP call is used to send an existing file directly to a print queue without recopying the file into a separate spool file.

Write to Spool File        0x2222     17       00

This NCP call is used to add data to the end of a client's current spool file.

## Queue Services

Queue services provide a holding place for various jobs that will be handled by job servers.

### Abort Servicing Queue Job          0x2222    23    132

This NCP is used to immediately halt a job that is in the queue. The NCP call requires the definition of a queue ID and a job number.

### Abort Servicing Queue Job (old)    0x2222    23    115

This NCP call has been replaced by Abort Servicing Queue Job (function 23, subfunction 132).

### Attach Queue Server to Queue       0x2222    23    111

This NCP call is used by a device to associate itself with a specific queue as a queue server. This enables the device to service jobs from the queue.

### Change Job Priority                0x2222    23    130

This NCP call is used to alter the priority of a job that is currently listed in a queue.

### Change Queue Job Entry             0x2222    23    123

This NCP call enables you to change certain aspects of a job that is currently in the queue. This includes target server ID number, target execution time, service restart flag, and operator hold flag.

### Change Queue Job Entry (old)       0x2222    23    109

This NCP call has been replaced by Change Queue Job Entry (function 23, subfunction 123).

### Change Queue Job Position          0x2222    23    110

This NCP call is used to change an existing job's position within a queue. When a job position has been changed, the job positions of all entries in the queue are updated to reflect their new positions.

Change to Client Rights          0x2222    23    133

This NCP call is used to allow a queue server to change its login identity to match that of a client.

Change to Client Rights (old)       0x2222    23    116

This NCP call has been replaced by Change to Client Rights (function 23, subfunction 133).

Close File and Start Queue Job      0x2222    23    127

This NCP call is used to close a client's queue job and mark it as ready for execution.

Close File and Start Queue Job (old)    0x2222    23    105

This NCP call has been replaced by Close File and Start Queue Job (function 23, subfunction 127).

Create Queue                           0x2222    23    100

This NCP call is used to create a queue. Associated properties include queue type, queue name, queue directory, queue servers, queue operators, and queue users.

Create Queue Job and File          0x2222    23    121

This NCP call enters a new job into a queue.

Create Queue Job and File (old)      0x2222    23    104

This NCP call has been replaced by Create Queue Job and File (function 23, subfunction 121).

Destroy Queue                         0x2222    23    101

This NCP call is used to destroy a queue based on its defined queue ID. Any active jobs in that queue are aborted.

Detach Queue Server from Queue        0x2222        23        112

This NCP call removes the device from a specified queues list of active queue servers.

Finish Servicing Queue Job        0x2222        23        131

This NCP call enables a queue server to signal the queue management process that a job has been successfully serviced.

Finish Servicing Queue Job (old)        0x2222        23        114

This NCP call has been replaced by Finish Servicing Queue Job (function 23, subfunction 131).

Get Queue Job File Size        0x2222        23        135

This NCP call is used to obtain the current length of a file associated with a queue entry.

Get Queue Job File Size (old)        0x2222        23        120

This NCP call has been replaced by Get Queue Job File Size (function 23, subfunction 135).

Get Queue Job List        0x2222        23        129

This NCP call is used to obtain the list of jobs currently held in a queue.

Get Queue Job List (old)        0x2222        23        107

This NCP call has been replaced by Get Queue Job List (function 23, subfunction 129).

Get Queue Jobs from Form List        0x2222        23        137

This NCP call is used to get a list of jobs in the queues, using a form-of-type match list. The requester sends the job form type along in the request and the queue server searches the current queue to see if any jobs match that form type.

| Move Queue Job from Src Q to Dst Q | 0x2222 | 23 | 136 |

This NCP call is used to move a queue job from a source queue to a destination queue. The queue job is provided a new job number after it has been moved.

| Read Queue Current Status | 0x2222 | 23 | 125 |

This NCP call is used to obtain the current status of a queue (queue hold, no queue job, queue servicing, queue not active, queue halted, and the like).

| Read Queue Current Status (old) | 0x2222 | 23 | 102 |

This NCP call has been replaced by Read Queue Current Status (function 23, subfunction 125).

| Read Queue Job Entry | 0x2222 | 23 | 122 |

This NCP call is used to obtain a job queue record. The job record includes the job ID number, job type, job position, job founding, and such.

| Read Queue Job Entry (old) | 0x2222 | 23 | 108 |

This NCP call is replaced by Read Queue Job Entry (function 23, subfunction 122).

| Read Queue Server Current Status | 0x2222 | 23 | 134 |

This NCP call is used to obtain the current status of the queue server. Status values include queue error, directory full error, queue not active, and such.

| Read Queue Server Current Status (old) | 0x2222 | 23 | 118 |

This NCP call has been replaced by Read Queue Server Current Status (function 23, subfunction 134).

| Remove Job from Queue | 0x2222 | 23 | 128 |

This NCP call is to remove a specific job from the queue based on its job number.

### Remove Job from Queue (old)     0x2222    23     106

This NCP call has been replaced by Remove Job from Queue (function 23, subfunction 128).

### Restore Queue Server Rights     0x2222    23     117

This NCP call is used to restore a queue server's identity (after it has assumed a client's identity by using Change to Client Rights [function 116]).

### Service Queue Job     0x2222    23     124

This NCP call enables a queue server client to select a new job for servicing.

### Service Queue Job (old)     0x2222    23     113

This NCP call has been replaced by Service Queue Job (function 23, subfunction 124).

### Service Queue Job by Form List     0x2222    23     138

This NCP call enables a server to retrieve a job for a service based on a form list. The form list is used to define a job queue specification to match in order for a job to be serviced.

### Set Queue Current Status     0x2222    23     126

This NCP call is used to enable an operator to control the addition of jobs in servers to a queue.

### Set Queue Current Status (old)     0x2222    23     103

This NCP call has been replaced by Set Queue Current Status (function 23, subfunction 126).

### Set Queue Server Current Status     0x2222    23     119

This NCP call enables a queue server to update a queue manager's copy of queue server status information.

## RPC Services NCPs

RPCs (Remote Procedure Calls) enable remote execution of specific tasks at a server.

### RPC Add Name Space to Volume     0x2222     131     05

This NCP call is used to remotely add a specific name space to a mounted volume on a server. The requesting client must be at least equivalent to supervisor. Name spaces available include DOS, MAC, NFS, FTAM, and OS/2 (long name space).

### RPC Dismount Volume     0x2222     131     04

This NCP call is used to remotely dismount a volume on a server.

### RPC Execute NCF File     0x2222     131     07

This NCP call is used to remotely execute an NCF file at the server.

### RPC Load an NLM     0x2222     131     01

This NCP call is used to load a specific NLM on a server.

### RPC Mount Volume     0x2222     131     03

This NCP call is used to remotely mount a volume on a server. Reply codes may indicate whether a volume is already mounted, the volume requested is unknown, or the RPC request was successfully completed.

### RPC Set SET Command Value     0x2222     131     06

This NCP call is used to remotely change the current status of a SET command on a server.

### RPC Unload an NLM     0x2222     131     02

This NCP call is used to remotely unload an NLM from a server. The requestor must be at least equivalent to supervisor.

## Statistical NCPs

Statistical NCPs provide information about the server, including the file protocol and LAN board statistics and performance.

### Active LAN Board List                    0x2222     123     20

This NCP call returns a basic list of active LAN boards in the server. It does not provide details on LAN board performance.

### Active Protocol Stacks                    0x2222     123     40

This NCP call provides a list of the protocol stacks that are currently active on the server. This NCP call does not provide detailed information on protocol performance.

### CPU Information                    0x2222     123     08

This NCP call provides basic server CPU information, such as bus type (ISA, Micro Channel, EISA, PCI, or PCMCIA). This NCP call also indicates whether a coprocessor is present.

### Garbage Collection Information          0x2222     123     07

This NCP call returns information about the garbage collection process of a server, including the number of times that allocation failed because no memory was available, the number of times garbage collection was invoked since the server started, and the number of times garbage collection reclaimed memory.

### Get Active Connection List by Type     0x2222     123     14

This NCP call provides a connection list based on type, such as NCP connection type, NLM connection type, AFP connection type, and the like.

### Get Cache Information                    0x2222     123     01

This NCP call is used to get cache memory and trend information. This information is similar to the information provided at the server monitor screen.

### Get Compression and Decompression Time and Count     0x2222    123    72

This NCP call provides compression and decompression information for the server on a selected volume.

### Get Current Compressing File     0x2222    123    70

This NCP call identifies the file currently being compressed on a specified volume.

### Get Current Decompressing File Info List    0x2222    123    71

This NCP call provides a list of files currently being decompressed on a selected volume.

### Get Directory Cache Information     0x2222    123    12

This NCP call provides directory cache information, such as minimum nonreferenced time, wait time before new buffer, and maximum concurrent rights.

### Get File Server Information     0x2222    123    02

This NCP call provides basic information about the server, including the operating system version number, the number of connections in use, and the reexecuted request count.

### Get General Router and SAP Information    0x2222    123    50

This NCP call is used to obtain basic SAP and Router information, such as the existing SAP socket, the router tracking state (TRACK ON), and the reply to nearest server flag setting.

### Get Known Networks Information     0x2222    123    53

This NCP call is used to provide the routing information table.

### Get Known Servers Information     0x2222    123    56

This NCP call is used to get the server information table.

Get Loaded Media Number List       0x2222    123    47

This NCP call is used to obtain basic information about loaded media.

Get Media Manager Object Children's List    0x2222    123    32

This NCP call is used to obtain a list of children belonging to a specific media manager parent object.

Get Media Manager Object Information      0x2222    123    30

This NCP call is used to obtain basic information about media manager objects, such as capacity, block size, type, and status.

Get Media Manager Objects List         0x2222    123    31

This NCP call is used to return a simple list of media manager objects.

Get Media Name by Media Number       0x2222    123    46

This NCP call is used to obtain a media name for a specific media number included in the request packet.

Get Network Router Information         0x2222    123    51

This NCP call provides information about network routing services on a server.

Get Network Routers Information        0x2222    123    52

This NCP call is used to obtain information about routers on a network.

Get NLM Loaded List                  0x2222    123    10

This NCP call is used to obtain a list of NLMs running on a server.

Get NLM Resource Tag List            0x2222    123    15

This NCP call is used to obtain a list of resources used by NLMs on a server.

Get Operating System Version Information     0x2222    123    13

This NCP call is used to obtain information about the NetWare operating system version running on a server. The reply packeting includes major version, minor version, volume support, connection support, and server serial number.

Get Protocol Stack Configuration Information     0x2222    123    41

This NCP call provides configuration information about protocols loaded on the server. This includes frame types being used by a specific protocol.

Get Protocol Stack Custom Information     0x2222    123    43

This NCP call provides custom information about a protocol stack on a server.

Get Protocol Stack Numbers by LAN
Board Number     0x2222    123    45

This NCP call is used to obtain a list of protocol stack ID numbers for a specific LAN board.

Get Protocol Stack Numbers by Media Number     0x2222    123    44

This NCP call is used to obtain the protocol stack ID numbers for a specific medium.

Get Protocol Stack Statistics Information     0x2222    123    42

This NCP call is used to obtain protocol statistics for a server. Statistics include transmit and receive count information.

Get Server Information     0x2222    123    54

This NCP call is used to obtain information about the server, such as server type, server name, current server time, server address, and hops to server.

Get Server Set Categories     0x2222    123    61

This NCP call is used to obtain information about the server SET categories.

### Get Server Set Commands Information 0x2222 123 60

This NCP call is used to obtain server SET command information.

### Get Server Sources Information 0x2222 123 55

This NCP call is used to obtain address information about other servers known to a specific server. The reply packet includes server type, server name, and current server time.

### Get Volume Information by Level 0x2222 123 34

This NCP call is used to obtain volume information, such as last modified date and time, and compression limits.

### Get Volume Segment List 0x2222 123 33

This NCP call is used to obtain the list of volume segments, including segment offset and segment size.

### IPX SPX Information 0x2222 123 06

This NCP call is used to obtain IPX and SPX information from the server. This information includes IPX malformed packet accounts, and SPX listen connection failures. These statistics are similar to the information gathered through the IPXCON utility.

### LAN Common Counters Information 0x2222 123 22

This NCP call is used to obtain common statistics for a specific LAN board, such as total transmitted packet count and total received packet count.

### LAN Configuration Information 0x2222 123 21

This NCP call is used to obtain LAN configuration information, such as LAN driver node address, LAN driver maximum received size, and LAN driver card name.

### LAN Custom Counters Information     0x2222    123    23

This NCP call is used to obtain the custom statistics for a LAN board, such as raw sends and fatal retransmissions.

### LAN Name Information     0x2222    123    24

This NCP call is used to obtain LAN name information, such as network board name and driver name.

### LSL Information     0x2222    123    25

This NCP call is used to obtain LSL information, such as get ECB buffers, get ECB fails, unclaimed packets, and maximum physical packet size.

### LSL Logical Board Statistics     0x2222    123    26

This NCP call provides information about LSL logical boards, such as LAN board number, and packets transmitted and received.

### MLID Board Information     0x2222    123    27

This NCP call is used to obtain MLID information, such as protocol number, protocol name, and protocol ID for the board in use.

### NetWare File Systems Information     0x2222    123    03

This NCP call is used to obtain information about the file system, such as FAT right error count, FAT moved count, and TURBO FAT build screwed up count.

### NLM Information     0x2222    123    11

This NCP call is used to obtain basic information about an NLM currently running on a server, such as NLM date, version information, and message language. This NCP call is also used to determine if this module is reentrant, can be loaded more than once, or allows forced preemption (pseudopreemption).

Packet Burst Information    0x2222    123    05

This NCP call is used to obtain packet burst information from the server, such as right time out count, control being torn down count, and out of order receipts count.

User Information    0x2222    123    04

This NCP call is used to obtain information for a specific connection in use, such as total bytes read, total bytes written, and login time.

Volume Switch Information  0x2222    123    09

This NCP call is used to obtain information about the number of times various code paths have been taken in the NetWare Operating System.

## Synchronization Services

Synchronization services are used to coordinate access to the files and records among users. File and record locking services are provided by this set of NCP calls.

Clear File    0x2222    87    38

This NCP call enables a client to release the locks on a file and close a file.

Clear File (old)    0x2222    07    —

This NCP call has been replaced by Clear File (function 87, subfunction 38).

Clear File Set    0x2222    08    —

This NCP call clears all files from a client's logged file table.

Clear Lock Wait Node    0x2222    112    —

This NCP call aborts an appending lock by clearing it.

Clear Logical Record       0x2222     11     —

This NCP call releases a synchronization string and removes it from a synchronization string table. A synchronization string is a logical record name used for locking.

Clear Logical Record Set       0x2222     14     —

This NCP call releases all of the client's logical record locks (synchronization strings) and clears the synchronization string table.

Clear Physical Record       0x2222     30     —

This NCP call removes a specific byte range from the client's byte range table.

Clear Physical Record Set       0x2222     31     —

This NCP call clears a client's byte range table, all bytes held by the server for a specific task. All locks are released.

Close Semaphore       0x2222     111     04

This NCP call is used to close a semaphore that is not needed any longer.

Close Semaphore (old)       0x2222     32     04

This NCP call has been replaced by Closed Semaphore (function 111, subfunction 04).

Examine Semaphore       0x2222     111     01

This NCP call is used to obtain the value of a target semaphore.

Examine Semaphore (old)       0x2222     32     01

This NCP call has been replaced by Examine Semaphore (function 111, subfunction 01).

File Release Lock       0x2222     02

This NCP call releases locks on shareable files.

File Set Lock (old)              0x2222    01

This NCP call has been replaced by File Release Lock (function 02).

Lock File Set                   0x2222    106    —

This NCP call locks all files locked by the current task.

Lock File Set (old)             0x2222    04     —

This NCP call is replaced by Lock File Set (function 106).

Lock Logical Record Set         0x2222    108    —

This NCP call is used to lock all of the client's logged synchronization strings (logical record set).

Lock Logical Record Set (old)   0x2222    10     —

This NCP call has been replaced by Lock Logical Record Set (function 108).

Lock Physical Record Set        0x2222    110    —

This NCP call is used to lock all byte ranges currently logged by the client.

Lock Physical Record Set (old)  0x2222    27     —

This NCP call has been replaced by Lock Physical Record Set (function 110).

Log File                        0x2222    87     36

This NCP call is used to log a file for exclusive use by a client.

Log File (old)                  0x2222    105    —

This NCP call has been replaced by Log File (function 87, subfunction 36).

Log File (old)                  0x2222    03     —

This NCP call has been replaced by Log File (function 87, subfunction 36).

**Log Logical Record**            0x2222     107     –

This NCP call logs a synchronization string for the client.

**Log Logical Record (old)**       0x2222     09      —

This NCP call has been replaced by Log Logical Record (function 107).

**Log Physical Record**           0x2222     109     —

This NCP call is used to lock a byte range within a file.

**Log Physical Record (old)**      0x2222     26      —

This NCP call has been replaced by Log Physical Record (function 109).

**Open/Create a Semaphore**       0x2222     111     00

This NCP call is used to open a named semaphore.

**Open Semaphore (old)**          0x2222     32      00

This NCP call has been replaced by Open/Create a Semaphore (function 111, subfunction 00).

**Release File**                  0x2222     87      37

This NCP call is used to release the locks on a file.

**Release File (old)**            0x2222     05      —

This NCP call has been replaced by Release File (function 87, subfunction 37).

**Release File Set**              0x2222     06      —

This NCP call is used to release all the client's currently logged or locked files.

**Release Logical Record**        0x2222     12      —

This NCP call is used to release a single synchronization string held by the client.

Release Logical Record Set    0x2222    13    —

This NCP call is used to release all of a client's locked synchronization strings.

Release Physical Record    0x2222    28    —

This NCP call is used to release a locked byte range.

Release Physical Record Set    0x2222    29    —

This NCP call is to release all of a client's locked byte ranges.

Signal Semaphore (old)    0x2222    32    03

This NCP call has been replaced by Signal (V) Semaphore (function 111, subfunction 03).

Signal (V) Semaphore    0x2222    111    03

This NCP call is used to increment the semaphore value by 1.

Wait on (P) Semaphore    0x2222    111    02

This NCP call enables a client to wait on a semaphore.

Wait on Semaphore (old)    0x2222    32    02

This NCP call has been replaced by Wait on (P) Semaphore (function 111, subfunction 02).

## Transaction Tracking Services

These NCP calls are used to maintain database integrity by ensuring that all elements of a database transaction are executed or the transactions will "roll back" to the last known-to-be-good spot in the database history.

TTS Abort Transaction    0x2222    34    03

This NCP call aborts explicit and implicit TTS transactions and cancels all rights made since the start of a transaction.

**TTS Begin Transaction**  0x2222  34  01

This NCP call begins an explicit TTS transaction and starts tracking all files currently opened.

**TTS End Transaction**  0x2222  34  02

This NCP call ends an explicit TTS transaction and returns a transaction number.

**TTS Get Application Thresholds**  0x2222  34  05

This NCP call is used to determine the number of logical and physical record locks allowed before an implicit transaction begins.

**TTS Get Transaction Bit**  0x2222  34  09

This NCP call is used to obtain the control flags for a task.

**TTS Get Workstation Thresholds**  0x2222  34  07

This NCP call is used to get TTS workstation threshold numbers through the SETTTS.EXE utility, as well.

**TTS Is Available**  0x2222  34  00

This NCP call verifies whether the file server supports transaction tracking.

**TTS Set Application Thresholds**  0x2222  34  06

This NCP call is used to specify the number of logical and physical record locks allowed before an implicit transaction occurs. This call can be used to change application thresholds and restore the thresholds later, if desired.

**TTS Set Transaction Bit**  0x2222  34  10

This NCP call enables a client to alter the TTS control flags.

**TTS Set Workstation Thresholds**  0x2222  34  08

This NCP call is used to set workstation TTS threshold values.

TTS Transaction Status     0x2222     34     04

This NCP call verifies whether a transaction has been written to disk.

# CD CONTENTS

**T**his CD contains a demo version of LANalyzer for Windows and a series of trace files that can be opened on the full-working LANalyzer for Windows product only.

## LANalyzer for Windows Demo

The demo version of LANalyzer for Windows will provide you with an overview of its functionality and interface. Several demo trace files have been provided to demonstrate how LANalyzer for Window can be used to troubleshoot network problems.

> **The demo version of LANalyzer for Windows cannot be used to open the separate book trace files located in the \TRACES directory. You must have the full working version of LANalyzer or EtherPeek to view those files.**

**NOTE**

This demo can be run on Windows 3.0, 3.1, 3.11 and Windows 95. The following is an overview of the steps to set up and run the demo:

**1** • Install from CD (run setup.exe); refer to readme.txt file for details.

**2** • Restart to DOS and load LZENET.BAT or LZTNET.BAT for either Ethernet or Token Ring simulation (refer to LZFW readme file Section 4 for details).

**3** • Launch Windows (type **WIN**).

**4** • Double-click the LZFW demo.

**5** • Skip through the marketing information to the demo and select the demo scenario.

> **Most people forget Step 2, so please read the readme file carefully for detailed installation instructions.**

**NOTE**

## Book Trace Files

Throughout the development of this book, we gathered numerous trace files, which are included on this book's CD-ROM. Trace files contain packets from the network—they are the files we open to look at the communications a packet at a time.

The following list of trace files and their descriptions should give you some idea of what you can find in each of the trace files enclosed. Remember that these trace files can be opened with the NCC LAN Network Probe and the AG Group Etherpeek products, but not with the LANalyzer for Windows demo included on the CD. The demo version has been altered so that it cannot be used as an external trace file reader.

### 07RETRY.TR1  NCP TIMEOUTS

This trace shows a client that makes the request to obtain files/subdirectory information (packet 111). The server was temporarily disconnected from the network, so the NCP request was not handled. Looking at the time stamps, we can see the client gradually increase its time-out parameter up to eight seconds (packet 123). Once the client has made numerous requests without an answer from the server, the client sends RIP broadcasts to identify if there is another network path available. After that the client attempts to perform a LIP echo test, which tests connectivity between a client and the server. The fourth LIP echo test is successful because the server has been plugged back into the network (packet 131). The remainder of the communications follow normally.

### 08SPX.TR1  RCONSOLE SPX

This trace shows a client setting up an SPX connection with a server to run RCONSOLE. The handshake can be seen in packets 5 and 6. This trace is a perfect example of how the sequence number and acknowledgment number fields increment with each data transfer sequence. Interestingly, the RCONSOLE session is not encrypted or hidden from view at the upper layers. In packet 37, for example, we can see in the data portion that the server screen is being downloaded to the client in ASCII text. Then, in packet 39, we can see a message that is on the console, indicating that this server is unable to communicate with another server at the current time. If you continue along with the larger packets (583 bytes each), you'll notice the data that comes down the cable during an RCONSOLE session. The SPX connection is terminated in packets 2,966 and 2,967.

### 10FSDOWN.TR1   FILE SERVER BROUGHT DOWN

This trace file shows what happens when a file server is "downed" using the DOWN command at the server console. Notice in packets 4 and 5 that the server sends an NCP call to connections 2 and 5 (the only active connections on this test network). This NCP call, Broadcast Message Waiting, indicates that the client should come pick up a message that is held at the server. In packets 6 and 7, the clients send requests to get their messages. Packets 8 and 9 show the server sending a message that "File server COMPAQ-FS2 is down." Packets 12 and 13 display the RIP broadcasts, indicating that the networks available through that server are now 16 hops away (unreachable). Packets 14 and 15 are SAP broadcasts indicating that services available on that server are 16 hops away (unreachable). We can also see the process of NLSP updating the link state database.

### 11NLSPUP.TR1   SECOND NLSP ROUTER COMING UP

This trace file starts with a network that has a single NLSP router on it. In packet 1, we can see the router's priority is set to 64, indicating that it has already bumped its priority level up by 20 to become the designated router. In packet 16, a second NLSP router is brought up on the network and it broadcasts a hello packet. In packet 22, you can see our original router sending a hello packet that contains a neighboring router's option entry for the new router.

### 13APPS.TR1   LAUNCHING PCONSOLE.EXE

In this trace file we see a client requesting to open PCONSOLE.EXE in packet 1. After obtaining the file and directory information, the client requests to open the file in packet 13. In packet 14, the server replies and allocates the file handle to the PCONSOLE.EXE. The file handle granted is 0x00002964.

**File handle names are reordered in different ways in the summary screen than in the actual packet. In the summary screen this file handle is 0x000064290000.**

NOTE

The client then makes a burst read request for the file in packet 15. During the launch sequence, the client looks for dependent files, such as PCONSOLE.PIF in packet 37, DEFAULT.PIF in packet 53, and PCONSOLE.ICO in packet 57. Each time the client reopens and reads a bit of PCONSOLE.EXE, the client is provided a new file handle, making each file close with different file handle names. Starting with packet 89, the client begins to completely read the PCONSOLE.EXE file using burst mode. Throughout the rest of the trace you will see additional supplemental files being located and downloaded by the client.

### 13LOGIN.TR1   LOGIN AS ADMIN

In this trace file, you log into a server using the ADMIN account. The login process begins in packet 23. The client reads the public key at packet 29 and again in packets 39 and 53, since there are various key operations. The authentication process can be seen in packets 55 through 58. The client begins to read its own property values (such as name information) starting at packet 59. The client checks for a container login script in packet 83 and for a profile login script in packet 89. Finally the client checks for a user login script in packet 93. Since the scripts do not exist, the client executes the default login script starting on packet 97. For a quick reference identifier, we can look at packet 151 to see the strange variable OS directory look-up that is contained in the default login script.

### 13 ADDREP.TR1   TRACE NDS ADD REPLICA

This trace file depicts the process of adding a replica for an NDS partition. In this trace you can go down to packet 182 and look inside the packet to see the NDS data replication process underway. Packet 401 contains the Add Replica NCP call (function code 104, subfunction 2, verb 25).

**NOTE**

**We can see in this trace that one of the replies is not decoded properly (packets 403 and 405). Looking at the text we can see that the tree information is being exchanged. It is always important to look in the data portion to try to figure out what is going on when an analyzer does not contain a complete decode of a packet.**

For information on additional trace files, refer to the author's Web site, www.imagitech.com.

# *I*ndex

**B**

## C

## E

*(continued)*

## N

(continued)

## O

### S

*(continued)*

*(continued)*

## X

## Z

# IDG BOOKS WORLDWIDE, INC.
# END-USER LICENSE AGREEMENT

<u>READ THIS.</u> You should carefully read these terms and conditions before opening the software packet(s) included with this book ("Book"). This is a license agreement ("Agreement") between you and IDG Books Worldwide, Inc. ("IDGB"). By opening the accompanying software packet(s), you acknowledge that you have read and accept the following terms and conditions. If you do not agree and do not want to be bound by such terms and conditions, promptly return the Book and the unopened software packet(s) to the place you obtained them for a full refund.

1. <u>License Grant.</u> IDGB grants to you (either an individual or entity) a nonexclusive license to use one copy of the enclosed software program(s) (collectively, the "Software") solely for your own personal or business purposes on a single computer (whether a standard computer or a workstation component of a multiuser network). The Software is in use on a computer when it is loaded into temporary memory (RAM) or installed into permanent memory (hard disk, CD-ROM, or other storage device). IDGB reserves all rights not expressly granted herein.

2. <u>Ownership.</u> IDGB is the owner of all right, title, and interest, including copyright, in and to the compilation of the Software recorded on the disk(s) or CD-ROM ("Software Media"). Copyright to the individual programs recorded on the Software Media is owned by the author or other authorized copyright owner of each program. Ownership of the Software and all proprietary rights relating thereto remain with IDGB and its licensers.

3. <u>Restrictions on Use and Transfer.</u>
   (a) You may only (i) make one copy of the Software for backup or archival purposes, or (ii) transfer the Software to a single hard disk, provided that you keep the original for backup or archival purposes. You may not (i) rent or lease the Software, (ii) copy or reproduce the Software through a LAN or other network system or through any computer subscriber system or bulletin-board

system, or (iii) modify, adapt, or create derivative works based on the Software.

**(b)** You may not reverse engineer, decompile, or disassemble the Software. You may transfer the Software and user documentation on a permanent basis, provided that the transferee agrees to accept the terms and conditions of this Agreement and you retain no copies. If the Software is an update or has been updated, any transfer must include the most recent update and all prior versions.

4. **<u>Restrictions on Use of Individual Programs.</u>** You must follow the individual requirements and restrictions detailed for each individual program in Appendix H of this Book. These limitations are also contained in the individual license agreements recorded on the Software Media. These limitations may include a requirement that after using the program for a specified period of time, the user must pay a registration fee or discontinue use. By opening the Software packet(s), you will be agreeing to abide by the licenses and restrictions for these individual programs that are detailed in Appendix H and on the Software Media. None of the material on this Software Media or listed in this Book may ever be redistributed, in original or modified form, for commercial purposes.

5. **<u>Limited Warranty.</u>**

   **(a)** IDGB warrants that the Software and Software Media are free from defects in materials and workmanship under normal use for a period of sixty (60) days from the date of purchase of this Book. If IDGB receives notification within the warranty period of defects in materials or workmanship, IDGB will replace the defective Software Media.

   **(b) IDGB AND THE AUTHOR OF THE BOOK DISCLAIM ALL OTHER WARRANTIES, EXPRESS OR IMPLIED, INCLUDING WITHOUT LIMITATION IMPLIED WARRANTIES OF MERCHANTABILITY AND FITNESS FOR A PARTICULAR PURPOSE, WITH RESPECT TO THE**

SOFTWARE, THE PROGRAMS, THE SOURCE CODE CONTAINED THEREIN, AND/OR THE TECHNIQUES DESCRIBED IN THIS BOOK. IDGB DOES NOT WARRANT THAT THE FUNCTIONS CONTAINED IN THE SOFTWARE WILL MEET YOUR REQUIREMENTS OR THAT THE OPERATION OF THE SOFTWARE WILL BE ERROR FREE.

(c) This limited warranty gives you specific legal rights, and you may have other rights that vary from jurisdiction to jurisdiction.

6. **Remedies.**

(a) IDGB's entire liability and your exclusive remedy for defects in materials and workmanship shall be limited to replacement of the Software Media, which may be returned to IDGB with a copy of your receipt at the following address: Software Media Fulfillment Department, Attn.:*Novell's Guide to LAN/WAN Analysis: IPX/SPX,* IDG Books Worldwide, Inc., 7260 Shadeland Station, Ste. 100, Indianapolis, IN 46256, or call 1-800-762-2974. Please allow three to four weeks for delivery. This Limited Warranty is void if failure of the Software Media has resulted from accident, abuse, or misapplication. Any replacement Software Media will be warranted for the remainder of the original warranty period or thirty (30) days, whichever is longer.

(b) In no event shall IDGB or the author be liable for any damages whatsoever (including without limitation damages for loss of business profits, business interruption, loss of business information, or any other pecuniary loss) arising from the use of or inability to use the Book or the Software, even if IDGB has been advised of the possibility of such damages.

(c) Because some jurisdictions do not allow the exclusion or limitation of liability for consequential or incidental damages, the above limitation or exclusion may not apply to you.

7. **U.S. Government Restricted Rights.** Use, duplication, or disclosure of the Software by the U.S. Government is subject to restrictions stated in paragraph (c)(1)(ii) of the Rights in Technical Data and Computer Software clause of DFARS 252.227-7013, and in subparagraphs (a) through (d) of the Commercial Computer @md Restricted Rights clause at FAR 52.227-19, and in similar clauses in the NASA FAR supplement, when applicable.

8. **General.** This Agreement constitutes the entire understanding of the parties and revokes and supersedes all prior agreements, oral or written, between them and may not be modified or amended except in a writing signed by both parties hereto that specifically refers to this Agreement. This Agreement shall take precedence over any other documents that may be in conflict herewith. If any one or more provisions contained in this Agreement are held by any court or tribunal to be invalid, illegal, or otherwise unenforceable, each and every other provision shall remain in full force and effect.

# my2cents.idgbooks.com

## Installation Instructions

This CD contains a demo version of LANalyzer for Windows and a series of trace files that can be opened on the full-working LANalyzer for Windows product only.

To install LANalyzer, run SETUP.EXE from the LANalyzer Demo CD ROM. The installation is a three-step process:

1 • LANalyzer for Windows software installation: The installation process expands and copies product files to the specified directory (hereafter referred to as <product> directory).

2 • Workstation software installation: The installation process copies the LANalyzer for Windows LZFW.INI file to the WINDOWS directory, and installs Windows 3.1 DLLs (COMMDLG.DLL, WINHELP.EXE, VER.DLL, WINHELP.HLP) as needed.

3 • System setup: After installing all necessary files, SETUP updates the following files: Modifies the Windows SYSTEM.INI file to include the one virtual driver, VCAFT.386.

For each file to be modified, you have two choices:

▸ Let SETUP back up the current file and update the file accordingly.

▸ Leave the file untouched and have SETUP provide a sample file.

SETUP creates a program group and icons for LANalyzer for Windows Demo. If they already exist, they are replaced.